# REPORT OF
# COMMISSION OF INQUIRY

UNIVERSITY OF OXFORD

# REPORT OF
# COMMISSION OF
# INQUIRY

## II · STATISTICAL APPENDIX

OXFORD

AT THE CLARENDON PRESS

1966

*Oxford University Press, Ely House, London W. 1*

GLASGOW NEW YORK TORONTO MELBOURNE WELLINGTON
CAPE TOWN SALISBURY IBADAN NAIROBI LUSAKA ADDIS ABABA
BOMBAY CALCUTTA MADRAS KARACHI LAHORE DACCA
KUALA LUMPUR HONG KONG

# CONTENTS

## PART III

### UNDERGRADUATES

## PART IV

## POSTGRADUATES

## PART V

### THE ACADEMIC STAFF

PART VI

THE MAIN SOURCES OF STATISTICAL INFORMATION

## PART VII

### OPINIONS OF THE ACADEMIC STAFF AND OF POSTGRADUATES

# LIST OF TABLES

PART II

UNDERGRADUATE ADMISSIONS PAGE

PART III

UNDERGRADUATES

## PART IV

### POSTGRADUATES

PART V

THE ACADEMIC STAFF

### PART VI

#### THE MAIN SOURCES OF STATISTICAL INFORMATION

# FIGURES

# DEFINITIONS

1. UNIVERSITIES. These are defined as universities and university colleges in receipt of Exchequer grant, but excluding the former colleges of advanced technology and the Heriot-Watt University. By *Oxford* is meant the University of Oxford and its colleges and other societies.

2. ACADEMIC YEAR. Dates expressed as 1964–5, etc., refer to the academic year October–September. At Oxford the three terms of the academic year (in order) are known as Michaelmas Term, Hilary Term, and Trinity Term. References to term at Oxford apply to Full Term which in each case lasts 8 weeks.

3. SOCIETIES is a generic term used only in relation to Oxford. It includes the colleges, Permanent Private Halls, and other societies (i.e. Linacre College, St. Cross College, and Iffley College) of Oxford. The colleges may be divided into the *men's colleges*, the *women's colleges*, and the *graduate colleges*. The men's colleges and women's colleges are referred to as the *traditional colleges* (or sometimes as the *undergraduate colleges*). Where the context does not require a distinction to be drawn between colleges and other societies, the term 'colleges' may be used and should be construed to include other societies where appropriate.

4. ACADEMIC STAFF. For universities other than Oxford, all full-time teaching and research staff paid directly from university funds financed by Exchequer grants to universities are included. These are the staff included in university returns to the University Grants Committee. For Oxford, in addition to the above, full-time teaching and research staff at the colleges and other societies are included, as are those holding part-time teaching and research posts with both the University and a college or other society. See para. 407 for further details. For some purposes a wider definition of *academic staff (including outside grants staff)* is adopted for Oxford. This comprises the academic staff as defined above together with others holding research posts who are paid through grants from outside bodies which are formally accepted by, and channelled through, the University.

5. ACADEMIC COMMUNITY. This term is used in respect of Oxford only. The academic community includes, besides the academic staff, others employed in Oxford who are members of the FSSU. They include heads of houses, library and museum staff, and administrative staff both in the University and in colleges. Members of the academic community are usually also members of Congregation.

6. STUDENTS are classified as *undergraduates* or *postgraduates* (except that for universities other than Oxford—and for Oxford in earlier years—some

students cannot be allocated to either group). All students at Oxford are full-time. In the statistics relating to other universities, full-time students only are included. For Oxford, matriculated students only are included, except that in Part I, para. 47 and Table 18 details are given of non-matriculated students and some are included in calculations of student/staff ratios in Part V.

7. UNDERGRADUATES. These comprise full-time students following courses for first degrees and diplomas. For universities other than Oxford the statistics are those returned by universities to the UGC, part-time students being excluded throughout. For Oxford, undergraduates comprise matriculated students in residence reading for a B.A. or B.M. (except Part II chemists and metallurgists); those reading for a second Honour School; and those taking an Overseas Service Course.

8. POSTGRADUATES. For universities other than Oxford postgraduates are defined as full-time students returned by universities to the UGC as taking advanced courses (for which a first degree is normally a necessary qualification) leading to higher degrees and diplomas, or doing advanced work not leading to a degree or diploma. Students reading for a fourth-year Certificate or Diploma in Education are included. For Oxford, all matriculated students in residence other than undergraduates are postgraduates.

9. GRADUATES. Students having a first degree are described as graduates. They may have obtained the degree at Oxford or elsewhere, and at Oxford they may be undergraduates or postgraduates.

10. OVERSEAS STUDENTS are students whose permanent home residence is outside the United Kingdom.

11. SUBJECT GROUP. The practice of the UGC until 1964–5 is followed. (The subject groupings adopted by the UGC for 1965–6 are different.) The UGC distinguished eight faculties thus:

> Arts (including Education)
> Social studies
> Pure science
> Applied science
> Agriculture
> Medicine
> Dentistry
> Veterinary medicine

For universities other than Oxford the division of subjects into faculties is that adopted for returns to the UGC. It is known that in some cases the allocation is made differently in different universities. For Oxford the subjects are divided thus:

(a) *Arts* include Philosophy, Theology, Languages and Literature, Oriental Studies, History, Geography, Music, and Education;

(b) *Social studies* include Law, Economics, Politics, Sociology, and Anthropology;

(c) *Pure science* includes Mathematics, Physics, Chemistry, Biochemistry, Physiology, Zoology, Botany, Geology, and Psychology;

(d) *Applied science* includes Engineering and Metallurgy;

(e) *Agriculture* includes Agriculture and Forestry;

(f) *Medicine* includes Pre-clinical and Clinical Medicine;

(g) *Dentistry* and *veterinary medicine* are not taught at Oxford.

For almost all purposes a less-detailed classification is used thus:

Arts
Social studies
Science, comprising pure science, applied science, and agriculture
Medicine (including dentistry and veterinary medicine where appropriate).

Posts are classified according to the faculty within which they are held for those with university appointments (posts in the Faculty of Anthropology and Geography being divided according to subject), and according to subject for others. Undergraduates are classified according to the Honour School for which they are reading (all those reading for the Pass School are allocated to arts since full details of their subjects are not available, and those taking Overseas Service Courses are also included under arts), except that in some tables in Part I undergraduates reading for the B.M. are shown under medicine. The Honour School of Philosophy, Politics, and Economics is included under social studies, and the Honour Schools of Psychology, Philosophy, and Physiology and of Engineering Science and Economics are included under science. Postgraduates are classified according to the faculty board under which they are registered (or by subject for those under the Committee for Advanced Studies, or under arts for those not reading for a degree or diploma).

12. ACCEPTANCE RATE. In Part II the number of candidates for admission who are given places expressed as a percentage of all applicants in the appropriate group is termed the *acceptance rate*.

13. TYPES OF TEACHING. Teaching at Oxford is divided into five categories: tutorials; classes and seminars; lectures; practicals; and postgraduate supervision. For statistical purposes tutorials are defined as teaching for groups of up to three students, while classes and seminars include teaching for larger groups (but excluding lectures and practicals).

Tutorials are normally given on behalf of a college (or other society) but classes and seminars may be organized on a college or a university basis. *Practicals* include practical instruction given to regular classes; this type of instruction is also referred to as *demonstrating*. Postgraduate supervision includes informal teaching for postgraduates, and discussion with postgraduates of their work.

# NOTES

1. In the tables each figure is rounded separately. Totals may not, therefore, be exactly equal to the sum of their components.

2. Dates expressed as 1964–5, etc., refer to the academic year.

3. The following symbols are used:

|  |  |
|---|---|
| Nil or negligible | — |
| Not applicable | . |
| Not available | .. |

4. The annual publication of the University Grants Committee, *Returns from universities and university colleges in receipt of Exchequer* [*Treasury* until 1961–2] *grant,* is referred to as 'UGC Returns'.

# STATISTICAL
# APPENDIX

# PART I

## THE DEVELOPMENT OF OXFORD SINCE 1923

### OXFORD IN 1923–4 AND IN 1963–4*

**Students**

1. In 1923–4 Oxford had about 4,000 students, of whom almost 90 per cent. were undergraduates, and four-fifths were reading arts and social studies subjects. By 1963–4 the size of the University, in terms of student numbers, had more than doubled; the proportion of undergraduates had dropped to four-fifths; and the proportion reading arts and social studies had dropped to two-thirds.

2. During the same period, the student population at other universities in Great Britain trebled;[1] there was a substantial increase in the proportion of postgraduates;[2] but there was no significant change in the proportion of students in arts and social studies (two-fifths) which was, and is, much lower than at Oxford.

3. Tables 1 and 2 set out the comparison of student numbers in more detail. They show that, at Oxford, the number of undergraduates has doubled and the number of postgraduates quadrupled. Comparable figures for other universities are not available since a large number of students in 1923–4 cannot be classified on the basis of current definitions, but the proportion of postgraduates in 1963–4 was rather higher at Oxford (20·6 per cent.) than at other universities (17·8 per cent.).

* In this and other sections where comparisons are made between Oxford and other universities in Great Britain, the comparisons are generally with the *average* of the other universities; there may also be considerable variations amongst them. The latest available data for other universities are for 1963–4. Where comparisons are made the latest year given is therefore 1963–4. Where no such comparisons are involved, statistics are given for Oxford in 1964–5 (and sometimes 1965–6) wherever available.

[1] The number of universities has also increased but the universities established since 1923–4 accounted for only 5·1 per cent. of all students in 1963–4. See Note 5 to Table 1.

[2] The proportion in 1923–4 cannot be calculated accurately, but it was only 10 per cent. in 1948–9 (Table 14).

**Table 1.** *Student numbers in 1923–4 and 1963–4*

NUMBER

| | Oxford | | | All universities in Great Britain except Oxford | | |
|---|---|---|---|---|---|---|
| | 1923–4 | 1963–4 | Column (2) as percentage of column (1) | 1923–4 | 1963–4 | Column (5) as percentage of column (4) |
| | (1) | (2) | (3) | (4) | (5) | (6) |
| Undergraduates | 3,709 | 7,118 | 192 | 29,840 | 95,781 | . |
| Postgraduates | 439 | 1,845 | 420 | 1,789 | 20,743 | . |
| Not classifiable | 15 | — | . | 7,100 | 958 | . |
| Men | 3,422 | 7,558 | 221 | 26,530 | 85,078 | 321 |
| Women | 741 | 1,405 | 190 | 12,199 | 32,404 | 266 |
| Arts | } 3,342 | 4,288 | } 176 | } 15,534 | 34,770 | } 313 |
| Social studies | | 1,601 | | | 13,870 | |
| Pure science | 536 | 2,363 | 441 | 7,011 | 31,952 | 456 |
| Applied science | 43 | 244 | 567 | 4,666 | 18,249 | 391 |
| Agriculture | 127 | 75 | 59 | 729 | 1,952 | 268 |
| Medicine | 115 | 392 | 341 | } 10,709 | 12,449 | } 156 |
| Dentistry | — | — | — | | 2,998 | |
| Veterinary science | — | — | — | | 1,242 | |
| Overseas students | 603 | 1,102 | 183 | 3,086 | 12,684 | 411 |
| All students | 4,163 | 8,963 | 215 | 38,729 | 117,482 | 303 |

Source: UGC Returns for 1923–4 and 1963–4; Registry.

NOTES

1. So far as possible the current definitions have been used in compiling the 1923–4 figures. But diploma students at universities other than Oxford and a few students at Oxford cannot be classified as undergraduates or postgraduates. Where percentages would be misleading for this reason, they are omitted.
2. For Oxford, in 1923–4, Part II chemists are included with undergraduates.
3. For Oxford, the distinction between science and medicine is not clear cut since medical students (concurrently with work for the First B.M.) read an Honour School, almost invariably in science, and usually Animal Physiology, before proceeding to work for the Second B.M. All candidates for the B.M. and postgraduates in medicine are included under medicine. All candidates for the Second B.M. are included with undergraduates, despite the fact that candidates for the Second B.M. have a first degree. This follows current UGC practice. See Table 13 for further details of medical students.
4. For 1923–4 the numbers are those in residence (in attendance at other universities) in the third term of the academic year. For 1963–4 they are of those in residence at any time during the academic year.
5. Institutions in receipt of grant through the UGC in 1963–4, but not in 1923–4, were the Universities of East Anglia, Essex, Hull, Keele, Kent, Lancaster, Leicester, Sussex, Warwick, and York, and (indirectly via University College, Cardiff) St. David's College, Lampeter. Of these the Universities of Essex, Kent, Lancaster, and Warwick were not yet generally open to students. The universities established since 1923–4 accounted for 5·1 per cent. of all full-time university students in 1963–4.
6. In 1923–4 there were 80 students at universities other than Oxford who cannot be classified by subject group.

**Table 2.** *The distribution of students in 1923–4 and 1963–4*

PERCENTAGE

| | Oxford | | All universities in Great Britain except Oxford | |
| --- | --- | --- | --- | --- |
| | 1923–4 | 1963–4 | 1923–4 | 1963–4 |
| Arts | } 80·3 | 47·8 | } 40·2 | 29·6 |
| Social studies | | 17·9 | | 11·8 |
| Pure science | 12·9 | 26·4 | 18·1 | 27·2 |
| Applied science | 1·0 | 2·7 | 12·1 | 15·5 |
| Agriculture | 3·1 | 0·8 | 1·9 | 1·7 |
| Medicine | 2·8 | 4·4 | } 27·7 | 10·6 |
| Dentistry | — | — | | 2·6 |
| Veterinary science | — | — | | 1·1 |
| All subjects | 100·0 | 100·0 | 100·0 | 100·0 |
| Postgraduates as percentage of undergraduates plus postgraduates | 10·6 | 20·6 | .. | 17·8 |
| Women as percentage of all students | 17·8 | 15·7 | 31·5 | 27·6 |
| Overseas students as percentage of all students | 14·5 | 12·3 | 8·0 | 10·8 |
| Oxford students as percentage of all university students in Great Britain | 9·7 | 7·1 | | |

SOURCE: Table 1.

4. Oxford has grown less rapidly than other universities, and the proportion of Oxford students among all university students has fallen from 9·7 per cent. to 7·1 per cent.

5. The fastest-growing subjects both at Oxford, and nationally, have been those comprising pure and applied science. In both these groups, the proportionate increase in relation to the over-all increase has been greater at Oxford than at other universities, and as a result the distribution of Oxford students between subject groups is now much closer to the distribution at other universities than in 1923–4. In fact, the proportion reading pure science at Oxford, 26·4 per cent., is almost the same as that elsewhere, 27·2 per cent. The concentration at Oxford on arts and social studies is balanced by the small proportions reading applied science and medicine.

6. Both at Oxford and at other universities the proportion of women students has fallen since 1923–4,[1] but the proportion at Oxford, 15·7 per cent. in 1963–4, is substantially less than the 27·6 per cent. at other universities.

7. In 1923–4, 14·5 per cent. of Oxford students came from overseas, against 8·0 per cent. at other universities. Since then, the proportion at Oxford has fallen, and that at other universities has risen, so that there is now little difference.

**Table 3.** *Income and staff of Oxford*

OXFORD

|  | 1920 | 1963–4 | Col. (2) as percentage of col. (1) |
|---|---|---|---|
|  | (1) | (2) | (3) |
| Income of University (£) | 260,000 | 6,328,000 | 2,433 |
| Income of colleges (£) | 565,000 | 4,168,000 | 738 |
| Total income (£) | 825,000 | 10,496,000 | 1,272 |
| University income as percentage of total | 31·5 | 60·3 | |
| Members of Congregation | 502 | 1,358 | 271 |
| Members of Congregation holding university posts | 166 | 986 | 594 |

SOURCE: 1920 income: Report of 1922 Royal Commission.
　　　　1963–4 income: Table I.
　　　　Members of Congregation: Registry.

NOTES

1. The details of Congregation relate to 1922 and 1962.
2. The income of colleges shown against 1963–4 is that for 1963.
3. Included as income of colleges are board and lodging and similar fees (except that for 1920 some of these fees cannot be included, so that the figures for the two dates are not strictly comparable). In 1963 they amounted to £1,832,000. If they are excluded, university income was 73 per cent. of total income.

## Income

8. Some idea of the change in the relative roles of the University and colleges can be obtained from Table 3. Between 1920 and 1963–4 the income of the University increased approximately twenty-fourfold (the income of other universities, except Cambridge, increased about thirtyfold

---

[1] But the proportion at both Oxford and other universities has been increasing since 1959–60.

in the same period). The income of the colleges increased only sevenfold, and the total income of Oxford increased thirteenfold. It is difficult to gauge how much of the increase in income has been necessary to keep pace with rising prices. But academic salaries account for approaching half the expenditure of universities, and the University Grants Committee Returns for 1923–4 give details of academic salaries in that year. The average salary of professors was £977 per annum; that of assistant professors, readers, and independent heads of departments was £582 per annum; and that of lecturers £444 per annum. This suggests that academic salaries (nationally, not necessarily at Oxford) have increased by a factor of $4\frac{1}{2}$–5, and that real expenditure in other universities increased about sixfold.

## Academic staff

9. Only an approximate measure of the change in the numbers of academic staff can be obtained, and the membership of Congregation provides the most convenient. As well as members of the academic staff, Congregation includes other members of the academic community such as heads of houses, and senior library, museum, and administrative staff. It also includes some who are not members of the academic community, but who are members by virtue of membership of a university board or committee. And some members of the academic staff will not be members either because they have not sufficient standing to qualify for the M.A. degree, or because they hold junior posts. The membership of Congregation has increased approximately $2\frac{3}{4}$ times and the academic staff must have increased by a similar factor.

10. Less than a third of the members of Congregation in 1922 held university posts, whereas in 1962–3 nearly three-quarters held at least a part-time university post.

## Colleges

11. Oxford has changed in other ways as well as in numbers of students and staff. The principal change in the collegiate structure has been the founding of the two graduate colleges, Nuffield and St. Antony's, and the establishment of three graduate societies, Linacre, St. Cross, and Iffley Colleges; the last two of which were established in 1965 and initially had senior members only. Among undergraduate societies, St. Peter's was established as a Permanent Private Hall in 1929 and achieved full college status in 1961, and three other Permanent Private Halls have been established since 1923–4. In addition, eight of the present undergraduate colleges have achieved full collegiate status since 1923–4. They are: Keble College; St. Edmund Hall; the five women's colleges, Lady Margaret Hall, and Somerville, St. Hugh's, St. Hilda's, and St. Anne's Colleges; and St. Catherine's College.

12. Other changes affecting the academic life of Oxford have been the increase in the number of faculties and departments, and of Honour Schools and of courses open to postgraduates.

## THE PRESENT ACADEMIC STRUCTURE OF OXFORD

13. There are three annual publications of the University which set out its constitution and academic structure. They are the *Statuta et Decreta Universitatis Oxoniensis* (referred to as *Statuta*) which gives the statutes (other than those regulating examinations) and some of the decrees currently in force; the *Examination Statutes* which give the statutes and regulations concerning examinations; and the *Oxford University Calendar* which gives, *inter alia*, details of university boards and committees, academic staff, university institutions, examination results, details of colleges and other societies and their members, and an alphabetical list of members of the University. In addition the *Oxford University Gazette* is published regularly through the academic year. It gives details of legislation before the University, and notices by faculty boards; professors, readers, and university lecturers; colleges and other societies; and other bodies. Published as supplements to the *Gazette* are examination entries and results, accounts, details of scholarships and prizes, the University's annual report, including an oration by the Vice-Chancellor, annual reports by other university bodies, statistics on student numbers, and other matters. In the following paragraphs some of the most important aspects of the academic structure in 1965–6 are set out.

14. In order to become a member of the University a person must become a member of a college or other society and be presented as a candidate for matriculation. All students reading for a degree, and almost all other students, must matriculate. It is possible to be a member of the academic staff without being a member of the University, but such a person could not be a member of a faculty[1] or of Congregation, the governing body of the University. In practice almost all members of the academic staff at the level of lecturer and above and many below that level are members of the University.

15. The colleges and other societies whose members may become members of the University comprise the colleges proper, the three new societies (which have power to admit postgraduates subject to regulation by the University), and the five Permanent Private Halls. The colleges proper comprise the traditional colleges (23 for men and 5 for women) which admit undergraduate and postgraduate students, two colleges for postgraduates, and All Souls College. The societies are:

---

[1] Here, and below, minor exceptions exist to the rules as set out. Reference should be made to the *Statuta* for full details.

*Men's colleges*

| | | |
|---|---|---|
| University College | Magdalen College | Pembroke College |
| Balliol College | Brasenose College | Worcester College |
| Merton College | Corpus Christi College | Hertford College |
| Exeter College | Christ Church | Keble College |
| Oriel College | Trinity College | St. Edmund Hall |
| Queen's College | St. John's College | St. Peter's College |
| New College | Jesus College | St. Catherine's College |
| Lincoln College | Wadham College | |

*Women's colleges*

Lady Margaret Hall
Somerville College
St. Hugh's College
St. Hilda's College
St. Anne's College

*Graduate colleges*

All Souls College
Nuffield College
St. Antony's College

*Other societies*

Linacre College
St. Cross College
Iffley College

*Permanent Private Halls*

Campion Hall
St. Benet's Hall
Mansfield College
Regent's Park College
Greyfriars

(Within each group, societies are shown in order of foundation.)

16. The principal governing body of the University is Congregation. Its membership is drawn from a wider body, Convocation, which comprises all holders of the Oxford degree of Master of Arts. Congregation consists of those members of the academic community who are members of Convocation.[1] There were 1,620 members at 31 December 1965. Members of the academic staff at the level of lecturer and above (and other members of the academic community) who are not Oxford graduates are on appointment granted an M.A. by decree (or by incorporation if graduates of Cambridge or Trinity College, Dublin) to qualify them for membership of Congregation and, where appropriate, of a faculty.

[1] Some other persons, such as external examiners and members of electoral boards (if Oxford M.A.s) are also members.

17. The studies of the University are organized in sixteen faculties. In order of creation they are:

Theology
Law
Medicine
Literae Humaniores
Modern History
English Language and Literature
Medieval and Modern European
    Languages and Literature other
    than English

Oriental Studies
Physical Sciences
Biological Sciences
Social Studies
Anthropology and Geography
Music
Agriculture and Forestry
Psychological Studies
Mathematics

The membership of a faculty consists mainly of teachers in the subject who are members of Convocation. All members of the academic staff who are members of Convocation are normally members of a faculty (some of more than one) except for some holders of junior posts. The administrative body in each faculty is the faculty board with (ordinarily) up to nineteen members.

18. There are two first degrees for which undergraduates may read: the Bachelor of Arts and the Bachelor of Medicine. The requirements for the B.A. are to keep residence for at least nine terms and to pass a First and Second Public Examination. (Or to keep six terms and to pass a Second Public Examination if a graduate of another university or in certain other circumstances.) Candidates for the B.M. are required to take a B.A. degree at Oxford. They are required to pass the First B.M. Examination, which also counts as a First Public Examination, and the Second B.M. Examination. In certain circumstances honours graduates of other universities who have passed an examination equivalent to the First B.M. can be admitted to read for the Second B.M.

19. The parts of the First Public Examination are five Honour Moderations (in which a class is awarded); Law Moderations; and fourteen Preliminary Examinations. Details are:

*Honour Moderations*

Greek and Latin Literature
Mathematics
Theology
Biochemistry
Physics, Mathematics, and Engineering Science

*Law Moderations*

*Preliminary Examinations*

Natural Science
Geography

Modern Languages
Modern History

English Language and Literature
Oriental Studies
Classical (Greek and Latin) Languages
Theology
Philosophy, Politics, and Economics

Music
Psychology, Philosophy, and Physiology
Physiology
Biology
Geology

20. The parts of the Second Public Examination are sixteen Honour Schools (in which a class is awarded) and the Pass School. The Honour Schools are:

Literae Humaniores
Mathematics
Natural Science
  Physics
  Chemistry
  Animal Physiology
  Zoology
  Botany
  Geology
  Engineering Science
  Biochemistry
  Metallurgy
Jurisprudence

Modern History
Theology
Oriental Studies
English Language and Literature
Modern Languages
Philosophy, Politics, and Economics
Geography
Agriculture
Forestry
Psychology, Philosophy, and Physiology
Music
Engineering Science and Economics

21. Postgraduates may read for a research degree, including the Doctorate of Philosophy; for an advanced degree by examination; or for a certificate or diploma. The degrees are described below in paras. 40–42. Details of the certificates and diplomas are given in the *Examination Statutes*.

THE DEVELOPMENT OF OXFORD 1923–4 TO 1964–5

## Students

22. In this section the changes in student numbers at Oxford outlined in the first section are analysed in more detail. Seven periods, at ten-year intervals except for the earliest and latest periods, are used to illustrate the long-term trends. But the trends have by no means been regular, particularly since 1948–9, and no particular significance attaches to the years chosen. Where there have been important changes which are not apparent from the long-term trends, they are noted.

23. The main statistical sources which are drawn on are, for universities other than Oxford, the University Grants Committee Returns; and for Oxford, the Registry records on which Oxford's returns to the UGC have been based, but which give more detail than is published by the UGC, and which in turn are based on returns made by the colleges and other societies to the University.

24. Tables 4 and 5 show that between 1923–4 and 1938–9 the number of

**Table 4.** *Student numbers at Oxford*

| OXFORD | 1923–4 | 1928–9 | 1938–9 | 1948–9 | 1958–9 | 1963–4 | 1964–5 | Percentage change | |
|---|---|---|---|---|---|---|---|---|---|
| | | | | | | | | 1958–9 to 1964–5 | 1963–4 to 1964–5 |
| Undergraduates | 3,709 | 4,116 | 4,391 | 6,159 | 7,436 | 7,118 | 7,297 | –2 | 2·5 |
| Postgraduates | 439 | 357 | 536 | 1,071 | 1,263 | 1,845 | 2,153 | 70 | 16·7 |
| Not classifiable | 15 | 86 | 96 | 64 | — | — | — | | |
| Arts | 3,342 | 3,797 | 4,090 | 5,460 | 6,325 | 4,288 | 4,395 | –3 | 2·5 |
| Social studies | | | | | | 1,601 | 1,747 | | 9·1 |
| Science | 706 | 652 | 701 | 1,480 | 2,072 | 2,682 | 2,882 | 39 | 7·5 |
| Medicine | 115 | 110 | 232 | 354 | 302 | 392 | 426 | 41 | 8·7 |
| Postgraduates in science | 63 | 47 | 142 | 343 | 369 | 684 | 790 | 114 | 15·5 |
| Men | 3,422 | 3,728 | 4,147 | 6,218 | 7,492 | 7,558 | 7,936 | 6 | 5·0 |
| Women | 741 | 831 | 876 | 1,076 | 1,207 | 1,405 | 1,514 | 25 | 7·8 |
| All students | 4,163 | 4,559 | 5,023 | 7,294 | 8,699 | 8,963 | 9,450 | 9 | 5·4 |

*(NUMBER)*

SOURCE: UGC Returns; Registry.

NOTES

1. Before 1954–5 those not reading for a degree or diploma cannot be classified as undergraduates or postgraduates.
2. In 1923–4, 1928–9, and 1938–9 Part II chemists are included with undergraduates.
3. Those reading for pass degrees, and those not reading for a degree or diploma are included in arts.
4. See Note 3 to Table I.
5. Because of adjustments to make figures for each period as comparable as possible, the figures in the table do not all agree with those published by the UGC.
6. For 1923–4 to 1948–9 the numbers are of those in residence in Trinity Term. For 1958–9 and later years the numbers are of those in residence at any time during the academic year. Despite this change in the figures (which took effect in 1950–1, and was the result of a change in the requirements of the UGC), it is believed that some college returns to the University, on which the numbers are based, continued to be made on the earlier definition after 1950–1.

students increased fairly slowly (by 21 per cent. over the period of 15 years), and that there was no great change in the balance of subjects.

25. By 1948–9 student numbers had increased to 45 per cent. above the 1938–9 figure; there was a marked increase to 15 per cent. in the proportion of postgraduates; and there was a substantial increase in the proportion of science students and a fall in the proportion reading arts and social studies.

**Table 5.** *The distribution of students at Oxford*

| OXFORD | | | | | | | PERCENTAGE |
|---|---|---|---|---|---|---|---|
| | 1923–4 | 1928–9 | 1938–9 | 1948–9 | 1958–9 | 1963–4 | 1964–5 |
| Undergraduates | 89 | 92 | 89 | 85 | 85 | 79 | 77 |
| Postgraduates | 11 | 8 | 11 | 15 | 15 | 21 | 23 |
| Arts | } 80 | 83 | 81 | 75 | 73 | 48 | 47 |
| Social studies | | | | | | 18 | 18 |
| Science | 17 | 14 | 14 | 20 | 24 | 30 | 30 |
| Medicine | 3 | 2 | 5 | 5 | 3 | 4 | 5 |
| Men | 82 | 82 | 83 | 85 | 86 | 84 | 84 |
| Women | 18 | 18 | 17 | 15 | 14 | 16 | 16 |
| All students | 100 | 100 | 100 | 100 | 100 | 100 | 100 |

SOURCE: Table 4.

26. Between 1948–9 and 1958–9 numbers grew by 19 per cent., but there was no great change in the distribution of students. Table 6 shows that the number of undergraduates reached a peak in 1949–50 and dropped thereafter, as the number of ex-service undergraduates decreased. But by 1954–5 undergraduate numbers were increasing, and there were very large increases in 1956–7 to 1958–9 as national service ended. Postgraduate numbers were around 1,100 until 1957–8, since which year they have increased steadily.

27. Between 1923–4 and 1958–9 there had been a gradual decline in the proportion of women students. It was in 1957 that the statutory limitation on the size of the women's colleges was removed, and since 1959–60 the proportion of women has increased. Table 7 gives details of student numbers in 1948–9, 1958–9, and the three most recent years showing men and women separately.

28. In the five years 1958–9 to 1963–4, total numbers increased very slowly (by 3 per cent.), but there were substantial changes in the distribution of students. Undergraduate numbers declined after the end of national service

**Table 6.** *Undergraduates and postgraduates by subject group 1948–9 to 1965–6*

OXFORD
NUMBER

| | Undergraduates | | | Postgraduates | | | All students | | |
|---|---|---|---|---|---|---|---|---|---|
| | Arts and social studies | Science and medicine | All subjects | Arts and social studies | Science and medicine | All subjects | Arts and social studies | Science and medicine | All subjects |
| 1948–9 | 4,679 | 1,480 | 6,159 | 717 | 354 | 1,071 | 5,460 | 1,834 | 7,294 |
| 1949–50 | 4,664 | 1,497 | 6,161 | 729 | 382 | 1,111 | 5,444 | 1,879 | 7,323 |
| 1950–1 | 4,505 | 1,463 | 5,968 | 755 | 379 | 1,134 | 5,365 | 1,842 | 7,207 |
| 1951–2 | 4,483 | 1,400 | 5,883 | 702 | 397 | 1,099 | 5,296 | 1,797 | 7,093 |
| 1952–3 | 4,400 | 1,292 | 5,692 | 683 | 409 | 1,092 | 5,177 | 1,701 | 6,878 |
| 1953–4 | 4,504 | 1,393 | 5,897 | 655 | 396 | 1,051 | 5,248 | 1,789 | 7,037 |
| 1954–5 | 4,655 | 1,424 | 6,079 | 707 | 401 | 1,108 | 5,362 | 1,825 | 7,187 |
| 1955–6 | 4,736 | 1,517 | 6,253 | 720 | 373 | 1,093 | 5,456 | 1,890 | 7,346 |
| 1956–7 | 4,942 | 1,608 | 6,550 | 785 | 373 | 1,158 | 5,727 | 1,981 | 7,708 |
| 1957–8 | 5,215 | 1,818 | 7,033 | 820 | 381 | 1,201 | 6,035 | 2,199 | 8,234 |
| 1958–9 | 5,471 | 1,965 | 7,436 | 854 | 409 | 1,263 | 6,325 | 2,374 | 8,699 |
| 1959–60 | **5,488** | 2,039 | 7,527 | 921 | 445 | 1,366 | **6,409** | 2,484 | 8,893 |
| 1960–1 | 5,383 | 2,056 | 7,439 | 988 | 548 | 1,536 | 6,371 | 2,604 | 8,975 |
| 1961–2 | 5,059 | 2,116 | 7,175 | 996 | 631 | 1,627 | 6,055 | 2,747 | 8,802 |
| 1962–3 | 4,844 | 2,191 | 7,035 | 1,031 | 723 | 1,754 | 5,875 | 2,914 | 8,789 |
| 1963–4 | 4,793 | 2,325 | 7,118 | 1,096 | 749 | 1,845 | 5,889 | 3,074 | 8,963 |
| 1964–5 | 4,850 | 2,447 | 7,297 | **1,292** | 861 | 2,153 | 6,142 | 3,308 | 9,450 |
| 1965–6 | 5,080 | **2,518** | **7,598** | 1,235 | **991** | **2,226** | 6,315 | **3,509** | **9,824** |

SOURCE: Registry.

NOTES
1. See Notes 1, 3–6 to Table 4.
2. For the years 1948–9 to 1953–4 the difference between the total of undergraduates and postgraduates, and the figure for all students is the number of students who cannot be classified as undergraduates or postgraduates.
3. The figures for 1965–6 are provisional, being based on the Michaelmas Term 1965 returns from colleges.
4. The maximum figure in each column is in bold type.

and the proportion of postgraduates reached 21 per cent. by 1963–4, when 30 per cent. of all students were reading science. The very large increase in the number of science postgraduates and the decline in the number of undergraduates[1] are the main explanations of the change in the subject balance.

29. Between 1963–4 and 1964–5 total numbers increased by 5·4 per cent., the largest percentage increase since 1958–9. Postgraduate numbers were up by 17 per cent. against 2·5 per cent. for undergraduates, and the proportion of postgraduates rose to 23 per cent. Students in social studies increased by 9 per cent., and those in science and medicine by 8 per cent.

**Table 7.** *Undergraduates and postgraduates by subject group and sex*

OXFORD                                                                                                    NUMBER

| | Arts and social studies | | | Science and medicine | | | All subjects | | |
|---|---|---|---|---|---|---|---|---|---|
| | Men | Women | All | Men | Women | All | Men | Women | All |
| **UNDERGRADUATES** | | | | | | | | | |
| 1948–9 | 3,909 | 770 | 4,679 | 1,318 | 162 | 1,480 | 5,227 | 932 | 6,159 |
| 1958–9 | 4,692 | 779 | 5,471 | 1,704 | 261 | 1,965 | 6,396 | 1,040 | 7,436 |
| 1963–4 | 3,960 | 833 | 4,793 | 1,997 | 328 | 2,325 | 5,957 | 1,161 | 7,118 |
| 1964–5 | 3,995 | 855 | 4,850 | 2,112 | 335 | 2,447 | 6,107 | 1,190 | 7,297 |
| 1965–6 | 4,168 | 912 | 5,080 | 2,152 | 366 | 2,518 | 6,320 | 1,278 | 7,598 |
| **POSTGRADUATES** | | | | | | | | | |
| 1948–9 | 609 | 108 | 717 | 320 | 34 | 354 | 929 | 142 | 1,071 |
| 1958–9 | 722 | 132 | 854 | 374 | 35 | 409 | 1,096 | 167 | 1,263 |
| 1963–4 | 904 | 192 | 1,096 | 697 | 52 | 749 | 1,601 | 244 | 1,845 |
| 1964–5 | 1,048 | 244 | 1,292 | 781 | 80 | 861 | 1,829 | 324 | 2,153 |
| 1965–6 | 983 | 252 | 1,235 | 893 | 98 | 991 | 1,876 | 350 | 2,226 |
| **ALL STUDENTS** | | | | | | | | | |
| 1948–9 | 4,580 | 880 | 5,460 | 1,638 | 196 | 1,834 | 6,218 | 1,076 | 7,294 |
| 1958–9 | 5,414 | 911 | 6,325 | 2,078 | 296 | 2,374 | 7,492 | 1,207 | 8,699 |
| 1963–4 | 4,864 | 1,025 | 5,889 | 2,694 | 380 | 3,074 | 7,558 | 1,405 | 8,963 |
| 1964–5 | 5,043 | 1,099 | 6,142 | 2,893 | 415 | 3,308 | 7,936 | 1,514 | 9,450 |
| 1965–6 | 5,151 | 1,164 | 6,315 | 3,045 | 464 | 3,509 | 8,196 | 1,628 | 9,824 |

SOURCE: Registry.
NOTE: See Notes 1–3 to Table 6.

30. Taking the period 1958–65, total numbers increased by 9 per cent. While undergraduate numbers declined slightly (by 2 per cent.), postgraduates increased by 70 per cent. Students in science and medicine increased by 39 per cent., while arts and social studies declined by 3 per cent. Separate figures are not available for arts and social studies up to 1958–9, but a comparison of 1959–60 with 1964–5 shows that (Table 8) the decline

[1] The proportion reading science subjects is lower among undergraduates than among postgraduates. See below, Tables 11 and 15.

in the proportion reading arts and social studies has been mainly at the expense of arts, and that the proportion for social studies has been increasing since 1962–3.

**Table 8.** *Social studies at Oxford*

OXFORD

|  | 1959–60 | 1960–1 | 1961–2 | 1962–3 | 1963–4 | 1964–5 |
|---|---|---|---|---|---|---|
| Number of students reading social studies | 1,736 | 1,721 | 1,648 | 1,530 | 1,601 | 1,747 |
| Students reading social studies as percentage of all students | 19·5 | 19·2 | 18·7 | 17·4 | 17·9 | 18·5 |

SOURCE: UGC Returns; Registry.

**Table 9.** *Percentage change in student numbers 1958–9 to 1963–4*

PERCENTAGE

| University | Undergraduates | Postgraduates | All students |
|---|---|---|---|
| Oxford | −4·3 | 46·1 | 3·0 |
| Cambridge | −2·4 | 44·8 | 3·7 |
| London | 6·5 | 40·1 | 14·1 |
| England, except Oxford | 21·7 | 53·0 | 27·2 |
| G.B., except Oxford | 23·8 | 52·5 | 28·4 |

SOURCE: Oxford: Table 4.
   Other universities: UGC Returns 1958–9 and 1963–4.

31. Table 9 compares the rates of growth for Oxford with those at Cambridge, London, other universities in England, and other universities in Great Britain. The percentage increase in postgraduate numbers at other universities generally was somewhat higher than at Oxford, but Cambridge showed about the same increase as Oxford, and London (which already had a very high proportion of postgraduates) had a smaller increase. Undergraduate numbers increased by less than postgraduates, and declined at Oxford and Cambridge.

## Undergraduates

32. Tables 10 and 11 give numbers and distributions of first-degree students (i.e. all undergraduates other than those taking Overseas Service Courses) by subject group and Honour School.[1] Table 11 shows a sharp fall in the proportion reading Literae Humaniores in 1948–9 (7·4 per cent.) compared

[1] Details for each year from 1951–2 to 1962–3 are given in *Gazette*, vol. xciv, pp. 306–7.

## Table 10. *Honour School of first-degree students*

OXFORD                                                                                    NUMBER

|  | 1923–4 | 1928–9 | 1938–9 | 1948–9 | 1958–9 | 1963–4 | 1964–5 |
|---|---|---|---|---|---|---|---|
| Literae Humaniores | 543 | 611 | 584 | 454 | 774 | 605 | 559 |
| Theology | 107 | 121 | 143 | 146 | 179 | 169 | 180 |
| Modern History | 849 | 889 | 869 | 1,148 | 1,150 | 930 | 939 |
| English | 412 | 393 | 360 | 722 | 700 | 690 | 685 |
| Modern Languages | 221 | 284 | 463 | 673 | 782 | 684 | 718 |
| Oriental Studies | 12 | 4 | 9 | 31 | 52 | 64 | 68 |
| Geography | . | . | 102 | 150 | 233 | 233 | 216 |
| Music | . | . | . | . | 48 | 71 | 80 |
| **Arts** | **2,144** | **2,302** | **2,530** | **3,324** | **3,918** | **3,446** | **3,445** |
| Jurisprudence | 382 | 509 | 464 | 535 | 703 | 535 | 581 |
| PPE | 178 | 350 | 495 | 798 | 751 | 740 | 761 |
| **Social studies** | **560** | **859** | **959** | **1,333** | **1,454** | **1,275** | **1,342** |
| Mathematics | 113 | 121 | 138 | 194 | 307 | 391 | 419 |
| Physics | 57 | 57 | 52 | 181 | 397 | 444 | 440 |
| Chemistry | 232 | 200 | 162 | 315 | 469 | 508 | 528 |
| Biochemistry | . | . | . | . | 50 | 83 | 74 |
| Physiology (other than B.M.) | 40 | 42 | 31 | 30 | 32 | 24 | 24 |
| Zoology | 19 | 28 | 33 | 53 | 78 | 119 | 105 |
| Botany | 17 | 18 | 19 | 28 | 35 | 41 | 54 |
| Geology | 12 | 6 | 7 | 43 | 61 | 38 | 27 |
| PPP | . | . | . | 34 | 56 | 97 | 137 |
| **Pure science** | **490** | **472** | **442** | **878** | **1,485** | **1,745** | **1,808** |
| Engineering Science | 43 | 33 | 40 | 79 | 141 | 174 | 190 |
| Engineering and Economics | . | . | . | . | . | 1 | 12 |
| Metallurgy | . | . | . | . | 6 | 31 | 34 |
| **Applied science** | **43** | **33** | **40** | **79** | **147** | **206** | **236** |
| Agriculture | 110 | 100 | 77 | 180 | 26 | 29 | 29 |
| Forestry | . | . | . | . | 45 | 18 | 19 |
| **Agriculture and forestry** | **110** | **100** | **77** | **180** | **71** | **47** | **48** |
| **Medicine (B.M.)** | **115** | **109** | **226** | **343** | **262** | **327** | **355** |
| **All Honours and B.M.** | **3,462** | **3,875** | **4,274** | **6,137** | **7,337** | **7,046** | **7,234** |
| **Pass School** | **247** | **241** | **117** | **22** | **33** | **32** | **33** |
| **All first-degree students** | **3,709** | **4,116** | **4,391** | **6,159** | **7,370** | **7,078** | **7,267** |

SOURCE: Registry.

NOTES

1. First degrees comprise B.A. and B.M. Only those reading an Honour School and the B.M. can be classified by subject.
2. In 1958–9 Metallurgy was called 'Science of Metals'.
3. See Notes 2 and 6 to Table 4.

## Table 11. *Honour School of first-degree students*

OXFORD                                                                                    PERCENTAGE

| | 1923–4 | 1928–9 | 1938–9 | 1948–9 | 1958–9 | 1963–4 | 1964–5 |
|---|---|---|---|---|---|---|---|
| Literae Humaniores | 14·6 | 14·8 | 13·3 | 7·4 | 10·5 | 8·5 | 7·7 |
| Theology | 2·9 | 2·9 | 3·3 | 2·4 | 2·4 | 2·4 | 2·5 |
| Modern History | 22·9 | 21·6 | 19·8 | 18·6 | 15·6 | 13·1 | 12·9 |
| English | 11·1 | 9·6 | 8·2 | 11·7 | 9·5 | 9·7 | 9·4 |
| Modern Languages | 5·9 | 6·9 | 10·5 | 10·9 | 10·6 | 9·7 | 9·9 |
| Oriental Studies | 0·3 | 0·1 | 0·2 | 0·5 | 0·7 | 0·9 | 0·9 |
| Geography | · | · | 2·3 | 2·4 | 3·2 | 3·3 | 3·0 |
| Music | · | · | · | · | 0·7 | 1·0 | 1·1 |
| | | | | | | | |
| Arts | 57·8 | 55·9 | 57·6 | 54·0 | 53·2 | 48·7 | 47·4 |
| | | | | | | | |
| Jurisprudence | 10·3 | 12·4 | 10·6 | 8·7 | 9·5 | 7·6 | 8·0 |
| PPE | 4·8 | 8·5 | 11·3 | 13·0 | 10·2 | 10·5 | 10·5 |
| | | | | | | | |
| Social studies | 15·1 | 20·9 | 21·8 | 21·6 | 19·7 | 18·0 | 18·5 |
| | | | | | | | |
| Mathematics | 3·0 | 2·9 | 3·1 | 3·1 | 4·2 | 5·5 | 5·8 |
| Physics | 1·5 | 1·4 | 1·2 | 2·9 | 5·4 | 6·3 | 6·1 |
| Chemistry | 6·3 | 4·9 | 3·7 | 5·1 | 6·4 | 7·2 | 7·3 |
| Biochemistry | · | · | · | · | 0·7 | 1·2 | 1·0 |
| Physiology (other than B.M.) | 1·1 | 1·0 | 0·7 | 0·5 | 0·4 | 0·3 | 0·3 |
| Zoology | 0·5 | 0·7 | 0·8 | 0·9 | 1·1 | 1·7 | 1·4 |
| Botany | 0·5 | 0·4 | 0·4 | 0·5 | 0·5 | 0·6 | 0·7 |
| Geology | 0·3 | 0·1 | 0·2 | 0·7 | 0·8 | 0·5 | 0·4 |
| PPP | · | · | · | 0·6 | 0·8 | 1·4 | 1·9 |
| | | | | | | | |
| Pure science | 13·2 | 11·5 | 10·1 | 14·3 | 20·1 | 24·7 | 24·9 |
| | | | | | | | |
| Engineering Science | 1·2 | 0·8 | 0·9 | 1·3 | 1·9 | 2·5 | 2·6 |
| Engineering and Economics | · | · | · | · | · | — | 0·2 |
| Metallurgy | · | · | · | · | 0·1 | 0·4 | 0·5 |
| | | | | | | | |
| Applied science | 1·2 | 0·8 | 0·9 | 1·3 | 2·0 | 2·9 | 3·2 |
| | | | | | | | |
| Agriculture | 3·0 | 2·4 | 1·8 | 2·9 | 0·4 | 0·4 | 0·4 |
| Forestry | · | · | · | · | 0·6 | 0·3 | 0·3 |
| | | | | | | | |
| Agriculture and forestry | 3·0 | 2·4 | 1·8 | 2·9 | 1·0 | 0·7 | 0·7 |
| | | | | | | | |
| Medicine (B.M.) | 3·1 | 2·6 | 5·1 | 5·6 | 3·6 | 4·6 | 4·9 |
| | | | | | | | |
| All Honours and B.M. | 93·3 | 94·1 | 97·3 | 99·6 | 99·6 | 99·5 | 99·5 |
| | | | | | | | |
| Pass School | 6·7 | 5·9 | 2·7 | 0·4 | 0·4 | 0·5 | 0·5 |
| | | | | | | | |
| All first-degree students | 100·0 | 100·0 | 100·0 | 100·0 | 100·0 | 100·0 | 100·0 |

SOURCE: Registry.

NOTE: See notes to Table 10.

with 1938–9 (13·3 per cent.). Since 1948–9 arts subjects whose share of undergraduates has increased are Oriental Studies and Geography. The swing to science subjects is strongest in the largest Honour Schools, Mathematics, Physics, and Chemistry, and in Zoology, the Honour School of Psychology, Philosophy, and Physiology (PPP), and the applied sciences. Those in Agriculture and Forestry have declined to little more than a quarter of the number in 1948–9.

33. There was a steady fall in the proportion reading for pass degrees up to 1948–9, since when it has been about 0·5 per cent.

34. The distribution by subject is different for men and women. Table 12 gives details for 1964–5. Subjects which are read by a relatively large proportion of women are English, Modern Languages, Mathematics, and the Biological Sciences. Those which are read by relatively few women are Theology, Oriental Studies, Jurisprudence, Physical Sciences, Geology, PPP, Applied Sciences, and Agriculture. The higher than average proportion of women reading Mathematics is not a freak for 1964–5, as the same held in 1948–9, 1958–9, and 1963–4.

35. Women formed 16 per cent. of all first-degree students in 1964–5. This is the same as their proportion of all students; there being little difference in the proportion of women for undergraduates and postgraduates. (For the latter the proportion was 15 per cent. in 1964–5.)

## Medical students

36. At Oxford medical students also read an Honour School (usually Animal Physiology) during the first three years of the course. In Tables 10 and 11 all such students are shown as undergraduates in medicine. Also shown under this head are students reading for the Second B.M. who will have already taken a first degree; this is in accordance with the practice of the UGC. Table 13 shows the various categories of medical student separately and also shows the actual size of the Animal Physiology School.

## Postgraduates

37. The effects of the changes in undergraduate and postgraduate numbers given in Table 9 on the proportion of all students who are postgraduates are set out in Table 14. London has the highest proportion of postgraduates (many of whom are in exclusively or predominantly postgraduate institutions), and this proportion reached 28 per cent. in 1963–4. The proportion at Oxford is slightly higher than at Cambridge, and, in 1963–4, than the average for all universities in England except Oxford. The proportion is lower for all universities in Great Britain than for universities in England. Figures for 1964–5 and 1965–6 are available for Oxford only. They show a

**Table 12.** *Honour School of first-degree students by sex, 1964–5*

OXFORD

| | Men | | Women | | Women as percentage of total |
|---|---|---|---|---|---|
| | Number | Percentage | Number | Percentage | |
| Literae Humaniores | 469 | 7·7 | 90 | 7·6 | 16 |
| Theology | 166 | 2·7 | 14 | 1·2 | 8 |
| Modern History | 768 | 12·6 | 171 | 14·4 | 18 |
| English | 472 | 7·8 | 213 | 17·9 | 31 |
| Modern Languages | 544 | 9·0 | 174 | 14·6 | 24 |
| Oriental Studies | 60 | 1·0 | 8 | 0·7 | 12 |
| Geography | 183 | 3·0 | 33 | 2·8 | 15 |
| Music | 70 | 1·2 | 10 | 0·8 | 13 |
| Arts | 2,732 | 45·0 | 713 | 60·0 | 21 |
| Jurisprudence | 547 | 9·0 | 34 | 2·9 | 6 |
| PPE | 654 | 10·8 | 107 | 9·0 | 14 |
| Social studies | 1,201 | 19·8 | 141 | 11·9 | 11 |
| Mathematics | 334 | 5·5 | 85 | 7·1 | 20 |
| Physics | 404 | 6·6 | 36 | 3·0 | 8 |
| Chemistry | 474 | 8·0 | 54 | 4·5 | 10 |
| Biochemistry | 60 | 1·0 | 14 | 1·2 | 19 |
| Physiology (other than B.M.) | 15 | 0·2 | 9 | 0·8 | 38 |
| Zoology | 67 | 1·1 | 38 | 3·2 | 36 |
| Botany | 36 | 0·6 | 18 | 1·5 | 33 |
| Geology | 25 | 0·4 | 2 | 0·2 | 7 |
| PPP | 124 | 2·0 | 13 | 1·1 | 9 |
| Pure science | 1,539 | 25·3 | 269 | 22·6 | 15 |
| Engineering Science | 190 | 3·1 | — | — | — |
| Engineering and Economics | 12 | 0·2 | — | — | — |
| Metallurgy | 34 | 0·6 | — | — | — |
| Applied science | 236 | 3·9 | — | — | — |
| Agriculture | 25 | 0·4 | 4 | 0·3 | 14 |
| Forestry | 19 | 0·3 | — | — | — |
| Agriculture and forestry | 44 | 0·7 | 4 | 0·3 | 8 |
| Medicine (B.M.) | 293 | 4·8 | 62 | 5·2 | 17 |
| All Honours and B.M. | 6,045 | 99·5 | 1,189 | 100·0 | 16 |
| Pass School | 33 | 0·5 | — | — | — |
| All first-degree students | 6,078 | 100·0 | 1,189 | 100·0 | 16 |

SOURCE: Registry.
NOTE: See notes to Table 10.

**Table 13.** *First-degree students in Animal Physiology and in Medicine*

OXFORD                                                                    NUMBER

|  | 1948–9 | 1958–9 | 1963–4 | 1964–5 |
|---|---|---|---|---|
| ANIMAL PHYSIOLOGY |  |  |  |  |
| B.M. students | 172 | 202 | 250 | 259 |
| Others | 30 | 32 | 24 | 24 |
| All Animal Physiology | 202 | 234 | 274 | 283 |
| MEDICINE—B.M. STUDENTS |  |  |  |  |
| Reading for Honour School | 188 | 206 | 229 | 260 |
| Taking courses in General Pathology, Bacteriology, and Pharmacology | .. | 53 | 69 | 50 |
| Reading for Second B.M. in the Clinical School | 45 | 42 | 60 | 63 |
| Average number of B.M. students (see Note 8) | .. | 275 | 324 | 348 |
| OTHER CLINICAL STUDENTS |  |  |  |  |
| Matriculated | 1 | 17 | 12 | 7 |
| Not matriculated | — | — | 5 | 8 |

SOURCE: Medical School; Registry.

NOTES

1. The numbers in Animal Physiology are those returned by colleges to the Registry.
2. The numbers in Medicine are based on the records of the Medical School, which keeps a Register of Medical Students; except that the figure for medical students reading for an Honour School in 1948–9 is that returned by colleges to the Registry.
3. Medical students take courses in General Pathology, Bacteriology, and Pharmacology during the first half of the academic year following their taking an Honour School. They then proceed either to the Oxford Clinical School, or to clinical schools in other universities.
4. There are two intakes to the Clinical School each year and the numbers consequently fluctuate during the year. The table gives the average for the four quarters of the academic year.
5. Shown against 'other clinical students' are students taking clinical courses in Oxford for a medical qualification of another university.
6. Oxford B.M. students taking clinical courses in other universities are not included.
7. The figures for B.M. students reading Animal Physiology and medical students reading for an Honour School in 1963–4 are not consistent. The explanation is presumably that colleges classified as B.M. students some undergraduates reading Animal Physiology who were not B.M. students.
8. The totals of the first-degree students shown in this table as reading for the B.M. do not agree with the figures in Table 10 for three reasons:
    (i) Because the two sets of figures were compiled in different ways. In particular the college returns do not distinguish B.M. students reading for Honour Schools other than Animal Physiology (and Chemistry in 1948–9); see also Note 7.
    (ii) Because there is double counting of those who take the six-month courses in General Pathology, Bacteriology, and Pharmacology and then enter the Clinical School. The line in the table giving the average number of B.M. students is calculated as those reading for an Honour School plus half those taking courses in General Pathology, Bacteriology, and Pharmacology, plus those reading for the Second B.M. in the Clinical School.
    (iii) Because Table 10 includes matriculated clinical students not reading for the B.M.

significant increase in the proportion between 1963–4 and 1964–5, but there was a very slight fall between 1964–5 and 1965–6.

38. Students taking a university teacher training course are included among postgraduates. They are not, however, doing advanced work in the subject of their first degrees. Some calculations for Oxford, London, and all universities in Great Britain except Oxford are therefore presented in Table 14 from which postgraduates in education are excluded.[1] The proportions are all reduced, but those for Oxford are reduced by less than for other universities.

39. The distribution of postgraduates by subject group is given in Table 15. Compared with undergraduates (Table 11) postgraduates are more concentrated in pure science, and over the past forty years the trend of the proportion in science has been strongly upward. It reached 37 per cent. in 1963–4 and 1964–5.[2]

40. Postgraduates may work for a research (thesis) degree, for an advanced degree involving an examination and perhaps the preparation of a thesis, or they may take an examination for an advanced diploma (or certificate).

41. The research degrees (apart from the higher doctorates) are, first, the D.Phil., involving a minimum of two years and in practice usually at least three years research. Candidates for the D.Phil. are known as Advanced Students. Secondly there is the B.Litt. (in arts) or B.Sc. (in science) which involves a minimum of one year and in practice usually at least two years research. Undergraduates reading Chemistry and Metallurgy take an examination (Part I) after three years on the result of which unclassified honours are awarded and the B.A. degree may be taken. They carry out a piece of research in the fourth year for Part II of the examination, and it is only after this has been examined that they are awarded a class on the results of both parts. Special arrangements exist whereby they may submit their Part II research for the B.Sc. degree and Part II candidates are classified as postgraduates.

42. The principal advanced degree not based solely on a thesis is the B.Phil. which was introduced in 1946. The B.Phil. can be taken in a number of arts and social studies subjects. It is awarded after an examination usually taken after two years. A short thesis is obligatory in most subjects and optional in the others. Three other degrees in particular subjects are included in advanced courses. They are the B.C.L. in Law, the B.D. in

[1] They are excluded from both the number of postgraduates and the total number of students on which the percentages are based. It is likely that some who are excluded were, in fact, doing advanced work.
[2] There was in fact a slight fall in the proportion in 1964–5. This may be an effect of the increasing popularity of the B.Phil., which is not available in science subjects.

**Table 14.** *Postgraduates as percentage of all students*

PERCENTAGE

|  | 1948–9 | 1958–9 | 1963–4 | 1964–5 | 1965–6 |
|---|---|---|---|---|---|
| **INCLUDING EDUCATION** | | | | | |
| Oxford | 14·8 | 14·5 | 20·6 | 22·8 | 22·7 |
| Cambridge | .. | 14·3 | 19·8 | .. | .. |
| London | 16·0 | 22·8 | 28·0 | .. | .. |
| England, excluding Oxford | 12·3 | 16·4 | 19·8 | .. | .. |
| G.B., excluding Oxford | 10·0 | 15·0 | 17·8 | .. | .. |
| **EXCLUDING EDUCATION** | | | | | |
| Oxford | 12·6 | 12·9 | 18·7 | 21·0 | .. |
| London | 13·0 | 19·1 | 25·1 | .. | .. |
| G.B., excluding Oxford | 7·6 | 11·4 | 14·5 | .. | .. |

SOURCE: Oxford: Registry and Table 4.
Other universities: UGC Returns

NOTES
1. Those who cannot be classified as undergraduates or postgraduates have been excluded.
2. Postgraduates in Education have been excluded from the calculations for the lower panel of the table. Details of those excluded are as follows:
Oxford: Matriculated students taking the Diploma in Education for teacher training.
London: Students at the Institute of Education.
G.B.: Advanced students in Education, as in Table 7 of UGC Returns (1958–9 and 1963–4); students taking teacher-training courses (1948–9) (but some such students in Scotland could not be excluded).
3. The figure for Oxford in 1965–6 is provisional, being based on the Michaelmas Term 1965 returns from colleges.

**Table 15.** *Subjects studied by postgraduates*

OXFORD                                                                    PERCENTAGE

|  | 1928–9 | 1938–9 | 1948–9 | 1958–9 | 1963–4 | 1964–5 |
|---|---|---|---|---|---|---|
| Arts ⎫ | 86·6 | 72·4 | 66·9 | 67·6 | 41·7 | 41·2 |
| Social studies ⎭ | | | | | 17·7 | 18·8 |
| Pure science | 11·8 | 23·5 | 28·5 | 25·1 | 33·5 | 31·9 |
| Applied science | — | 1·3 | 0·5 | 1·0 | 2·1 | 3·0 |
| Agriculture | 1·4 | 1·7 | 3·1 | 3·1 | 1·5 | 1·8 |
| Medicine | 0·3 | 1·1 | 1·0 | 3·2 | 3·5 | 3·3 |
| All subjects | 100·0 | 100·0 | 100·0 | 100·0 | 100·0 | 100·0 |
| *Number* | *357* | *536* | *1,071* | *1,263* | *1,845* | *2,153* |

SOURCE: Registry.

NOTE: See notes to Table 4.

Theology, and the B.Mus. in Music. The B.C.L. is an examination degree, the B.D. involves a thesis and a qualifying examination (from which some candidates may be dispensed). The B.Mus. is open to Oxford graduates with a first- or second-class degree in Music, and involves an examination and a musical composition.

**Table 16.** *Course taken by postgraduates*

OXFORD                                                                          PERCENTAGE

| | 1923–4 | 1928–9 | 1938–9 | 1948–9 | 1958–9 | 1963–4 | 1964–5 |
|---|---|---|---|---|---|---|---|
| D.Phil. | 12·1 | 15·1 | 22·6 | 34·2 | .. | 39·8 | 36·1 |
| B.Litt. | 22·6 | 18·2 | 18·3 | 21·5 | .. | 20·9 | 21·4 |
| B.Sc. (with Part II) | .. | .. | .. | 5·8 | 7·1 | 6·8 | 7·4 |
| B.Sc. (other) | 10·5 | 7·0 | 14·0 | 4·1 | .. | 4·5 | 4·2 |
| All research degrees | 45·1 | 40·3 | 54·9 | 65·5 | 72·8 | 72·0 | 69·1 |
| B.C.L. | 6·4 | 10·9 | 4·7 | 3·6 | .. | 0·8 | 0·9 |
| B.D. | 1·6 | 0·6 | 0·7 | 0·4 | .. | 0·1 | 0·2 |
| B.Mus. | 3·4 | 3·6 | 3·0 | 3·3 | .. | 0·2 | 0·2 |
| B.Phil. | · | · | · | 4·1 | .. | 6·6 | 8·9 |
| All advanced courses | 11·4 | 15·1 | 8·4 | 11·4 | 6·1 | 7·6 | 10·2 |
| Diploma in Education | 13·4 | 27·2 | 22·6 | 17·1 | 12·7 | 11·3 | 10·2 |
| Other diplomas | 30·1 | 17·4 | 14·2 | 6·0 | 6·2 | 7·2 | 8·9 |
| No degree or diploma | .. | .. | .. | .. | 2·1 | 1·8 | 1·7 |
| All postgraduates | 100·0 | 100·0 | 100·0 | 100·0 | 100·0 | 100·0 | 100·0 |
| *Number* | *439* | *357* | *536* | *1,071* | *1,263* | *1,845* | *2,153* |

SOURCE: Registry.

NOTES

1. See notes to Table 4.
2. For the years in which the number reading for Part II Chemistry or not reading for any degree or diploma cannot be determined, the percentages are based on the number of postgraduates excluding these categories.

43. Table 16 sets out the distribution of postgraduates according to the course taken. It should be noted that (except for most diplomas and the B.C.L., B.D., and B.Mus.), though a student is at any time registered as a candidate for one or other of the degrees, and is included under this degree in the statistics, all would-be D.Phil. candidates in arts and social studies and some in science are not admitted initially to this status. They become Probationer B.Litt. or B.Sc. candidates and subsequently transfer if their work is satisfactory. Table 16 therefore understates the proportion of postgraduates who may be aiming at a D.Phil.

44. The proportion of postgraduates working for research degrees increased very considerably between the twenties and 1958–9. Since then it has declined somewhat as the B.Phil. has become established and popular. Among the research degrees, the D.Phil. appears to have increased in popularity relative to the B.Litt. and B.Sc. But for the reasons given in the previous paragraph, the results in Table 16 may reflect changes in practice by faculty boards as well as genuine changes in the proportions taking each degree.

45. There is a marked difference between the proportion of men and of women working for the D.Phil. In 1964–5, 39 per cent. of men postgraduates were working for the D.Phil. For women the figure was 19 per cent.

**Table 17.** *Overseas students 1964–5*

OXFORD                                                                    PERCENTAGE

| | Overseas students from | | | All overseas students | *Number* | Percentage of total | Overseas students as percentage of all students |
| | Common-wealth | U.S.A. | Other countries | | | | |
|---|---|---|---|---|---|---|---|
| Undergraduates | 47 | 33 | 19 | 100 | *430* | 40·4 | 5·9 |
| Postgraduates | 48 | 28 | 24 | 100 | *634* | 59·6 | 29·4 |
| Arts | 45 | 41 | 14 | 100 | *402* | 37·8 | 9·1 |
| Social studies | 45 | 28 | 27 | 100 | *390* | 36·7 | 22·3 |
| Science | 57 | 18 | 25 | 100 | *225* | 21·1 | 7·8 |
| Medicine | 47 | 19 | 34 | 100 | *47* | 4·4 | 11·0 |
| All overseas students | 48 | 30 | 22 | 100 | *1,064* | 100·0 | 11·3 |

SOURCE: Registry.

NOTE: This table relates to the number of overseas students at 31 October 1964.

## Overseas students

46. In 1964–5, 11 per cent. of students were from overseas. Nearly half the overseas students were from Commonwealth countries, and a further 30 per cent. were from the U.S.A. (Table 17). The proportion from the Commonwealth was highest in science, and that from the U.S.A. was highest in arts. 60 per cent. of overseas students were postgraduates; 29 per cent. of all postgraduates being from overseas.

## Non-matriculated students

47. In order to matriculate, and thus become a member of the University, a student must be a member of a college or other society. Only matriculated students may take a degree, but certain diplomas are open to specific classes

of non-matriculated students (as well as to matriculated students) and in addition non-matriculated students working for medical qualifications of other universities may be accepted to take the course in Clinical Medicine. Details for 1964–5 are given in Table 18. Elsewhere in this Appendix, unless specified to the contrary, non-matriculated students are excluded. Rather more than half the non-matriculated students were at Ruskin College and Plater College (formerly Catholic Workers' College) which are not constituent societies of the University, and which make their own provision for much of the teaching for their students.

**Table 18.** *Non-matriculated students 1964–5*

OXFORD                                                                    NUMBER

| Course for which non-matriculated students may be accepted | Number of non-matriculated students | | |
| --- | --- | --- | --- |
| | Men | Women | All |
| Diploma in Philology (Professor of Comparative Philology) | — | — | — |
| Certificate in Fine Art (Ruskin School of Drawing and Fine Art) | 10 | 38 | 48 |
| Diploma in Education (Department of Education) | 21 | 40 | 61 |
| Diploma in Economics and Political Science (Ruskin College and Plater College) | 124 | 7 | 131 |
| Diploma in Public and Social Administration (Department of Social and Administrative Studies) | 5 | 10 | 15 |
| (Ruskin College and Plater College) | 10 | 17 | 27 |
| Diplomas in Human Biology, Prehistoric Archaeology, Ethnology, and Social Anthropology (Institute of Social Anthropology) | — | — | — |
| Diploma in Forestry (Department of Forestry) | 4 | — | 4 |
| Clinical Medicine (Clinical Medical School) | 5 | 3 | 8 |
| All non-matriculated students | 179 | 115 | 294 |

SOURCE: Registry.

NOTE: The department or institution to which the students are attached is shown in brackets.

## Financial assistance for students

48. The great majority of students in 1964–5 received some form of financial assistance other than from their family, relatives, or friends (Tables 19 and 20). Among undergraduates, 94 per cent. had some assistance, 29 per cent. having a college award (usually supplemented by the state), and 50 per cent. having a Local Education Authority award. For 82 per cent. the amount of the award was £75 and over per annum, while 12 per cent.

**Table 19.** *Type of financial assistance for students 1964–5*

OXFORD                                                                                              PERCENTAGE

| Source of financial assistance | Undergraduates | | | Postgraduates | | |
|---|---|---|---|---|---|---|
| | Men | Women | All | Men | Women | All |
| A college scholarship or exhibition and a State Scholarship or LEA award | 28·4 | 20·2 | 27·1 | 3·3 | 1·9 | 3·1 |
| A college scholarship or exhibition | 1·8 | 0·9 | 1·6 | 3·0 | 2·2 | 2·8 |
| A Local Education Authority award | 48·4 | 55·7 | 49·6 | 13·3 | 14·5 | 13·5 |
| A State Scholarship | 8·4 | 15·8 | 9·6 | 4·2 | 1·2 | 3·8 |
| A State Studentship | — | — | — | 14·0 | 18·5 | 14·7 |
| A DSIR Studentship | — | — | — | 13·8 | 8·6 | 13·0 |
| Any other type of award or grant (other than contributions from family, relatives, or friends) | 6·9 | 2·4 | 6·2 | 34·3 | 25·9 | 33·0 |
| No assistance (other than from family, relatives, or friends) | 6·0 | 5·0 | 5·9 | 14·2 | 27·2 | 16·1 |
| All in residence | 100·0 | 100·0 | 100·0 | 100·0 | 100·0 | 100·0 |
| *Number in residence* | *6,107* | *1,190* | *7,297* | *1,829* | *324* | *2,153* |

SOURCE: *Gazette*, No. 3259, of 9 December 1965, pp. 419–20.

NOTE: A student is included once only, in the highest appropriate category.

**Table 20.** *Amount of financial assistance for students 1964–5*

OXFORD                                                                                              PERCENTAGE

| Amount of financial assistance (other than from family, relatives, or friends) (£ per annum) | Undergraduates | | | Postgraduates | | | All students | | |
|---|---|---|---|---|---|---|---|---|---|
| | Men | Women | All | Men | Women | All | Men | Women | All |
| None | 6·0 | 5·0 | 5·9 | 14·2 | 27·2 | 16·1 | 7·9 | 9·8 | 8·2 |
| 10 or less | 0·9 | 0·3 | 0·8 | 1·7 | 0·3 | 1·5 | 1·1 | 0·3 | 1·0 |
| Over 10 but less than 75 | 12·0 | 9·4 | 11·6 | 8·6 | 2·2 | 7·6 | 11·2 | 7·9 | 10·7 |
| 75 and over | 81·1 | 85·2 | 81·7 | 75·6 | 70·4 | 74·8 | 79·8 | 82·0 | 80·1 |
| All in residence | 100·0 | 100·0 | 100·0 | 100·0 | 100·0 | 100·0 | 100·0 | 100·0 | 100·0 |
| *Number in residence* | *6,107* | *1,190* | *7,297* | *1,829* | *324* | *2,153* | *7,936* | *1,514* | *9,450* |

SOURCE: *Gazette*, No. 3259, of 9 December 1965, pp. 419–20.

received between £10 and £75. The proportion of postgraduates receiving assistance was somewhat less (84 per cent.). Local Education Awards, State Studentships, and DSIR Studentships each accounted for 13–15 per cent. College awards accounted for a further 6 per cent. and there was a large residual category (33 per cent.) consisting largely of students from overseas holding awards made by governments and other institutions in their home countries.

## Colleges

49. As has been stated above, St. Peter's and the graduate societies are the only additions to the societies of Oxford since 1923–4,[1] and the main change affecting undergraduate societies has been that the societies which were not full colleges in 1923–4 have now achieved that status. It follows that student numbers per college must have increased considerably. No reliable data which give students in residence by college are available for the pre-war period. Table 21 gives a summary of student numbers by college groups since 1948–9. Table 22 gives details of student numbers, and the proportion of postgraduates, by colleges for 1948–9 and later years. The percentage change in numbers shows that since 1958–9 larger increases have been made by the less well-endowed colleges, and especially by the women's colleges. Nine men's colleges reduced their numbers. Of the increase of 890 in postgraduates, 221, or 25 per cent., were taken by the graduate societies. Linacre College, which was established in 1962, accounts for most of these.

50. Nearly all the undergraduate colleges have increased the proportion of postgraduates among their students since 1958–9. The undergraduate societies with the highest proportions (over 23 per cent.) in 1964–5 were Balliol, Jesus, Merton, New College, St. Catherine's, St. John's, Wadham, Greyfriars, Mansfield, and Somerville.

51. An approximate measure of the number of college fellows is given in Table 23. It is approximate because the published *Calendar* cannot be completely up to date, and because of difficulty in interpreting some entries in the *Calendar*, especially for the earlier years.[2]

52. The number of fellows at the undergraduate colleges has rather more than doubled since 1926. Over the same period the number of students has increased in about the same proportion. The proportional increase in fellows was rather higher at the women's colleges than at the men's.

---

[1] Except that the number of Permanent Private Halls has increased from two to five.
[2] It is likely that the number of fellows is understated. For instance, the total number of tutorial fellows for 1964–5 is given in the table as 497, whereas the number reported by the colleges at 1 January 1965 is 506. To a certain extent this is because of late elections which may have been exceptionally numerous in 1964–5 when colleges appointed an unusual number of non-fellows holding university posts during the course of the year.

**Table 21.** *Student numbers by college group, sex, and whether undergraduates or postgraduates*

OXFORD                                                                                                          NUMBER

| | Men's societies | | | Women's colleges | | | Graduate societies | | |
|---|---|---|---|---|---|---|---|---|---|
| | Under-graduates | Post-graduates | All students | Under-graduates | Post-graduates | All students | Men | Women | All students |
| 1948–9 | 5,258 | 960 | 6,218 | 933 | 143 | 1,076 | · | · | · |
| 1958–9 | 6,394 | 1,011 | 7,405 | 1,040 | 167 | 1,207 | 87 | — | 87 |
| 1963–4 | 5,934 | 1,391 | 7,325 | 1,155 | 211 | 1,366 | 233 | 39 | 272 |
| 1964–5 | 6,090 | 1,590 | 7,680 | 1,190 | 272 | 1,462 | 256 | 52 | 308 |
| 1965–6 | 6,303 | 1,664 | 7,967 | 1,278 | 293 | 1,571 | 229 | 57 | 286 |

SOURCE: Registry.

NOTES

1. Undergraduates included under graduate societies are as follows:

    1958–9    2 men
    1963–4    23 men, 6 women
    1964–5    17 men
    1965–6    17 men

2. For 1948–9 students who cannot be classified as undergraduates and postgraduates have been divided equally between the two categories.
3. See Notes 1 and 3 to Table 6.

**Table 22.** *Students by college*

OXFORD

| | 1948–9 | | 1958–9 | | 1963–4 | | 1964–5 | | Percentage change in numbers 1958–9 to 1964–5 |
|---|---|---|---|---|---|---|---|---|---|
| | No. of students | Post-graduates as percentage of all students | No. of students | Post-graduates as percentage of all students | No. of students | Post-graduates as percentage of all students | No. of students | Post-graduates as percentage of all students | |
| Balliol | 350 | 15·7 | 436 | 17·7 | 410 | 22·4 | 415 | 28·7 | −4·8 |
| Brasenose | 356 | 16·5 | 354 | 11·6 | 336 | 21·1 | 348 | 22·7 | −1·7 |
| Christ Church | 337 | 12·9 | 454 | 8·4 | 429 | 11·9 | 429 | 12·1 | −5·5 |
| Corpus Christi | 135 | 3·8 | 183 | 9·3 | 192 | 16·7 | 202 | 18·8 | 10·4 |
| Exeter | 305 | 17·8 | 312 | 12·2 | 292 | 17·5 | 309 | 19·7 | −1·0 |
| Hertford | 175 | 11·4 | 178 | 7·9 | 196 | 8·7 | 210 | 15·7 | 18·0 |
| Jesus | 266 | 20·0 | 266 | 18·8 | 278 | 23·4 | 295 | 26·1 | 10·9 |
| Keble | 290 | 13·7 | 360 | 9·7 | 366 | 13·4 | 380 | 16·1 | 5·6 |
| Lincoln | 268 | 20·2 | 305 | 11·8 | 246 | 19·5 | 271 | 20·7 | −11·1 |
| Magdalen | 340 | 16·3 | 441 | 15·9 | 366 | 23·2 | 376 | 22·6 | −14·7 |
| Merton | 237 | 18·5 | 292 | 17·5 | 271 | 28·4 | 279 | 24·7 | −4·5 |
| New College | 390 | 16·4 | 398 | 9·8 | 398 | 21·9 | 426 | 23·2 | 7·0 |
| Oriel | 260 | 17·0 | 263 | 13·3 | 251 | 18·7 | 266 | 17·7 | 1·1 |
| Pembroke | 159 | 10·1 | 245 | 7·3 | 311 | 19·9 | 318 | 16·4 | 29·8 |
| Queen's | 289 | 16·5 | 329 | 10·6 | 304 | 17·4 | 314 | 21·7 | −4·6 |
| St. Catherine's | 344 | 26·0 | 360 | 27·5 | 371 | 20·5 | 415 | 24·3 | 15·3 |
| St. Edmund Hall | 229 | 14·8 | 348 | 9·5 | 386 | 19·9 | 382 | 21·7 | 9·8 |
| St. John's | 218 | 11·5 | 295 | 13·9 | 309 | 24·3 | 313 | 24·3 | 6·1 |
| St. Peter's | 133 | 11·5 | 234 | 11·5 | 257 | 16·7 | 278 | 19·4 | 18·8 |
| Trinity | 270 | 5·3 | 241 | 15·4 | 220 | 14·5 | 225 | 14·7 | −6·6 |
| University | 281 | 17·2 | 338 | 14·5 | 322 | 17·1 | 361 | 15·5 | 6·8 |
| Wadham | 336 | 12·3 | 329 | 23·1 | 311 | 20·9 | 335 | 27·2 | 1·8 |
| Worcester | 212 | 4·3 | 291 | 6·5 | 327 | 15·9 | 334 | 16·8 | 14·8 |
| Men's colleges | 6,180 | 15·1 | 7,252 | 13·4 | 7,149 | 19·1 | 7,481 | 20·7 | 3·2 |

[continued

# Table 22 (continued). Students by college

OXFORD

| | 1948–9 | | 1958–9 | | 1963–4 | | 1964–5 | | Percentage change in numbers 1958–9 to 1964–5 |
|---|---|---|---|---|---|---|---|---|---|
| | No. of students | Post-graduates as percentage of all students | No. of students | Post-graduates as percentage of all students | No. of students | Post-graduates as percentage of all students | No. of students | Post-graduates as percentage of all students | |
| Campion Hall | 30 | 21·4 | 52 | 13·5 | 41 | 19·5 | 45 | 22·2 | –13·5 |
| Greyfriars | · | · | 13 | 15·4 | 20 | 25·0 | 16 | 31·3 | 23·1 |
| Mansfield | · | · | 39 | 35·9 | 54 | 16·7 | 73 | 26·0 | 87·2 |
| Regent's Park | · | · | 27 | 37·0 | 43 | 14·0 | 44 | 18·2 | 63·0 |
| St. Benet's Hall | 8 | — | 22 | 13·6 | 18 | 5·6 | 21 | 9·5 | –4·5 |
| Permanent Private Halls | 38 | 16·7 | 153 | 23·5 | 176 | 16·5 | 199 | 22·1 | 30·1 |
| Men's societies | 6,218 | 15·1 | 7,405 | 13·7 | 7,325 | 19·0 | 7,680 | 20·7 | 3·7 |
| Lady Margaret Hall | 226 | 17·3 | 239 | 12·6 | 292 | 16·1 | 304 | 21·1 | 27·2 |
| St. Anne's | 277 | 11·6 | 277 | 11·9 | 297 | 15·8 | 309 | 16·5 | 11·6 |
| St. Hilda's | 185 | 17·3 | 229 | 15·3 | 259 | 10·4 | 282 | 13·1 | 23·1 |
| St. Hugh's | 167 | 7·2 | 208 | 8·7 | 254 | 17·3 | 283 | 17·3 | 36·1 |
| Somerville | 221 | 12·3 | 254 | 20·1 | 264 | 17·4 | 284 | 25·0 | 11·8 |
| Women's colleges | 1,076 | 13·2 | 1,207 | 13·8 | 1,366 | 15·4 | 1,462 | 18·6 | 21·1 |
| All undergraduate societies | 7,294 | 14·8 | 8,612 | 13·7 | 8,691 | 18·4 | 9,142 | 20·4 | 6·2 |
| Linacre | · | · | · | · | 178 | 84·3 | 195 | 91·3 | · |
| Nuffield | · | · | 35 | 100·0 | 41 | 100·0 | 49 | 100·0 | 40·0 |
| St. Antony's | · | · | 52 | 96·2 | 53 | 98·1 | 64 | 100·0 | 23·1 |
| Graduate societies | · | · | 87 | 97·7 | 272 | 89·3 | 308 | 94·5 | 254·0 |
| All societies | 7,294 | 14·8 | 8,699 | 14·5 | 8,963 | 20·6 | 9,450 | 22·8 | 8·6 |

SOURCE: Registry.

NOTES

1. For 1948–9 students not reading for a degree or diploma are excluded from the calculation of postgraduates as a percentage of all students.
2. Nuffield College did not matriculate its students until 1958 when it received its Charter of Incorporation. For 1948–9, therefore, students at Nuffield are included under the college through which they were matriculated. They were about 14 in number.

## Table 23. *College fellows*

OXFORD                                                                                                    NUMBER

| | 1925–6 All fellows on academic staff | 1948–9 Tutorial fellows | 1948–9 All fellows on academic staff | 1958–9 Tutorial fellows | 1958–9 All fellows on academic staff | 1964–5 Tutorial fellows | 1964–5 All fellows on academic staff |
|---|---|---|---|---|---|---|---|
| Balliol | 17 | 19 | 25 | 22 | 32 | 27 | 45 |
| Brasenose | 14 | 11 | 18 | 13 | 21 | 15 | 22 |
| Christ Church | 27 | 17 | 30 | 24 | 34 | 26 | 39 |
| Corpus Christi | 10 | 5 | 13 | 9 | 14 | 12 | 19 |
| Exeter | 10 | 8 | 12 | 12 | 17 | 15 | 20 |
| Hertford | 10 | 6 | 8 | 7 | 10 | 12 | 16 |
| Jesus | 10 | 11 | 13 | 12 | 16 | 19 | 25 |
| Keble | 8 | 9 | 10 | 13 | 14 | 17 | 20 |
| Lincoln | 7 | 7 | 16 | 11 | 17 | 15 | 22 |
| Magdalen | 28 | 20 | 39 | 22 | 40 | 26 | 46 |
| Merton | 18 | 8 | 18 | 15 | 25 | 17 | 29 |
| New College | 26 | 14 | 27 | 15 | 28 | 20 | 35 |
| Oriel | 14 | 11 | 17 | 12 | 17 | 16 | 23 |
| Pembroke | 4 | 6 | 8 | 10 | 14 | 14 | 18 |
| Queen's | 20 | 11 | 21 | 21 | 30 | 23 | 34 |
| St. Catherine's | 11 | 8 | 8 | 10 | 10 | 19 | 29 |
| St. Edmund Hall | 3 | 3 | 3 | 12 | 13 | 17 | 20 |
| St. John's | 15 | 12 | 19 | 14 | 19 | 20 | 33 |
| St. Peter's | . | 4 | 4 | 6 | 6 | 11 | 16 |
| Trinity | 10 | 10 | 12 | 11 | 16 | 13 | 21 |
| University | 14 | 10 | 16 | 13 | 21 | 19 | 29 |
| Wadham | 9 | 7 | 10 | 12 | 15 | 16 | 21 |
| Worcester | 6 | 8 | 10 | 10 | 14 | 19 | 25 |
| Men's colleges | 291 | 225 | 357 | 306 | 443 | 408 | 607 |
| Lady Margaret Hall | 8 | 7 | 10 | 11 | 15 | 14 | 21 |
| St. Anne's | 12 | 8 | 8 | 12 | 12 | 16 | 19 |
| St. Hilda's | 5 | 8 | 10 | 7 | 9 | 13 | 19 |
| St. Hugh's | 9 | 8 | 10 | 11 | 14 | 14 | 18 |
| Somerville | 10 | 8 | 11 | 13 | 18 | 13 | 24 |
| Women's colleges | 44 | 39 | 49 | 54 | 68 | 70 | 101 |
| All Souls | 25 | — | .. | — | .. | — | 40 |
| Nuffield | . | 8 | 15 | 9 | 25 | 11 | 32 |
| St. Antony's | . | . | . | 3 | 19 | 8 | 29 |
| All colleges | 360 | 272 | .. | 372 | .. | 497 | 809 |

SOURCE: *Calendar.*

NOTES

1. The table is based on counts of names published in the *Calendar*, and should be regarded as approximate only. Besides the fact that some fellows are appointed too late to be included in the *Calendar* for their first year, the arrangement of the entries, and the terminology used, vary from college to college. It is therefore likely that complete consistency has not been achieved.
2. Fellows who are described as 'tutor' or 'lecturer' or the equivalent are counted as tutorial fellows; except that senior research fellows and supernumerary fellows also holding lecturerships are not included.
3. Some colleges which had not achieved that status at the earlier dates did not have fellows as such (e.g. St. Catherine's Society). In such cases the tutors and lecturers listed in the *Calendar* have been counted as fellows.

53. Since 1948–9 the number of fellows has increased by 70 per cent. at the men's colleges, and by 106 per cent. at the women's colleges. The corresponding percentages for tutorial fellows are 81 and 79 respectively. Over this period the number of students at the colleges has increased by 21 per cent. for men and by 36 per cent. for women.

54. Thus the number of tutorial fellows has increased faster than the number of students since 1948–9.[1] How this is reflected in a reduction in the number of students per tutorial fellow is shown in Table 24.

55. The only other university with a collegiate structure similar to Oxford's is Cambridge. But Cambridge is a slightly larger university with fewer colleges, and thus the colleges on average are larger. Including both fellows and students, no Oxford college is larger than 500 persons, whereas a quarter of Cambridge colleges are above that size, and two have over 700 persons. The median total size is about 325 for Oxford, and about 430 for Cambridge. Similar differences exist in terms of undergraduates, and of all students, as can be seen from Table 25.

## Accommodation in colleges for students

56. In 1964–5 half of the men students and over two-thirds of the women lived in college or in a college hostel (Table 26). Separate figures for undergraduates and postgraduates are not available, but the proportion of undergraduates living in college is almost certain to be higher than for postgraduates. The policy of about two-thirds of the men's colleges is to give undergraduates two years in college, while the remainder usually give half their undergraduates one year and half two years in college. Where a choice has to be made, nearly all colleges give preference to scholars and exhibitioners, and then to secretaries of the main clubs; and preference against those who fail Preliminary Examinations. The women's colleges give nearly all their undergraduates three years in college. At least half the colleges try to give unmarried postgraduates (other than those who were undergraduates at the college) rooms in college for a year.

57. The proportion of students in college is lower than it was pre-war, though it is higher than in 1948–9. But because the proportion of postgraduates has increased, it does not follow that the average time that undergraduates can expect to spend in college is lower than it was pre-war.

58. The forms of college accommodation for students are shown in Table 27. In 1965 there were 5,100 accommodation units, providing for

[1] The number of undergraduates was high in 1948–9 because of the influx of ex-servicemen.

**Table 24.** *Students per tutorial fellow by colleges*

| OXFORD | 1948–9 | 1958–9 | RATIO 1964–5 |
|---|---|---|---|
| Balliol | 18 | 20 | 15 |
| Brasenose | 32 | 27 | 23 |
| Christ Church | 20 | 19 | 17 |
| Corpus Christi | 27 | 20 | 17 |
| Exeter | 38 | 26 | 21 |
| Hertford | 29 | 25 | 18 |
| Jesus | 24 | 22 | 16 |
| Keble | 32 | 28 | 22 |
| Lincoln | 38 | 28 | 18 |
| Magdalen | 17 | 20 | 14 |
| Merton | 30 | 19 | 16 |
| New College | 28 | 27 | 21 |
| Oriel | 24 | 22 | 17 |
| Pembroke | 27 | 25 | 23 |
| Queen's | 26 | 16 | 14 |
| St. Catherine's | 43 | 36 | 22 |
| St. Edmund Hall | 76 | 29 | 22 |
| St. John's | 18 | 21 | 16 |
| St. Peter's | 33 | 39 | 25 |
| Trinity | 27 | 22 | 17 |
| University | 28 | 26 | 19 |
| Wadham | 48 | 27 | 21 |
| Worcester | 27 | 29 | 18 |
| Men's colleges | 27 | 24 | 18 |
| Lady Margaret Hall | 32 | 22 | 22 |
| St. Anne's | 35 | 23 | 19 |
| St. Hilda's | 23 | 33 | 22 |
| St. Hugh's | 21 | 19 | 20 |
| Somerville | 28 | 20 | 22 |
| Women's colleges | 28 | 22 | 21 |
| All undergraduate colleges | 28 | 23 | 19 |
| Nuffield | 2 | 4 | 4 |
| St. Antony's | . | 17 | 8 |
| Graduate colleges | 2 | 7 | 6 |
| All colleges | 27 | 23 | 18 |

SOURCE: Tables 22 and 23.

NOTE: The figure for Nuffield in 1948–9 is based on the number of students (14) listed in the *Calendar* for 1949. These students are also included under the colleges through which they had matriculated.

**Table 25.** *The size of Oxford and Cambridge colleges, 1963–4. Undergraduate colleges*

NUMBER

| | Oxford | | | Cambridge | | |
|---|---|---|---|---|---|---|
| | Under-graduates | All students | Fellows and students | Under-graduates | All students | Fellows and students |
| Under 200 | 5 | 2 | — | 3 | 1 | 1 |
| 200–49 | 11 | 2 | 3 | 1 | 1 | — |
| 250–99 | 7 | 10 | 7 | 6 | 2 | 2 |
| 300–49 | 4 | 7 | 9 | 6 | 3 | 2 |
| 350–99 | 1 | 5 | 3 | 5 | 6 | 5 |
| 400–49 | — | 2 | 4 | — | 4 | 4 |
| 450–99 | — | — | 2 | — | 3 | 3 |
| 500–99 | — | — | — | 1 | 1 | 4 |
| 600–99 | — | — | — | 1 | 1 | — |
| 700–99 | — | — | — | — | — | 1 |
| 800–99 | — | — | — | — | 1 | — |
| 900–99 | — | — | — | — | — | 1 |
| All | 28 | 28 | 28 | 23 | 23 | 23 |

SOURCE: Oxford:  Students from college returns to the University.
Fellows from *Calendar*.
Cambridge: *Commonwealth Universities Year Book 1965*.

**Table 26.** *Accommodation for students in colleges*

OXFORD                                    PERCENTAGE

| Year | Students in college or college hostels as percentage of all students | | |
|---|---|---|---|
| | Men | Women | All students |
| 1923–4 | 57·9 | 52·4 | 56·9 |
| 1928–9 | 56·0 | 67·4 | 58·1 |
| 1938–9 | 57·9 | 74·4 | 60·8 |
| 1948–9 | 47·5 | 57·3 | 49·0 |
| 1958–9 | 46·2 | 71·7 | 49·7 |
| 1963–4 | 52·8 | 72·7 | 55·9 |
| 1964–5 | 50·4 | 69·7 | 53·5 |

SOURCE: Registry (1964–5); UGC Returns (other years).

nearly 5,400 students. 56 per cent. of the units were bedsitters, and 37 per cent. were two-room sets. In the men's colleges, 43 per cent. were bedsitters, and 49 per cent. were two-room sets.

59. In the period 1955–65, 1,661 units of accommodation for students were brought into use by colleges.[1] The net increase was less than this since much of the accommodation was brought into use by conversions. Of the accommodation brought into use, 85 per cent. was in the form of bedsitters. 14 per cent. of the units were primarily for postgraduates. New building accounted for 996 of the units (60 per cent. of the total). The largest single item was the new St. Catherine's College which provided 285 bedsitters.

## Academic staff

60. The structure of the academic staff is more complicated than at other universities (except perhaps for Cambridge) because of the existence of both university and college teaching posts. It is described in detail in Part V.

61. There are full-time university posts similar to those in other universities.[2] And there are college teaching posts which comprise tutorial fellowships and college lecturerships.[3] Most members of the academic staff (80 per cent.) hold both a university and a college post. The main teaching duties attached to the university posts are lecturing and (where appropriate) demonstrating. Those attaching to college posts are the tutorial teaching and general academic welfare of undergraduates. The supervision of postgraduates on behalf of the University is not part of the formal duties of holders of university or college posts, and separate payment is made for such supervision. But holders of college posts may have responsibility for postgraduates within their college, and this is an important duty of official fellows at Nuffield and St. Antony's.

62. In addition to teaching posts, both the University and colleges have a number of research posts.

63. In 1922 most members of the academic staff held either a university post, or a college post, but not both. There were, however, 5 readers and 35 lecturers and equivalent holding fellowships. Since then, there has grown up a system of part-time university posts which are held in conjunction with college tutorial posts. The CUF lecturership is the chief example of such posts, but others are faculty lecturerships and special lecturerships.

[1] In addition the University has built Summertown House which provides 132 flats for postgraduates.
[2] Except that there is no grade of senior lecturer, and to compensate for this the lecturer scale has three increments above the national scale.
[3] That is, lecturerships with which no fellowship is associated.

Table 27. *Student accommodation, 1965*

OXFORD                                                                          NUMBER

| Type of accommodation | Accommodation provided by | | | | | | |
| --- | --- | --- | --- | --- | --- | --- | --- |
| | Men's colleges | Permanent Private Halls | Men's societies | Women's colleges | All undergraduate societies | Graduate societies | All societies |
| In college | 3,250 | 165 | 3,415 | 945 | 4,360 | 31 | 4,391 |
| In *aedes annexae* and in other buildings | 478 | 7 | 485 | 130 | 615 | 94 | 709 |
| Bedsitters | 1,609 | 130 | 1,739 | 1,074 | 2,813 | 58 | 2,871 |
| Three-room sets for two students | 281 | 2 | 283 | — | 283 | — | 283 |
| Two-room sets | 1,828 | 40 | 1,868 | 1 | 1,869 | 43 | 1,912 |
| Flats | 10 | — | 10 | — | 10 | 24 | 34 |
| All units | 3,728 | 172 | 3,900 | 1,075 | 4,975 | 125 | 5,100 |

SOURCE: Colleges.

NOTE: The figures give the number of accommodation units, *not* the number of students who can be accommodated. The latter is greater by the number of three-room sets for two students.

## Table 28. Student accommodation which came into use 1955–65

OXFORD    NUMBER

| | Accommodation provided by | | | | | | |
|---|---|---|---|---|---|---|---|
| | Men's colleges | Permanent Private Halls | Men's societies | Women's colleges | All under-graduate societies | Graduate societies | All societies |
| *Bedsitters brought into use 1955–65 by:* | | | | | | | |
| Conversion of double sets | 257 | — | 257 | — | 257 | — | 257 |
| Other conversions | 207 | 8 | 215 | 77 | 292 | 28 | 320 |
| New building | 612 | 33 | 645 | 176 | 821 | 7 | 828 |
| *Three-room sets for two students brought into use 1955–65 by:* | | | | | | | |
| Conversion of double sets | 15 | — | 15 | — | 15 | — | 15 |
| Other conversions | 14 | — | 14 | — | 14 | — | 14 |
| *Two-room sets brought into use 1955–65 by:* | | | | | | | |
| Conversions | 35 | — | 35 | — | 35 | 6 | 41 |
| New building | 94 | 38 | 132 | — | 132 | 26 | 158 |
| *Flats brought into use 1955–65 by:* | | | | | | | |
| Conversions | 10 | — | 10 | — | 10 | 8 | 18 |
| New building | — | — | — | — | — | 10 | 10 |
| *Accommodation brought into use 1955–65 primarily for postgraduates:* | | | | | | | |
| Bedsitters | 84 | — | 84 | 31 | 115 | 35 | 150 |
| Three-room sets for two students | 4 | — | 4 | — | 4 | — | 4 |
| Two-room sets | 17 | — | 17 | — | 17 | 32 | 49 |
| Flats | 10 | — | 10 | — | 10 | 18 | 28 |
| All accommodation brought into use 1955–65 primarily for postgraduates | 115 | — | 115 | 31 | 146 | 85 | 231 |
| All student accommodation brought into use 1955–65 | 1,244 | 79 | 1,323 | 253 | 1,576 | 85 | 1,661 |

SOURCE: Colleges.

NOTE: See note to Table 27.

As a result, the proportion of the academic staff holding no university post decreased from over half in 1922 to 14 per cent. in 1964–5. If teaching staff only are included, the proportion in 1964–5 is 6 per cent. and at least half those with no university post are new appointees who may expect to receive one within one or two years of appointment. Thus the proportion of teachers with no university post in 1964–5 was insignificant. Although details are not available for earlier years, much the same probably applies to 1958–9 but not to 1948–9 or earlier.[1]

**Table 29.** *Academic staff*

OXFORD                                                                   NUMBER

|  | 1922 | 1938–9 | 1948–9 | 1958–9 | 1964–5 |
|---|---|---|---|---|---|
| Professors | 66 | 74 | 84 | 93 | 104 |
| Readers and equivalent | 11 | 9 | 46 | 82 | 84 |
| Lecturers and equivalent | 64 | } | 136 | 275 | 332 |
| Part-time lecturers holding college teaching posts | — | 421 | 152 | 314 | 350 |
| Other full-time university academic staff | 2 | } | 155 | 78 | 103 |
| College tutorial fellows not holding a university post | 214 | .. | .. | .. | 43 |
| Other college academic staff not holding a university post | .. | .. | .. | .. | 111 |
| All university staff | 143 | 504 | 573 | 842 | 973 |
| All academic staff | 357 | .. | .. | .. | 1,127 |

SOURCE

1922: An analysis of the membership of Congregation using university records and the *Calendar*.

1938–9, 1948–9, 1958–9: Staff returns made to the UGC and university records of part-time lecturers.

1964–5: Table 235.

NOTES

1. The figures for different years are not all comparable. Those for professors and readers should be comparable; so should those for lecturers except for 1938–9. The figures for part-time lecturers in 1948–9 and 1964–5 are reasonably comparable in coverage but a smaller proportion of tutorial fellows held such posts in 1948–9 than in 1964–5. The figure for 1958–9 includes only CUF lecturers. There were no such part-time posts in 1922, while the number in 1938–9 cannot be shown separately.
2. Canon professors are included among professors.
3. In 1948–9, eight senior lecturers are included among readers.
4. Holders of posts financed by outside grants are not included unless another qualifying post is held.

[1] To compile figures for earlier years would have involved the laborious collation of several sets of records. This has not been attempted, but an approximate method based on membership of Congregation has been applied to 1922.

64. It should be noted that there is a distinct contrast between posts in arts and social studies and in science subjects. In the former most posts are college tutorships (held with part-time lecturerships in more recent years) or professorships. In science subjects most teachers hold university posts, many in conjunction with a college post. The usual arrangement is for a full-time university post to be held with a 'part-time' college post which involves a lighter college teaching load than applies to tutors in arts subjects.

65. Table 29 presents some details of the academic staff. Full-time members of the academic staff holding a university post (full-time or part-time) increased over threefold between 1922 and 1938–9. Between 1948–9 and 1958–9 the increase was 47 per cent., and in the six years since 1958–9 it was 16 per cent., but in the latter period most of the growth represented a net expansion of the academic staff of Oxford, whereas in the earlier period part of the expansion in university posts represents the appointment of existing college tutors to CUF lecturerships. (There were 107 CUF lecturers in 1948–9 and 271 in 1958–9.)

66. The estimate of the total academic staff of Oxford for 1922 is 357; it is likely to be a slight underestimate as members of Congregation (who must be M.A.s) only are included, and some younger staff may not have achieved that status. By 1964–5 the total had grown to 1,127, a threefold increase.

FUTURE STUDENT NUMBERS

### Undergraduates

67. Most of the evidence on future student numbers presented to the Commission envisaged a fairly static number of undergraduates, except for an increase in the number of women. The Commission endorses this position with the qualification that the number of undergraduates in applied science and clinical medicine should increase, and that there should be some increase in social studies and pure science probably at the expense of arts subjects. The number of undergraduates in 1964–5 was 7,300 and provisional figures for 1965–6 show a rise to 7,600. If the number reading applied science and clinical medicine increases by 400, and the number of women by 700, the total might be expected to grow to 8,500–9,000 in 15 to 20 years, of whom nearly a quarter would be women.

### Postgraduates

68. Two approaches to the forecasting of postgraduate numbers suggest that over the next 15 years present trends might lead to an increase to about 3,500.

69. One is based on the statistics in the Robbins Report.[1] First, the output of graduates from Oxford and Cambridge might be taken at their present

---

[1] We are grateful to Professor C. A. Moser and Mr. P. R. G. Layard for the analysis in paras. 69–75.

level, while the output of graduates from other universities in Great Britain is forecast to increase by a factor of 2·2 by 1980.[1] The number of post-graduates coming from overseas is highly problematical, but it is assumed that overseas postgraduates will form a constant proportion of all post-graduates at Oxford.

70. Secondly, the proportion of graduates going on to postgraduate work must be estimated. This is about 20 per cent. and does not vary much between the university groups distinguished in the Robbins Report. It has increased from 18·4 per cent. in 1958 to 21·3 per cent. in 1962, and the increase has affected all the major subject groups.[2] Partly on this evidence and partly because it was thought to be intrinsically desirable the Robbins Committee recommended a figure of 30 per cent. for 1980, and this could be assumed to affect all universities alike.

71. Finally, the proportion of postgraduates going to Oxford must be estimated. The statistics produced by the Robbins Committee did not distinguish between Oxford and Cambridge, and what applies to the two universities together has been assumed to apply to them separately.

72. Of all postgraduates in Great Britain in 1961–2 who had graduated from Oxford or Cambridge, 61 per cent. were studying at the university from which they graduated and 5 per cent. had transferred to the 'other place' (Oxford or Cambridge as appropriate). In addition, 3·5 per cent. of post-graduates who had graduated at other universities in Great Britain were studying at Oxford or Cambridge. Taking account of the numbers at differ-ent university groups it follows that the percentage of postgraduates at Oxford and Cambridge in 1961–2 who graduated from the relevant uni-versity groups was as follows:

| | |
|---|---|
| Same university | 51 |
| The 'other place' | 4 |
| Another university in Great Britain | 12 |
| Overseas | 33 |
| Total | 100 |

73. If it is assumed that the output of graduates from Oxford and Cam-bridge will not increase materially, but that the national trend for a larger proportion of graduates to go on to postgraduate work is followed, there will be an increase by a factor of 1·5 from graduates of Oxford and Cam-bridge.

74. The output of graduates from other universities may rise by a factor of 2·2, and the proportion staying on as postgraduates may rise by a factor

[1] Robbins Report, Appendix One, Annex Table Z. 1. This table relates to all universities in Great Britain, but for present purposes it is necessary to distinguish Oxford and Cambridge.
[2] Robbins Report, Appendix Two (A), pp. 51 and 304.

of 1·5. Assuming that the same proportion go to Oxford as in 1961–2 the supply from this source will grow by a factor of $2·2 \times 1·5 = 3·3$.

75. Thus the number of home postgraduates at Oxford would rise by a weighted average which is equal to a factor of 1·8. Assuming that the proportion of overseas postgraduates remains the same, the factor of 1·8 would apply to all postgraduates. Applied to the 1963–4 number of postgraduates this would give some 3,300 in 1980. This projection rests on many assumptions which cannot be tested, and should not be taken as more than an order of magnitude of what might result from current trends and the projection by the Robbins Committee of undergraduate numbers in 1980.

76. The second approach consisted in asking the representatives of each faculty board to forecast likely numbers when they gave oral evidence to the Commission.[1] The answers are obviously no more than an assessment of probabilities, but in total they amounted to about 3,500 distributed roughly thus:[2]

| | |
|---|---:|
| Arts | 1,200 |
| Social studies | 650 |
| Science | 1,500 |
| Medicine | 150 |
| Total | 3,500 |

77. These estimates are therefore comparable. The Commission recommends that deliberate attempts should be made to develop postgraduate studies, and recommends that a doubling of the present figure to 4,000–4,500 (including Recognized Students) in 1980–5 should be planned for. Included in this total would be 700 women—double the present figure. Given that the number of undergraduates is recommended to increase by over 1,000 rather than remain static, and that the time span is 15–20 years, the figure of 4,000–4,500 (including 500 or so Recognized Students not taking advanced courses) is broadly in line with the analysis in paras. 69–75.

## Implications of the projected student numbers

78. In round figures, numbers in 1965–6 and those projected for 1980–5 are:

| | 1965–6 | 1980–5 |
|---|---|---|
| Undergraduates | 7,600 | 8,750 |
| Postgraduates | 2,200 | 4,250 |
| All students | 9,800 | 13,000 |

and of the increase, some 1,050 would be women (700 undergraduates and 350 postgraduates). To avoid the danger of colleges growing too big the Commission considers the founding of a new undergraduate college, either for women or mixed, may be necessary over the next 15–20 years.

[1] See Oral Evidence, Part 45, pp. 13–16; Part 46, pp. 21–24; Part 47, pp. 28–29; Part 48, pp. 24–26; Part 50, pp. 31–33; Part 53, pp. 28–29.
[2] Certain students (such as those in Education) for whom faculty boards are not directly responsible are included in the figures.

79. Over-all, the proportion of postgraduates would rise from 23 per cent. to 33 per cent. However, the postgraduate societies (including St. Cross and Iffley) would account for some 1,100 assuming 300 at each of the new societies.[1] A further 500 included under postgraduates would be Recognized Students without college membership. This would give, say, 2,650 postgraduates at the traditional societies, i.e. 23 per cent. of all their students. The proportion would be higher in the men's societies and lower in the women's colleges. In 1964–5 the proportion of postgraduates at the traditional societies was 20 per cent. and for eight colleges it was over 23 per cent.

80. There would be over 10,000 men students altogether. Allowing for the postgraduate societies and the Recognized Students, the men's societies would have about 9,000 students. This is just over 1,000 more than in 1965–6, or an average of about 40 extra students for each of the men's colleges (assuming a small increase at the Permanent Private Halls). This would include 25–30 postgraduates and 10–15 undergraduates. The average number of students at the men's colleges would be about 375.

81. Postgraduates at the graduate societies would include up to 200 women (against 60 in 1965–6) if the proportion of women at these societies is to be similar to that among all postgraduates. The five existing women's colleges and the proposed undergraduate college would therefore have a total of about 2,400 students. This would lead to an average size for the six colleges of about 400 students.

82. The recommendations would thus not lead to excessive numbers or a substantial change in the balance of undergraduates and postgraduates in the traditional colleges.

[1] The Principal of Linacre College considers 250–350 as the optimum size for his own society. See *Oral Evidence*, Part 67, p. 6.

# PART II

---

# UNDERGRADUATE ADMISSIONS

---

83. Admissions of undergraduates are made by individual colleges, and the University has not accumulated detailed records about them. But each undergraduate must matriculate in his first term to become a member of the University, and must complete a matriculation form. The analyses given below of those entering before October 1965 are based on the matriculation forms.[1]

84. In 1961 the Universities Central Council on Admissions (UCCA) was set up to co-ordinate admissions to universities nationally. Oxford co-operated with the scheme which was subsequently implemented, and for admissions for 1966–7 has joined the scheme. Partly as a result of the establishment of UCCA, the men's colleges set up the Oxford Colleges Admissions Office in 1962 to facilitate co-operation with UCCA and reorganize admissions to Oxford. This has led to much more complete information about Oxford admissions of men becoming available, and many of the recent data presented below have been supplied by the Admissions Office.

85. Both the pattern of admissions and current procedures are different for men and for women. Accordingly, most of the analyses are given separately for men and women.

### MATRICULATIONS 1938–9 TO 1964–5[2]

86. Matriculations have been analysed where possible by the type of school or university previously attended; whether a holder of a college entrance award (scholarship or exhibition), or a commoner; home address;[3] and the proposed course of study. Only matriculants intending to read for a first degree have been included.[4]

---

[1] Except for Table 43 on entrants in October 1964.

[2] In some of the tables, figures for 1965–6 are included. They are not completely comparable with those for earlier years, being derived from the admissions competition. See below, paras. 103 ff.

[3] 'Home address' is the term used, but the address recorded on matriculation forms has been the address of parent or guardian.

[4] Postgraduates who come to Oxford from another university and members of the staff who do not have an Oxford degree also matriculate.

87. Schools are classified as independent, direct-grant, or maintained according to their status in the year in question.[1] Independent schools are subdivided into independent boarding and independent day schools according to whether the majority of pupils were boarders or day pupils. In some tables a further distinction is made for independent and direct-grant schools according to whether or not the headmaster was a member of the Headmasters' Conference. Overseas schools, schools which did not fit any of the categories or which could not be identified, and other institutions such as technical colleges or Ruskin College, or private tuition are included in a category termed 'Other schools'. In some tables this is divided into 'Other U.K. schools' and 'Overseas schools'.

88. Home address has been grouped in eight regions; seven for United Kingdom, and one for overseas.[2]

## Award holders

89. Table 30 shows undergraduate entrants classified by status as award holders or commoners entering from schools, or as graduates of U.K. or other universities.

90. The proportion of award holders is higher among men than among women. Among men it has increased from under one-quarter in 1923–4 to over one-third in 1964–5. Among women it has remained a little under one-fifth. The proportion of overseas graduates is also higher for men than for women, but is lower in 1958–9 and 1964–5 than earlier.

[1] Direct-grant schools include grant-aided schools in Scotland. Maintained schools include voluntary aided, voluntary controlled and transitionally assisted schools. The basic sources of information for classifying schools were the annual *Register of Members* of the Incorporated Association of Head Masters for the appropriate years. The contemporary edition of *Whitaker's Almanack* was used to obtain the members of the Headmasters' Conference. Some schools were not listed in the IAHM *Register of Members* and where adequate contemporary information was lacking the information available at the closest point in time to the date concerned was used. Some changes in classification of schools took place. For example, there were about seventeen schools not in the Headmasters' Conference in 1948 which were members in 1963 and nineteen which were members in 1948 but not in 1963. For 1964–5 and 1965–6, information from the Department of Education and Science and the *Education Authorities Directory and Annual 1964* were also used.

[2] The regions in the U.K. are defined as follows:
*Scotland*
*North:* Cumberland, Durham, Isle of Man, Lancashire, Northumberland, Westmorland, Yorkshire.
*Midlands:* Cheshire, Derbyshire, Herefordshire, Leicestershire, Lincolnshire, Nottinghamshire, Rutland, Shropshire, Staffordshire, Warwickshire, Worcestershire.
*Wales:* Wales and Monmouthshire.
*South-east:* Bedfordshire, Berkshire, Buckinghamshire, Cambridgeshire, Channel Islands, Essex, Hampshire and Isle of Wight, Hertfordshire, Huntingdonshire, Kent, London, Middlesex, Norfolk, Northamptonshire, Oxfordshire, Suffolk, Surrey, Sussex.
*South-west:* Cornwall, Devonshire, Dorset, Gloucestershire, Somerset, Wiltshire.
*Northern Ireland*

**Table 30.** *Status as award holder, commoner, or graduate by sex. Entrants to read for first degrees*

| OXFORD | | | | | PERCENTAGE |
|---|---|---|---|---|---|
| | | 1938–9 | 1948–9 | 1958–9 | 1964–5 |
| Men | Award holders | 23·7 | 16·9 | 31·2 | 34·3 |
| | Commoners | 62·3 | 63·2 | 62·9 | 57·8 |
| | U.K. universities | 4·0 | 6·1 | 0·8 | 1·4 |
| | Other universities | 10·0 | 13·8 | 5·1 | 6·5 |
| | All men | 100·0 | 100·0 | 100·0 | 100·0 |
| | *Number* | *1,436* | *1,847* | *2,185* | *2,051* |
| Women | Award holders | 17·7 | 19·7 | 20·0 | 17·8 |
| | Commoners | 73·8 | 71·7 | 75·6 | 76·9 |
| | U.K. universities | 3·2 | 4·0 | 1·2 | 1·7 |
| | Other universities | 5·3 | 4·6 | 3·2 | 3·6 |
| | All women | 100·0 | 100·0 | 100·0 | 100·0 |
| | *Number* | *282* | *325* | *340* | *411* |
| Men and women | Award holders | 22·7 | 17·3 | 29·7 | 31·6 |
| | Commoners | 64·2 | 64·5 | 64·6 | 61·0 |
| | U.K. universities | 3·8 | 5·8 | 0·9 | 1·5 |
| | Other universities | 9·3 | 12·4 | 4·8 | 6·0 |
| | All entrants | 100·0 | 100·0 | 100·0 | 100·0 |
| | *Number* | *1,718* | *2,172* | *2,525* | *2,462* |

SOURCE: Matriculation forms.

NOTE: The figures for award holders and commoners exclude those entrants who held a degree at time of matriculation. The latter are shown separately under U.K. universities and other universities. It is unlikely that many graduate entrants held awards, but accurate figures cannot be obtained as some holders of Rhodes Scholarships, etc., have been recorded as award holders on matriculation forms.

## Type of school

91. Entrants from schools are classified by type of school in Tables 31 and 32. For both men and women the proportion from independent schools has fallen over time, while that from both direct-grant and maintained schools has increased. An exception to the trend is 1948–9 for men, when the proportion from maintained schools was just higher than in 1964–5, and that from independent schools was correspondingly lower. This is very likely a reflection of the special circumstances of the time when there were many ex-servicemen in residence.

**Table 31.** *Type of school of entrants to read for first degrees. Men non-graduates*

OXFORD PERCENTAGE

| Type of school | 1938–9 | 1948–9 | 1958–9 | 1964–5 | 1965–6 |
|---|---|---|---|---|---|
| HMC independent boarding | 55·2 | 39·1 | 42·2 | 32·7 | 31·1 |
| Independent boarding | 2·3 | 1·3 | 1·1 | 1·6 | 1·6 |
| HMC independent day | 4·0 | 4·5 | 8·3 | 9·5 | 8·1 |
| Independent day | 0·6 | 0·5 | 0·8 | 1·2 | 0·6 |
| All independent | 62·0 | 45·2 | 52·4 | 45·0 | 41·3 |
| HMC direct-grant | 10·9 | 12·1 | 14·0 | 14·8 | 14·9 |
| Direct-grant | 1·6 | 2·8 | 1·5 | 2·3 | 2·2 |
| All direct-grant | 12·6 | 14·9 | 15·4 | 17·2 | 17·1 |
| Maintained | 19·2 | 35·2 | 30·1 | 34·3 | 40·2 |
| Other U.K. schools | 4·5 | 1·0 | 0·7 | 2·0 | 0·6 |
| Overseas schools | 1·7 | 3·6 | 1·3 | 1·5 | 0·8 |
| All schools | 100·0 | 100·0 | 100·0 | 100·0 | 100·0 |
| *Number* | *1,235* | *1,480* | *2,056* | *1,889* | *1,912* |

SOURCE: Matriculation forms except for 1965–6.
Admissions Office for 1965–6.

NOTE: The figures for 1965–6 are not fully comparable with those for earlier years as they are based on places offered and accepted, not on actual matriculations.

**Table 32.** *Type of school of entrants to read for first degrees. Women non-graduates*

OXFORD PERCENTAGE

| Type of school | 1938–9 | 1948–9 | 1958–9 | 1964–5 | 1965–6 |
|---|---|---|---|---|---|
| Independent boarding | 36·0 | 31·6 | 21·5 | 19·8 | 19·2 |
| Independent day | 14·7 | 14·1 | 15·7 | 8·5 | 12·2 |
| Direct-grant | 13·2 | 16·5 | 24·3 | 28·8 | 23·9 |
| Maintained | 32·6 | 31·3 | 36·6 | 38·3 | 42·7 |
| Other schools | 3·5 | 6·4 | 1·8 | 4·6 | 2·0 |
| All independent | 50·8 | 45·8 | 37·2 | 28·3 | 31·4 |
| All schools | 100·0 | 100·0 | 100·0 | 100·0 | 100·0 |
| *Number* | *258* | *297* | *325* | *389* | *443* |

SOURCE: Matriculation forms except for 1965–6.
Women's colleges for 1965–6.

NOTE: See note to Table 31.

92. The proportion of women from maintained schools is higher than for men, but the difference has been growing smaller in recent years. The proportion is now a little over 40 per cent. for each sex. The proportion of women from direct-grant schools is also higher but has been growing faster than for men.

93. Among men from independent schools, the great majority are from HMC schools.[1]

94. Independent schools are divided into boarding and day schools since a number of independent day schools have a proportion of places which are paid for by local authorities, and have strong similarities with direct-grant schools. The proportion of men from independent day schools has been increasing, at least up to 1964–5, while that from independent boarding schools has been falling. The proportion of women from independent boarding schools has also fallen, and so has that from day schools since 1958–9.

**Table 33.** *Holders of entrance awards as percentage of all entrants to read for first degrees by type of school. Men non-graduates*

| OXFORD | | | | | PERCENTAGE |
| --- | --- | --- | --- | --- | --- |
| Type of school | 1938–9 | 1948–9 | 1958–9 | 1964–5 | 1965–6 |
| Independent boarding | 20·7 | 19·8 | 30·8 | 34·1 | 35·9 |
| Independent day | 42·9 | 24·7 | 41·7 | 41·3 | 49·1 |
| Direct-grant | 46·5 | 29·5 | 42·3 | 45·7 | 46·5 |
| Maintained | 40·9 | 21·3 | 31·3 | 38·1 | 41·4 |
| Other | — | — | 4·8 | 7·5 | 25·9 |
| All schools | 27·5 | 21·1 | 33·2 | 37·3 | 40·9 |

SOURCE: Matriculation forms except for 1965–6.
          Admissions Office for 1965–6.
NOTE: See note to Table 31.

95. Holders of college entrance awards (open and closed scholars and exhibitioners) now account for 41 per cent. of men and 19 per cent. of women entering from schools (Tables 33 and 34). The proportion of women award holders has not changed appreciably since 1938–9, but that of men has increased from 28 per cent. in 1938–9. Throughout the period the proportion of award holders from independent boarding schools has been lower, for both men and women, than for other types of school, but the contrast was greatest in 1938–9. The highest proportions of award holders are for independent day and direct-grant schools.

[1] i.e. schools whose headmaster is a member of the Headmasters' Conference.

**Table 34.** *Holders of entrance awards as percentage of all entrants to read for first degrees by type of school. Women non-graduates*

OXFORD                                                          PERCENTAGE

| Type of school | 1938–9 | 1948–9 | 1958–9 | 1964–5 | 1965–6 |
|---|---|---|---|---|---|
| Independent boarding | 9·7 | 22·3 | 18·6 | 15·6 | 9·4 |
| Independent day | 21·1 | 26·2 | 19·6 | 24·2 | 20·4 |
| Direct-grant | 29·4 | 20·4 | 27·8 | 22·3 | 31·1 |
| Maintained | 26·2 | 19·4 | 19·3 | 17·4 | 17·5 |
| Other | 11·1 | 21·1 | — | 11·1 | 11·1 |
| All schools | 19·4 | 21·5 | 20·9 | 18·8 | 19·4 |

SOURCE: Matriculation forms except for 1965–6.
Women's colleges for 1965–6.
NOTE: See note to Table 31.

## Home address

96. Table 35 shows the distribution of entrants according to home address. There is no systematic difference between men and women, except that the proportion of men from the south-east has risen, while that for women has been fairly steady. The proportion of entrants drawn from the north and midlands has increased over the period, while that from overseas has fallen.

## Analyses by subject group

97. Tables 36 and 37 show distributions by type of school within subject groups. Among men, entrants from independent boarding schools are most strongly represented in social studies, and least in science, while the opposite holds for entrants from maintained schools. Between the two dates there has been a strong swing from arts to science. There has thus been an increased representation of entrants from maintained schools in the arts and science (but not social studies) subjects, and a swing to science in which the proportion from maintained schools is above average.

98. For women also, entrants from independent boarding schools are more strongly represented, and those from maintained schools are less strongly represented in social studies, but there is no significant difference for either group between arts and science. However, the proportion in social studies from maintained schools increased sharply between 1958–9 and 1964–5.

99. Table 30 shows that among men the proportion of graduates reading first degrees was high in 1938–9 (14 per cent.) and in 1948–9 (20 per cent.),

**Table 35.** *Home address of entrants to read for first degrees by sex. Non-graduates*

| OXFORD | | | PERCENTAGE | |
|---|---|---|---|---|
| | 1938–9 | 1948–9 | 1958–9 | 1964–5 |
| MEN | | | | |
| Scotland | 2·5 | 2·9 | 1·8 | 1·3 |
| North | 15·1 | 14·9 | 15·1 | 17·2 |
| Midlands | 13·0 | 13·2 | 14·7 | 14·8 |
| Wales | 4·6 | 3·9 | 3·1 | 2·5 |
| South-east | 48·1 | 50·1 | 52·0 | 51·5 |
| South-west | 8·7 | 9·7 | 9·2 | 8·0 |
| Northern Ireland | 0·1 | 0·3 | 0·2 | 0·6 |
| Overseas | 7·9 | 4·9 | 3·7 | 4·1 |
| All men | 100·0 | 100·0 | 100·0 | 100·0 |
| *Number* | *1,235* | *1,480* | *2,056* | *1,889* |
| WOMEN | | | | |
| Scotland | 1·6 | 2·0 | 1·8 | 1·5 |
| North | 14·7 | 13·8 | 13·5 | 18·0 |
| Midlands | 12·4 | 10·8 | 15·4 | 15·2 |
| Wales | 3·5 | 3·0 | 3·4 | 2·1 |
| South-east | 51·2 | 53·9 | 50·5 | 50·4 |
| South-west | 11·2 | 10·1 | 9·5 | 8·2 |
| Northern Ireland | — | — | 1·8 | 1·5 |
| Overseas | 5·4 | 6·4 | 4·0 | 3·1 |
| All women | 100·0 | 100·0 | 100·0 | 100·0 |
| *Number* | *258* | *297* | *325* | *389* |
| MEN AND WOMEN | | | | |
| Scotland | 2·3 | 2·8 | 1·8 | 1·3 |
| North | 15·0 | 14·7 | 14·9 | 17·3 |
| Midlands | 12·9 | 12·8 | 14·8 | 14·9 |
| Wales | 4·4 | 3·8 | 3·1 | 2·5 |
| South-east | 48·6 | 50·8 | 51·8 | 51·3 |
| South-west | 9·2 | 9·7 | 9·3 | 8·0 |
| Northern Ireland | 0·1 | 0·3 | 0·5 | 0·7 |
| Overseas | 7·4 | 5·2 | 3·7 | 3·9 |
| All entrants | 100·0 | 100·0 | 100·0 | 100·0 |
| *Number* | *1,493* | *1,777* | *2,381* | *2,278* |

SOURCE: Matriculation forms.

**Table 36.** *Type of school of entrants to read for first degrees by subject group. Men non-graduates*

| OXFORD | | | PERCENTAGE | |
|---|---|---|---|---|
| Subject group and type of school | 1958–9 | | 1964–5 | |
| ARTS | | | | |
| Independent boarding | 40·4 | | 35·0 | |
| Independent day | 9·6 | | 10·4 | |
| Direct-grant | 16·6 | | 16·4 | |
| Maintained | 31·8 | | 35·1 | |
| Other schools | 1·7 | | 3·1 | |
| All schools | 100·0 | 52·8 | 100·0 | 43·1 |
| *Number* | *1,086* | | *815* | |
| SOCIAL STUDIES | | | | |
| Independent boarding | 57·8 | | 46·3 | |
| Independent day | 7·5 | | 11·7 | |
| Direct-grant | 9·4 | | 12·7 | |
| Maintained | 21·5 | | 21·6 | |
| Other schools | 3·9 | | 7·7 | |
| All schools | 100·0 | 21·3 | 100·0 | 21·3 |
| *Number* | *438* | | *402* | |
| SCIENCE | | | | |
| Independent boarding | 37·4 | | 26·3 | |
| Independent day | 9·4 | | 10·2 | |
| Direct-grant | 18·0 | | 20·7 | |
| Maintained | 33·8 | | 41·1 | |
| Other schools | 1·3 | | 1·6 | |
| All schools | 100·0 | 25·9 | 100·0 | 35·6 |
| *Number* | *532* | | *672* | |
| ALL SUBJECTS | | | | |
| Independent boarding | 43·3 | | 34·3 | |
| Independent day | 9·1 | | 10·6 | |
| Direct-grant | 15·4 | | 17·2 | |
| Maintained | 30·1 | | 34·3 | |
| Other schools | 2·0 | | 3·5 | |
| All schools | 100·0 | 100·0 | 100·0 | 100·0 |
| *Total number* | | *2,056* | | *1,889* |

SOURCE: Matriculation forms.

**Table 37.** *Type of school of entrants to read for first degrees by subject group. Women non-graduates*

| OXFORD | | | PERCENTAGE | |
|---|---|---|---|---|
| Subject group and type of school | 1958–9 | | 1964–5 | |
| ARTS | | | | |
| Independent boarding | 21·6 | | 17·2 | |
| Independent day | 15·5 | | 8·8 | |
| Direct-grant | 22·5 | | 31·9 | |
| Maintained | 39·4 | | 36·6 | |
| Other schools | 0·9 | | 5·5 | |
| All schools | 100·0 | 65·5 | 100·0 | 61·2 |
| *Number* | *213* | | *238* | |
| SOCIAL STUDIES | | | | |
| Independent boarding | 24·3 | | 32·6 | |
| Independent day | 24·3 | | 8·7 | |
| Direct-grant | 21·6 | | 15·2 | |
| Maintained | 21·6 | | 32·6 | |
| Other schools | 8·1 | | 10·9 | |
| All schools | 100.0 | 11·4 | 100·0 | 11·8 |
| *Number* | *37* | | *46* | |
| SCIENCE | | | | |
| Independent boarding | 20·0 | | 20·0 | |
| Independent day | 12·0 | | 7·6 | |
| Direct-grant | 30·7 | | 27·6 | |
| Maintained | 36·0 | | 44·8 | |
| Other schools | 1·3 | | — | |
| All schools | 100·0 | 23·1 | 100·0 | 27·0 |
| *Number* | *75* | | *105* | |
| ALL SUBJECTS | | | | |
| Independent boarding | 21·5 | | 19·8 | |
| Independent day | 15·7 | | 8·5 | |
| Direct-grant | 24·3 | | 28·8 | |
| Maintained | 36·6 | | 38·3 | |
| Other schools | 1·8 | | 4·6 | |
| All schools | 100·0 | 100·0 | 100·0 | 100·0 |
| *Total number* | | *325* | | *389* |

SOURCE: Matriculation forms.

was much lower in 1958–9 (6 per cent.), but rose to 8 per cent. in 1964–5. Table 38 gives a breakdown by subject group for the two last periods. The increase has occurred in arts and social studies, the latter having the heaviest concentration, almost all being foreign graduates (many American) most of whom probably read PPE.

**Table 38.** *Graduates as percentage of all entrants to read for first degrees by subject group. Men*

OXFORD    PERCENTAGE

| | U.K. universities | Other universities | All universities |
|---|---|---|---|
| ARTS | | | |
| 1958–9 | 1·1 | 3·4 | 4·6 |
| 1964–5 | 2·7 | 5·6 | 8·3 |
| SOCIAL STUDIES | | | |
| 1958–9 | 0·6 | 10·9 | 11·5 |
| 1964–5 | 0·2 | 13·9 | 14·1 |
| SCIENCE | | | |
| 1958–9 | 0·4 | 3·3 | 3·6 |
| 1964–5 | 0·6 | 2·6 | 3·2 |
| ALL SUBJECTS | | | |
| 1958–9 | 0·8 | 5·1 | 5·9 |
| 1964–5 | 1·4 | 6·5 | 7·9 |

SOURCE: Matriculation forms.

100. Among women the over-all proportion of graduates is smaller (Table 39), and a larger proportion of them come from U.K. universities. Otherwise, the pattern is similar to that for men. (The number of women graduates reading first degrees is small, and the proportions within subject groups are likely to fluctuate widely from year to year.)

101. Table 40 shows that for men in recent years the proportion of award holders was lower in social studies than in arts and science. This need not reflect a lower quality of entry in social studies since a large proportion of the men's awards are tied to particular subjects. For women the figures are liable to greater erratic fluctuations because of the small numbers involved, and because awards for women are not usually tied to subjects in the same way as those for men, but it appears that the proportion of award holders was highest in arts.

**Table 39.** *Graduates as percentage of all entrants to read for first degrees by subject group. Women*

|  | U.K. universities | Other universities | All universities |
|---|---|---|---|
| **ARTS** | | | |
| 1958–9 | 0·5 | 2·7 | 3·2 |
| 1964–5 | 1·6 | 4·0 | 5·6 |
| **SOCIAL STUDIES** | | | |
| 1958–9 | 4·8 | 7·1 | 11·9 |
| 1964–5 | 3·8 | 7·7 | 11·5 |
| **SCIENCE** | | | |
| 1958–9 | 1·3 | 2·6 | 3·8 |
| 1964–5 | 0·9 | 0·9 | 1·9 |
| **ALL SUBJECTS** | | | |
| 1958–9 | 1·2 | 3·2 | 4·4 |
| 1964–5 | 1·7 | 3·6 | 5·4 |

SOURCE: Matriculation forms.

**Table 40.** *Award holders as percentage of all entrants to read for first degrees by subject group and sex. Non-graduates*

|  | Arts | Social studies | Science | All subjects |
|---|---|---|---|---|
| **MEN** | | | | |
| 1958–9 | 37·7 | 17·1 | 37·2 | 33·2 |
| 1964–5 | 38·0 | 25·6 | 43·3 | 37·3 |
| **WOMEN** | | | | |
| 1958–9 | 23·5 | 10·8 | 18·7 | 20·9 |
| 1964–5 | 21·4 | 19·6 | 12·4 | 18·8 |

SOURCE: Matriculation forms.

**Table 41.** *Type of school by home address. Men non-graduate entrants to read for first degrees*

OXFORD                                                                      PERCENTAGE

| Home address | Independent boarding | Independent day | Direct-grant | Maintained | Other schools | All schools | *Number* |
|---|---|---|---|---|---|---|---|
| *1958–9* | | | | | | | |
| Scotland | 86 | 11 | — | 3 | — | 100 | *37* |
| North | 22 | 2 | 34 | 40 | 1 | 100 | *311* |
| Midlands | 33 | 9 | 23 | 35 | — | 100 | *303* |
| Wales | 47 | — | 8 | 45 | — | 100 | *64* |
| South-east | 48 | 14 | 8 | 29 | 1 | 100 | *1,070* |
| South-west | 53 | 3 | 22 | 22 | 1 | 100 | *190* |
| Northern Ireland | 100 | — | — | — | — | 100 | *5* |
| Overseas | 61 | 1 | 4 | 3 | 32 | 100 | *76* |
| All regions | 43 | 9 | 15 | 30 | 2 | 100 | *2,056* |
| *1964–5* | | | | | | | |
| Scotland | 42 | 29 | 8 | 13 | 8 | 100 | *24* |
| North | 16 | 2 | 32 | 47 | 2 | 100 | *325* |
| Midlands | 19 | 7 | 29 | 43 | 3 | 100 | *280* |
| Wales | 31 | — | 10 | 50 | 8 | 100 | *48* |
| South-east | 41 | 16 | 9 | 32 | 1 | 100 | *973* |
| South-west | 51 | 2 | 23 | 23 | 2 | 100 | *151* |
| Northern Ireland | 18 | — | 45 | 27 | 9 | 100 | *11* |
| Overseas | 52 | 4 | 4 | 3 | 38 | 100 | *77* |
| All regions | 34 | 11 | 17 | 34 | 4 | 100 | *1,889* |

SOURCE: Matriculation forms.

## Home address and type of school

102. Distributions showing type of school within regions are given in Tables 41 and 42. They are heavily dependent on the geographical distribution of independent and direct-grant schools. The region is that in which an individual's home address lies, not that of his school. In a number of cases, particularly for women, the numbers involved are small and firm conclusions cannot be drawn. However, it appears that the proportion of entrants from independent boarding and day schools is above average for the south-east, the south-west (boarding schools only), and probably Scotland. The proportion from direct-grant schools is above average for the north, the midlands, and the south-west (but not for women). The proportion from direct-grant schools in the south-east is low for men, but about average for women. The proportion from maintained schools is above average for the north, the midlands, and Wales.

**Table 42.** *Type of school by home address. Women non-graduate entrants to read for first degrees*

OXFORD                                                 PERCENTAGE

| Home address | Independent boarding | Independent day | Direct-grant | Main-tained | Other schools | All schools | *Number* |
|---|---|---|---|---|---|---|---|
| *1958–9* | | | | | | | |
| Scotland | 33 | 50 | 17 | — | — | 100 | *6* |
| North | 16 | 2 | 34 | 45 | 2 | 100 | *44* |
| Midlands | 10 | 4 | 44 | 42 | — | 100 | *50* |
| Wales | 9 | 9 | 9 | 73 | — | 100 | *11* |
| South-east | 25 | 24 | 19 | 32 | — | 100 | *164* |
| South-west | 26 | 6 | 19 | 45 | 3 | 100 | *31* |
| Northern Ireland | 50 | — | 33 | 17 | — | 100 | *6* |
| Overseas | 23 | 23 | 8 | 15 | 31 | 100 | *13* |
| All regions | 22 | 16 | 24 | 37 | 2 | 100 | *325* |
| *1964–5* | | | | | | | |
| Scotland | 67 | — | 33 | — | — | 100 | *6* |
| North | 6 | 7 | 43 | 41 | 3 | 100 | *70* |
| Midlands | 17 | 5 | 31 | 44 | 3 | 100 | *59* |
| Wales | 25 | — | 13 | 63 | — | 100 | *8* |
| South-east | 17 | 11 | 30 | 38 | 3 | 100 | *196* |
| South-west | 53 | 9 | 3 | 25 | 9 | 100 | *32* |
| Northern Ireland | 17 | — | — | 83 | — | 100 | *6* |
| Overseas | 42 | — | 8 | 8 | 42 | 100 | *12* |
| All regions | 20 | 8 | 29 | 38 | 5 | 100 | *389* |

SOURCE: Matriculation forms.

## THE ADMISSIONS COMPETITIONS FOR ENTRY IN 1965–6

103. The Oxford Colleges Admissions Office began operating for the competition in December 1963 for entry to the men's colleges in October 1964. It serves primarily as a clearing house, receiving applications, reproducing and distributing them to colleges, and keeping colleges informed on the 'state of play' on each candidate. In its first year it did not handle all applications and the arrangements *vis-à-vis* Cambridge were different from those in the following year. The tables given below are based on the December 1964 competition for entry in October 1965, except for Table 43 which gives some details of the 1964–5 entry for comparative purposes.

104. The women's colleges do not use the Admissions Office, and details of their competition for entry in 1965–6 were supplied by the individual colleges.

# Men

105. Table 43 shows the distribution of applications and admissions, and gives the acceptance rates by type of school for the December 1963 competition for entry in October 1964. The distribution of admissions is close to that based on matriculations (after 'other schools' are removed) except for the division between independent boarding and day schools. Some schools may have been classified differently in the analysis of matriculation forms. The table shows that the distribution of applications and admissions were different to the extent that the acceptance rate for independent boarding schools was below the average, and that for independent day schools was above average.

106. In the December 1963 competition, candidates could apply separately to Oxford and to Cambridge. The large number of withdrawals is a reflection of this. In the following year, candidates could make only one application in which Oxford and Cambridge were listed in order of preference, and the application was sent to the university of first choice. The papers of candidates unsuccessful at their university of first choice were then considered by the other university; such candidates for Oxford are termed the 'Cambridge pool', while applications from first choice candidates are termed 'central applications'.

107. The remainder of this survey covers all applications and admissions of non-graduates in the December 1964 competition. Applications from graduates, and from most mature students, are not included. There were 4,011 central applications, of whom 1,818 were given places. In addition to the central admissions, 63 unsuccessful candidates at Cambridge were given a place, and there were 31 direct admissions to colleges under schemes which earmark places for particular schools or groups of schools.[1] Thus, including the Cambridge pool and direct admissions, there were 1,912 admissions. These admissions are referred to as those for entry in 1965–6, but they include 95 places for entry in October 1966. (There were similarly 109 boys offered places as a result of the previous year's competition to come up in October 1965 who are excluded from the analyses unless they reapplied for an award.)

108. In making admissions, the men's colleges operate in three groups (see Tables 45 and 46), although a common examination has been used since December 1964. In making his application a candidate lists the colleges of the group to which he applies in order of preference. He is considered by these colleges and, if unsuccessful, details of his performance are passed to the remaining colleges for consideration. This procedure applies in all

---

[1] The principal such scheme is that associated with maintained schools in the West Riding (*Written Evidence*, Part XI, p. 26). The direct admissions (unlike those referred to in para. 109 below) did not pass through the machinery of the Admissions Office.

**Table 43.** Type of school of applicants and admissions. Men non-graduate candidates for admission in 1964–5 to read for first degrees

OXFORD

| Type of school | Applications | | Applications excluding those with-drawing before competition | | Admissions | | Acceptance rate | |
| --- | --- | --- | --- | --- | --- | --- | --- | --- |
| | Number (1) | Percentage (2) | Number (3) | Percentage (4) | Number (5) | Percentage (6) | Col. (5) as percentage of col. (1) | Col. (5) as percentage of col. (3) |
| Independent boarding | 2,302 | 40·4 | 2,044 | 41·4 | 678 | 37·3 | 29·5 | 33·2 |
| Independent day | 345 | 6·0 | 317 | 6·4 | 148 | 8·2 | 42·9 | 46·7 |
| Direct-grant | 990 | 17·4 | 846 | 17·1 | 325 | 17·9 | 32·7 | 38·4 |
| Maintained | 2,065 | 36·2 | 1,726 | 35·0 | 665 | 36·6 | 32·2 | 38·5 |
| All schools | 5,702 | 100·0 | 4,933 | 100·0 | 1,816 | 100·0 | 31·9 | 36·8 |

SOURCE: Styler, L. M., *Oxford Magazine*, 12 March 1964.

NOTES

1. The total of admissions is not the same as that shown in Table 31 as matriculating in 1964–5, since not all applications were handled by the Admissions Office, on whose information this table is based. In addition, some successful candidates may subsequently have withdrawn. It is therefore possible that the totals for this table was carried out independently of that for Tables 31, 44, and related tables. It is therefore possible that some schools have been classified differently in different tables; this applies particularly to the division of independent schools into boarding and day categories.
2. The classification of schools for this table was carried out independently of that for Tables 31, 44, and related tables. It is therefore possible that some schools have been classified differently in different tables; this applies particularly to the division of independent schools into boarding and day categories.

**Table 44.** *Type of school of applicants and admissions. Men non-graduate candidates for admission in 1965–6 to read for first degrees*

OXFORD

| Type of school | Excluding Cambridge pool and direct admissions | | | | | Including Cambridge pool and direct admissions | | | | |
|---|---|---|---|---|---|---|---|---|---|---|
| | Applications | | Admissions | | Acceptance rate Col. (3) as percentage of col. (1) | Applications | | Admissions | | Acceptance rate Col. (8) as percentage of col. (6) |
| | Number | Percentage | Number | Percentage | | Number | Percentage | Number | Percentage | |
| | (1) | (2) | (3) | (4) | (5) | (6) | (7) | (8) | (9) | (10) |
| Independent boarding | 1,370 | 34·2 | 600 | 33·0 | 43·8 | 1,394 | 34·0 | 624 | 32·6 | 44·8 |
| Independent day | 340 | 8·5 | 156 | 8·6 | 45·9 | 349 | 8·5 | 165 | 8·6 | 47·3 |
| Direct-grant | 618 | 15·4 | 314 | 17·3 | 50·8 | 631 | 15·4 | 327 | 17·1 | 51·8 |
| Maintained | 1,576 | 39·3 | 724 | 39·8 | 45·9 | 1,621 | 39·5 | 769 | 40·2 | 47·4 |
| Overseas | 61 | 1·5 | 16 | 0·9 | 26·2 | 61 | 1·5 | 16 | 0·8 | 26·2 |
| Other | 46 | 1·1 | 8 | 0·4 | 17·4 | 49 | 1·2 | 11 | 0·6 | 22·4 |
| All independent | 1,710 | 42·6 | 756 | 41·6 | 44·2 | 1,743 | 42·5 | 789 | 41·3 | 45·3 |
| All schools | 4,011 | 100·0 | 1,818 | 100·0 | 45·3 | 4,105 | 100·0 | 1,912 | 100·0 | 46·6 |

SOURCE: Admissions Office.

NOTE: Included in this table are those taking part in the December 1964 competition, and the total of 1,912 admissions will differ from non-graduates matriculating in 1965–6 in the following ways:

1. 109 candidates in the previous year were offered places for 1965–6, and are not included in the table unless they reapplied for an award;
2. 95 candidates were offered places for 1966–7 and are included under 'admissions' in the table;
3. Some of those offered and accepting places may have subsequently withdrawn;
4. Some mature students will have been admitted by colleges subsequently to the competition and are not included in the table.

subjects except Geography, Music, and Mathematics, candidates in which may apply to any men's college. Of the 1,912 admissions:

1,560 or 82 per cent. were at college of first choice;

208 or 11 per cent. were at other colleges in the same group;

50 or 3 per cent. were at colleges in other groups;

63 or 3 per cent. were from Cambridge;

31 or 2 per cent. were direct college admissions.

109. Before the examination took place, 216 places were offered in addition to the 109 offered places as a result of the previous year's competition. Of the total number of 325 pre-examination admissions, 103 subsequently won awards (70 scholarships and 33 exhibitions).

## Men : type of school

110. Table 44 gives details of applications, admissions, and acceptance rates by type of school. Compared with the previous year there was a marked fall in the number of applications (in part because of the elimination of double applications to Oxford and Cambridge). Applications from independent boarding schools fell particularly sharply. There was rather less variation in the acceptance rates between types of school than in the previous year; and the proportion of admissions from independent boarding schools was lower for 1965–6 than for 1964–5, while the proportion from maintained schools was markedly higher.[1]

111. Tables 45 and 46 give the type of school of applicants and admissions by colleges. Within colleges there are likely to be considerable year-to-year fluctuations in the proportion of both applicants and admissions from different types of school.

[1] Provisional details of the 1965 competition for admission in 1966–7 show a rise in the number of applications to 4,219 and a slight fall in total admissions to 1,850. Details by type of school are:

|  | Central applications | | Admissions (including Cambridge pool and direct admissions) | |
|---|---|---|---|---|
|  | Number | Percentage | Number | Percentage |
| Independent boarding | 1,297 | 30·7 | 541 | 29·2 |
| Independent day | 387 | 9·2 | 180 | 9·7 |
| Direct-grant | 663 | 15·7 | 324 | 17·5 |
| Maintained | 1,737 | 41·1 | 776 | 41·9 |
| Other | 135 | 3·2 | 29 | 1·6 |
| All | 4,219 | 100·0 | 1,850 | 100·0 |

Compared with the previous year the number of applications from independent boarding schools is down, whereas more applied from each of the other three main types of school. The proportions of applications from each of these types of school also increased at the expense of that from independent boarding schools. Admissions of candidates from independent boarding schools fell. The proportion of admissions, compared with the previous year, was lower for independent boarding schools, and slightly higher for independent day and maintained schools.

**Table 45.** *Type of school of applicants by college. Men non-graduate candidates for admission in 1965–6 to read for first degrees*

OXFORD                                                                PERCENTAGE

| College and college group | Independent | Direct-grant | Maintained | Other schools | All schools | *Number* |
|---|---|---|---|---|---|---|
| Corpus Christi | 45 | 21 | 34 | 1 | 100 | *92* |
| Hertford | 43 | 18 | 35 | 4 | 100 | *160* |
| New College | 60 | 10 | 30 | 1 | 100 | *179* |
| Queen's | 23 | 19 | 56 | 2 | 100 | *169* |
| St. Catherine's | 27 | 16 | 56 | 2 | 100 | *257* |
| Trinity | 66 | 11 | 22 | — | 100 | *122* |
| University | 40 | 13 | 43 | 4 | 100 | *178* |
| Worcester | 49 | 14 | 35 | 2 | 100 | *204* |
| All Group I | 42 | 15 | 41 | 2 | 100 | *1,361* |
| Balliol | 43 | 15 | 36 | 6 | 100 | *149* |
| Exeter | 38 | 19 | 41 | 2 | 100 | *210* |
| Keble | 43 | 15 | 41 | 1 | 100 | *215* |
| Pembroke | 35 | 17 | 48 | 1 | 100 | *204* |
| St. Edmund Hall | 39 | 14 | 43 | 4 | 100 | *244* |
| St. John's | 45 | 18 | 34 | 2 | 100 | *158* |
| St. Peter's | 34 | 20 | 44 | 2 | 100 | *162* |
| Wadham | 29 | 12 | 58 | 1 | 100 | *184* |
| All Group II | 38 | 16 | 43 | 2 | 100 | *1,526* |
| Brasenose | 49 | 20 | 29 | 3 | 100 | *189* |
| Christ Church | 70 | 10 | 18 | 2 | 100 | *225* |
| Jesus | 33 | 16 | 50 | 1 | 100 | *168* |
| Lincoln | 38 | 12 | 48 | 3 | 100 | *155* |
| Magdalen | 50 | 17 | 26 | 6 | 100 | *172* |
| Merton | 36 | 18 | 45 | 1 | 100 | *164* |
| Oriel | 57 | 12 | 31 | 1 | 100 | *145* |
| All Group III | 48 | 15 | 34 | 3 | 100 | *1,218* |
| All colleges | 42 | 15 | 39 | 3 | 100 | *4,105* |

SOURCE: Admissions Office.

NOTES:

1. Cambridge pool and direct admissions are included.
2. See note to Table 44.
3. The college is that of first choice.

**Table 46.** *Type of school of admissions by college. Men non-graduate admissions in 1965–6 to read for first degrees*

OXFORD                                                PERCENTAGE

| College and college group | Independent | Direct-grant | Maintained | Other schools | All schools | *Number* |
|---|---|---|---|---|---|---|
| Corpus Christi | 46 | 17 | 37 | — | 100 | 46 |
| Hertford | 40 | 16 | 44 | — | 100 | 63 |
| New College | 56 | 11 | 33 | — | 100 | 98 |
| Queen's | 25 | 25 | 49 | — | 100 | 67 |
| St. Catherine's | 23 | 17 | 59 | 1 | 100 | 115 |
| Trinity | 62 | 12 | 27 | — | 100 | 60 |
| University | 36 | 13 | 48 | 2 | 100 | 83 |
| Worcester | 40 | 24 | 35 | 1 | 100 | 83 |
| All Group I | 40 | 17 | 43 | 1 | 100 | 615 |
| Balliol | 43 | 18 | 36 | 3 | 100 | 91 |
| Exeter | 31 | 21 | 46 | 1 | 100 | 84 |
| Keble | 42 | 13 | 45 | — | 100 | 102 |
| Pembroke | 29 | 17 | 53 | 1 | 100 | 96 |
| St. Edmund Hall | 41 | 15 | 42 | 3 | 100 | 106 |
| St. John's | 53 | 17 | 31 | — | 100 | 78 |
| St. Peter's | 26 | 23 | 49 | 1 | 100 | 73 |
| Wadham | 31 | 12 | 57 | — | 100 | 83 |
| All Group II | 37 | 17 | 45 | 1 | 100 | 713 |
| Brasenose | 46 | 30 | 25 | — | 100 | 81 |
| Christ Church | 71 | 7 | 21 | 1 | 100 | 123 |
| Jesus | 27 | 18 | 55 | — | 100 | 77 |
| Lincoln | 38 | 17 | 41 | 5 | 100 | 63 |
| Magdalen | 45 | 21 | 33 | 1 | 100 | 95 |
| Merton | 32 | 21 | 47 | — | 100 | 66 |
| Oriel | 57 | 15 | 28 | — | 100 | 79 |
| All Group III | 48 | 18 | 34 | 1 | 100 | 584 |
| All colleges | 41 | 17 | 40 | 1 | 100 | 1,912 |

SOURCE: Admissions Office.

NOTE: See Notes 1–2 to Table 45.

## Men : subject

112. The subjects which attracted the largest number of applicants were Modern History, Jurisprudence, and PPE (Table 47). In the first of these, the acceptance rate was above average, but in the other two it was well below the average. Among the other subjects (other than the smaller subjects with less than 50 applicants), the acceptance rate was very high for Literae Humaniores and was high for Physics, while it was below average for Geography, Animal Physiology, and Engineering Science.

**Table 47.** *Proposed Honour School of applicants and admissions. Men non-graduate candidates for admission in 1965–6 to read for first degrees*

OXFORD NUMBER

| Honour School | Excluding Cambridge and direct admissions | | | Including Cambridge and direct admissions | | |
|---|---|---|---|---|---|---|
| | Applications | Admissions | *Acceptance rate (percentage)* | Applications | Admissions | *Acceptance rate (percentage)* |
| Literae Humaniores | 235 | 154 | *65·5* | 236 | 155 | *65·7* |
| Theology | 24 | 18 | *75·0* | 28 | 22 | *78·6* |
| Modern History | 502 | 252 | *50·2* | 507 | 257 | *50·7* |
| English | 295 | 129 | *43·7* | 298 | 132 | *44·3* |
| Modern Languages | 446 | 193 | *43·3* | 454 | 201 | *44·3* |
| Oriental Studies | 16 | 7 | *43·8* | 16 | 7 | *43·8* |
| Geography | 136 | 53 | *39·0* | 137 | 54 | *39·4* |
| Music | 38 | 20 | *52·6* | 40 | 22 | *55·0* |
| Jurisprudence | 465 | 175 | *37·6* | 468 | 178 | *38·0* |
| PPE | 472 | 176 | *37·3* | 477 | 181 | *37·9* |
| Mathematics | 235 | 109 | *46·4* | 244 | 118 | *48·4* |
| Physics | 214 | 123 | *57·5* | 231 | 140 | *60·6* |
| Chemistry | 335 | 157 | *46·9* | 342 | 164 | *48·0* |
| Biochemistry | 47 | 25 | *53·2* | 48 | 26 | *54·2* |
| Animal Physiology | 217 | 83 | *38·2* | 220 | 86 | *39·1* |
| Zoology | 40 | 19 | *47·5* | 40 | 19 | *47·5* |
| Botany | 8 | 6 | *75·0* | 9 | 7 | *77·8* |
| Geology | 7 | 7 | *100·0* | 11 | 11 | *100·0* |
| PPP | 31 | 10 | *32·3* | 32 | 11 | *34·4* |
| Engineering | 171 | 71 | *41·5* | 187 | 87 | *46·5* |
| Engineering and Economics | 36 | 10 | *27·8* | 36 | 10 | *27·8* |
| Metallurgy | 20 | 11 | *55·0* | 21 | 12 | *57·1* |
| Agriculture | 15 | 8 | *53·3* | 16 | 9 | *56·3* |
| Forestry | 6 | 2 | *33·0* | 6 | 2 | *33·0* |
| Subject not known | — | — | *.* | 1 | 1 | *100·0* |
| All Honour Schools | 4,011 | 1,818 | *45·3* | 4,105 | 1,912 | *46·6* |

SOURCE: Admissions Office.
NOTE: See note to Table 44.

**Table 48.** *Schools submitting candidates and gaining places. Men non-graduate candidates for admission in 1965–6 to read for first degrees*

OXFORD NUMBER

| Type of school | Number of schools | | *Col. (2) as percentage of col. (1)* |
|---|---|---|---|
| | Submitting candidates (1) | Gaining places (2) | |
| Independent boarding | 130 | 92 | *70·8* |
| Independent day | 33 | 32 | *97·0* |
| Direct-grant | 72 | 66 | *91·7* |
| Maintained | 497 | 357 | *71·8* |
| All schools | 732 | 547 | *74·7* |

SOURCE: Admissions Office.
NOTES
1. The Cambridge pool and direct admissions are included.
2. See note to Table 44.

## Men : schools submitting candidates

113. The number of schools of each type submitting candidates and the number of places gained are given in Tables 48 and 49. 75 per cent. of all schools submitting candidates gained at least one place, but the proportion was much higher for independent day (97 per cent.) and direct-grant (92 per cent.) schools, and was 71 and 72 per cent. for independent boarding and maintained schools. But the independent boarding schools which gained places gained on average 6·8 places, more than at other types of school. The average was even higher, 7·9, at HMC independent boarding schools, and 8 such schools gained over 20 places each. The average was 5·2 for all independent day schools, 5·0 for all direct-grant schools, and 2·2 for maintained schools. Just over half the admissions came from the 87 schools gaining 6 or more places each, which comprised 37 independent boarding, 12 independent day, 19 direct-grant, and 19 maintained schools.

## Men : time in sixth form

114. Some further analyses have been carried out on those direct applications and admissions from the four main types of school.[1] The Oxford entrance competition takes place in December, and most candidates enter for it in their seventh term in the sixth form.[2] Tables 50 and 51 show that 69 per cent. of applicants and 71 per cent. of admissions in fact did this, but there were wide variations between types of school. At independent schools a substantial proportion (28 per cent. at independent boarding schools) entered the competition after three complete years and a term in the sixth form. From maintained schools only was there a substantial proportion (28 per cent.) of applicants from the second-year sixth. Among admissions, compared with all applicants, there was a lower proportion from the second-year sixth, and a higher proportion from the fourth-year sixth, and 34 per cent. of all admissions from independent boarding schools were from the fourth-year sixth.

115. Pupils who enter the competition from the third-(or fourth-)year sixth may either be older, or have entered the sixth form early via an 'express stream'. That the latter is the preponderant explanation, not only for independent and direct-grant schools, but also for maintained schools gaining places at Oxford, is strongly suggested by Table 52. The differences in average age (for admissions) between those from second- and third-, and between those from third- and fourth-year sixth forms are each considerably less than one year. There is no substantial difference between

---

[1] Those with qualifications other than GCE A level (e.g. Scottish Higher Leaving Certificate) have been excluded.

[2] That is, from the 'third-year sixth'. This term is used, although candidates may leave school after the entrance examination, thus spending only two years and one term in the sixth form. The number of terms in the sixth form is defined as the number of terms spent on A level (or more advanced) work.

*1965-6 to read for first degrees*

OXFORD

NUMBER

| Number of admissions per school | HMC independent boarding | Independent boarding | HMC independent day | Independent day | HMC direct-grant | Direct-grant | Maintained | All schools — Number of schools | All schools — Number of admissions |
|---|---|---|---|---|---|---|---|---|---|
| 39 | 1 |  |  |  | 1 |  |  | 2 | 78 |
| 29 | 1 |  |  |  |  |  |  | 1 | 29 |
| 28 | 1 |  |  |  |  |  |  | 1 | 28 |
| 23 | 2 |  |  |  | 1 |  |  | 3 | 69 |
| 22 | 1 |  |  |  |  |  |  | 1 | 22 |
| 21 | 2 |  |  |  |  |  |  | 2 | 42 |
| 17 | 2 |  | 2 |  | 1 |  |  | 5 | 85 |
| 16 | 1 |  |  |  | 1 |  | 1 | 3 | 48 |
| 14 | 2 |  | 1 |  |  |  |  | 3 | 42 |
| 13 | 3 |  |  |  | 1 |  |  | 4 | 52 |
| 12 |  |  |  |  | 1 |  | 1 | 2 | 24 |
| 11 | 2 |  |  |  | 1 |  | 1 | 4 | 44 |
| 10 |  |  |  |  | 2 |  | 1 | 3 | 30 |
| 9 | 6 |  | 1 |  |  |  |  | 7 | 63 |
| 8 | 3 |  | 1 |  |  |  |  | 4 | 32 |
| 7 | 2 |  | 4 |  | 4 | 1 | 5 | 16 | 112 |
| 6 | 8 |  | 3 |  | 4 | 1 | 10 | 26 | 156 |
| 5 | 3 |  | 2 |  | 6 | 2 | 9 | 22 | 110 |
| 4 | 11 | 2 | 6 |  | 4 |  | 28 | 51 | 204 |
| 3 | 10 | 2 | 1 | 1 | 4 | 2 | 43 | 63 | 189 |
| 2 | 6 | 3 | 2 | 2 | 7 | 2 | 80 | 102 | 204 |
| 1 | 8 | 10 | 2 | 4 | 11 | 9 | 178 | 222 | 222 |
| *Schools* | | | | | | | | | |
| Number | 75 | 17 | 25 | 7 | 49 | 17 | 357 | 547 | |
| *Percentage* | *13·7* | *3·1* | *4·6* | *1·3* | *9·0* | *3·1* | *65·3* | *100·0* | |
| *Admissions* | | | | | | | | | |
| Number | 594 | 30 | 154 | 11 | 285 | 42 | 769 | | 1,885 |
| *Percentage* | *31·5* | *1·6* | *8·2* | *0·6* | *15·1* | *2·2* | *40·8* | | *100·0* |
| Average number of places per school | 7·9 | 1·8 | 6·2 | 1·6 | 5·8 | 2·5 | 2·2 | 3·4 | |

SOURCE: Admissions Office.

NOTES

1. The Cambridge pool and direct admissions are included, but 27 admissions from overseas and other schools are excluded.
2. See note to Table 44.

**Table 50.** *Time in sixth form of applicants by type of school. Men non-graduate candidates for admission in 1965–6 to read for first degrees*

OXFORD                                                                    PERCENTAGE

| Terms in sixth form at time of entrance competition | Independent boarding | Independent day | Direct-grant | Maintained | All schools |
|---|---|---|---|---|---|
| 4 | 6·5 | 9·5 | 9·9 | 28·0 | 15·9 |
| 7 | 65·2 | 70·6 | 82·0 | 67·6 | 69·3 |
| 10 or more | 28·4 | 19·9 | 8·1 | 4·4 | 14·8 |
| All | 100·0 | 100·0 | 100·0 | 100·0 | 100·0 |
| *Number* | *1,359* | *326* | *616* | *1,555* | *3,856* |
| Percentage of total | 35·2 | 8·5 | 16·0 | 40·3 | 100·0 |

SOURCE: Admissions Office.

NOTES
1. Central applications only are included, and of these 155 from other types of school, or with qualifications other than GCE are excluded.
2. 'Terms in sixth form' are the terms spent on A level (or more advanced) work.

**Table 51.** *Time in sixth form of admissions by type of school. Men non-graduate admissions in 1965–6 to read for first degrees*

OXFORD                                                                    PERCENTAGE

| Terms in sixth form at time of entrance competition | Independent boarding | Independent day | Direct-grant | Maintained | All schools |
|---|---|---|---|---|---|
| 4 | 3·2 | 8·5 | 4·5 | 23·7 | 12·1 |
| 7 | 62·8 | 68·3 | 85·6 | 71·6 | 70·9 |
| 10 or more | 34·0 | 23·2 | 9·9 | 4·6 | 17·1 |
| All | 100·0 | 100·0 | 100·0 | 100·0 | 100·0 |
| *Number* | *597* | *142* | *313* | *712* | *1,764* |
| Percentage of total | 33·8 | 8·0 | 17·7 | 40·4 | 100·0 |

SOURCE: Admissions Office.

NOTES
1. Central admissions only are included, and of these 54 from other types of school, or with qualifications other than GCE are excluded.
2. Those included will not correspond exactly with those matriculating in 1965–6 for the reasons stated in Note 1 above and in the note to Table 44.
3. 'Terms in sixth form' are the terms spent on A level (or more advanced) work.

maintained and other schools. The average age and the proportion aged 18 and over were the same for all applicants as for admissions. The pattern was very similar except that applicants from independent boarding schools, for each length of time in the sixth form, were slightly older than those admitted.

**Table 52.** *Average age by time in sixth form and type of school. Men non-graduate admissions in 1965–6 to read for first degrees*

OXFORD                                                                                                                      YEARS

| Terms in sixth form at time of entrance competition | Independent boarding | Independent day | Direct-grant | Maintained | All schools |
|---|---|---|---|---|---|
| 4 | 17·3 | 17·2 | 17·5 | 17·6 | 17·5 |
|   | (21) | (—) | (29) | (17) | (17) |
| 7 | 17·7 | 17·8 | 17·8 | 17·9 | 17·8 |
|   | (30) | (31) | (35) | (47) | (38) |
| 10 or more | 18·1 | 18·3 | 18·4 | 18·3 | 18·2 |
|   | (60) | (75) | (90) | (71) | (66) |
| All | 17·8 | 17·8 | 17·8 | 17·9 | 17·9 |
|   | (41) | (39) | (40) | (41) | (41) |

SOURCE: Admissions Office.

NOTES
1. See notes to Table 51.
2. Age is that at 1 November 1964, i.e. shortly before the entrance competition.
3. The percentage of those in each group who were aged 18 and over at 1 November 1964 is shown in brackets.

## Men: GCE qualifications

116. The GCE A level attainments of applicants and admissions at the time of the competition have been given ratings of 'very good', 'good', or 'pass', following the scheme used by UCCA[1] (Tables 53 and 54). Among applicants, of those having taken two or more A levels, the proportion rated 'very good' was highest for direct-grant and maintained schools, and lowest for independent boarding schools. And the proportion rated 'pass' was lowest for maintained schools and highest for independent boarding

[1] The ratings are based on the detailed classification used by UCCA, but the grouping of the classes is different in two respects. First, UCCA do not distinguish a group 'very good' (see *Second Report 1963–4*, UCCA, 1965, Table 11A). Secondly, their group 'good' is more selective than ours for those with two A levels. Our ratings have been chosen so that candidates with two A levels can achieve the highest rating of 'very good' and the definition of the rating 'good' on two A levels is adjusted accordingly. Only 4 per cent. of candidates who had taken A levels had a rating of 'very good' or 'good' on two A levels, however (they were mainly from independent boarding schools, and almost all were in arts and social studies), and the results would have been very similar had the UCCA convention been followed strictly.

**Table 53.** *GCE A level rating of applicants by type of school. Men non-graduate candidates for admission in 1965–6 to read for first degrees*

OXFORD                                                                    PERCENTAGE

| A level rating | Independent boarding | Independent day | Direct-grant | Maintained | All schools |
|---|---|---|---|---|---|
| Very good | 17·3 | 26·4 | 33·8 | 34·2 | 26·8 |
| Good | 35·8 | 40·0 | 37·2 | 39·7 | 37·8 |
| Pass | 38·9 | 30·8 | 27·1 | 23·8 | 30·9 |
| Fail | 8·0 | 2·7 | 2·0 | 2·3 | 4·5 |
| All having taken A levels | 100·0 | 100·0 | 100·0 | 100·0 | 100·0 |
| *Number having taken A levels* | *1,269* | *295* | *557* | *1,123* | *3,244* |
| *Total number* | *1,359* | *326* | *616* | *1,555* | *3,856* |
| Percentage having taken A levels | 93·4 | 90·5 | 90·4 | 72·2 | 84·1 |

SOURCE: Admissions Office.

NOTES

1. The A level rating (but not the nomenclature) is based on the classification scheme used by UCCA. The rating 'very good' corresponds to UCCA groups 1.3 and 1.2; and 'good' corresponds to UCCA groups 2.3, 3.3, and 2.2. (See *Second Report 1963–4*, UCCA, London, 1965, p. 13.) 'Very good' is defined as an average performance in three subjects better than three B grades or in two subjects better than two B grades. 'Good' is defined as an average performance below 'very good' but in three subjects equal to or better than three C grades; or, in two subjects, better than two C grades. 'Fail' means that at least two A levels had been taken, but fewer than two passes (grade E or better) had been obtained. 'Pass' is a performance between 'Good' and 'Fail'. No significance attaches to the nomenclature except that it gives a readily recognizable ordering of the groups.
2. Where more than three A levels in different subjects had been taken, the rating is based on the three best grades.
3. Where A level passes had been obtained in any subject on more than one occasion, the *latest* grade has been taken.
4. A few candidates had only one A level pass. In almost all cases this was taken in the first year of the sixth-form course. Such candidates have been counted as not having A level.
5. The rating applies to A level passes at the time of the entrance competition.
6. See Note 1 to Table 50.

schools. 8 per cent. from independent boarding schools had failed to obtain two A level passes, and 2 per cent. from the other types of school. Among admissions the relative positions of the different types of school was similar, but the proportion rated 'very good' was much higher. Among both applicants and admissions, the proportion not having taken A levels is, of course, closely related to the proportion from the second-year sixth form.

**Table 54.** *GCE A level rating of admissions by type of school. Men non-graduate admissions in 1965–6 to read for first degrees*

OXFORD                                                                    PERCENTAGE

| A level rating | Independent boarding | Independent day | Direct-grant | Maintained | All schools |
|---|---|---|---|---|---|
| Very good | 33·3 | 51·6 | 50·8 | 56·4 | 46·3 |
| Good | 42·7 | 35·2 | 34·3 | 33·8 | 37·3 |
| Pass | 22·9 | 12·5 | 14·1 | 9·1 | 15·5 |
| Fail | 1·1 | 0·8 | 0·7 | 0·7 | 0·8 |
| All having taken A levels | 100·0 | 100·0 | 100·0 | 100·0 | 100·0 |
| *Number having taken A levels* | *571* | *128* | *297* | *539* | *1,535* |
| *Total number* | *597* | *142* | *313* | *712* | *1,764* |
| Percentage having taken A levels | 95·6 | 90·1 | 94·9 | 75·7 | 87·0 |

SOURCE: Admissions Office.

NOTE: See Notes 1 and 2 to Table 51 and Notes 1–5 to Table 53.

117. A similar analysis of GCE S level passes is given in Tables 55 and 56. The distributions are based on all those having taken two or more A levels. Of these, 70 per cent. of the applicants and 81 per cent. of the admissions had taken S levels. Among applicants, the proportion having taken S levels was slightly lower for independent boarding schools than for other types of school. Having taken A levels but not S levels could be related to the ability of the candidate, but it could also reflect his school's policy or teaching arrangements and resources. No account can be taken of these factors. The S level ratings are more selective than the A level ratings, and only 11 per cent. of applicants who had taken A levels fell in the two highest S level categories. The proportion with an S level rating of 'good' or better was very close to the proportion with an A level rating of 'very good' for both applicants and admissions. Judged in terms of the two highest S level ratings, applicants and admissions from independent day and direct-grant schools had the highest qualifications, followed by those from independent boarding schools, with those from maintained schools having the lowest qualifications.[1] But if those with a 'good' rating or better are considered, the ranking is maintained schools in the third position, followed by independent boarding schools.

[1] It should be noted that candidates for the London University GCE may take one S level only, and therefore cannot appear in the two highest categories.

**Table 55.** *GCE S level rating of applicants by type of school. Men non-graduate candidates for admission in 1965–6 to read for first degrees*

OXFORD                                                                                      PERCENTAGE

| S level rating | Inde-pendent boarding | Inde-pendent day | Direct-grant | Maintained | All schools |
|---|---|---|---|---|---|
| Excellent | 4·2 | 5·8 | 6·6 | 3·5 | 4·5 |
| Very good | 6·9 | 9·2 | 6·8 | 5·9 | 6·7 |
| Good | 12·2 | 16·9 | 17·1 | 19·5 | 16·0 |
| Pass | 33·6 | 34·6 | 40·0 | 42·0 | 37·7 |
| All having taken S levels | 66·4 | 73·9 | 72·4 | 72·6 | 70·2 |
| Having taken A levels but not S levels | 33·6 | 26·1 | 27·6 | 27·4 | 29·8 |
| All having taken A levels | 100·0 | 100·0 | 100·0 | 100·0 | 100·0 |
| *Number having taken A levels* | *1,269* | *295* | *557* | *1,123* | *3,244* |

SOURCE: Admissions Office.

NOTES

1. S level passes are graded 1, 2, U in descending order of merit. The rating is based on the two best S level passes in different subjects, the most recent grade being taken where a subject had been taken more than once. The ratings are defined as follows:

    Excellent   Two grade 1 passes
    Very good   One grade 1 pass and one grade 2 pass
    Good   One grade 1 pass (and possibly a U grade) or two grade 2 passes
    Pass   Any other combination of grades.

    No significance attaches to the nomenclature except that it gives a readily recognizable ordering of the groups.

2. The rating applies to S level passes at the time of the entrance competition.

3. A number are included under 'All having taken S levels' who had taken S level papers none of which were classified since the necessary qualifying marks at A level (grade C or better) had not been obtained.

4. Only those having taken two A levels at the time of the competition are included.

5. See Note 1 to Table 50.

118. A similar analysis by subject group (Tables 57 and 58) shows that both applicants and admissions in science subjects had better A level qualifications than those in arts and social studies and a higher proportion had taken S level, but their S level qualifications were only slightly better. A larger proportion of applicants and admissions from maintained schools than from independent boarding schools are in science subjects. Part of the difference in A level qualifications of these two groups is thus accounted for by a difference in subject, but there are also substantial differences between the two types of school within the main subject groups.

**Table 56.** *GCE S level rating of admissions by type of school. Men non-graduate admissions in 1965–6 to read for first degrees*

OXFORD PERCENTAGE

| S level rating | Independent boarding | Independent day | Direct-grant | Maintained | All schools |
|---|---|---|---|---|---|
| Excellent | 8·9 | 13·3 | 12·1 | 6·7 | 9·1 |
| Very good | 13·5 | 15·6 | 11·8 | 10·2 | 12·2 |
| Good | 19·8 | 22·7 | 22·9 | 30·1 | 24·2 |
| Pass | 33·8 | 30·5 | 34·0 | 35·1 | 34·0 |
| All having taken S levels | 78·8 | 85·9 | 81·5 | 82·6 | 81·2 |
| Having taken A levels but not S levels | 21·2 | 14·1 | 18·5 | 17·4 | 18·8 |
| All having taken A levels | 100·0 | 100·0 | 100·0 | 100·0 | 100·0 |
| *Number having taken A levels* | *571* | *128* | *297* | *539* | *1,535* |

SOURCE: Admissions Office.
NOTE: See Notes 1–2 to Table 51 and Notes 1–4 to Table 55.

**Table 57.** *GCE A level rating by subject group. Men non-graduate candidates for admission in 1965–6 to read for first degrees*

OXFORD PERCENTAGE

| A level rating | Applications | | Admissions | |
|---|---|---|---|---|
| | Arts and social studies | Science | Arts and social studies | Science |
| Very good | 21·4 | 37·0 | 38·7 | 59·7 |
| Good | 39·4 | 34·8 | 42·1 | 29·0 |
| Pass | 34·1 | 24·9 | 18·1 | 11·0 |
| Fail | 5·2 | 3·4 | 1·1 | 0·4 |
| All having taken A levels | 100·0 | 100·0 | 100·0 | 100·0 |
| *Number having taken A levels* | *2,116* | *1,128* | *979* | *556* |
| *Total number* | *2,514* | *1,342* | *1,127* | *637* |
| Percentage having taken A levels | 84·2 | 84·1 | 86·9 | 87·3 |

SOURCE: Admissions Office.
NOTE: See notes to Tables 53 and 54.

**Table 58.** *GCE S level rating by subject group. Men non-graduate candidates for admission in 1965–6 to read for first degrees*

OXFORD                                                        PERCENTAGE

| S level rating | Applications | | Admissions | |
|---|---|---|---|---|
| | Arts and social studies | Science | Arts and social studies | Science |
| Excellent | 4·4 | 4·7 | 9·3 | 8·8 |
| Very good | 5·6 | 8·9 | 10·1 | 15·8 |
| Good | 15·5 | 17·0 | 23·6 | 25·4 |
| Pass | 37·0 | 39·2 | 33·8 | 34·4 |
| All having taken S levels | 68·4 | 73·7 | 79·0 | 85·3 |
| Having taken A levels but not S levels | 31·6 | 26·3 | 21·0 | 14·7 |
| All having taken A levels | 100·0 | 100·0 | 100·0 | 100·0 |
| *Number having taken A levels* | *2,116* | *1,128* | *979* | *556* |

SOURCE: Admissions Office.

NOTE: See notes to Tables 55 and 56.

119. There is an apparent inconsistency between the A level and S level ratings in the highest ranges for maintained schools. The two examinations are often thought to test different things—achievement in the former case, and 'promise' in the latter—so it is possible that they should give conflicting results. But the apparent inconsistency may be a result of the particular ratings adopted. The 'very good' rating for A level is the highest group used by UCCA. But it covers a wide range of results from three good A grades to (for example) a weak A and two B grades. The S level ratings, on the other hand, have as the two highest groups the two highest possible results. If a more selective top rating had been used for A levels it is possible that a relatively small proportion of those from maintained schools would have been found in it.

120. The proportion of admissions gaining open scholarships, or any entrance award, was highest for independent day schools. Next were direct-grant schools followed by maintained schools, while the proportion was lowest for independent boarding schools (Table 59). There was a definite relationship between the proportions gaining open scholarships and all awards, and both A level and S level ratings (Tables 60 and 61). Of those with a rating of 'excellent' at S level, 80 per cent. gained awards. Apart from the over-all difference between schools set out in Table 59, there was no systematic difference between types of schools at different A and S level ratings.

**Table 59.** *Open scholars and all award holders as percentage of all admissions by type of school. Men non-graduate admissions in 1965–6 to read for first degrees*

OXFORD                                                                    PERCENTAGE

|  | Independent boarding | Independent day | Direct-grant | Maintained | All schools |
|---|---|---|---|---|---|
| Open scholars | 18 | 33 | 24 | 21 | 21 |
| All award holders | 37 | 54 | 46 | 43 | 42 |

SOURCE: Admissions Office.

NOTES
1. See Notes 1–2 to Table 51.
2. Because of the differences in coverage explained in Notes 1–2 to Table 51, the figures for award holders in this table are slightly different from those in Table 33.
3. Holders of closed scholarships and exhibitions are included under all award holders.

**Table 60.** *Open scholars and all award holders as percentage of all admissions by GCE A level rating and subject group. Men non-graduate admissions in 1965–6 to read for first degrees*

OXFORD                                                                    PERCENTAGE

|  | GCE A level rating | | | | All |
|---|---|---|---|---|---|
|  | Very good | Good | Pass or fail | Not having taken A levels | |
| **ARTS AND SOCIAL STUDIES** | | | | | |
| Open scholars | 34 | 13 | 8 | 17 | 20 |
| All award holders | 55 | 33 | 23 | 33 | 39 |
| **SCIENCE** | | | | | |
| Open scholars | 35 | 14 | 10 | 16 | 25 |
| All award holders | 65 | 30 | 24 | 28 | 48 |
| **ALL SUBJECTS** | | | | | |
| Open scholars | 34 | 13 | 8 | 17 | 21 |
| All award holders | 60 | 32 | 24 | 31 | 42 |

SOURCE: Admissions Office.

NOTES
1. Holders of closed scholarships and exhibitions are included under all award holders.
2. See Notes 1–2 to Table 51 and Notes 1–5 to Table 53.

**Table 61.** *Open scholars and all award holders as percentage of all admissions by GCE S level rating and subject group. Men non-graduate admissions in 1965–6 to read for first degrees*

OXFORD                                                                 PERCENTAGE

|  | GCE S level rating | | | | | |
|---|---|---|---|---|---|---|
|  | Excellent | Very good | Good | Pass | Having taken A but not S levels | All having taken A levels |
| ARTS AND SOCIAL STUDIES | | | | | | |
| Open scholars | 55 | 29 | 20 | 11 | 16 | 20 |
| All award holders | 76 | 56 | 44 | 29 | 33 | 40 |
| SCIENCE | | | | | | |
| Open scholars | 55 | 42 | 25 | 17 | 16 | 26 |
| All award holders | 88 | 69 | 57 | 37 | 30 | 50 |
| ALL SUBJECTS | | | | | | |
| Open scholars | 55 | 35 | 22 | 14 | 16 | 22 |
| All award holders | 80 | 62 | 49 | 32 | 32 | 44 |

SOURCE: Admissions Office.

NOTE: See Notes 1–2 to Table 51, Notes 1–2 and 4 to Table 55, and Note 1 to Table 60.

121. The less selective nature of the A level ratings compared with the S level ratings is illustrated by the fact that the proportions of open scholars and of all award holders among those with S level ratings of 'good' or better were 32 per cent. and 59 per cent. respectively—almost as high as among those with A level ratings 'very good'.

## Women

122. The information on women's admissions relates to the December 1964 competition for admission in October 1965 and covers applications from non-graduates only.

123. Two important points of difference from the men's admissions are that there was no formal central admissions scheme, and that candidates could apply separately to Cambridge. There were a number of applicants who declined places when offered, presumably because a place or award had been accepted at Cambridge.

124. There were 1,842 applications, of whom 443 were admitted (i.e. were offered and accepted places), 86 with awards. A further 89 declined places offered, 22 of whom also refused awards. No candidate was offered a place before the special examination.

**Table 62.** *Type of school of applicants and admissions. Women non-graduate candidates for admission in 1965–6 to read for first degrees*

OXFORD

| Type of school | Applications (including those who declined a place) | | Applications (excluding those who declined a place) | | Admissions | | Acceptance rate | |
|---|---|---|---|---|---|---|---|---|
| | Number (1) | Percentage (2) | Number (3) | Percentage (4) | Number (5) | Percentage (6) | Col. (5) as percentage of col. (1) | Col. (5) as percentage of col. (3) |
| Independent boarding | 318 | 17·3 | .. | .. | 85 | 19·2 | 26·7 | .. |
| Independent day | 205 | 11·1 | .. | .. | 54 | 12·2 | 26·3 | .. |
| Direct-grant | 382 | 20·7 | 362 | 20·7 | 106 | 23·9 | 27·7 | 29·3 |
| Maintained | 874 | 47·5 | 832 | 47·5 | 189 | 42·7 | 21·6 | 22·7 |
| Others | 63 | 3·4 | 63 | 3·6 | 9 | 2·0 | 14·3 | 14·3 |
| All independent | 523 | 28·4 | 496 | 28·3 | 139 | 31·4 | 26·6 | 28·0 |
| All schools | 1,842 | 100·0 | 1,753 | 100·0 | 443 | 100·0 | 24·0 | 25·3 |

SOURCE: Women's colleges.

NOTES

1. Those included in this table are those taking part in the December 1964 competition, and the total of 443 admissions will differ from non-graduates matriculating in 1965–6 in so far as some of those accepting places may have subsequently withdrawn.

2. There may be a small amount of double counting in the applications.

## Women : type of school

125. Table 62 shows applications, admissions, and acceptance[1] rates by type of school. Compared with the men, the over-all acceptance rate was much lower, and that for applicants from maintained schools was below the average whereas for men it was a little above the average. But nearly half the applications came from maintained schools, and in the distribution of admissions there was a marginally higher proportion from maintained schools than for men.

**Table 63.** *Type of school of applicants and admissions by college. Women non-graduate candidates for admission in 1965–6 to read for first degrees*

OXFORD                                                                                          PERCENTAGE

| College | Independent boarding | Independent day | Direct-grant | Maintained | Other schools | All schools | *Number* |
|---|---|---|---|---|---|---|---|
| **APPLICATIONS** | | | | | | | |
| Lady Margaret Hall | 22 | 10 | 20 | 39 | 9 | 100 | *311* |
| St. Anne's | 19 | 12 | 27 | 40 | 1 | 100 | *478* |
| St. Hilda's | 16 | 9 | 15 | 57 | 2 | 100 | *414* |
| St. Hugh's | 19 | 7 | 19 | 53 | 3 | 100 | *323* |
| Somerville | 9 | 17 | 22 | 48 | 3 | 100 | *316* |
| All colleges | 17 | 11 | 21 | 48 | 3 | 100 | *1,842* |
| **ADMISSIONS** | | | | | | | |
| Lady Margaret Hall | 25 | 4 | 29 | 39 | 4 | 100 | *85* |
| St. Anne's | 26 | 16 | 25 | 32 | 1 | 100 | *103* |
| St. Hilda's | 17 | 12 | 12 | 56 | 2 | 100 | *89* |
| St. Hugh's | 17 | 9 | 23 | 48 | 2 | 100 | *81* |
| Somerville | 9 | 20 | 29 | 40 | 1 | 100 | *85* |
| All colleges | 19 | 12 | 24 | 43 | 2 | 100 | *443* |

SOURCE: Women's colleges.

NOTES
1. Those who declined a place are included among applicants.
2. Applicants are included under their college of first choice.
3. See notes to Table 62.

126. Table 63 gives type of school of applicants and admissions by college. Within colleges there are likely to be considerable year-to-year fluctuations in the proportions of both applicants and admissions from different types of school.

[1] Acceptance, that is, by the colleges. One set of acceptance rates includes among applicants those who subsequently declined a place; the other does not.

## Women : subject

127. Table 64 gives applications, admissions, and acceptance rates by subject of proposed degree course. The Schools attracting the largest numbers of applicants were Modern History, English, and Modern Languages. In Modern History the acceptance rate was average, and in the other two it was well below average. Among the remaining larger subjects above average acceptance rates obtained for Literae Humaniores, PPE, Physics, Chemistry, and Zoology, while in Jurisprudence the acceptance rate was below average. The acceptance rates might, however, be affected by the teaching resources of the colleges as well as the quality of the applicants.

**Table 64.** *Proposed Honour School of applicants and admissions. Women non-graduate candidates for admission in 1965–6 to read for first degrees*

OXFORD                                                                    NUMBER

| Honour School | Applications (including those who declined a place) (1) | Applications (excluding those who declined a place) (2) | Admissions (3) | Acceptance rate Col. (3) as percentage of col. (1) (4) | Col. (3) as percentage of col. (2) (5) |
|---|---|---|---|---|---|
| Literae Humaniores | 80 | 68 | 31 | 39 | 46 |
| Theology | 4 | 4 | 1 | 25 | 25 |
| Modern History | 249 | 241 | 60 | 24 | 25 |
| English | 366 | 358 | 68 | 19 | 19 |
| Modern Languages | 377 | 367 | 68 | 18 | 19 |
| Oriental Studies | 10 | 10 | 5 | 50 | 50 |
| Geography | 51 | 49 | 13 | 25 | 27 |
| Music | 23 | 22 | 7 | 30 | 32 |
| Jurisprudence | 58 | 55 | 10 | 17 | 18 |
| PPE | 115 | 112 | 37 | 32 | 33 |
| Mathematics | 158 | 147 | 36 | 23 | 24 |
| Physics | 51 | 46 | 18 | 35 | 39 |
| Chemistry | 84 | 73 | 25 | 30 | 34 |
| Biochemistry | 35 | 32 | 7 | 20 | 22 |
| Animal Physiology | 108 | 102 | 26 | 24 | 25 |
| Zoology | 40 | 35 | 19 | 48 | 54 |
| Botany | 10 | 10 | 3 | 30 | 30 |
| Geology | — | — | — | . | . |
| PPP | 17 | 16 | 7 | 41 | 44 |
| Engineering | 5 | 5 | 1 | 20 | 20 |
| Engineering and Economics | — | — | — | . | . |
| Metallurgy | — | — | — | . | . |
| Agriculture | 1 | 1 | 1 | 100 | 100 |
| Forestry | — | — | — | . | . |
| All Honour Schools | 1,842 | 1,753 | 443 | 24 | 25 |

SOURCE: Women's colleges.

NOTE: See notes to Table 62.

**Table 65**. *GCE A level qualifications. Women non-graduate candidates for admission in 1965–6 to read for first degrees*

OXFORD                   PERCENTAGE

| | With A level passes | Without A level passes | All | *Number* |
|---|---|---|---|---|
| Applicants | 65·9 | 34·1 | 100·0 | *1,842* |
| Admissions | 75·4 | 24·6 | 100·0 | *443* |
| Admissions as percentage of applicants (acceptance rate) | 27·5 | 17·3 | 24·0 | |

SOURCE: Women's colleges.

NOTES
1. The applicants include those who subsequently withdrew.
2. See notes to Table 62.

## Women : GCE qualifications

128. The proportion of admissions without A level passes was 25 per cent., twice that for men. The acceptance rate was 28 per cent. among applicants with A levels, and 17 per cent. among those without A levels. The differential between the acceptance rates for those with, and those without, A levels was higher than for men.

### THE ACADEMIC EFFICIENCY OF OXFORD ADMISSIONS

129. In the present context academic efficiency is defined (but not precisely) in terms of Oxford obtaining the highest quality of entrants; the prime criterion of quality being performance in the Honour Schools.

130. Selection procedures for university admissions are far from perfect, and it is clearly impossible to ensure that no weak individuals are admitted. But it is obviously desirable to discover systematic biases if they exist. Three possible kinds of bias[1] are considered here; that operating against women, regionally, or against candidates from maintained schools.

131. Any investigation of this kind must use criteria by which to judge the quality of candidates for admission. As already stated, class of Oxford degree is the prime criterion. But at least three years must pass before this criterion can be applied,[2] and it cannot be applied at all to those who fail to gain admission. An attempt has therefore been made to use other criteria for which evidence is available. Admission to another university is one measure of quality. Attainment as measured by GCE A and S levels is another, and so is a career in a school sixth form. None of these criteria is ideal, but the first two are preferred to the last.

[1] The word is used in a technical sense, not as a synonym of 'prejudice'.
[2] Except for graduates of other universities, with whom we are not concerned here.

132. Biases in admissions, if they exist, may occur in two ways. First, they may occur in the application rate. If would-be applicants whom Oxford would like to accept are deterred by the impression that they stand no chance of admission, or by the nature of the admissions competition, then it should be possible to remove some of the hindrances, and hence improve the entry. Secondly, there may be biases (conscious or unconscious) in the process of selecting from applicants. Both these possible sources of bias are considered where appropriate, and where suitable data are available.

133. The main conclusion from the analyses that follow is that Oxford has admitted disproportionately few men undergraduates from maintained schools, though the proportion has increased strikingly in recent years. The main reason has been that the application rate from such schools has been low, but it is also true that the acceptance rate for candidates with given levels of qualifications appears to be lower for candidates from maintained schools than for candidates from independent boarding schools. The application rate from maintained schools is low largely because candidates from such schools whose sixth-form work is organized on a two-year basis rather than a three-year basis find themselves at a disadvantage in the admissions competition. It has not been possible to determine the size of this group of schools with any precision. Apart from any disadvantage connected with type of school, there does not appear to be any significant regional bias. There is a bias against women in the sense that it should be possible to increase the admissions of women while keeping their quality at least as high as that of the men.

## Region

134. England and Wales only are considered.

135. The figures given in Tables 66 and 67 are in terms of entries per 1,000 sixth-form pupils. They take no account of possible variations between the regions in the proportions of sixth formers going on to university. Separate figures are given for the main types of schools, and there is a difficulty in interpreting those for independent schools. For entrants are classified according to home address, whereas sixth formers are classified according to address of school. To the extent that pupils attend schools in a region other than that in which they live, like is not being compared with like. (This difficulty could also occur with maintained and direct-grant schools, but it is unlikely to have a significant effect as there are few boarding pupils at these schools.) In so far as independent schools are concentrated in the south-east, and draw pupils from other regions, the figure in the table will be lower than if entrants had been classified by the region of their school.[1]

---

[1] Forty-four per cent. of all sixth-form boys were in the south-east, but 57 per cent. of sixth-form boys at independent schools were in the south-east.

**Table 66.** *Number of entrants to read for first degrees, 1964–5, per 1,000 pupils in sixth forms by region and type of school. Men non-graduates from England and Wales*

RATIO

|  | Independent | Direct-grant | Maintained | All |
|---|---|---|---|---|
| North | 27·8 | 18·9 | 7·3 | 11·1 |
| Midlands | 19·5 | 37·1 | 6·8 | 11·6 |
| Wales | 44·2 | (40·7) | 3·7 | 6·3 |
| South-east | 41·0 | 26·1 | 7·7 | 16·7 |
| South-west | 19·2 | 21·6 | 4·9 | 11·7 |
| England and Wales | 32·7 | 24·4 | 7·0 | 13·5 |

SOURCE: Sixth-form pupils: Department of Education and Science.
Entrants: matriculation forms.
NOTES:
1. Those from other types of schools are excluded.
2. The numbers of sixth-form pupils are those at January 1964.
3. All entrants from independent schools are included, but sixth-form pupils at independent schools recognized as efficient only are included.
4. Where entrants were 5 or less, the entry in the table is in brackets.

**Table 67.** *Number of entrants to read for first degrees, 1964–5, per 1,000 pupils in sixth forms by region and type of school. Women non-graduates from England and Wales*

RATIO

|  | Independent | Direct-grant | Maintained | All |
|---|---|---|---|---|
| North | 5·8 | 7·7 | 1·8 | 3·2 |
| Midlands | 8·5 | 15·4 | 2·0 | 3·7 |
| Wales | (4·3) | (3·8) | (0·9) | 1·3 |
| South-east | 8·3 | 18·9 | 2·5 | 4·8 |
| South-west | 10·7 | (1·7) | 1·6 | 3·8 |
| England and Wales | 8·2 | 12·0 | 2·1 | 3·9 |

SOURCE: Sixth-form pupils: Department of Education and Science.
Entrants: matriculation forms.
NOTE: See notes to Table 66.

136. Although the numbers from Wales are small, they suggest marked under-representation compared with England; but Wales, like Scotland, has its 'own' university system.

137. From maintained schools, the largest entry (in proportion to sixth formers) came from the south-east, followed by the north and midlands. It was smallest from the south-west. The differences are not large, however. The pattern is similar for men and women.

138. The midlands entry from direct-grant schools was high (the highest for men) and so was that of the south-east (the highest for women).

139. The main feature of the entry from independent schools is that for men it was much higher for the south-east than for other parts of England, and would probably be higher still if entrants were classified by the region of their school.

140. The over-all figures show a higher entry for the south-east, and not a great deal of difference between the other regions of England. For men the higher entry from the south-east is largely due to the position at independent schools.

141. Thus, if there is a definite regional bias in entries, it would appear to be in favour of the south-east, largely because of the high proportion of sixth formers at independent schools who enter. But reaching the sixth form is not in itself a qualification to enter Oxford, and no account has been taken of the proportion of sixth formers who might be so qualified. Those who go on to any university would be a better guide, and if the proportion of sixth formers going on to university were higher in the south-east, this would account for some of the apparent bias shown in Tables 66 and 67.

## Sex

142. The proportion of women undergraduates at universities other than Oxford and Cambridge is 31 per cent.; at Oxford it is 16 per cent. This suggests that it should be possible to increase the proportion of women at Oxford unless a higher proportion of women than of men at other universities gain poor degrees or no degrees, and would not be regarded as potential entrants to Oxford. The evidence on this point is threefold.

143. First, the statistics collected by the Robbins Committee show the wastage rate is much the same for men as for women, and that of those graduating in Great Britain in 1958 (and receiving honours or pass degrees) 59 per cent. of the men and 57 per cent. of the women received first- or second-class honours.[1] There was more difference between men and women receiving firsts or upper seconds (36 per cent. and 29 per cent. respectively); but this will be partly accounted for by there being a higher proportion of firsts and upper seconds in science, while a lower proportion of women than of men read science. There was also a lower than average proportion of firsts and seconds among women from maintained schools.

144. Secondly, there is the evidence on the class of degree obtained by men and women at Oxford. Table 68 shows that over the past decade a

[1] Robbins Report, Appendix Two (A), Part IV, p. 133, and Table 31, p. 155.

substantially higher proportion of women than of men have gained firsts
or seconds, though the proportion of women gaining firsts has been lower.
The proportion of Oxford men gaining firsts or seconds has been about the
same as the national proportion in 1958, but the proportion for Oxford
women is well above the national proportion.

**Table 68.** *Percentage of those graduating who gained first- and second-class
honours*

OXFORD                                                                    PERCENTAGE

| | Men | | Women | | Men and women | |
|---|---|---|---|---|---|---|
| | Firsts | Firsts and seconds | Firsts | Firsts and seconds | Firsts | Firsts and seconds |
| 1955 | 7·5 | 61·1 | 4·2 | 82·4 | 7·0 | 64·7 |
| 1956 | 9·0 | 59·2 | 6·0 | 78·1 | 8·5 | 62·4 |
| 1957 | 8·0 | 58·3 | 6·6 | 76·2 | 7·7 | 61·3 |
| 1958 | 8·1 | 59·0 | 7·9 | 79·4 | 8·1 | 62·2 |
| 1959 | 7·6 | 59·2 | 8·5 | 73·1 | 7·7 | 61·2 |
| 1960 | 8·4 | 57·5 | 7·9 | 78·7 | 8·3 | 60·4 |
| 1961 | 8·9 | 63·2 | 4·5 | 71·4 | 8·3 | 64·3 |
| 1962 | 8·3 | 62·9 | 6·2 | 69·1 | 8·0 | 63·7 |
| 1963 | 8·7 | 62·2 | 7·5 | 78·4 | 8·5 | 64·6 |
| 1964 | 9·1 | 63·2 | 9·0 | 79·2 | 9·1 | 65·9 |

SOURCE: *Oxford Magazine* (annual articles).

NOTES
1. For 1955–8 the figures are the percentage of all those obtaining a class; for 1959–64
   they are the percentage of all those obtaining a class, an *aegrotat*, a pass degree, or
   failing in Honours examinations.
2. The results of the B.C.L. are included.

145. These two pieces of evidence suggest that women entering Oxford
are on average of higher intellectual calibre than men, whereas there is little
to choose between the sexes nationally.[1] If a larger proportion of places
were available for women at Oxford it should therefore be possible to
increase the Oxford intake of women without their performance falling
below that of men.

146. This evidence is buttressed by an analysis of the A level performance
of applicants and admissions to universities in October 1964 made through
UCCA. Table 69 shows that women applicants were rather better qualified
than men; that the acceptance rates were very similar; and thus among
admissions, the women were rather better qualified.

[1] These statements are based on those gaining firsts or seconds. They do not apply to
those gaining firsts.

**Table 69.** *Applicants and admissions through UCCA for entry to universities in October 1964, by A level qualifications, subject group, and sex*

PERCENTAGE

| | Applicants (excluding those who withdrew) | | | | | Admissions | | | | Acceptance rates (admissions as percentage of applicants) | | | |
| --- | --- | --- | --- | --- | --- | --- | --- | --- | --- | --- | --- | --- | --- |
| | A level rating | | | | Number | A level rating | | | Number | A level rating | | | All |
| | Very good | Good | Pass | Fail | | Very good | Good | Pass | | Very good | Good | Pass | |
| **MEN** | | | | | | | | | | | | | |
| Arts | 9·1 | 34·2 | 49·2 | 7·5 | 5,209 | 15·6 | 53·5 | 30·9 | 2,906 | 95·6 | 87·4 | 35·0 | 55·8 |
| Social studies | 7·2 | 30·6 | 53·6 | 8·5 | 4,194 | 14·1 | 53·0 | 32·9 | 2,105 | 98·0 | 86·8 | 30·8 | 50·2 |
| Science | 13·9 | 30·8 | 47·5 | 7·8 | 12,181 | 19·8 | 42·1 | 38·1 | 8,472 | 98·9 | 95·0 | 55·9 | 69·6 |
| Medicine | 4·8 | 23·0 | 58·7 | 13·4 | 2,315 | 10·7 | 42·4 | 46·9 | 988 | 94·6 | 78·8 | 34·0 | 42·7 |
| All subjects | 10·8 | 30·8 | 50·0 | 8·4 | 23,899 | 17·5 | 46·0 | 36·5 | 14,471 | 98·0 | 90·6 | 44·2 | 60·6 |
| **WOMEN** | | | | | | | | | | | | | |
| Arts | 15·7 | 38·5 | 41·4 | 4·4 | 6,092 | 24·0 | 54·5 | 21·5 | 3,915 | 98·5 | 91·0 | 33·3 | 64·3 |
| Social studies | 8·4 | 32·2 | 51·7 | 7·7 | 1,732 | 15·8 | 53·6 | 30·6 | 899 | 97·3 | 86·4 | 30·7 | 51·9 |
| Science | 12·4 | 32·3 | 47·0 | 8·4 | 3,072 | 17·4 | 44·2 | 38·4 | 2,150 | 98·4 | 96·0 | 57·1 | 70·0 |
| Medicine | 8·4 | 29·3 | 49·9 | 12·4 | 910 | 16·3 | 48·1 | 35·6 | 405 | 86·8 | 73·0 | 31·7 | 44·5 |
| All subjects | 13·2 | 35·2 | 45·0 | 6·5 | 11,806 | 20·7 | 51·0 | 28·3 | 7,369 | 97·8 | 90·4 | 39·2 | 62·4 |
| **MEN AND WOMEN** | | | | | | | | | | | | | |
| Arts | 12·6 | 36·5 | 45·0 | 5·8 | 11,301 | 20·4 | 54·1 | 25·5 | 6,821 | 97·5 | 89·4 | 34·2 | 60·4 |
| Social studies | 7·6 | 31·1 | 53·1 | 8·3 | 5,926 | 14·6 | 53·2 | 32·2 | 3,004 | 97·8 | 86·7 | 30·8 | 50·7 |
| Science | 13·6 | 31·1 | 47·4 | 7·9 | 15,253 | 19·3 | 42·5 | 38·2 | 10,622 | 98·8 | 95·2 | 56·1 | 69·6 |
| Medicine | 5·8 | 24·8 | 56·2 | 13·1 | 3,225 | 12·3 | 44·1 | 43·6 | 1,393 | 91·5 | 76·8 | 33·5 | 43·2 |
| All subjects | 11·6 | 32·2 | 48·4 | 7·8 | 35,705 | 18·6 | 47·7 | 33·8 | 21,840 | 97·9 | 90·5 | 42·7 | 61·2 |

SOURCE: *Second Report 1963–4*, UCCA, Tables 15–25.

NOTES

1. Those with A levels which could not be classified (UCCA groups U.2, U.3, and U) are excluded.
2. The A level ratings are described in Note 1 to Table 53.
3. This table is based on a large sample of all applicants. See source for details.

147. It should thus be possible to increase the proportion of women under-graduates to the 20–25 per cent. recommended as a planning figure by the Commission. This would depend on sufficient suitably qualified women applying for admission, but since the number of applicants per place is roughly twice that for men, some increase should be possible as soon as places are made available.

**Table 70.** *Applicants and admissions for entry to read first degrees at Oxford in October 1965 by subject. Women non-graduates*

OXFORD                                                          PERCENTAGE

|  | Applicants (excluding those who declined a place) | Admissions | Acceptance rate |
|---|---|---|---|
| Arts | 63·8 | 57·1 | 22·6 |
| Social studies | 9·5 | 10·6 | 28·1 |
| Science and medicine | 26·6 | 32·3 | 30·6 |
| All subjects | 100·0 | 100·0 | 25·3 |
| *Number* | *1,753* | *443* | · |

SOURCE: Table 64.
NOTE: See notes to Table 62.

**Table 71.** *Applicants and admissions through UCCA for entry to universities in October 1964 by subject. Women*

PERCENTAGE

|  | Applicants (excluding those who withdrew) | Admissions | Acceptance rate |
|---|---|---|---|
| Arts | 51·0 | 53·2 | 59·8 |
| Social studies | 15·3 | 12·4 | 46·6 |
| Science | 25·6 | 28·9 | 64·8 |
| Medicine | 8·0 | 5·5 | 39·2 |
| All subjects | 100·0 | 100·0 | 57·4 |
| *Number* | *13,086* | *7,512* | · |

SOURCE: *Second Report 1963–4*, UCCA, Tables 15–25.
NOTE: This table is based on a large sample of all applicants through UCCA. See source for details.

148. A further important consideration is the balance of subjects. The proportion of women undergraduates reading arts at Oxford is already higher than for men (Table 12) and it would lead to an unsatisfactory balance of subjects in the women's colleges if the untapped 'pool' consisted mainly of those wishing to read arts subjects. Tables 70 and 71 compare admissions by subject at Oxford with those at other universities. They show that a slightly higher proportion are admitted nationally than at Oxford to read social studies, and science and medicine, while in arts the proportion is slightly lower. It would appear that, although Oxford has not much leeway, increasing the entry of women need not lead to a worsening of the balance of subjects. One potential problem would be to persuade more suitably qualified girls wishing to read science to apply to Oxford, since the acceptance rate in science is at present well above that in arts.

## Type of school

149. Entrants to university in 1961 from England and Wales were much the same proportion of school leavers who were formally qualified (with at least two A levels) for each type of school. For men, the over-all proportion was 66 per cent.; it was 63 per cent. for maintained, and 69 per cent. for independent schools. The corresponding figures for women were 48 per cent., 49 per cent., and 51 per cent. But the proportions going to Oxford or Cambridge were very different. Of all men with two or more A levels, 14 per cent. went to Oxford or Cambridge; but of those from maintained schools the figure was 7 per cent., while it was 33 per cent. for those from independent schools. 2 per cent. of 'qualified' women from maintained schools went to Oxford or Cambridge, compared with 7 per cent. from independent schools, the over-all figure being 4 per cent.[1] Undergraduates from maintained schools were thus less well represented at Oxford than at other universities.

150. In 1961 60 per cent. of all men undergraduates at universities in England and Wales were from maintained schools, whereas for Oxford the figure was 33 per cent. At London it was 58 per cent. The position was similar for women for whom the proportions were 67 per cent., 40 per cent., and 56 per cent. respectively.[2]

151. Since 1961 there has been an increase in the proportion of undergraduates from maintained schools both at Oxford and nationally, but the increase in the proportion of men from maintained schools appears to have been considerably less at other universities than it was at Oxford. Tables 31 and 32 show that for entrants to Oxford from schools in 1965–6, 40

[1] Robbins Report, Appendix Two (B), Part I, Table 14, p. 13.
[2] Robbins Report, Appendix Two (B), Part I, Table 11, p. 9. The figures for Oxford are consistent with Tables 31 and 32, making allowance for sampling fluctuations and the difference in date.

**Table 72.** *Type of school of school leavers in 1963–4 who intended going on to university. England and Wales*

PERCENTAGE

|  | Independent | Direct-grant | Maintained | All schools | *Number* |
|---|---|---|---|---|---|
| Men | 21 | 15 | 64 | 100 | *17,520* |
| Women | 13 | 15 | 72 | 100 | *8,090* |
| Men and women | 18 | 15 | 67 | 100 | *25,610* |

SOURCE: Department of Education and Science.

NOTES
1. Independent schools not recognized as efficient are excluded.
2. Included in this table are school leavers in 1963–4 who intended going on to university within 12 months of leaving school.

per cent. of the men and 43 per cent. of the women were from maintained schools (and if entrants from overseas and 'other' schools are excluded, the proportions are 41 per cent. and 44 per cent. respectively). Table 72 gives the distribution of school leavers in 1963–4 from schools in England and Wales[1] who intended to go on to university, and shows that 64 per cent. of men and 72 per cent. of women were from maintained schools. This is only an approximation to the distribution of all entrants in 1964–5 for a number of reasons. The proportion from independent schools is slightly understated since leavers from independent schools not recognized as efficient are excluded. Entrants to universities in England and Wales in 1964–5 will also be different to the extent that some came from schools outside England and Wales; that some school leavers went to universities outside England and Wales; and some entrants to universities left school before 1963–4. However, these differences in coverage will affect the pattern only to the extent that they affect leavers from the various types of school differently. And similar figures for two previous years show a lower proportion from maintained schools. Of school leavers in 1960–1 who intended to go on to university, 62 per cent. of the men and 66 per cent. of the women were from maintained schools; the corresponding figures for school leavers in 1962–3 were 62 per cent. and 67 per cent.[2]

[1] Except from independent schools not recognized as efficient.
[2] *Statistics of Education*, 1961, Part II, Table 7; and 1963, Part III, Table 9. There is one difference between the compilation of these figures and those of school leavers in 1963–4. The category 'leaving to enter temporary employment', which includes leavers intending eventually to enter universities, was defined precisely for 1963–4 leavers, but not for earlier years. The definition embraces leavers whose intended entry to full-time further education was 13 or more months after leaving school, but was not later than September/October 1965. In earlier years the interpretation of the term was at the discretion of the schools making returns.

152. In the Robbins Report this situation is analysed further and in particular in terms of the qualifications of entrants, and of the relation between applications and admissions.[1] The main results are summarized in paras. 153 and 154 and 164–72 below.

153. In the latter half of the fifties the relative position of the maintained schools declined (Table R. 15). The number of university places did not rise as fast as the number of school children aged 17, and in this sense there was a decline in opportunity. (It is possible that the increase in the number of school children aged 17 merely reflects a change in the composition of sixth forms. Evidence examined by the Robbins Committee suggests, however, that in the case of boys the number qualified for university entry rose at the same rate as the number at school aged 17, and in the case of girls, the number so qualified rose more quickly.)[2] The relative decline in 'opportunity' for men was greater for pupils from maintained schools (since the number of 17-year-olds increased more rapidly at this type of school), and was especially great with respect to Oxford and Cambridge (which did not expand as fast as other universities).

154. At the national level the qualifications (in terms of A levels) were not significantly different for undergraduates from different types of school in 1961–2 (Table R. 21), but entrants to Oxford and Cambridge were better qualified than entrants to other universities (Table R. 25), and among undergraduates at Oxford and Cambridge significant differences emerged when they were classified by type of school (Table R. 26). 22 per cent. of all undergraduates with two or more A levels had three or more at grades A or B.[3] 43 per cent. at Oxford and Cambridge came into this category, compared with 26 per cent. at London and 16 per cent. at other English universities. At Oxford and Cambridge, 58 per cent. from maintained schools had three or more A levels at grades A or B, compared with 50 per cent. from direct-grant schools and 30 per cent. from independent schools. Similar but smaller differences by type of school apply to London and other universities.[4] These results are in line with our findings on Oxford, but the differences between entrants from the different types of school have either narrowed somewhat since 1961–2 or were less at Oxford than at Cambridge in 1961–2. (See Table 54 which relates, however, to qualifications of men at the time of the admissions competition, not on entry.)

[1] See Robbins Report, Appendix Two (B), Part I, pp. 14–25, 34–44, 46–51, and, in particular, Tables 15, 21, 25, 26, 40, 42, 43, 48–53. For brevity, tables from this part of the report will be referred to as Table R. 15, etc., in the following paragraphs.

[2] Robbins Report, Appendix One, Annex R, pp. 253–6.

[3] This category is similar to our category 'very good'. It includes all those rated 'very good' in our classification except those with AAC, AA, or AB, and some rated as 'good' (i.e. the combination BBB).

[4] This holds despite there being no appreciable over-all difference as is shown in Table R. 21.

**Table 73.** *Percentage of those having three complete years in the sixth form who sat A or S levels a second time at end of third year, by sex and type of school. Undergraduates entering in October 1962*

OXFORD                                        PERCENTAGE

|         | Independent | Direct-grant | Maintained |
|---------|-------------|--------------|------------|
| Men     | 64          | 35           | 44         |
| Women   | 16          | 9            | 39         |

SOURCE: Peterson, A. D. C., 'The sixth form experience of Oxford entrants', *Oxford Magazine*, 6 February 1964.

155. Part of the difference in A level qualifications could be that independent schools lay less stress on them. There is little statistical evidence on this, but a survey of entrants to Oxford in October 1962 by Mr. A. D. C. Peterson showed that among those men completing a third year in the sixth form, the proportion resitting A levels was higher for independent than for maintained or direct-grant schools (Table 73). This does not suggest that A levels are considered less important in independent boys' schools but the proportion resitting A levels need not indicate the extent to which the schools aim to achieve the best possible A level grades. For women, the proportions were lower, and the highest proportion was among those from maintained schools.

156. The evidence from the Robbins Report, and that in Tables 33, 34, and 59 (on award holders), and 54 and 56 (on GCE qualifications of men), shows that the qualifications of men entrants from maintained schools (except at the highest ratings of S level) have been better than those of entrants from independent boarding schools, while the qualifications of entrants from independent day and direct-grant schools are either superior to those of entrants from maintained schools, or lie between those of entrants from maintained and independent boarding schools. But it is likely that the differential between independent boarding and maintained schools was smaller for entrants in 1965–6 than in earlier years.

157. Some further evidence on the calibre of undergraduates from different types of school can be obtained by comparing degree results. Tables 74 and 75 summarize some results from a one-in-two sample of matriculations in 1958–9 (fuller results are given in Part III, paras. 283–7) and also give results compiled by Mr. W. A. Hayward, Mr. J. Muschamp, the Revd. L. M. Styler, and Mr. G. D. N. Worswick. This evidence, which for men spans graduations between 1951 and 1965, will not, of course, reflect any changes that have occurred in the composition of the entry in the most recent two or three years.

158. The distribution of the 1958 matriculations in respect of type of school and proportion of award holders is not exactly the same as in Tables 31–34 because of sampling fluctuations and wastage, but the differences are small.

159. Among the 1958 matriculations of men (most of whom graduated in 1961) the highest proportion of firsts went to those from independent day and direct-grant schools, but the highest proportion of firsts or seconds went to those from maintained schools. In each case those from independent boarding schools gained the smallest proportion. The other data on men are consistent with this except for Merton graduations, where independent schools did slightly better than maintained schools on firsts,[1] and direct-grant schools did better than maintained schools on firsts or seconds.

160. Thus three samples from single years, and four samples covering a number of years lead broadly to the conclusion that in the fifties and early sixties independent day and direct-grant schools have provided the highest, and independent boarding the lowest, proportions of firsts among men, while maintained schools have provided the smallest, and independent boarding schools the largest, proportions of thirds among men. It may also be noted that, despite this finding, entrants from maintained schools have gained only a slightly larger proportion of awards than have entrants from independent boarding schools.[2]

161. Among women the position is less clear. The numbers are smaller, and the 1961 degree results were something of a freak, as Table 68 shows. Less firm conclusions can therefore be drawn. Worswick's analysis shows women from independent schools gaining more firsts, but fewer firsts or seconds than women from maintained schools. In the 1958 matriculations sample, however, the performance of women from maintained schools is very poor, while that of women from independent boarding schools is the best.

162. The better-than-average degree performance of men from maintained schools need not imply that the calibre of *entrants* from maintained schools has been above average if the wastage amongst such men has been higher than average. But such evidence as is available suggests that this is not so, and that wastage amongst men from maintained schools is below average. (That for women from maintained schools is about average.) And wastage of entrants from independent boarding schools is above average. The evidence is provided by a survey of 1955 entrants quoted by the Robbins Committee, which takes account of wastage before the final examination, but not of failures in finals, and by our sample of 1958 matriculations.[3]

---

[1] But independent day schools are not distinguished.
[2] See Table 33. In the sample of 1958 matriculations, men from maintained schools had a slightly *lower* proportion of awards than men from independent boarding schools.
[3] Robbins Report, Appendix Two (A), Part IV, Table 11, p. 134; and Part III, paras. 257–9 below.

**Table 74.** *Degree performance and holders of awards by type of school. Men non-graduates*

OXFORD                                                                                   PERCENTAGE

| Source | Type of school | Percentage in | | Percentage of | | Percentage of total |
|---|---|---|---|---|---|---|
| | | 1st class | 1st or 2nd class | Scholars | Award holders | |
| 1958 matriculations (one-in-two sample) | Independent boarding | 7·8 | 55·7 | 20·6 | 32·4 | 41·8 |
| | Independent day | 11·5 | 69·0 | 23·0 | 44·8 | 9·1 |
| | All independent | 8·4 | 58·0 | 21·0 | 34·6 | 50·9 |
| | Direct-grant | 12·1 | 66·0 | 23·4 | 40·4 | 14·8 |
| | Maintained | 9·8 | 71·6 | 18·9 | 31·5 | 33·2 |
| *Number = 954* | All schools | 9·4 | 63·6 | 20·6 | 34·3 | 100·0 |
| 1965 Class Lists | Independent | 8·0 | 63·2 | .. | .. | 47·4 |
| | Direct-grant | 16·0 | 74·2 | .. | .. | 17·1 |
| | Maintained | 10·0 | 76·8 | .. | .. | 33·5 |
| *Number = 1,604* | All schools | 10·0 | 69·3 | .. | .. | 100·0 |
| 1956 Class Lists | Independent (HMC) | 7·8 | 52·4 | .. | .. | .. |
| | Direct-grant (HMC) | 13·9 | 68·1 | .. | .. | .. |
| *Number = 1,100* | Maintained | 9·5 | 69·0 | .. | .. | .. |
| Balliol admissions (1950–62) | Independent | 15·3 | .. | .. | .. | 52·8 |
| | Direct-grant | 20·0 | .. | .. | .. | 14·2 |
| | Maintained | 16·1 | .. | .. | .. | 33·0 |
| *Number = 1,018* | All schools | 16·2 | .. | .. | 35·3 | 100·0 |
| Keble admissions (1950–62) | Independent | 1·5 | .. | .. | 15·2 | 41·5 |
| | Direct-grant | 2·6 | .. | .. | 17·7 | 16·8 |
| | Maintained | 5·9 | .. | .. | 13·0 | 41·7 |
| *Number = 1,145* | All schools | 3·5 | .. | .. | 14·7 | 100·0 |
| Merton graduations (1951–62) | Independent | 11·6 | 68·1 | .. | 40·4 | 53·2 |
| | Direct-grant | 15·5 | 78·3 | .. | 60·6 | 15·6 |
| | Maintained | 11·1 | 70·3 | .. | 37·0 | 31·2 |
| *Number = 605* | All schools | 12·2 | 70·5 | .. | 42·5 | 100·0 |
| Wadham admissions (1950–62) | Independent | 9·1 | .. | .. | 19·9 | 36·9 |
| | Direct-grant | 12·2 | .. | .. | 29·4 | 18·2 |
| | Maintained | 10·4 | .. | .. | 17·4 | 44·9 |
| *Number = 897* | All schools | 10·3 | .. | .. | 20·5 | 100·0 |

SOURCE: 1958 matriculations: Registry.

1965 Class Lists: Styler, L. M., *Oxford Magazine*, 3 December 1965.

1956 Class Lists: Worswick, G. D. N., 'Anatomy of Oxbridge', *The Times Educational Supplement*, 3 May 1957.

College admissions and graduations: the colleges concerned. The data were compiled by Mr. W. A. Hayward and Mr. J. Muschamp.

NOTES

1. The 'all schools' row for 1958 matriculations and for 1965 Class Lists includes those from other types of schools.
2. Graduates, and those from overseas or other types of school are excluded, except as in Note 1.
3. It is not possible to obtain figures for all schools from the source on 1956 Class Lists. The numbers in the categories given were: independent, 628; direct, grant, 144, and maintained, 328.

**Table 75.** *Degree performance and holders of awards by type of school. Women non-graduates*

OXFORD                                                                    PERCENTAGE

| Source | Type of school | Percentage in | | Percentage of | | Percentage of total |
|---|---|---|---|---|---|---|
| | | 1st class | 1st or 2nd class | Scholars | Award holders | |
| 1958 matriculations (one-in-two sample) | Independent boarding | 10·0 | 70·0 | 10·0 | 10·0 | 19·0 |
| | Independent day | 5·6 | 61·2 | 16·7 | 27·8 | 11·4 |
| | All independent | 8·3 | 66·7 | 12·5 | 16·7 | 30·4 |
| | Direct-grant | 7·0 | 69·8 | 14·0 | 32·6 | 27·2 |
| | Maintained | — | 55·4 | 7·7 | 16·9 | 41·1 |
| *Number = 156* | All schools | 4·4 | 63·3 | 10·8 | 20·9 | 100·0 |
| 1956 Class Lists | Independent | 5·8 | 73·3 | .. | .. | .. |
| | Maintained | 3·0 | 82·1 | .. | .. | .. |
| *Number = 187* | | | | | | |

SOURCE: 1958 matriculations: Registry.
          1956 Class Lists: Worswick, G. D. N., 'Anatomy of Oxbridge', *The Times Educational Supplement*, 3 May 1957.
NOTES
1. The 'all schools' row for 1958 matriculations includes those from other types of schools.
2. In the data on 1956 Class Lists only schools listed as Principal Girls' Schools in *Whitaker's Almanack* are included as independent schools.
3. Those from overseas or other types of school are excluded from the data on 1956 Class Lists.
4. It is not possible to obtain figures for all schools from the source on 1956 Class Lists. The numbers in the categories given were: independent, 120; maintained, 67.

163. If entrants from maintained schools are of higher than average, and entrants from independent boarding schools are of lower than average, calibre,[1] either fewer potential entrants are applying from maintained schools (the application rate is low), or the selection process is, in effect, more stringent when applied to applicants from maintained schools (the acceptance rate is low), or both.

164. An examination of the position by the Robbins Committee, based on their survey of undergraduates in 1961–2, led to the conclusion that the difference between the distribution of men undergraduates by type of school at all universities, and that at Oxford and Cambridge[2] could be attributed to both the application rates and the acceptance rates, but that differences in the application rates were far more important than differences in the acceptance rates (Table R. 53).

[1] Particularly for men.
[2] It should be borne in mind that the proportion of men undergraduates from maintained schools was substantially higher at Oxford than at Cambridge. See Table R. 11.

165. A third of all undergraduates in 1961–2 had applied to Oxford or Cambridge (37 per cent. of men and 22 per cent. of women), but there were large differences by type of school. Among men, 67 per cent. from independent schools, 43 per cent. from direct-grant schools, and 22 per cent. from maintained schools had applied. The corresponding figures for women were 34 per cent., 30 per cent., and 16 per cent. (see Table R. 48).

166. This indicates large differences in the application rates. These differences persist when undergraduates are classified by their A levels (Table R. 49), but the differences were greater for those with the lower grades of A levels. Among men with two or more A levels,[1] the proportion of undergraduates with three or more A levels at grades A or B who had applied to Oxford or Cambridge was 76 per cent. from independent schools and 43 per cent. from maintained schools, but the proportions for those with no more than one A level at grades A or B were 58 per cent. from independent schools and 13 per cent. from maintained schools. Thus the differences in the application rates were greater among the more marginal candidates.

167. There were also considerable differences in the acceptance rates of applicants from different types of school, especially among men (see Table R. 50). Of all men undergraduates in 1961 who had applied to Oxford or Cambridge, 78 per cent. of those from independent, 66 per cent. of those from direct-grant, and 52 per cent. of those from maintained schools were accepted. Among women the acceptance rates from independent (39 per cent.) and maintained (37 per cent.) schools were much the same, and less than from direct-grant schools (53 per cent.).

168. These differences do not appear to be due to candidates from maintained schools having been less well qualified, since among men 44 per cent. of applicants from maintained schools had three or more grade A or B passes in A level (when at university, not necessarily at the time of applying) against 27 per cent. of applicants from independent schools (Table R. 51).

169. The position had changed among men entrants by 1965–6. In the first place there was little difference between the over-all acceptance rates (Tables 43 and 44), in contrast to the position in 1961–2 as shown in Table R. 50. But although it is likely there have been changes in the underlying pattern of admissions, of which the increased proportion of entrants from maintained schools is one manifestation, part of the difference between the two sets of figures is due to differences in the ways in which they were compiled.[2] The Robbins Committee statistics are restricted to applicants to Oxford or Cambridge who entered some university or other. In effect,

---

[1] Separate figures are not given for women.
[2] See Robbins Report, Appendix Two (B), Annex I, pp. 438–9.

potential entrants to Oxford and Cambridge are assumed to be restricted to those who do gain a university place somewhere in Great Britain. This means excluding any well-qualified candidates who prefer to go to no university, or to go to a university abroad, if they cannot obtain a place at Oxford or Cambridge, and this may be thought a disadvantage. But it also excludes weak candidates who are rejected by any other university to which they apply, and this may be thought an advantage. If candidates in these two categories are drawn more than proportionately from independent schools (and the relatively high proportion of candidates from independent boarding schools who had failed A levels, as shown in Table 53, is a pointer in this direction), part of the discrepancy between Tables 43 and 44 and the Robbins Committee statistics would be explained. Further, candidates for entry may apply in more than one year. No account of this is taken in Tables 43 and 44, which do not, therefore, give the chances of eventually gaining admission for candidates from the different types of school. Some evidence that reapplications are less frequent among candidates from maintained schools is given in the following paragraph. Another difference between Table R. 50 and Table 43 is that Table R. 50 treated Oxford and Cambridge as a single category, and to the extent that some candidates applied to both Oxford and Cambridge for admission in 1964–5 the tables are not comparable. But this difference can hardly have been significant in the following year, when candidates made a single application putting Oxford and Cambridge in an order of preference, and Oxford admissions from the Cambridge pool were only 3 per cent. of all admissions.

**Table 76.** *Candidates for admission in 1965–6 who failed to gain a place and who reapplied for admission in 1966–7, by type of school and subject group. Men non-graduates*

OXFORD

| | Number who failed to gain a place for 1965–6 (1) | Number who reapplied for admission in 1966–7 (2) | Number who gained a place for 1966–7 (3) | Percentage reapplying col. (2) as percentage of col. (1) (4) | Acceptance rate for those reapplying col. (3) as percentage of col. (2) (5) | Col. (3) as percentage of col. (1) (6) |
|---|---|---|---|---|---|---|
| TYPE OF SCHOOL | | | | | | |
| Independent boarding | 762 | 119 | 40 | 16 | 34 | 5·2 |
| Independent day | 184 | 23 | 13 | 13 | 57 | 7·1 |
| Direct-grant | 303 | 41 | 19 | 14 | 46 | 6·3 |
| Maintained | 843 | 77 | 37 | 9 | 48 | 4·4 |
| SUBJECT GROUP | | | | | | |
| Arts and social studies | 1,387 | 198 | 86 | 14 | 43 | 6·2 |
| Science | 705 | 62 | 23 | 9 | 37 | 3·3 |
| All | 2,092 | 260 | 109 | 12 | 42 | 5·2 |

SOURCE: Admissions Office.

NOTE: See Note 1 to Table 50.

170. Of the applicants in the December 1964 competition who failed to gain a place, 260 applied again in the following year, of whom 109 (42 per cent.) gained a place. 36, or 33 per cent. of those gaining a place, won an award. These include 12 who won an open scholarship. The proportions of reapplicants who were in the second-year sixth form in December 1964 were 20 per cent. for independent boarding schools, 17 per cent. for independent day schools, 34 per cent. for direct-grant schools, and 69 per cent. for maintained schools. The acceptance rate for the reapplicants was only marginally lower than the over-all acceptance rate of 44 per cent. (see note to para. 110). Table 76 gives some further details about the reapplicants. The acceptance rate was lowest for reapplicants from independent boarding schools. Of those who failed to gain a place in December 1964, the proportion reapplying was 12 per cent.; it was above average for candidates from independent boarding schools, and below average for those from maintained schools. But because the acceptance rate for candidates from independent boarding schools was relatively low, there was less difference between these schools and maintained schools in the number who gained a place at the second attempt expressed as a percentage of all who failed to gain a place in December 1964 (see column (6) of Table 76). These details of reapplicants suggest that a part, but only a relatively small part, of the differences between Table 44 and Table R. 50 can be explained in terms of differential reapplication rates.[1]

171. Men applicants from maintained schools for admission in 1965–6 were better qualified, in terms of A levels, than those from independent boarding schools. Comparison of Table 53 and Table R. 51 suggests that the position had not altered substantially since the years in which those who were undergraduates in 1961–2 entered universities.

172. Acceptance rates were found by the Robbins Committee to vary with A level qualifications, as well as with type of school (Table R. 52). As was noted with application rates, the differences for men between independent and maintained schools were greater at the lower grades of A levels. Among undergraduates in 1961–2, acceptance rates at Oxford and Cambridge for men from independent schools were 87 per cent. for those with three or more A level passes at grades A or B, and 71 per cent. for those with no more than one such pass. The corresponding figures for men from maintained schools were 65 per cent. and 35 per cent. respectively.

173. The acceptance rates in Table 77 are also systematically lower for maintained than for independent boarding schools[2] and the differences are greater at the lower ratings, but they are smaller than in Table R. 52. Thus,

---

[1] The calculations given here do not take account of the proportion of applicants in December 1964 who were then applying for a second time. It is unlikely that an allowance for this would substantially alter the results.

[2] Except among the very small number who had failed A levels.

Table 77 shows acceptance rates for independent boarding schools of 87 per cent. at the 'very good' A level rating and 27 per cent. at the 'pass' rating.[1] The corresponding figures for maintained schools were 79 per cent. and 18 per cent.

**Table 77.** *Acceptance rate by GCE A level rating and type of school. Men non-graduate candidates for admission in 1965–6 to read for first degrees*

OXFORD                                                                 PERCENTAGE

| A level rating | Independent boarding | Independent day | Direct-grant | Maintained | All schools |
|---|---|---|---|---|---|
| Very good | 86·8 | 84·6 | 80·3 | 79·2 | 81·8 |
| Good | 53·7 | 38·1 | 49·3 | 40·8 | 46·8 |
| Pass | 26·5 | 17·6 | 27·8 | 18·4 | 23·7 |
| Fail | 5·9 | 12·5 | 18·2 | 15·4 | 8·8 |
| All having taken A levels | 45·0 | 43·4 | 53·3 | 48·0 | 47·3 |
| Not having taken A levels | 28·9 | 45·2 | 27·1 | 40·0 | 37·4 |
| All | 43·9 | 43·6 | 50·8 | 45·8 | 45·7 |

SOURCE: Admissions Office.
NOTE: See notes to Tables 53 and 54.

174. In these comparisons the criterion of quality is (perforce) A level qualifications, and it may be objected that A level performance is not a reliable indicator of academic promise. No final answer can be given on this point until the Admissions Office has accumulated records over at least three years, when A level qualifications and performance in the entrance competition can both be compared with degree performance. However, the results in Tables 54, 74, and R. 26 show that men entrants from maintained schools had, on average, better A level qualifications than men from independent boarding schools, and they achieved better degrees.[2] Although this evidence does not throw much light on the value of A levels as a measure of academic promise in individuals, it suggests that A level qualifications are useful in an aggregative sense, and that the higher the proportion of good A levels in a group, the higher the proportion who will achieve a good (first- or second-class) degree. In the absence of any better measure it seems reasonable to use A levels as an approximate measure of academic promise in this aggregative sense.

[1] For all independent schools the figures were 86 per cent. and 26 per cent.
[2] It should be noted, however, that the three tables referred to relate to different individuals.

**Table 78.** *Acceptance rate by GCE S level rating and type of school. Men non-graduate candidates for admission in 1965–6 to read for first degrees*

OXFORD                                                                    PERCENTAGE

| S level rating | Independent boarding | Independent day | Direct-grant | Maintained | All schools |
|---|---|---|---|---|---|
| Excellent | 96·2 | 100·0 | 97·3 | 92·3 | 95·9 |
| Very good | 88·5 | 74·1 | 92·1 | 83·3 | 85·8 |
| Good | 72·9 | 58·0 | 71·6 | 74·0 | 71·7 |
| Pass | 45·2 | 38·2 | 45·3 | 40·0 | 42·6 |
| All having taken S levels | 53·4 | 50·5 | 60·0 | 54·6 | 54·7 |
| Having taken A levels but not S levels | 28·3 | 23·4 | 35·7 | 30·5 | 29·8 |
| All having taken A levels | 45·0 | 43·4 | 53·3 | 48·0 | 47·3 |

SOURCE: Admissions Office.

NOTE: See notes to Tables 55 and 56.

175. Table 78 shows acceptance rates analysed by S level ratings. At the two highest and the lowest ratings, the acceptance rate was higher for independent boarding than for maintained schools, but the differences are smaller than in the case of A levels. At the 'good' rating, the acceptance rate was marginally higher for maintained schools. There is at present no adequate evidence on the relative merits of A and S levels as predictors of academic performance.[1]

176. The preceding paragraphs may be summarized as follows. First, acceptance rates at a given level of GCE qualifications have been lower (with the exception given in the previous paragraph), for men applicants from maintained schools than for candidates from independent boarding schools, with the differences tending to be greater at the lower levels of qualifications. Secondly, the differences in the acceptance rates have diminished considerably in the past five years. Thirdly, the differences are smaller when candidates are classified by S levels than when they are classified by A levels.

177. Acceptance rates when candidates are classified by their time in the sixth form are given in Table 79. There were considerable differences both between candidates from the second-year sixth and the third-year sixth,

[1] It may be noted, however, that among the top 46 per cent. of admissions, the proportions of open scholars (and of all award holders) were practically the same when admissions were ranked by A levels as when they were ranked by S levels. See para. 121 and Tables 54, 56, and 60.

and between candidates from the third-year sixth and the fourth-year sixth. A lower than average acceptance rate might be expected for candidates from the second-year sixth form. This is partly because some such candidates are having a 'trial run', and partly because the entrance examination is designed more with candidates from the third-year sixth in mind (although allowance is made for candidates from the second-year sixth form, and their schools are invited to show on the application form the parts of the A level syllabus which such candidates will not have covered). The acceptance rate for candidates from the second-year sixth form of maintained schools was above the average for all from the second-year sixth. The difference between the acceptance rates for candidates from the third- and fourth-year sixth forms of independent schools was large; the corresponding difference for maintained schools was small.

**Table 79.** *Acceptance rates by time in sixth form and type of school. Men non-graduate candidates for admission in 1965–6 to read for first degrees*

OXFORD                                                                  PERCENTAGE

| Terms in sixth form at time of entrance competition | Independent boarding | Independent day | Direct-grant | Maintained | All schools |
|---|---|---|---|---|---|
| 4 | 15·9 | 38·7 | 23·0 | 38·6 | 33·8 |
| 7 | 40·7 | 41·1 | 53·0 | 48·4 | 46·1 |
| 10 or more | 58·0 | 55·4 | 62·0 | 50·7 | 57·2 |
| All | 43·9 | 43·6 | 50·8 | 45·8 | 45·7 |

SOURCE: Admissions Office.
NOTE: See notes to Tables 50 and 51.

178. The acceptance rate was higher in science than in arts and social studies. But the candidates were better qualified in terms of A levels (see Table 57 above) and the acceptance rates at each A level rating were lower in science (Table 80). In terms of S levels, the acceptance rates were higher in science at each rating except the highest. In both subject groups the acceptance rate was higher for those with a 'pass' rating than for those with A levels who had not taken S level papers. This, however, may be partly a reflection of the rule in force in 1964 that S level papers were not given a grade unless the corresponding A level was grade C or better.

179. The application rate was discussed in paras. 163–6 above. It is lower from maintained schools than from direct-grant and independent schools, and this is the most important reason for the relatively small proportion of undergraduates from maintained schools at Oxford compared with other universities.[1] The low application rate could be a result of either or both

[1] The Robbins Committee statistics show that this was so in the years immediately preceding 1961–2 (see paras. 165–6 above); Table 44 taken together with Table 72 suggests strongly that it is still so.

**Table 80.** *Acceptance rate by GCE A level rating and subject group. Men non-graduate candidates for admission in 1965–6 to read for first degrees*

OXFORD                                                          PERCENTAGE

| A level rating | Arts and social studies | Science | All subjects |
|---|---|---|---|
| Very good | 83·8 | 79·6 | 81·8 |
| Good | 49·5 | 41·1 | 46·8 |
| Pass | 24·5 | 21·7 | 23·7 |
| Fail | 10·1 | 5·3 | 8·8 |
| All having taken A levels | 46·3 | 49·3 | 47·3 |
| Not having taken A levels | 37·2 | 37·9 | 37·4 |
| All | 44·8 | 47·5 | 45·7 |

SOURCE: Admissions Office.
NOTE: See notes to Tables 53 and 54.


**Table 81.** *Acceptance rate by GCE S level rating and subject group. Men non-graduate candidates for admission in 1965–6 to read for first degrees*

OXFORD                                                          PERCENTAGE

| S level rating | Arts and social studies | Science | All subjects |
|---|---|---|---|
| Excellent | 97·8 | 92·5 | 95·9 |
| Very good | 83·9 | 88·0 | 85·8 |
| Good | 70·6 | 73·4 | 71·7 |
| Pass | 42·3 | 43·2 | 42·6 |
| All having taken S levels | 53·4 | 57·0 | 54·7 |
| Having taken A levels but not S levels | 30·8 | 27·6 | 29·8 |
| All having taken A levels | 46·3 | 49·3 | 47·3 |

SOURCE: Admissions Office.
NOTE: See notes to Tables 55 and 56.

of two factors: a more stringent pre-selection of candidates generally; and a failure to attract candidates in any numbers from some of the maintained schools, in particular those whose sixth-form organization is based on a two-year course directed towards A levels, rather than a three-year (or at least seven-term) course with preparation for the Oxford and Cambridge entrance competitions a regular part of sixth-form work. The formulation of policies to improve the application rate from maintained schools requires information on the structure, size, and number of schools which do not regularly submit candidates to Oxford, and on the methods of those which do. Some evidence on these topics is presented below.

180. Tables 51 and 65 showed that 12 per cent. of men and 25 per cent. of women entering Oxford in 1965–6 spent no more than two years in the sixth form.[1] Surveys of entrants in 1962–3 and 1963–4 by Mr. A. D. C. Peterson are similar, but suggest that the proportion of women entrants from the second-year sixth form has been increasing (Table 82), while that for men may have declined slightly.

**Table 82.** *Entrants from the second-year sixth form as percentage of all entrants by sex*

| OXFORD | | PERCENTAGE | |
| --- | --- | --- | --- |
| Men entering in | | Women entering in | |
| 1962–3 | 1963–4 | 1962–3 | 1963–4 |
| 15 | 13 | 18 | 21 |

SOURCE: Surveys carried out by Mr. A. D. C. Peterson, Director of the Institute of Education, Oxford. For results of the survey in 1962–3 see Peterson, A. D. C. 'The sixth form experience of Oxford entrants', *Oxford Magazine*, 6 February 1964.

181. In many boys' schools, a third (or fourth) year in the sixth form is achieved, not by staying at school longer, but by means of an 'express stream' in the middle school so that the sixth form is reached at an early age. The average ages in Table 52 illustrate this.

182. In order to discover more about the schools which do not regularly submit candidates to Oxford, the Commission selected 13 such schools (Group A), and 11 schools which do regularly submit candidates to Oxford (Group B). A questionnaire was completed by each school, and the heads subsequently gave oral evidence (*Oral Evidence*, Part 102).

183. Schools in Group A were all maintained; they had between 500 and 1,000 pupils. Six were boys' schools, two were girls' schools, and five were mixed. The average number of pupils was 760.

[1] The figure for women relates to those who had no A level passes at the time of the entrance competition.

184. Three of the schools in Group B were independent, two were direct-grant schools, and of the six maintained schools, two were voluntary aided schools, and one was a voluntary controlled school. There were eight boys' and three girls' schools, ranging in size from 440 to 1,100 pupils. The average size was 660 pupils.

185. Table 83 gives a summary of some of the characteristics of the two groups of schools in the autumn term 1964. In Group B 17 per cent. of the sixth formers were in the third or subsequent years, compared with 6 per cent. in Group A. Candidates for any U.K. university formed much the same proportion of sixth formers beyond the first year for each group, but the proportion aiming at Oxford or Cambridge was over three times as high for Group B as for Group A. There was a much greater concentration of Oxford and Cambridge graduates on the staffs of schools in Group B.

186. Some further facts which emerged from the questionnaire are that 70 per cent. of the sixth formers in Group B schools had two O levels in languages against only 30 per cent. for Group A. Eight of the schools in Group B had an 'express stream'[1] who took O level at age 15+; only two of the schools in Group A appear to have a regular 'express stream', but three others bring small selected groups of pupils to O levels at age 15+. In ten of the Group B schools, four or more periods per week of special teaching is given to pupils in the third- and fourth-year sixth form in most subjects. Five of the Group A schools certainly provide such teaching, with two more being marginal cases. None of the schools provides special teaching for the Oxford and Cambridge entrance examinations in the second-year sixth form (except possibly for a few individual pupils unable to stay for a third year). All the schools in Group B provide such special teaching in the third year. One school in Group A provides such teaching and four or five others make *ad hoc* arrangements as the need arises.

187. Although the samples were not representative, the inquiry demonstrates the existence of maintained schools preparing a high proportion of their sixth formers for university entrance, but submitting relatively few candidates to Oxford and Cambridge. The evidence of their heads makes clear the difficulties which such schools have, both in persuading promising pupils to stay on for an extra year to try for Oxford and Cambridge, and in properly preparing candidates for the entrance examinations.

188. It is extremely difficult to determine how many schools in England and Wales might fall into Group A, and harder still to determine how many of their candidates for other universities would prefer to try for Oxford or Cambridge if the admissions procedure were modified.

---

[1] The 'express stream' may apply to the whole intake of the school.

**Table 83.** *Results from the survey of schools. Autumn Term 1964*

| | Number of schools | Average number of sixth-form pupils | Year of course of sixth-form pupils (percentage) | | | | | Candidates for U.K. universities as percentage of sixth formers in all years except first | Candidates for Oxford or Cambridge as percentage of sixth formers by year of course | | | | Number of Oxford or Cambridge graduates on staff per 100 pupils | |
| --- | --- | --- | --- | --- | --- | --- | --- | --- | --- | --- | --- | --- | --- | --- |
| | | | 1 | 2 | 3 | 4 or more | All | | 2 | 3 | 4 or more | All except first | Sixth form | All pupils |
| Schools which do not regularly submit candidates to Oxford (Group A) | 13 | 139 | 51 | 43 | 6 | — | 100 | 55 | 2 | 31 | . | 6 | 3·3 | 0·6 |
| Schools which regularly submit candidates to Oxford (Group B) | 11 | 261 | 41 | 41 | 15 | 2 | 100 | 52 | 1 | 62 | 100 | 22 | 9·8 | 3·8 |

SOURCE: Schools questionnaire.

**Table 84.** *Schools with sixth forms and with third-year sixth forms by type of school. England and Wales, January 1965*

NUMBER

| | Boys' schools with | | Mixed schools with | | Girls' schools with | |
|---|---|---|---|---|---|---|
| | Sixth form | Third-year sixth | Sixth form | Third-year sixth | Sixth form | Third-year sixth |
| Independent | 197 | 148 | 72 | 19 | 359 | 73 |
| Direct-grant | 82 | 81 | 2 | 2 | 95 | 47 |
| Maintained | 600 | 390 | 912 | 426 | 596 | 222 |
| All schools | 879 | 619 | 986 | 447 | 1,050 | 342 |

SOURCE: Department of Education and Science.

NOTES
1. Independent schools not recognized as efficient are excluded.
2. Schools with third-year sixth forms are defined as schools having sixth-form pupils who are following GCE A level courses in the third or subsequent year of the course. By 'year of course' is meant the level of study as determined by the curriculum and not the time spent in the course by an individual pupil.

**Table 85.** *Number of pupils in sixth forms by type of school. England and Wales, January 1965*

NUMBER

| | Boys | | | Girls | | |
|---|---|---|---|---|---|---|
| | Number in sixth forms | Number in third-year sixth | *Percentage of sixth formers in third year* | Number in sixth forms | Number in third-year sixth | *Percentage of sixth formers in third year* |
| Independent | 24,053 | 2,892 | *12·0* | 10,828 | 178 | *1·6* |
| Direct-grant | 13,305 | 1,835 | *13·8* | 9,097 | 175 | *1·9* |
| Maintained | 92,587 | 6,517 | *7·0* | 66,666 | 1,532 | *2·3* |
| All schools | 129,945 | 11,244 | *8·7* | 86,591 | 1,885 | *2·2* |

SOURCE: Department of Education and Science.

NOTES
1. Pupils not following GCE A level courses (almost all of whom are in the first-year sixth form) are excluded.
2. See notes to Table 84.

189. One difficulty lies in determining how many schools have a third-year sixth in the special sense used here of a third year largely concerned with preparation for entry to Oxford and Cambridge. The Department of Education and Science compiles statistics of sixth forms divided by year of course. A large majority of boys' schools have pupils in the third year of the sixth, as can be seen from Table 86, and such schools account for almost all sixth formers at boys' schools (Table 87). The proportions of mixed and girls' schools with sixth forms which have a third-year sixth form are lower, and less than half. But among mixed and girls' maintained schools, those with a third-year sixth form account for about 90 per cent. of all sixth formers. (Some information on sixth forms and sixth-form pupils is given in Tables 84 and 85 to which further reference is made below.) Thus, the overwhelming majority of men applying to Oxford must come from schools with a third-year sixth form of some kind, but among an unknown number of these schools, particularly the maintained schools, the third-year sixth is not specially geared to the Oxford examination (and it may be very small).

**Table 86.** *Schools with third-year sixth forms as percentage of all schools with sixth form by type of school. England and Wales, January 1965*

PERCENTAGE

|  | Boys' schools | Mixed schools | Girls' schools |
|---|---|---|---|
| Independent | 75 | 26 | 20 |
| Direct-grant | 99 | 100 | 49 |
| Maintained | 65 | 47 | 37 |
| All schools | 70 | 45 | 33 |

SOURCE: Table 84.
NOTE: See notes to Table 84.

**Table 87.** *Sixth-form pupils at schools with third-year sixth form as percentage of all sixth-form pupils, by type of school. England and Wales, January 1965*

PERCENTAGE

|  | Boys' schools | Mixed schools | Girls' schools |
|---|---|---|---|
| Independent | 92 | 46 | 27 |
| Direct-grant | 99 | 100 | 51 |
| Maintained | 97 | 91 | 89 |
| All schools | 96 | 90 | 73 |

SOURCE: Department of Education and Science.
NOTE: See notes to Table 84.

190. The total third-year sixth form does not consist entirely of candidates for Oxford and Cambridge, but they probably constitute a substantial proportion of it, even for maintained schools. But there is a complication which makes an estimate difficult. The statistics in Table 85 were collected in January 1965, and successful candidates for Oxford and Cambridge who left school when they were sure of a place would not be included. It is impossible to say how many of these there were; but Peterson's surveys of entrants to Oxford (see para. 95) showed that of those spending at least seven terms in the sixth form, 91 per cent. of entrants in 1962–3 completed nine terms, but only 48 per cent. of entrants in 1963–4 (56 per cent. of men and 23 per cent. of women) did so. The Robbins Committee found that 29 per cent. of undergraduates at Oxford and Cambridge in 1961–2 had spent over six months but under a year between leaving school and entering university.[1] The survey of schools (see para. 182) showed that of the third- and fourth-year sixth formers at schools in Group B in the Autumn Term 1964, 57 per cent. had left before the end of the academic year 1964–5 (some having left at Easter). The corresponding figure for schools in Group A was 36 per cent.

191. Applicants to Oxford and Cambridge probably numbered rather more than 8,000 in December 1964. If none left in the December, these candidates would account for almost all boys in third-year sixth forms at independent schools, between half and three-quarters at direct-grant schools, and between a third and half at maintained schools.[2] Since some will have left in the December the actual proportions will be lower than this, but by an unknown amount.

192. In passing, it may be noted that the statistics of the Department of Education and Science suggest that the third-year sixth form is not increasing in numbers, although total sixth-form numbers[3] (and entrants to universities) are increasing. In January 1963 12,600 boys were in the third year of sixth forms, out of 107,500 altogether, or 11·7 per cent. In January 1964 the corresponding figures were 11,200 out of 121,500, or 9·2 per cent.[4] The decline between January 1963 and January 1964 in both absolute numbers and the proportion in the third-year sixth is similar for each type of school and for girls. By January 1965 the number of boys in sixth forms had increased to 129,900 (Table 85) while the number in the third year of sixth forms remained at 11,200, a fall in independent schools

---

[1] Robbins Report, Appendix Two (B), Part I, Table 42, p. 40.

[2] A rough allowance has been made for those applying from the second-year sixth.

[3] Pupils not following GCE A level courses are excluded from the calculations in this paragraph.

[4] See *Statistics of Education*, 1963, Part I, Tables 14 and 21; and 1964, Part I, Table 7. There was a minor change in the compilation of the statistics between the two years. For January 1964 a definition of the year of a sixth-form course was given (see Note 2 to Table 84); for January 1963 no definition was given.

being off-set by a rise in direct-grant schools. But it does not follow that the same pattern applies among those third-year sixth formers seeking entrance to Oxford or Cambridge.

193. A different approach to the question of the balance of admissions is via the concentration of applications and admissions at only a fraction of the schools of any type. Table 88 brings together, for men, the information in Tables 48 and 49 on schools submitting candidates and gaining places[1] with that in Table 84 on total numbers of schools.

**Table 88.** *Schools with sixth forms, submitting candidates for Oxford and gaining places, by type of school. Men: schools in England and Wales*

NUMBER

| | Boys' and mixed schools | | | | | |
|---|---|---|---|---|---|---|
| | With sixth form | With third-year sixth form | With male applicants to Oxford for 1965–6 entry | Gaining at least one place for 1965–6 | Gaining at least three places for 1965–6 | Gaining at least four places for 1965–6 |
| | (1) | (2) | (3) | (4) | (5) | (6) |
| INDEPENDENT | | | | | | |
| Number | 269 | 167 | 156 | 117 | 83 | 71 |
| Percentage of col. 2 | | 100 | 93 | 70 | 50 | 43 |
| DIRECT-GRANT | | | | | | |
| Number | 84 | 83 | 71 | 65 | 37 | 31 |
| Percentage of col. 2 | | 100 | 86 | 78 | 45 | 37 |
| MAINTAINED | | | | | | |
| Number | 1,512 | 816 | 490 | 350 | 98 | 56 |
| Percentage of col. 2 | | 100 | 60 | 43 | 12 | 7 |
| ALL SCHOOLS | | | | | | |
| Number | 1,865 | 1,066 | 717 | 532 | 218 | 158 |
| Percentage of col. 2 | | 100 | 67 | 50 | 20 | 15 |

SOURCE: Table 84 and Admissions Office.

NOTES
1. The number of schools with sixth forms and with third-year sixth forms relates to January 1965.
2. Independent schools not recognized as efficient are *excluded* from the number of schools with sixth forms and with third-year sixth forms, but *included* among schools with applicants and gaining places.
3. A very small number of schools in Scotland and Northern Ireland which submitted candidates but did not gain any places may be included in column 3.
4. See Note 2 to Table 84.

194. First, attention may be restricted to schools with third-year sixth forms (in the wider sense), since these schools account for the great majority of boys in sixth forms. This has the effect of leaving out of account over half the mixed maintained schools with sixth forms.

[1] But for schools in England and Wales only.

195. About 90 per cent. of the independent and direct-grant schools submitted candidates; 60 per cent. of the maintained schools did so. 70 per cent. of independent schools and 78 per cent. of direct-grant schools gained at least one place against 43 per cent. for maintained schools. Thus the discrepancy between maintained and other schools is greater in terms of gaining places than in terms of applicants. The discrepancy is even greater when schools gaining a number of places are considered, and details are given in Table 88 for three or more, and four or more places.

196. This analysis is based on one year, so it cannot pick out schools regularly submitting candidates or gaining places with any certainty or accuracy. But it seems reasonable that most schools gaining, say, three places for 1965–6 gain at least one place fairly regularly. And it is plausible that there are other schools which regularly gain at least one place, and that these would outnumber those with an unusually good performance in the year analysed. If so, at least 40 per cent. of independent and direct-grant schools, and perhaps over 50 per cent., regularly gain places at Oxford. The proportion for maintained schools is almost certainly considerably lower. Until the Admissions Office has been operating longer it will not be possible to refine an analysis along these lines.

197. To identify the number of schools rarely gaining places at Oxford could contribute to the discussion of one of the important questions about admissions; namely the extent to which some schools are not at present in the running for places. But it does not contribute to consideration of how many individual pupils choose not to apply solely because to do so would defer for a year their entry to a university.

### SCHOLARSHIPS AND EXHIBITIONS[1]

198. Details of the proportion of entrance award holders, which has increased for men since 1948–9, and which is now about twice as high for men as for women, have been given in Tables 30, 33, 34, 40, 59, 60, 61, and 74. It was shown that the proportion of award holders among men is correlated with GCE ratings in Tables 60 and 61. Three sets of figures enable a comparison of the degree performance of award holders and commoners to be made. The results are given in more detail in Part III, but Table 89 summarizes the results. The data are provided by the sample of 1958 matriculations, the analyses of four colleges' admissions, and evidence submitted by Mr. T. W. H. Holland. The table shows that the proportion of good degrees (especially of firsts) is much higher for award holders and especially for scholars.

---

[1] No details of awards won by individual schools are given. Mr. G. D. N. Worswick has published such details in articles in *The Times Educational Supplement*, and in the issue of 4 February 1966 he summarizes his results for 1956–7 to 1959–60 and 1961–2 to 1964–5. See also his letter in the issue of 25 February 1966.

**Table 89.** *Degree performance by status as scholar, exhibitioner, or commoner*

OXFORD                                                                    PERCENTAGE

| Source | | Percentage in | |
|---|---|---|---|
| | | 1st class | 1st or 2nd class |
| 1958 matriculations (men) | Scholars | 23·2 | 79·4 |
| (one-in-two sample) | Exhibitioners | 12·2 | 72·5 |
| | All award holders | 18·9 | 76·6 |
| | Commoners | 4·8 | 57·6 |
| *Number = 1,006* | All undergraduates | 9·4 | 63·9 |
| 1958 matriculations (women) | Scholars | 27·8 | 88·9 |
| (one-in-two sample) | Exhibitioners | 6·3 | 56·3 |
| | All award holders | 17·6 | 73·5 |
| | Commoners | 1·6 | 61·0 |
| *Number = 162* | All undergraduates | 4·9 | 63·5 |
| 1962 Class Lists (men and women) | Award holders | 16·0 | 77·3 |
| | Commoners | 5·8 | 60·7 |
| *Number = 1,896* | All undergraduates | 8·4 | 65·0 |
| Balliol admissions 1950–62 | Award holders | 30·6 | 80·7 |
| | Open award holders | 33·7 | 85·6 |
| | Closed award holders | 18·9 | 62·1 |
| | Commoners | 8·3 | .. |
| *Number = 1,018* | All undergraduates | 16·2 | .. |
| Keble admissions 1950–62 | Award holders | 9·5 | 77·4 |
| | Commoners | 2·6 | .. |
| *Number = 1,145* | All undergraduates | 3·6 | .. |
| Merton graduations 1951–62 | Scholars | 23·4 | 88·6 |
| | Exhibitioners | 21·1 | 81·1 |
| | All award holders | 22·6 | 86·0 |
| | Commoners | 4·3 | 58·9 |
| *Number = 605* | All undergraduates | 12·1 | 70·4 |
| Wadham admissions 1950–62 | Open award holders | 26·6 | 82·6 |
| | All award holders | 25·9 | 80·8 |
| | Commoners | 6·0 | .. |
| *Number = 897* | All undergraduates | 10·3 | .. |

SOURCE: 1958 matriculations: Registry.
  1962 Class Lists: Holland, T. W. H., *Written Evidence*, Part IV, p. 93 and Part XIV, p. 36.
  Colleges: the colleges concerned. The data were compiled by Mr. W. A. Hayward and Mr. J. Muschamp.

NOTES
1. Status is that on admission, not that at the time of graduation.
2. The figures for the four colleges include only undergraduates from schools in the United Kingdom.

**Table 90.** *Open and closed college entrance awards. Awards made for entry in 1965–6 to men's colleges*

| OXFORD | | | PERCENTAGE |
|---|---|---|---|
| Type of school | Open awards | Closed awards | All awards |
| Independent boarding | 26·5 | 45·1 | 28·6 |
| Independent day | 11·3 | 3·3 | 10·4 |
| Direct-grant | 18·7 | 25·3 | 19·4 |
| Maintained | 42·5 | 26·4 | 40·7 |
| Overseas | 0·4 | — | 0·4 |
| Other | 0·6 | — | 0·5 |
| All schools | 100·0 | 100·0 | 100·0 |
| *Number* | *691* | *91* | *782* |

SOURCE: Admissions Office.

199. The entrance awards offered by colleges are of two types: open and closed. Open awards (which include the great majority of all awards) are open to any candidate except that many (especially in the men's colleges) are offered in particular subjects. Closed awards are subject to conditions other than subject. The conditions may relate to birth-place, domicile, father's profession, and a miscellany of other restrictions, but the most common condition is that the candidate must have been a pupil of a specified school or group of schools. Not only is there this wide variety in the kind of restrictions imposed, but some closed awards are thrown open if no suitable 'closed' candidate appears, while others are not. There is thus a wide spectrum of closed awards, and the number fluctuates from year to year. The number of closed awards (including those closed as to parentage, area, etc., as well as those closed as to school) won by men candidates for entry in October 1964 was 93; candidates from independent schools won 49; those from direct-grant schools won 26; and 18 went to candidates from maintained schools. The men's colleges offered a total of about 190 closed awards for entry in October 1965.[1] But many of these were either thrown open (and awarded as open awards) or were not awarded, and only 91 closed scholarships and exhibitions were awarded as such. Table 90 shows their distribution.

[1] Some closed awards are offered only once in every two or three years. Such awards have been included as one-half or one-third in calculating the total.

# PART III

---

# UNDERGRADUATES

---

200. In this Part the teaching received by undergraduates in Michaelmas Term 1964 is analysed; and information is given on the academic performance of undergraduates and on a number of other topics such as the use of libraries by undergraduates, their financial support at university, and their subsequent careers.

## TEACHING

201. The information on teaching is derived from two surveys carried out by the Commission during Michaelmas Term 1964. One was addressed to one-sixth of all undergraduates in their first, second, or third years and was mainly concerned with the teaching they received during the third week of term. The other was addressed to all organizers of tutorial work in the colleges and other societies, and covered the arrangements for the Michaelmas Term of tutorials and college classes and seminars for undergraduates reading Honour Schools.

202. It should be noted that the teaching can be regarded in two different ways: from the point of view of the undergraduates, or of the teachers. For example, the number of tutorials received by undergraduates will exceed the number of tutorials given by teachers, to the extent that tutorials are given to two or three undergraduates at a time. In the Undergraduate Survey teaching is approached from the undergraduates' point of view. In the Tutorial Organizers Survey it is approached from the teachers' point of view.

203. The response rate in the Undergraduate Survey was 94 per cent., and all organizers of tutorial work made a return. Further details of response and of other aspects of the surveys are given in Part VI.

## Background

204. The distribution of the sample of undergraduates by subject group and year is given in Table 91. A comparison of these distributions with

those from the Tutorial Organizers Survey and from official university statistics is given in Part VI and shows the three sources to be in close agreement.

**Table 91.** *Undergraduates by subject group and year. Michaelmas Term 1964*

OXFORD                                                              PERCENTAGE

|  | Year | | | All years | Number in sample |
|---|---|---|---|---|---|
|  | First | Second | Third |  |  |
| Arts | 35 | 35 | 30 | 100 | *496* |
| Social studies | 37 | 30 | 33 | 100 | *216* |
| Science | 36 | 35 | 30 | 100 | *357* |
| All subjects | 35 | 34 | 31 | 100 | *1,069* |
| Arts | 46 | 48 | 46 | 46 | . |
| Social studies | 21 | 18 | 22 | 20 | . |
| Science | 34 | 34 | 32 | 33 | . |
| All subjects | 100 | 100 | 100 | 100 | . |
| *Number in sample* | 379 | 361 | 329 | *1,069* | . |

SOURCE: Undergraduate Survey.

**Table 92.** *Examination undergraduates were working for, by year. Michaelmas Term 1964*

OXFORD                                                              PERCENTAGE

| Examination | Year | | | All years |
|---|---|---|---|---|
|  | First | Second | Third |  |
| Preliminary examination | 57 | 1 | — | 21 |
| Moderations | 33 | 8 | 1 | 14 |
| Honour School | 10 | 91 | 99 | 65 |
| Pass School | — | 1 | — | — |
| All examinations | 100 | 100 | 100 | 100 |
| *Number in sample* | 379 | 361 | 329 | *1,069* |

SOURCE: Undergraduate Survey.

205. The distribution of undergraduates according to the type of examination for which they were working is given in Table 92. A negligible number were reading for the Pass School, and about two-thirds had passed a First Public Examination and were reading for an Honour School. Preliminary Examinations and Law Moderations are usually taken during the first year, and Honour Moderations either at the end of the first year or during the second year. One-third of first-year undergraduates were reading for Moderations (including Law Moderations). The remainder were reading for, or had already taken, a Preliminary Examination.[1]

**Table 93.** *Undergraduates by subject group and type of society. Michaelmas Term 1964*

OXFORD                                                              PERCENTAGE

|  | Men's colleges | Permanent Private Halls | Women's colleges | All societies | *Number in sample* |
|---|---|---|---|---|---|
| Arts | 74 | 4 | 22 | 100 | *496* |
| Social studies | 89 | 1 | 9 | 100 | *216* |
| Science | 86 | — | 13 | 100 | *357* |
| All subjects | 81 | 2 | 16 | 100 | *1,069* |
| Arts | 42 | 85 | 61 | 46 | · |
| Social studies | 22 | 12 | 11 | 20 | · |
| Science | 35 | 4 | 27 | 33 | · |
| All subjects | 100 | 100 | 100 | 100 | · |
| *Number in sample* | *868* | *26* | *175* | *1,069* | · |

SOURCE: Undergraduate Survey.

NOTE: Two undergraduates at Linacre College are included under 'men's colleges'.

206. Table 93 gives the distribution of undergraduates in the survey by subject group and college group (men's and women's colleges and Permanent Private Halls). It is in close agreement with the distributions by subject in Table 12, and in addition it shows that the great majority of undergraduates at Permanent Private Halls were reading arts subjects.

[1] Most of those who had taken a Preliminary Examination were chemists. In the second year a few were still reading for a Preliminary Examination. The great majority of the 8 per cent. reading for Moderations were reading for Classical Honour Moderations which is normally taken after five terms. See Part I, paras. 18–20 for details of the First and Second Public Examinations.

**Table 94.** *Undergraduates in their second and third years with Senior Status by subject group. Michaelmas Term 1964*

OXFORD                                                                    PERCENTAGE

|                                                      | Arts | Social studies | Science | All subjects |
|------------------------------------------------------|------|----------------|---------|--------------|
| Graduates of U.K. universities with Senior Status    | 3    | 1              | —       | 1            |
| Graduates of overseas universities with Senior Status| 4    | 10             | 1       | 3            |
| Others with Senior Status                            | 2    | 2              | 1       | 1            |
| Without Senior Status                                | 92   | 87             | 98      | 95           |
| All undergraduates in second or third years          | 100  | 100            | 100     | 100          |

SOURCE: Undergraduate Survey.

207. Suitably qualified undergraduates are given Senior Status. This dispenses them from the First Public Examination, and enables them to take a degree in two years instead of three. Senior Status is usually granted only to graduates of other universities and to undergraduates who have previously passed a university diploma while at Ruskin College or Plater College. In the Undergraduate and Tutorial Organizers Surveys undergraduates with Senior Status have been treated as second year in their first year of residence, etc. Table 94 shows their distribution by subject group among all second- and third-year undergraduates. Graduates of overseas universities form the majority of undergraduates with Senior Status, who were most heavily represented in social studies. There were very few in science.

## Average amounts of teaching received

208. Table 95 gives the weekly averages for the main forms of teaching by subject group and year. On average, undergraduates attended 1·5 tutorials, 0·8 classes and seminars, and 4·7 lectures. Scientists spent an average of 7·5 hours doing practical work in laboratories. But there were considerable variations about the averages, both between years and between subject groups. In arts and social studies the number of tutorials increased with year, the average being rather higher in social studies than in arts. The relatively small number of tutorials in the first year corresponded with a high figure for classes and seminars. In science, classes and seminars were used less, and the number of tutorials decreased with year, the over-all average being the same as in arts.

**Table 95.** *Average per week of teaching received by undergraduates by subject group and year. Michaelmas Term 1964*

OXFORD

NUMBER

| Subject group | | Year | | | All years |
|---|---|---|---|---|---|
| | | First | Second | Third | |
| Arts | Tutorials | 1·1 | 1·6 | 1·6 | 1·4 |
| | Classes or seminars | 2·4 | 0·7 | 0·8 | 1·3 |
| | Lectures | 5·2 | 2·7 | 2·7 | 3·6 |
| | Practicals (hours) | 0·2 | — | — | 0·1 |
| Social studies | Tutorials | 1·5 | 1·7 | 1·9 | 1·7 |
| | Classes or seminars | 1·2 | 0·2 | 0·4 | 0·6 |
| | Lectures | 5·2 | 2·5 | 3·1 | 3·7 |
| | Practicals (hours) | — | — | — | — |
| Science | Tutorials | 1·6 | 1·4 | 1·3 | 1·4 |
| | Classes or seminars | 0·4 | 0·1 | 0·3 | 0·3 |
| | Lectures | 8·6 | 5·5 | 6·1 | 6·8 |
| | Practicals (hours) | 9·0 | 8·2 | 4·8 | 7·5 |
| All subjects | Tutorials | 1·3 | 1·5 | 1·6 | 1·5 |
| | Classes or seminars | 1·5 | 0·4 | 0·6 | 0·8 |
| | Lectures | 6·3 | 3·6 | 3·9 | 4·7 |
| | Practicals (hours) | 3·1 | 2·8 | 1·5 | 2·5 |

SOURCE: Undergraduate Survey.

NOTES

1. Tutorials which undergraduates should have attended but which were missed during the survey week are included.
2. The sample numbers corresponding to the breakdown in this table are given in Table 365.

209. The average for lectures was highest in the first year, followed by the third year. There was little difference between arts and social studies in the number of lectures attended, but about twice as many were attended in science.

210. There are two ways in which the survey results are not typical of the whole academic year. Most important, they relate to the Michaelmas Term only, and it could well be that the amount and distribution of teaching (and of class teaching in particular) would be different in other terms. Partly because of the different timing of the First Public Examination in different subjects, the weight of the various forms of teaching falling in Michaelmas Term is likely to vary between subjects, and to this extent the survey is not representative. Secondly, lecture audiences fall off as a term progresses. Although the averages for the third week of the term should provide a valid basis for comparisons between subjects, years, etc., they do not provide reliable estimates of the average for the whole term.

211. In the subsequent sections the various forms of teaching are analysed in more detail.

**Table 96.** *Number of tutorials attended by undergraduates per week, by subject group and year. Michaelmas Term 1964*

| Subject group | Number of tutorials attended per week | Year | | | All years |
|---|---|---|---|---|---|
| | | First | Second | Third | |
| Arts | None | 24 | 2 | 3 | 10 |
| | One | 51 | 45 | 32 | 43 |
| | Two | 20 | 49 | 62 | 43 |
| | Three and over | 6 | 3 | 3 | 4 |
| | All | 100 | 100 | 100 | 100 |
| Social studies | None | 10 | 2 | — | 4 |
| | One | 37 | 29 | 21 | 29 |
| | Two | 48 | 68 | 72 | 62 |
| | Three and over | 5 | 2 | 7 | 5 |
| | All | 100 | 100 | 100 | 100 |
| Science | None | 1 | — | — | — |
| | One | 50 | 66 | 71 | 62 |
| | Two | 43 | 33 | 25 | 34 |
| | Three and over | 7 | 1 | 4 | 4 |
| | All | 100 | 100 | 100 | 100 |
| All subjects | None | 13 | 1 | 1 | 5 |
| | One | 47 | 50 | 42 | 47 |
| | Two | 33 | 47 | 53 | 44 |
| | Three and over | 6 | 2 | 4 | 4 |
| | All | 100 | 100 | 100 | 100 |

SOURCE: Undergraduate Survey.

NOTE: Tutorials which undergraduates should have attended but which were missed during the survey week are included.

## Tutorials attended

212. Table 96 shows the number of tutorials attended by undergraduates. The low average in Table 95 for first-year undergraduates in arts and social studies can be seen to correspond with a sizeable proportion not attending any tutorials. In interpreting the figures in this table, it should be remembered that the survey related to one week only, whereas tutorials are sometimes arranged at the rate of three a fortnight. Therefore an approximately equal, but unknown, number of those attending one or two tutorials in the survey week were attending three a fortnight.

**Table 97.** *Number of undergraduates attending tutorials by subject group and year. Michaelmas Term 1964*

OXFORD                                                                    PERCENTAGE

| Subject group | Number attending tutorials received by undergraduates | Year | | | All years |
| --- | --- | --- | --- | --- | --- |
| | | First | Second | Third | |
| Arts | One | 22 | 49 | 47 | 41 |
| | Two | 40 | 44 | 47 | 44 |
| | Three | 37 | 7 | 6 | 15 |
| | All | 100 | 100 | 100 | 100 |
| Social studies | One | 13 | 37 | 44 | 32 |
| | Two | 50 | 57 | 50 | 52 |
| | Three | 37 | 6 | 6 | 16 |
| | All | 100 | 100 | 100 | 100 |
| Science | One | 23 | 45 | 55 | 39 |
| | Two | 69 | 51 | 41 | 55 |
| | Three | 9 | 4 | 4 | 6 |
| | All | 100 | 100 | 100 | 100 |
| All subjects | One | 20 | 45 | 48 | 38 |
| | Two | 54 | 49 | 46 | 50 |
| | Three | 26 | 6 | 6 | 12 |
| | All | 100 | 100 | 100 | 100 |

SOURCE: Undergraduate Survey.

213. Half the tutorials were attended in pairs; 38 per cent. were attended alone; and the remaining 12 per cent. were attended by three undergraduates. There was a decrease in the average number attending with increasing year, the biggest difference being between the first and second years. The lowest proportion of solo tutorials was in social studies, and tutorials in threes were relatively uncommon in science (Table 97). 62 per cent. of the tutorials reported by undergraduates were in pairs or threes, but a rather smaller proportion, 55 per cent., of undergraduates had no tutorial alone during the week (Table 98). This is to be expected since an undergraduate having two tutorials has two chances of one being alone.[1]

214. The great majority of tutorials attended by more than one undergraduate were attended by undergraduates from one college only; an even larger majority were attended by undergraduates of one sex only. Table 99 shows that 6 per cent. of such tutorials were attended by members of more than one college. The proportion was slightly higher in arts, and was higher in the third year than in the first or second years.

[1] In fact, only 52 per cent. of undergraduates would have had no tutorial alone if the chance of a tutorial being alone had been the same for each tutorial, so there was a slightly greater chance of a second tutorial being alone if the first one was than if the first one was not.

**Table 98.** *Number of tutorials attended alone by undergraduates per week by subject group and year. Michaelmas Term 1964*

OXFORD                                                                    PERCENTAGE

| Subject group | Number of tutorials attended alone per week | Year | | | All years |
|---|---|---|---|---|---|
| | | First | Second | Third | |
| Arts | None | 78 | 41 | 39 | 53 |
| | One | 20 | 45 | 46 | 37 |
| | Two | 1 | 14 | 15 | 10 |
| | Three and over | 1 | — | — | — |
| | All | 100 | 100 | 100 | 100 |
| Social studies | None | 82 | 51 | 43 | 60 |
| | One | 16 | 37 | 36 | 29 |
| | Two | 1 | 12 | 19 | 11 |
| | Three and over | — | — | 1 | — |
| | All | 100 | 100 | 100 | 100 |
| Science | None | 71 | 46 | 41 | 53 |
| | One | 22 | 48 | 47 | 39 |
| | Two | 7 | 5 | 11 | 8 |
| | Three and over | — | 1 | 1 | 1 |
| | All | 100 | 100 | 100 | 100 |
| All subjects | None | 77 | 45 | 40 | 55 |
| | One | 20 | 45 | 44 | 36 |
| | Two | 3 | 11 | 15 | 9 |
| | Three and over | — | — | 1 | — |
| | All | 100 | 100 | 100 | 100 |

SOURCE: Undergraduate Survey.

215. Tables 100 and 101 give details of tutorials by subject. The subjects are those of Honour Schools (and branches of the Honour School of Natural Science) wherever possible, and undergraduates reading for a First Public Examination are included under the corresponding Honour School. But certain First Public Examinations in science subjects do not correspond with a single Honour School, and must be shown separately. Classical Honour Moderations (under which undergraduates reading for the Preliminary Examination in Classical (Greek and Latin) Languages are also included) is also shown separately.

216. For the sake of completeness, each subject is shown.[1] But a number of subjects, especially in science, are small and the numbers in the sample are very small. For such subjects the survey results will not be reliable and are usually disregarded in the commentary. The sample numbers are given in Table 100.

[1] Except that Engineering, and Engineering and Economics are combined, and Agriculture and Forestry are combined.

**Table 99.** *Percentage of tutorials attended by undergraduates in pairs or threes which were attended by members of one college or one sex only. Michaelmas Term 1964*

OXFORD                                                                      PERCENTAGE

| Subject group | Percentage of tutorials in pairs or threes which were attended by: | Year | | | All years |
|---|---|---|---|---|---|
| | | First | Second | Third | |
| Arts | Members of one college only | 97 | 93 | 86 | 92 |
| | Members of one sex only | 99 | 98 | 95 | 97 |
| Social studies | Members of one college only | 95 | 99 | 91 | 95 |
| | Members of one sex only | 95 | 100 | 96 | 97 |
| Science | Members of one college only | 97 | 93 | 91 | 94 |
| | Members of one sex only | 99 | 99 | 95 | 98 |
| All subjects | Members of one college only | 96 | 94 | 88 | 94 |
| | Members of one sex only | 98 | 99 | 96 | 97 |

SOURCE: Undergraduate Survey.

217. Among arts subjects, the average number of tutorials was above the over-all average in Literae Humaniores (even after allowing for the fact that these undergraduates were in their third year) and in English. It was below the over-all average in Theology and Geography.

218. In science, tutorials were below average in Chemistry and a number of the smaller subjects, and above average in PPP and perhaps in Biochemistry. The average for Honour Moderations in Physics, Mathematics, and Engineering was above the first-year average in science.

219. There were considerable variations between subjects in the proportion of tutorials attended by one undergraduate only. Among the larger subjects the proportion was high in Literae Humaniores and Classical Honour Moderations, and low in Jurisprudence and Chemistry.

**Table 100.** *Tutorials attended by undergraduates by subject. Michaelmas Term 1964*

OXFORD                                                                    PERCENTAGE

| Subject | Percentage of undergraduates attending stated number of tutorials per week | | | | *Average number of tutorials attended per week* | *Number in sample* |
|---|---|---|---|---|---|---|
| | None | One | Two or more | All | | |
| Literae Humaniores | — | 10 | 90 | 100 | 2·0 | 20 |
| Classical Honour Mods. | 4 | 80 | 15 | 100 | 1·2 | 45 |
| Theology | 22 | 65 | 13 | 100 | 1·0 | 23 |
| Modern History | 16 | 41 | 43 | 100 | 1·3 | 158 |
| English | 4 | 16 | 80 | 100 | 1·8 | 99 |
| Modern Languages | 8 | 51 | 41 | 100 | 1·3 | 102 |
| Oriental Studies | — | 43 | 57 | 100 | 1·6 | 7 |
| Geography | 9 | 71 | 21 | 100 | 1·1 | 34 |
| Music | — | 25 | 75 | 100 | 1·8 | 8 |
| Jurisprudence | 5 | 36 | 59 | 100 | 1·6 | 97 |
| PPE | 3 | 24 | 73 | 100 | 1·7 | 119 |
| Mathematics | — | 62 | 38 | 100 | 1·4 | 69 |
| Physics | — | 76 | 24 | 100 | 1·3 | 49 |
| Chemistry | 1 | 84 | 15 | 100 | 1·1 | 82 |
| Biochemistry | — | 20 | 80 | 100 | 1·8 | 10 |
| Animal Physiology | — | 59 | 41 | 100 | 1·5 | 39 |
| Zoology | — | 86 | 14 | 100 | 1·1 | 14 |
| Botany | — | 80 | 20 | 100 | 1·2 | 5 |
| Geology | — | 100 | — | 100 | 1·0 | 2 |
| PPP | — | — | 100 | 100 | 2·5 | 15 |
| Natural Science | — | — | 100 | 100 | 2·0 | 4 |
| Physics, Mathematics, and Engineering | — | 9 | 91 | 100 | 1·9 | 34 |
| Biology | — | 88 | 13 | 100 | 1·1 | 8 |
| Engineering | — | 56 | 44 | 100 | 1·4 | 16 |
| Metallurgy | — | 83 | 17 | 100 | 1·2 | 6 |
| Agriculture and Forestry | — | 100 | — | 100 | 1·0 | 4 |
| All subjects | 5 | 47 | 48 | 100 | 1·5 | 1,069 |

SOURCE: Undergraduate Survey.

NOTES

1. Engineering includes Engineering and Economics.
2. Natural Science, Physics, Mathematics, and Engineering, and Biology are First Public Examinations.

220. Subjects in which a comparatively large proportion of tutorials were attended by members of more than one college were mainly the smaller arts subjects, in which not every college has a tutor. There was also an above average proportion of 'mixed tutorials' in Engineering.

**Table 101.** *Number, college, and sex of undergraduates attending tutorials, by subject. Michaelmas Term 1964*

OXFORD                                                                 PERCENTAGE

| Subject | Percentage of tutorials which were attended by stated number of persons | | | | Percentage of tutorials attended by undergraduates in pairs or threes which were attended by members of | |
| --- | --- | --- | --- | --- | --- | --- |
| | One | Two | Three | All | One college only | One sex only |
| Literae Humaniores | 53 | 45 | 3 | 100 | 100 | 100 |
| Classical Honour | | | | | | |
| Mods. | 77 | 11 | 11 | 100 | 100 | 100 |
| Theology | 59 | 32 | 9 | 100 | 56 | 100 |
| Modern History | 36 | 44 | 20 | 100 | 97 | 98 |
| English | 34 | 52 | 14 | 100 | 98 | 98 |
| Modern Languages | 34 | 51 | 15 | 100 | 90 | 94 |
| Oriental Studies | 64 | 18 | 18 | 100 | 50 | 100 |
| Geography | 30 | 53 | 18 | 100 | 63 | 96 |
| Music | 69 | 31 | — | 100 | 75 | 100 |
| Jurisprudence | 18 | 61 | 22 | 100 | 94 | 96 |
| PPE | 42 | 46 | 12 | 100 | 95 | 97 |
| Mathematics | 39 | 58 | 3 | 100 | 93 | 97 |
| Physics | 47 | 45 | 8 | 100 | 97 | 100 |
| Chemistry | 17 | 77 | 5 | 100 | 99 | 99 |
| Biochemistry | 44 | 44 | 11 | 100 | 100 | 100 |
| Animal Physiology | 47 | 41 | 12 | 100 | 97 | 100 |
| Zoology | 100 | — | — | 100 | . | . |
| Botany | 100 | — | — | 100 | . | . |
| Geology | 100 | — | — | 100 | . | . |
| PPP | 64 | 28 | 8 | 100 | 92 | 100 |
| Natural Science | 14 | 86 | — | 100 | 83 | 100 |
| Physics, Mathematics, | | | | | | |
| and Engineering | 15 | 83 | 2 | 100 | 100 | 100 |
| Biology | 56 | 22 | 22 | 100 | 50 | 100 |
| Engineering | 43 | 57 | — | 100 | 62 | 100 |
| Metallurgy | 29 | 57 | 14 | — | 80 | 100 |
| Agriculture and | | | | | | |
| Forestry | 100 | — | — | 100 | . | . |
| All subjects | 38 | 50 | 12 | 100 | 94 | 97 |

SOURCE: Undergraduate Survey.
NOTE: See notes to Table 100.

221. Table 102 shows that the average number of tutorials was higher for the women's colleges than for the men's colleges. The average number attending tutorials was slightly higher for the women's colleges than for the men's colleges, and there was considerable variation between individual colleges, particularly in the proportion of solo tutorials (see Table 103).

**Table 102.** *Tutorials attended by undergraduates by college. Michaelmas Term 1964*

OXFORD                                             PERCENTAGE

| College | Percentage of undergraduates attending stated number of tutorials per week | | | | | *Average number of tutorials received per week* | *Number in sample* |
|---|---|---|---|---|---|---|---|
| | None | One | Two | Three or more | All | | |
| Balliol | 2 | 50 | 43 | 5 | 100 | 1·5 | 44 |
| Brasenose | 7 | 60 | 25 | 7 | 100 | 1·3 | 40 |
| Christ Church | 4 | 56 | 38 | 2 | 100 | 1·4 | 52 |
| Corpus Christi | — | 39 | 61 | — | 100 | 1·6 | 23 |
| Exeter | 8 | 45 | 45 | 3 | 100 | 1·4 | 38 |
| Hertford | 4 | 67 | 26 | 4 | 100 | 1·3 | 27 |
| Jesus | 9 | 48 | 33 | 9 | 100 | 1·5 | 33 |
| Keble | 5 | 44 | 46 | 5 | 100 | 1·5 | 41 |
| Lincoln | 11 | 36 | 46 | 7 | 100 | 1·5 | 28 |
| Magdalen | 2 | 43 | 52 | 2 | 100 | 1·5 | 46 |
| Merton | — | 61 | 39 | — | 100 | 1·4 | 31 |
| New College | 9 | 40 | 51 | — | 100 | 1·4 | 53 |
| Oriel | 13 | 42 | 42 | 3 | 100 | 1·4 | 31 |
| Pembroke | 5 | 49 | 41 | 5 | 100 | 1·5 | 39 |
| Queen's | 11 | 57 | 31 | — | 100 | 1·2 | 35 |
| St. Catherine's | 7 | 40 | 53 | — | 100 | 1·5 | 45 |
| St. Edmund Hall | 13 | 42 | 42 | 2 | 100 | 1·3 | 45 |
| St. John's | — | 65 | 29 | 6 | 100 | 1·5 | 34 |
| St. Peter's | 3 | 53 | 41 | 3 | 100 | 1·4 | 32 |
| Trinity | 7 | 48 | 37 | 7 | 100 | 1·5 | 27 |
| University | — | 49 | 36 | 15 | 100 | 1·7 | 47 |
| Wadham | 9 | 38 | 44 | 9 | 100 | 1·5 | 34 |
| Worcester | 2 | 46 | 51 | — | 100 | 1·5 | 41 |
| Men's colleges | 6 | 48 | 42 | 4 | 100 | 1·4 | 866 |
| Permanent Private Halls | — | 50 | 38 | 12 | 100 | 1·7 | 26 |
| Men's societies | 6 | 48 | 42 | 4 | 100 | 1·5 | 894 |
| Lady Margaret Hall | — | 43 | 54 | 3 | 100 | 1·6 | 35 |
| St. Anne's | 3 | 37 | 61 | — | 100 | 1·6 | 38 |
| St. Hilda's | 6 | 17 | 74 | 3 | 100 | 1·7 | 35 |
| St. Hugh's | 6 | 47 | 36 | 11 | 100 | 1·5 | 36 |
| Somerville | 6 | 42 | 52 | — | 100 | 1·5 | 31 |
| Women's colleges | 4 | 37 | 55 | 3 | 100 | 1·6 | 175 |
| All societies | 5 | 47 | 44 | 4 | 100 | 1·5 | 1,069 |

SOURCE: Undergraduate Survey.

NOTE: Two undergraduates at Linacre College are not shown separately, but are included in the total for men's societies.

**Table 103.** *Number, college, and sex of undergraduates attending tutorials, by college. Michaelmas Term 1964*

OXFORD PERCENTAGE

| College | Percentage of tutorials which were attended by stated number of persons | | | | Percentage of tutorials attended by undergraduates in pairs or threes which were attended by members of | |
|---|---|---|---|---|---|---|
| | One | Two | Three | All | One college only | One sex only |
| Balliol | 33 | 52 | 14 | 100 | 90 | 95 |
| Brasenose | 36 | 51 | 13 | 100 | 97 | 97 |
| Christ Church | 46 | 42 | 13 | 100 | 95 | 95 |
| Corpus Christi | 62 | 22 | 16 | 100 | 93 | 93 |
| Exeter | 50 | 37 | 13 | 100 | 88 | 100 |
| Hertford | 49 | 40 | 11 | 100 | 83 | 100 |
| Jesus | 36 | 53 | 11 | 100 | 100 | 100 |
| Keble | 24 | 53 | 24 | 100 | 96 | 98 |
| Lincoln | 24 | 69 | 7 | 100 | 100 | 100 |
| Magdalen | 56 | 38 | 6 | 100 | 100 | 100 |
| Merton | 63 | 35 | 2 | 100 | 94 | 100 |
| New College | 41 | 54 | 5 | 100 | 86 | 98 |
| Oriel | 50 | 40 | 10 | 100 | 95 | 100 |
| Pembroke | 24 | 62 | 14 | 100 | 95 | 98 |
| Queen's | 48 | 45 | 8 | 100 | 100 | 100 |
| St. Catherine's | 35 | 53 | 11 | 100 | 95 | 100 |
| St. Edmund Hall | 14 | 69 | 17 | 100 | 96 | 100 |
| St. John's | 27 | 58 | 15 | 100 | 94 | 100 |
| St. Peter's | 41 | 39 | 20 | 100 | 96 | 100 |
| Trinity | 26 | 59 | 15 | 100 | 90 | 97 |
| University | 39 | 44 | 17 | 100 | 94 | 96 |
| Wadham | 41 | 43 | 16 | 100 | 100 | 100 |
| Worcester | 52 | 40 | 8 | 100 | 90 | 97 |
| Men's colleges | 39 | 48 | 12 | 100 | 94 | 98 |
| Permanent Private Halls | 50 | 36 | 14 | 100 | 68 | 100 |
| Men's societies | 40 | 48 | 12 | 100 | 94 | 98 |
| Lady Margaret Hall | 27 | 63 | 11 | 100 | 88 | 93 |
| St. Anne's | 30 | 58 | 12 | 100 | 98 | 100 |
| St. Hilda's | 20 | 75 | 5 | 100 | 96 | 96 |
| St. Hugh's | 39 | 50 | 11 | 100 | 88 | 97 |
| Somerville | 38 | 44 | 18 | 100 | 96 | 96 |
| Women's colleges | 30 | 59 | 11 | 100 | 93 | 96 |
| All societies | 38 | 50 | 12 | 100 | 94 | 97 |

SOURCE: Undergraduate Survey.

NOTE: See note to Table 102.

## Persons giving tutorials

222. The Undergraduate Survey did not inquire into the persons giving tutorials: whether they were fellows or lecturers of the undergraduate's college, fellows of other colleges, etc. The Tutorial Organizers Survey was designed to elicit this information. It shows the distribution of (teachers') tutorial hours according to the persons giving the tutorials, the total of teachers' time expended, and the teachers' hours per undergraduate. In addition, where teaching was given outside an undergraduate's college, the tutor was asked to give the reason. The main analyses given below are for undergraduates at the men's and women's colleges. The Permanent Private Halls are treated separately and results are given in Tables 108 and 109. While the survey was being carried out it was pointed out to us that tutorial arrangements in Oriental Studies are not on a college basis, and undergraduates in Oriental Studies are therefore excluded. Their teaching arrangements are summarized in Table 132.

223. Tables 104 and 105 give results for the main subject groups subdivided between men and women. Between 50 per cent. and 60 per cent. of tutorials at the men's colleges were given by fellows of the undergraduates' own college, the proportion being lowest in science. At the women's colleges, the corresponding proportions were lower, the difference being largest in science. When teaching by lecturers of the undergraduates' college is added, to give in-college teaching, the proportion rises to around 70 per cent. for the men's colleges and 50–60 per cent. for the women's colleges. Much of the remaining tutorials were given by fellows or lecturers of other colleges. The proportion from this source is higher for the women's than the men's colleges, and this largely compensates for the smaller proportion from in-college teachers. Persons holding a university but not a college post provide a substantial amount of teaching only in science, and postgraduates are used more in science than in other subjects.

224. Of all out-college teaching, about 40 per cent. was sent out either because the college had no teacher in the subject, or because the college teacher was on leave. The proportion accounted for in this way was higher in arts (because the college teacher being on leave was more often mentioned) and a good deal lower in social studies. The college teacher having reached his maximum hours accounted for a quarter of out-college teaching in social studies, a fifth in science, and a tenth in arts. The first three reasons given in the table are all involuntary, and together account for more than half of all out-college teaching. Teaching for optional or special papers accounted for a substantial proportion (39 per cent.) of out-college teaching in social studies, for 26 per cent. in arts, but for only 16 per cent. in science. The remainder, around a fifth, was accounted for by other reasons, of which details are given in Table 106.

**Table 104.** Persons giving tutorials to undergraduates (except those at Permanent Private Halls) by subject group and sex of undergraduates. Tutorial hours: Michaelmas Term 1964

OXFORD

PERCENTAGE

| Tutorial hours given by | Tutorial hours given for undergraduates in | | | | | | | | | | | |
| --- | --- | --- | --- | --- | --- | --- | --- | --- | --- | --- | --- | --- |
| | Arts | | | Social studies | | | Science | | | All subjects | | |
| | Men | Women | All | Men | Women | All | Men | Women | All | Men | Women | All |
| Fellows of undergraduates' college | 59 | 48 | 56 | 55 | 50 | 54 | 51 | 34 | 49 | 55 | 45 | 53 |
| Lecturers of undergraduates' college | 13 | 10 | 12 | 16 | 11 | 15 | 15 | 13 | 14 | 14 | 11 | 14 |
| Fellows or lecturers of other colleges | 17 | 28 | 19 | 16 | 27 | 18 | 11 | 23 | 13 | 15 | 26 | 17 |
| Persons holding a university but not a college post | 2 | 2 | 2 | 3 | 6 | 3 | 13 | 14 | 13 | 6 | 6 | 6 |
| Postgraduates | 4 | 5 | 4 | 6 | 5 | 6 | 8 | 8 | 8 | 6 | 6 | 6 |
| Other persons not holding a university or college post | 6 | 7 | 6 | 4 | 2 | 4 | 3 | 7 | 3 | 4 | 6 | 5 |
| All in-college teachers | 72 | 58 | 69 | 71 | 60 | 69 | 66 | 47 | 63 | 69 | 56 | 67 |
| All out-college teachers | 28 | 42 | 31 | 29 | 40 | 31 | 34 | 53 | 37 | 31 | 44 | 33 |
| All teachers | 100 | 100 | 100 | 100 | 100 | 100 | 100 | 100 | 100 | 100 | 100 | 100 |
| Total tutorial hours | 2,681 | 708 | 3,389 | 1,247 | 192 | 1,440 | 2,033 | 327 | 2,360 | 5,961 | 1,227 | 7,188 |
| Tutorial hours per undergraduate | 1·1 | 1·0 | 1·0 | 1·0 | 1·4 | 1·1 | 1·0 | 1·1 | 1·0 | 1·0 | 1·1 | 1·0 |

SOURCE: Tutorial Organizers Survey.

**Table 105.** *Reason for out-college tutorial teaching by subject group and sex. Undergraduate out-college tutorials except at Permanent Private Halls. Michaelmas Term 1964*

OXFORD      PERCENTAGE

| Reason for out-college tutorial teaching | Out-college tutorial hours given for undergraduates in | | | | | | | | | | | |
|---|---|---|---|---|---|---|---|---|---|---|---|---|
| | Arts | | | Social studies | | | Science | | | All subjects | | |
| | Men | Women | All | Men | Women | All | Men | Women | All | Men | Women | All |
| No teacher in the subject | 30 | 31 | 30 | 5 | 13 | 7 | 35 | 44 | 37 | 27 | 32 | 28 |
| College teacher on leave | 18 | 12 | 16 | 7 | 5 | 7 | 6 | 1 | 5 | 11 | 8 | 10 |
| College teacher had reached his maximum hours | 10 | 9 | 9 | 27 | 19 | 25 | 19 | 16 | 19 | 17 | 12 | 16 |
| For teaching for optional or special papers | 27 | 25 | 26 | 37 | 47 | 39 | 14 | 23 | 16 | 24 | 28 | 25 |
| For other reasons | 16 | 23 | 18 | 24 | 15 | 22 | 25 | 16 | 23 | 21 | 20 | 21 |
| All | 100 | 100 | 100 | 100 | 100 | 100 | 100 | 100 | 100 | 100 | 100 | 100 |

SOURCE: Tutorial Organizers Survey.

**Table 106.** *Reason for out-college tutorial teaching included under 'other reasons' in Table 105. Tutorial organizers except those at Permanent Private Halls: Michaelmas Term 1964*

OXFORD                                                              PERCENTAGE

| Reason for out-college tutorial teaching | Tutorial organizers for undergraduates in | | | | | |
|---|---|---|---|---|---|---|
| | Arts | Social studies | Science | Men's colleges | Women's colleges | All colleges |
| For variety | 14 | 4 | 9 | 7 | 24 | 9 |
| For teaching by a relative specialist | 50 | 52 | 72 | 60 | 74 | 62 |
| For miscellaneous reasons or no reason given | 42 | 44 | 25 | 36 | 20 | 33 |
| All tutors specifying 'other reasons' in Table 105 | 100 | 100 | 100 | 100 | 100 | 100 |
| Percentage of all out-college tutorial hours specified under 'other reasons' in Table 105 | 18 | 22 | 23 | 21 | 20 | 21 |

SOURCE: Tutorial Organizers Survey.

NOTES

1. This table gives the distribution of returns made by tutors, not that of the tutorial hours given to undergraduates. In comparison with Table 105, therefore, small subjects (having a small number of undergraduates per tutor) will be relatively heavily weighted.
2. The columns do not all add to 100 per cent. since some tutors specified more than one reason.

225. Unlike Table 105, Table 106 is based on the number of tutors replying, not on the number of tutorial hours involved. In comparison with Table 105, therefore, subjects with relatively few undergraduates per tutor are more heavily weighted. The most frequent 'other reason' given for out-college teaching was that it is preferable for undergraduates to go to a teacher who is something of a specialist on the subject-matter of a particular paper. Although the borderline is not clear, an attempt was made in editing the answers to distinguish between this situation in teaching for main line subjects, which is referred to as teaching by 'relative specialists', and teaching by specialists for special subjects. Teaching by 'relative specialists' accounted for 62 per cent. of 'other reasons' for out-college teaching, or about 13 per cent. of all out-college teaching. It was mentioned

more often in science than in arts or social studies, and more often by women than by men.[1] The next most frequent single reason was that undergraduates were sent out for the sake of variety.

**Table 107.** *Persons giving tutorials to undergraduates (except those at Permanent Private Halls) by year of undergraduates. Tutorial hours: Michaelmas Term 1964*

OXFORD                                                                                                    PERCENTAGE

| Tutorial hours given by | Tutorial hours given for under-graduates in | | | | |
|---|---|---|---|---|---|
| | 1st year | 2nd year | 3rd year | 4th and subsequent years | All years |
| Fellows of undergraduates' college | 54 | 56 | 51 | 48 | 53 |
| Lecturers of undergraduates' college | 15 | 16 | 11 | 9 | 14 |
| Fellows or lecturers of other colleges | 7 | 15 | 24 | 28 | 17 |
| Persons holding a university but not a college post | 7 | 5 | 6 | 6 | 6 |
| Postgraduates | 8 | 5 | 5 | 7 | 6 |
| Other persons not holding a university or college post | 10 | 3 | 3 | 3 | 5 |
| All in-college teachers | 68 | 72 | 63 | 57 | 67 |
| All out-college teachers | 32 | 28 | 37 | 43 | 33 |
| All teachers | 100 | 100 | 100 | 100 | 100 |
| *Total tutorial hours* | *1,818* | *2,542* | *2,384* | *445* | *7,188* |
| *Tutorial hours per undergraduate* | *0·8* | *1·1* | *1·2* | *1·6* | *1·0* |

SOURCE: Tutorial Organizers Survey.

226. The proportion of in-college teaching was highest for the second year and lowest for the third and fourth years (Table 107). This decline was matched by an increased use of fellows and lecturers of other colleges, but not of other categories of teachers.[2]

227. Tutorial arrangements at Permanent Private Halls are summarized in Tables 108 and 109. These societies have few tutors, and the bulk of their

[1] It was mentioned more often in the 'small' sciences having few undergraduates per tutor. If the replies had been weighted according to the number of tutorial hours involved, the proportion would probably have been lower in science and over-all.

[2] There is a difference between the men's and women's colleges. The proportion of in-college teaching at the women's colleges declines from 65 per cent. for the first year, to 59 per cent. for the second year, 48 per cent. for the third year, and 42 per cent. for the fourth and subsequent years.

teaching was done either by their own lecturers or by fellows or lecturers of other colleges. Of the 15 per cent. of teaching done outside the society for 'other reasons', 63 per cent. (in terms of tutors, not of tutorial hours) was sent out for the sake of variety, and 25 per cent. for teaching by a 'relative specialist'.

**Table 108.** *Persons giving tutorials to undergraduates in Permanent Private Halls by year of undergraduates. Tutorial hours: Michaelmas Term 1964*

OXFORD                                                                                            PERCENTAGE

| Tutorial hours given by | Tutorial hours given for undergraduates in | | | | |
|---|---|---|---|---|---|
| | 1st year | 2nd year | 3rd year | 4th and subsequent years | All years |
| Tutors of undergraduates' society | 13 | 12 | 12 | 48 | 15 |
| Lecturers of undergraduates' society | 18 | 25 | 29 | 6 | 23 |
| Fellows or lecturers of other colleges | 50 | 52 | 45 | 42 | 49 |
| Persons holding a university but not a college post | 1 | 7 | 5 | 3 | 4 |
| Postgraduates | 10 | 3 | 8 | — | 6 |
| Other persons not holding a university or college post | 7 | 1 | 2 | — | 3 |
| All in-college teachers | 31 | 37 | 41 | 55 | 38 |
| All out-college teachers | 69 | 63 | 59 | 45 | 62 |
| All teachers | 100 | 100 | 100 | 100 | 100 |
| Total tutorial hours | 73 | 69 | 64 | 17 | 223 |
| Tutorial hours per undergraduate | 1·6 | 1·1 | 1·5 | 1·2 | 1·4 |

SOURCE: Tutorial Organizers Survey.

**Table 109.** *Reason for out-college tutorial teaching for undergraduates in Permanent Private Halls. Undergraduate out-college tutorials at Permanent Private Halls: Michaelmas Term 1964*

| OXFORD | PERCENTAGE |
|---|---|
| No teacher in the subject | 78 |
| College teacher on leave | — |
| College teacher had reached his maximum hours | 1 |
| For teaching for optional or special papers | 6 |
| For other reasons | 15 |
| All | 100 |

SOURCE: Tutorial Organizers Survey.

228. Tables 110 and 111 show tutorial arrangements by subjects, and it can be seen that there were considerable differences between subjects, which fall broadly into two groups: 'large' subjects in which most colleges have a tutor; and 'small' subjects where this is not so.

229. Table 112 shows that it is the less well-endowed colleges which tend to have the highest proportions of out-college teaching.

## Tutorial teaching at Cambridge

230. Cambridge University is the only university in Great Britain with a structure similar to that of Oxford, and with undergraduate teaching based on a tutorial system. But the organization of tutorial teaching at Cambridge is different from that at Oxford.

231. The term 'supervision' is used at Cambridge in place of 'tutorial'. Details of supervisions in 1961–2 in six selected subjects were collected by a Committee on Teaching set up by Cambridge University, and some of their results are reproduced in Table 114. Several qualifications must be mentioned before considering these results. In the table a column for all six subjects is shown. This simply summarizes the results for the six subjects, and should not be taken as representative of all subjects. Secondly, the figures are for teaching in the various subjects, and not for teaching given to particular undergraduates. To the extent that undergraduates receive teaching in more than one subject, these are different, and the last line in Table 114 on teachers' hours per undergraduate is not comparable with similar figures quoted above for Oxford. A Cambridge undergraduate reading English or Law spends his whole time on his subject, but an undergraduate during his first two years at least may spend only half his time on French or Russian, and only a third or a quarter of his time on Physics or Biochemistry, the rest of his time being spent on other subjects. Thirdly, the returns from colleges on which the figures are based were not quite complete (one college did not reply to the inquiry and the returns of four other colleges were incomplete), so that the total amount of teaching is understated. This may, but need not, also lead to some distortion of the distribution of teaching according to categories of teacher.

232. Table 114 shows that in-college teaching (in the six subjects) accounted for a much smaller proportion of all teaching than is the average at Oxford. The figures for teachers' hours per undergraduate in English and Law should be comparable with those for Oxford. In English the average was 0·8 hours for Cambridge and 1·1 hours for Oxford. In Law the average was 0·9 hours at each university. In the other subjects, as explained in the previous paragraph, the figures are not comparable.

**Table 110.** *Persons giving tutorials to undergraduates (except those at Permanent Private Halls), by subject of undergraduates. Tutorial hours: Michaelmas Term 1964*

OXFORD

PERCENTAGE

| Subject | Tutorial hours given by | | | | | | | | | Total tutorial hours | Tutorial hours per under-graduate |
| --- | --- | --- | --- | --- | --- | --- | --- | --- | --- | --- | --- |
| | Fellows of under-graduates' college | Lecturers of under-graduates' college | Fellows or lecturers of other colleges | Persons holding a university but not a college post | Post-graduates | Other persons not holding a university or a college post | All in-college teachers | All out-college teachers | All teachers | | |
| Literae Humaniores | 69 | 7 | 15 | — | 8 | 1 | 76 | 24 | 100 | 446 | 1·7 |
| Classical Honour Mods | 86 | 8 | 5 | 1 | — | — | 94 | 6 | 100 | 308 | 1·1 |
| Theology | 33 | 1 | 63 | 1 | — | 2 | 34 | 66 | 100 | 159 | 1·4 |
| Modern History | 62 | 5 | 20 | 1 | 5 | 7 | 67 | 33 | 100 | 808 | 0·9 |
| English | 56 | 20 | 9 | 1 | 5 | 10 | 75 | 25 | 100 | 699 | 1·1 |
| Modern Languages | 47 | 19 | 24 | 4 | 1 | 5 | 65 | 35 | 100 | 681 | 1·0 |
| Geography | 31 | 19 | 30 | 15 | 2 | 2 | 51 | 49 | 100 | 155 | 0·7 |
| Music | 26 | 18 | 22 | 9 | 8 | 17 | 44 | 56 | 100 | 132 | 1·6 |
| Jurisprudence | 53 | 18 | 23 | — | — | 6 | 71 | 29 | 100 | 528 | 0·9 |
| PPE | 55 | 14 | 15 | 5 | 9 | 3 | 68 | 32 | 100 | 912 | 1·2 |
| Mathematics | 62 | 8 | 14 | 14 | 10 | 1 | 70 | 30 | 100 | 452 | 1·1 |
| Physics | 64 | 14 | 3 | 6 | 8 | 5 | 78 | 22 | 100 | 426 | 1·0 |
| Chemistry | 67 | 13 | 7 | 5 | 4 | 4 | 80 | 20 | 100 | 339 | 0·7 |
| Biochemistry | 53 | 10 | 16 | 8 | 13 | 6 | 63 | 37 | 100 | 78 | 1·0 |
| Animal Physiology | 54 | 17 | 10 | 7 | 7 | 3 | 70 | 30 | 100 | 303 | 1·0 |
| Zoology | 18 | 23 | 10 | 33 | 13 | 4 | 42 | 58 | 100 | 96 | 1·0 |
| Botany | 5 | 10 | 37 | 44 | — | — | 15 | 85 | 100 | 114 | 2·0 |
| Geology | 2 | 37 | 31 | 30 | — | — | 39 | 61 | 100 | 27 | 1·0 |
| PPP | 28 | 15 | 8 | 28 | 17 | 5 | 42 | 58 | 100 | 204 | 1·7 |
| Engineering | 28 | 28 | 25 | 10 | 7 | 3 | 56 | 44 | 100 | 185 | 1·0 |
| Engineering and Economics | 67 | 12 | 18 | 2 | — | — | 79 | 21 | 100 | 21 | 1·5 |
| Metallurgy | 59 | 7 | 11 | 11 | 11 | — | 66 | 34 | 100 | 35 | 1·0 |
| Agriculture | 1 | 15 | 32 | 50 | 2 | — | 16 | 84 | 100 | 68 | 2·4 |
| Forestry | 4 | 28 | — | 69 | — | — | 31 | 69 | 100 | 14 | 1·0 |
| All subjects | 53 | 14 | 17 | 6 | 6 | 5 | 67 | 33 | 100 | 7,188 | 1·0 |

SOURCE: Tutorial Organizers Survey.

952425.2

F

**Table 111.** *Reason for out-college tutorial teaching, by subject. All undergraduate out-college tutorials except at Permanent Private Halls: Michaelmas Term 1964*

OXFORD                                                         PERCENTAGE

| Subject | No college teacher in the subject | College teacher on leave | College teacher had reached his maximum hours | For teaching for optional or special papers | For other reasons | All |
|---|---|---|---|---|---|---|
| Literae Humaniores | 12 | 38 | 7 | 7 | 36 | 100 |
| Classical Honour Mods. | 5 | 5 | 57 | 32 | — | 100 |
| Theology | 45 | — | 2 | 23 | 31 | 100 |
| Modern History | 6 | 19 | 2 | 61 | 12 | 100 |
| English | 28 | 16 | 25 | 6 | 24 | 100 |
| Modern Languages | 48 | 14 | 9 | 10 | 19 | 100 |
| Geography | 37 | — | — | 58 | 5 | 100 |
| Music | 63 | 12 | 8 | 10 | 7 | 100 |
| Jurisprudence | 10 | — | 30 | 22 | 37 | 100 |
| PPE | 5 | 11 | 23 | 48 | 13 | 100 |
| Mathematics | 21 | 4 | 24 | 41 | 11 | 100 |
| Physics | 15 | 6 | 49 | 6 | 23 | 100 |
| Chemistry | 29 | 8 | 10 | 18 | 36 | 100 |
| Biochemistry | 42 | 11 | 25 | 5 | 18 | 100 |
| Animal Physiology | 31 | 2 | 25 | 16 | 26 | 100 |
| Zoology | 40 | — | 7 | 26 | 27 | 100 |
| Botany | 77 | — | — | 7 | 16 | 100 |
| Geology | 30 | — | — | 12 | 58 | 100 |
| PPP | 52 | 8 | 3 | 11 | 25 | 100 |
| Engineering | 16 | 12 | 35 | 7 | 31 | 100 |
| Engineering and Economics | — | — | 70 | 23 | 7 | 100 |
| Metallurgy | 67 | — | 25 | — | 8 | 100 |
| Agriculture | 55 | — | — | 11 | 33 | 100 |
| Forestry | 89 | — | — | — | 11 | 100 |
| All subjects | 28 | 10 | 16 | 25 | 21 | 100 |

SOURCE: Tutorial Organizers Survey.

## Classes and seminars

233. Classes and seminars are organized for undergraduates both on a college and on a university basis, but the majority (probably about three-quarters) are on a college (or inter-college) basis. The Undergraduate Survey covered all classes and seminars; the Tutorial Organizers Survey covered college and inter-college classes and seminars.

OXFORD

PERCENTAGE

*... giving tuition to undergraduates, by college of undergraduates. Tutorial hours: Michaelmas Term 1904*

| College | Tutorial hours given by | | | | | | | | | Total tutorial hours | Tutorial hours per under-graduate |
| --- | --- | --- | --- | --- | --- | --- | --- | --- | --- | --- | --- |
| | Fellows of under-graduates' college | Lecturers of under-graduates' college | Fellows or lecturers of other colleges | Persons holding a university but not a college post | Post-graduates | Other persons not holding a university or a college post | All in-college teachers | All out-college teachers | All teachers | | |
| Balliol | 75 | 12 | 11 | 1 | 1 | — | 86 | 14 | 100 | 303 | 1·0 |
| Brasenose | 47 | 31 | 8 | 4 | 7 | 3 | 78 | 22 | 100 | 232 | 0·9 |
| Christ Church | 48 | 21 | 6 | 5 | 2 | 19 | 68 | 32 | 100 | 419 | 1·1 |
| Corpus Christi | 59 | 17 | 13 | 3 | 5 | 4 | 75 | 25 | 100 | 203 | 1·3 |
| Exeter | 62 | 15 | 11 | 5 | 7 | — | 77 | 23 | 100 | 298 | 1·2 |
| Hertford | 38 | 9 | 16 | 14 | 12 | 10 | 48 | 52 | 100 | 178 | 1·0 |
| Jesus | 67 | 10 | 17 | 1 | 4 | — | 77 | 23 | 100 | 215 | 1·0 |
| Keble | 53 | 17 | 16 | 7 | 2 | 4 | 70 | 30 | 100 | 281 | 0·9 |
| Lincoln | 58 | 9 | 19 | 5 | 8 | 1 | 67 | 33 | 100 | 195 | 1·0 |
| Magdalen | 62 | 16 | 13 | 3 | 3 | 3 | 78 | 22 | 100 | 302 | 1·0 |
| Merton | 57 | 19 | 12 | 7 | 5 | — | 75 | 25 | 100 | 226 | 1·1 |
| New College | 55 | 18 | 8 | 4 | 6 | 8 | 73 | 27 | 100 | 340 | 1·1 |
| Oriel | 66 | 11 | 11 | 4 | 7 | 1 | 77 | 23 | 100 | 212 | 1·0 |
| Pembroke | 42 | 22 | 18 | 11 | 2 | 5 | 63 | 37 | 100 | 232 | 0·9 |
| Queen's | 70 | 1 | 11 | 8 | 6 | 4 | 70 | 30 | 100 | 221 | 0·9 |
| St. Catherine's | 42 | 5 | 23 | 16 | 9 | 5 | 47 | 53 | 100 | 359 | 1·2 |
| St. Edmund Hall | 50 | 8 | 17 | 6 | 11 | 8 | 58 | 42 | 100 | 240 | 0·8 |
| St. John's | 67 | 15 | 11 | 5 | 2 | — | 83 | 17 | 100 | 209 | 0·9 |
| St. Peter's | 42 | 9 | 34 | 7 | 5 | 3 | 51 | 49 | 100 | 255 | 1·2 |
| Trinity | 43 | 21 | 21 | 3 | 8 | 4 | 64 | 36 | 100 | 177 | 1·0 |
| University | 53 | 9 | 20 | 2 | 11 | 3 | 63 | 37 | 100 | 306 | 1·1 |
| Wadham | 51 | 17 | 17 | 10 | 3 | 3 | 68 | 32 | 100 | 274 | 1·1 |
| Worcester | 66 | 11 | 10 | 4 | 7 | 3 | 77 | 23 | 100 | 286 | 1·0 |
| Lady Margaret Hall | 53 | 8 | 28 | 3 | 5 | 3 | 61 | 39 | 100 | 245 | 1·0 |
| St. Anne's | 49 | 12 | 23 | 4 | 3 | 9 | 61 | 39 | 100 | 280 | 1·1 |
| St. Hilda's | 50 | 7 | 21 | 9 | 4 | 9 | 57 | 43 | 100 | 255 | 1·1 |
| St. Hugh's | 29 | 13 | 38 | 5 | 12 | 2 | 42 | 58 | 100 | 221 | 1·0 |
| Somerville | 40 | 15 | 24 | 9 | 6 | 6 | 55 | 45 | 100 | 227 | 1·2 |
| All colleges | 53 | 14 | 17 | 6 | 6 | 5 | 67 | 33 | 100 | 7,188 | 1·0 |

SOURCE: Tutorial Organizers Survey.

**Table 113.** *Reason for out-college tutorial teaching, by college. Under-graduate out-college tutorials: Michaelmas Term 1964*

    PERCENTAGE

| College | No college teacher in the subject | College teacher on leave | College teacher had reached his maximum hours | For teaching for optional or special papers | For other reasons | All out-college tutorial hours |
|---|---|---|---|---|---|---|
| Balliol | 17 | 24 | 3 | 33 | 23 | 100 |
| Brasenose | 18 | 19 | 7 | 15 | 42 | 100 |
| Christ Church | 9 | 24 | 36 | 19 | 13 | 100 |
| Corpus Christi | 22 | — | 28 | 38 | 12 | 100 |
| Exeter | 12 | — | 17 | 45 | 26 | 100 |
| Hertford | 27 | 7 | 23 | 26 | 19 | 100 |
| Jesus | 44 | — | 2 | 19 | 35 | 100 |
| Keble | 28 | — | 6 | 26 | 40 | 100 |
| Lincoln | 20 | 8 | 16 | 25 | 32 | 100 |
| Magdalen | 22 | 3 | 22 | 34 | 19 | 100 |
| Merton | 27 | 9 | 14 | 29 | 20 | 100 |
| New College | 17 | 6 | 28 | 24 | 25 | 100 |
| Oriel | 15 | — | 21 | 47 | 18 | 100 |
| Pembroke | 20 | 1 | 39 | 28 | 11 | 100 |
| Queen's | 35 | 20 | 11 | 19 | 15 | 100 |
| St. Catherine's | 43 | 17 | 24 | 6 | 9 | 100 |
| St. Edmund Hall | 38 | 24 | 6 | 15 | 16 | 100 |
| St. John's | 27 | 14 | 5 | 40 | 14 | 100 |
| St. Peter's | 23 | — | 15 | 27 | 35 | 100 |
| Trinity | 11 | 41 | — | 38 | 9 | 100 |
| University | 28 | — | 17 | 18 | 37 | 100 |
| Wadham | 22 | 22 | 13 | 22 | 21 | 100 |
| Worcester | 62 | — | 6 | 17 | 15 | 100 |
| Lady Margaret Hall | 44 | 3 | 10 | 32 | 10 | 100 |
| St. Anne's | 30 | 4 | 12 | 32 | 23 | 100 |
| St. Hilda's | 37 | — | 6 | 24 | 34 | 100 |
| St. Hugh's | 37 | 12 | 16 | 30 | 5 | 100 |
| Somerville | 13 | 20 | 16 | 21 | 30 | 100 |
| All colleges | 28 | 10 | 16 | 25 | 21 | 100 |

SOURCE: Tutorial Organizers Survey.

**Table 114.** *Persons giving supervisions in certain subjects at Cambridge. 1961–2*

    PERCENTAGE

| Persons giving supervisions to undergraduates | English | Law | French | Russian | Physics | Bio-chemistry | All six subjects |
|---|---|---|---|---|---|---|---|
| Fellows of under-graduates' college | 44 | 39 | 48 | 6 | 34 | 30 | 39 |
| Fellows of other colleges | 9 | 13 | 14 | 21 | 4 | 14 | 10 |
| University staff, not fellows of any college | 6 | 3 | 4 | 56 | 6 | 10 | 7 |
| Postgraduates of undergraduates' college | 9 | 1 | 4 | 5 | 29 | 26 | 11 |
| Postgraduates of other colleges | 6 | — | 2 | — | 21 | 14 | 7 |
| Other persons | 27 | 44 | 28 | 12 | 7 | 7 | 25 |
| All | 100 | 100 | 100 | 100 | 100 | 100 | 100 |
| *Supervisors' hours per undergraduate per week in the subject* | 0·8 | 0·9 | 0·7 | 0·9 | 0·5 | 0·3 | 0·6 |

SOURCE: 'Report to the General Board of the Committee on Teaching', *Cambridge University Reporter*, 1 May 1964.

**Table 115.** *Number of classes or seminars attended by undergraduates per week, by subject group and year. Michaelmas Term 1964*

OXFORD                                                                PERCENTAGE

| Subject group | Number of classes or seminars attended per week | Year | | | All years |
|---|---|---|---|---|---|
| | | First | Second | Third | |
| Arts | None | 12 | 56 | 47 | 38 |
| | One | 18 | 22 | 34 | 24 |
| | Two | 23 | 16 | 15 | 18 |
| | Three and over | 47 | 5 | 4 | 19 |
| | All | 100 | 100 | 100 | 100 |
| Social studies | None | 39 | 83 | 68 | 62 |
| | One | 27 | 15 | 22 | 22 |
| | Two | 19 | 2 | 7 | 10 |
| | Three and over | 15 | — | 3 | 6 |
| | All | 100 | 100 | 100 | 100 |
| Science | None | 72 | 90 | 77 | 80 |
| | One | 20 | 9 | 20 | 16 |
| | Two | 7 | 2 | 2 | 4 |
| | Three and over | 1 | — | 1 | 1 |
| | All | 100 | 100 | 100 | 100 |
| All subjects | None | 38 | 73 | 61 | 57 |
| | One | 21 | 16 | 27 | 21 |
| | Two | 17 | 9 | 9 | 12 |
| | Three and over | 25 | 2 | 3 | 10 |
| | All | 100 | 100 | 100 | 100 |

SOURCE: Undergraduate Survey.

234. The average number of classes and seminars (given in Table 95) was 0·8, but over half the sample did not attend any, and 10 per cent. attended three or more (Table 115). It was only in arts that a majority attended any classes or seminars, and only among first-year arts undergraduates that most did so. It should be noted that classes and seminars may not have the same form or the same purpose in different subjects and at different stages of an undergraduate's career. A common procedure is for one of a small group of undergraduates to present a paper which is then discussed by the group with one or two tutors controlling the argument. This procedure is more often used in classes for second- and third-year undergraduates. Classes in which direct instruction plays a greater part are used for those at the beginning of their first year who are working for the First Public Examination.

**Table 116.** *Size of classes or seminars attended by undergraduates by subject group and year. Michaelmas Term 1964*

OXFORD                                                                PERCENTAGE

| Subject group | Classes or seminars attended by stated number of persons | Year | | | All years |
| | | First | Second | Third | |
|---|---|---|---|---|---|
| Arts | 4–5 | 28 | 26 | 23 | 27 |
| | 6–10 | 47 | 33 | 49 | 44 |
| | 11 and over | 26 | 40 | 28 | 29 |
| | All | 100 | 100 | 100 | 100 |
| Social studies | 4–5 | 26 | 25 | 9 | 22 |
| | 6–10 | 43 | 58 | 28 | 41 |
| | 11 and over | 31 | 17 | 63 | 37 |
| | All | 100 | 100 | 100 | 100 |
| Science | 4–5 | 22 | 33 | 21 | 23 |
| | 6–10 | 36 | 40 | 28 | 34 |
| | 11 and over | 42 | 27 | 52 | 43 |
| | All | 100 | 100 | 100 | 100 |
| All subjects | 4–5 | 27 | 27 | 20 | 26 |
| | 6–10 | 45 | 36 | 42 | 43 |
| | 11 and over | 28 | 37 | 38 | 32 |
| | All | 100 | 100 | 100 | 100 |

SOURCE: Undergraduate Survey.

235. About a quarter of the classes and seminars were small, with four or five attending. Nearly half were attended by 6–10 persons, and a third were larger than this. The average number attending was probably about nine. The average number attending was smallest in arts and for first-year undergraduates, and was largest in science and for the third year.

236. Table 117 shows that a substantial proportion of classes and seminars in arts were for proses in languages. Of all classes and seminars, those for ancillary subjects accounted for 20 per cent., and those for optional and special subject papers accounted for a further 14 per cent. The bulk of the remainder were devoted to main-subject teaching (see Table 118). There was little difference between the over-all figures for social studies and science, although there were differences between years, and in each of these subject groups about half the classes and seminars were devoted to main-subject teaching. Ancillary subjects accounted for some 21 per cent. and special subjects some 14 per cent. If proses are counted as main-subject teaching, the position was similar in arts.

**Table 117.** *Type of classes or seminars attended by undergraduates by subject group and year. Michaelmas Term 1964*

OXFORD                                                                          PERCENTAGE

| Subject group | Classes or seminars for | Year | | | All years |
|---|---|---|---|---|---|
| | | First | Second | Third | |
| Arts | Proses | 32 | 59 | 40 | 39 |
| | Ancillary subjects | 30 | 3 | 3 | 20 |
| | Optional or special subject papers | 9 | 16 | 29 | 14 |
| | Other purposes | 28 | 22 | 28 | 27 |
| | All purposes | 100 | 100 | 100 | 100 |
| Social studies | Ancillary subjects | 30 | — | 6 | 22 |
| | Optional or special subject papers | 8 | 8 | 41 | 15 |
| | Other purposes | 62 | 92 | 53 | 63 |
| | All purposes | 100 | 100 | 100 | 100 |
| Science | Ancillary subjects | 35 | 13 | — | 21 |
| | Optional or special subject papers | 2 | 27 | 24 | 13 |
| | Other purposes | 63 | 60 | 76 | 66 |
| | All purposes | 100 | 100 | 100 | 100 |
| All subjects | Proses | 24 | 49 | 27 | 29 |
| | Ancillary subjects | 31 | 4 | 3 | 20 |
| | Optional or special subject papers | 8 | 16 | 30 | 14 |
| | Other purposes | 37 | 31 | 40 | 37 |
| | All purposes | 100 | 100 | 100 | 100 |

SOURCE: Undergraduate Survey.

237. Sixty-one per cent. of classes and seminars were attended by members of one college only. This could be taken as a minimum figure for the proportion of college-based classes and seminars. The proportion attended by members of one college only was much higher for the first year than for subsequent years. It was highest in social studies and lowest in science. Three-quarters of the classes and seminars were attended by members of one sex only. (Table 119.)

238. Tables 120–2 give details of classes and seminars by subject. Although no great reliance can be placed on the results for 'small' subjects, there seems to be no science subject in which classes and seminars were extensively used. They were used most in arts subjects and PPE.

**Table 118.** *Type of classes or seminars attended by undergraduates shown as attending classes or seminars for 'other purposes' in Table 117, by subject group and year. Michaelmas Term 1964*

OXFORD                                                                    PERCENTAGE

| Subject group | Type of classes or seminars for 'other purposes' | Year | | | All years |
|---|---|---|---|---|---|
| | | First | Second | Third | |
| Arts | Main subject teaching | 74 | 90 | 74 | 77 |
| | Revision | — | — | 11 | 3 |
| | Miscellaneous | 3 | 5 | 7 | 4 |
| | Not ascertained | 23 | 5 | 7 | 16 |
| | All types | 100 | 100 | 100 | 100 |
| Social studies | Main subject teaching | 81 | 90 | 54 | 77 |
| | Revision | — | — | 31 | 7 |
| | Miscellaneous | 3 | — | 15 | 5 |
| | Not ascertained | 16 | 10 | — | 12 |
| | All types | 100 | 100 | 100 | 100 |
| Science | Main subject teaching | 95 | 75 | 56 | 76 |
| | Revision | — | — | 33 | 13 |
| | Miscellaneous | 5 | 13 | 6 | 7 |
| | Not ascertained | — | 13 | 6 | 4 |
| | All types | 100 | 100 | 100 | 100 |
| All subjects | Main subject teaching | 80 | 87 | 64 | 77 |
| | Revision | — | — | 22 | 6 |
| | Miscellaneous | 3 | 5 | 9 | 5 |
| | Not ascertained | 17 | 8 | 5 | 12 |
| | All types | 100 | 100 | 100 | 100 |

SOURCE: Undergraduate Survey.

239. A higher than average proportion of classes and seminars in Modern History, English, Jurisprudence, and Physics, Mathematics, and Engineering appear to be college organized. In the other arts subjects, except for Modern Languages (in which classes in French are predominantly college based, while classes in other languages are mainly university organized), the proportion of college organized classes and seminars appears to be below average.

240. Similar details by college are given in Tables 123 and 124. The average number of classes and seminars attended by women is nearly twice that

for men. This is because a larger proportion of women attend at least one class or seminar; the average attendance for those attending at least one being much the same for men and women.

**Table 119.** *Percentage of classes or seminars attended by undergraduates which were attended by members of one college or one sex only, by subject group and year. Michaelmas Term 1964*

OXFORD                                                                                                    PERCENTAGE

| Subject group | Percentage of classes or seminars which were attended by | Year | | | All years |
|---|---|---|---|---|---|
| | | First | Second | Third | |
| Arts | Members of one college only | 76 | 38 | 36 | 61 |
| | Members of one sex only | 86 | 64 | 56 | 76 |
| Social studies | Members of one college only | 75 | 83 | 38 | 67 |
| | Members of one sex only | 84 | 92 | 41 | 74 |
| Science | Members of one college only | 68 | 47 | 34 | 54 |
| | Members of one sex only | 72 | 53 | 48 | 62 |
| All subjects | Members of one college only | 75 | 42 | 36 | 61 |
| | Members of one sex only | 85 | 65 | 52 | 75 |

SOURCE: Undergraduate Survey.

## College classes and seminars

241. A rough calculation based on the Undergraduate Survey and Tutorial Organizers Survey suggests that about 70 per cent. of classes and seminars for undergraduates were organized on a college or inter-college basis. In the Undergraduate Survey, 61 per cent. of the classes attended had under-graduates from one college only. In the Tutorial Organizers Survey, tutors reported about 720 teachers' hours for college classes and seminars attended by undergraduates of one college only. They also reported about 230 teachers' hours giving inter-college classes and seminars (i.e. college organized classes and seminars attended by undergraduates of more than one college). Each of these hours should have been reported by as many tutors as there were colleges represented; thus each hour should have been reported at least twice. Therefore 100 teachers' hours might be taken as a

**Table 120.** *Classes or seminars attended by undergraduates per week by subject. Michaelmas Term 1964*

OXFORD

PERCENTAGE

| Subject | Percentage of undergraduates attending stated number of classes or seminars per week | | | | | Average number of classes or seminars attended per week by | |
|---|---|---|---|---|---|---|---|
| | None | One | Two | Three and over | All | *All under-graduates* | *Undergraduates attending at least one class or seminar* |
| Literae Humaniores | 75 | 25 | — | — | 100 | 0·3 | 1·0 |
| Classical Honour Mods. | 33 | 38 | 22 | 7 | 100 | 1·0 | 1·5 |
| Theology | 35 | 35 | 13 | 17 | 100 | 1·6 | 2·4 |
| Modern History | 46 | 22 | 8 | 23 | 100 | 1·3 | 2·3 |
| English | 51 | 20 | 17 | 12 | 100 | 1·0 | 2·0 |
| Modern Languages | 3 | 24 | 41 | 32 | 100 | 2·2 | 2·3 |
| Oriental Studies | 14 | — | 14 | 71 | 100 | 3·6 | 4·2 |
| Geography | 62 | 32 | 6 | — | 100 | 0·4 | 1·2 |
| Music | 38 | 13 | 25 | 25 | 100 | 1·4 | 2·2 |
| Jurisprudence | 76 | 18 | 6 | — | 100 | 0·3 | 1·3 |
| PPE | 50 | 25 | 13 | 12 | 100 | 0·9 | 1·8 |
| Mathematics | 81 | 16 | 3 | — | 100 | 0·2 | 1·2 |
| Physics | 90 | 8 | 2 | — | 100 | 0·1 | 1·2 |
| Chemistry | 73 | 23 | 4 | — | 100 | 0·3 | 1·1 |
| Biochemistry | 90 | 10 | — | — | 100 | 0·1 | 1·0 |
| Animal Physiology | 90 | 5 | 3 | 3 | 100 | 0·3 | 2·0 |
| Zoology | 100 | — | — | — | 100 | — | . |
| Botany | 80 | 20 | — | — | 100 | 0·2 | 1·0 |
| Geology | 100 | — | — | — | 100 | — | . |
| PPP | 67 | 13 | 20 | — | 100 | 0·5 | 1·6 |
| Natural Science | 75 | — | 25 | — | 100 | 0·5 | 2·0 |
| Physics, Mathematics, and Engineering | 65 | 29 | 6 | — | 100 | 0·4 | 1·2 |
| Biology | 63 | 25 | — | 13 | 100 | 1·1 | 3·0 |
| Engineering | 94 | 6 | — | — | 100 | 0·1 | 1·0 |
| Metallurgy | 50 | 50 | — | — | 100 | 0·5 | 1·0 |
| Agriculture and Forestry | 75 | 25 | — | — | 100 | 0·2 | 1·0 |
| All subjects | 57 | 21 | 12 | 10 | 100 | 0·8 | 1·9 |

SOURCE: Undergraduate Survey.

NOTE: See notes to Table 100.

reasonable figure for inter-college classes.[1] This gives a total of 820 teachers' hours for all college and inter-college classes and seminars which would have comprised about 70 per cent. of all classes and seminars for undergraduates.

[1] Classes given to third-year undergraduates in Modern History for special subject teaching are listed in the lecture list, and were therefore not included in the Tutorial Organizers Survey. But these classes are, in effect, college classes, and therefore the extent of college class teaching in Modern History is understated. Most of these classes are attended by undergraduates of more than one college.

**Table 121.** *Classes or seminars attended by undergraduates (number, college, and sex of those attending) by subject. Michaelmas Term 1964*

OXFORD                                                                    PERCENTAGE

| Subject | Percentage of classes or seminars which were attended by stated number of persons | | | | Percentage of classes or seminars which were attended by members of | |
|---|---|---|---|---|---|---|
| | 4–5 | 6–10 | 11 and over | All | One college only | One sex only |
| Literae Humaniores | 20 | 40 | 40 | 100 | 40 | 60 |
| Classical Honour Mods. | 33 | 35 | 33 | 100 | 43 | 63 |
| Theology | 28 | 28 | 44 | 100 | 8 | 31 |
| Modern History | 29 | 55 | 16 | 100 | 82 | 88 |
| English | 22 | 41 | 37 | 100 | 85 | 93 |
| Modern Languages | 21 | 47 | 32 | 100 | 54 | 74 |
| Oriental Studies | 52 | 8 | 40 | 100 | 8 | 64 |
| Geography | 27 | 53 | 20 | 100 | 20 | 60 |
| Music | 36 | — | 64 | 100 | 18 | 36 |
| Jurisprudence | 38 | 38 | 24 | 100 | 83 | 93 |
| PPE | 18 | 42 | 41 | 100 | 63 | 69 |
| Mathematics | 20 | 40 | 40 | 100 | 60 | 60 |
| Physics | 33 | 33 | 33 | 100 | 67 | 67 |
| Chemistry | 40 | 48 | 12 | 100 | 64 | 80 |
| Biochemistry | — | — | 100 | 100 | — | — |
| Animal Physiology | — | — | 100 | 100 | — | — |
| Zoology | . | . | . | . | . | . |
| Botany | 100 | — | — | 100 | — | 100 |
| Geology | . | . | . | . | . | . |
| PPP | 13 | 25 | 63 | 100 | 50 | 50 |
| Natural Science | — | 100 | — | 100 | 100 | 100 |
| Physics, Mathematics, and Engineering | 14 | 43 | 43 | 100 | 93 | 100 |
| Biology | 11 | 11 | 78 | 100 | 11 | 22 |
| Engineering | — | — | 100 | 100 | — | 100 |
| Metallurgy | 67 | — | 33 | 100 | 67 | 67 |
| Agriculture and Forestry | — | 100 | — | 100 | — | — |
| All subjects | 26 | 43 | 32 | 100 | 61 | 75 |

SOURCE: Undergraduate Survey.
NOTE: See notes to Table 100.

242. Tables 125–30 give details of the persons giving college classes and seminars attended by undergraduates of one college only in a form similar to the tables about the organization of tutorial teaching. Table 125 shows that the proportion of in-college teaching in arts and social studies was much the same as for tutorials but that in science it was higher than in

**Table 122.** *Type of classes or seminars attended by undergraduates by subject. Michaelmas Term 1964*

OXFORD                                                                PERCENTAGE

| Subject | Classes or seminars for | | | | |
|---|---|---|---|---|---|
| | Proses | Ancillary subjects | Optional or special subjects | Other purposes | All purposes |
| Literae Humaniores | — | — | — | 100 | 100 |
| Classical Honour Mods. | 33 | — | 57 | 11 | 100 |
| Theology | 8 | 56 | 11 | 25 | 100 |
| Modern History | 1 | 45 | 26 | 29 | 100 |
| English | 19 | 17 | 4 | 59 | 100 |
| Modern Languages | 90 | — | 1 | 9 | 100 |
| Oriental Studies | 56 | — | 12 | 32 | 100 |
| Geography | — | 40 | 13 | 47 | 100 |
| Music | — | 9 | — | 91 | 100 |
| Jurisprudence | — | 11 | 11 | 79 | 100 |
| PPE | — | 25 | 17 | 58 | 100 |
| Mathematics | — | — | 40 | 60 | 100 |
| Physics | — | — | — | 100 | 100 |
| Chemistry | — | 31 | 19 | 50 | 100 |
| Biochemistry | — | — | — | 100 | 100 |
| Animal Physiology | — | — | — | 100 | 100 |
| Zoology | . | . | . | . | . |
| Botany | — | 100 | — | — | 100 |
| Geology | . | . | . | . | . |
| PPP | — | 25 | — | 75 | 100 |
| Natural Science | — | — | — | 100 | 100 |
| Physics, Mathematics, and Engineering | — | 36 | 7 | 57 | 100 |
| Biology | — | 33 | — | 67 | 100 |
| Engineering | — | — | — | 100 | 100 |
| Metallurgy | — | 33 | — | 67 | 100 |
| Agriculture and Forestry | — | — | — | 100 | 100 |
| All subjects | 29 | 20 | 14 | 37 | 100 |

SOURCE: Undergraduate Survey.
NOTE: See notes to Table 100.

other subject groups, and much higher than for tutorials. Again in contrast with tutorial teaching, fellows and lecturers of other colleges were used very little, and there was more extensive employment of persons without a college or a university post. (Here, this group includes postgraduates.)

**Table 123.** *Classes or seminars attended by undergraduates per week by college. Michaelmas Term 1964*

OXFORD                                                                    PERCENTAGE

| College | Percentage of undergraduates attending stated number of classes or seminars per week | | | | | Average number of classes or seminars attended per week by | |
| --- | --- | --- | --- | --- | --- | --- | --- |
| | None | One | Two | Three and over | All | All undergraduates | Undergraduates attending at least one class or seminar |
| Balliol | 64 | 27 | 5 | 5 | 100 | 0·6 | 1·6 |
| Brasenose | 57 | 15 | 15 | 12 | 100 | 0·8 | 2·0 |
| Christ Church | 63 | 15 | 12 | 10 | 100 | 0·7 | 1·9 |
| Corpus Christi | 74 | 17 | 9 | — | 100 | 0·3 | 1·3 |
| Exeter | 63 | 13 | 16 | 8 | 100 | 0·8 | 2·1 |
| Hertford | 59 | 30 | 4 | 7 | 100 | 0·7 | 1·6 |
| Jesus | 58 | 9 | 15 | 18 | 100 | 1·1 | 2·5 |
| Keble | 68 | 15 | 10 | 7 | 100 | 0·6 | 2·0 |
| Lincoln | 64 | 14 | 7 | 14 | 100 | 0·8 | 2·3 |
| Magdalen | 54 | 26 | 15 | 4 | 100 | 0·7 | 1·6 |
| Merton | 45 | 39 | 6 | 10 | 100 | 0·8 | 1·5 |
| New College | 72 | 13 | 6 | 9 | 100 | 0·6 | 2·1 |
| Oriel | 55 | 19 | 13 | 13 | 100 | 1·0 | 2·2 |
| Pembroke | 62 | 26 | 8 | 5 | 100 | 0·7 | 1·8 |
| Queen's | 63 | 14 | 17 | 6 | 100 | 0·7 | 1·9 |
| St. Catherine's | 58 | 27 | — | 16 | 100 | 0·8 | 2·0 |
| St. Edmund Hall | 40 | 29 | 13 | 18 | 100 | 1·3 | 2·1 |
| St. John's | 71 | 9 | 12 | 9 | 100 | 0·6 | 2·0 |
| St. Peter's | 78 | 6 | 9 | 6 | 100 | 0·6 | 2·7 |
| Trinity | 59 | 11 | 15 | 15 | 100 | 0·9 | 2·2 |
| University | 64 | 34 | 2 | — | 100 | 0·4 | 1·1 |
| Wadham | 56 | 24 | 12 | 9 | 100 | 0·8 | 1·8 |
| Worcester | 63 | 15 | 12 | 10 | 100 | 0·8 | 2·3 |
| Men's colleges | 61 | 20 | 10 | 9 | 100 | 0·7 | 1·9 |
| Permanent Private Halls | 46 | 38 | 8 | 8 | 100 | 0·8 | 1·4 |
| Men's societies | 61 | 20 | 10 | 9 | 100 | 0·7 | 1·9 |
| Lady Margaret Hall | 20 | 43 | 23 | 14 | 100 | 1·4 | 1·7 |
| St. Anne's | 45 | 16 | 16 | 24 | 100 | 1·4 | 2·5 |
| St. Hilda's | 54 | 23 | 11 | 11 | 100 | 0·9 | 2·0 |
| St. Hugh's | 39 | 19 | 25 | 17 | 100 | 1·3 | 2·1 |
| Somerville | 29 | 19 | 29 | 23 | 100 | 1·5 | 2·1 |
| Women's colleges | 38 | 24 | 21 | 18 | 100 | 1·3 | 2·1 |
| All societies | 57 | 21 | 12 | 10 | 100 | 0·8 | 1·9 |

SOURCE: Undergraduate Survey.

NOTE: See note to Table 102.

**Table 124.** *Classes or seminars attended by undergraduates (number, college, and sex of those attending) by college. Michaelmas Term 1964*

| College | Percentage of classes or seminars which were attended by stated number of persons | | | | Percentage of classes or seminars which were attended by members of | |
|---|---|---|---|---|---|---|
| | 4–5 | 6–10 | 11 and over | All | One college only | One sex only |
| Balliol | 38 | 23 | 38 | 100 | 58 | 62 |
| Brasenose | 6 | 68 | 26 | 100 | 62 | 74 |
| Christ Church | 8 | 33 | 58 | 100 | 61 | 83 |
| Corpus Christi | — | 50 | 50 | 100 | 25 | 50 |
| Exeter | 14 | 41 | 45 | 100 | 55 | 69 |
| Hertford | 28 | 33 | 39 | 100 | 28 | 56 |
| Jesus | 31 | 57 | 11 | 100 | 71 | 80 |
| Keble | 23 | 31 | 46 | 100 | 38 | 46 |
| Lincoln | 17 | 52 | 30 | 100 | 57 | 83 |
| Magdalen | 12 | 39 | 48 | 100 | 64 | 70 |
| Merton | 24 | 44 | 32 | 100 | 48 | 76 |
| New College | 31 | 59 | 9 | 100 | 78 | 88 |
| Oriel | 19 | 29 | 52 | 100 | 39 | 84 |
| Pembroke | 41 | 26 | 33 | 100 | 52 | 70 |
| Queen's | 32 | 56 | 12 | 100 | 88 | 88 |
| St. Catherine's | 29 | 42 | 29 | 100 | 61 | 79 |
| St. Edmund Hall | 26 | 56 | 18 | 100 | 65 | 82 |
| St. John's | 40 | 45 | 15 | 100 | 60 | 85 |
| St. Peter's | 21 | 63 | 16 | 100 | 68 | 89 |
| Trinity | 17 | 50 | 33 | 100 | 58 | 63 |
| University | 28 | 50 | 22 | 100 | 83 | 89 |
| Wadham | 44 | 30 | 26 | 100 | 78 | 78 |
| Worcester | 15 | 26 | 59 | 100 | 44 | 53 |
| Men's colleges | 24 | 44 | 32 | 100 | 60 | 75 |
| Permanent Private Halls | 5 | 55 | 40 | 100 | 10 | 65 |
| Men's societies | 23 | 44 | 32 | 100 | 58 | 74 |
| Lady Margaret Hall | 31 | 46 | 23 | 100 | 81 | 83 |
| St. Anne's | 28 | 28 | 43 | 100 | 68 | 75 |
| St. Hilda's | 53 | 34 | 13 | 100 | 84 | 88 |
| St. Hugh's | 28 | 30 | 43 | 100 | 49 | 60 |
| Somerville | 26 | 55 | 19 | 100 | 74 | 74 |
| Women's colleges | 32 | 39 | 30 | 100 | 70 | 75 |
| All societies | 26 | 43 | 32 | 100 | 61 | 75 |

SOURCE: Undergraduate Survey.

NOTE: See note to Table 102.

**Table 125.** *Persons giving college classes or seminars attended by under-graduates (except those at Permanent Private Halls) from one college only, by subject group of undergraduates. Teachers' hours: Michaelmas Term 1964*

| College class or seminar teaching hours given by | For undergraduates in | | | |
|---|---|---|---|---|
| | Arts | Social studies | Science | All subjects |
| Fellows or lecturers of undergraduates' college | 70 | 72 | 85 | 73 |
| Fellows or lecturers of other colleges | 5 | 6 | 2 | 5 |
| Persons holding a university but not a college post | 1 | 3 | 1 | 1 |
| Persons not holding any university or college post | 23 | 19 | 12 | 21 |
| Jointly | 1 | 1 | — | 1 |
| All out-college teachers | 30 | 28 | 15 | 27 |
| All teachers | 100 | 100 | 100 | 100 |
| *Total teachers' hours per week* | *477* | *127* | *98* | *702* |
| *Teachers' hours per 10 undergraduates* | *1·5* | *1·0* | *0·4* | *1·0* |

SOURCE: Tutorial Organizers Survey.

NOTE: Classes or seminars shown as given jointly were given by persons from any two of the categories of the teacher, except that none was given jointly by members of the first two categories.

243. Also in contrast with tutorials, the use of in-college teachers increased with the year of the undergraduates, as Table 126 shows. The proportion of college classes and seminars given by fellows of other colleges increased with year, while that for persons not holding a college or university post declined.

244. As with tutorials, a smaller proportion of college classes and seminars were given by in-college teachers for women than men, but the deficiency was made up, not by greater use of fellows or lecturers of other colleges, as with tutorials, but by greater use of persons with no college or university post (Table 127).

**Table 126.** *Persons giving college classes or seminars attended by undergraduates (except those at Permanent Private Halls) from one college only, by year of undergraduates. Teachers' hours: Michaelmas Term 1964*

OXFORD　　　　　　　　　　　　　　　　　　　　　　　　　　PERCENTAGE

| College class or seminar teaching hours given by | For undergraduates in | | | | |
| --- | --- | --- | --- | --- | --- |
| | 1st year | 2nd year | 3rd year | 4th and subsequent years | All years |
| Fellows or lecturers of undergraduates' college | 68 | 77 | 82 | 100 | 73 |
| Fellows or lecturers of other colleges | 3 | 6 | 10 | — | 5 |
| Persons holding a university but not a college post | 1 | 1 | 1 | — | 1 |
| Persons not holding any university or college post | 27 | 13 | 6 | — | 21 |
| Jointly | — | 3 | 1 | — | 1 |
| All out-college teachers | 32 | 23 | 18 | — | 27 |
| All teachers | 100 | 100 | 100 | 100 | 100 |
| *Total teachers' hours per week* | *460* | *119* | *112* | *11* | *702* |
| *Teachers' hours per 10 undergraduates* | 2·0 | 0·5 | 0·5 | 0·4 | 1·0 |

SOURCE: Tutorial Organizers Survey.
NOTE: See note to Table 125.

245. College classes and seminars for undergraduates at Permanent Private Halls were almost all given by fellows or lecturers of other colleges. Details of the hours given are in Table 128.

246. Tables 129 and 130 give details of college class and seminar teaching by subject and college.

## Inter-college classes and seminars

247. These comprise college classes and seminars attended by undergraduates of more than one college. Since each tutor returned any classes or seminars attended by undergraduates of his own college, inter-college classes and seminars should have been returned more than once, but it is

**Table 127.** *Persons giving college classes or seminars attended by under-graduates (except those at Permanent Private Halls) from one college only, by sex of undergraduates. Teachers' hours: Michaelmas Term 1964*

OXFORD             PERCENTAGE

| College class or seminar teaching hours given by | For undergraduates at | | |
|---|---|---|---|
| | Men's colleges | Women's colleges | All colleges |
| Fellows or lecturers of under-graduates' college | 75 | 63 | 73 |
| Fellows or lecturers of other colleges | 5 | 3 | 5 |
| Persons holding a university but not a college post | 1 | 1 | 1 |
| Persons not holding any univer-sity or college post | 18 | 33 | 21 |
| Jointly | 1 | — | 1 |
| All out-college teachers | 25 | 37 | 27 |
| All teachers | 100 | 100 | 100 |
| *Total teachers' hours per week* | *563* | *139* | *702* |
| *Teachers' hours per 10 under-graduates* | *1·0* | *1·2* | *1·0* |

SOURCE: Tutorial Organizers Survey.
NOTE: See note to Table 125.

**Table 128.** *Persons giving college classes or seminars attended by under-graduates at Permanent Private Halls, from one society only, by year of undergraduates. Michaelmas Term 1964*

OXFORD             HOURS

| College classes or seminars attended by undergraduates from one society only | Class or seminar teaching hours given for undergraduates in | | | | |
|---|---|---|---|---|---|
| | 1st year | 2nd year | 3rd year | 4th and subsequent years | All years |
| Total teachers' hours per week | 3 | 5 | 4 | 2 | 14 |
| Teachers' hours per 10 under-graduates | 0·7 | 0·8 | 0·9 | 1·4 | 0·9 |

SOURCE: Tutorial Organizers Survey.

**Table 129.** *Persons giving college classes or seminars attended by undergraduates (except those at Permanent Private Halls) from one college only, by subject of undergraduates. Teachers' hours: Michaelmas Term 1964*

OXFORD

| Subject | College class or seminar teaching hours given by | | | | | | | Total teachers' hours | PERCENTAGE Teachers' hours per 10 undergraduates |
|---|---|---|---|---|---|---|---|---|---|
| | Fellows or lecturers of undergraduates' college | Fellows or lecturers of other colleges | Persons holding a university but not a college post | Persons not holding any university or college post | Jointly | All out-college teachers | All teachers | | |
| Literae Humaniores | 100 | — | — | — | — | — | 100 | 18 | 0.7 |
| Classical Honour Mods. | 92 | — | — | — | 8 | 8 | 100 | 50 | 1.7 |
| Theology | 100 | — | — | — | — | — | 100 | 3 | 0.3 |
| Modern History | 66 | 3 | — | 30 | — | 34 | 100 | 178 | 1.9 |
| English | 77 | 1 | 1 | 21 | — | 23 | 100 | 90 | 1.4 |
| Modern Languages | 58 | 13 | 2 | 27 | — | 42 | 100 | 131 | 1.9 |
| Geography | 71 | — | — | 29 | — | 29 | 100 | 7 | 0.3 |
| Jurisprudence | 100 | — | — | — | — | — | 100 | 26 | 0.4 |
| PPE | 64 | 7 | 4 | 24 | 1 | 36 | 100 | 101 | 1.3 |
| Mathematics | 89 | 6 | — | 6 | — | 11 | 100 | 18 | 0.4 |
| Physics | 87 | — | — | 13 | — | 13 | 100 | 23 | 0.5 |
| Chemistry | 84 | — | — | 16 | — | 16 | 100 | 25 | 0.5 |
| Animal Physiology | 50 | — | — | 50 | — | 50 | 100 | 2 | 0.1 |
| Zoology | 67 | 33 | — | — | — | 33 | 100 | 3 | 0.3 |
| PPP | 82 | — | 6 | 12 | — | 18 | 100 | 17 | 1.4 |
| Engineering | 100 | — | — | — | — | — | 100 | 5 | 0.3 |
| Metallurgy | 80 | — | — | 20 | — | 20 | 100 | 5 | 1.4 |
| All subjects | 73 | 5 | 1 | 21 | 1 | 27 | 100 | 702 | 1.0 |

SOURCE: Tutorial Organizers Survey.

NOTE: See notes to Table 100 and note to Table 125.

*graduates. Teachers' hours: Michaelmas Term 1964*

OXFORD

PERCENTAGE

| College | College class or seminar teaching hours given by | | | | | All out-college teachers | All teachers | Total teachers' hours | Teachers' hours per 10 undergraduates |
|---|---|---|---|---|---|---|---|---|---|
| | Fellows or lecturers of undergraduates' college | Fellows or lecturers of other colleges | Persons holding a university but not a college post | Persons not holding any university or college post | Jointly | | | | |
| Balliol | 94 | — | — | 6 | — | 6 | 100 | 35 | 1·2 |
| Brasenose | 85 | 11 | — | 4 | — | 15 | 100 | 27 | 1·0 |
| Christ Church | 79 | — | — | 7 | 14 | 21 | 100 | 29 | 0·8 |
| Corpus Christi | 100 | — | — | — | — | — | 100 | 7 | 0·4 |
| Exeter | 75 | 4 | — | 21 | — | 25 | 100 | 24 | 1·0 |
| Hertford | 88 | — | — | 13 | — | 13 | 100 | 8 | 0·5 |
| Jesus | 70 | 5 | — | 20 | 5 | 30 | 100 | 20 | 0·9 |
| Keble | 66 | 16 | — | 18 | — | 34 | 100 | 29 | 0·9 |
| Lincoln | 74 | — | — | 26 | — | 26 | 100 | 19 | 0·9 |
| Magdalen | 88 | 7 | — | 6 | — | 13 | 100 | 24 | 0·9 |
| Merton | 80 | 4 | — | 16 | — | 20 | 100 | 15 | 0·7 |
| New College | 78 | — | — | 22 | — | 22 | 100 | 46 | 1·4 |
| Oriel | 58 | — | — | 42 | — | 42 | 100 | 12 | 0·6 |
| Pembroke | 79 | 16 | — | 5 | — | 21 | 100 | 19 | 0·7 |
| Queen's | 71 | 8 | — | 21 | — | 29 | 100 | 38 | 1·6 |
| St. Catherine's | 81 | 8 | — | 12 | — | 19 | 100 | 26 | 1·6 |
| St. Edmund Hall | 40 | 6 | — | 54 | — | 60 | 100 | 48 | 1·6 |
| St. John's | 62 | 19 | — | 19 | — | 38 | 100 | 21 | 0·9 |
| St. Peter's | 80 | — | — | 20 | — | 20 | 100 | 15 | 0·7 |
| Trinity | 76 | 4 | 4 | 16 | — | 24 | 100 | 25 | 1·3 |
| University | 85 | — | — | 15 | — | 15 | 100 | 27 | 1·0 |
| Wadham | 82 | — | — | 18 | — | 18 | 100 | 28 | 1·2 |
| Worcester | 71 | 10 | 19 | — | — | 29 | 100 | 21 | 0·8 |
| Lady Margaret Hall | 58 | — | — | 42 | — | 42 | 100 | 40 | 1·7 |
| St. Anne's | 53 | 3 | — | 44 | — | 47 | 100 | 30 | 1·2 |
| St. Hilda's | 76 | 3 | — | 21 | — | 24 | 100 | 21 | 0·9 |
| St. Hugh's | 64 | 9 | — | 27 | — | 36 | 100 | 22 | 1·0 |
| Somerville | 73 | — | 5 | 22 | — | 27 | 100 | 26 | 1·3 |
| All colleges | 73 | 5 | 1 | 21 | 1 | 27 | 100 | 702 | 1·0 |

SOURCE: Tutorial Organizers Survey.

NOTE: See note to Table 102 and note to Table 125.

impossible to tell how many times. Further, the distinction between in-college and out-college teachers does not apply. It is not possible, therefore, to give tables in the same form as for college classes and seminars, and the distributions in Table 131 are approximate since there may be differences between the categories of teacher in the extent of double counting. The totals of hours (including the double counting) were 150 in arts; 16 in social studies; and 41 in science, giving 207 in all. These totals exclude Permanent Private Halls. Totals by college groups were 155 for men's colleges; 52 for women's colleges; and 19 for Permanent Private Halls. Most of the inter-college classes and seminars were given for undergraduates in their first year (89 hours) or third year (79 hours).

248. Table 131 shows that about 80 per cent. of inter-college classes and seminars[1] were given by fellows or lecturers of colleges and some 12 per cent. by persons not holding any university or college post. A higher than average proportion was given by college fellows and lecturers for women and for third-year undergraduates. This proportion was below average in science.

## Teaching arrangements in Oriental Studies

249. There are few college posts in Oriental Studies, and teaching is organized by the faculty.[2] Table 132 gives details of the tutorial and class teaching. This shows that in terms of teaching hours per undergraduate, tutorials are slightly below the average, but class teaching is very much more used than the average.

## Written work by undergraduates

250. Undergraduates were asked how many essays and other written exercises they had written in the survey week. Over all, undergraduates wrote an average of 1·1 essays, compared with an average of 1·5 tutorials. In arts, the average number of essays was the same as the average number of tutorials in the first year, but in subsequent years there were fewer essays than tutorials. In social studies there were rather more essays than tutorials in the first year, and about the same number in subsequent years.[3] In science the number of essays was considerably less than the number of tutorials, although the difference decreased with year. But in science other written exercises (such as solving problems in mathematics) replace essays to a much greater extent than in arts and social studies. (Table 133.)

---

[1] Those reported by tutors at Permanent Private Halls are excluded, although some attended by their undergraduates will be included if also attended by undergraduates at the colleges proper.

[2] We are grateful to Professor A. F. L. Beeston, Laudian Professor of Arabic, for pointing this out, and for supplying the information presented here.

[3] Although the number of essays is here compared with the number of tutorials, some of the essays were no doubt written for classes and seminars.

**Table 131.** *Persons giving college classes and seminars attended by undergraduates (except those at Permanent Private Halls) of more than one college. Teachers' hours: Michaelmas Term 1964*

OXFORD      PERCENTAGE

| College class or seminar teaching hours given by | For undergraduates in | | | | | 1st year | 2nd year | 3rd year | 4th and subsequent years | All under-graduates |
| --- | --- | --- | --- | --- | --- | --- | --- | --- | --- | --- |
| | Arts | Social studies | Science | Men's colleges | Women's colleges | | | | | |
| Fellows or lecturers of colleges | 85 | 81 | 63 | 77 | 90 | 75 | 79 | 90 | 50 | 81 |
| Persons holding a university but not a college post | 4 | — | 12 | 6 | 2 | 3 | 6 | 5 | 33 | 5 |
| Persons not holding any university or college post | 9 | 19 | 20 | 14 | 6 | 21 | 12 | 3 | — | 12 |
| Jointly | 1 | — | 5 | 2 | 2 | — | 3 | 3 | 17 | 2 |
| All teachers | 100 | 100 | 100 | 100 | 100 | 100 | 100 | 100 | 100 | 100 |

SOURCE: Tutorial Organizers Survey.

NOTE: The figures in this table are approximate only, as a result of double counting. See para. 247.

**Table 132.** *Tutorial and class arrangements in Oriental Studies. Michaelmas Term 1964*

OXFORD

| | For undergraduates in year | | | | | | | All under-graduates |
|---|---|---|---|---|---|---|---|---|
| | 1 | 1+2 | 2 | 2+3 | 3 | 3+4 | 4 and over | |
| Number of under-graduates (by year of residence) | 14 | — | 20 | — | 17 | — | 12 | 63 |
| (by year in Oriental Studies School) | 17 | — | 25 | — | 17 | — | 4 | 63 |
| Tutorial hours by Holders of university post | 3 | — | 17 | — | 18 | — | 7 | 45 |
| Postgraduates | — | — | 1 | — | 1 | — | — | 2 |
| Others | — | — | 5 | 2 | 1 | — | 1 | 9 |
| All teachers | 3 | — | 23 | 2 | 20 | — | 8 | 56 |
| Tutorial hours per undergraduate | 0·2 | . | 1·0 | . | 1·2 | . | 2·0 | 0·9 |
| Class hours by Holders of university post | 15 | 2 | 6 | — | 3 | 1 | — | 27 |
| Postgraduates | 3 | 2 | — | — | — | — | — | 5 |
| Others | 2 | — | — | — | — | — | — | 2 |
| All teachers | 20 | 4 | 6 | — | 3 | 1 | — | 34 |
| Class teachers' hours per 10 under-graduates | 12·9 | . | 3·2 | . | 2·1 | . | 1·3 | 5·4 |

SOURCE: Professor A. F. L. Beeston.

NOTES
1. Years are based on time actually spent in Oxford (except that undergraduates with Senior Status are treated in the same way as in the Tutorial Organizers Survey); no account is taken of years spent away from Oxford.
2. Since a number of undergraduates change to Oriental Studies from other Schools, undergraduates are classified both by their year of residence and their year in the Oriental Studies School. For the details of teaching, undergraduates are classified by the latter.
3. 1+2 indicates that first- and second-year undergraduates are taken together.
4. Two of the holders of university posts held college lecturerships with tutorial, but not teaching, duties; two held professorial fellowships; and none of the remainder held a college post.
5. The category 'other teachers' comprises a man holding no post in Oxford who was doing substitute teaching for a university lecturer on leave of absence, and a junior research fellow.
6. In calculating teachers' hours per undergraduate, teaching given to groups of undergraduates from two years is divided equally between the two years.

**Table 133.** *Average number of essays and other exercises written by under-graduates per week by subject group and year. Michaelmas Term 1964.*

OXFORD NUMBER

| Subject group | | Year | | | All years |
|---|---|---|---|---|---|
| | | First | Second | Third | |
| Arts | Essays | 1·1 | 1·2 | 1·4 | 1·2 |
| | Other written exercises | 2·1 | 0·9 | 0·8 | 1·3 |
| Social studies | Essays | 1·7 | 1·7 | 1·8 | 1·8 |
| | Other written exercises | 1·2 | 0·5 | 0·2 | 0·6 |
| Science | Essays | 0·5 | 0·6 | 0·8 | 0·6 |
| | Other written exercises | 1·2 | 1·0 | 0·9 | 1·0 |
| All subjects | Essays | 1·0 | 1·1 | 1·3 | 1·1 |
| | Other written exercises | 1·6 | 0·9 | 0·7 | 1·1 |

SOURCE: Undergraduate Survey.

251. It is much more difficult to interpret the figures for 'other written exercises' since this includes a wide range of different kinds of work, and it is not clear what constitutes an appropriate unit in the different cases. It is likely that undergraduates doing a particular type of work did not all adopt the same unit, and, even if they had, the problem of comparing different types of written work remains. (For example, how many mathematical problems equals one prose?) For these reasons the only fairly firm conclusion about 'other written exercises' which can be drawn from Table 133 is that in arts and social studies they were much less important in the second and third years than in the first year. In science there was only a small decline with year.

252. Tables 134 and 135 give similar details by subject and college.

## Lectures

253. The average number of lectures attended is given in Table 95 above. Tables 136 and 137 give distributions of undergraduates according to the number of lectures attended.

## Practicals

254. Table 138 gives the average hours of practical work in subjects in which some practical work was reported.

**Table 134.** *Average number of essays and other exercises written by undergraduates per week by subject. Michaelmas Term 1964*

| OXFORD | NUMBER | |
|---|---|---|
| Subject | Average number per undergraduate per week of | |
| | Essays | Other written exercises |
| Literae Humaniores | 1·8 | 0·2 |
| Classical Honour Mods. | 0·4 | 1·8 |
| Theology | 0·8 | 1·2 |
| Modern History | 1·4 | 1·1 |
| English | 1·4 | 0·8 |
| Modern Languages | 1·3 | 2·2 |
| Oriental Studies | 0·9 | 1·2 |
| Geography | 0·9 | 0·6 |
| Music | 1·1 | 2·9 |
| Jurisprudence | 1·9 | 0·6 |
| PPE | 1·6 | 0·6 |
| Mathematics | — | 1·3 |
| Physics | 0·4 | 1·7 |
| Chemistry | 1·0 | 0·7 |
| Biochemistry | 1·6 | 0·2 |
| Animal Physiology | 1·0 | 0·8 |
| Zoology | 1·1 | 0·1 |
| Botany | 1·0 | 0·8 |
| Geology | 1·0 | 1·0 |
| PPP | 1·4 | 1·0 |
| Natural Science | 0·5 | 1·8 |
| Physics, Mathematics, and Engineering | 0·1 | 1·7 |
| Biology | 0·9 | 0·2 |
| Engineering | 0·2 | 1·7 |
| Metallurgy | 1·0 | 0·5 |
| Agriculture and Forestry | 1·0 | 0·5 |
| All subjects | 1·1 | 1·1 |

SOURCE: Undergraduate Survey.
NOTE: See notes to Table 100.

## Collections

255. Collections are college examinations, usually sat at the beginning of a term, which are used to test undergraduates' progress. Tutorial organizers were asked whether they set Collections and, if so, whether penalties were imposed for bad performance. The replies are summarized in Table 139. This table gives distributions of tutors rather than of the undergraduates for whom they organize teaching. Therefore, as in Table 106, 'small' subjects will have a relatively high weighting. Caution is needed in interpreting

**Table 135.** *Average number of essays and other exercises written by under-graduates per week by college. Michaelmas Term 1964*

OXFORD                                                    NUMBER

| College | Average number per under-graduate per week of | |
| --- | --- | --- |
| | Essays | Other written exercises |
| Balliol | 1·1 | 0·6 |
| Brasenose | 1·0 | 1·0 |
| Christ Church | 1·3 | 0·8 |
| Corpus Christi | 1·2 | 0·6 |
| Exeter | 1·0 | 1·1 |
| Hertford | 1·0 | 1·6 |
| Jesus | 1·0 | 1·2 |
| Keble | 1·0 | 0·7 |
| Lincoln | 1·1 | 1·1 |
| Magdalen | 1·3 | 1·1 |
| Merton | 0·8 | 1·0 |
| New College | 1·1 | 1·0 |
| Oriel | 0·8 | 1·7 |
| Pembroke | 0·9 | 1·4 |
| Queen's | 0·9 | 1·1 |
| St. Catherine's | 1·2 | 1·0 |
| St. Edmund Hall | 1·2 | 1·4 |
| St. John's | 1·0 | 1·0 |
| St. Peter's | 1·3 | 0·8 |
| Trinity | 1·0 | 1·0 |
| University | 1·1 | 1·1 |
| Wadham | 1·2 | 1·0 |
| Worcester | 1·3 | 0·8 |
| Men's colleges | 1·1 | 1·0 |
| Permanent Private Halls | 1·3 | 0·8 |
| Men's societies | 1·1 | 1·0 |
| Lady Margaret Hall | 1·6 | 1·7 |
| St. Anne's | 1·3 | 1·1 |
| St. Hilda's | 1·3 | 1·4 |
| St. Hugh's | 1·0 | 1·6 |
| Somerville | 1·2 | 1·4 |
| Women's colleges | 1·3 | 1·4 |
| All societies | 1·1 | 1·1 |

SOURCE: Undergraduate Survey.
NOTE: See note to Table 102.

**Table 136.** *Number of lectures attended by undergraduates per week, by subject group and year. Michaelmas Term 1964*

OXFORD                                                   PERCENTAGE

| Subject group | Number of lectures attended per week | Year | | | All years |
|---|---|---|---|---|---|
| | | First | Second | Third | |
| Arts | None | 2 | 25 | 25 | 17 |
| | 1–2 | 11 | 37 | 30 | 26 |
| | 3–5 | 48 | 22 | 28 | 33 |
| | 6–9 | 32 | 12 | 16 | 20 |
| | 10 and over | 7 | 4 | 1 | 4 |
| | All | 100 | 100 | 100 | 100 |
| Social studies | None | 4 | 28 | 22 | 17 |
| | 1–2 | 8 | 28 | 26 | 20 |
| | 3–5 | 34 | 32 | 33 | 33 |
| | 6–9 | 54 | 9 | 15 | 28 |
| | 10 and over | — | 3 | 3 | 2 |
| | All | 100 | 100 | 100 | 100 |
| Science | None | — | 8 | 6 | 4 |
| | 1–2 | 2 | 14 | 9 | 8 |
| | 3–5 | 11 | 27 | 30 | 22 |
| | 6–9 | 48 | 39 | 35 | 41 |
| | 10 and over | 39 | 13 | 20 | 24 |
| | All | 100 | 100 | 100 | 100 |
| All subjects | None | 2 | 19 | 18 | 13 |
| | 1–2 | 7 | 28 | 22 | 19 |
| | 3–5 | 33 | 26 | 30 | 29 |
| | 6–9 | 42 | 21 | 22 | 29 |
| | 10 and over | 16 | 7 | 8 | 10 |
| | All | 100 | 100 | 100 | 100 |

SOURCE: Undergraduate Survey.

NOTE: The data relate to the third week in the term.

the replies, since many tutors stated that although penalties may be imposed as a result of performance in Collections, such performance is only one of a number of factors taken into account in considering whether to impose penalties. Where mild penalties (such as having to resit the Collection) were mentioned they were recorded as such. But where the penalty was not specified, it may have been a mild one and may only be imposed where other adverse evidence about an undergraduate's progress is available. A fifth of the replies reported no Collections, and a further fifth reported no penalties. The latter proportion was much higher (36 per cent.) for the women's colleges. About half (a third for women's colleges) reported penalties were applied when appropriate, and a tenth mentioned mild penalties, or penalties for scholars.

**Table 137.** *Number of lectures attended by undergraduates per week by subject. Michaelmas Term 1964*

OXFORD  PERCENTAGE

| Subject | Percentage of undergraduates attending stated number of lectures per week | | | | | | Average number of lectures attended per week |
|---|---|---|---|---|---|---|---|
| | None | 1–2 | 3–5 | 6–9 | 10 and over | All | |
| Literae Humaniores | 15 | 15 | 10 | 50 | 10 | 100 | 4·9 |
| Classical Honour Mods. | 11 | 38 | 7 | 22 | 22 | 100 | 5·1 |
| Theology | — | 13 | 26 | 43 | 17 | 100 | 6·1 |
| Modern History | 20 | 30 | 41 | 9 | — | 100 | 2·6 |
| English | 29 | 26 | 33 | 11 | — | 100 | 2·5 |
| Modern Languages | 11 | 22 | 45 | 21 | 2 | 100 | 3·8 |
| Oriental Studies | 29 | 14 | — | 43 | 14 | 100 | 4·6 |
| Geography | 6 | 15 | 26 | 47 | 6 | 100 | 5·6 |
| Music | — | 38 | 13 | 50 | — | 100 | 4·5 |
| Jurisprudence | 20 | 19 | 24 | 35 | 3 | 100 | 3·9 |
| PPE | 15 | 21 | 41 | 22 | 1 | 100 | 3·5 |
| Mathematics | 7 | 7 | 26 | 29 | 30 | 100 | 6·9 |
| Physics | 10 | 18 | 33 | 29 | 10 | 100 | 5·1 |
| Chemistry | — | 7 | 16 | 48 | 29 | 100 | 7·4 |
| Biochemistry | 10 | — | 40 | 50 | — | 100 | 5·1 |
| Animal Physiology | 5 | 10 | 41 | 44 | — | 100 | 4·9 |
| Zoology | — | — | 29 | 57 | 14 | 100 | 6·5 |
| Botany | — | — | 60 | 40 | — | 100 | 5·4 |
| Geology | — | — | — | 50 | 50 | 100 | 8·5 |
| PPP | 13 | 33 | 13 | 40 | — | 100 | 3·5 |
| Natural Science | — | — | — | 75 | 25 | 100 | 9·2 |
| Physics, Mathematics, and Engineering | — | — | — | 35 | 65 | 100 | 10·2 |
| Biology | — | — | 13 | 88 | — | 100 | 7·4 |
| Engineering | 6 | — | — | 44 | 50 | 100 | 8·3 |
| Metallurgy | — | — | — | 67 | 33 | 100 | 8·5 |
| Agriculture and Forestry | — | — | 50 | 25 | 25 | 100 | 6·3 |
| All subjects | 13 | 19 | 29 | 29 | 10 | 100 | 4·7 |

SOURCE: Undergraduate Survey.

NOTE: See notes to Table 100 and note to Table 136.

## WASTAGE AND CHANGE OF COURSE

## Wastage

256. At the request of the University Grants Committee, the University has twice collected information from colleges about undergraduate wastage. The results are summarized in Tables 140 and 141. The first table relates to undergraduates matriculating in 1952–3, and the second to 1957–8 matriculations. Each inquiry was carried out after four years, and in each

**Table 138.** *Average number of hours per week spent by undergraduates doing practical work in laboratories by subject. Michaelmas Term 1964*

| OXFORD | HOURS |
|---|---|
| Subject | Average hours doing practical work |
| Geography | 0·9 |
| Physics | 11·4 |
| Chemistry | 9·1 |
| Biochemistry | 13·8 |
| Animal Physiology | 11·0 |
| Zoology | 5·0 |
| Botany | 10·6 |
| Geology | 7·5 |
| PPP | 1·6 |
| Natural Science | 14·2 |
| Physics, Mathematics, and Engineering | 8·9 |
| Biology | 18·7 |
| Engineering | 3·7 |
| Metallurgy | 7·5 |
| Agriculture and Forestry | 5·8 |

SOURCE: Undergraduate Survey.

NOTE: See notes to Table 100.

**Table 139.** *Use made of Collections. Michaelmas Term 1964*

OXFORD                                                                                                      PERCENTAGE

| Use made of Collections | Percentage of tutorial organizers (except those in Permanent Private Halls) in | | | | | | Percentage of tutorial organizers in Permanent Private Halls |
|---|---|---|---|---|---|---|---|
| | Arts | Social studies | Science | Men's colleges | Women's colleges | All colleges | |
| No Collections | 14 | 2 | 26 | 18 | 24 | 19 | 34 |
| No penalties | 23 | 23 | 18 | 18 | 36 | 20 | 30 |
| Penalties (not specified) | 53 | 61 | 50 | 56 | 31 | 52 | 34 |
| Mild penalties | 3 | 4 | — | 1 | 3 | 2 | 2 |
| Penalties for scholars | 7 | 11 | 6 | 7 | 6 | 7 | — |
| All | 100 | 100 | 100 | 100 | 100 | 100 | 100 |

SOURCE: Tutorial Organizers Survey.

NOTES

1. A very small number of replies stating that rewards are given as a result of Collections are included under 'no penalties'.
2. A very small number of replies stating that Collections are organized by the department concerned are included under 'no Collections'.
3. This table gives the distribution of returns made by tutors, and is not weighted by the number of undergraduates in each return. It therefore gives the distribution of subjects within colleges, and not that of undergraduates, according to the treatment of Collections.

case 1 per cent. of undergraduates were still reading for their degree. In a number of respects a similar pattern emerged from each inquiry. Wastage, i.e. those who had left without obtaining a degree, amounted to 7 per cent. for each inquiry, while wastage for academic reasons was $4\frac{1}{2}$–5 per cent. Wastage for academic reasons was higher for men than for women. It was slightly higher in arts and social studies than in science. The close similarity between the two sets of figures suggests that wastage rates did not change appreciably during the nineteen-fifties.

**Table 140.** *Reasons for wastage by subject group and sex. First-degree students entering in October 1952*

OXFORD                                                                                           PERCENTAGE

|  | Arts and social studies | Science | Men | Women | All |
|---|---|---|---|---|---|
| Completed course successfully | 92·1 | 93·1 | 91·8 | 95·1 | 92·3 |
| Course not completed by October 1956 | 1·0 | 0·8 | 1·1 | 0·3 | 1·0 |
| Left without success: | | | | | |
| sent down for academic failure | 2·7 | 1·1 | 2·7 | 1·0 | 2·4 |
| left for other reasons | 2·5 | 1·9 | 2·2 | 3·3 | 2·4 |
| completed course but failed | 1·6 | 3·0 | 2·2 | 0·3 | 1·9 |
| All entrants | 100 | 100 | 100 | 100 | 100 |
| *Number* | *1,460* | *364* | *1,518* | *306* | *1,824* |

SOURCE: Registry.

NOTES
1. Those who were sent down for disciplinary reasons (4 men and 4 women) are included under 'left for other reasons'.
2. Those shown as completing their course successfully include some who took longer than the normal period.

257. A slightly different analysis of wastage (and change of course) among undergraduates matriculating in 1958–9 is given in Table 142. Being based on university records only, it is not possible to specify reasons for wastage, nor to separate those who sat a Second Public Examination and failed from those who went down without doing so. However, it is possible to distinguish between those who did, and did not, pass a First Public Examination, and it is also possible to classify by type of school.

258. The proportion who achieved a degree (including pass degrees) was 92 per cent. This is in good agreement with Tables 140 and 141 and so are

the differences between subjects and between men and women. About a third of the wastage took place without a pass having been obtained in a First Public Examination (there is, of course, a causal connexion); this must correspond closely with wastage in the first year. Wastage was below average for undergraduates from direct-grant and maintained schools, and above average (and twice as great as for direct-grant and maintained schools) for those from independent schools.[1] Among other undergraduates (from other types of school, from overseas, and from universities) wastage was high.

**Table 141.** *Reasons for wastage by subject group and sex. First-degree students entering in October 1957*

OXFORD                                                                    PERCENTAGE

|  | Arts | Social studies | Science | Men | Women | All |
|---|---|---|---|---|---|---|
| Completed course successfully | 92·5 | 90·5 | 92·0 | 91·9 | 92·2 | 91·9 |
| Course not completed by October 1961 | 0·5 | 0·8 | 2·0 | 1·1 | — | 1·0 |
| Left without success: sent down for academic failure | 3·7 | 4·0 | 2·6 | 3·8 | 1·2 | 3·5 |
| left for other reasons | 2·4 | 2·3 | 1·8 | 1·7 | 5·8 | 2·2 |
| completed course but failed | 1·0 | 2·5 | 1·5 | 1·5 | 0·9 | 1·4 |
| All entrants | 100 | 100 | 100 | 100 | 100 | 100 |
| *Number* | *1,342* | *528* | *650* | *2,176* | *344* | *2,520* |

SOURCE: Registry.

NOTES

1. Those who were sent down for disciplinary reasons (5 men) are included under 'left for other reasons'.
2. See Note 2 to Table 140.

259. Statistics presented by the Robbins Committee[2] show that nationally the wastage rate is about twice that at Oxford and, in contrast to the position at Oxford, is higher in science than in arts and social studies. A survey quoted by the Robbins Committee showed a very similar relationship between wastage and type of school for Oxford and Cambridge as that in Table 142.

[1] The figures in Table 142 are for men and women together. For men alone the proportions who obtained a first degree are the same except that 95 per cent. from direct-grant schools achieved a degree, and 78 per cent. of 'others' did so.
[2] Undergraduate wastage is discussed in Robbins Report, Appendix Two (A), Part IV, Section 1, pp. 125–38.

**Table 142.** *Wastage and change of course, by subject group, sex, and type of school. Undergraduates entering in 1958–9*

OXFORD

PERCENTAGE

| | Arts | Social studies | Science | Men | Women | Independent boarding | Independent day | Direct-grant | Maintained | Other | All |
|---|---|---|---|---|---|---|---|---|---|---|---|
| No change in subject | 84 | 78 | 81 | 81 | 88 | 77 | 82 | 92 | 86 | 70 | 82 |
| Changed before First Public Examination | 3 | 3 | 8 | 4 | 5 | 5 | 4 | 3 | 4 | 1 | 4 |
| Changed after First Public Examination | 6 | 7 | 4 | 6 | 2 | 8 | 4 | 2 | 6 | 8 | 6 |
| All obtaining a first degree | 93 | 88 | 94 | 92 | 96 | 90 | 91 | 96 | 96 | 79 | 92 |
| Did not take, or did not pass a Second Public Examination and: passed a First Public Examination (or had Senior Status) | 5 | 7 | 5 | 6 | 3 | 6 | 6 | 4 | 3 | 15 | 5 |
| did not pass a First Public Examination | 3 | 5 | 1 | 3 | 1 | 4 | 3 | 1 | 1 | 6 | 3 |
| All undergraduates entering in 1958–9 | 100 | 100 | 100 | 100 | 100 | 100 | 100 | 100 | 100 | 100 | 100 |
| *Number in sample* | 678 | 268 | 321 | 1,098 | 169 | 476 | 116 | 192 | 397 | 86 | 1,267 |

SOURCE: 1958–9 matriculations sample.

## Change of course

260. Table 142 also gives a summary of change of course by undergraduates who entered in 1958–9. Some 10 per cent. of undergraduate entrants changed their course of study, 4 per cent. before the First Public Examination, and 6 per cent. after it. The 'course' is here defined as an Honour School, and an undergraduate is regarded as having changed his course unless the School he states he proposes to read when he matriculates and his Second Public Examination are the same, and his First Public Examination is in the same subject.[1] If the First Public Examination for an undergraduate who changed course was not in the same subject as his proposed course, he is recorded in the table as changing before the First Public Examination, and as after it otherwise.[2] The proportion changing subject in science was slightly higher than in other subjects, and was higher among men than among women.

261. The numbers of those changing course are given in Table 143. The total of 128 comprises the 10 per cent. of all undergraduates shown as changing course in Table 142. Since the sample was one-half of all undergraduates entering in 1958–9, estimates of the total numbers can be obtained by doubling the figures in the table. But the numbers are small, and the breakdown is detailed, so such estimates would be very approximate.

262. About a tenth of the changes were from an Honour School to the Pass School. About a quarter were from Literae Humaniores to other Schools. Most of the undergraduates concerned took Classical Honour Moderations and then changed. A third are accounted for by other changes within the arts and social studies group of subjects and a further fifth by changes within the science group. Changes from science to arts and social studies and vice versa (including those from Literae Humaniores) each accounted for about a tenth of the changes.

263. A question was asked in the Undergraduate Survey about change of course. The results are not directly comparable with those for entrants in 1958–9 because some first- (and perhaps second-) year undergraduates will have changed after replying to the questionnaire, and the dividing line between early and late changes was drawn differently. In the survey, 8 per cent. of the sample said they had changed or intended to change, 4 per cent. having changed within four weeks of coming up. The 4 per cent. saying

---

[1] The various branches of the Honour School of Natural Science are treated as different courses.

[2] The First Public Examinations in science are not single subject examinations, and there were a few cases where it was doubtful when the change in course took place. In such cases it was assumed to have occurred before the First Public Examination.

## Table 143. Original and final subject of undergraduates who changed course. Undergraduates entering in 1958–9

OXFORD     SAMPLE NUMBER

| Original subject | Changed to → Literae Humaniores | Theology | Modern History | English | Modern Languages | Oriental Studies | Geography | Music | Jurisprudence | PPE | Mathematics | Physics | Chemistry | Animal Physiology | Zoology | Geology | PPP | Engineering | Metallurgy | Forestry | Pass School | All subjects |
|---|---|---|---|---|---|---|---|---|---|---|---|---|---|---|---|---|---|---|---|---|---|---|
| Literae Humaniores |  | 1 | 1 | 7* | 2 | 5 |  |  | 3 | 5 |  |  |  | 1 |  |  | 6 |  |  |  |  | 31 |
| Theology |  |  |  |  |  |  |  |  |  |  |  |  |  |  |  |  |  |  |  |  | 1 | 1 |
| Modern History | 1 | 1 |  | 1 |  | 1 | 1 |  |  | 3 |  |  |  |  |  |  |  |  |  |  | 3 | 10 |
| English | 1 |  | 3 |  | 1 |  | 1 |  | 1 | 1 |  |  |  |  |  |  |  |  |  |  | 1 | 9 |
| Modern Languages |  |  | 1 | 2 |  | 2 |  |  |  |  |  |  |  |  |  |  |  |  |  |  | 1 | 6 |
| Geography | 1 |  | 1 | 1 |  |  |  |  |  |  |  |  |  |  |  |  |  |  |  |  | 1 | 3 |
| Jurisprudence | 1 |  | 4 | 1†† |  |  |  |  |  | 3 |  |  |  |  |  |  | 3 |  |  |  | 2 | 14 |
| PPE |  |  | 3 |  | 2 |  | 2 | 1 | 2 |  | 1 | 1** |  |  |  |  |  |  |  |  | 1 | 13 |
| Mathematics |  |  |  |  |  |  |  |  |  | 1 |  | 1 | 1 | 1 |  |  |  | 1 |  |  |  | 5 |
| Physics |  |  |  |  |  |  |  |  |  | 1** | 1 | 1 |  | 1 |  | 1 |  | 4 | 2 |  |  | 11 |
| Chemistry |  |  |  |  |  |  |  |  |  | 1** | 1 | 2 |  |  | 1 | 2 |  | 1 |  |  |  | 12 |
| Biochemistry |  |  |  |  |  |  |  |  |  | 1 |  |  |  |  |  |  |  |  |  |  |  | 2 |
| Animal Physiology |  |  |  |  |  |  |  |  |  |  |  |  |  | 1 | 1 |  |  |  |  |  |  | 1 |
| Zoology |  |  |  |  |  |  |  |  |  |  |  |  |  | 1 | 1 |  |  |  |  |  |  | 2 |
| PPP |  |  |  |  |  |  |  |  |  | 1 |  |  |  |  |  |  |  |  |  |  |  | 1 |
| Geology |  |  |  |  |  |  |  |  |  |  |  |  |  |  |  |  |  |  |  | 1 |  | 2 |
| Engineering |  |  |  |  |  |  |  |  |  |  |  | 2 |  |  |  |  |  |  | 1 |  |  | 1 |
| Forestry |  |  |  | 2 |  |  |  |  |  |  |  |  |  |  |  | 1 |  |  |  |  | 1† | 4 |
| **All subjects** | 4 | 2 | 13 | 14 | 7 | 8 | 3 | 1 | 7 | 18 | 2 | 6 | 1 | 4 | 2 | 4 | 11 | 6 | 2 | 1 | 12 | 128 |

SOURCE: 1958–9 matriculations sample.

NOTES

\* One had proposed course D.Phil.
\*\* Proposed course B.Sc.
† Proposed course diploma.
†† Proposed course B.Litt.
1. The sample on which the numbers are based was one-half of undergraduates.

Table 144. *Change of course by undergraduates by subject group. Undergraduates in residence in Michaelmas Term 1964*

OXFORD
SAMPLE NUMBER

| Subject group (before change) | Undergraduates who changed or intended to change | | | | Wished to change but could not because | | | All who changed or wished to change | |
|---|---|---|---|---|---|---|---|---|---|
| | Changed in first 4 weeks | Changed after first 4 weeks | Intended to change | All | Insufficient knowledge | Too late | Other reasons | Number | Percentage of all undergraduates in sample |
| Arts | 17 | 20 | 3 | 40 | 6 | 4 | 12 | 62 | 12 |
| Social studies | 8 | 6 | — | 14 | 2 | 4 | 2 | 22 | 10 |
| Science | 16 | 13 | 1 | 30 | 3 | 1 | 11 | 45 | 12 |
| All subjects | 41 | 39 | 4 | 84 | 11 | 9 | 25 | 129 | 12 |

SOURCE: Undergraduate Survey.

NOTE: The sample on which the table is based was one-sixth of undergraduates in their first, second, or third years in Michaelmas Term 1964.

they changed after four weeks must have come from the second and third years, so that if later changes occur with the same frequency among the freshmen, the total number changing will have been 10 per cent., as for entrants in 1958–9.

264. Undergraduates were also asked whether they had wished to change, but had been unable to do so. About half as many as had actually changed had wanted to do so, this proportion being the same in the three subject groups. (See Table 144.)

265. Table 145 gives for the Undergraduate Survey a detailed breakdown on the lines of Table 143. The general pattern of changes in these two tables are similar. Table 146 gives details of the way in which undergraduates *wished* to change subject, and it shows that the desired changes were realistic in that they broadly followed the pattern of actual changes.

## Preliminary Examinations

266. Two topics related to undergraduate wastage are the number of times Preliminary Examinations are taken before a pass is achieved, and the number of undergraduates taking longer than three years to achieve a degree.

267. The number of times undergraduates in the sample of 1958–9 matriculations took the various Preliminary Examinations is shown in Table 147. This table underestimates the number of attempts a candidate makes, as he is only recorded if he achieves success in part of the examination. It is the usual practice in Oxford to send down an undergraduate who has twice failed a First Public Examination. In several subjects the numbers were small, but in the larger subjects the best performances were in English and Modern Languages, and the worst in Geography and Natural Science.

## Undergraduates taking over three years

268. In 1963–4, 2·7 per cent. of undergraduates were in their fourth or subsequent years, excluding those in four-year Schools. Undergraduates spend four or more years for a number of reasons, of which the most important are: to catch up after changing subject (likely to affect Oriental Studies and PPP); because a year was spent abroad, especially by those reading Modern Languages or Oriental Studies; and because of illness or for other non-academic reasons.[1] Table 148 suggests that the last reason accounts on average for $1\frac{1}{2}$–2 per cent. of undergraduates.

[1] In 1963–4 the proportion of undergraduates taking four years in biological subjects was unusually high as a consequence of the reorganization of courses in biology which took place.

Table 145. *Original subject and changed subject of undergraduates who had changed course, or who intended to change. Undergraduates in residence in Michaelmas Term 1964*

OXFORD

| Original subject | Theology | Modern History | English | Modern Languages | Oriental Studies | Geography | Music | Jurisprudence | PPE | Mathematics | Physics | Chemistry | Biochemistry | Animal Physiology | Zoology | Botany | PPP | Engineering | Engineering and Economics | Agriculture | All subjects |
|---|---|---|---|---|---|---|---|---|---|---|---|---|---|---|---|---|---|---|---|---|---|
| | | | | | | | | *Changed (or intended to change) to* | | | | | | | | | | | | | SAMPLE NUMBER |
| Literae Humaniores | — | 1 | 2 | 2 | — | — | — | 2 | 5 | — | — | — | — | — | — | — | 4 | — | — | — | 18 |
| Theology | 1 | — | 1 | — | — | — | — | — | — | — | — | — | — | — | — | — | 1 | — | — | — | 1 |
| Modern History | 1 | — | 1 | 1 | — | — | — | 1 | 2 | — | — | — | — | — | — | — | 2 | — | — | — | 6 |
| English | — | 1 | — | 1 | — | — | — | 1 | 1 | — | — | — | — | — | — | — | 1 | — | — | — | 5 |
| Modern Languages | — | — | 2 | — | 1* | — | — | — | 4 | — | — | — | — | — | — | — | — | — | — | — | 8 |
| Geography | — | 2 | 2 | — | — | — | — | — | 1 | — | — | — | — | — | — | — | — | — | — | — | — |
| Music | — | — | — | — | — | — | — | — | — | — | — | — | — | — | — | — | — | — | — | — | — |
| Jurisprudence | — | 1 | 1 | — | — | — | — | 1 | 1* | — | — | — | — | — | — | — | 1 | — | — | — | 6 |
| PPE | — | 1 | — | — | — | — | — | — | 2 | — | 2 | 2 | — | — | — | — | 1 | — | — | — | 8 |
| Mathematics | — | — | — | — | — | — | — | — | — | — | 2 | — | — | — | — | — | — | — | — | — | — |
| Physics | — | — | — | — | — | — | — | — | — | 2 | — | 1 | — | — | — | — | — | — | — | — | 3 |
| Chemistry | — | — | — | — | — | — | — | — | — | 1 | — | — | 1 | 2 | 1 | — | — | 1 | — | — | 7 |
| Biochemistry | — | — | — | — | — | — | — | — | — | — | — | — | 1 | — | — | — | — | — | — | — | 3 |
| Animal Physiology | — | — | — | — | — | — | — | — | — | — | — | — | — | — | — | — | — | — | — | — | 1 |
| Zoology | — | — | — | — | — | — | — | — | — | — | — | — | — | — | — | 1 | — | — | — | — | 2 |
| Botany | — | — | — | — | — | — | — | — | — | — | — | — | — | — | — | — | — | — | — | 1 | — |
| Geology | — | — | — | — | — | — | — | — | — | — | — | — | — | — | — | — | — | — | — | — | 1 |
| PPP | — | — | — | 1** | — | — | — | — | — | — | — | — | — | — | — | — | — | — | — | — | 3 |
| Engineering | — | — | — | — | — | — | — | — | — | — | — | — | — | — | — | — | — | — | 2 | — | 1 |
| Agriculture | — | — | 1 | — | — | — | — | — | — | — | — | — | — | — | — | — | — | — | — | — | 1 |
| All subjects | 2 | 11 | 10 | 4 | 1 | — | — | 6 | 20 | 3 | 2 | 1 | 1 | 3 | 1 | 1 | 8 | 3 | 3 | 2 | 84 |

SOURCE: Undergraduate Survey.

NOTES. * Originally D.Phil. student in Physics.    ** Originally D.Phil. student in Physics.

**Table 146.** *Subject and desired subject of undergraduates who wished to change course but could not. Undergraduates in residence in Michaelmas Term 1964*

OXFORD

| Subject | Wished to change to | | | | | | | | | | | | | SAMPLE NUMBER |
|---|---|---|---|---|---|---|---|---|---|---|---|---|---|---|
| | Literae Humaniores | Theology | Modern History | English | Modern Languages | Oriental Studies | Music | Jurisprudence | PPE | Chemistry | Medicine | PPP | Engineering | All subjects |
| Theology | | | | | | | | | 1 | | | | | 1 |
| Modern History | 1 | | | 3 | | | | 1 | 4 | | | | | 9 |
| English | | | | | | | | | 3 | | | | | 3 |
| Modern Languages | | 1 | 1 | 2 | 1* | | | 1 | 1 | | | | | 7 |
| Geography | | | | | | | | | 2 | | | | | 2 |
| Jurisprudence | 1 | | | 2 | | 1 | | | 1 | | | | | 5 |
| PPE | | | 1 | 1 | | | 1 | | | | | | | 3 |
| Mathematics | | | 1 | 1 | | | 1 | | 1 | | | | | 4 |
| Physics | | | | | 1 | | 1 | | | 2 | 1 | | 1 | 6 |
| Chemistry | | | | | | | | | | | 1 | | | 1 |
| Animal Physiology | | | | | | | | | | | | 2 | | 2 |
| Zoology | | | | | | | | | 1 | | | 1 | | 2 |
| All subjects | 2 | 1 | 3 | 9 | 2 | 1 | 3 | 2 | 14 | 2 | 2 | 3 | 1 | 45 |

SOURCE: Undergraduate Survey.

NOTES

* A different main language.

1. See note to Table 144.

**Table 147.** *Number of times Preliminary Examinations were taken. Undergraduates who matriculated in 1958–9 and who took a Preliminary Examination*

OXFORD                                                                    PERCENTAGE

| Subject | Number of times taken with some success | | | All | Number in sample |
|---------|---|---|---|-----|-------------------|
| | 1 | 2 | 3 | | |
| Theology | 50 | 50 | — | 100 | 10 |
| Modern History | 81 | 19 | — | 100 | 194 |
| Classical Languages | 100 | — | — | 100 | 9 |
| English Language and Literature | 88 | 12 | — | 100 | 95 |
| Modern Languages | 89 | 11 | — | 100 | 141 |
| Oriental Studies | 100 | — | — | 100 | 7 |
| Geography | 73 | 27 | — | 100 | 48 |
| Music | 71 | 29 | — | 100 | 7 |
| PPE | 82 | 18 | — | 100 | 119 |
| Geology | 100 | — | — | 100 | 1 |
| Natural Science | 57 | 36 | 7 | 100 | 198 |
| Physiology | 100 | — | — | 100 | 1 |

SOURCE: 1958–9 matriculations sample.

NOTES
1. Outright failures are not included.
2. Only those who subsequently passed a Second Public Examination are included above. Of others who took a Preliminary Examination, the proportion taking the examination with some success once only is at least as high as above, except for PPE where the percentage was 71. But it is impossible to tell from the information abstracted whether a pass in the whole examination was obtained by those who did not subsequently pass a Second Public Examination.

DEGREE PERFORMANCE

269. A number of forms of variability can be observed in degree results. There are definite trends over time; there can be quite large year-to-year fluctuations in particular subjects; and there are systematic differences between subjects.

270. The trend has been for the proportion of 'good' degrees (firsts and seconds) to increase over time. Table 149 gives figures (prepared by the Kneale Committee) for a selection of the major subjects in arts and social studies spanning twenty years. There is an increasing proportion of firsts and seconds over all, and in each subject except Literae Humaniores and PPE. The proportion has been stable in PPE but has declined considerably in Literae Humaniores. Since competition for entry to Oxford has become increasingly severe, it is not surprising that the degree performance of undergraduates should have improved. The decline in performance in Literae Humaniores (assuming that the years quoted are not exceptional)

**Table 148.** *Percentage of first-degree students in more than their third year by course and sex. 1963-4*

| OXFORD | | PERCENTAGE | |
| --- | --- | --- | --- |
| Course | Men | Women | Men and Women |
| Literae Humaniores | — | 2·2 | 0·3 |
| Theology | 8·2 | — | 7·7 |
| Modern History | 2·1 | 1·3 | 1·9 |
| English | 1·9 | 0·9 | 1·6 |
| Modern Languages | 7·0 | 1·2 | 5·6 |
| Oriental Studies | 5·0 | 50·0 | 7·8 |
| Geography | 1·5 | 2·9 | 1·7 |
| Music | — | — | — |
| Jurisprudence | 2·6 | — | 2·4 |
| PPE | 1·4 | 4·8 | 1·9 |
| Mathematics | 1·0 | 3·6 | 1·5 |
| Physics | 0·7 | — | 0·7 |
| Chemistry | 2·0 | — | 1·8 |
| Biochemistry | — | — | — |
| Animal Physiology | 8·1 | — | 6·9 |
| Zoology | 6·4 | 7·3 | 6·7 |
| Botany | 8·3 | 11·8 | 9·8 |
| Geology | 2·8 | — | 2·6 |
| PPP | 10·3 | 10·0 | 10·3 |
| Engineering | — | · | — |
| Engineering and Economics | — | · | — |
| Metallurgy | 3·2 | · | 3·2 |
| Agriculture | 3·8 | — | 3·4 |
| Forestry | — | · | — |
| Pass School | 22·6 | — | 21·9 |
| All courses | 2·8 | 2·2 | 2·7 |

SOURCE: Registry.

NOTES

1. Fourth-year students in subjects in which the normal course lasts for four years (Literae Humaniores, Biochemistry, and Forestry) are counted as in their third year for this table.
2. Students taking the Second B.M. are excluded.
3. A student's standing for this table is based on years of study for a particular course. Therefore, students reading a second Honour School would not necessarily be counted as in their fourth or subsequent year.

might be a result of the expansion of science; able pupils who in the past would have taken classics at school may now take science, and the entry to the School of Literae Humaniores may have declined in quality.[1] Nevertheless, it is surprising that the proportion of firsts and seconds in 1959 was less than in Modern History, English, and Modern Languages.

[1] It should, however, be noted that the proportion of firsts in Literae Humaniores is high compared with other arts subjects. See Tables 150 and 151.

**Table 149.** *Percentage of those classed gaining first- or second-class honours*

| OXFORD | | PERCENTAGE | |
| --- | --- | --- | --- |
| Subject | 1938 | 1954 | 1959 |
| Literae Humaniores | 69·7 | 65·7 | 61·5 |
| Modern History | 52·8 | 65·7 | 67·0 |
| English | 57·9 | 68·8 | 74·1 |
| Modern Languages | 67·7 | 72·6 | 73·1 |
| Jurisprudence | 44·9 | 54·9 | 56·7 |
| PPE | 56·4 | 56·6 | 55·8 |
| Total of the above six Schools | 57·6 | 64·0 | 65·4 |

SOURCE: *Report of the Committee on the Structure of the First and Second Public Examinations,* Supplement\* No. 3 to the *University Gazette* (March 1965).

271. The position with regard to firsts is different. The long-term trend has been for the proportion of firsts to fall. Miss Tomlinson and Mrs. Paul of St. Hilda's, in a letter to the *Oxford Magazine*, 29 October 1959, cite statistics showing that, for men, the proportion of firsts was about 15 per cent. in the 1920's, and has fallen steadily since then to about 8 per cent. at the end of the 1950's. (But it rose slightly in 1960–4; see para. 274 below.) For women the proportion has remained steady. Nationally there has also been a long-term fall in the proportion gaining firsts.

272. Each year the *Oxford Magazine* publishes details of degree results. A comparison of successive years shows some quite large year-to-year variations, even in the larger Schools. The fluctuations in Modern History in recent years are an example of this. The proportions of firsts, and of firsts and seconds, among all those classed in the Modern History School, were 4·4 per cent. and 61·1 per cent. in 1962; 7·8 per cent. and 62·9 per cent. in 1963; 3·7 per cent. and 55·0 per cent. in 1964; and 8·1 per cent. and 75·8 per cent. in 1965.

273. Because of the irregular year-to-year fluctuations, results for 1955–64 have been aggregated into two sets, each spanning five years. Results for 1955–9 appear in Table 150, which is based on those receiving a class. Since 1959 the *Oxford Magazine* has published more detailed figures, showing those who receive an *aegrotat*, are overstanding for honours, or who fail. The results for 1960–4 are therefore presented in two ways. Table 151 is drawn up in the same way as Table 150, and Table 152 shows the fails, etc. These tables should give a picture of the recent trends and of differences between subjects.

**Table 150.** *Class of degree by Honour School. Undergraduates classed in* *1955–9*

OXFORD                                       PERCENTAGE

| Subject | Class of degree | | | | All | Number |
|---|---|---|---|---|---|---|
| | 1st | 2nd | 3rd | 4th | | |
| Literae Humaniores | 12·4 | 53·8 | 30·7 | 3·1 | 100 | 716 |
| Theology | 3·3 | 49·8 | 40·0 | 6·9 | 100 | 305 |
| Modern History | 5·7 | 61·8 | 30·5 | 1·9 | 100 | 1,604 |
| English | 6·8 | 60·2 | 29·7 | 3·4 | 100 | 1,059 |
| Modern Languages | 4·5 | 67·0 | 26·7 | 1·8 | 100 | 1,123 |
| Oriental Studies | 17·9 | 56·4 | 20·5 | 5·1 | 100 | 39 |
| Geography | 2·6 | 49·1 | 44·7 | 3·5 | 100 | 340 |
| Music | 16·9 | 42·4 | 35·6 | 5·1 | 100 | 59 |
| Arts | 6·5 | 59·7 | 31·0 | 2·8 | 100 | 5,245 |
| Jurisprudence | 4·6 | 48·2 | 38·3 | 8·9 | 100 | 955 |
| PPE | 8·0 | 44·0 | 40·5 | 7·6 | 100 | 1,005 |
| Social studies | 6·3 | 46·0 | 39·4 | 8·2 | 100 | 1,960 |
| Arts and social studies | 6·4 | 55·9 | 33·3 | 4·3 | 100 | 7,205 |
| Mathematics | 15·3 | 48·7 | 30·3 | 5·7 | 100 | 353 |
| Physics | 11·9 | 57·2 | 25·7 | 5·1 | 100 | 369 |
| Chemistry | 15·2 | 62·0 | 20·9 | 2·0 | 100 | 460 |
| Biochemistry | 15·6 | 59·4 | 21·9 | 3·1 | 100 | 32 |
| Animal Physiology | 5·9 | 49·3 | 39·8 | 5·0 | 100 | 337 |
| Zoology | 15·2 | 51·4 | 29·5 | 3·8 | 100 | 105 |
| Botany | 14·3 | 63·3 | 16·3 | 6·1 | 100 | 49 |
| Geology | 14·9 | 42·6 | 34·0 | 8·5 | 100 | 47 |
| PPP | 14·0 | 53·0 | 31·0 | 2·0 | 100 | 100 |
| Engineering | 12·7 | 20·4 | 37·6 | 29·3 | 100 | 157 |
| Metallurgy | · | · | · | · | · | — |
| Agriculture | 2·8 | 50·0 | 41·7 | 5·6 | 100 | 36 |
| Forestry | 3·3 | 37·7 | 47·5 | 11·5 | 100 | 61 |
| Science | 12·3 | 51·5 | 29·8 | 6·4 | 100 | 2,106 |
| All subjects | 7·8 | 55·0 | 32·5 | 4·7 | 100 | 9,311 |

SOURCE: *Oxford Magazine.*

**Table 151.** *Class of degree by Honour School. Undergraduates classed in* *1960–4*

| Subject | Class of degree | | | | All | *Number* |
|---|---|---|---|---|---|---|
| | 1st | 2nd | 3rd | 4th | | |
| Literae Humaniores | 12·8 | 51·1 | 33·7 | 2·5 | 100 | *814* |
| Theology | 3·4 | 52·5 | 35·4 | 8·7 | 100 | *322* |
| Modern History | 5·2 | 55·6 | 36·5 | 2·7 | 100 | *1,749* |
| English | 6·4 | 61·5 | 29·1 | 3·0 | 100 | *1,126* |
| Modern Languages | 5·9 | 67·6 | 24·9 | 1·6 | 100 | *1,127* |
| Oriental Studies | 15·4 | 54·9 | 20·9 | 8·8 | 100 | *91* |
| Geography | 5·8 | 58·6 | 31·5 | 4·1 | 100 | *362* |
| Music | 17·6 | 61·5 | 19·8 | 1·1 | 100 | *91* |
| Arts | 7·0 | 58·6 | 31·4 | 3·0 | 100 | *5,682* |
| Jurisprudence | 6·1 | 57·5 | 30·9 | 5·5 | 100 | *938* |
| PPE | 6·6 | 53·3 | 35·8 | 4·2 | 100 | *1,324* |
| Social studies | 6·4 | 55·0 | 33·8 | 4·8 | 100 | *2,262* |
| Arts and social studies | 6·8 | 57·6 | 32·1 | 3·5 | 100 | *7,944* |
| Mathematics | 17·6 | 50·3 | 26·3 | 5·9 | 100 | *495* |
| Physics | 12·4 | 51·5 | 34·1 | 2·0 | 100 | *660* |
| Chemistry | 14·5 | 61·4 | 20·4 | 3·7 | 100 | *627* |
| Biochemistry | 13·9 | 65·3 | 19·4 | 1·4 | 100 | *72* |
| Animal Physiology | 10·6 | 65·0 | 21·0 | 3·3 | 100 | *329* |
| Zoology | 11·3 | 74·5 | 11·3 | 2·8 | 100 | *141* |
| Botany | 12·5 | 68·8 | 16·7 | 2·1 | 100 | *48* |
| Geology | 14·6 | 41·6 | 32·6 | 11·2 | 100 | *89* |
| PPP | 12·0 | 50·4 | 34·4 | 3·2 | 100 | *125* |
| Engineering | 12·1 | 33·1 | 33·9 | 20·9 | 100 | *239* |
| Metallurgy | 9·1 | 68·2 | 22·7 | — | 100 | *22* |
| Agriculture | 8·3 | 56·3 | 31·3 | 4·2 | 100 | *48* |
| Forestry | 9·3 | 20·9 | 46·5 | 23·3 | 100 | *43* |
| Science | 13·4 | 54·6 | 26·7 | 5·4 | 100 | *2,938* |
| All subjects | 8·6 | 56·8 | 30·6 | 4·0 | 100 | *10,882* |

SOURCE: *Oxford Magazine.*

**Table 152.** *Result of Second Public Examination by Honour School. Undergraduates taking Second Public Examination in 1960–4*

OXFORD                                                                    PERCENTAGE

| Subject | 1st class | 2nd class | 3rd class | 4th class | Fail | aegrotat or overstanding | All | Number |
|---|---|---|---|---|---|---|---|---|
| Literae Humaniores | 12·6 | 50·5 | 33·3 | 2·4 | 0·7 | 0·4 | 100 | *823* |
| Theology | 3·2 | 49·7 | 33·5 | 8·2 | 4·7 | 0·6 | 100 | *340* |
| Modern History | 5·1 | 54·9 | 36·0 | 2·7 | 1·1 | 0·3 | 100 | *1,773* |
| English | 6·3 | 60·3 | 28·6 | 3·0 | 1·0 | 0·9 | 100 | *1,148* |
| Modern Languages | 5·8 | 66·4 | 24·5 | 1·6 | 1·5 | 0·3 | 100 | *1,147* |
| Oriental Studies | 14·6 | 52·1 | 19·8 | 8·3 | 4·2 | 1·0 | 100 | *96* |
| Geography | 5·8 | 58·4 | 31·4 | 4·1 | 0·3 | — | 100 | *363* |
| Music | 17·4 | 60·9 | 19·6 | 1·1 | — | 1·1 | 100 | *92* |
| Arts | 6·8 | 57·6 | 30·9 | 3·0 | 1·3 | 0·4 | 100 | *5,782* |
| Jurisprudence | 5·6 | 53·3 | 28·7 | 5·1 | 5·9 | 1·4 | 100 | *1,012* |
| PPE | 6·6 | 52·8 | 35·5 | 4·2 | 0·7 | 0·2 | 100 | *1,336* |
| Social studies | 6·2 | 53·0 | 32·5 | 4·6 | 2·9 | 0·7 | 100 | *2,348* |
| Arts and social studies | 6·6 | 56·3 | 31·4 | 3·4 | 1·8 | 0·5 | 100 | *8,130* |
| Mathematics | 17·3 | 49·6 | 25·9 | 5·8 | 1·0 | 0·4 | 100 | *502* |
| Physics | 11·6 | 48·2 | 31·9 | 1·8 | 5·1 | 1·4 | 100 | *706* |
| Chemistry | 14·4 | 61·1 | 20·3 | 3·7 | 0·5 | — | 100 | *630* |
| Biochemistry | 13·9 | 65·3 | 19·4 | 1·4 | — | — | 100 | *72* |
| Animal Physiology | 10·5 | 64·1 | 20·7 | 3·3 | 0·3 | 1·2 | 100 | *334* |
| Zoology | 11·2 | 73·4 | 11·2 | 2·8 | — | 1·4 | 100 | *143* |
| Botany | 12·5 | 68·8 | 16·7 | 2·1 | — | — | 100 | *48* |
| Geology | 14·3 | 40·7 | 31·9 | 11·0 | 2·2 | — | 100 | *91* |
| PPP | 11·8 | 49·6 | 33·9 | 3·1 | 0·8 | 0·8 | 100 | *127* |
| Engineering | 10·3 | 28·1 | 28·8 | 17·8 | 13·5 | 1·4 | 100 | *281* |
| Metallurgy | 9·1 | 68·2 | 22·7 | — | — | — | 100 | *22* |
| Agriculture | 8·0 | 54·0 | 30·0 | 4·0 | 2·0 | 2·0 | 100 | *50* |
| Forestry | 8·5 | 19·1 | 42·6 | 21·3 | 8·5 | — | 100 | *47* |
| Science | 12·9 | 52·5 | 25·6 | 5·2 | 3·0 | 0·8 | 100 | *3,053* |
| All subjects | 8·4 | 55·2 | 29·8 | 3·9 | 2·1 | 0·6 | 100 | *11,183* |

SOURCE: *Oxford Magazine.*

NOTES

1. In Chemistry and Metallurgy, undergraduates spend a year doing research after the Second Public Examination, and do not receive a class until this has been examined. This table relates to chemists and metallurgists who obtained a class (or failed to obtain one) in 1960–4.

2. A candidate who has passed his twelfth term since matriculation cannot (with certain exceptions) be awarded an honours degree, and is said to be 'overstanding'.

3. In 1964, Examiners could award a Pass Degree on the Honour School examination. Such degrees are included under 'aegrotat or overstanding'. In previous years, it is likely that many such candidates were included under 'fail'.

274. Over all there was an increase over the period in the proportions of firsts, and of firsts and seconds. The proportion of firsts rose in each subject group, and in half the individual subjects. The proportion of firsts and seconds fell slightly in arts, and rose in social studies and science. Most of the major subjects were close to the trend of their subject group, but there was a fall in the proportion of firsts and seconds in Physics, from 69 per cent. to 64 per cent.

**Table 153.** *Result of Second Public Examination by Honour School. Undergraduates taking Second Public Examination in 1960–4*

OXFORD                                                                          PERCENTAGE

| Subject | 1st class | 1st or 2nd class | 3rd class | 4th class, aegrotat, over-standing, or fail | All | Number |
|---|---|---|---|---|---|---|
| Literae Humaniores | 12·6 | 63·1 | 33·3 | 3·5 | 100 | 823 |
| Theology | 3·2 | 52·9 | 33·5 | 13·5 | 100 | 340 |
| Modern History | 5·1 | 60·0 | 36·0 | 4·1 | 100 | 1,773 |
| English | 6·3 | 66·6 | 28·6 | 4·9 | 100 | 1,148 |
| Modern Languages | 5·8 | 72·2 | 24·5 | 3·4 | 100 | 1,147 |
| Oriental Studies | 14·6 | 66·7 | 19·8 | 13·5 | 100 | 96 |
| Geography | 5·8 | 64·2 | 31·4 | 4·4 | 100 | 363 |
| Music | 17·4 | 78·3 | 19·6 | 2·2 | 100 | 92 |
| Arts | 6·8 | 64·4 | 30·9 | 4·7 | 100 | 5,782 |
| Jurisprudence | 5·6 | 58·9 | 28·7 | 12·4 | 100 | 1,012 |
| PPE | 6·6 | 59·4 | 35·5 | 5·1 | 100 | 1,336 |
| Social studies | 6·2 | 59·2 | 32·5 | 8·2 | 100 | 2,348 |
| Arts and social studies | 6·6 | 62·9 | 31·4 | 5·7 | 100 | 8,130 |
| Mathematics | 17·3 | 66·9 | 25·9 | 7·2 | 100 | 502 |
| Physics | 11·6 | 59·8 | 31·9 | 8·3 | 100 | 706 |
| Chemistry | 14·4 | 75·5 | 20·3 | 4·2 | 100 | 630 |
| Biochemistry | 13·9 | 79·2 | 19·4 | 1·4 | 100 | 72 |
| Animal Physiology | 10·5 | 74·6 | 20·7 | 4·8 | 100 | 334 |
| Zoology | 11·2 | 84·6 | 11·2 | 4·2 | 100 | 143 |
| Botany | 12·5 | 81·3 | 16·7 | 2·1 | 100 | 48 |
| Geology | 14·3 | 55·0 | 31·9 | 13·2 | 100 | 91 |
| PPP | 11·8 | 61·4 | 33·9 | 4·7 | 100 | 127 |
| Engineering | 10·3 | 38·4 | 28·8 | 32·7 | 100 | 281 |
| Metallurgy | 9·1 | 77·3 | 22·7 | — | 100 | 22 |
| Agriculture | 8·0 | 62·0 | 30·0 | 8·0 | 100 | 50 |
| Forestry | 8·5 | 27·6 | 42·6 | 29·8 | 100 | 47 |
| Science | 12·9 | 65·4 | 25·6 | 9·0 | 100 | 3,053 |
| All subjects | 8·4 | 63·6 | 29·8 | 6·6 | 100 | 11,183 |

SOURCE: *Oxford Magazine.*

NOTE: See notes to Table 152.

275. A simplified form of the information on 1960–4 is given in Table 153. This shows the proportion of firsts, of firsts and seconds, of thirds, and of fourths, *aegrotats*, overstanding for honours, and fails.

### Differences between subjects

276. The proportion of firsts was much higher in science than in arts and social studies. This holds good not only for Oxford, but nationally.[1] Among arts subjects, a high proportion of firsts were awarded in Literae Humaniores, Oriental Studies, and Music. The proportion of firsts in Mathematics was also high.

277. In terms of firsts and seconds, the difference between science and other subjects was much smaller. (Nationally the proportion of firsts and seconds was lower in science in 1959.[1]) The proportion of firsts and seconds was well above average in Modern Languages, Music, Chemistry, Biochemistry, Animal Physiology, Zoology, Botany, and Metallurgy (but the total number of candidates was small in Biochemistry, Botany, and Metallurgy). It was below average in Theology, Physics, Geology, Engineering, and Forestry (in the last of which numbers were small).

278. Table 153 thus shows wide variations in degree results between subjects. But considerable variations occur nationally.[2]

279. There were 3·9 per cent. in the fourth class; 2·1 per cent. failed; and 0·6 per cent. received *aegrotats* or were overstanding for honours. That is, 6·6 per cent. of candidates failed to achieve at least a third-class degree. This proportion was highest in science, due mainly to the very high proportion, 33 per cent., in Engineering. In arts it was high in Theology and Oriental Studies with 13·5 per cent. each, but was less than 5 per cent. in other arts subjects. Other subjects in which there were more than 5 per cent. weak candidates were Jurisprudence, PPE (but only just), Mathematics, Physics, Geology, Agriculture, and Forestry. Of these, there were more than 10 per cent. in Jurisprudence, Geology, and Forestry.

### Factors affecting degree performance

280. The class of degree awarded can be used as a criterion by which different groups of undergraduates may be compared, and this approach has been used in Part II. Four factors which may have a bearing on degree performance are considered here. They are: whether there was a change of subject; whether a scholar, exhibitioner, or commoner; sex; and type of school attended.

---

[1] Robbins Report, Appendix Two (A), Part IV, Section 2, Table 21, p. 144.
[2] Robbins Report, Appendix Two (A), Part IV, Section 2, Table 22, p. 146. In two cases at least, the pattern is similar to that at Oxford. In classics and mathematics the proportion of firsts is high both nationally and at Oxford, but in neither case is the proportion of firsts and seconds especially high.

**Table 154.** *Degree performance by change of course. All undergraduates entering in 1958–9 who obtained a degree*

OXFORD                                                                    PERCENTAGE

| Undergraduates who | 1st class | 2nd class | 3rd class | 4th class | Other | All | Number in sample |
|---|---|---|---|---|---|---|---|
| Did not change course | 9 | 56 | 30 | 3 | 1 | 100 | 1,040 |
| Changed before First Public Examination | 8 | 43 | 43 | 2 | 4 | 100 | 53 |
| Changed after First Public Examination | 4 | 45 | 32 | 5 | 13 | 100 | 75 |
| All | 9 | 55 | 31 | 3 | 2 | 100 | 1,168 |

SOURCE: 1958–9 matriculations sample.

## Change of course

281. The 10 per cent. of undergraduates who changed course obtained less good degrees than those who did not change. There are two possible explanations of this: that the weaker candidates changed course; or that changing in itself had an adverse effect on an undergraduate's chance of a good (first- or second-class) degree. Any undergraduate who changes his subject is likely to find himself somewhat behind those who have not changed. This applies to those who change early in their undergraduate career if their work in the sixth form was directed towards the subject they originally intended to read. For those who change after the First Public Examination, both explanations are likely to apply; they include some who fail to live up to their earlier promise and others who change for other reasons, and are somewhat handicapped thereby.

282. It is impossible to determine how many undergraduates in the sample changed course because they failed to live up to their earlier promise. But the proportion of award holders (though not the proportion of scholars) was higher among those who changed than among those who did not. Thus those who changed course did not consist mainly of the weakest undergraduates (as judged at the time of admission). Both award holders and commoners in both groups changing course obtained a lower proportion of firsts and seconds than did their counterparts who did not change.

## Scholars, exhibitioners, and commoners

283. Tables 155 and 156 show in detail the performance of award holders, undergraduates in the main subject groups, and men and women. Throughout, scholars obtained a much greater, and exhibitioners a considerably

greater, proportion of firsts than did commoners. In all subjects award holders obtained 67 per cent. of all firsts. When firsts and seconds are considered, substantial differences persist between the three groups.

**Table 155.** *Degree performance by subject group and status as scholar, exhibitioner, or commoner. All undergraduates entering in 1958–9 who obtained a degree*

OXFORD                                                                    PERCENTAGE

| Subject group | Scholar, exhibitioner, or commoner | 1st class | 2nd class | 3rd class | 4th class | Other | All | *Number in sample* |
|---|---|---|---|---|---|---|---|---|
| Arts | Scholar | 19·8 | 60·3 | 18·3 | 0·8 | 0·8 | 100 | *131* |
| | Exhibitioner | 11·1 | 55·6 | 30·0 | 1·1 | 2·2 | 100 | *90* |
| | Commoner | 2·2 | 54·2 | 37·5 | 3·9 | 2·2 | 100 | *408* |
| | All | 7·2 | 55·6 | 32·4 | 2·9 | 1·9 | 100 | *629* |
| Social studies | Scholar | 26·3 | 57·9 | 15·8 | — | — | 100 | *19* |
| | Exhibitioner | 8·7 | 65·2 | 21·7 | 4·3 | — | 100 | *23* |
| | Commoner | 4·1 | 56·9 | 36·4 | 2·6 | — | 100 | *195* |
| | All | 6·3 | 57·8 | 33·3 | 2·5 | — | 100 | *237* |
| Science | Scholar | 29·6 | 49·3 | 18·3 | 1·4 | 1·4 | 100 | *71* |
| | Exhibitioner | 14·7 | 64·7 | 20·6 | — | — | 100 | *34* |
| | Commoner | 8·6 | 50·3 | 30·5 | 7·6 | 3·0 | 100 | *197* |
| | All | 14·2 | 51·7 | 26·5 | 5·3 | 2·3 | 100 | *302* |
| All subjects | Scholar | 23·5 | 56·6 | 18·1 | 0·9 | 0·9 | 100 | *221* |
| | Exhibitioner | 11·6 | 59·2 | 26·5 | 1·4 | 1·4 | 100 | *147* |
| | Commoner | 4·3 | 53·9 | 35·5 | 4·5 | 1·9 | 100 | *800* |
| | All | 8·8 | 55·1 | 31·1 | 3·4 | 1·6 | 100 | *1,168* |

SOURCE: 1958–9 matriculations sample.

NOTE: Status as scholar, exhibitioner, or commoner relates to awards held on entrance.

## Sex

284. Women who matriculated in 1958–9 obtained an unusually low proportion of firsts, and those in our sample had a lower proportion of firsts and seconds combined than did all women graduating in 1961 (see Tables 68 and 75). This latter result is a consequence of sampling fluctuations. Table 68 shows that in other years there was a markedly better performance from women, and that women consistently gain a higher proportion of firsts and seconds than do men.

**Table 156.** *Degree performance by status as scholar, exhibitioner, or commoner, and sex. Undergraduates entering in 1958–9 who obtained a degree*

OXFORD                                                                      PERCENTAGE

|  | 1st class | 2nd class | 3rd class | 4th class | Other | All | Number in sample |
|---|---|---|---|---|---|---|---|
| **MEN** | | | | | | | |
| Scholar | 23·2 | 56·2 | 18·7 | 1·0 | 1·0 | 100 | *203* |
| Exhibitioner | 12·2 | 60·3 | 25·2 | 0·8 | 1·5 | 100 | *131* |
| Commoner | 4·8 | 52·8 | 36·0 | 4·6 | 1·8 | 100 | *672* |
| All men | 9·4 | 54·5 | 31·1 | 3·4 | 1·6 | 100 | *1,006* |
| **WOMEN** | | | | | | | |
| Scholar | 27·8 | 61·1 | 11·1 | — | — | 100 | *18* |
| Exhibitioner | 6·3 | 50·0 | 37·5 | 6·3 | — | 100 | *16* |
| Commoner | 1·6 | 59·4 | 32·8 | 3·9 | 2·3 | 100 | *128* |
| All women | 4·9 | 58·6 | 30·9 | 3·7 | 1·9 | 100 | *162* |
| **ALL UNDERGRADUATES** | | | | | | | |
| Scholar | 23·5 | 56·6 | 18·1 | 0·9 | 0·9 | 100 | *221* |
| Exhibitioner | 11·6 | 59·2 | 26·5 | 1·4 | 1·4 | 100 | *147* |
| Commoner | 4·3 | 53·9 | 35·5 | 4·5 | 1·9 | 100 | *800* |
| All undergraduates | 8·8 | 55·1 | 31·1 | 3·4 | 1·6 | 100 | *1,168* |

SOURCE: 1958–9 matriculations sample.
NOTE: See note to Table 155.

## Type of school

285. The performance of men when classified by the type of school they attended is given in Table 157. In terms of firsts alone, those from independent day and direct-grant schools with 12 per cent. had the best performance, followed by those from maintained schools with 10 per cent. When firsts and seconds are considered, undergraduates who attended maintained schools had the best performance. They had 72 per cent. against an over-all figure of 64 per cent. This high performance is largely a result of the much above average performance of commoners from maintained schools; scholars from these schools did not do as well as other scholars.

286. The number of women is too small to permit such a detailed breakdown. Table 158 gives a breakdown by type of school, and Table 159 is similar to Table 157 but for men and women.

**Table 157.** *Degree performance by type of school and status as scholar, exhibitioner, or commoner. Men undergraduates entering in 1958–9 who obtained a degree*

OXFORD                                                                                          PERCENTAGE

| Type of school (or university) | Scholar, exhibitioner, or commoner | 1st class | 2nd class | 3rd class | 4th class | Other | All | *Number in sample* |
|---|---|---|---|---|---|---|---|---|
| Independent boarding | Scholar | 23·2 | 53·7 | 20·7 | 1·2 | 1·2 | 100 | *82* |
| | Exhibitioner | 8·5 | 48·9 | 38·3 | — | 4·3 | 100 | *47* |
| | Commoner | 3·0 | 45·9 | 42·2 | 5·2 | 3·7 | 100 | *270* |
| | All | 7·8 | 47·9 | 37·3 | 3·8 | 3·3 | 100 | *399* |
| Independent day | Scholar | 25·0 | 60·0 | 10·0 | — | 5·0 | 100 | *20* |
| | Exhibitioner | 10·5 | 63·2 | 26·3 | — | — | 100 | *19* |
| | Commoner | 6·2 | 54·2 | 35·4 | 4·2 | — | 100 | *48* |
| | All | 11·5 | 57·5 | 27·6 | 2·3 | 1·1 | 100 | *87* |
| Direct-grant | Scholar | 24·2 | 63·6 | 9·1 | 3·0 | — | 100 | *33* |
| | Exhibitioner | 25·0 | 58·3 | 16·7 | — | — | 100 | *24* |
| | Commoner | 3·6 | 48·8 | 41·7 | 4·8 | 1·2 | 100 | *84* |
| | All | 12·1 | 53·9 | 29·8 | 3·5 | 0·7 | 100 | *141* |
| Maintained | Scholar | 21·7 | 58·3 | 20·0 | — | — | 100 | *60* |
| | Exhibitioner | 10·0 | 72·5 | 15·0 | 2·5 | — | 100 | *40* |
| | Commoner | 6·5 | 60·8 | 27·6 | 4·7 | 0·5 | 100 | *217* |
| | All | 9·8 | 61·8 | 24·6 | 3·5 | 0·3 | 100 | *317* |
| University | All | 9·6 | 59·6 | 28·8 | 1·9 | — | 100 | *52* |
| All | Scholar | 23·2 | 56·2 | 18·7 | 1·0 | 1·0 | 100 | *203* |
| | Exhibitioner | 12·2 | 60·3 | 25·2 | 0·8 | 1·5 | 100 | *131* |
| | Commoner | 4·8 | 52·8 | 36·0 | 4·6 | 1·8 | 100 | *672* |
| | All | 9·4 | 54·5 | 31·1 | 3·4 | 1·6 | 100 | *1,006* |

SOURCE: 1958–9 matriculations sample.

NOTES
1. The last panel of the table includes ten undergraduates from other types of school.
2. See note to Table 155.

**Table 158.** *Degree performance by type of school. Women undergraduates entering in 1958–9 who obtained a degree*

OXFORD                                                                      PERCENTAGE

| Type of school | 1st class | 2nd class | 3rd class | 4th class | Other | All | *Number in sample* |
|---|---|---|---|---|---|---|---|
| Independent boarding | 10·0 | 60·0 | 26·7 | 3·3 | — | 100 | *30* |
| Independent day | 5·6 | 55·6 | 27·8 | 5·6 | 5·6 | 100 | *18* |
| Direct-grant | 7·0 | 62·8 | 18·6 | 7·0 | 4·7 | 100 | *43* |
| Maintained | — | 55·4 | 43·1 | 1·5 | — | 100 | *65* |
| All undergraduates | 4·9 | 58·6 | 30·9 | 3·7 | 1·9 | 100 | *162* |

SOURCE: 1958–9 matriculations sample.

NOTE: The last line of the table includes two undergraduates from other types of school, and four from universities.

287. The performance of women in the sample is the reverse of that of men, with the best performance from women who attended independent boarding schools, followed by those from direct-grant, independent day, and maintained schools.[1]

## Comparisons with other universities

288. A comparison of 1959 degree results at different universities was made by the Robbins Committee.[2] The over-all comparison shows that 7·5 per cent. gained firsts at Oxford, compared with 6·4 per cent. at Cambridge, 8·4 per cent. at London, 7·9 per cent. at the larger civic universities, and 4·4 per cent. at the smaller civic universities in England. At Oxford 65·4 per cent. gained firsts or seconds. This was more than at civic universities, but less than at Cambridge (68·2 per cent.) and London (68·0 per cent.). But there are two difficulties about this comparison. First, there is a significantly smaller proportion of firsts in arts and social studies than in science, and Oxford is more heavily weighted in the former subjects. Secondly, the percentages quoted above are of all students graduating, not of all gaining honours degrees, and the proportion of honours degrees is higher at Oxford than at other universities. The proportions obtaining ordinary or pass degrees was 0·5 per cent. at Oxford; 9·4 per cent. at Cambridge; 14·5 per cent. at London; 30·2 per cent. at the larger civic universities; and 19·3 per cent. at the smaller civic universities. Some of these will have been reading for ordinary or pass degrees, and others will have been awarded them on the results of an honours examination. The Robbins Committee reported

---

[1] But, as noted in paragraph 284, the sample of women is not representative of all women in the year in question, which was itself an unusual one so far as women's degree results are concerned. There is no reason to suppose that the sample of men is atypical in this way.

[2] Robbins Report, Appendix Two (A), Part IV, Section 2, Tables 23 and 24, pp. 147–8.

**Table 159.** *Degree performance by type of school and status as scholar, exhibitioner, or commoner. All undergraduates entering in 1958–9 who obtained a degree*

OXFORD                                                                    PERCENTAGE

| Type of school (or university) | Scholar, exhibitioner, or commoner | 1st class | 2nd class | 3rd class | 4th class | Other | All | *Number in sample* |
|---|---|---|---|---|---|---|---|---|
| Independent boarding | Scholar | 23·5 | 54·1 | 20·0 | 1·2 | 1·2 | 100 | *85* |
| | Exhibitioner | 8·5 | 48·9 | 38·3 | — | 4·3 | 100 | *47* |
| | Commoner | 3·4 | 47·1 | 41·1 | 5·1 | 3·4 | 100 | *297* |
| | All | 7·9 | 48·7 | 36·6 | 3·7 | 3·0 | 100 | *429* |
| Independent day | Scholar | 26·1 | 60·9 | 8·7 | — | 4·3 | 100 | *23* |
| | Exhibitioner | 9·5 | 66·7 | 23·8 | — | — | 100 | *21* |
| | Commoner | 4·9 | 52·5 | 36·1 | 4·9 | 1·6 | 100 | *61* |
| | All | 10·5 | 57·1 | 27·6 | 2·9 | 1·9 | 100 | *105* |
| Direct-grant | Scholar | 25·6 | 64·1 | 7·7 | 2·6 | — | 100 | *39* |
| | Exhibitioner | 21·9 | 56·3 | 18·8 | 3·1 | — | 100 | *32* |
| | Commoner | 2·7 | 53·1 | 36·3 | 5·3 | 2·7 | 100 | *113* |
| | All | 10·9 | 56·0 | 27·2 | 4·3 | 1·6 | 100 | *184* |
| Maintained | Scholar | 20·0 | 58·5 | 21·5 | — | — | 100 | *65* |
| | Exhibitioner | 8·7 | 67·4 | 21·7 | 2·2 | — | 100 | *46* |
| | Commoner | 5·2 | 60·1 | 30·3 | 4·1 | 0·4 | 100 | *271* |
| | All | 8·1 | 60·7 | 27·7 | 3·1 | 0·3 | 100 | *382* |
| University | All | 10·7 | 58·9 | 28·6 | 1·8 | — | 100 | *56* |
| All | Scholar | 23·5 | 56·6 | 18·1 | 0·9 | 0·9 | 100 | *221* |
| | Exhibitioner | 11·6 | 59·2 | 26·5 | 1·4 | 1·4 | 100 | *147* |
| | Commoner | 4·3 | 53·9 | 35·5 | 4·5 | 1·9 | 100 | *800* |
| | All | 8·8 | 55·1 | 31·1 | 3·4 | 1·6 | 100 | *1,168* |

SOURCE: 1958–9 matriculations sample.

NOTES
1. The last panel of the table includes 12 undergraduates from other types of school.
2. See note to Table 155.

that two-thirds to three-quarters of those obtaining pass degrees in Great Britain did so after taking pass courses.[1] But the proportion taking pass courses is much higher in Scottish universities[2] and will be correspondingly lower in universities in England and Wales.

[1] Robbins Report, Appendix Two (A), Part IV, Section 2, para. 38, p. 139. Medical subjects are excluded.
[2] Forty-four per cent. of third-year students (excluding medical students) were taking pass courses in Scottish universities in 1961–2. Robbins Report, Appendix Two (B), Part III, Section 1, Table 5, p. 211.

289. In making inter-university comparisons of degree results, to exclude those who receive ordinary or pass degrees is appropriate if universities have a common standard for distinguishing between honours and pass work. It is by no means obvious that this is so, for a university with relatively large pass schools alongside its honour schools may be more likely to insist that weak candidates take a pass course and to give a pass degree to weak honours candidates than one with no separate pass schools. And a university such as Oxford, with a fourth class, may be more likely to give an honours degree to weak candidates than other universities.

**Table 160.** *Class of degree of undergraduates receiving honours degrees, by subject group and university group. England, 1959*

PERCENTAGE

|  | Percentage in | | All honours degrees |
|---|---|---|---|
|  | 1st class | 1st or 2nd class | |
| ARTS AND SOCIAL STUDIES | | | |
| Oxford | 7 | 67 | 100 |
| Oxford and Cambridge | 6 | 70 | 100 |
| London | 5 | 85 | 100 |
| Larger civic | 5 | 84 | 100 |
| Smaller civic | 3 | 79 | 100 |
| SCIENCE (EXCLUDING APPLIED SCIENCE) | | | |
| Oxford | 13 | 67 | 100 |
| Oxford and Cambridge | 10 | 74 | 100 |
| London | 13 | 76 | 100 |
| Larger civic | 15 | 84 | 100 |
| Smaller civic | 8 | 72 | 100 |
| ALL SUBJECTS | | | |
| Oxford | 8 | 67 | 100 |
| Cambridge | 7 | 75 | 100 |
| Oxford and Cambridge | 7 | 70 | 100 |
| London | 10 | 80 | 100 |
| Larger civic | 11 | 85 | 100 |
| Smaller civic | 5 | 78 | 100 |

SOURCE: Robbins Report, Appendix Two (A), Part IV, Section 2, Tables 23 and 24.
Oxford Magazine, 15 October 1959 (Oxford only).
NOTES
1. Medical subjects are excluded.
2. In the figures for Oxford (but not for Oxford and Cambridge) the fourth class is excluded.

290. In the absence of detailed information on the way in which universities draw the line between honours and pass degrees, it seems more reasonable, however, to base a comparison of the size of the classes on undergraduates achieving honours degrees rather than on all those graduating,

and this is done in Table 160. But for Oxford the fourth class is also excluded. On this basis, the proportion of firsts at Oxford was above that at other universities in arts and social studies. In pure science the proportion of firsts at Oxford was the same as at London, higher than at Cambridge, but lower than at larger civic universities.[1] But the proportion of firsts and seconds was considerably below that at other universities in both subject groups.

291. Differences in degree results could be due to differences in the calibre of undergraduates or to differences of standards. They could also result, in part, from differences in wastage rates. And it is possible that the collegiate structure at Oxford enables a larger proportion of the weaker undergraduates to achieve a third-class honours degree.

292. The Robbins Committee cite statistics on a different basis which show that of all *entrants* in 1956 to universities in England, 7 per cent. obtained firsts at Oxford and Cambridge, London, and the larger civic universities, and 3 per cent. at the smaller civic universities. The proportions obtaining firsts or seconds were 63 per cent. at Oxford and Cambridge, 56 per cent. at London, 50 per cent. at larger civic, and 48 per cent. at smaller civic universities. The A level qualifications of entrants to Oxford and Cambridge were better than those of entrants to London, which, in turn, were better than those of entrants to civic universities. Thus, looked at in this way, undergraduates at Oxford and Cambridge (who were better qualified on entry than undergraduates at other universities) obtained no more firsts than at London or larger civic universities, but more firsts and seconds. And the A level qualifications correlate with the proportion of firsts and seconds, but not with the proportion of firsts.[2] Comparisons on this basis would be appropriate if universities have the same minimum standard for admission.

293. Thus both Table 160 and the previous paragraph show that the proportion of firsts at Oxford was as high as, or slightly higher than, the proportion at other universities. But Table 160 shows the proportion of firsts and seconds to be considerably below that at other English universities (including Cambridge), whereas the approach on which the previous paragraph is based shows Oxford and Cambridge with a higher proportion of firsts and seconds than other universities. Neither approach, however, leads to conclusions about the relative standards at different universities, since the calibre of the undergraduates could differ. To meet this difficulty,

[1] Pure science and applied science are shown separately in the Robbins Report as the pattern of degree results is different in the two cases. Applied science is not shown in Table 160 as the numbers at Oxford are small. Performance in applied science at Oxford was somewhat lower than at other universities in terms of firsts, and much lower in terms of firsts and seconds.

[2] Robbins Report, Appendix Two (A), Part IV, Tables 27 and 28, p. 151. Medical students are excluded.

the Robbins Committee examined the degree performance of State Scholars, who form a reasonably homogeneous group.[1] All State Scholars, whether or not they obtained degrees, who went down in 1956–7 to 1959–60 were included. In arts, the proportion who obtained firsts was the same at Oxford and Cambridge as at all universities (12 per cent.); the proportion of firsts and seconds was 81 per cent. at Oxford and Cambridge, and 83 per cent. at all universities. In pure science the corresponding figures were (with those for Oxford and Cambridge given first): 18 per cent. and 21 per cent. for firsts; and 73 per cent. and 74 per cent. for firsts and seconds. There is no reason to suppose that the calibre of State Scholars at Oxford and Cambridge was lower than at other universities, nor that there was an appreciable difference in their calibre as between Oxford and Cambridge. These results, taken together with those in Table 160 (which show Oxford with a higher proportion of firsts, and a lower proportion of firsts and seconds than for Oxford and Cambridge together) therefore suggest that the standard for a first at Oxford is not very different from the average for all universities,[2] but that the standard for a second at Oxford is higher.

**Table 161.** *Awards held by undergraduates in 1964*

OXFORD

| Awards made by | Number of under-graduates receiving financial benefit from awards in Michaelmas Term 1964 | Amount paid in 1964 to under-graduates in respect of awards held | | |
| --- | --- | --- | --- | --- |
| | | Derived from Trust funds £ | Other £ | Total amount £ |
| Men's colleges | 2,206 | 71,718 | 48,866 | 120,584 |
| Permanent Private Halls | 8 | 1,245 | — | 1,245 |
| Men's societies | 2,214 | 72,963 | 48,866 | 121,829 |
| Women's colleges | 231 | 7,710 | 1,544 | 9,254 |
| Undergraduate societies | 2,445 | 80,673 | 50,410 | 131,083 |
| University | 43 | 3,859 | — | 3,859 |

SOURCE: Registry and colleges.

NOTES
1. Open and closed scholarships and exhibitions are included, whether awarded on entrance or subsequently. Prizes, grants, or awards for travelling are not included.
2. Awards held by Part II chemists and metallurgists are not included. For details see Table 232.
3. For one college the amount derived from Trust Funds is an estimated figure.

[1] Robbins Report, Appendix Two (A), Part IV, Table 29, p. 153.
[2] Unless the calibre of State Scholars who went to Oxford was above average, in which case the evidence would suggest that the standard for a first at Oxford is higher than the average for all universities.

AWARDS HELD BY UNDERGRADUATES

294. Table 161 shows the number of awards (other than honorary awards) held by undergraduates in Michaelmas Term 1964. Most of the awards had been made on entrance but those made subsequently are also included. The total amount paid out in 1964 is given, and also the amounts derived from Trust Funds. The average value of awards was £55 a year for the men's societies, £40 for the women's colleges, and £90 for the university awards.

**Table 162.** *Oxford graduates who read for advanced degrees as percentage of all graduating. Undergraduates matriculating in 1958–9*

| OXFORD | PERCENTAGE |
|---|---|
| B.A. subject | Percentage of those graduating who read for advanced degrees |
| Literae Humaniores | 6 |
| Theology | — |
| Modern History | 5 |
| English | 6 |
| Modern Languages | 8 |
| Oriental Studies | — |
| Geography | 6 |
| Music | 29 |
| Jurisprudence | 2 |
| PPE | 4 |
| Mathematics | 12 |
| Physics | 18 |
| Chemistry | 43 |
| Biochemistry | 63 |
| Animal Physiology | 6 |
| Zoology | 8 |
| Botany | 25 |
| Geology | — |
| PPP | 15 |
| Engineering | 13 |
| Metallurgy | 100 |
| Agriculture | 13 |
| Forestry | — |
| Arts and social studies | 5 |
| Science | 22 |
| All subjects | 10 |

SOURCE: 1958–9 matriculations sample.

NOTES
1. Most of those included above graduated in 1961.
2. Candidates for Part II Chemistry are automatically registered for a B.Sc. In this table only those who had taken a B.Sc. by 1964, or who were registered for a D.Phil. are included.
3. The table includes those who came up to begin to read for the degrees of B.Litt., B.Sc., B.Phil., B.C.L., and D.Phil.

## UNDERGRADUATES WHO SUBSEQUENTLY READ FOR ADVANCED DEGREES

295. Of the undergraduates who matriculated in 1958–9 and who received a first degree, 10 per cent. returned to Oxford to read for an advanced degree. (The proportion who continued with any kind of postgraduate study at Oxford will have been somewhat higher.) Details are given in Table 162. The proportion who read for advanced degrees was much higher in science (22 per cent.) than in arts and social studies (5 per cent.).

### USE OF LIBRARIES AND PURCHASE OF BOOKS

296. During the third week of Michaelmas Term 1964, 53 per cent. of undergraduates used the Bodleian Library, 40 per cent. used departmental and faculty libraries, and 85 per cent. used college libraries (Tables 163–5). Undergraduates used libraries least in their first year, and most in their third year, but in the case of college libraries there were comparatively small differences between undergraduates in different years. There is a great deal of variation between subjects which reflects the particular library facilities available in them.

297. The City libraries were used by only 6 per cent. of undergraduates, while other libraries (of which the Union Library was the most important) were used by 8 per cent. (Table 166).

298. In the Undergraduate Survey undergraduates were asked about their purchases of books since the beginning of the term. It is likely that a considerable proportion of the books bought during the term were bought in this period, but total purchases during the year cannot be inferred from these figures. Table 167 gives the number of books and Table 168 the expenditure. Nearly twice as many books were bought in arts as in science, with social studies lying between. But average expenditure was highest in social studies and lowest in arts.

299. The average number of books, average expenditure, and the percentage of undergraduates buying some books were all highest for first-year undergraduates.

### SUBSEQUENT CAREERS

300. This section relates to men who matriculated in 1958–9 only. Their first occupation after graduation is analysed by the subject and class of their degree (the three main subject groups are shown and also the two large mixed-subject Schools of Literae Humaniores and PPE).[1] It is based on the sample of 1958 matriculations.

---

[1] The numbers are relatively small, and the results for Literae Humaniores and PPE will be subject to greater sampling fluctuations than will those for the larger groupings. These Schools are also included in the figures for the appropriate subject group.

**Table 163.** *Percentage of undergraduates using the Bodleian Library, by subject and year. Third week, Michaelmas Term 1964*

OXFORD                                                        PERCENTAGE

| Subject | Year | | | All years |
|---|---|---|---|---|
| | First | Second | Third | |
| Literae Humaniores | . | — | 79 | 75 |
| Classical Honour Mods. | 45 | 23 | — | 33 |
| Theology | 17 | 40 | 29 | 30 |
| Modern History | 56 | 85 | 80 | 73 |
| English | 41 | 69 | 74 | 63 |
| Modern Languages | 7 | 6 | 12 | 8 |
| Oriental Studies | . | — | 100 | 43 |
| Geography | 40 | 33 | 67 | 47 |
| Music | — | — | . | — |
| Jurisprudence | 69 | 72 | 67 | 69 |
| PPE | 27 | 75 | 77 | 60 |
| Mathematics | 64 | 12 | 42 | 39 |
| Physics | 50 | 46 | 57 | 51 |
| Chemistry | 46 | 58 | 87 | 65 |
| Biochemistry | 50 | 100 | 100 | 80 |
| Animal Physiology | 73 | 64 | 80 | 72 |
| Zoology | . | 100 | 100 | 100 |
| Botany | . | 50 | — | 40 |
| Geology | . | 50 | . | 50 |
| PPP | 67 | 83 | 100 | 80 |
| Natural Science | 67 | — | . | 50 |
| Physics, Mathematics, and Engineering | 35 | . | . | 35 |
| Biology | 71 | — | . | 63 |
| Engineering | . | — | 29 | 13 |
| Metallurgy | 33 | 100 | 50 | 50 |
| Agriculture and Forestry | . | . | — | — |
| All subjects | 43 | 53 | 66 | 53 |

SOURCE: Undergraduate Survey.
NOTE: See notes to Table 100.

**Table 164.** *Percentage of undergraduates using departmental and faculty libraries, by subject and year. Third week, Michaelmas Term 1964*

OXFORD                                                                    PERCENTAGE

| Subject | Year | | | All years |
|---|---|---|---|---|
| | First | Second | Third | |
| Literae Humaniores | . | — | 26 | 25 |
| Classical Honour Mods. | — | 14 | — | 7 |
| Theology | 83 | 60 | 57 | 65 |
| Modern History | 4 | 56 | 78 | 44 |
| English | 69 | 56 | 58 | 61 |
| Modern Languages | 89 | 97 | 96 | 93 |
| Oriental Studies | . | 100 | 100 | 100 |
| Geography | 70 | 100 | 92 | 88 |
| Music | 100 | 100 | . | 100 |
| Jurisprudence | 3 | 4 | 3 | 3 |
| PPE | 35 | 62 | 79 | 59 |
| Mathematics | — | 4 | 5 | 3 |
| Physics | — | — | — | — |
| Chemistry | — | 13 | — | 4 |
| Biochemistry | — | — | — | — |
| Animal Physiology | 7 | — | — | 3 |
| Zoology | . | 57 | 100 | 79 |
| Botany | . | 100 | 100 | 100 |
| Geology | . | 100 | . | 100 |
| PPP | 100 | 83 | 100 | 93 |
| Natural Science | 33 | 100 | . | 50 |
| Physics, Mathematics, and Engineering | 21 | . | . | 21 |
| Biology | 57 | 100 | . | 63 |
| Engineering | . | 67 | 100 | 81 |
| Metallurgy | — | — | 100 | 33 |
| Agriculture and Forestry | . | . | 100 | 100 |
| All subjects | 28 | 45 | 49 | 40 |

SOURCE: Undergraduate Survey.

NOTE: See notes to Table 100.

**Table 165.** *Percentage of undergraduates using college libraries, by subject and year. Third week, Michaelmas Term 1964*

OXFORD                                                           PERCENTAGE

| Subject | Year | | | All years |
|---|---|---|---|---|
| | First | Second | Third | |
| Literae Humaniores | . | 100 | 95 | 95 |
| Classical Honour Mods. | 91 | 95 | 100 | 93 |
| Theology | 83 | 60 | 86 | 74 |
| Modern History | 95 | 96 | 91 | 94 |
| English | 97 | 97 | 89 | 94 |
| Modern Languages | 84 | 91 | 84 | 86 |
| Oriental Studies | . | 50 | 33 | 43 |
| Geography | 60 | 83 | 83 | 76 |
| Music | 25 | 50 | . | 38 |
| Jurisprudence | 90 | 84 | 94 | 90 |
| PPE | 80 | 85 | 97 | 87 |
| Mathematics | 60 | 64 | 89 | 70 |
| Physics | 50 | 88 | 86 | 86 |
| Chemistry | 89 | 96 | 93 | 93 |
| Biochemistry | 75 | 75 | 50 | 70 |
| Animal Physiology | 60 | 79 | 80 | 72 |
| Zoology | . | 71 | 71 | 71 |
| Botany | . | 50 | — | 40 |
| Geology | . | 50 | . | 50 |
| PPP | 50 | 100 | 100 | 80 |
| Natural Science | 67 | 100 | . | 75 |
| Physics, Mathematics, and Engineering | 91 | . | . | 91 |
| Biology | 71 | 100 | . | 75 |
| Engineering | . | 78 | 100 | 88 |
| Metallurgy | 100 | — | 100 | 83 |
| Agriculture and Forestry | . | . | — | — |
| All subjects | 82 | 85 | 88 | 85 |

SOURCE: Undergraduate Survey.

NOTE: See notes to Table 100.

**Table 166.** *Percentage of undergraduates using City and other libraries by subject. Third week, Michaelmas Term 1964*

| OXFORD | PERCENTAGE | |
| --- | --- | --- |
| Subject | City libraries | Other libraries |
| Literae Humaniores | — | 15 |
| Classical Honour Mods. | 7 | 9 |
| Theology | 4 | 43 |
| Modern History | 6 | 9 |
| English | 15 | 9 |
| Modern Languages | 4 | 5 |
| Oriental Studies | 14 | — |
| Geography | 3 | 9 |
| Music | — | — |
| Jurisprudence | 1 | 7 |
| PPE | 7 | 10 |
| Mathematics | — | 9 |
| Physics | 8 | 8 |
| Chemistry | 2 | 6 |
| Biochemistry | 10 | — |
| Animal Physiology | 5 | — |
| Zoology | 7 | 7 |
| Botany | — | 20 |
| Geology | — | — |
| PPP | 20 | 7 |
| Natural Science | — | — |
| Physics, Mathematics, and Engineering | 3 | — |
| Biology | 25 | — |
| Engineering | 6 | — |
| Metallurgy | — | — |
| Agriculture and Forestry | — | — |
| All subjects | 6 | 8 |

SOURCE: Undergraduate Survey.
NOTE: See notes to Table 100.

**Table 167.** *Average number of books bought by undergraduates by subject group and year. First three weeks of Michaelmas Term 1964*

OXFORD                                                                    NUMBER

| Subject group | Books bought during first three weeks of term | Year | | | All years |
| --- | --- | --- | --- | --- | --- |
| | | First | Second | Third | |
| Arts | Average number for all undergraduates | 10·4 | 4·2 | 4·3 | 6·4 |
| | Average number for undergraduates buying at least one book | 10·8 | 5·4 | 5·9 | 7·7 |
| | *Percentage of undergraduates buying at least one book* | 97 | 77 | 74 | *83* |
| Social studies | Average number for all undergraduates | 6·9 | 3·7 | 4·1 | 5·0 |
| | Average number for undergraduates buying at least one book | 7·1 | 4·5 | 5·1 | 5·7 |
| | *Percentage of undergraduates buying at least one book* | 97 | 82 | 81 | 87 |
| Science | Average number for all undergraduates | 6·8 | 2·0 | 1·4 | 3·5 |
| | Average number for undergraduates buying at least one book | 7·0 | 2·7 | 2·3 | 4·5 |
| | *Percentage of undergraduates buying at least one book* | 97 | 75 | 63 | 79 |
| All subjects | Average number for all undergraduates | 8·4 | 3·4 | 3·4 | 5·2 |
| | Average number for undergraduates buying at least one book | 8·7 | 4·3 | 4·7 | 6·3 |
| | *Percentage of undergraduates buying at least one book* | 97 | 77 | 72 | 83 |

SOURCE: Undergraduate Survey.

**Table 168.** *Average expenditure by undergraduates on books, by subject group and year. First three weeks of Michaelmas Term 1964*

OXFORD                                                                                    £

| Subject group | Expenditure on books bought during first three weeks of term | Year | | | All years |
| --- | --- | --- | --- | --- | --- |
| | | First | Second | Third | |
| Arts | Average expenditure for all undergraduates | 6·6 | 3·7 | 3·7 | 4·7 |
| | Average expenditure for undergraduates buying at least one book | 6·9 | 4·8 | 5·2 | 5·8 |
| Social studies | Average expenditure for all undergraduates | 9·6 | 4·6 | 4·8 | 6·5 |
| | Average expenditure for undergraduates buying at least one book | 10·0 | 5·9 | 6·2 | 7·7 |
| Science | Average expenditure for all undergraduates | 11·3 | 3·7 | 2·8 | 6·2 |
| | Average expenditure for undergraduates buying at least one book | 11·9 | 5·1 | 4·5 | 8·0 |
| All subjects | Average expenditure for all undergraduates | 8·9 | 3·9 | 3·6 | 5·6 |
| | Average expenditure for undergraduates buying at least one book | 9·2 | 5·1 | 5·3 | 6·9 |

SOURCE: Undergraduate Survey.

301. About half the men who entered as undergraduates in 1958–9 and who received a degree entered employment following graduation. A third undertook further study or training (Tables 169 and 170). Most of the remainder were not in employment at the time the records were completed (about six months after graduation), i.e. they were seeking employment or were not available for it.

302. The proportion entering employment was average in arts (but was above average in Literae Humaniores); was above average in social studies (mainly because of the high proportion reading Jurisprudence entering employment); and was below average in science (in which 33 per cent. continued with academic study).

**Table 169.** *First occupation of graduates by subject. Men who entered in 1958–9*

OXFORD                                                    PERCENTAGE

|  | Arts | Lit. Hum. | Social studies | PPE | Science | All subjects |
|---|---|---|---|---|---|---|
| Academic study—home | 10 | 13 | 1 | 3 | 30 | 13 |
| Academic study—overseas | 3 | 1 | 5 | 7 | 3 | 3 |
| Teacher training | 13 | 4 | 4 | 6 | 4 | 9 |
| Other specialized training | 5 | 3 | 7 | 7 | 12 | 7 |
| Returned to own country overseas | 1 | — | 7 | 8 | 2 | 2 |
| Entered employment—home | 44 | 58 | 58 | 49 | 38 | 45 |
| Entered employment— overseas | 4 | 1 | 4 | 5 | 2 | 4 |
| Other | 18 | 17 | 13 | 15 | 8 | 15 |
| Not known | 2 | 3 | — | 1 | 2 | 2 |
| **All** | **100** | **100** | **100** | **100** | **100** | **100** |
| *Number in sample graduating* | *530* | *72* | *215* | *119* | *261* | *1,006* |

SOURCE: Appointments Committee and 1958–9 matriculations sample.

NOTE: The category 'other' includes those already in employment or not available for employment; and those seeking employment at the time the records were completed (about six months after graduation).

**Table 170.** *First occupation of graduates by degree performance. Men who entered in 1958–9*

OXFORD                                                    PERCENTAGE

|  | Degree | | | | |
|---|---|---|---|---|---|
|  | 1st class | 2nd class | 3rd class | Others | All |
| Academic study—home | 42 | 14 | 4 | 4 | 13 |
| Academic study—overseas | 12 | 4 | — | — | 3 |
| Teacher training | 4 | 10 | 9 | — | 9 |
| Other specialized training | 6 | 8 | 7 | 8 | 7 |
| Returned to own country overseas | 3 | 2 | 3 | — | 2 |
| Entered employment—home | 21 | 45 | 54 | 42 | 45 |
| Entered employment—overseas | 1 | 4 | 3 | 8 | 4 |
| Other | 9 | 11 | 19 | 28 | 15 |
| Not known | 1 | 1 | 1 | 10 | 2 |
| **All** | **100** | **100** | **100** | **100** | **100** |
| *Number in sample graduating* | *95* | *548* | *313* | *50* | *1,006* |

SOURCE: Appointments Committee and 1958–9 matriculations sample.

NOTE: See note to Table 169.

303. Not surprisingly, the proportion continuing with academic study was highest among firsts, only 22 per cent. of whom entered employment.

**Table 171.** *Type of employer by subject. Men entering in 1958–9 who entered employment on graduation*

OXFORD                                                                    PERCENTAGE

| Type of employer | Arts | Lit. Hum. | Social studies | PPE | Science | All subjects |
|---|---|---|---|---|---|---|
| Home Civil Service and Foreign Service | 10 | 24 | 4 | 9 | 8 | 8 |
| Overseas Civil Service | 2 | — | — | — | 5 | 2 |
| Local government | 3 | 2 | 5 | — | — | 3 |
| Schools | 19 | 26 | 2 | 5 | 13 | 13 |
| Universities | — | — | 2 | 2 | 2 | 1 |
| Agriculture | 1 | 2 | 2 | — | 1 | 1 |
| Industry | 26 | 14 | 23 | 34 | 52 | 31 |
| Commerce | 16 | 21 | 24 | 33 | 5 | 16 |
| Legal | 3 | 2 | 28 | 3 | 4 | 10 |
| Public authorities and services | 1 | 2 | 2 | 2 | 3 | 2 |
| Publishing | 4 | — | 4 | 7 | 2 | 4 |
| Entertainment and cultural | 5 | 2 | 2 | 2 | 1 | 3 |
| Other | 9 | 2 | 3 | 3 | 4 | 6 |
| All | 100 | 100 | 100 | 100 | 100 | 100 |
| *Number in sample entering employment* | *233* | *42* | *125* | *58* | *100* | *458* |

SOURCE: Appointments Committee and 1958–9 matriculations sample.

304. Those who entered employment are further analysed in Tables 171–4. The Home Civil Service and Foreign Service accounted for 8 per cent. of all undergraduates, but for 24 per cent. of those who read Literae Humaniores. 13 per cent. became school teachers (and a further 9 per cent. of all who graduated entered teacher training). About a quarter of graduates in arts and social studies entered industry, compared with half the science graduates.[1] Industry and commerce together accounted for around 45 per cent. in arts and social studies, and for 57 per cent. in science. The main features of Table 172 are the high proportion of those with firsts entering the Home Civil Service and Foreign Service (this figure is, however, based on a small number), and the high proportion of those with thirds entering industry and commerce.

[1] As throughout this paragraph, these are the proportions of those who entered employment. Since the proportion of those graduating who entered employment was higher in arts and social studies than in science, the differences between the subject groups in the proportions of those *graduating* who entered industry (12 per cent. in arts and social studies and 20 per cent. in science) is smaller.

**Table 172.** *Type of employer by degree performance. Men entering in 1958–9 who entered employment on graduation*

OXFORD                                       PERCENTAGE

| Type of employer | Degree | | | | |
| --- | --- | --- | --- | --- | --- |
| | 1st class | 2nd class | 3rd class | Others | All |
| Home Civil Service and Foreign Service | 35 | 12 | 1 | — | 8 |
| Overseas Civil Service | — | 2 | 1 | 9 | 2 |
| Local government | — | 4 | 2 | — | 3 |
| Schools | 20 | 12 | 12 | 23 | 13 |
| Universities | — | 2 | 1 | — | 1 |
| Agriculture | — | 1 | 1 | 5 | 1 |
| Industry | 10 | 31 | 34 | 27 | 31 |
| Commerce | 15 | 13 | 21 | 14 | 16 |
| Legal | 5 | 15 | 6 | — | 10 |
| Public authorities and services | 5 | 1 | 2 | 5 | 2 |
| Publishing | — | 3 | 5 | 5 | 4 |
| Entertainment and cultural | 5 | 2 | 5 | 9 | 3 |
| Other | 5 | 4 | 10 | 5 | 6 |
| All | 100 | 100 | 100 | 100 | 100 |
| *No. in sample entering employment* | 20 | 247 | 169 | 22 | 458 |

SOURCE: Appointments Committee and 1958–9 matriculations sample.

**Table 173.** *Type of work by subject. Men entering in 1958–9 who entered employment on graduation*

OXFORD                                       PERCENTAGE

| Type of work | Arts | Lit. Hum. | Social studies | PPE | Science | All subjects |
| --- | --- | --- | --- | --- | --- | --- |
| Administration | 18 | 19 | 8 | 12 | — | 12 |
| Teaching | 20 | 29 | 4 | 7 | 14 | 14 |
| Scientific research | 1 | — | — | — | 24 | 6 |
| Design, development, routine analysis, etc. | 1 | 2 | 4 | 9 | 17 | 5 |
| Production, operation, and maintenance | 1 | — | 2 | — | 6 | 2 |
| Buying and selling | 12 | 5 | 10 | 16 | 1 | 9 |
| Financial | 11 | 29 | 18 | 24 | 2 | 11 |
| Legal | 3 | 2 | 34 | 3 | 6 | 12 |
| Social and personnel | 2 | 2 | — | — | — | 1 |
| Editing, journalism, libraries, museums | 5 | — | 4 | 7 | 2 | 4 |
| Films, TV, radio, and drama | 3 | 2 | 1 | 2 | 1 | 2 |
| Other | 22 | 10 | 15 | 21 | 27 | 21 |
| All | 100 | 100 | 100 | 100 | 100 | 100 |
| *No. in sample entering employment* | 233 | 42 | 125 | 58 | 100 | 458 |

SOURCE: Appointments Committee and 1958–9 matriculations sample.

NOTE: The category 'other' includes general traineeships and postgraduate apprenticeships.

**Table 174.** *Type of work by degree performance. Men entering in 1958-9 who entered employment on graduation*

OXFORD                                                   PERCENTAGE

| Type of work | Degree | | | | |
| --- | --- | --- | --- | --- | --- |
| | 1st class | 2nd class | 3rd class | Others | All |
| Administration | 35 | 13 | 8 | — | 12 |
| Teaching | 25 | 14 | 12 | 23 | 14 |
| Scientific research | 5 | 6 | 6 | — | 6 |
| Design, development, routine analysis, etc. | 5 | 5 | 5 | 9 | 5 |
| Production, operation, and maintenance | — | 2 | 3 | 9 | 2 |
| Buying and selling | — | 7 | 13 | 9 | 9 |
| Financial | 10 | 10 | 12 | 14 | 11 |
| Legal | 5 | 17 | 8 | — | 12 |
| Social and personnel | — | — | 2 | — | 1 |
| Editing, journalism, libraries, museums | 5 | 4 | 4 | 9 | 4 |
| Films, TV, radio, and drama | — | 1 | 3 | 5 | 2 |
| Other | 10 | 21 | 24 | 23 | 21 |
| All | 100 | 100 | 100 | 100 | 100 |
| *No. in sample entering employment* | 20 | 247 | 169 | 22 | 458 |

SOURCE: Appointments Committee and 1958-9 matriculations sample.

NOTE: See note to Table 173.

305. Tables 173 and 174 give the type of work taken up by those who entered employment. This is closely related to the type of employer in many cases, but the tables show separately the main types of work in industry and commerce.

306. Most of those in the sample graduated in 1961. For similar details of the employment of those graduating in later years see the Annual Reports of the Appointments Committee.

# PART IV

---

# POSTGRADUATES

---

307. In Part I the numbers of postgraduates were given, together with their distribution between subject groups and the various qualifications for which they were reading. Here attention is focused on their academic life, and on the non-academic matters which may affect the quality of their academic life.

## THE POSTGRADUATE SURVEY

308. To collect information on these matters, the Commission carried out a sample survey of postgraduates early in Michaelmas Term 1964, and most of the material presented here is based on that survey. In order to achieve its aims, this survey could not be representative of all postgraduates. There was no point in including first-year postgraduates, who would not be able to give useful information on the supervision they received. Nor would they have had time to form views on the position of postgraduates. The great majority of postgraduates who spend at least two years at Oxford are those reading for higher degrees, most diploma courses lasting one year. Accordingly, the survey was restricted to postgraduates reading for higher degrees in their second and subsequent years. References to postgraduates in the following sections should be construed in this sense unless it is explicitly stated to the contrary.

309. A sample of 50 per cent. was taken and the response rate was high, 86 per cent. This figure may understate the true response since some of those who did not reply may not have been in residence. The total number of replies was 386. Further details about the survey and of the sample numbers in the main categories are given in Part VI.

## BACKGROUND
### University of previous study

310. In Table 175 postgraduates are classified according to whether they were graduates of Oxford, of other U.K. universities, or of universities overseas. The picture is complicated by the fact that 22 per cent. (mainly

**Table 175.** *Universities at which postgraduates obtained their degrees, by subject group*

OXFORD                                                                    PERCENTAGE

| Universities at which postgraduates obtained degrees | Arts and social studies | Science and medicine | All subjects |
|---|---|---|---|
| Oxford | 28 | 57 | 43 |
| Oxford and another U.K. university | 3 | 2 | 3 |
| Another U.K. university | 16 | 16 | 16 |
| Other U.K. universities (two degrees) | 2 | 1 | 2 |
| Overseas | 23 | 13 | 18 |
| Overseas and Oxford | 5 | — | 3 |
| Overseas and another U.K. university | 1 | 1 | 1 |
| Overseas (two degrees) | 21 | 8 | 14 |
| No degree | 2 | — | 1 |
| All | 100 | 100 | 100 |

SOURCE: Postgraduate Survey.

**Table 176.** *Universities at which postgraduates obtained their degrees, by subject group (summary table)*

OXFORD                                                                    PERCENTAGE

| Universities at which postgraduates obtained degrees | Arts and social studies | Science and medicine | All subjects |
|---|---|---|---|
| Oxford | 31 | 60 | 46 |
| Other U.K. universities | 20 | 17 | 19 |
| Overseas universities | 49 | 23 | 35 |
| All | 100 | 100 | 100 |

SOURCE: Postgraduate Survey.

NOTES
1. Those with a degree at Oxford and another U.K. university are included under Oxford in this table.
2. Those with no degrees are included under other U.K. universities in this table.
3. All postgraduates with at least one degree at an overseas university are included under overseas universities in this table.

from overseas) had taken at least two degrees before embarking on post-graduate work at Oxford.[1] The proportion of Oxford graduates was much higher, and the proportion of overseas graduates much lower, in science and medicine than in arts and social studies. Over all, 35 per cent. had a degree from a university overseas. The proportion of graduates of other U.K. universities was about a fifth in each of the two subject groups. Table 176 gives the same information in the simplified form which is usually used below.

**Table 177.** *Universities at which postgraduates obtained their degrees, by college group*

OXFORD                                              PERCENTAGE

| Universities at which postgraduates obtained degrees | Men's societies | Women's colleges | Graduate societies | All societies |
|---|---|---|---|---|
| Oxford | 53 | 32 | 7 | 43 |
| Oxford and another U.K. university | 2 | — | 5 | 3 |
| Another U.K. university | 12 | 27 | 26 | 16 |
| Other U.K. universities (two degrees) | 2 | 2 | — | 2 |
| Overseas | 15 | 23 | 26 | 18 |
| Overseas and Oxford | 2 | 2 | 3 | 3 |
| Overseas and another U.K. university | — | — | 3 | 1 |
| Overseas (two degrees) | 12 | 11 | 28 | 14 |
| No degree | — | 2 | 2 | 1 |
| All | 100 | 100 | 100 | 100 |

SOURCE: Postgraduate Survey.

311. Almost exactly half the sample had an Oxford degree, including 6 per cent. who also had a degree at another university. The proportion of Oxford graduates was considerably less in the women's colleges (about a third) and was only 15 per cent. in the graduate societies (Table 177). Over a quarter in the women's colleges and a third in the graduate societies were graduates of other U.K. universities, compared with 14 per cent. in the men's societies. There was a very high proportion of overseas graduates in the graduate societies (60 per cent.) compared with 29 per cent. at the men's societies and 36 per cent. at the women's colleges. (Postgraduates with degrees at more than one of the university groups have been counted twice in these figures.)

[1] This may be an understatement. Most of those with more than one degree had a higher degree of some kind, but the questionnaire asked for details of 'first degree'. It is possible that some interpreted this strictly to mean a bachelor's or undergraduate degree, and did not record their higher degree.

**Table 178.** *Country in which postgraduates obtained their degrees, by subject group*

OXFORD                                                                                      PERCENTAGE

|  | U.K. | Australia Canada New Zealand South Africa | Other Common-wealth countries | U.S.A. | Europe | Other countries | No degree | All |
|---|---|---|---|---|---|---|---|---|
| **DEGREE 1** | | | | | | | | |
| Arts and social studies | 49 | 21 | 3 | 16 | 3 | 6 | 2 | 100 |
| Science and medicine | 77 | 9 | 5 | 4 | 1 | 2 | — | 100 |
| All subjects | 64 | 15 | 4 | 10 | 2 | 4 | 1 | 100 |
| **DEGREE 2** | | | | | | | | |
| Arts and social studies | 10 | 9 | 2 | 9 | 2 | 1 | 69 | 100 |
| Science and medicine | 5 | 4 | 2 | 2 | — | — | 87 | 100 |
| All subjects | 7 | 6 | 2 | 5 | 1 | — | 78 | 100 |

SOURCE: Postgraduate Survey.

NOTES
1. The subject group is that of the subject studied at Oxford.
2. Degree 1 and Degree 2 refer to degrees taken before embarking on postgraduate work at Oxford, in chronological order. They are referred to as 'first degrees' although some, particularly those under Degree 2, are not first (or undergraduate) degrees. A very small number in the sample had taken three degrees before becoming postgraduates at Oxford.

## Country of previous study

312. The first degree (Degree 1 in Table 178) was taken overseas by 35 per cent. of postgraduates, Australia, Canada, New Zealand, South Africa, and the U.S.A. accounting for 25 per cent. Postgraduates who had studied in the U.S.A. were concentrated in arts and social studies. Under Degree 2 in Table 178 is shown the countries in which the 14 per cent. who had taken two degrees overseas obtained their second degree.

313. Table 179 gives a similar analysis by college group. The proportions from Australia, Canada, New Zealand, South Africa, and the U.S.A. did not vary greatly between the college groups. The proportion from Commonwealth countries other than Australia, Canada, and New Zealand, from Europe, and from other countries was higher for the graduate societies than for the other college groups.

**Table 179.** *Country in which postgraduates obtained their degrees, by college group*

OXFORD                                                                                    PERCENTAGE

|  | U.K. | Australia Canada New Zealand South Africa | Other Common-wealth countries | U.S.A. | Europe | Other countries | No degree | All |
|---|---|---|---|---|---|---|---|---|
| **DEGREE 1** | | | | | | | | |
| Men's societies | 70 | 14 | 3 | 10 | 1 | 1 | — | 100 |
| Women's colleges | 61 | 18 | 5 | 7 | 2 | 5 | 2 | 100 |
| Graduate societies | 36 | 16 | 10 | 11 | 8 | 16 | 2 | 100 |
| **All societies** | 64 | 15 | 4 | 10 | 2 | 4 | 1 | 100 |
| **DEGREE 2** | | | | | | | | |
| Men's societies | 7 | 6 | 1 | 5 | 1 | — | 81 | 100 |
| Women's colleges | 5 | 7 | 2 | — | 2 | — | 84 | 100 |
| Graduate societies | 11 | 10 | 7 | 10 | — | 2 | 61 | 100 |
| **All societies** | 7 | 6 | 2 | 5 | 1 | — | 78 | 100 |

SOURCE: Postgraduate Survey.
NOTE: See notes to Table 178.

## Marital status

314. Thirty-seven per cent. of postgraduates were married, and 33 per cent. had their husband or wife in Oxford (Table 180). 16 per cent. had children, and 15 per cent. had their children in Oxford. The proportion of married postgraduates was highest (45 per cent.) among overseas graduates, 21 per cent. of whom had children with them in Oxford. The proportion of graduates of U.K. universities other than Oxford who were married was low, but the proportion with children was average.

315. Table 181 shows that the proportion of postgraduates who were married was just over a third in the men's societies and in the women's colleges. In each case 13 per cent. had children. In the graduate societies half were married, and 37 per cent. had children (though only 30 per cent. had their children with them in Oxford).

## Age

316. An undergraduate who enters university at 18 could begin post-graduate work after a three-year degree course at 21, and would be 22 in his second year. He would be up to 25 in his fourth postgraduate year if he had entered at 19, or spent four years on his first degree. 75 per cent. of

**Table 180.** *Marital status of postgraduates, by university of first degree.* *Michaelmas Term 1964*

OXFORD                                                                        PERCENTAGE

| | Postgraduates with first degrees from | | | All universities |
| --- | --- | --- | --- | --- |
| | Oxford | Other U.K. universities | Overseas universities | |
| Single | 65 | 73 | 55 | 63 |
| Married, husband or wife not in Oxford | 2 | 1 | 2 | 2 |
| Married with children, family not in Oxford | 1 | 4 | 2 | 2 |
| Married, husband or wife in Oxford | 22 | 9 | 20 | 19 |
| Married with children, family in Oxford | 10 | 13 | 21 | 15 |
| All | 100 | 100 | 100 | 100 |

SOURCE: Postgraduate Survey.

**Table 181.** *Marital status of postgraduates, by college group. Michaelmas Term 1964*

OXFORD                                                                        PERCENTAGE

| | Men's societies | Women's colleges | Graduate societies | All societies |
| --- | --- | --- | --- | --- |
| Single | 65 | 64 | 51 | 63 |
| Married, husband or wife not in Oxford | 1 | 7 | 2 | 2 |
| Married with children, family not in Oxford | 1 | 2 | 7 | 2 |
| Married, husband or wife in Oxford | 21 | 16 | 11 | 19 |
| Married with children, family in Oxford | 12 | 11 | 30 | 15 |
| All | 100 | 100 | 100 | 100 |

SOURCE: Postgraduate Survey.

**Table 182.** *Age of postgraduates, by university of first degrees and number of degrees held. Michaelmas Term 1964*

OXFORD                                                                          PERCENTAGE

| Age | Postgraduates with first degrees from | | | Postgraduates with | | All post-graduates |
|---|---|---|---|---|---|---|
| | Oxford | Other U.K. universities | Overseas universities | One or no degree | Two degrees | |
| Under 22 | I | — | I | I | — | I |
| 22–25 | 75 | 51 | 46 | 66 | 40 | 60 |
| 26–29 | 22 | 22 | 31 | 22 | 37 | 25 |
| 30 and over | 2 | 26 | 21 | 11 | 23 | 13 |
| All | 100 | 100 | 100 | 100 | 100 | 100 |

SOURCE: Postgraduate Survey.

Oxford graduates were in this age group, most of the remainder being aged 26–29. Graduates of overseas universities may be expected to be older, since the normal age of graduation is often higher than in the U.K. and because many had two degrees. This was so (Table 182), and just over half were 26 and over. Graduates of other U.K. universities rather surprisingly had the highest average age: 51 per cent. were under 26 and 26 per cent. were 30 and over. This group included a number of postgraduates who had interrupted a career later in life to work for a higher degree. Not surprisingly, those with two degrees were older than those with only one.

**Table 183.** *Age of postgraduates, by marital status. Michaelmas Term 1964*

OXFORD                                              PERCENTAGE

| Age | Single | Married without children | Married with children | All |
|---|---|---|---|---|
| Under 22 | I | I | — | I |
| 22–25 | 70 | 63 | 21 | 60 |
| 26–29 | 20 | 29 | 41 | 25 |
| 30 and over | 9 | 8 | 38 | 13 |
| All | 100 | 100 | 100 | 100 |

SOURCE: Postgraduate Survey.

317. Table 183 shows that there was not a great deal of difference between the age distributions for single postgraduates, and for those who were married without children. Those with children were older, 38 per cent. being 30 and over.

**Table 184.** *Type of degree held by postgraduates, by subject group*

OXFORD                                                                          PERCENTAGE

| | Type of degree | | | | All |
|---|---|---|---|---|---|
| | Bachelor's | Master's | Other | None | |
| **DEGREE 1** | | | | | |
| Arts and social studies | 91 | 5 | 2 | 2 | 100 |
| Science and medicine | 95 | 2 | 3 | — | 100 |
| All | 93 | 4 | 3 | 1 | 100 |
| **DEGREE 2** | | | | | |
| Arts and social studies | 8 | 16 | 7 | 69 | 100 |
| Science and medicine | 3 | 7 | 2 | 87 | 100 |
| All | 6 | 11 | 5 | 78 | 100 |

SOURCE: Postgraduate Survey.

NOTE: Three members of the sample who already possessed a doctorate are included under 'master's'.

## Degrees held

318. It is difficult to fit degrees into a simple classification because of the great variety of degrees and of their nomenclature. In Table 184 they are classified broadly as bachelor's (or undergraduate) and master's (i.e. degrees below doctorates and usually taken after one or two years of postgraduate work) degrees. The great majority of first degrees were bachelor's. Some were recorded as master's. Confusing nomenclature and a failure of some holding two degrees to record their bachelor's degree are likely explanations. Half those holding two degrees had a master's degree or its equivalent, a quarter had a second bachelor's degree (mainly an Oxford B.A.), and the remainder had other types of degrees, or degrees which could not be classified.

319. Table 185 shows the class of degree held. Bachelor's degrees are, in general, the only degrees which are classed, and for many of these (particularly in the U.S.A.) a class is not awarded. This accounts for the large proportion under 'others' for Degree 1 in Table 185. Very few in this category held lower second- or third-class degrees. In arts and social studies there were more firsts than upper seconds,[1] the position was reversed in science and medicine.

[1] Under Degree 1.

**Table 185.** *Class of degree held by postgraduates, by subject group*

PERCENTAGE

| | Class of degree | | | All |
|---|---|---|---|---|
| | First | Upper second | Other degrees | |
| **DEGREE 1** | | | | |
| Arts and social studies | 41 | 31 | 29 | 100 |
| Science and medicine | 36 | 52 | 12 | 100 |
| All subjects | 38 | 42 | 20 | 100 |
| **DEGREE 2** | | | | |
| Arts and social studies | 8 | 3 | 89 | 100 |
| Science and medicine | 1 | 1 | 97 | 100 |
| All subjects | 5 | 2 | 93 | 100 |

SOURCE: Postgraduate Survey.
NOTE: Undivided seconds are included under 'upper second'.

## COURSE TAKEN AT OXFORD

**Subject**

320. Postgraduates in the sample were roughly equally divided between arts and social studies on the one hand, and science and medicine on the other (Table 186). There were 37 per cent. in arts and 11 per cent. in social studies. This may be compared with Table 15 which shows that of all postgraduates in 1964–5 (including diploma students and first-year post-graduates) 41 per cent. were in arts, 19 per cent. in social studies, and 40 per cent. in science. There was also a marked difference in the subject groups of postgraduates in their second year and those in subsequent years. Among the second year, 39 per cent. were in science and medicine, compared with 65 per cent. in subsequent years. The proportions in arts and in social studies declined accordingly. There are two explanations of this. First, degrees other than the doctorate, which can be earned in a shorter time, are more frequently taken in arts and social studies than in science and medicine. Secondly, wastage is less in science and medicine (see paras. 379–82 below).

321. As already noted, a higher than average proportion (68 per cent.) of Oxford graduates were in science and medicine. This proportion was lowest for graduates of universities overseas of whom twice the average proportion were in social studies.

**Table 186.** *Subject group of postgraduates, by year and university of first degrees. Michaelmas Term 1964*

OXFORD                                                                                    PERCENTAGE

| | Postgraduates in their | | Postgraduates with first degrees from | | | All post-graduates |
|---|---|---|---|---|---|---|
| | 2nd year | 3rd and subsequent years | Oxford | Other U.K. universities | Overseas universities | |
| Arts | 46 | 28 | 29 | 43 | 45 | 37 |
| Social studies | 15 | 7 | 3 | 8 | 21 | 11 |
| Arts and social studies | 61 | 35 | 32 | 51 | 66 | 48 |
| Science and medicine | 39 | 65 | 68 | 49 | 34 | 52 |
| All subjects | 100 | 100 | 100 | 100 | 100 | 100 |

SOURCE: Postgraduate Survey.

**Table 187.** *Year of postgraduates, by subject group. Michaelmas Term 1964*

OXFORD                                                                                    PERCENTAGE

| Year of postgraduate work | Arts | Social studies | Arts and social studies | Science and medicine | All subjects |
|---|---|---|---|---|---|
| Second | 62 | 68 | 63 | 37 | 50 |
| Third | 28 | 27 | 28 | 43 | 36 |
| Fourth | 7 | 5 | 6 | 14 | 10 |
| Fifth and subsequent | 3 | — | 3 | 5 | 4 |
| All years | 100 | 100 | 100 | 100 | 100 |

SOURCE: Postgraduate Survey.

322. Table 187 shows the same position in a different way. In arts and social studies 63 per cent. were in their second year, but only 28 per cent. in their third year. In science and medicine the two proportions were roughly equal.[1]

### Degree

323. The degrees other than the D.Phil. are the B.Litt. and B.Sc. (research degrees) and the B.Phil. and B.C.L. (examination degrees).[2] The per-

[1] Sampling fluctuations are probably the explanation of a slightly higher proportion in the third year.

[2] The B.Mus. and B.D. are also higher degrees, but the numbers reading them are very small, and there was no one reading them in the sample.

centages aiming at these degrees, by subject group, are given in Table 188. Here an important distinction must be made. Postgraduates reading for the degrees of B.Litt., B.Sc., B.Phil., and D.Phil. must apply to a faculty board or the Committee for Advanced Studies for permission to read for one of these degrees.[1] But a student is not necessarily admitted in the first instance to read for the degree he hopes eventually to take. In arts and social studies a student aiming at a D.Phil. must initially be registered as a Probationer B.Litt. student (unless he already holds a B.Litt., B.Sc., B.Phil., or Diploma in Law), and can proceed to D.Phil. status only after serving a probationary period. Table 188 is in terms of the degree post-graduates stated they were aiming at, not the degree for which they were registered. In arts and social studies, 16 per cent. were aiming for a B.Litt., and 17 per cent. for examination degrees. Two-thirds were aiming at a D.Phil., compared with 97 per cent. in science and medicine.

**Table 188.** *Degree aimed at by postgraduates, by subject group. Michaelmas Term 1964*

OXFORD                                                              PERCENTAGE

| Degree aimed at | Arts | Social studies | Arts and social studies | Science and medicine | All subjects |
|---|---|---|---|---|---|
| B.Litt. | 15 | 20 | 16 | — | 8 |
| B.Sc. | — | — | — | 3 | 2 |
| B.Phil. | 17 | 10 | 15 | — | 7 |
| B.C.L. | — | 7 | 2 | — | 1 |
| D.Phil. | 68 | 63 | 67 | 97 | 82 |
| All degrees | 100 | 100 | 100 | 100 | 100 |

SOURCE: Postgraduate Survey.

**Table 189.** *Degree aimed at by postgraduates, by university of first degrees. Michaelmas Term 1964*

OXFORD                                                              PERCENTAGE

| Degree aimed at | Postgraduates with first degrees from | | | All postgraduates |
|---|---|---|---|---|
| | Oxford | Other U.K. universities | Overseas universities | |
| B.Litt. and B.Sc. | 6 | 13 | 13 | 10 |
| B.Phil. and B.C.L. | 3 | 11 | 13 | 8 |
| D.Phil. | 90 | 76 | 75 | 82 |
| All degrees | 100 | 100 | 100 | 100 |

SOURCE: Postgraduate Survey.

[1] Candidates for the B.C.L., other than Oxford graduates with first- or second-class degrees in Jurisprudence, must be admitted by the faculty board to read for the degree.

324. The results in Table 189, showing the degree aimed at according to university of first degree, are implied in what has been shown above: that a high proportion of Oxford graduates were doing postgraduate work in science and medicine, and the proportion aiming at a D.Phil. was very high in science and medicine. 90 per cent. of Oxford graduates were aiming at a D.Phil. For others the proportion was about three-quarters.

**Table 190.** *Degree registered for, by subject group. Michaelmas Term 1964*

OXFORD                                                                    PERCENTAGE

| Degree registered for | Arts | Social studies | Arts and social studies | Science and medicine | All subjects |
|---|---|---|---|---|---|
| Probationer B.Litt. | 7 | 17 | 9 | — | 5 |
| B.Litt. | 37 | 39 | 37 | — | 18 |
| B.Sc. | 1 | — | 1 | 13 | 7 |
| B.Phil. and B.C.L. | 19 | 20 | 19 | — | 9 |
| D.Phil. | 36 | 24 | 34 | 86 | 61 |
| All degrees | 100 | 100 | 100 | 100 | 100 |

SOURCE: Postgraduate Survey.

325. The degree for which postgraduates were registered is given in Table 190. Before being registered for a B.Litt. (which may itself be only a stage before transferring to D.Phil. status) there is a probationer stage. Comparing this table with Table 188, it can be seen that in science and medicine about 10 per cent. were registered for a B.Sc. but were aiming at a D.Phil. In arts and social studies 33 per cent. (half those aiming for a D.Phil) were aiming at a D.Phil. but registered for a lower degree. The proportion was higher in social studies than in arts. A very small number registered for a B.Phil. (or admitted to read for a B.C.L.) were aiming at a D.Phil.

### RESIDENCE IN OXFORD

326. A third of the postgraduates in the survey had spent virtually the whole of the previous academic year (at least 47 weeks) in Oxford, and three-quarters had spent at least 38 weeks. On average, those in science and medicine spent 6 weeks more in Oxford than those in arts and social studies. There was a difference in the average of 3 weeks between the first and subsequent years (see Table 191).

### TEACHING RECEIVED BY POSTGRADUATES

327. The faculty board or the Committee for Advanced Studies appoints a supervisor (sometimes described here as a faculty supervisor to

Table 191. *Number of weeks postgraduates were in residence, by subject group, year, and university of first degree. October 1963–September 1964*

OXFORD
PERCENTAGE

| Number of weeks residence in the year | Postgraduates in | | Postgraduates in their | | Postgraduates with first degrees from | | | All post-graduates |
|---|---|---|---|---|---|---|---|---|
| | Arts and social studies | Science and medicine | 1st year | 2nd and subsequent years | Oxford | Other U.K. universities | Overseas universities | |
| 24 or less | 15 | 3 | 8 | 9 | 8 | 10 | 8 | 8 |
| 25–28 | 8 | — | 7 | 1 | 2 | 1 | 7 | 4 |
| 29–37 | 19 | 7 | 19 | 7 | 8 | 17 | 17 | 13 |
| 38–46 | 30 | 56 | 43 | 44 | 53 | 46 | 30 | 44 |
| 47–52 | 29 | 34 | 23 | 40 | 30 | 26 | 38 | 32 |
| All | 100 | 100 | 100 | 100 | 100 | 100 | 100 | 100 |
| *Average number of weeks of residence* | 38 | 44 | 40 | 43 | 42 | 40 | 41 | 41 |

SOURCE: Postgraduate Survey.

distinguish him from the college supervisor appointed by some colleges) for each postgraduate reading for higher degrees other than the B.C.L., B.D., and B.Mus.[1] The supervisor's duties are to direct and superintend the postgraduate's work (though not to give systematic instruction), and to make a report on his progress to the faculty board each term and at any other time when the board requests or he deems it expedient.

328. Postgraduates reading for the examination degrees (B.Phil. and B.C.L.) often receive regular tuition in the form of tutorials, and attend seminars which are organized to meet their needs.

329. Postgraduates reading for the research degrees are much less likely to have tutorials (those who do may be filling in particular gaps in their knowledge), but they quite frequently attend seminars.

330. Lectures are also provided for postgraduates. Some are on research methods and techniques. Others are on advanced topics.

## Supervision

331. The system of supervision is the most important element in postgraduate training, for the research degrees at least. There are great variations in the amount and form of supervision given, and the picture given here, based on supervision in Trinity Term 1964, is far from a complete one. In particular, it does not bring out the stages a postgraduate goes through, and the differing needs for supervision in these stages. In arts and social studies, at the beginning he will be deciding on his topic, doing a lot of reading, and probably needing frequent consultation with his supervisor. There may follow a lengthy period of assembling his material, during which he will have less contact with his supervisor. But when he comes to develop and clarify his ideas he may spend long sessions with his supervisor discussing them. While he is writing his thesis he will want his supervisor's criticisms as each chapter is written, and when he is putting the finishing touches to his thesis he may be in very frequent contact with him. There are two important differences in science. First, there will be a laboratory where the postgraduate will work alongside other postgraduates and members of the academic staff including his supervisor. Much of his supervision may take place through this day-to-day contact and the amount of supervision is very difficult to estimate. Secondly, the piece of research undertaken is more likely to form part of the department's general scheme of research, and it may well be closely related to the supervisor's own research.

---

[1] The appointment of a supervisor for candidates for the B.Phil. is not obligatory, but one is normally appointed.

332. The differences in the pattern of supervision between arts and social studies, and science and medicine are brought out by the statistics. But the variations over a postgraduate's career are not brought out clearly, and the Trinity Term is not representative of the whole year (for example, few postgraduates would have been at the beginning of their research). To a certain extent the variation in the amount of supervision received reflects the differing needs of postgraduates, but it also reflects the fact that some postgraduates received less supervision than they would have liked.

**Table 192.** *Frequency of visits to faculty supervisor, by subject group and year. Trinity Term 1964*

OXFORD                                                                           PERCENTAGE

| Subject group | Visits to faculty supervisor during the term | Postgraduates in their | | All years |
|---|---|---|---|---|
| | | 1st year | 2nd and subsequent years | |
| Arts and social studies | None | 6 | 18 | 10 |
| | One | 21 | 16 | 19 |
| | Monthly | 23 | 40 | 29 |
| | Fortnightly | 33 | 22 | 29 |
| | Weekly | 13 | 3 | 9 |
| | In day-to-day contact | 4 | 1 | 3 |
| | All | 100 | 100 | 100 |
| Science and medicine | None | 3 | 5 | 4 |
| | One | 5 | 6 | 6 |
| | Monthly | 8 | 8 | 8 |
| | Fortnightly | 14 | 5 | 8 |
| | Weekly | 27 | 20 | 22 |
| | In day-to-day contact | 43 | 56 | 52 |
| | All | 100 | 100 | 100 |
| All subjects | None | 5 | 9 | 7 |
| | One | 15 | 10 | 12 |
| | Monthly | 17 | 19 | 18 |
| | Fortnightly | 25 | 11 | 18 |
| | Weekly | 19 | 14 | 16 |
| | In day-to-day contact | 20 | 37 | 28 |
| | All | 100 | 100 | 100 |

SOURCE: Postgraduate Survey.

333. In arts and social studies postgraduates in their first year received more supervision than those in their second and subsequent years (Table 192). But even in the first year 27 per cent. had not visited their supervisors more than once. The corresponding figure for later years was 34 per cent., with 18 per cent. having had no visits. The most usual arrangements were monthly or fortnightly visits.

334. In science and medicine about half were in day-to-day contact with their supervisors, and three-quarters met them to discuss their work at least weekly.

**Table 193.** *Time spent with faculty supervisor, by subject group and year. Trinity Term 1964*

OXFORD                                                                                                    PERCENTAGE

| Subject group | Time spent with faculty supervisor during the term | Postgraduates in their | | All years |
|---|---|---|---|---|
| | | 1st year | 2nd and subsequent years | |
| Arts and social studies | Under 4 hours | 55 | 56 | 55 |
| | 4 but under 8 hours | 25 | 25 | 25 |
| | 8 but under 16 hours | 14 | 12 | 13 |
| | 16 hours and over | 2 | 6 | 3 |
| | In day-to-day contact | 4 | 1 | 3 |
| | All | 100 | 100 | 100 |
| Science and medicine | Under 4 hours | 18 | 20 | 19 |
| | 4 but under 8 hours | 18 | 17 | 17 |
| | 8 but under 16 hours | 12 | 4 | 7 |
| | 16 hours and over | 9 | 6 | 7 |
| | In day-to-day contact | 43 | 53 | 50 |
| | All | 100 | 100 | 100 |
| All subjects | Under 4 hours | 40 | 32 | 36 |
| | 4 but under 8 hours | 22 | 20 | 21 |
| | 8 but under 16 hours | 13 | 7 | 10 |
| | 16 hours and over | 5 | 6 | 5 |
| | In day-to-day contact | 20 | 35 | 27 |
| | All | 100 | 100 | 100 |

SOURCE: Postgraduate Survey.

NOTE: The proportions in day-to-day contact are slightly different from those in Table 192 since a few in that position gave an estimate of the hours involved.

335. The time spent with the supervisor is more difficult to estimate, and Table 193 may be less accurate than Table 192.[1] It shows less difference between the first and subsequent years in terms of time than was found in frequency of visits. It is quite plausible that postgraduates in their first year made more frequent, but shorter, visits than those in their second year, many of whom would have been settling on the main lines of argument for their theses. Assuming that day-to-day contact amounts to a fairly high number of hours over a term, postgraduates in science and medicine spent considerably longer with their supervisors than did those in arts and social studies, over half of whom spent under four hours.

[1] Estimates of the amount of postgraduate supervision from the Academic Staff Survey were higher than those from the Postgraduate Survey. See Part VI, para. 627.

**Table 194.** *Supervision received by postgraduates, by type of degree aimed at. Trinity Term 1964*

PERCENTAGE

| | Postgraduates reading for | | | |
| --- | --- | --- | --- | --- |
| | B.Litt. and B.Sc. | B.Phil and B.C.L. | D.Phil. | All degrees |
| **VISITS TO FACULTY SUPERVISOR DURING THE TERM** | | | | |
| None | 8 | 13 | 6 | 7 |
| One | 14 | 26 | 11 | 12 |
| Monthly | 27 | 26 | 17 | 18 |
| Fortnightly | 27 | 26 | 16 | 18 |
| Weekly | 5 | 10 | 18 | 16 |
| In day-to-day contact | 19 | — | 32 | 28 |
| All | 100 | 100 | 100 | 100 |
| **TIME SPENT WITH FACULTY SUPERVISOR DURING THE TERM** | | | | |
| Under 4 hours | 46 | 68 | 32 | 36 |
| 4 but under 8 hours | 35 | 23 | 19 | 21 |
| 8 but under 16 hours | 3 | 10 | 11 | 10 |
| 16 hours and over | 3 | — | 6 | 5 |
| In day-to-day contact | 14 | — | 32 | 27 |
| All | 100 | 100 | 100 | 100 |

SOURCE: Postgraduate Survey.

336. Candidates for the B.Phil. and B.C.L. received less supervision than those reading for research degrees, but more provision of other forms of teaching is made for them. The differences in Table 194 between the B.Litt. and B.Sc., and the D.Phil. are largely a result of the concentration of the former in arts and social studies, and of the latter in science and medicine. There were very few B.Sc. students and all received supervision at least weekly. And there were no significant differences between B.Litt. candidates and D.Phil. candidates in arts and social studies.

337. From Table 195 it can be seen that the duration of visits to supervisors was very variable. If the subject groups are considered separately, there was a tendency for the average length of visit, at a given frequency, to be slightly lower in science and medicine than in arts and social studies.

338. The degree of satisfaction with the amount of supervision was high, but was related to the amount received. Of the whole sample, 77 per cent. were satisfied (Table 196). There was a higher level of satisfaction in

**Table 195.** *Time spent with faculty supervisor, by frequency of visits to faculty supervisor. Trinity Term 1964*

OXFORD                                                                                                    PERCENTAGE

| Time spent with faculty supervisor | Visits to faculty supervisor during the term | | | | | |
| | None or one | Monthly | Fort-nightly | Weekly | In day-to-day contact | All |
| --- | --- | --- | --- | --- | --- | --- |
| Under 4 hours | 93 | 67 | 25 | 11 | — | 37 |
| 4 but under 8 hours | 7 | 29 | 54 | 26 | 2 | 21 |
| 8 but under 16 hours | — | 4 | 14 | 37 | 2 | 10 |
| 16 hours and over | — | — | 7 | 24 | 1 | 5 |
| In day-to-day contact | — | — | — | 2 | 95 | 27 |
| All | 100 | 100 | 100 | 100 | 100 | 100 |

SOURCE: Postgraduate Survey.

NOTE: A few postgraduates in day-to-day contact with their supervisor gave an estimate of the total number of hours spent with him.

**Table 196.** *Percentage of postgraduates who were satisfied with the amount of supervision received. Trinity Term 1964*

OXFORD                                                                                    PERCENTAGE

| | Percentage of postgraduates satisfied with amount of supervision received |
| --- | --- |
| Arts and social studies | 76 |
| Science and medicine | 79 |
| 1st year | 79 |
| 2nd and subsequent years | 76 |
| B.Litt. and B.Sc. | 78 |
| B.Phil. and B.C.L. | 65 |
| D.Phil. | 79 |
| Oxford graduates | 80 |
| Graduates of other universities in U.K. | 77 |
| Graduates of overseas universities | 75 |
| All postgraduates | 77 |

SOURCE: Postgraduate Survey.

NOTE: The degree is that aimed at.

science and medicine than in arts and social studies; among the first year than among later years; among candidates for research degrees than among candidates for examination degrees; and among Oxford graduates than among the graduates of other universities.

**Table 197.** *Percentage of postgraduates who were satisfied with the amount of supervision received, by subject group and frequency of visits to faculty supervisor. Trinity Term 1964*

OXFORD                                    PERCENTAGE

| Visits to faculty supervisor during the term | Arts and social studies | Science and medicine | All subjects |
|---|---|---|---|
| None or one | 54 | 35 | 49 |
| Monthly | 84 | 53 | 76 |
| Fortnightly | 79 | 81 | 80 |
| Weekly | 100 | 69 | 77 |
| In day-to-day contact | 100 | 96 | 96 |
| All | 76 | 79 | 77 |

SOURCE: Postgraduate Survey.

339. Only half those with no more than one visit to their supervisor during the term were satisfied, whereas 96 per cent. of those in day-to-day contact were satisfied (Table 197). Between these two extremes the average level of satisfaction was in the region of 75–80 per cent. At each frequency except one the level of satisfaction was lower in science and medicine than in arts and social studies. (The higher over-all level of satisfaction in science and medicine is not inconsistent with this finding, since the average amount of supervision was higher in science and medicine than in arts and social studies.)

340. It was shown in Table 191 that many postgraduates spend much of the vacations in Oxford. Table 198 shows that many also receive supervision during vacations. 50 per cent. received at least 5 hours' supervision during vacations. D.Phil. students received a comparatively large amount of vacation supervision, 26 per cent. receiving 20 hours or more. Candidates for the B.Phil. and B.C.L. received comparatively little. Those in their first year received less than others, and there was a very marked difference between the subject groups. 63 per cent. in science and medicine received 10 hours or more, against 10 per cent. in arts and social studies.

## Other teaching

341. Table 199 summarizes the other forms of teaching received, tutorials, seminars and classes, and lectures, giving averages per week.

Table 198. *Supervision during vacations, by subject group, year, and degree aimed at. Vacations October 1963–September 1964*

OXFORD          PERCENTAGE

| Hours spent with faculty supervisor during vacations | Postgraduates in | | Postgraduates in their | | Postgraduates reading for | | | All post-graduates |
|---|---|---|---|---|---|---|---|---|
| | Arts and social studies | Science and medicine | 1st year | 2nd and subsequent years | B.Litt. and B.Sc. | B.Phil. and B.C.L. | D.Phil. | |
| Less than 1 | 43 | 7 | 34 | 14 | 43 | 65 | 18 | 24 |
| 1 but less than 5 | 33 | 20 | 25 | 28 | 38 | 23 | 26 | 26 |
| 5 but less than 10 | 15 | 10 | 13 | 12 | 5 | 13 | 13 | 13 |
| 10 but less than 20 | 8 | 22 | 14 | 16 | 8 | — | 17 | 15 |
| 20 or more | 2 | 41 | 14 | 30 | 5 | — | 26 | 22 |
| All | 100 | 100 | 100 | 100 | 100 | 100 | 100 | 100 |

SOURCE: Postgraduate Survey.

**Table 199.** *Average number of tutorials, seminars and classes, and lectures attended by postgraduates per week, by subject group, year, and degree aimed at. Michaelmas Term 1964*

OXFORD                                                                                   NUMBER

| | Postgraduates in | | Postgraduates in their | | Postgraduates reading for | | | All post-graduates |
| --- | --- | --- | --- | --- | --- | --- | --- | --- |
| | Arts and social studies | Science and medicine | 2nd year | 3rd and subsequent years | B.Litt. and B.Sc. | B.Phil. and B.C.L. | D.Phil. | |
| Tutorials | 0·20 | 0·03 | 0·18 | 0·04 | 0·09 | 0·52 | 0·07 | 0·11 |
| Seminars and classes | 0·8 | 0·6 | 0·8 | 0·5 | 0·5 | 1·5 | 0·6 | 0·7 |
| Lectures | 1·2 | 0·9 | 1·5 | 0·6 | 1·4 | 3·2 | 0·7 | 1·0 |

SOURCE: Postgraduate Survey.
NOTE: The number of tutorials relates to Trinity Term 1964.

**Table 200.** *Tutorials received by postgraduates, by subject group, year, and degree aimed at. Trinity Term 1964*

OXFORD                                                          PERCENTAGE

| | Frequency of tutorials | | | |
| --- | --- | --- | --- | --- |
| | Not at all | Fortnightly | Weekly | All |
| Arts and social studies | 77 | 11 | 11 | 100 |
| Science and medicine | 97 | 1 | 2 | 100 |
| 1st year | 80 | 9 | 11 | 100 |
| 2nd and subsequent years | 94 | 3 | 3 | 100 |
| B.Litt. and B.Sc. | 86 | 8 | 5 | 100 |
| B.Phil. and B.C.L. | 45 | 23 | 32 | 100 |
| D.Phil. | 91 | 4 | 4 | 100 |
| All postgraduates | 87 | 6 | 7 | 100 |

SOURCE: Postgraduate Survey.

## Tutorials

342. Tutorials were very rare in science and medicine (Table 200). 23 per cent. had regular tutorials in arts and social studies, and a majority of those reading for the B.Phil. and B.C.L. had regular tutorials, a third having them weekly. A slightly higher proportion of those reading for the B.Litt. and B.Sc. had regular tutorials than among doctoral students.

**Table 201.** *Number attending tutorials, by subject group, year, and degree aimed at. Trinity Term 1964*

OXFORD                                                          PERCENTAGE

| | Number attending tutorials | | No tutorials attended | All |
|---|---|---|---|---|
| | 1 | 2 or more | | |
| Arts and social studies | 17 | 5 | 77 | 100 |
| Science and medicine | 2 | 1 | 97 | 100 |
| 1st year | 14 | 6 | 80 | 100 |
| 2nd and subsequent years | 6 | — | 94 | 100 |
| B.Litt. and B.Sc. | 14 | — | 86 | 100 |
| B.Phil. and B.C.L. | 39 | 16 | 45 | 100 |
| D.Phil. | 6 | 2 | 91 | 100 |
| All postgraduates | 10 | 3 | 87 | 100 |

SOURCE: Postgraduate Survey.

343. Table 201 shows that about three-quarters of the tutorials were given singly.

**Table 202.** *Percentage of postgraduates who would prefer more tutorials, by subject group, year, and degree aimed at. Trinity Term 1964*

OXFORD                                                          PERCENTAGE

| | Percentage of postgraduates who would prefer more tutorials than they received in Trinity Term 1964 |
|---|---|
| Arts and social studies | 14 |
| Science and medicine | 14 |
| 1st year | 15 |
| 2nd and subsequent years | 13 |
| B.Litt and B.Sc. | 19 |
| B.Phil. and B.C.L. | 35 |
| D.Phil. | 11 |
| All postgraduates | 14 |

SOURCE: Postgraduate Survey.

344. Table 202 shows that 14 per cent. would have preferred more tutorials (a further 1 per cent. would have preferred fewer). There was no difference between subject groups, despite the wide difference in the proportions receiving tutorials. But there were differences between the different degrees. 35 per cent. of those reading for the B.Phil. and B.C.L. would have preferred more tutorials.

**Table 203.** *Seminars and classes attended by postgraduates, by subject group, year, and degree aimed at. Michaelmas Term 1964*

OXFORD                                                                                   PERCENTAGE

| Number of seminars and classes attended per week | Postgraduates in | | Postgraduates in their | | Postgraduates reading for | | | All post-graduates |
|---|---|---|---|---|---|---|---|---|
| | Arts and social studies | Science and medicine | 2nd year | 3rd and subsequent years | B.Litt. and B.Sc. | B.Phil. and B.C.L. | D.Phil. | |
| None | 55 | 63 | 54 | 64 | 68 | 23 | 62 | 59 |
| 1 | 22 | 23 | 20 | 24 | 19 | 23 | 23 | 22 |
| 2 | 14 | 11 | 16 | 8 | 8 | 39 | 10 | 12 |
| 3 | 8 | 3 | 7 | 3 | 3 | 10 | 5 | 5 |
| 4 or more | 2 | 1 | 2 | 1 | 3 | 6 | 1 | 1 |
| All | 100 | 100 | 100 | 100 | 100 | 100 | 100 | 100 |

SOURCE: Postgraduate Survey.

## Seminars and classes

345. Forty-one per cent. of the sample had attended at least one seminar or class in the week before the survey. Attendance at seminars and classes was rather higher in arts and social studies than in science and medicine; in the second year than in subsequent years; and was much higher (77 per cent.) for B.Phil. and B.C.L. candidates.[1] Table 203 gives details.

## Lectures

346. The pattern for lecture attendances was very similar to that for seminars and classes (Table 204) but the average number attended was slightly higher (see Table 199).

## Opinions on teaching adequacy

347. When asked about the adequacy of seminars, classes, and lectures, about a third expressed a need for more teaching in these forms (Table 205). The main demand was for more seminars. There was less satisfaction in arts and social studies than in science and medicine, and those reading for the B.Phil. and B.C.L. were less satisfied than others.

[1] All B.Phil. candidates in social studies attended at least one seminar.

**Table 204.** *Lectures attended by postgraduates, by subject group, year, and degree aimed at. Michaelmas Term 1964*

OXFORD                                                                PERCENTAGE

| Number of lectures attended per week | Postgraduates in | | Postgraduates in their | | Postgraduates reading for | | | All post-graduates |
|---|---|---|---|---|---|---|---|---|
| | Arts and social studies | Science and medicine | 2nd year | 3rd and subsequent years | B.Litt. and B.Sc. | B.Phil. and B.C.L. | D.Phil. | |
| None | 56 | 61 | 48 | 70 | 49 | 13 | 65 | 59 |
| 1–2 | 25 | 28 | 29 | 24 | 27 | 32 | 26 | 27 |
| 3–5 | 13 | 10 | 17 | 6 | 19 | 35 | 8 | 11 |
| 6–9 | 5 | 1 | 6 | 1 | 5 | 19 | 1 | 3 |
| All | 100 | 100 | 100 | 100 | 100 | 100 | 100 | 100 |

SOURCE: Postgraduate Survey.

## OTHER ACADEMIC MATTERS

### Preparation for postgraduate work

348. Postgraduates were asked whether they had needed any instruction for postgraduate work subsequent to their first degrees. Because a considerable proportion had taken a second degree before coming to Oxford, some of the answers were difficult to interpret. So far as possible Tables 206 and 207 are based on the needs for further instruction on commencing postgraduate work at Oxford. A majority considered they needed no further instruction, and of those who felt some need the most important single one was for instruction in research methods, particularly in arts and social studies. In science and medicine there was a need for instruction in special subjects.

349. A larger proportion of Oxford graduates than of graduates of other universities expressed a need for further instruction. In part, but only in part, this is due to the concentration of Oxford graduates in science and medicine. Graduates of universities overseas expressed the least need for further instruction.

350. When asked whether they had received any instruction in research methods and sources at Oxford,[1] 45 per cent. said they had received none, but had not needed any. A further 25 per cent. had received none, and most of these had expressed some need. The 30 per cent. who had received some instruction specified it in various ways, some by the form of instruction, and some by the subject-matter (Table 208). For scientists, the

---

[1] The question was framed in this way, but it is possible that some respondents interpreted it in a wider sense and included, for instance, instruction in special subjects.

**Table 205.** *Opinions of postgraduates on adequacy of seminars, classes, and lectures, by subject group, year, and degree aimed at. Michaelmas Term 1964*

OXFORD | | | | | | | | PERCENTAGE

| Opinion on adequacy of seminars, classes, and lectures | Postgraduates in | | Postgraduates in their | | Postgraduates reading for | | | All post-graduates |
|---|---|---|---|---|---|---|---|---|
| | Arts and social studies | Science and medicine | 2nd year | 3rd and subsequent years | B.Litt. and B.Sc. | B.Phil. and B.C.L. | D.Phil. | |
| Adequate | 40 | 53 | 50 | 44 | 49 | 39 | 47 | 47 |
| Fairly adequate | 22 | 18 | 20 | 20 | 19 | 19 | 20 | 20 |
| Lectures inadequate | 7 | 8 | 7 | 8 | 11 | 6 | 7 | 8 |
| More general seminars needed | 16 | 14 | 13 | 18 | 14 | 19 | 15 | 15 |
| More advanced seminars needed | 10 | 5 | 6 | 8 | 5 | 6 | 8 | 7 |
| More individual tuition needed | 3 | — | 3 | 1 | — | 6 | 1 | 2 |
| More ancillary teaching needed | 2 | 2 | 2 | 2 | 3 | 3 | 2 | 2 |
| All | 100 | 100 | 100 | 100 | 100 | 100 | 100 | 100 |

SOURCE: Postgraduate Survey.

**Table 206.** *Instruction for postgraduate work needed subsequent to first degree, by subject group and degree aimed at*

OXFORD                                                                PERCENTAGE

| Instruction needed | Postgraduates in | | Postgraduates reading for | | | All postgraduates |
|---|---|---|---|---|---|---|
| | Arts and social studies | Science and medicine | B.Litt. and B.Sc. | B.Phil. and B.C.L. | D.Phil. | |
| None needed | 61 | 57 | 57 | 81 | 57 | 59 |
| Some needed | 9 | 16 | 14 | 6 | 13 | 13 |
| Needed in special subjects | 5 | 15 | 14 | — | 11 | 10 |
| Needed in research methods | 19 | 7 | 14 | 13 | 13 | 13 |
| Needed to catch up with other students | 1 | 2 | — | — | 2 | 2 |
| Needed because embarked on new subject | 4 | 2 | 3 | — | 4 | 3 |
| All | 100 | 100 | 100 | 100 | 100 | 100 |

SOURCE: Postgraduate Survey.

**Table 207.** *Instruction for postgraduate work needed subsequent to first degree, by university of first degree*

OXFORD                                              PERCENTAGE

| Instruction needed | Graduates of | | | All postgraduates |
|---|---|---|---|---|
| | Oxford | Other U.K. universities | Overseas universities | |
| None needed | 51 | 57 | 71 | 59 |
| Some needed | 13 | 16 | 11 | 13 |
| Needed in special subjects | 16 | 13 | 1 | 10 |
| Needed in research methods | 16 | 9 | 11 | 13 |
| Needed to catch up with other students | — | — | 4 | 2 |
| Needed because embarked on new subject | 3 | 6 | 1 | 3 |
| All | 100 | 100 | 100 | 100 |

SOURCE: Postgraduate Survey.

**Table 208.** *Instruction in research methods and sources received at Oxford, by subject group and degree aimed at*

OXFORD                                                                                          PERCENTAGE

| Instruction in research methods and sources received at Oxford | Postgraduates in | | Postgraduates reading for | | | All post-graduates |
|---|---|---|---|---|---|---|
| | Arts and social studies | Science and medicine | B.Litt. and B.Sc. | B.Phil. and B.C.L. | D.Phil. | |
| None | 20 | 29 | 19 | 13 | 27 | 25 |
| None needed or received | 49 | 41 | 43 | 74 | 42 | 45 |
| Informal instruction | 3 | 10 | 11 | — | 7 | 7 |
| Lectures | 7 | 8 | 5 | 6 | 8 | 7 |
| Classes | 7 | 3 | 3 | — | 6 | 5 |
| Other instruction | 3 | 3 | 3 | — | 3 | 3 |
| In research methods | 11 | 5 | 16 | 6 | 7 | 8 |
| All | 100 | 100 | 100 | 100 | 100 | 100 |

SOURCE: Postgraduate Survey.

informal instruction resulting from working alongside experienced researchers was an important component. In arts and social studies 11 per cent. had received instruction in research methods, but some of the 14 per cent. attending lectures and classes almost certainly also received such instruction. There was no difference between the subject groups in the proportion receiving some instruction.

## Opportunities to meet staff and students

351. Postgraduates were asked whether there were senior members other than their faculty supervisor whom they consulted about their work. Only 40 per cent. stated that there were any, the proportion being higher in science and medicine than in arts and social studies, and slightly higher in the third and subsequent years than in the second year.[1] The proportion was particularly low (22 per cent.) among candidates for the B.Litt. and B.Sc. Table 209 gives an indication of how many, and how often senior members were consulted, but the figures should be treated cautiously, as many of the replies were difficult to interpret. For example, 1 per cent. specifically mentioned their college supervisor and are shown accordingly. But it does not follow that only 1 per cent. had a college supervisor, as some may not have mentioned him specifically.

[1] In arts and social studies it was higher (43 per cent.) for those in their third and subsequent years than for those in their second year (33 per cent.). But in science and medicine it was slightly higher (46 per cent. compared with 40 per cent.) for those in their second year.

**Table 209.** *Senior members (other than faculty supervisor) whom postgraduates consult about their work, by subject group, year, and degree aimed at. Michaelmas Term 1964*

OXFORD

PERCENTAGE

| Senior members (other than faculty supervisor) consulted about work | Postgraduates in | | Postgraduates in their | | Postgraduates reading for | | | All post-graduates |
|---|---|---|---|---|---|---|---|---|
| | Arts and social studies | Science and medicine | 2nd year | 3rd and subsequent years | B.Litt. and B.Sc. | B.Phil. and B.C.L. | D.Phil. | |
| None | 63 | 58 | 62 | 59 | 78 | 55 | 59 | 60 |
| One sometimes | 5 | 5 | 5 | 5 | 8 | 6 | 5 | 5 |
| One regularly | 8 | 12 | 11 | 10 | 11 | 16 | 10 | 10 |
| Two or more sometimes | 14 | 12 | 10 | 15 | 3 | 10 | 14 | 13 |
| Two or more regularly | 7 | 13 | 10 | 10 | — | 6 | 11 | 10 |
| College supervisor | 3 | — | 2 | 1 | — | 6 | 1 | 1 |
| All | 100 | 100 | 100 | 100 | 100 | 100 | 100 | 100 |

SOURCE: Postgraduate Survey.

**Table 210.** *Percentage of postgraduates considering that opportunities to meet members of the academic staff and other students in their fields are adequate, by subject group and year. Michaelmas Term 1964*

OXFORD                                                                    PERCENTAGE

| Those considering adequate opportunities exist to meet | Postgraduates in | | Postgraduates in their | | All post-graduates |
|---|---|---|---|---|---|
| | Arts and social studies | Science and medicine | 2nd year | 3rd and subsequent years | |
| Academic staff in their field | 49 | 76 | 57 | 69 | 63 |
| Other students in their field | 56 | 81 | 63 | 74 | 69 |

SOURCE: Postgraduate Survey.

352. Table 210 shows the extent to which postgraduates considered they had sufficient opportunities to meet academic staff and other students in their field. About two-thirds were satisfied, with rather more of them satisfied with opportunities to meet students than with opportunities to meet staff. Over three-quarters in science and medicine were satisfied with opportunities to meet academic staff, against half in arts and social studies. Those who had spent longer in Oxford had more contacts, and were more satisfied.[1]

TEACHING GIVEN BY POSTGRADUATES

353. Postgraduates give university teaching in the form of tutorials and classes for undergraduates and, in science, assist with demonstrating in laboratories. In addition, some give various forms of teaching outside the University.

354. Table 211 shows that 37 per cent. of postgraduates in the survey gave some teaching,[2] 16 per cent. giving up to 3 hours a week, 17 per cent. giving 4–6 hours a week, and 5 per cent. giving over 6 hours a week. There was a big difference between the proportion teaching in arts and social studies and in science and medicine, and also between those in their second year and those in subsequent years.

355. There was a striking difference between the proportion of Oxford graduates teaching and that for other graduates. The proportion of students who taught was higher among D.Phil. students than among candidates for the other degrees (Table 212).

[1] If the subject groups are considered separately, however, it is seen that in arts and social studies the proportion who were satisfied was lower for postgraduates in their second year than for those in subsequent years, but in science and medicine there was no significant difference.

[2] The proportion among all postgraduates, including those in their first year, would doubtless be considerably less.

**Table 211.** *Total teaching given by postgraduates, by subject group and year. Michaelmas Term 1964*

OXFORD                                                                    PERCENTAGE

| Total hours of teaching given per week by post-graduates | Postgraduates in | | Postgraduates in their | | All post-graduates |
|---|---|---|---|---|---|
| | Arts and social studies | Science and medicine | 2nd year | 3rd and subsequent years | |
| None | 75 | 52 | 74 | 53 | 63 |
| 1–3 | 13 | 18 | 13 | 18 | 16 |
| 4–6 | 9 | 23 | 11 | 23 | 17 |
| 7 and over | 3 | 6 | 3 | 6 | 5 |
| All | 100 | 100 | 100 | 100 | 100 |

SOURCE: Postgraduate Survey.

**Table 212.** *Total teaching given by postgraduates, by degree aimed at and university of first degree. Michaelmas Term 1964*

OXFORD                                                                    PERCENTAGE

| Total hours of teaching given per week | Postgraduates reading for | | | Postgraduates with first degrees from | | | All post-graduates |
|---|---|---|---|---|---|---|---|
| | B.Litt. and B.Sc. | B.Phil. and B.C.L. | D.Phil. | Oxford | Other U.K. univer-sities | Overseas univer-sities | |
| None | 78 | 71 | 61 | 47 | 74 | 79 | 63 |
| 1–3 | 8 | 19 | 16 | 25 | 7 | 7 | 16 |
| 4–6 | 11 | 10 | 18 | 23 | 13 | 10 | 17 |
| 7 and over | 3 | — | 5 | 5 | 6 | 4 | 5 |
| All | 100 | 100 | 100 | 100 | 100 | 100 | 100 |

SOURCE: Postgraduate Survey.

356. The way in which the total teaching was made up is given in Table 213. Tables 214–17 give details of the various components.

357. The total hours of teaching were about equally divided between tutorials and classes, demonstrating, and teaching outside the University. Demonstrating only applies in science and medicine, and accounts for the higher average in these subjects compared with arts and social studies. Postgraduates in their third and subsequent years did twice as much teaching as those in their second year, but, again, the difference in demonstrating accounted for much of the difference. D.Phil. students did about twice as much teaching as others.

**Table 213.** *Average hours of teaching given by postgraduates per week, by subject group, year, and degree aimed at. Michaelmas Term 1964*

OXFORD                                                                         HOURS

| | Postgraduates in | | Postgraduates in their | | Postgraduates reading for | | | All post-graduates |
|---|---|---|---|---|---|---|---|---|
| | Arts and social studies | Science and medicine | 2nd year | 3rd and subsequent years | B.Litt. and B.Sc. | B.Phil. and B.C.L. | D.Phil. | |
| Tutorials and classes | 0·7 | 0·6 | 0·5 | 0·7 | 0·2 | 0·5 | 0·6 | 0·6 |
| Demonstrating | — | 1·1 | 0·2 | 1·0 | 0·3 | — | 0·6 | 0·6 |
| Teaching outside the University | 0·4 | 0·6 | 0·4 | 0·6 | 0·5 | 0·4 | 0·5 | 0·5 |
| All teaching | 1·0 | 2·3 | 1·1 | 2·2 | 1·0 | 0·9 | 1·8 | 1·7 |

SOURCE: Postgraduate Survey.

Table 214. *Tutorials and classes given by postgraduates, by subject group, year, and degree aimed at. Michaelmas Term 1964*

OXFORD

PERCENTAGE

| Hours giving tutorials and classes per week | Postgraduates in | | Postgraduates in their | | Postgraduates reading for | | | All post-graduates |
|---|---|---|---|---|---|---|---|---|
| | Arts and social studies | Science and medicine | 2nd year | 3rd and subsequent years | B.Litt. and B.Sc. | B.Phil. and B.C.L. | D.Phil. | |
| None | 83 | 82 | 85 | 80 | 95 | 77 | 81 | 83 |
| 1–3 | 9 | 13 | 10 | 12 | 3 | 19 | 11 | 11 |
| 4–6 | 6 | 4 | 4 | 6 | 3 | 3 | 6 | 5 |
| 7–10 | 2 | 1 | 1 | 2 | — | — | 2 | 1 |
| All | 100 | 100 | 100 | 100 | 100 | 100 | 100 | 100 |

SOURCE: Postgraduate Survey.

358. Tutorials were given by 17 per cent., there being little difference between the two subject groups, or between second and subsequent years.[1] Very few candidates for the B.Litt. or B.Sc. gave tutorials (Table 214).

**Table 215.** *Demonstrating in laboratories by postgraduates, by year. Postgraduates in science and medicine. Michaelmas Term 1964*

OXFORD PERCENTAGE

| Hours of demonstrating in laboratories per week | Postgraduates in science and medicine in | | |
|---|---|---|---|
| | 2nd year | 3rd and subsequent years | All years |
| None | 89 | 71 | 77 |
| 1–3 | 1 | 6 | 5 |
| 4–6 | 9 | 23 | 18 |
| All | 100 | 100 | 100 |

SOURCE: Postgraduate Survey.

359. In science and medicine, 23 per cent. did demonstrating, the proportion being higher (29 per cent.) for those in their third and subsequent years.

**Table 216.** *Teaching outside the University by postgraduates, by subject group. Michaelmas Term 1964*

OXFORD PERCENTAGE

| Hours teaching outside the University per week | Postgraduates in | | |
|---|---|---|---|
| | Arts and social studies | Science and medicine | All subjects |
| None | 91 | 83 | 87 |
| 1–3 | 5 | 10 | 7 |
| 4 or more | 4 | 7 | 6 |
| All | 100 | 100 | 100 |

SOURCE: Postgraduate Survey.

[1] But in science and medicine there was no significant difference between the proportion giving tutorials in the second year, and in subsequent years; whereas in arts and social studies it was 11 per cent. in the second year, and 28 per cent. for subsequent years.

360. Teaching outside the University was done by 13 per cent. The proportion was higher in science and medicine (17 per cent.) than in arts and social studies (9 per cent.). There were no significant differences between postgraduates in different years, or taking different degrees.

361. Table 217 shows the type of teaching given outside the University. The most frequent type of teaching was private tuition, and this was more frequent in science and medicine than in arts and social studies.

**Table 217.** *Type of teaching given outside the University by postgraduates, by subject group. Michaelmas Term 1964*

| OXFORD | | | PERCENTAGE |
|---|---|---|---|
| Type of teaching given outside the University | Postgraduates in | | |
| | Arts and social studies | Science and medicine | All subjects |
| None | 90 | 83 | 87 |
| Schools | 1 | 2 | 1 |
| Technical colleges | 2 | 2 | 2 |
| LEA evening classes | — | 1 | 1 |
| WEA evening classes | 1 | 2 | 1 |
| Private tuition | 2 | 7 | 5 |
| Other | 4 | 4 | 4 |
| All | 100 | 100 | 100 |

SOURCE: Postgraduate Survey.

### POSTS HELD BY POSTGRADUATES

362. There is a certain amount of overlapping between the academic staff and postgraduates registered as reading for a higher degree, and details are given in Part VI, para. 602. Anyone in the original sample for the Postgraduate Survey who was a full-time teacher (such as university lecturer, CUF lecturer, or full-time departmental demonstrator) was excluded from the tabulations. But included in the survey were research fellows of colleges, holders of departmental research and similar posts, and part-time departmental demonstrators. 10 per cent. of the sample held such posts, the proportion being 14 per cent. in science, and 15 per cent. for those in their third and subsequent years. Table 218 gives details.

### ADVICE ON NON-ACADEMIC MATTERS

363. Only 18 per cent. of postgraduates considered they had no one to turn to with problems of a non-academic nature. This proportion was lowest for Oxford graduates, and highest (24 per cent.) for graduates of overseas

**Table 218.** *Posts held by postgraduates. Michaelmas Term 1964*

OXFORD

| | Postgraduates in | | Postgraduates in their | | Postgraduates with first degrees from | | | PERCENTAGE |
| --- | --- | --- | --- | --- | --- | --- | --- | --- |
| | Arts and social studies | Science and medicine | 2nd year | 3rd and subsequent years | Oxford | Other U.K. universities | Overseas universities | All postgraduates |
| No post | 96 | 86 | 96 | 85 | 88 | 90 | 94 | 90 |
| Research fellow | 2 | 1 | 1 | 3 | 2 | 1 | 1 | 2 |
| Part-time departmental demonstrator | — | 10 | 2 | 9 | 10 | 1 | 2 | 5 |
| Research assistant | 1 | 3 | 2 | 2 | 1 | 7 | 1 | 2 |
| Other posts | 2 | — | — | 2 | 1 | — | 1 | 1 |
| All | 100 | 100 | 100 | 100 | 100 | 100 | 100 | 100 |

SOURCE: Postgraduate Survey.

NOTE: The graduates of overseas universities holding research fellowships were also graduates of Oxford.

universities. Nearly a quarter mentioned someone in his college as being available, and 9 per cent. mentioned someone elsewhere (in departments, friends outside the University, etc.). Half the sample said there was someone, but did not specify who it was. There was little difference between postgraduates in different years (and even less between subject groups). (See Tables 219 and 220.)

**Table 219.** *Persons postgraduates can consult* (*other than their supervisor*) *for non-academic advice, by year and university of first degree. Michaelmas Term 1964*

OXFORD                                                                                          PERCENTAGE

| Persons postgraduates can consult (other than their supervisor) on non-academic problems | Postgraduates in their | | Postgraduates with first degrees from | | | All postgraduates |
|---|---|---|---|---|---|---|
| | 2nd year | 3rd and subsequent years | Oxford | Other U.K. universities | Overseas universities | |
| No one | 19 | 18 | 14 | 17 | 24 | 18 |
| Someone (not specified) | 53 | 47 | 48 | 53 | 52 | 50 |
| Someone in college | 23 | 22 | 26 | 26 | 17 | 22 |
| Someone elsewhere | 5 | 13 | 12 | 4 | 7 | 9 |
| All | 100 | 100 | 100 | 100 | 100 | 100 |

SOURCE: Postgraduate Survey.

**Table 220.** *Persons postgraduates can consult* (*other than their supervisor*) *for non-academic advice, by college group. Michaelmas Term 1964*

OXFORD                                                                                          PERCENTAGE

| Persons postgraduates can consult (other than their supervisor) on non-academic problems | Men's societies | Women's colleges | Graduate societies | All societies |
|---|---|---|---|---|
| No one | 19 | 20 | 15 | 18 |
| Someone (not specified) | 48 | 45 | 64 | 50 |
| Someone in college | 24 | 25 | 15 | 22 |
| Someone elsewhere | 10 | 9 | 7 | 9 |
| All | 100 | 100 | 100 | 100 |

SOURCE: Postgraduate Survey.

## POSTGRADUATES AND THE COLLEGES

364. All postgraduates must matriculate and must therefore become members of a college or other society.[1] Postgraduates in the survey were asked a number of questions about the provisions their college made for them, and about their preferences for different forms of college organization.

365. The distribution of postgraduates in the sample between the different types of society is given in Table 221. Nearly three-quarters were in the men's societies, a tenth in the women's colleges, and a sixth in the graduate societies. (In 1964-5 the distribution of all postgraduates was 73·9 per cent. at the men's societies, 12·6 per cent. at the women's colleges, and 13·5 per cent. at the graduate societies.) In science and medicine there were 84 per cent. at the men's societies. The proportion at the men's societies was lower for second than for subsequent years. Of Oxford graduates, 88 per cent. were at the men's societies. Nearly a fifth of other postgraduates were at Linacre College (Table 221).

## College accommodation

366. Colleges provided accommodation for 15 per cent. of the postgraduates. This is the figure for a particular year, and since few postgraduates spend all their time at Oxford in college accommodation, the proportion of postgraduates spending at least a year in college accommodation will be considerably higher. A majority of colleges have adopted a policy of giving unmarried postgraduates from other, and especially overseas, universities their first year at Oxford in college. Hence the figure of 15 per cent. would certainly have been higher if first-year postgraduates could have been included. 38 per cent. of postgraduates at the graduate societies were in college accommodation, these being almost all at Nuffield College and St. Antony's College. The least accommodation was provided by the women's colleges. Colleges made more provision for graduates of overseas universities than for those from the U.K. (See Table 222.)

367. The proportion in college or college accommodation was higher for postgraduates in their second than for those in subsequent years (Table 223). None of those who were married with their family in Oxford was in college, but 6 per cent. lived in college accommodation.

## College facilities

368. Postgraduates were asked what facilities their college provided for them and how much they used the facilities. The answers are tabulated in

---

[1] Except for certain diploma students who were not included in the Postgraduate Survey.

**Table 221.** *College group of postgraduates, by subject group, year, and university of first degree. Michaelmas Term 1964*

OXFORD

PERCENTAGE

| | Postgraduates in | | Postgraduates in their | | Postgraduates with first degrees from | | | All post-graduates |
|---|---|---|---|---|---|---|---|---|
| | Arts and social studies | Science and medicine | 2nd year | 3rd and subsequent years | Oxford | Other U.K. universities | Overseas universities | |
| Men's societies | 61 | 84 | 69 | 76 | 88 | 57 | 61 | 73 |
| Women's colleges | 16 | 7 | 13 | 10 | 8 | 19 | 12 | 11 |
| Nuffield and St. Antony's | 12 | — | 7 | 5 | 4 | 4 | 9 | 6 |
| Linacre | 11 | 9 | 10 | 9 | — | 19 | 18 | 10 |
| Graduate societies | 23 | 9 | 18 | 14 | 4 | 24 | 27 | 16 |
| All societies | 100 | 100 | 100 | 100 | 100 | 100 | 100 | 100 |

SOURCE: Postgraduate Survey.

**Table 222.** *Where postgraduates live in Oxford, by college group and university of first degree. Michaelmas Term 1964*

OXFORD

PERCENTAGE

| | Postgraduates in | | | Postgraduates with first degrees from | | | All post-graduates |
|---|---|---|---|---|---|---|---|
| Postgraduates living | Men's societies | Women's colleges | Graduate societies | Oxford | Other U.K. universities | Overseas universities | |
| In college | 10 | 5 | 23 | 9 | 7 | 16 | 11 |
| In college accommodation | 2 | — | 15 | 2 | — | 7 | 4 |
| Elsewhere | 89 | 95 | 62 | 89 | 93 | 76 | 85 |
| All | 100 | 100 | 100 | 100 | 100 | 100 | 100 |

SOURCE: Postgraduate Survey.

**Table 223.** *Where postgraduates live in Oxford, by year and marital status.*
*Michaelmas Term 1964*

OXFORD                                                                    PERCENTAGE

| Postgraduates living | Postgraduates in their | | Postgraduates who were | | All post-graduates |
|---|---|---|---|---|---|
| | 2nd year | 3rd and subsequent years | Single or married, family not in Oxford | Married, family in Oxford | |
| In college | 13 | 9 | 16 | — | 11 |
| In college accommodation | 5 | 2 | 3 | 6 | 4 |
| Elsewhere | 82 | 89 | 81 | 94 | 85 |
| All | 100 | 100 | 100 | 100 | 100 |

SOURCE: Postgraduate Survey.

Tables 224–8. The facilities are as the postgraduates recorded them, not
necessarily the facilities actually provided. It was clear from inspection
of the replies that some did not record facilities which were recorded by
others at the same college, and which therefore presumably existed. This
could be because the person was not aware of the facilities, or because he
did not think they amounted to anything worth recording.

**Table 224.** *College facilities specified by postgraduates, by college group.*
*Michaelmas Term 1964*

OXFORD                                                                    PERCENTAGE

| College facilities specified | Men's societies | Women's colleges | Graduate societies | All societies |
|---|---|---|---|---|
| None or same as for undergraduates | 24 | 32 | 30 | 26 |
| Middle Common Room, etc. | 76 | 68 | 13 | 65 |
| Graduate society | — | — | 57 | 9 |
| All | 100 | 100 | 100 | 100 |

SOURCE: Postgraduate Survey.

369. The facilities have been divided into three groups as in Table 224.
The main provision made for postgraduates by the undergraduate colleges
was a Middle Common Room. Because of the varying amount of detail it
might be misleading to subdivide the facilities in the tables. But over all
54 per cent. simply mentioned a MCR; 5 per cent. mentioned a graduate

building (and perhaps a MCR also); 4 per cent. said facilities were planned;[1] and 3 per cent. mentioned academic facilities such as lectures, seminars, or a college supervisor (and perhaps a MCR also). Three-quarters of those at the men's societies specified a MCR and related facilities. The corresponding figure for the women's colleges was two-thirds. Only 57 per cent. at the graduate societies described the facilities in terms indicating facilities differing from those in traditional societies.[2]

**Table 225.** *College facilities specified by postgraduates, by university of first degree. Michaelmas Term 1964*

| OXFORD | | | | PERCENTAGE |
|---|---|---|---|---|
| College facilities specified | Postgraduates with first degrees from | | | All post-graduates |
| | Oxford | Other U.K. universities | Overseas universities | |
| None or same as for undergraduates | 20 | 26 | 33 | 26 |
| Middle Common Room, etc. | 77 | 60 | 54 | 65 |
| Graduate society | 3 | 14 | 13 | 9 |
| All | 100 | 100 | 100 | 100 |

SOURCE: Postgraduate Survey.

370. When postgraduates are classified according to where they obtained their degrees, they show very differing assessments of the facilities provided. Oxford graduates were more aware of college facilities, or attached a greater value to them, than did graduates from other universities. Graduates of overseas universities reported fewest facilities.

371. Of postgraduates reporting no college facilities specifically for postgraduates, 11 per cent. used undergraduate facilities (often for sports), 5 per cent. regularly ate in college, and 2 per cent. used academic facilities (usually the college library). Of those reporting facilities for postgraduates, 37 per cent. made little or no use of the facilities. 56 per cent. made use of the MCR (or ate in college regularly), 31 per cent. doing so regularly.[3] 4 per cent. used academic facilities. Of those stating their college was a graduate society and provided the corresponding facilities, 20 per cent. made little or no use of their college's facilities.[4] (Table 226.)

[1] These are included as existing facilities, as respondents mentioning planned facilities indicated they were due to come into operation shortly after the survey.
[2] Postgraduates at Nuffield College and St. Antony's College almost all described their college's facilities in these terms.
[3] i.e. where postgraduates described their use as regular, weekly, or in similar terms.
[4] Almost all these 20 per cent. were at Linacre College.

**Table 226.** *College facilities used by postgraduates, by facilities specified. Michaelmas Term 1964*

OXFORD                                                                                PERCENTAGE

| Use of college facilities | Postgraduates specifying stated college facilities | | | All postgraduates |
|---|---|---|---|---|
|  | None or same as for undergraduates | MCR etc. | Graduate college |  |
| Little or no use | 82 | 37 | 20 | 47 |
| Use of undergraduate facilities | 11 | 2 | — | 4 |
| Some use of MCR | — | 25 | — | 17 |
| Regular use of MCR and/or regular meals | 5 | 31 | — | 22 |
| Use of academic facilities | 2 | 4 | — | 3 |
| Use of all facilities (graduate society) | — | — | 80 | 7 |
| All | 100 | 100 | 100 | 100 |

SOURCE: Postgraduate Survey.

372. A smaller than average proportion of those living in college accommodation made little or no use of their college's facilities, but this is largely because a considerable proportion of such postgraduates were at graduate societies. For the remainder there would be much less difference from those not living in college accommodation, except that where college facilities were used they were more likely to be used regularly. There was not a great deal of difference in the use of college facilities between Oxford and other graduates, except that overseas graduates were less likely to use their MCR regularly (Table 227). Married postgraduates with their families in Oxford were less likely to use their college facilities than were others, and when they used them were less likely to do so regularly (Table 228). Nevertheless, over two-fifths did use college facilities.

## Preferences for college organization

373. Postgraduates were asked to state a preference between a number of alternative forms of college organization for postgraduates.[1] The results are in Tables 229–31. Rather less than half chose the existing system in which there is a choice of traditional societies, specialized (as to fields of study) graduate colleges (Nuffield and St. Antony's), and an unspecialized graduate society (Linacre), and in which college membership is obligatory.

[1] The question is reproduced in Part VI. It is question 27 in the Postgraduate Survey questionnaire.

**Table 227.** *College facilities used by postgraduates, by where living and university of first degree. Michaelmas Term 1964*

OXFORD

PERCENTAGE

| Use of college facilities | Postgraduates who live | | Postgraduates with first degrees from | | | All postgraduates |
|---|---|---|---|---|---|---|
| | In college or college accommodation | Elsewhere | Oxford | Other U.K. universities | Overseas universities | |
| Little or no use | 33 | 50 | 45 | 43 | 52 | 47 |
| Use of undergraduate facilities | 2 | 5 | 7 | 3 | 2 | 4 |
| Some use of MCR | 7 | 18 | 16 | 16 | 18 | 17 |
| Regular use of MCR and/or regular meals | 25 | 21 | 28 | 27 | 11 | 22 |
| Use of academic facilities | 5 | 3 | 2 | 1 | 6 | 3 |
| Use of all facilities (graduate society) | 28 | 4 | 3 | 10 | 11 | 7 |
| All | 100 | 100 | 100 | 100 | 100 | 100 |

SOURCE: Postgraduate Survey.

22 per cent. chose postgraduate societies, with the primary academic responsibility remaining (as it is now) with the University; 9 per cent. chose postgraduate societies with full academic responsibility; and 21 per cent. chose university academic responsibility with optional membership of a social centre (2 per cent.), a postgraduate society (8 per cent.), or a traditional society (11 per cent.). Of those preferring postgraduate societies, only a quarter wanted them specialized as to fields of study.

**Table 228.** *College facilities used by postgraduates, by marital status. Michaelmas Term 1964*

OXFORD                                                          PERCENTAGE

| Use of college facilities | Postgraduates who were | | All postgraduates |
| --- | --- | --- | --- |
| | Single or married, family not in Oxford | Married, family in Oxford | |
| Little or none | 44 | 54 | 47 |
| Use of undergraduate facilities | 5 | 2 | 4 |
| Some use of MCR | 15 | 20 | 17 |
| Regular use of MCR and/or regular meals | 26 | 12 | 22 |
| Use of academic facilities | 2 | 5 | 3 |
| Use of all facilities (graduate society) | 7 | 7 | 7 |
| All | 100 | 100 | 100 |

SOURCE: Postgraduate Survey.

374. The chief features of Table 229 are that women were the least in favour of the existing situation, and voted heavily for postgraduate societies. It was amongst members of the graduate societies that the largest proportion were in favour of the primary academic responsibility being with the college rather than the University, but the proportion was only 16 per cent. For each of the college groups, about two-thirds were either in favour of the existing system, or of postgraduate societies, the University having the primary academic responsibility. A quarter of those at the men's societies chose the alternative under which college membership would be optional.

375. The main differences between the subject groups (see Table 230) were that there was a greater preference for postgraduate societies taking full academic responsibility in arts and social studies (the fact that students at Nuffield and St. Antony's were in these subjects explains some but not all of this), and for optional college membership in science and medicine.

**Table 229.** *Postgraduates' preferences for college organization, by college group and where living. Michaelmas Term 1964*

OXFORD                                                                                    PERCENTAGE

| Preference for college organization for postgraduates | Postgraduates in | | | Postgraduates living | | All post-graduates |
|---|---|---|---|---|---|---|
| | Men's societies | Women's colleges | Graduate societies | In college or college accommodation | Else-where | |
| 1. Existing choice | 52 | 27 | 33 | 37 | 48 | 46 |
| 2. Postgraduate societies, with primary academic responsibility with the University | 16 | 43 | 34 | 28 | 21 | 22 |
| 3. Postgraduate societies, with primary academic responsibility with the society | 6 | 14 | 16 | 14 | 8 | 9 |
| 4. All academic responsibility with the University and optional membership of: | | | | | | |
| a social centre | 2 | 5 | 3 | 2 | 2 | 2 |
| a postgraduate society | 8 | 9 | 7 | 4 | 8 | 8 |
| a combined postgraduate and undergraduate society | 14 | — | 2 | 14 | 10 | 11 |
| 5. No answer | 2 | 2 | 5 | 2 | 3 | 3 |
| Those preferring 2 or 3 who prefer postgraduate societies to be: | | | | | | |
| specialized as to fields of study | 5 | 16 | 13 | 12 | 6 | 7 |
| not specialized as to fields of study | 16 | 39 | 31 | 25 | 20 | 21 |
| All | 100 | 100 | 100 | 100 | 100 | 100 |

SOURCE: Postgraduate Survey.

NOTE: Some who chose 4 did not specify any of the three sub-groups. They have been allocated to these groups in the same proportion as others choosing 4.

376. A larger proportion of those in their third and subsequent years chose the existing situation, compared with second-year postgraduates, but this was partly due to those reading science and medicine being more strongly represented in the later years.[1]

377. A high proportion of Oxford graduates chose the existing situation (59 per cent.). But Table 231 shows that the proportion choosing either this or postgraduate societies with the primary academic responsibility with the University was not so much above the average. Graduates of overseas universities were more strongly in favour of postgraduate societies carrying the primary academic responsibility than were graduates of Oxford or of other U.K. universities.

[1] There was a slightly smaller proportion in favour of optional college membership in the third and subsequent years. This is the opposite of what might have been expected in view of the greater concentration of scientists in these years.

**Table 230.** *Postgraduates' preferences for college organization, by subject group and year. Michaelmas Term 1964*

OXFORD                                                                    PERCENTAGE

| Preference for college organization for postgraduates | Postgraduates in | | Postgraduates in their | | All post-graduates |
|---|---|---|---|---|---|
| | Arts and social studies | Science and medicine | 2nd year | 3rd and subsequent years | |
| 1. Existing choice | 39 | 53 | 41 | 51 | 46 |
| 2. Postgraduate societies, with primary academic responsibility with the University | 28 | 16 | 24 | 20 | 22 |
| 3. Postgraduate societies, with primary academic responsibility with the society | 15 | 3 | 9 | 9 | 9 |
| 4. All academic responsibility with the University and optional membership of: | | | | | |
| a social centre | 2 | 2 | 2 | 2 | 2 |
| a postgraduate society | 5 | 10 | 8 | 7 | 8 |
| a combined postgraduate and undergraduate society | 9 | 12 | 13 | 9 | 11 |
| 5. No answer | 2 | 3 | 3 | 3 | 3 |
| Those preferring 2 or 3 who prefer postgraduate societies to be: | | | | | |
| specialized as to fields of study | 15 | — | 10 | 4 | 7 |
| not specialized as to fields of study | 27 | 16 | 21 | 21 | 21 |
| All | 100 | 100 | 100 | 100 | 100 |

SOURCE: Postgraduate Survey.
NOTE: See note to Table 229.

## AWARDS HELD BY POSTGRADUATES

378. This paragraph is not based on the Postgraduate Survey, and refers to all postgraduates. The proportion of postgraduates who held awards (mainly from colleges) was small—about 10 per cent. of postgraduates other than Part II chemists and metallurgists in 1964—but the average value was high: £286 for college awards and £328 for university awards held by postgraduates other than Part II chemists and metallurgists. Table 232 gives details. The awards held by Part II chemists and metallurgists may be presumed to have been undergraduate awards extended for a fourth year, and had an average value of £60. (See Part III, para. 294 for details of undergraduate awards.)

**Table 231.** *Postgraduates' preferences for college organization by university of first degree. Michaelmas Term 1964*

OXFORD

PERCENTAGE

| Preference for college organization for postgraduates | Postgraduates with first degrees from | | | All post-graduates |
|---|---|---|---|---|
| | Oxford | Other U.K. universities | Overseas universities | |
| 1. Existing choice | 59 | 37 | 35 | 46 |
| 2. Postgraduate societies, with primary academic responsibility with the University | 17 | 30 | 24 | 22 |
| 3. Postgraduate societies, with primary academic responsibility with the society | 5 | 4 | 17 | 9 |
| 4. All academic responsibility with the University and optional membership of: | | | | |
| a social centre | 2 | 6 | 1 | 2 |
| a postgraduate society | 4 | 11 | 10 | 8 |
| a combined postgraduate and undergraduate society | 13 | 7 | 10 | 11 |
| 5. No answer | 1 | 4 | 4 | 3 |
| Those preferring 2 or 3 who prefer postgraduate societies to be: | | | | |
| specialized as to fields of study | 3 | 6 | 13 | 7 |
| not specialized as to fields of study | 17 | 29 | 23 | 21 |
| All | 100 | 100 | 100 | 100 |

SOURCE: Postgraduate Survey.

NOTE: See note to Table 229.

**Table 232.** *Awards held by postgraduates in 1964*

OXFORD

| Awards made by | Number of postgraduates receiving financial benefit from awards in Michaelmas Term 1964 | | Total amount paid in 1964 to postgraduates in respect of awards held | | Amount derived from Trust Funds only |
|---|---|---|---|---|---|
| | Part II chemists and metallurgists | Other post-graduates | Part II chemists and metallurgists | Other post-graduates | |
| | | | £ | £ | £ |
| Men's colleges | 71 | 80 | 4,328 | 15,390 | 10,883 |
| Permanent Private Halls | — | — | — | — | — |
| Men's societies | 71 | 80 | 4,328 | 15,390 | 10,883 |
| Women's colleges | 4 | 13 | 156 | 1,595 | 1,725 |
| Undergraduate societies | 75 | 93 | 4,484 | 16,985 | 12,608 |
| Graduate societies | — | 47 | — | 23,006 | 4,335 |
| All societies | 75 | 140 | 4,484 | 39,991 | 16,943 |
| University | — | 32 | — | 10,498 | 10,498 |

SOURCE: Registry and colleges.

NOTE: For one college the amount derived from Trust Funds is an estimated figure.

**Table 233.** *Time taken for, and proportion completing, research degrees. Postgraduates admitted in 1953–4*

OXFORD     PERCENTAGE

| Degree, subject, and university of first degree | Degree obtained in | | | | | Total obtaining degree | Obtained bachelor's degree | Withdrawn or failed by 1960 | Outstanding in 1960 | All | Number | Percentage of total |
|---|---|---|---|---|---|---|---|---|---|---|---|---|
| | 1st or 2nd year | 3rd year | 4th year | 5th year | 6th or 7th year | | | | | | | |
| B.Litt. | 6 | 13 | 9 | 4 | 5 | 37 | — | 61 | 3 | 100 | 112 | 32 |
| B.Sc. | 13 | 27 | 9 | — | 5 | 54 | — | 46 | — | 100 | 22 | 6 |
| D.Phil.: arts and social studies | 1 | 13 | 17 | 11 | 13 | 55 | 9 | 26 | 11 | 100 | 93 | 26 |
| D.Phil.: science and medicine | 3 | 28 | 26 | 12 | 11 | 80 | 3 | 13 | 4 | 100 | 125 | 36 |
| Arts and social studies | 4 | 13 | 13 | 7 | 9 | 45 | 4 | 45 | 6 | 100 | 205 | 58 |
| Science and medicine | 5 | 28 | 23 | 10 | 10 | 76 | 3 | 18 | 3 | 100 | 147 | 42 |
| Oxford | .. | .. | .. | .. | .. | 61 | 2 | 33 | 4 | 100 | 166 | 47 |
| Other U.K. universities | .. | .. | .. | .. | .. | 57 | 5 | 33 | 5 | 100 | 60 | 17 |
| Overseas universities | .. | .. | .. | .. | .. | 55 | 4 | 35 | 6 | 100 | 126 | 36 |
| All | 4 | 19 | 17 | 8 | 9 | 58 | 3 | 34 | 5 | 100 | 352 | 100 |

SOURCE: Report of the Committee on Postgraduate Studies, in Supplement* No. 2 to the *University Gazette* (February 1964), Annex B.
NOTE: The degree is that entered for.

**Table 234.** *Time taken for, and proportion completing, advanced courses. Graduates of other universities matriculating in 1958–9*

OXFORD          PERCENTAGE

| Degree and subject | Degree obtained in | | | | | Total obtaining degree by Sept. 1964 | Not obtaining degree | All | Number in sample | Percentage of total |
|---|---|---|---|---|---|---|---|---|---|---|
| | 2nd year | 3rd year | 4th year | 5th year | 6th year | | | | | |
| B.Litt. | — | 13 | 13 | 9 | — | 34 | 66 | 100 | 32 | 33 |
| B.Sc. | 20 | 20 | — | 40 | — | 80 | 20 | 100 | 5 | 5 |
| B.Phil. | 43 | 29 | 14 | — | — | 86 | 14 | 100 | 7 | 7 |
| B.C.L. | 33 | 67 | — | — | — | 100 | — | 100 | 3 | 3 |
| D.Phil.: arts and social studies | — | 5 | 5 | 11 | 21 | 42 | 58 | 100 | 19 | 20 |
| D.Phil.: science and medicine | 7 | 23 | 40 | 20 | 3 | 93 | 7 | 100 | 30 | 31 |
| Arts and social studies | 7 | 15 | 10 | 8 | 7 | 46 | 54 | 100 | 61 | 64 |
| Science and medicine | 9 | 23 | 34 | 23 | 3 | 91 | 9 | 100 | 35 | 36 |
| All | 7 | 18 | 19 | 14 | 5 | 63 | 38 | 100 | 96 | 100 |

SOURCE: 1958–9 matriculations sample.

NOTE: The degree is that obtained, not necessarily that entered for.

PERFORMANCE AND WASTAGE OF POSTGRADUATES

379. The University Committee on Postgraduate Studies compiled some statistics on postgraduates who were admitted to read for research degrees in 1953–4, and these are summarized in Table 233. The proportion who obtained the degree they were entered for by 1960 was 58 per cent., a further 3 per cent. having submitted for a doctorate being awarded a B.Litt. or B.Sc. The proportion obtaining a degree was much higher in science and medicine than in arts and social studies. This was partly because of the very low proportion obtaining the B.Litt., but there was also a large difference between the two subject groups when doctoral students only are considered. The proportion obtaining a degree was highest for Oxford graduates, and lowest for overseas graduates. But if the high concentration of Oxford graduates in science and medicine observed in the Postgraduate Survey held for postgraduates admitted in 1953–4, this could well explain the difference in the proportion obtaining a degree between Oxford and other graduates.

380. The average time taken to obtain a degree was shorter in science and medicine than in arts and social studies, for both the bachelor's degrees and the D.Phil.

381. Some similar data for 1958–9 entrants from universities other than Oxford are given in Table 234. They are derived from the sample of 1958–9 matriculations, and therefore do not include Oxford graduates beginning postgraduate work in 1958–9. Being a sample, and excluding Oxford graduates, the numbers are much smaller than in Table 233.

382. The main differences between Tables 233 and 234 are that the proportion obtaining a degree was higher in science and medicine for 1958–9 entrants than for 1953–4 entrants, while it fell a little in arts and social studies. The average time spent over a D.Phil. increased a little in arts and social studies, but remained steady in science and medicine. These results should be treated with caution, however, because the number of 1958–9 entrants is small, and the two sets of figures are not fully comparable.

# PART V

---

# THE ACADEMIC STAFF

---

383. The classification of the various academic posts at Oxford is complicated by the college system, and it is different from that of any other
British university. If Cambridge (which has arrangements similar to, but
by no means identical with, those at Oxford) is excluded, the chief
differences are:

(a) that all professors receive the same salary[2] (though some do also
receive allowances for departmental responsibilities);

(b) that there is no grade of senior lecturer;

(c) that, as a corollary to (b), the lecturers' scale rises to £2,760, three
increments above the national maximum of £2,505;[3]

(d) that the lecturers' scale is a rigid age-wage scale;

(e) that any university post save that of professor may be held together
with a paid college post, and that there are a considerable number
of part-time university posts which are tenable *only* by those who
also hold a paid college post;

(f) that there is no grade of assistant lecturer (the grade of departmental
demonstrator is analogous to it; but it exists only in the science
faculties, and the number of full-time departmental demonstrators
is small);

(g) that some members of the academic staff are employed only by the
colleges and hold no university post.

## University posts

384. A list of the University's academic posts at 1 January 1965 at the level
of lecturer and above,[4] except those in clinical medicine, is contained in

---

[1] The description relates to 1964–5. Since then there has been a change which is
described in para. 409.

[2] Except for a differential between clinical and other professors.

[3] Throughout this Part, salaries and salary scales are those in force in 1964–5.

[4] The list includes statutory posts charged against the General Board's budget, and
all those where appointment is made by, or must be approved by, the General Board.

evidence from the General Board (*Written Evidence*, Part XII, pp. 25-39). The main posts are:

(*a*) professor;
(*b*) reader;
(*c*) university lecturer;
(*d*) senior research officer;
(*e*) Common University Fund (CUF)
(*f*) special lecturer;
(*g*) faculty lecturer.

385. Professors hold *ex officio* non-stipendiary college fellowships; (*b*)-(*d*) may be held together with a paid college post; (*e*)-(*g*) are part-time posts which are peculiar to Oxford and are designed to meet its special needs and can only be held together with a paid college post. There are also certain special grades in particular university institutions. They include tutors in the Department and Institute of Education and in the Department of Social and Administrative Studies, and certain research posts. These posts may be held together with a paid college post.

386. Posts in clinical medicine (apart from statutory ones) are administered by the Nuffield Committee for the Advancement of Medicine (Nuffield Committee) rather than the General Board, although the General Board provides the funds for some of them. The posts in clinical medicine include five statutory professorships which are a charge on the funds of the Nuffield Medical Benefaction. The main posts are:

(*a*) professor;
(*b*) reader and first assistant;
(*c*) lecturer;
(*d*) research officer.

For grades (*b*)-(*d*) there are separate salary scales for those with and those without medical qualifications; these posts may be held together with a paid college post. The *title* of university lecturer or clinical lecturer (without stipend) may be conferred on members of hospital staffs who contribute to the work of the Medical School, but these persons do not fall within our definition of the academic staff.

387. There are also junior posts to which appointment is made departmentally. They may be held together with a paid college post. Most are short-term research posts. Departmental demonstratorships are short-term teaching posts;[1] they may be full-time or part-time and they carry no automatic or even semi-automatic prospect of promotion to a permanent post.

[1] Junior lecturerships in Mathematics are similar.

## College posts

388. The most common college post is that of tutorial fellow, a main duty of which is to teach undergraduates in the college. (Official Fellows of Nuffield College and St. Antony's College are here regarded as tutorial fellows; they have similar responsibilities towards the postgraduates in their colleges.) But there are also research fellows—short-term junior research fellows or longer-term senior research fellows.[1] There are also college lecturers, i.e. persons who are employed by a college to do some of the college's undergraduate teaching but who are not made fellows. Normally the lecturers are responsible only for teaching in smaller Schools or in particular subjects in larger Schools, where the teaching needs in any one college would not justify the appointment of a tutorial fellow, and they are paid a modest retaining fee plus piece-rates for the teaching they actually do. Sometimes, however, the college (either alone or in conjunction with another college) will pay a definite salary to a lecturer; a particular example of this is where small groups of colleges have combined to appoint a person to be a tutorial fellow of one of the colleges and to have teaching responsibilities in the other colleges as a lecturer. Most, but not all, college fellows and lecturers also hold a university post. A college is bound by its statutes to inform the appropriate faculty board when it intends to elect a tutorial fellow, and the board may make representations about the needs of the subject; but the college is under no obligation to give effect to these representations, and there is no need for it to consult the faculty board about the actual person to be elected. Since colleges may wish to appoint to tutorial fellowships persons appointed to university posts such as university lecturerships, the University has established the practice of notifying colleges when there are vacancies in appropriate grades of university posts.

389. The type of university post likely to be held by a college tutorial fellow is largely determined by his subject, mainly for historical reasons. Before 1939 the majority of fellows were in arts and social studies subjects, and received their salaries solely from their college. After 1945 many of the colleges could no longer afford, because of the decline in the value of money, to give adequate salaries to the number of fellows they now required to teach the increased number of undergraduates; the university therefore greatly increased the number of CUF lecturerships, and this is the university post normally held by a tutorial fellow in arts or social studies (though a few hold a full university lecturership or a readership). The growth of science at Oxford, however, was increasingly a university activity because of the need to provide centrally expensive laboratories and equipment; and gradually, in parallel with this, most appointments in

---

[1] Research and faculty fellows of St. Antony's College often have responsibilities towards postgraduates in the college similar to those of Official Fellows.

science subjects became primarily university appointments. The holders may or may not also hold tutorial fellowships in colleges; if they do, the college makes a comparatively small addition to their university salary, within a maximum jointly agreed by the colleges and the University. The great majority of science tutorial fellows are therefore university lecturers. However, the University (on which the greater expense falls) has in recent years been unable to create posts at the rate necessary to keep pace with the needs of colleges, and in a number of cases college fellowships in science have been awarded to people holding junior appointments, e.g. to departmental demonstrators.

## Professors

390. Appointments to statutory professorships are made by special electoral boards. Professors normally hold office until retiring age. Their duties include original work and the general supervision of research and advanced work in the particular subject of their chair; residence within 10 miles of Carfax for a certain part of the year; (for arts professors generally) the giving of at least 36 lectures or classes a year (of which not less than 28 must be lectures); (for science professors generally) the giving of 28 lectures or classes a year, and (in appropriate cases) responsibility for departments assigned to them.

391. Professorial salaries at 1 January 1965 were:[1]

|  | Oxford (£ per annum) | National (£ per annum) |
|---|---|---|
| Non-medical and pre-clinical | 4,100 (plus allowances for departmental responsibility of 300, 400 or 600 in 22 cases). | Within range 3,400–4,750 subject to a maximum average of 4,200 in each university. |
| Clinical | 3,875 or 4,445 according to whether or not the professor retains fees for attending on patients in hospitals associated with the Nuffield scheme. | Within range 3,150–4,445. |

## Readers and first assistants

392. Readers are appointed either by special electoral boards of the same kind as appoint professors or by the General Board, usually on the recommendation of a faculty board. (First assistants in clinical medicine, who are paid on the same scale as readers, are appointed by the Nuffield Committee.) Readerships filled in the first way are those established by statute or decree; those filled in the second way are normally *ad hominem* posts given to an existing member of the academic staff in recognition of

---

[1] The salaries and duties attaching to professorships, and the salary scales and outlines of the duties of readers, university lecturers, and CUF lecturers are published annually in the *Statuta*. The salary scales published are for the university appointment, and do not include any payments by colleges.

particular personal distinction. Their duties are to engage in advanced study and research, and normally (in the case of arts readers) to give not less than 36 lectures or classes a year or (in science and medicine) to co-operate as required in the teaching and administrative work of the department. They are normally appointed for 5 years in the first instance and then (if re-appointed) confirmed to retiring age. Appointment to a college post is a separate procedure; but whether or not such an appointment (which may or may not be stipendiary) is made, not more than 6 hours a week of college teaching may be done. First assistants are appointed or reappointed by the Nuffield Committee, on the recommendation of a specially consti-tuted subcommittee. Tenure is normally for a period of 5 years in the first instance. Their duties are to work under the direction of the head of the department, and they may hold a paid college post. They may be re-appointed for a second period of not more than 5 years, after which (if reappointed) their appointments may be confirmed until the retiring age (in the latter case they then become subject to the disciplinary powers of the Visitatorial Board).

393. Salary scales for readers (and first assistants in clinical medicine) at 1 January 1965 were:

|  | Oxford (£ per annum) | National (£ per annum) |
| --- | --- | --- |
| Non-medical and pre-clinical | $2,800 \times 75\text{--}3,250$. Where a college post is also held the joint stipend may not exceed 3,675. | Scales with maxima up to 3,250. |
| Clinical | $2,975 \times 110\text{--}3,195 \times 220\text{--}3,415 \times 115\text{--}3,645$ if medically quali-fied. $2,800 \times 75\text{--}3,250$ if not medi-cally qualified. | Scales within the range 2,500–3,600 (or 3,990 for posts of special responsibility). |

394. There is no post of senior lecturer at Oxford. The national scales for senior lecturers are subject to the same limits as those for readers.

## University lecturers and senior research officers

395. University lecturers are appointed by the faculty boards, subject to the approval of the General Board (in the case of appointments in science departments, on the recommendation of a specially constituted committee). Their duties are to engage in advanced study or research and (in the case of arts lecturers) normally to give not less than 36 lectures or classes a year or (in the case of lecturers in science and medical departments) to co-operate as required in the teaching and administrative work of the depart-ment in both term and vacation under the direction of the head of the department. Senior research officers (who are mainly in science depart-ments) are appointed in a similar way (though the committee procedure is not statutorily required in their case) and are paid on the same scale; their

duties are to engage in advanced study or research in both term and vacation under the direction of the head of the department (and in some cases they may also be required to assist in the teaching work of the department). University lecturers and senior research officers are normally appointed for 5 years in the first instance and then (if reappointed) confirmed to retiring age. They may do up to 12 hours a week of college teaching. Appointment to a college post is formally a separate procedure from the university appointment; but such appointments are subject to the limit of not more than 12 hours a week of college teaching (11 in the case of tutorial fellows holding university lecturerships in science departments).

396. Salary scales for university lecturers (and senior research officers at Oxford[1]) at 1 January 1965 were:

|  | Oxford (£ per annum) | National (£ per annum) |
| --- | --- | --- |
| Non-medical | 1,400 (under age 28); 1,485 (at age 28) × 85– 2,760 (at age 43 and over). Where a college post is held the joint stipend may not exceed 3,450. | 1,400 × 85–2,505 |
| Pre-clinical | 1,400 × 85–2,760 if medically qualified;[1] otherwise as for non-medical. Where a college post is held the joint stipend may not exceed 3,450. | 1,400 to maxima ranging from 2,505 to 3,250 (increments of 100–120). |

## Lecturers in clinical medicine

397. Lecturers and research officers in clinical departments are appointed by the Nuffield Committee, on the recommendation of heads of departments. The title lecturer is used for those primarily carrying out formal teaching duties (lectures, seminars, ward classes) and the title research officer for those primarily engaged in research. In both cases the duties are to work under the direction of the head of the department. These appointments are tenable with paid college posts. Tenure is normally for not more than 3 years at a time, but the appointment of a lecturer or research officer who has served for at least 5 years is reviewed, on the expiry of his current period of office, by a specially constituted sub-committee, to determine whether (if reappointed) he should be reappointed for a further limited term or until the retiring age (those reappointed until the retiring age become subject to the disciplinary powers of the Visitatorial Board). Junior lecturers and junior research officers are normally appointed for not more than 2 years at a time.

[1] The age-tie at Oxford is statutory in the case of non-medical lecturers, and is also applied in practice to pre-clinical lecturers and senior research officers.

398. Salary scales for lecturers in clinical medicine at 1 January 1965 were:

|  | Oxford (£ per annum) | National (£ per annum) |
|---|---|---|
| Scale III | 1,635 × 115–1,750 × 55– | 1,400 to maxima ranging from |
|  | 1,805 × 60–1,865 × 55– | 2,500 to 3,600 (or 3,990 for |
|  | 1,920 × 115–2,035 × 60– | posts of special responsibility). |
|  | 2,095 × 55–2,205 × 110– |  |
|  | 2,315 × 55–2,480 × 110– |  |
|  | 2,700 if medically qualified. |  |
|  | 2,420 × 85–2,760 if not medically qualified. |  |
| Scale II | 1,580 × 55–1,635; thence as Scale |  |
|  | III to 2,205 if medically qualified. |  |
|  | 1,400 × 85–2,335 if not medically qualified. |  |

## Departmental demonstrators

399. Departmental demonstrators are appointed in certain faculties by heads of departments, and their duties (including the college teaching they may do) are determined by the head of the department. They may be appointed for up to 3 years, and may be reappointed except that their total service as a departmental demonstrator may not normally exceed 6 years. Their salary may not normally exceed £1,325 *per annum* (£1,470 for those medically qualified in medical departments). The national scale for assistant lecturers was £1,050 × £75–£1,275 *per annum* at 1 January 1965.

## CUF lecturers[1]

400. CUF lecturers, as has been explained, owe their primary appointment in Oxford not to the university but to their college. When a college elects an arts tutorial fellow, it will usually put his name forward to the university for appointment as a CUF lecturer, and the fellow (and his college) may normally expect appointment within a year or so of his election as fellow.[2] A CUF lecturer's university duties are to give 16 lectures or classes a year and to engage in advanced study or research; and he will be eligible to continue to hold his lecturership for as long as he is doing at least 6 hours' college teaching a week in respect of a college appointment or appointments (no maximum is laid down by the university), subject only to a formal reappointment at the end of the first 5 years.

401. The salary scale for CUF lecturers at 1 January 1965 was:

| Age | Salary (£ per annum) |
|---|---|
| Under 30 | 950 |
| 30–34 | 1,050 |
| 35–39 | 1,150 |
| 40–44 | 1,250 |
| 45 and over | 1,350 |

[1] See also the evidence of the General Board, *Written Evidence*, Part XII.

[2] Fellows other than tutorial fellows, and college lecturers are also eligible to hold CUF lecturerships provided they do a minimum of 6 hours a week of undergraduate teaching either for the society at which a fellowship (if any) is held, or in respect of college lecturerships held.

Some fellows of the graduate colleges hold 'special CUF lecturerships' carrying a stipend £50 less at each age. These posts are included among CUF lecturerships in the statistics given below.

## Special lecturers[1]

402. Special lecturerships are found in arts subjects. They are posts of limited tenure, nominated by the faculty boards for those making, or being expected to make, some outstanding contribution to learning, and are designed to permit the holder to reduce his college teaching commitments. These lecturerships are usually held by CUF lecturers, who revert to being CUF lecturers when the tenure of the special lecturership comes to an end. Special lecturers are required to give at least 16 lectures or classes a year; the amount of college teaching permitted to them is restricted to 10 hours a week. The stipend at 1 January 1965 was £1,740 *per annum*.

## Faculty lecturers[1]

403. The faculty lecturership was created as one of the ways of solving the problems caused by the making of university appointments of which the holders were not elected to college fellowships. A faculty lecturer is appointed as a result of joint action between a faculty board and an interested college, and is usually required to give 24 lectures or classes a year for the faculty board. The amount of teaching available to the college is normally 12 hours a week. This type of appointment has been used particularly for some of the less studied modern languages, but has recently been extended to other faculties.[2]

404. The salary scale for faculty lecturers at 1 January 1965 was £1,200 × £50 (biennially)–£1,400 × £85 (biennially)–£1,570 *per annum*.

## College emoluments

405. Details of the stipends and other emoluments paid by colleges are given below, paras. 555–68.

## Outside grants staff

406. In addition to academic staff paid directly from university funds, or employed by colleges, there are others who are paid through grants from outside bodies which are formally accepted by, and channelled through, the University. They are referred to as outside grants staff. Such staff are not included in statistics returned by universities to the UGC since their salaries are not paid out of grants from the UGC.[3] But they are academic

---

[1] See also the evidence of the General Board, *Written Evidence*, Part XII.

[2] The college post held may be a tutorial fellowship, a non-tutorial fellowship, or a lecturership.

[3] Information about the number of holders of posts on outside grants in other universities is not available. One of the larger London colleges has told us that in 1964–5 such staff numbered 28 per cent. of the academic staff proper. The corresponding figure for Oxford was 11 per cent. The UGC is collecting information about the staff in 1965–6.

employees of the University and they contribute to research and in some cases to teaching. At Oxford, they are to be found mainly in science departments, and they nearly all hold short-term research posts. Outside grants staff should not be confused with staff employed directly by research councils (such as the Medical Research Council) who are accommodated in university premises. For several purposes, particularly where comparisons with other universities are concerned, it is not appropriate to include outside grants posts, and they are excluded from the definition of the academic staff. But for some purposes they are included, and an alternative definition 'academic staff (including outside grants staff)' is used.

### ACADEMIC STAFF NUMBERS

407. Table 235 gives the number of academic staff at 1 January 1965 according to university and college post. Only full-time staff are included. That is to say, holders of a full-time university or college teaching or research post, and holders of a part-time university and a part-time college teaching or research post. Among those *excluded* are heads of houses, other members of the academic community such as library staff who may, however, engage in both teaching and research for part of their working time, staff of the Extra-Mural Delegacy, and approximately 50 persons who are regarded as part-time. These last include those who hold a college non-stipendiary lecturership (or a stipendiary lecturership with stipend below £500 *per annum*) but no other post; tutorial fellows with stipends considerably below the usual rates in their colleges and with no university post; and those holding a college post with a university post other than a teaching or research post. Included as full-time are all those with a university and/or college teaching or research post, even where a substantial part of their total emoluments is derived from a college office, such as bursar, which is not directly concerned with teaching and research. But bursars, etc., who hold no teaching or research post in the University or their college are excluded. Included are 14 holders of outside grants posts who also held a stipendiary college fellowship. Academic staff on leave of absence on 1 January 1965 are included.

408. The total academic staff numbered 1,127. Nearly half were tutorial fellows or tutors at Permanent Private Halls. The main career grades of professor, reader, lecturer, and senior research officer accounted for 870, or 77 per cent. of the total. The junior teaching grades accounted for a further 38, or 3 per cent. Of the remaining 219 posts, about a fifth were tutorial fellows, most of whom could expect to obtain a university or CUF lecturership in due course. About a half were college lecturers and research fellows holding no university post. The remaining 65 held directorships or special teaching posts (see para. 385) or departmental research posts.

409. Since January 1965 the University has passed statutes to make provision of fellowships (which need not be stipendiary) for members of

**Table 235.** *Academic staff by university and college post held. 1 January 1965*

OXFORD · NUMBER

| College post | University post | | | | | | Other posts | None | All |
|---|---|---|---|---|---|---|---|---|---|
| | Professor | Reader and first assistant | University lecturer | Departmental demonstrator and equivalent | Part-time lecturer* | Senior research officer and equivalent | | | |
| Tutorial fellowship | — | 21 | 98 | 9 | 328 | 14 | 3 | 43 | 516 |
| Non-tutorial fellowship | 104 | 36 | 33 | 1 | 10 | 5 | 16 | 87 | 292 |
| Lecturership but not fellowship | — | — | 46 | 4 | 12 | 3 | 1 | 24 | 90 |
| None | — | 27 | 91 | 24 | — | 42 | 45 | — | 229 |
| All | 104 | 84 | 268 | 38 | 350 | 64 | 65 | 154 | 1,127 |

SOURCE: Registry; Chest; 1965 *Calendar*; colleges; Academic Staff Survey.

NOTES

*1. Part-time lecturers comprise 4 part-time university lecturers (of whom 3 were tutorial fellows, and 1 was a non-tutorial fellow); 309 CUF lecturers; 11 special lecturers; and 26 faculty lecturers (of whom 17 were tutorial fellows and 6 were non-tutorial fellows).

2. Included among tutorial fellows are 10 tutors at Permanent Private Halls.

3. Of the 24 holding a college lecturership and no university post, 7 held research lecturerships.

4. 'University lecturer' comprises full-time university lecturers and lecturers in clinical medicine on Scales II and III.

5. Departmental demonstrators and equivalent comprise departmental demonstrators, junior lecturers in mathematics, and lecturers in clinical medicine on Scale I.

6. Senior research officers and equivalent comprise senior research officers, graduate assistants, other research workers on the same scale, and research officers in clinical medicine on Scales II and III.

7. Those under 'other posts' include directors, tutors in the Department and Institute of Education, the Department of Social and Administrative Studies, and in clinical medicine, and holders of departmental research posts.

the academic staff in the main career grades. Two new societies—St. Cross College and Iffley College—were established in 1965 and on 1 June 1965 a statute was passed which provided that titular professors (by decree), readers, and holders of certain other specified posts should be entitled to fellowships, and that first assistants, university lecturers (including CUF lecturers, faculty lecturers, and special lecturers), senior research officers, and lecturers and research officers in clinical medicine paid on Scale III should be entitled to fellowships when their appointments have been confirmed to retiring age.[1] As a result there have been considerable changes in the numbers holding fellowships since 1 January 1965. St. Cross College and Iffley College in 1965–6 had 83 (non-tutorial) fellows drawn from those who previously had no fellowship. In addition, other colleges have elected to fellowships a considerable number of those shown as non-fellows in Table 235.

410. A breakdown of posts by subject groups is given in Table 236. Table 237 gives the subject groups of the 129 outside grants staff (other than the 14 referred to in para. 407) in post at 1 October 1964 (the available information being more complete for this date than for 1 January 1965). This gives a total academic staff (including outside grants staff) of about 1,256 for 1964–5.

411. Table 235 shows 90 persons holding college lecturerships but not fellowships. In addition, 80 college fellows held college lecturerships as well as their fellowships. The 170 members of the academic staff holding college lecturerships held altogether 220 such lecturerships. Tables 238 and 239 give details according to posts held. An analysis by subject group shows that 18 per cent. of the academic staff in arts were college lecturers; 13 per cent. in social studies; 17 per cent. in science; and 4 per cent. in medicine.

412. The proportion of women in the academic staff (including outside grants posts) was 13 per cent. It was highest in arts and medicine (17 per cent. and 18 per cent. respectively); was 14 per cent. in social studies, and 8 per cent. in science. The proportion of women was high among college teachers with no university post (28 per cent.), CUF lecturers (19 per cent.), and other university and outside grants staff (18 per cent.). It was 7 per cent. among readers and university lecturers, and 1 per cent. among professors.

## Comparisons with other universities

413. The special structure of posts at Oxford makes comparisons of the composition of the academic staff with other universities difficult. However, the grades of professor and reader are common to Oxford and other universities, and the proportions in these grades may be compared. Table 240

[1] Statt. Tit. XXIV, Sect. 1 (*Statuta*, 1965, p. 533).

**Table 236.** *Academic staff by post and subject group. 1 January 1965*

OXFORD

NUMBER

| Subject group | Professor | Reader and first assistant | University lecturer with tutorial fellowship | University lecturer without tutorial fellowship | CUF and special lecturer | Other university staff with tutorial fellowship | Other senior research staff | Other university staff | College post only: teaching | College post only: research | All posts |
|---|---|---|---|---|---|---|---|---|---|---|---|
| Arts | 51 | 19 | 19 | 46 | 234 | 13 | 1 | 23 | 31 | 45 | 482 |
| Social studies | 15 | 12 | 1 | 11 | 61 | 5 | 2 | 17 | 18 | 26 | 168 |
| Science | 28 | 33 | 71 | 84 | 25 | 28 | 27 | 45 | 11 | 22 | 374 |
| Pre-clinical medicine | 4 | 8 | 6 | 6 | — | — | 7 | 7 | — | 1 | 39 |
| Clinical medicine | 6 | 12 | 1 | 23 | — | — | 13 | 9 | — | — | 64 |
| All subjects | 104 | 84 | 98 | 170 | 320 | 46 | 50 | 101 | 60 | 94 | 1,127 |

SOURCE: Registry; Chest; 1965 *Calendar*; colleges; Academic Staff Survey.

NOTE: The category 'university lecturer' is defined as in Table 235; the category 'other senior research staff' is the same as the category 'senior research officer and equivalent' in Table 235 except that holders of tutorial fellowships are not included.

**Table 237.** *Holders of posts on outside grants. 1 October 1964*

| OXFORD | NUMBER |
|---|---|
| Arts | 6 |
| Social studies | 9 |
| Science | 90 |
| Medicine | 24 |
| All | 129 |

SOURCE: Chest; university departments.

NOTES
1. This table is based on information which was probably incomplete.
2. Holders of posts on outside grants who also held a stipendiary college fellowship are not included.

gives some details for 1964–5. Distributions are given for non-medical and for all subjects. The UGC has laid down for non-medical subjects a limit of two-ninths on the number of senior non-professorial posts as a proportion of all non-professorial posts. The limit does not apply in medical subjects and non-medical subjects are therefore shown separately. For Oxford, distributions are given for full-time university staff, all university staff, and all academic staff.

414. In terms of all academic staff, Oxford had a lower proportion of professors, and a slightly higher proportion of readers compared with the national distribution. The proportion of lecturers at Oxford is slightly higher than the proportion of senior lecturers and lecturers at all universities, and the proportion in the assistant lecturer and 'others' categories is marginally higher. Although these groups are not exactly comparable, they are broadly so. Almost all in the lecturer category at Oxford are on scales which go into the senior lecturer range, and about two-thirds are tutorial fellows whose combined university and college scales usually go at least to the top of the senior lecturer range. (See below, paras. 555–61.) Both nationally and at Oxford a very large proportion of 'other' posts are junior posts carrying a salary similar to that of an assistant lecturership. In paras. 532–45 a further comparison is made between Oxford and other universities on the basis of salary instead of grade.

415. There is considerable variation about the national average. Figures on individual universities have not yet been published for 1964–5, but in 1963–4 the proportion of professors at the universities and colleges shown in Table 241 ranged from 10·1 per cent. to 19·5 per cent. compared with the national average of 11·6 per cent., and the proportion of readers ranged from 4·9 per cent. to 18·1 per cent. compared with the national average of 6·8 per cent.

**Table 238.** *Members of the academic staff holding college lecturerships. 1 January 1965*

OXFORD

| Fellowship | College lecturerships | University post | | | | | No university post | NUMBER All |
|---|---|---|---|---|---|---|---|---|
| | | Reader | University lecturer and senior research officer | Departmental demonstrator and equivalent | Part-time lecturers | Other university and outside grants posts | | |
| Tutorial | 1 non-stipendiary | — | 13 | — | 17 | 1 | 2 | 33 |
| | 2 or more non-stipendiary | — | 3 | — | 3 | — | — | 6 |
| | 1 stipendiary | — | — | — | 12 | — | 5 | 17 |
| | Other combinations | — | 4 | — | 3 | — | — | 7 |
| | All | — | 20 | — | 35 | 1 | 7 | 63 |
| Non-tutorial | 1 non-stipendiary | 4 | 3 | 1 | 1 | — | 3 | 12 |
| | 2 or more non-stipendiary | — | 2 | — | 1 | — | — | 2 |
| | 1 stipendiary | — | 3 | — | — | — | — | 3 |
| | All | 4 | 8 | 1 | 1 | — | 3 | 17 |
| None | 1 non-stipendiary | — | 34 | 1 | 1 | 1 | — | 37 |
| | 2 or more non-stipendiary | — | 12 | 1 | — | — | — | 13 |
| | 1 stipendiary | — | 2 | 2 | 3 | — | 18 | 25 |
| | Other combinations | — | 1 | — | 8 | — | 6 | 15 |
| | All | — | 49 | 4 | 12 | 1 | 24 | 90 |
| All | 1 non-stipendiary | 4 | 50 | 2 | 19 | 2 | 5 | 82 |
| | 2 or more non-stipendiary | — | 17 | 1 | 3 | — | — | 21 |
| | 1 stipendiary | — | 5 | 2 | 15 | — | 23 | 45 |
| | Other combinations | — | 5 | — | 11 | — | 6 | 22 |
| | All | 4 | 77 | 5 | 48 | 2 | 34 | 170 |

SOURCE: See source to Table 235.

NOTES

1. Seven research lecturerships are included among the stipendiary lecturerships.
2. College lecturerships were also held by holders of outside grants posts and by others as follows:

| | 1 non-stipendiary | 1 stipendiary |
|---|---|---|
| Outside grants posts | 6 | 2 |
| Others | 19 | 5 |

**Table 239.** *Persons holding college lecturerships by number held. 1 January 1965*

OXFORD                                                                    NUMBER

| | Number of college lecturerships held | | | | Total number of college lecturerships |
|---|---|---|---|---|---|
| | 1 | 2 | 3 | 4 | |
| Academic staff | 127 | 37 | 5 | 1 | 220 |
| Others | 32 | — | — | — | 32 |
| All holding college lecturerships | 159 | 37 | 5 | 1 | 252 |

SOURCE: See source to Table 235.

**Table 240.** *Academic staff by grades. Oxford and all universities in Great Britain: 1964–5*

PERCENTAGE

| | Pro-fessor | Reader | Senior lecturer | Lecturer | Assistant lecturer | Other | All | *Number* |
|---|---|---|---|---|---|---|---|---|
| **NON-MEDICAL SUBJECTS** | | | | | | | | |
| Oxford: full-time university staff | 18·0 | 12·3 | — | 53·0 | 6·3 | 10·4 | 100 | *521* |
| Oxford: university staff | 10·8 | 7·3 | — | 71·9 | 3·8 | 6·2 | 100 | *871* |
| Oxford: all academic staff | 9·2 | 6·3 | — | 61·1 | 3·2 | 20·2 | 100 | *1,024* |
| All universities in Great Britain | 11·6 | 6·1 | 10·9 | 48·9 | 12·2 | 10·3 | 100 | *14,983* |
| **ALL SUBJECTS** | | | | | | | | |
| Oxford: full-time university staff | 16·7 | 13·5 | — | 53·3 | 6·1 | 10·4 | 100 | *623* |
| Oxford: university staff | 10·7 | 8·6 | — | 70·1 | 3·9 | 6·7 | 100 | *973* |
| Oxford: all academic staff | 9·2 | 7·5 | — | 60·5 | 3·4 | 19·4 | 100 | *1,127* |
| All universities in Great Britain | 11·8 | 6·5 | 12·6 | 46·6 | 12·0 | 10·5 | 100 | *18,375* |

SOURCE: Oxford: See source to Table 235.
         All universities in Great Britain: UGC.
NOTES
1. First assistants at Oxford are included under reader. If they were not, the percentages for readers at Oxford in all subjects would be 12·0, 7·7, and 6·7.
2. Senior research officers at Oxford are included under lecturer.
3. Departmental demonstrators and junior lecturers at Oxford are included under assistant lecturer.
4. Figures for Oxford alone relate to 1 January 1965; for all universities in Great Britain to 1964–5.
5. In the figures for all universities in Great Britain the staff included for Oxford and Cambridge are all full-time university staff.

**Table 241.** *Academic staff at certain universities and colleges by grades. 1963-4*

PERCENTAGE

| University or college | Pro-fessor | Reader | Senior lecturer | Lecturer | Assis-tant lec-turer | Other | All | *Number* |
|---|---|---|---|---|---|---|---|---|
| Bristol | 10·2 | 6·4 | 8·3 | 51·2 | 8·7 | 15·2 | 100 | 551 |
| Cambridge | 10·1 | 7·5 | — | 82·4 | | | 100 | 932 |
| Durham | 14·0 | 7·2 | 8·1 | 61·3 | 2·6 | 6·8 | 100 | 235 |
| Imperial College | 11·4 | 13·6 | 10·3 | 48·6 | 5·0 | 11·0 | 100 | 516 |
| Kings College | 19·5 | 15·9 | 6·0 | 41·0 | 12·0 | 5·6 | 100 | 251 |
| London School of Economics | 16·1 | 18·1 | 4·8 | 34·7 | 14·9 | 11·3 | 100 | 248 |
| University College | 14·3 | 17·6 | 5·9 | 40·5 | 7·2 | 14·5 | 100 | 511 |
| London | 14·3 | 14·2 | 11·5 | 40·5 | 9·7 | 9·8 | 100 | 3,750 |
| Manchester | 10·1 | 4·9 | 12·9 | 46·5 | 14·1 | 11·4 | 100 | 858 |
| All universities in Great Britain | 11·6 | 6·8 | 11·6 | 49·0 | 9·3 | 11·7 | 100 | 16,444 |

SOURCE: UGC Returns, 1963-4.

NOTES

1. Demonstrators are included under assistant lecturer for the individual colleges of London University (though not for London University as a whole).
2. In the figures for all universities in Great Britain the staff included for Oxford and Cambridge are all full-time university staff. Of these 1,185 lecturers, assistant lecturers, demonstrators, etc., at Oxford and Cambridge shown in Note 15 to the UGC Returns but not in its Table 9, are included under 'lecturer'.

## STUDENT/STAFF RATIOS[1]

416. The UGC calculates student/staff ratios in two ways. In both, only full-time staff and students enter into the calculations, and in both an attempt is made to confine the staff figures to teaching staff. The difference between the two methods is that in one all students are given the same weight, whereas in the other postgraduates are given a greater weight than undergraduates, on the grounds that they absorb more teaching resources per student.

417. These ratios can provide only a rough measure of the adequacy of staffing and should be interpreted with caution. One difficulty is that there is wide variation in the amount of teaching individuals do, and there is no clear-cut distinction between teaching and other academic staff. In addition, a certain amount of teaching at Oxford is done by persons other than the academic staff, and the same may apply in other universities. In making comparisons between subject groups it must be remembered that some staff teach in more than one of the groups.[2] In comparing universities it

[1] Throughout this section, student/staff ratios are expressed as the number of students per member of the staff, the student and staff numbers being calculated as explained below.
[2] And students may receive teaching in more than one subject group.

must be remembered that the size of departments, the methods of teaching (especially the size of the groups in which students are taught) and the type of courses (e.g. pass or honours) are also relevant to an assessment of relative staffing positions. And when weighted ratios are calculated, the weights must to a large extent be arbitrary. The practice of the UGC in this respect is to give postgraduates a weight of three, except in arts and social studies, where the weight is one for postgraduates taking a one-year certificate or diploma course in Education, and two for others. Undergraduates have a weight of one.

418. The UGC has published figures for 1964–5 for each university except Oxford and Cambridge[1] and a selection of the results is given in Tables 242 and 243. Some figures for Cambridge, calculated on as closely comparable a basis as possible are also given.

**Table 242.** *Student/staff ratios (unweighted) for certain universities in Great Britain. Autumn Term 1964*

RATIO

| University | Arts | Social studies | Arts and social studies | Science | Medicine (including dentistry) | All except medicine | All subjects |
|---|---|---|---|---|---|---|---|
| Bristol | 9·4 | 10·0 | 9·5 | 8·4 | 5·9 | 9·0 | 8·4 |
| Cambridge | 12·1 | 14·6 | 12·7 | 9·3 | | .. | 10·8 |
| Durham | 10·9 | 10·1 | 10·8 | 7·4 | . | 9·4 | 9·4 |
| London | 7·9 | 8·9 | 8·3 | 5·8 | 5·9 | 6·8 | 6·5 |
| Manchester | 7·8 | 10·3 | 8·6 | 6·4 | 4·8 | 7·4 | 7·0 |
| All universities in Great Britain except Oxford, Cambridge, and six new universities | 9·8 | 8·8 | 9·5 | 7·1 | 5·6 | 8·1 | 7·6 |

SOURCE
> Universities other than Cambridge: *Fifth Report from the Estimates Committee*, HMSO 1965, Appendix D. (UGC for certain details not given therein).
> Cambridge: Cambridge University.

NOTES
1. Staff figures on which the ratios are based are calculated as explained in para. 419.
2. The entries for Cambridge are provisional figures for the autumn term of 1965. The staff numbers on which they are based exclude a small number holding college but not university posts.

419. In calculating teaching staff, the UGC includes the main teaching grades (from professor to assistant lecturer) and half the 'other' academic staff.[2] Because of the different structure of posts, this approach has not been followed for Oxford, and instead an attempt has been made to

---

[1] *Fifth Report from the Estimates Committee*, HMSO 1965, Appendix D.
[2] After excluding all staff in the Provincial Agricultural Economics Service, the Extra-mural Delegacies, Institutes of Education, and certain research institutes attached to universities.

**Table 243.** *Student/staff ratios (weighted) for certain universities in Great Britain. Autumn Term 1964*

RATIO

| University | Arts | Social studies | Arts and social studies | Science | Medicine (including dentistry) | All except medicine | All subjects |
|---|---|---|---|---|---|---|---|
| Bristol | 10·6 | 12·6 | 11·0 | 11·0 | 6·7 | 11·0 | 10·3 |
| Cambridge | 13·6 | 17·2 | 14·5 | 13·1 | | .. | 13·7 |
| Durham | 11·8 | 10·6 | 11·6 | 11·7 | . | 11·7 | 11·7 |
| London | 10·7 | 15·8 | 11·9 | 9·5 | 8·3 | 10·5 | 9·8 |
| Manchester | 9·1 | 14·1 | 10·6 | 9·2 | 4·8 | 9·9 | 9·0 |
| All universities in Great Britain except Oxford, Cambridge, and six new universities | 10·6 | 13·0 | 11·2 | 9·8 | 6·9 | 10·7 | 9·9 |

SOURCE: See source to Table 242.

NOTES

1. The system of weighting is that used by the UGC. Postgraduates in arts and social studies (except those taking a diploma course in Education) are given a weight of two. Postgraduates in science and medicine are given a weight of three. Other students are given a weight of one. See main source for details.
2. See notes to Table 242.

classify each member of the academic staff as primarily a teacher or not. Included as teachers are professors, readers, all lecturers, all tutorial fellows, senior research officers and equivalent, tutors in the Department of Education and the Department of Social and Administrative Studies, departmental demonstrators, tutors at Permanent Private Halls, and stipendiary college lecturers. Of the total academic staff of 1,127, this gives 989 teaching and 138 research staff (mainly college research fellows and holders of departmental research posts).[1] Senior research officers are included among teachers since there is often little difference in practice between them and university lecturers. In several departments they can be required to assist in the teaching in their department, and there are fairly frequent redesignations of senior research officers as university lecturers. The amount of college teaching they may undertake is almost invariably the same as for university lecturers. Although the average amount of teaching reported by them in the Academic Staff Survey was less than for university lecturers over half did some teaching, and on balance it seems more appropriate to regard them as teachers than as non-teachers.[2]

[1] The total of 989 teaching staff is made up as follows: 434 in arts; 133 in social studies; 329 in science; and 93 in medicine. It may be noted that the alternative approach of taking all professors, readers, lecturers, and departmental demonstrators, and half the remaining staff (this corresponds as closely as possible to applying the UGC rules) gives an almost identical result of 986 teaching and 141 research staff.

[2] About a quarter of them held tutorial fellowships and are included among teachers on that ground.

**Table 244.** *Student/staff ratios for Oxford. 1964–5*

OXFORD                                                                    RATIO

| Subject group | Undergraduates | Postgraduates (unweighted) | All students (unweighted) | All students (weighted) |
|---|---|---|---|---|
| Arts | 8·1 | 2·1 | 10·2 | 11·7 |
| Social studies | 10·4 | 2·8 | 13·2 | 16·0 |
| Arts and social studies | 8·6 | 2·3 | 10·9 | 12·7 |
| Science | 6·3 | 2·4 | 8·7 | 13·5 |
| Medicine | 3·9 | 0·7 | 4·5 | 5·9 |
| All except medicine | 7·8 | 2·3 | 10·1 | 13·0 |
| All subjects | 7·4 | 2·2 | 9·6 | 12·3 |

SOURCE: Students: Registry and certain departments for non-matriculated students.
Staff: See source to Table 235.
NOTES
1. Non-matriculated students attached to departments (but not those at Ruskin College and Plater College) are included.
2. Student numbers relate to October 1964. Staff numbers relate to 1 January 1965.
3. For details of the weighting, and of the staff included see paras. 417 and 419.

420. Table 244 gives student/staff ratios for Oxford calculated in the way described above. The weighted ratio was 12·3 for Oxford, compared with the over-all national figure of 9·9, and of the universities shown in Tables 242 and 243, only Cambridge had a higher ratio.[1] The less favourable over-all ratio for Oxford is partly a consequence of the balance of subjects being different at Oxford than at other universities, but differences persist when the subject groups are compared. The weighted average in arts and social studies is 12·7 for Oxford against the national figure of 11·2. Corresponding figures for science show a bigger disparity: 13·5 for Oxford and 9·8 nationally. Only in medicine is the Oxford ratio (5·9) more favourable than the national figure (6·9). One factor which is relevant to the interpretation of these figures is the extent to which teaching is given by persons other than the academic staff. It is possible to estimate this for Oxford though not for other universities. The teaching given by persons other than the academic staff is mainly in the form of tutorials for undergraduates, and demonstrating in laboratories. Tutorials for undergraduates occupy about 62 per cent. of the total teaching hours of the academic staff, and demonstrating about 11 per cent.[2] Of undergraduate tutorials we estimate that

[1] Exeter and Southampton also had higher student/staff ratios.
[2] These figures are based on the same data as Tables 263 and 264, but outside grants staff are excluded.

6 per cent. are given by postgraduates, and 5 per cent. by other persons holding no university or college post. The evidence from heads of Science Departments (*Written Evidence*, Part VIII) suggests that about 30 per cent. of all demonstrating is done by persons not holding a university or departmental post. Thus, approximately 89 per cent. of the teaching (other than postgraduate supervision) is done by the academic staff.

**Table 245.** *Academic staff needed for Oxford to achieve the national student/ staff ratios. 1964–5*

| OXFORD | | | NUMBER |
|---|---|---|---|
| Subject group | Existing teaching staff | Staff needed to achieve national student/staff ratio (weighted) | Difference (col. (2)–col. (1)) |
| | (1) | (2) | (3) |
| Arts and social studies | 567 | 642 | 75 |
| Science | 329 | 453 | 124 |
| Medicine | 93 | 79 | −14 |
| All subjects | 989 | 1,174 | 185 |

SOURCE: Tables 243 and 244 and source to Table 235.

421. Table 245 shows the number of staff which would be needed if Oxford were to achieve the national ratios in each major subject group. It shows that an extra 185 teaching staff would be needed, of whom two-thirds would be in science.

422. Student/staff ratios are measures which cannot take account of the many variations in conditions and circumstances between universities and between subjects. And it is evident from Tables 242 and 243 and the data from which they have been compiled that inter-subject variations are by no means uniform in the universities. Too much significance should not, therefore, be attached to the figures given here, especially those in Table 245. This table does not purport to give, in column (2), the 'correct' or 'right' size of Oxford's total teaching staff (let alone that in particular subjects) since many of the relevant factors are not taken into account. It is merely intended to show the implications in terms of staff numbers of the difference between Oxford's and the national student/staff ratio, taking into account the relative size of the main subject groups. The figures do suggest, however, that Oxford is further from the average student/staff ratio than most universities; that extra staff of the order of 150–200 would be needed to bring Oxford close to the average; and that the science subjects are those which are most under-staffed.

423. A survey of all members of the academic staff (including holders of outside grants posts) was carried out during Michaelmas Term 1964. A very high response rate of 97 per cent. was achieved and 1,154 completed questionnaires were received (in addition 36 questionnaires were received from part-time academic staff). The survey did not include staff on leave of absence. The bulk of the results given below on the background, teaching, work, and publications of the academic staff have been derived from this survey, and they include holders of posts on outside grants unless specified to the contrary. Details of the survey, of the classification of posts (which is slightly different from that adopted for Table 236), and of the sample numbers corresponding to the main breakdowns used, are given in Part VI.

### Age

BACKGROUND

424. The average age of the staff was 41 years; it was lowest in science and highest in arts subjects (Table 246). The average age of professors was 55 years, of readers 51 years, and of lecturers and senior research officers about 42 years. Those with other university and outside grants posts and with college posts only had an average age in the low or mid thirties. Those with outside grants posts had an average age of 31 years. If they are excluded, the over-all average age is 43 years, and that in science is 40 years.

425. Age distributions are given in Tables 247 and 248. Only 5 per cent. were aged under 26 years, most of whom held junior research posts and junior research fellowships. In the lecturer grades the proportion aged under 30 was 5–8 per cent. About a quarter of the staff were aged 40–49, and a further quarter were 50 and over. The distribution when outside grants staff are excluded is given in Table 247. The national pattern is very different from that in Table 247. The Association of University Teachers found, in a remuneration survey[1] carried out in 1964–5, that 54 per cent. of professors and 73 per cent. of readers were under 51 years. Taking senior lecturers and lecturers together, the Association of University Teachers found 25 per cent. under 31 years and 71 per cent. under 41 years. Only 8 per cent. were 51 and over. Among assistant lecturers, 44 per cent. were 25 and under, and 93 per cent. were under 31. Although the age groupings are slightly different, it is clear that at each level of post the average age at Oxford was higher.

### Length of service

426. Table 249 gives the average time staff had spent in academic life, and in an academic post at Oxford. On average staff had spent 12·5 years in

[1] *The remuneration of university teachers, 1964–5*, AUT 1965. The survey covered the grades of professor, reader, senior lecturer, lecturer, and assistant lecturer only.

Table 246. *Average age of academic staff (including outside grants staff) by post and subject group. Michaelmas Term 1964*

OXFORD                                                                                     YEARS

| Subject group | Professor | Reader | University lecturer with tutorial fellowship | University lecturer without tutorial fellowship | CUF and special lecturer | Other university staff with tutorial fellowship | Other senior research staff | Other university and outside grants staff | College post only: teaching | College post only: research | All posts |
|---|---|---|---|---|---|---|---|---|---|---|---|
| Arts | 55 | 52 | 44 | 45 | 43 | 42 | 60 | 38 | 37 | 35 | 43 |
| Social studies | 56 | 47 | · | 43 | 41 | 38 | 48 | 35 | 34 | 33 | 40 |
| Science | 54 | 51 | 40 | 44 | 34 | 35 | 39 | 30 | 28 | 29 | 38 |
| Medicine | 57 | 57 | 42 | 39 | · | · | 43 | 37 | · | · | 42 |
| All subjects | 55 | 51 | 41 | 43 | 42 | 37 | 42 | 33 | 35 | 33 | 41 |

SOURCE: Academic Staff Survey.

# THE ACADEMIC STAFF

**Table 247.** *Age of academic staff (including outside grants staff) by post. Michaelmas Term 1964*

OXFORD  PERCENTAGE

| Age | Professor | Reader | University lecturer with tutorial fellowship | University lecturer without tutorial fellowship | CUF and special lecturer | Other university staff with tutorial fellowship | Other senior research staff | Other university and outside grants staff | College post only: teaching | College post only: research | All posts | All posts except outside grants posts |
|---|---|---|---|---|---|---|---|---|---|---|---|---|
| 25 and under | — | — | — | 1 | — | — | — | 15 | 14 | 22 | 5 | 5 |
| 26–29 | — | 1 | 6 | 4 | 8 | 19 | 8 | 37 | 27 | 31 | 14 | 11 |
| 30–39 | 2 | 16 | 43 | 38 | 36 | 46 | 37 | 32 | 30 | 27 | 32 | 31 |
| 40–49 | 19 | 19 | 37 | 33 | 32 | 30 | 35 | 7 | 22 | 10 | 24 | 26 |
| 50 and over | 79 | 63 | 15 | 25 | 24 | 5 | 20 | 9 | 8 | 10 | 24 | 27 |
| All | 100 | 100 | 100 | 100 | 100 | 100 | 100 | 100 | 100 | 100 | 100 | 100 |

SOURCE: Academic Staff Survey.

academic life and 9·8 years at Oxford. They must have entered the profession on average at about 29 years, an age which is in close agreement
with the national figure implied by the Association of University Teachers
survey.[1] On average, 2·7 years had been spent in academic life outside
Oxford.[2] For professors the average time spent away from Oxford was
9·8 years, and for readers it was 5·7 years. For other posts it was close to
2 years. It was slightly higher in arts and medicine than in social studies
and science.

**Table 248.** *Age of academic staff (including outside grants staff) by subject
group. Michaelmas Term 1964*

OXFORD                                                          PERCENTAGE

| Age | Arts | Social studies | Science | Medicine | All subjects |
|-----|------|----------------|---------|----------|--------------|
| 25 and under | 3 | 7 | 8 | 2 | 5 |
| 26–29 | 11 | 12 | 21 | 9 | 14 |
| 30–39 | 28 | 33 | 33 | 38 | 32 |
| 40–49 | 28 | 28 | 18 | 26 | 24 |
| 50 and over | 31 | 19 | 19 | 25 | 24 |
| All | 100 | 100 | 100 | 100 | 100 |

SOURCE: Academic Staff Survey.

427. Although the average age of CUF lecturers was similar to that of
other lecturers, they had spent a longer time in academic life, which they
had entered, on average, at about 26½ years. Table 250 shows that 69 per
cent. had spent at least 11 years, and 21 per cent. at least 21 years in
academic life. Table 251 shows a considerable difference between arts and
other subjects, particularly in the proportion having spent at least 21
years in academic life (24 per cent.) which was about twice that in other
subjects.

428. Table 252 shows the relation between age and years in academic life.

429. On average, readers had spent the longest time in Oxford, and Table
253 shows that a third had spent 21 years and over. 27 per cent. of professors and 18 per cent. of CUF lecturers had spent 21 years and over in
Oxford. There was a substantial difference between arts and other subjects.

[1] The average age corresponding to the distribution in Table 13 of the AUT survey is
about 29 years.
[2] This is an overstatement since the average time spent in Oxford relates only to posts
held continuously. References to time in Oxford should be read in this sense.

Table 249. *Average years in academic life and at Oxford by post and subject group. Michaelmas Term 1964*

OXFORD  
YEARS

| Subject group | Average years in | Professor | Reader | University lecturer with tutorial fellowship | University lecturer without tutorial fellowship | CUF and special lecturer | Other university staff with tutorial fellowship | Other senior research staff | Other university and outside grants staff | College post only: teaching | College post only: research | All posts |
|---|---|---|---|---|---|---|---|---|---|---|---|---|
| Arts | Academic life | 27.7 | 22.0 | 18.0 | 15.1 | 16.2 | 13.9 | 17.3 | 5.2 | 6.2 | 6.2 | 15.1 |
| | Academic post at Oxford | 18.1 | 13.3 | 14.8 | 11.1 | 14.2 | 10.6 | 17.3 | 3.7 | 4.2 | 4.1 | 11.9 |
| Social studies | Academic life | 27.7 | 18.5 | . | 11.3 | 14.2 | 5.8 | 11.5 | 6.0 | 6.9 | 4.0 | 11.3 |
| | Academic post at Oxford | 17.2 | 15.4 | . | 9.8 | 12.8 | 4.5 | 6.5 | 5.4 | 2.3 | 1.9 | 8.8 |
| Science | Academic life | 23.1 | 23.9 | 13.9 | 13.8 | 14.5 | 9.1 | 8.4 | 3.4 | 7.3 | 2.9 | 10.7 |
| | Academic post at Oxford | 12.6 | 19.1 | 12.1 | 11.6 | 12.9 | 7.4 | 7.5 | 2.5 | 4.1 | 1.5 | 8.4 |
| Medicine | Academic life | 22.4 | 26.5 | 14.0 | 8.4 | . | . | 12.1 | 6.2 | . | . | 11.4 |
| | Academic post at Oxford | 13.9 | 20.6 | 9.4 | 6.4 | . | . | 10.1 | 4.0 | . | . | 8.3 |
| All subjects | Academic life | 25.9 | 23.0 | 14.5 | 12.7 | 15.7 | 9.8 | 10.3 | 4.4 | 6.6 | 4.8 | 12.5 |
| | Academic post at Oxford | 16.1 | 17.3 | 12.6 | 10.3 | 13.8 | 7.8 | 8.8 | 3.2 | 3.6 | 2.9 | 9.8 |

SOURCE: Academic Staff Survey.

**Table 250.** *Years in academic life by post. Michaelmas Term 1964*

OXFORD

PERCENTAGE

| Years in academic life | Professor | Reader | University lecturer with tutorial fellowship | University lecturer without tutorial fellowship | CUF and special lecturer | Other university staff with tutorial fellowship | Other senior research staff | Other university and outside grants staff | College post only: teaching | College post only: research | All posts |
|---|---|---|---|---|---|---|---|---|---|---|---|
| None | — | — | — | 1 | — | — | 5 | 14 | 13 | 24 | 6 |
| 1-5 | 3 | 3 | 17 | 21 | 10 | 35 | 27 | 61 | 47 | 51 | 27 |
| 6-10 | 1 | 9 | 19 | 23 | 21 | 24 | 22 | 14 | 17 | 11 | 17 |
| 11-20 | 30 | 36 | 48 | 43 | 48 | 38 | 38 | 7 | 20 | 11 | 32 |
| 21 and over | 65 | 52 | 16 | 13 | 21 | 3 | 8 | 3 | 3 | 3 | 18 |
| All | 100 | 100 | 100 | 100 | 100 | 100 | 100 | 100 | 100 | 100 | 100 |

SOURCE: Academic Staff Survey.

**Table 251.** *Years in academic life by subject group. Michaelmas Term 1964*

OXFORD                                                                    PERCENTAGE

| Years in academic life | Arts | Social studies | Science | Medicine | All subjects |
|---|---|---|---|---|---|
| None | 3 | 7 | 7 | 4 | 6 |
| 1–5 | 19 | 24 | 34 | 36 | 27 |
| 6–10 | 14 | 23 | 18 | 15 | 17 |
| 11–20 | 39 | 34 | 27 | 25 | 32 |
| 21 and over | 24 | 12 | 14 | 19 | 18 |
| All | 100 | 100 | 100 | 100 | 100 |

SOURCE: Academic Staff Survey.

**Table 252.** *Years in academic life by age. Michaelmas Term 1964*

OXFORD                                                                    PERCENTAGE

| Years in academic life | Age | | | | | All ages |
|---|---|---|---|---|---|---|
| | Under 26 | 26–29 | 30–39 | 40–49 | 50 and over | |
| None | 49 | 13 | 3 | 1 | — | 6 |
| 1–5 | 51 | 81 | 32 | 8 | 4 | 27 |
| 6–10 | — | 6 | 40 | 12 | 2 | 17 |
| 11–20 | — | — | 25 | 74 | 25 | 32 |
| 21 and over | — | — | — | 5 | 68 | 18 |
| All | 100 | 100 | 100 | 100 | 100 | 100 |
| *Average years* | 0·7 | 2·4 | 7·7 | 14·3 | 25·6 | 12·5 |
| *Number* | 61 | 165 | 362 | 275 | 278 | 1,141 |

SOURCE: Academic Staff Survey.

OXFORD

PERCENTAGE

**Table 253.** *Years in academic post at Oxford by post. Michaelmas Term 1964*

| Years in academic post at Oxford | Professor | Reader | University lecturer with tutorial fellowship | University lecturer without tutorial fellowship | CUF and special lecturer | Other university staff with tutorial fellowship | Other senior research staff | Other university and outside grants staff | College post only: teaching | College post only: research | All posts |
|---|---|---|---|---|---|---|---|---|---|---|---|
| None | 2 | 3 | 2 | 4 | — | — | 7 | 21 | 31 | 32 | 9 |
| 1–5 | 21 | 16 | 21 | 31 | 20 | 54 | 30 | 64 | 55 | 55 | 36 |
| 6–10 | 13 | 12 | 22 | 23 | 22 | 14 | 25 | 9 | 5 | 7 | 16 |
| 11–20 | 37 | 36 | 42 | 36 | 40 | 30 | 35 | 4 | 6 | 4 | 27 |
| 21 and over | 27 | 33 | 12 | 8 | 18 | 3 | 3 | 2 | 3 | 2 | 11 |
| All | 100 | 100 | 100 | 100 | 100 | 100 | 100 | 100 | 100 | 100 | 100 |
| Percentage having spent all academic career at Oxford | 36 | 37 | 54 | 54 | 64 | 54 | 75 | 67 | 47 | 70 | 58 |

SOURCE: Academic Staff Survey.

**Table 254.** *Years in academic post at Oxford by subject group. Michaelmas Term 1964*

OXFORD                                                                          PERCENTAGE

| Years in academic post at Oxford | Arts | Social studies | Science | Medicine | All subjects |
|---|---|---|---|---|---|
| None | 6 | 12 | 11 | 10 | 9 |
| 1–5 | 29 | 33 | 41 | 43 | 36 |
| 6–10 | 15 | 20 | 16 | 14 | 16 |
| 11–20 | 33 | 26 | 24 | 22 | 27 |
| 21 and over | 16 | 9 | 8 | 11 | 11 |
| All | 100 | 100 | 100 | 100 | 100 |
| Percentage having spent all academic career at Oxford | 56 | 62 | 61 | 50 | 58 |

SOURCE: Academic Staff Survey.

In arts, half had spent 11 years and over in Oxford, against about a third in other subjects. Over all, 58 per cent. had spent all their academic career in Oxford.[1] The proportion was higher for CUF lecturers (64 per cent.) and for research staff, while only 36 per cent. of professors and 37 per cent. of readers had spent all their academic career in Oxford. It was highest in social studies and science, and lowest in medicine (Table 254).

430. Table 249 shows that, on average, over three-quarters of the academic staff's career had been spent in Oxford. Table 255 shows the relation between years in academic life and years in Oxford. The bulk of the entries lie on the diagonal of the table, but the proportion who had spent all their academic career in Oxford falls from 75 per cent. for those with 1–5 years in academic life to 41 per cent. for those with 21 years and over as academics.

**College fellowships**

431. Of the entire academic staff (including outside grants posts), 64 per cent. held college fellowships (Table 256). If those holding outside grants posts are excluded, the figure was 71 per cent.[2] Among university lecturers, senior research officers, and the equivalent who were not tutorial fellows, 20 per cent. held fellowships of other types (mainly research fellowships and fellowships at Linacre College). Two-thirds of college teachers with

[1] Because moves do not all take place at the beginning of the academic year some who spent up to a year elsewhere are included in this group.
[2] The proportion in 1965–6 would be higher. See para. 409 above.

**Table 255.** *Years in academic post at Oxford by years in academic life. Michaelmas Term 1964*

OXFORD                                                                    PERCENTAGE

| Years in academic post at Oxford | Years in academic life | | | | | |
|---|---|---|---|---|---|---|
| | None | 1–5 | 6–10 | 11–20 | 21 and over | All |
| None | 100 | 9 | 4 | 2 | — | 9 |
| 1–5 | — | 91 | 33 | 14 | 4 | 36 |
| 6–10 | — | — | 63 | 14 | 5 | 16 |
| 11–20 | — | — | — | 69 | 26 | 27 |
| 21 and over | — | — | — | — | 63 | 11 |
| All | 100 | 100 | 100 | 100 | 100 | 100 |
| Percentage having spent all academic career at Oxford | 100 | 75 | 51 | 54 | 41 | 58 |
| *Number* | *62* | *310* | *192* | *372* | *206* | *1,142* |

SOURCE: Academic Staff Survey.

no university post were fellows, the remaining third being stipendiary lecturers. The proportion of fellows was much lower in science than in arts and social studies. It was very low in medicine (very few staff in clinical medicine held a fellowship).

432. Tables 257 and 258 show, for college fellows, for how long they had held a fellowship at their present college. CUF lecturers had the highest average (12·0 years), followed by readers (11·1 years). The average for professors of 10·2 years must reflect fairly accurately the average time professors had held their chair in Oxford; it may be compared with the average of 16·1 years that professors had spent in an academic post at Oxford. The average in arts (9·8 years) was higher than in social studies or science.

### Appointments 1961–5

433. A separate and rather more detailed analysis has been made of appointments between October 1961 and January 1965 (i.e. effectively spanning the most recent four academic years) to posts at the level of lecturer or tutorial fellow and above. The purpose was to discover the current position in relation to the proportion of recruits who are Oxford graduates; who have held a post in another university; who are internally promoted (to reader or professor); and, for tutorial fellows, the extent to which college appointments are made before university appointments and vice versa.

**Table 256.** *Percentage holding college fellowships by post and subject group. Michaelmas Term 1964.*

OXFORD        PERCENTAGE

| Subject group | Professor | Reader | University lecturer with tutorial fellowship | University lecturer without tutorial fellowship | CUF and special lecturer | Other university staff with tutorial fellowship | Other senior research staff | Other university and outside grants staff | College post only: teaching | College post only: research | All posts | All posts except outside grants posts |
|---|---|---|---|---|---|---|---|---|---|---|---|---|
| Arts | 100 | 63 | 100 | 27 | 96 | 100 | — | 12 | 61 | 91 | 81 | 82 |
| Social studies | 100 | 91 | · | 33 | 100 | 100 | 50 | 15 | 83 | 100 | 78 | 82 |
| Science | 100 | 72 | 100 | 17 | 100 | 100 | 15 | 9 | 53 | 91 | 49 | 62 |
| Medicine | 100 | 55 | 100 | 13 | · | · | 25 | 8 | · | · | 28 | 33 |
| All subjects | 100 | 70 | 100 | 20 | 97 | 100 | 20 | 10 | 66 | 93 | 64 | 71 |

SOURCE: Academic Staff Survey.

**Table 257.** *Years college fellows have held a fellowship by post. College fellows: Michaelmas Term 1964*

OXFORD

PERCENTAGE

| Years a fellow | Professor | Reader | University lecturer with tutorial fellowship | University lecturer without tutorial fellowship | CUF and special lecturer | Other university staff with tutorial fellowship | Other senior research staff | Other university and outside grants staff | College post only: teaching | College post only: research | All posts |
|---|---|---|---|---|---|---|---|---|---|---|---|
| New appointment | 4 | 9 | 12 | 31 | 4 | 19 | 17 | 30 | 48 | 34 | 14 |
| 1–5 | 31 | 38 | 34 | 41 | 26 | 68 | 50 | 60 | 43 | 54 | 37 |
| 6–10 | 20 | 13 | 27 | 6 | 20 | 5 | 17 | 5 | 7 | 6 | 16 |
| 11–20 | 40 | 26 | 21 | 13 | 33 | 8 | 17 | 5 | 2 | 2 | 23 |
| 21 and over | 6 | 15 | 6 | 9 | 16 | — | — | — | — | 4 | 9 |
| All | 100 | 100 | 100 | 100 | 100 | 100 | 100 | 100 | 100 | 100 | 100 |
| Average years a fellow | 10·2 | 11·1 | 8·3 | 6·0 | 12·0 | 3·3 | 5·4 | 2·1 | 2·1 | 2·9 | 8·5 |

SOURCE: Academic Staff Survey.

**Table 258.** *Years college fellows have held a fellowship by subject group. College fellows: Michaelmas Term 1964*

OXFORD                                                                    PERCENTAGE

| Years a fellow | Arts | Social studies | Science | Medicine | All subjects |
|---|---|---|---|---|---|
| New appointment | 10 | 20 | 18 | 9 | 14 |
| 1–5 | 34 | 33 | 44 | 38 | 37 |
| 6–10 | 15 | 17 | 17 | 16 | 16 |
| 11–20 | 28 | 23 | 15 | 28 | 23 |
| 21 and over | 12 | 6 | 7 | 9 | 9 |
| All | 100 | 100 | 100 | 100 | 100 |
| *Average years a fellow* | 9·8 | 7·5 | 7·0 | 9·4 | 8·5 |

SOURCE: Academic Staff Survey.

**Table 259.** *Previous experience of professors and readers by subject group. Professors and readers appointed October 1961–January 1965*

OXFORD                                                                    PERCENTAGE

| Percentage in stated category | Arts and social studies | Science and medicine | All subjects |
|---|---|---|---|
| PROFESSORS | | | |
| Oxford graduates | 40 | 31 | 35 |
| Immediately previous post in Oxford | 40 | 31 | 35 |
| Had held post in another university | 70 | 62 | 65 |
| *Number* | *10* | *13* | *23* |
| READERS | | | |
| Oxford graduates | 56 | 35 | 42 |
| Immediately previous post in Oxford | 44 | 59 | 54 |
| Had held post in another university | 89 | 71 | 77 |
| *Number* | *9* | *17* | *26* |

SOURCE: Registry.
NOTE: Professors and readers in post on 1 January 1965 only are included.

434. The numbers of professors and readers are small and the results in Table 259 must therefore be generalized cautiously. In the four years considered, 35 per cent. of appointments to professorships were internal promotions. For readers the figure was 54 per cent. 35 per cent. of professors were Oxford graduates, compared with 42 per cent. of readers. More readers (77 per cent.) than professors (65 per cent.) had held a post

in another university. The proportion of Oxford graduates was smaller in science and medicine than in arts and social studies, but so was the proportion who had held a post in another university. In science and medicine there were relatively fewer internal promotions to chairs but relatively more to readerships, than in arts and social studies.

435. The numbers are too small to detect any time trend with accuracy, but for both professors and readers the proportion of internal promotions increased over the period.

436. Table 260 gives some similar figures for lecturers (including CUF lecturers, faculty lecturers, and senior research officers) and others with a tutorial fellowship at 1 January 1965 who were appointed between 1 October 1961 and 1 January 1965. There were 56 per cent. Oxford graduates, the proportion being higher than average for those under 30 years, in arts, and for CUF lecturers and tutorial fellows with no university post (other, possibly, than a junior post). Just over half had previously held a junior Oxford post,[1] there not being much variation about this figure, except that it was 60 per cent. for those under 30 years. Nearly two-thirds had been in Oxford either in a junior post or as research students. A substantially larger proportion of CUF lecturers and tutorial fellows without a university post came into this category, whereas only 48 per cent. of university lecturers without a tutorial fellowship did so.

437. Just over half the recruits had held a post in another university.[2] The proportion was, naturally, less for those aged under 30 years, and was higher in arts than in the other subject groups. It was lower than average for university lecturers without a tutorial fellowship.

438. The proportion who were aged under 30 years on appointment was slightly above the average of 41 per cent. in arts (45 per cent.) and below it in science and medicine (38 per cent.); it was substantially above average for CUF lecturers (57 per cent.), and for tutorial fellows without a university post (51 per cent.); while for university lecturers without a tutorial fellowship it was only 24 per cent.

439. Two interesting contrasts are apparent from this analysis. The first is between arts, and science and medicine. In the former both the proportion of Oxford graduates and the proportion who had held a post in another university were above the average; in the latter they were both below the average. The second (not altogether unrelated to the first) is

---

[1] This is likely to be an understatement, as records may not be complete for the older recruits.

[2] The proportion may be slightly higher than in the table as not all the records were complete. In addition some had held research posts other than in universities.

**Table 260.** *Previous experience of recruits by post, subject group, and age. Lecturers and tutorial fellows appointed October 1961–January 1965*

OXFORD — PERCENTAGE

| | Percentage of recruits who | | | | | Number |
|---|---|---|---|---|---|---|
| | Were Oxford graduates | Had held junior post in Oxford | Had held junior post or been research student in Oxford | Had held a post in another university | Were aged under 30 years | |
| **POST** | | | | | | |
| CUF lecturer | 75 | 59 | 75 | 51 | 57 | 51 |
| University lecturer with tutorial fellowship | 48 | 52 | 70 | 64 | 39 | 33 |
| University lecturer without tutorial fellowship | 41 | 42 | 48 | 45 | 24 | 71 |
| Tutorial fellow: no university post | 63 | 54 | 78 | 54 | 51 | 41 |
| **SUBJECT GROUP** | | | | | | |
| Arts | 82 | 44 | 63 | 61 | 45 | 57 |
| Social studies | 49 | 46 | 71 | 46 | 41 | 41 |
| Science and medicine | 43 | 56 | 63 | 48 | 38 | 98 |
| **AGE AT APPOINTMENT** | | | | | | |
| Under 30 | 60 | 60 | 71 | 34 | 100 | 80 |
| 30 and over | 53 | 44 | 60 | 64 | — | 116 |
| **All** | 56 | 51 | 65 | 52 | 41 | 196 |

SOURCE: See source to Table 235.

NOTES

1. Included are university lecturers, CUF lecturers, faculty lecturers, senior research officers, and others with a tutorial fellowship, in post at 1 January 1965 who did not hold any of these posts at 1 October 1961, and who were appointed to one of these posts between 1 October 1961 and 1 January 1965. Faculty lecturers are included with university lecturers.

2. The category 'tutorial fellow: no university post' includes some holding a junior post such as departmental demonstrator.

between tutorial fellows and university lecturers without a tutorial fellowship. The latter were less likely than the former to be Oxford graduates, or to have spent time in Oxford in a junior post or as a research student, but they were also less likely to have held a post in another university.

440. In comparing the different posts, however, it must be remembered that the last two listed in Table 260 are not static categories. University lecturers without a tutorial fellowship may subsequently be appointed to one, and most tutorial fellows without a university post (other than a junior one) will eventually achieve a lecturership. In arts and social studies they may expect to receive a CUF lecturership within a year or so of appointment by the college. In science and medicine they will usually be appointed to a university lecturership or senior research officership.

441. Table 261 gives some details of the order in which tutorial fellows received their university and college posts. CUF lecturers are excluded since the procedure is almost always for appointment to a tutorial fellowship to precede appointment to a CUF lecturership. Exceptions occur where a college lecturer or research fellow is made a CUF lecturer and is subsequently elected to a tutorial fellowship. The chief interest of Table 261 is the position in science and medicine where the usual university appointment is a university lecturership (CUF lecturerships are restricted almost entirely to Mathematics and Theoretical Physics). Half the appointments in science and medicine were made by the college before the University. A quarter were made within the same academic year. Not all these were necessarily made concurrently but the appointments include three faculty lecturers whose appointments were made jointly by the University and a college, and it is likely that most of the others in this group were appointed as a result of the simultaneous advertising of posts by the University and a college. In only a quarter of the cases did colleges appoint to a tutorial fellowship an existing university lecturer, though they may during this period have appointed to tutorial fellowships some whose appointment as university lecturer was before October 1961.[1] In arts and social studies, most of those with a college post before a university post were tutorial fellows in the 'queue' for a CUF lecturership. Those appointed to a university and a college post together were all faculty lecturers.

442. The proportion receiving a college appointment before a university appointment was higher for those aged under 30 years (who comprised 42 per cent. of those in arts and social studies, and 49 per cent. of those in science and medicine) than for those aged 30 years and over.

443. There was no systematic trend over the four years which have been analysed.

---

[1] There were in addition, 50 university lecturers appointed in science and medicine who were not tutorial fellows (and 11 in arts and 10 in social studies) some of whom may subsequently become tutorial fellows.

**Table 261.** *Order of appointment to university and college post by subject group and age at appointment. Tutorial fellows (other than CUF lecturers) appointed to a 'career' post between 1 October 1961 and 1 January 1965*

OXFORD                                                                    PERCENTAGE

| | Tutorial fellows (other than CUF lecturers) who were appointed to | | | All | Number |
|---|---|---|---|---|---|
| | University post before college post | University and college post together | College post before university post (or with no university post) | | |
| SUBJECT GROUP | | | | | |
| Arts | 20 | 7 | 73 | 100 | *15* |
| Social studies | — | 17 | 83 | 100 | *18* |
| Science and medicine | 27 | 24 | 49 | 100 | *41* |
| AGE AT APPOINTMENT | | | | | |
| Under 30 | 15 | 12 | 74 | 100 | *34* |
| 30 and over | 23 | 25 | 53 | 100 | *40* |
| All | 19 | 19 | 62 | 100 | *74* |

SOURCE: See source to Table 235.

NOTES
1. University and college appointments within the same academic year are counted as being made together.
2. Included are tutorial fellows (other than CUF lecturers) in post at 1 January 1965 whose appointment to a tutorial fellowship or to a university lecturership, faculty lecturership, or senior research officership (whichever was the earlier) was between 1 October 1961 and 1 January 1965.
3. Tutorial fellows holding a junior university post such as departmental demonstrator are counted as holding no university post in this table.


**Table 262.** *Recruits October 1961–January 1965 as percentage of all in post at 1 January 1965*

OXFORD                                                                    PERCENTAGE

| | Arts | Social studies | Science and medicine | All subjects |
|---|---|---|---|---|
| Professors and readers | 14 | 33 | 33 | 26 |
| Lecturers and tutorial fellows | 17 | 36 | 34 | 27 |
| All | 17 | 36 | 34 | 27 |

SOURCE: See source to Table 235.

444. The recruits to posts at the level of lecturer or tutorial fellow and above represent 27 per cent. of the total number of such staff in post at 1 January 1965 (Table 262). The rate of recruitment in relation to posts was highest in social studies and lowest in arts. Expansion probably accounts for 5–10 per cent. and replacement for 17–22 per cent. of the 27 per cent.

## TEACHING

445. This section is about teaching (other than postgraduate supervision) in Michaelmas Term 1964 and postgraduate supervision in Trinity Term 1964. Throughout, teaching hours are the hours given by the teachers, not those received by the taught, and time spent preparing teaching and correcting work is excluded. The tables are based on all members of the full-time academic staff (including outside grants staff) who returned a questionnaire in the Academic Staff Survey. They should, therefore, be representative of the over-all pattern of teaching at Oxford by the full-time academic staff,[1] except that the terms to which the statistics relate may not be representative of the rest of the year. But they will not exactly reflect the position of individuals. At any time some individuals will be teaching more than usual and others less than usual. There are several reasons for this. For example, the number of undergraduates taking particular subjects within a college fluctuates from year to year; colleagues take leave of absence; there may be a delay in filling posts which become vacant; pressure of other work may require a reduction in teaching. Therefore, averaged over a longer period it might be expected that a smaller proportion of the staff would be teaching relatively short hours or relatively long hours than in a single term. The evidence from the survey suggests, however, that the difference would be small. Apart from random fluctuations in the number of pupils, 4 per cent. reported they were teaching less than usual, and 1 per cent. that they were teaching more than usual. There were no marked differences between grades or between subject groups. If those who said the term was not typical are omitted, the average hours (to one decimal place) for each kind of teaching are unaltered.

446. Teaching at Oxford is carried out during the 8 weeks of each Full Term, except that teaching ends after 6 or 7 weeks for some undergraduates taking First Public Examinations and after 5 or 6 weeks for undergraduates taking Finals. An inquiry by the Committee on Teaching at Cambridge University[2] showed that the total number of days per year available for teaching was slightly higher at Oxford than the average of the universities surveyed.

[1] As noted in para. 420, some 11 per cent. of all teaching is given by other persons.
[2] *Cambridge University Reporter*, 1 May 1964, p. 1636.

**Table 263.** *Average hours per week spent on teaching for undergraduates by post and subject group. Michaelmas Term 1964*

OXFORD

| Subject group | Teaching for undergraduates (hours per week) | Professor | Reader | University lecturer with tutorial fellowship | University lecturer without tutorial fellowship | CUF and special lecturer | Other university staff with tutorial fellowship | Other senior research staff | Other university and outside grants staff | College post only: teaching | College post only: research | All posts |
|---|---|---|---|---|---|---|---|---|---|---|---|---|
| Arts | Tutorials | 0·4 | 2·0 | 9·8 | 4·8 | 11·1 | 11·6 | — | 2·0 | 9·1 | 3·3 | 7·6 |
| | Classes and seminars | 0·6 | 0·6 | 1·3 | 1·1 | 1·7 | 2·8 | — | 0·2 | 1·9 | 0·3 | 1·3 |
| | Lectures | 2·1 | 1·1 | 1·3 | 1·7 | 0·7 | 1·4 | — | 0·3 | 0·4 | 0·2 | 0·9 |
| | Practicals | — | — | 0·2 | 0·1 | 0·1 | — | 0·3 | 0·2 | — | — | 0·1 |
| | All teaching | 3·2 | 3·6 | 12·7 | 7·6 | 13·6 | 15·8 | 0·3 | 2·7 | 11·4 | 3·7 | 9·8 |
| Social studies | Tutorials | — | 4·0 | · | 2·7 | 9·9 | 8·0 | 2·0 | 2·4 | 7·9 | 2·3 | 5·7 |
| | Classes and seminars | — | 0·7 | · | 0·2 | 1·0 | 0·8 | 0·8 | 0·1 | 0·8 | 0·3 | 0·6 |
| | Lectures | 1·8 | 1·3 | · | 0·7 | 0·6 | 1·0 | 0·5 | — | 0·1 | — | 0·5 |
| | Practicals | — | — | · | 0·4 | — | — | — | — | 0·1 | — | 0·1 |
| | All teaching | 1·8 | 6·0 | · | 4·1 | 11·5 | 9·8 | 3·2 | 2·5 | 8·8 | 2·6 | 6·8 |
| Science | Tutorials | — | 3·3 | 7·5 | 3·6 | 12·3 | 7·1 | 2·3 | 2·0 | 7·7 | 2·9 | 4·1 |
| | Classes and seminars | 0·1 | 0·2 | 0·3 | 0·2 | 0·7 | 0·6 | — | 0·1 | 0·4 | 0·2 | 0·2 |
| | Lectures | 2·1 | 1·8 | 0·9 | 1·2 | 1·1 | 1·0 | 0·3 | 0·3 | 0·1 | 0·6 | 0·8 |
| | Practicals | 1·7 | 4·3 | 4·9 | 3·3 | — | 2·8 | 1·2 | 1·2 | 0·7 | — | 2·3 |
| | All teaching | 4·0 | 9·6 | 13·6 | 8·2 | 14·1 | 11·5 | 3·9 | 3·5 | 8·9 | 3·7 | 7·5 |
| Medicine | Tutorials | 0·2 | 1·3 | 9·6 | 1·6 | · | · | 0·7 | 0·7 | · | · | 1·3 |
| | Classes and seminars | 0·1 | 1·3 | · | 0·4 | · | · | — | 0·4 | · | · | 0·4 |
| | Lectures | 1·6 | 1·2 | 0·8 | 0·3 | · | · | 0·8 | 0·5 | · | · | 0·7 |
| | Practicals | 1·3 | 0·3 | 4·6 | 1·2 | — | · | — | 1·9 | · | · | 1·3 |
| | All teaching | 3·2 | 4·0 | 15·0 | 3·6 | · | · | 1·5 | 3·4 | · | · | 3·7 |
| All subjects | Tutorials | 0·3 | 2·8 | 8·1 | 3·4 | 11·0 | 8·2 | 1·6 | 1·8 | 8·4 | 2·9 | 5·4 |
| | Classes and seminars | 0·4 | 0·5 | 0·5 | 0·4 | 1·5 | 1·1 | 0·1 | 0·1 | 1·2 | 0·3 | 0·7 |
| | Lectures | 2·0 | 1·4 | 1·0 | 1·1 | 0·7 | 1·1 | 0·5 | 0·3 | 0·2 | 0·1 | 0·8 |
| | Practicals | 0·6 | 1·9 | 3·8 | 1·9 | — | 1·9 | 0·7 | 1·1 | 0·2 | 0·1 | 1·0 |
| | All teaching | 3·2 | 6·7 | 13·4 | 6·7 | 13·2 | 12·2 | 2·9 | 3·3 | 10·1 | 3·4 | 7·9 |

SOURCE: Academic Staff Survey.

Average hours per week spent on teaching for postgraduates (except supervision) by post and subject group.
Michaelmas Term 1964

OXFORD

HOURS

| Subject group | Teaching for postgraduates (hours per week) | Professor | Reader | University lecturer with tutorial fellowship | University lecturer without tutorial fellowship | CUF and special lecturer | Other university staff with tutorial fellowship | Other senior research staff | Other university and outside grants staff | College post only: teaching | College post only: research | All posts |
|---|---|---|---|---|---|---|---|---|---|---|---|---|
| Arts | Tutorials | 1·1 | 0·7 | 0·5 | 0·7 | 0·3 | 0·1 | 3·0 | 1·9 | 0·5 | 0·1 | 0·5 |
| | Classes and seminars | 0·5 | 1·0 | 0·3 | 0·6 | 0·1 | — | 1·0 | 1·3 | — | 0·1 | 0·3 |
| | Lectures | 0·2 | 1·4 | 0·1 | 0·2 | — | — | 1·3 | 1·0 | — | — | 0·2 |
| | Practicals | — | — | — | — | — | — | — | 0·3 | — | — | — |
| | All teaching | 1·8 | 3·1 | 1·0 | 1·4 | 0·4 | 0·1 | 5·3 | 4·5 | 0·5 | 0·2 | 1·0 |
| Social studies | Tutorials | 0·6 | 0·9 | . | 2·9 | 0·7 | — | 0·3 | 1·6 | 0·3 | 0·4 | 1·0 |
| | Classes and seminars | 1·2 | 0·9 | . | 0·8 | 0·5 | — | 0·5 | 0·4 | 0·7 | 0·1 | 0·6 |
| | Lectures | 0·3 | 0·5 | . | 0·4 | 0·1 | — | — | 0·2 | 0·1 | — | 0·2 |
| | Practicals | — | — | . | 0·3 | — | — | — | — | — | — | — |
| | All teaching | 2·1 | 2·4 | . | 4·4 | 1·3 | — | 0·8 | 2·1 | 1·2 | 0·5 | 1·7 |
| Science | Tutorials | 0·1 | 0·4 | 0·1 | 0·3 | 0·2 | — | — | 0·1 | 0·2 | — | 0·1 |
| | Classes and seminars | 0·5 | 0·1 | 0·1 | 0·3 | — | 0·1 | 0·2 | 0·1 | — | 0·2 | 0·2 |
| | Lectures | 0·2 | 0·3 | 0·1 | 0·2 | 0·2 | — | 0·1 | 0·2 | — | — | 0·1 |
| | Practicals | — | 0·1 | — | 0·1 | — | — | — | 0·1 | — | — | — |
| | All teaching | 0·8 | 0·9 | 0·3 | 0·9 | 0·4 | 0·2 | 0·3 | 0·4 | 0·2 | 0·2 | 0·5 |
| Medicine | Tutorials | 0·2 | — | — | 0·1 | . | . | — | 0·1 | . | . | 0·1 |
| | Classes and seminars | 0·3 | 0·2 | — | 0·4 | . | . | — | 0·4 | . | . | 0·3 |
| | Lectures | 0·3 | 0·5 | — | 0·3 | . | — | 0·1 | 0·2 | . | . | 0·2 |
| | Practicals | 0·8 | 0·5 | — | 0·7 | — | — | 0·1 | 0·2 | — | — | 0·4 |
| | All teaching | 1·6 | 1·2 | — | 1·5 | . | . | 0·1 | 0·8 | . | . | 0·9 |
| All subjects | Tutorials | 0·7 | 0·5 | 0·2 | 0·6 | 0·4 | 0·1 | 0·2 | 0·4 | 0·4 | 0·2 | 0·4 |
| | Classes and seminars | 0·6 | 0·5 | 0·2 | 0·4 | 0·2 | 0·1 | 0·2 | 0·3 | 0·2 | 0·1 | 0·3 |
| | Lectures | 0·2 | 0·6 | 0·2 | 0·3 | — | — | 0·2 | 0·3 | — | — | 0·2 |
| | Practicals | 0·1 | 0·1 | — | 0·2 | — | — | — | 0·1 | — | — | 0·1 |
| | All teaching | 1·6 | 1·7 | 0·4 | 1·5 | 0·6 | 0·1 | 0·5 | 1·2 | 0·6 | 0·3 | 0·9 |

SOURCE: Academic Staff Survey.

## Table 265. Time spent on teaching (excluding postgraduate supervision) by post and subject group. Michaelmas Term 1964

OXFORD     PERCENTAGE

| Subject group | Total teaching (hours per week) | Professor | Reader | University lecturer with tutorial fellowship | University lecturer without tutorial fellowship | CUF and special lecturer | Other university staff with tutorial fellowship | Other senior research staff | Other university and outside grants staff | College post only: teaching | College post only: research | All posts |
|---|---|---|---|---|---|---|---|---|---|---|---|---|
| Arts | None | — | — | — | — | — | — | — | 19 | — | 27 | 4 |
| | 1–4 | 62 | 25 | — | 18 | 1 | — | 33 | 12 | 16 | 27 | 14 |
| | 5–8 | 20 | 50 | — | 30 | 8 | — | 67 | 31 | 13 | 34 | 16 |
| | 9–12 | 13 | 19 | 33 | 27 | 25 | 13 | — | 27 | 25 | 11 | 22 |
| | 13–16 | 2 | — | 52 | 15 | 41 | 50 | — | 4 | 28 | — | 27 |
| | 17–20 | 2 | 6 | 14 | 9 | 20 | 38 | — | 8 | 13 | — | 14 |
| | 21 and over | — | — | — | — | 5 | — | — | — | 6 | — | 3 |
| | All | 100 | 100 | 100 | 100 | 100 | 100 | 100 | 100 | 100 | 100 | 100 |
| Social studies | None | — | — | . | — | 2 | — | — | 20 | — | 38 | 9 |
| | 1–4 | 78 | 9 | . | 22 | — | 25 | 75 | 20 | 21 | 21 | 18 |
| | 5–8 | 22 | 45 | . | 22 | 13 | 50 | 25 | 50 | 21 | 42 | 26 |
| | 9–12 | — | 36 | . | 39 | 31 | 25 | — | 10 | 16 | — | 21 |
| | 13–16 | — | 9 | . | 11 | 24 | — | — | — | 32 | — | 14 |
| | 17–20 | — | — | . | 6 | 28 | — | — | — | 11 | — | 11 |
| | 21 and over | — | — | . | — | 2 | — | — | — | — | — | 1 |
| | All | 100 | 100 | . | 100 | 100 | 100 | 100 | 100 | 100 | 100 | 100 |
| Science | None | 9 | — | — | 4 | — | — | 36 | 39 | — | 17 | 16 |
| | 1–4 | 65 | 14 | — | 15 | — | 4 | 24 | 24 | 7 | 48 | 19 |
| | 5–8 | 13 | 34 | 6 | 31 | — | 16 | 18 | 22 | 53 | 30 | 21 |
| | 9–12 | 9 | 17 | 21 | 28 | 23 | 36 | 9 | 6 | 13 | 4 | 16 |
| | 13–16 | — | 28 | 56 | 13 | 59 | 44 | 12 | 6 | 20 | — | 21 |
| | 17–20 | — | 3 | 17 | 6 | 14 | — | — | 3 | 7 | — | 6 |
| | 21 and over | 4 | 3 | — | 3 | 5 | — | — | — | — | — | 1 |
| | All | 100 | 100 | 100 | 100 | 100 | 100 | 100 | 100 | 100 | 100 | 100 |

[continued

# Table 265. (*continued*)

PERCENTAGE

| Subject group | Total teaching (hours per week) | Professor | Reader | University lecturer with tutorial fellowship | University lecturer without tutorial fellowship | CUF and special lecturer | Other university staff with tutorial fellowship | Other senior research staff | Other university and outside grants staff | College post only: teaching | College post only: research | All posts |
|---|---|---|---|---|---|---|---|---|---|---|---|---|
| Medicine | None | — | — | — | 19 | · | · | 80 | 45 | · | · | 34 |
| | 1–4 | 60 | 64 | — | 45 | · | · | 10 | 23 | · | · | 32 |
| | 5–8 | 30 | 18 | — | 13 | · | · | — | 13 | · | · | 12 |
| | 9–12 | 10 | 9 | 20 | 10 | · | · | 5 | 8 | · | · | 9 |
| | 13–16 | — | — | 40 | 10 | · | · | 5 | 8 | · | · | 7 |
| | 17–20 | — | 9 | 40 | 3 | · | · | — | 3 | · | · | 5 |
| | 21 and over | — | — | — | | · | · | — | 3 | · | · | 1 |
| | All | 100 | 100 | 100 | 100 | · | · | 100 | 100 | · | · | 100 |
| All subjects | None | 2 | — | — | 6 | — | — | 47 | 36 | — | 27 | 12 |
| | 1–4 | 64 | 24 | — | 23 | 1 | 5 | 23 | 22 | 15 | 31 | 18 |
| | 5–8 | 20 | 37 | 4 | 26 | 8 | 11 | 15 | 24 | 24 | 35 | 19 |
| | 9–12 | 10 | 19 | 24 | 26 | 26 | 32 | 7 | 9 | 20 | 7 | 18 |
| | 13–16 | 1 | 13 | 54 | 13 | 39 | 43 | 8 | 5 | 27 | — | 21 |
| | 17–20 | 1 | 4 | 18 | 6 | 21 | 8 | — | 3 | 11 | — | 9 |
| | 21 and over | 1 | 1 | — | 1 | 4 | — | — | — | 3 | — | 2 |
| | All | 100 | 100 | 100 | 100 | 100 | 100 | 100 | 100 | 100 | 100 | 100 |

SOURCE: Academic Staff Survey.

## Teaching for undergraduates (average hours)

447. On average, 7·9 hours were spent teaching undergraduates, 5·4 hours, or two-thirds, being accounted for by tutorials (Table 263). Classes and seminars accounted for 0·7 hours, lectures for 0·8 hours, and practical instruction for 1·0 hours. The average hours and their composition varied between subject groups. The average was highest in arts and lowest in medicine. Time spent on both tutorials and classes and seminars was highest in arts. The average of hours given to undergraduate teaching was significantly higher for college teachers than for others. It was 13·2 hours for CUF lecturers, 13·4 hours for university lecturers with a tutorial fellowship, 12·2 hours for other university staff with a tutorial fellowship, and 10·1 hours for college teachers with no university post. The high average in these cases was due to the high average for tutorials (but, in addition, in science and medicine university lecturers with a tutorial fellowship spent considerably more time giving practical instruction than did lecturers without a tutorial fellowship). Professors spent an average of 3·2 hours teaching undergraduates, mainly in the form of lectures. If outside grants staff are excluded, the average is 8·6 hours, of which 5·9 hours are accounted for by tutorials; the corresponding figures for science become 9·0 hours and 4·8 hours respectively.

## Teaching for postgraduates (average hours)

448. Teaching for postgraduates (excluding supervision which is considered in paras. 459–62) occupied an average of 0·9 hours per week (Table 264). Tutorials accounted for 0·4 hours, classes and seminars for 0·3 hours, lectures for 0·2 hours, and practical instruction (all in medicine) for 0·1 hours. The average was higher in social studies (1·7 hours), where tutorials and classes and seminars occupied about twice the average time, and lower in science. Professors, readers, and university lecturers without a tutorial fellowship spent more time on teaching for postgraduates than did other grades. If outside grants staff are excluded, the average for all subjects is 1·0 hours, and in science it is 0·6 hours.

## The distribution of teaching

449. Total teaching averaged 8·8 hours (9·6 hours if outside grants staff are excluded). The distribution of the staff according to the amount of teaching is given in Table 265. It shows that 12 per cent. did no teaching, while 11 per cent. did 17 hours and over, and 58 per cent. did between 5 and 16 hours. In arts, half spent between 9 and 16 hours on teaching, and 17 per cent. spent longer. In social studies nearly half spent between 5 and 12 hours, and 26 per cent. spent longer. In science there was no clear peak to the distribution; 58 per cent. spent between 5 and 16 hours and 7 per cent. spent longer. In medicine, a third did no teaching, and a third did between 1 and 4 hours. The peak of the distribution for all subjects

**Table 266.** *Time spent on teaching for undergraduates by post. Michaelmas Term 1964*

OXFORD

PERCENTAGE

| Teaching for undergraduates (hours per week) | Professor | Reader | University lecturer with tutorial fellowship | University lecturer without tutorial fellowship | CUF and special lecturer | Other university staff with tutorial fellowship | Other senior research staff | Other university and outside grants staff | College post only: teaching | College post only: research | All posts |
|---|---|---|---|---|---|---|---|---|---|---|---|
| None | 13 | 18 | — | 18 | 1 | — | 55 | 47 | 2 | 33 | 19 |
| 1–4 | 69 | 18 | — | 22 | 2 | 5 | 18 | 22 | 17 | 27 | 18 |
| 5–8 | 13 | 36 | 7 | 28 | 8 | 11 | 12 | 19 | 23 | 34 | 18 |
| 9–12 | 5 | 15 | 28 | 16 | 30 | 35 | 10 | 4 | 21 | 5 | 17 |
| 13–16 | — | 12 | 51 | 10 | 39 | 43 | 5 | 5 | 27 | — | 20 |
| 17 and over | 1 | 1 | 15 | 6 | 21 | 5 | — | 3 | 11 | — | 9 |
| All | 100 | 100 | 100 | 100 | 100 | 100 | 100 | 100 | 100 | 100 | 100 |

SOURCE: Academic Staff Survey.

was in the range 1–4 hours for professors, 5–8 hours for readers, 13–16 hours for tutorial fellows, and 5–12 hours for other university lecturers. Excluding outside grants staff, 92 per cent. did some teaching (93 per cent. in science) and 35 per cent. in science and in all subjects did 13 hours and over.

**Table 267.** *Time spent on teaching for undergraduates by subject group. Michaelmas Term 1964*

| OXFORD | | | | | PERCENTAGE |
|---|---|---|---|---|---|
| Teaching for undergraduates (hours per week) | Arts | Social studies | Science | Medicine | All subjects |
| None | 11 | 21 | 18 | 45 | 19 |
| 1–4 | 14 | 19 | 19 | 26 | 18 |
| 5–8 | 14 | 22 | 22 | 11 | 18 |
| 9–12 | 22 | 18 | 14 | 9 | 17 |
| 13–16 | 25 | 13 | 21 | 4 | 20 |
| 17 and over | 14 | 6 | 6 | 4 | 9 |
| All | 100 | 100 | 100 | 100 | 100 |

SOURCE: Academic Staff Survey.

450. Distributions for time spent on teaching for undergraduates are given in Tables 266 and 267 and for postgraduates (excluding supervision) in Tables 268 and 269. The general pattern for undergraduates is similar to that in Table 265. 28 per cent. gave some teaching for postgraduates (excluding supervision), the proportion being over a half for professors and readers, and higher than average (46 per cent.) in social studies.

451. When all forms of teaching, including postgraduate supervision, are considered, only 10 per cent. were doing no teaching at the time of the Academic Staff Survey.[1] 46 per cent. taught both undergraduates and postgraduates; 35 per cent. taught undergraduates only; and 9 per cent. taught postgraduates only (Tables 270 and 271). When outside grants staff are excluded just half taught both undergraduates and postgraduates; 35 per cent. taught undergraduates only; 9 per cent. taught postgraduates only; and 6 per cent. did no teaching. (And in science the corresponding figures were 57 per cent.; 34 per cent.; 5 per cent.; and 4 per cent. respectively.) The proportion teaching both undergraduates and postgraduates was highest for professors, readers, and university lecturers with tutorial fellowships. It was lowest for research staff, a higher than average proportion of whom taught postgraduates only.

[1] That is, were doing no teaching (other than supervision) in Michaelmas Term 1964, and had supervised no postgraduates in Trinity Term 1964.

PERCENTAGE

**Table 268.** *Time spent on teaching for postgraduates (excluding supervision) by post. Michaelmas Term 1964*

OXFORD

| Teaching for postgraduates (excluding supervision) (hours per week) | Professor | Reader | University lecturer with tutorial fellowship | University lecturer without tutorial fellowship | CUF and special lecturer | Other university staff with tutorial fellowship | Other senior research staff | Other university and outside grants staff | College post only: teaching | College post only: research | All posts |
|---|---|---|---|---|---|---|---|---|---|---|---|
| None | 49 | 48 | 81 | 62 | 72 | 89 | 80 | 78 | 77 | 88 | 72 |
| 1–3 | 37 | 37 | 16 | 19 | 24 | 11 | 13 | 9 | 18 | 10 | 19 |
| 4–6 | 7 | 12 | 2 | 12 | 4 | — | 5 | 4 | 3 | 2 | 5 |
| 7 and over | 7 | 3 | 1 | 7 | 1 | — | 2 | 9 | 2 | — | 3 |
| All | 100 | 100 | 100 | 100 | 100 | 100 | 100 | 100 | 100 | 100 | 100 |

SOURCE: Academic Staff Survey.

L

**Table 269.** *Time spent on teaching for postgraduates (excluding supervision) by subject group. Michaelmas Term 1964*

OXFORD                                                                    PERCENTAGE

| Teaching for post-graduates (excluding supervision) (hours per week) | Arts | Social studies | Science | Medicine | All subjects |
|---|---|---|---|---|---|
| None | 69 | 54 | 80 | 77 | 72 |
| 1–3 | 22 | 29 | 14 | 13 | 19 |
| 4–6 | 4 | 10 | 4 | 7 | 5 |
| 7 and over | 5 | 7 | 1 | 3 | 3 |
| All | 100 | 100 | 100 | 100 | 100 |

SOURCE: Academic Staff Survey.

## Tutorial teaching

452. The tutorial teaching of undergraduates is a main duty of tutorial fellows, and this form of teaching is undertaken by many other members of the academic staff. The average time spent in this way was 5·4 hours per week and Table 272 gives detailed distributions. 31 per cent. gave no tutorials to undergraduates (in medicine only 30 per cent. did give any), the grades containing a large proportion not giving tutorials to under-graduates being professors (who may not receive payment for this teaching), readers, university lecturers without a tutorial fellowship, and university or college research staff. There was a substantial minority amongst uni-versity lecturers without a tutorial fellowship who gave a considerable number of tutorials. A third gave at least 5 hours, and 11 per cent. gave at least 9 hours. About half the university lecturers with a tutorial fellowship gave 8 hours or less. Most CUF lecturers gave at least 9 hours, and 35 per cent. gave 13 hours and over. When outside grants staff are excluded, the proportion giving some tutorials for undergraduates is 75 per cent. in science and 72 per cent. in all subjects. The proportion spending at least 9 hours per week is 20 per cent. in science and 33 per cent. in all subjects.

453. Tutorial fellows are concentrated in the group spending 9–12 hours per week giving tutorials to undergraduates, and their distribution within this group is of some interest. Two-thirds of university lecturers with a tutorial fellowship in the 9–12 hours group gave 9 hours. College teachers with no university post were fairly evenly spread over the group. CUF lec-turers were also fairly evenly spread, but there were more at 9 or 12 hours than at 10 or 11 hours. There were 42 per cent. in the group. A detailed breakdown gives: 11 per cent. gave 9 hours; 9 per cent. gave 10 hours; 10 per cent. gave 11 hours; and 13 per cent. gave 12 hours.

**Table 270.** *Percentage of academic staff teaching undergraduates, postgraduates, or both, by post. Michaelmas Term 1964*

OXFORD PERCENTAGE

| Teaching given: | Professor | Reader | University lecturer with tutorial fellowship | University lecturer without tutorial fellowship | CUF and special lecturer | Other university staff with tutorial fellowship | Other senior research staff | Other university and outside grants staff | College post only: teaching | College post only: research | All posts |
|---|---|---|---|---|---|---|---|---|---|---|---|
| For undergraduates and postgraduates | 75 | 72 | 73 | 53 | 56 | 51 | 25 | 17 | 39 | 15 | 46 |
| For undergraduates only | 13 | 10 | 27 | 29 | 43 | 49 | 20 | 36 | 59 | 53 | 35 |
| For postgraduates only | 13 | 18 | — | 13 | 1 | — | 23 | 15 | 2 | 7 | 9 |
| No teaching given | — | — | — | 5 | — | — | 32 | 33 | — | 26 | 10 |
| All | 100 | 100 | 100 | 100 | 100 | 100 | 100 | 100 | 100 | 100 | 100 |

SOURCE: Academic Staff Survey.

NOTE: Tutorials, classes and seminars, lectures, and practical instruction given in Michaelmas Term 1964, and postgraduate supervision in Trinity Term 1964 are included.

**Table 271.** *Percentage of academic staff teaching undergraduates, post-graduates, or both, by subject group. Michaelmas Term 1964*

OXFORD                                                        PERCENTAGE

| Teaching given: | Arts | Social studies | Science | Medicine | All subjects |
|---|---|---|---|---|---|
| For undergraduates and postgraduates | 48 | 51 | 47 | 29 | 46 |
| For undergraduates only | 41 | 28 | 34 | 26 | 35 |
| For postgraduates only | 8 | 13 | 6 | 15 | 9 |
| No teaching given | 3 | 9 | 12 | 31 | 10 |
| All | 100 | 100 | 100 | 100 | 100 |

SOURCE: Academic Staff Survey.
NOTE: See note to Table 270.

454. Tables 273 and 274 give similar distributions for all tutorial teaching.

455. Table 275 shows the relative number of tutorial hours given to groups of one, two, or three pupils. Over all, 59 per cent. of tutorials for under-graduates were given singly, and 36 per cent. to pairs. The proportion given singly was highest in medicine (72 per cent.) and lowest in social studies (47 per cent.). Those without tutorial fellowships tended to give a higher proportion of tutorials singly. This was probably because their pupils often come from a number of colleges, and it is therefore less con-venient to group them in pairs or threes.

456. Those who taught in pairs and threes were asked for their reasons for doing so (Tables 276 and 277). Of those who gave tutorials, 33 per cent. gave none to pairs or threes, 33 per cent. taught pairs or threes by prefer-ence, 22 per cent. did so because they had not enough time to do otherwise, 5 per cent. did so because it was college policy, and the remainder either gave other reasons or no reply. Among other university and outside grants staff, and those with a college research post, at least as many taught pairs or threes for lack of time or because of college policy as did so by preference. For other grades, more did so by preference than for other reasons. The pressure of time was more in evidence in social studies (in which 81 per cent. gave some tutorials to pairs or threes) than in other subject groups.

457. A comparison of tutorial teaching in Oxford with supervision in Cam-bridge, according to the persons giving the teaching, was made in Part III. Table 278 gives some details of the amount of supervision given in Cam-bridge in six subjects in 1961–2. These figures cannot be directly compared

OXFORD

PERCENTAGE

**Table 272.** *Time spent giving tutorials to undergraduates by post and subject group. Michaelmas Term 1964*

| Subject group | Tutorials to undergraduates (hours per week) | Professor | Reader | University lecturer with tutorial fellowship | University lecturer without tutorial fellowship | CUF and special lecturer | Other university staff with tutorial fellowship | Other senior research staff | Other university and outside grants staff | College post only: teaching | College post only: research | All posts |
|---|---|---|---|---|---|---|---|---|---|---|---|---|
| Arts | None | 89 | 44 | — | 21 | — | — | 100 | 69 | — | 36 | 21 |
| | 1–4 | 9 | 38 | — | 30 | 7 | — | — | 15 | 16 | 20 | 12 |
| | 5–8 | — | 19 | 29 | 27 | 13 | — | — | 8 | 38 | 36 | 17 |
| | 9–12 | 2 | — | 57 | 18 | 44 | 75 | — | — | 25 | 7 | 30 |
| | 13–16 | — | — | 14 | 3 | 27 | 25 | — | 8 | 16 | — | 16 |
| | 17 and over | — | — | — | — | 8 | — | — | — | 6 | — | 4 |
| | All | 100 | 100 | 100 | 100 | 100 | 100 | 100 | 100 | 100 | 100 | 100 |
| Social studies | None | 100 | 18 | · · · | 56 | 6 | — | 50 | 45 | 11 | 54 | 31 |
| | 1–4 | — | 27 | · · · | 17 | 2 | 25 | 25 | 30 | 26 | 17 | 15 |
| | 5–8 | — | 55 | · · · | 17 | 28 | 50 | 25 | 25 | 11 | 29 | 25 |
| | 9–12 | — | — | · · · | 11 | 35 | — | — | — | 26 | — | 16 |
| | 13–16 | — | — | · · · | — | 24 | 25 | — | — | 16 | — | 10 |
| | 17 and over | — | — | · · · | — | 6 | — | — | — | 11 | — | 3 |
| | All | 100 | 100 | · · · | 100 | 100 | 100 | 100 | 100 | 100 | 100 | 100 |
| Science | None | 96 | 38 | — | 24 | — | — | 52 | 50 | — | 30 | 32 |
| | 1–4 | 4 | 24 | 6 | 41 | — | 16 | 21 | 32 | 13 | 48 | 25 |
| | 5–8 | — | 31 | 56 | 24 | 5 | 60 | 24 | 15 | 60 | 17 | 27 |
| | 9–12 | — | 7 | 38 | 9 | 41 | 24 | 3 | 2 | 20 | 4 | 13 |
| | 13–16 | — | — | — | 1 | 55 | — | — | 1 | 7 | — | 3 |
| | 17 and over | — | — | — | — | — | — | — | — | — | — | — |
| | All | 100 | 100 | 100 | 100 | 100 | 100 | 100 | 100 | 100 | 100 | 100 |
| Medicine | None | 90 | 73 | — | 68 | · · · | · · · | 90 | 65 | · · · | · · · | 70 |
| | 1–4 | 10 | 9 | 20 | 16 | · · · | · · · | 5 | 35 | · · · | · · · | 19 |
| | 5–8 | — | 18 | 80 | 13 | · · · | · · · | — | — | · · · | · · · | 6 |
| | 9–12 | — | — | — | 3 | · · · | · · · | 5 | — | · · · | · · · | 5 |
| | 13–16 | — | — | — | — | · · · | · · · | — | — | · · · | · · · | — |
| | 17 and over | — | — | — | — | · · · | · · · | — | — | · · · | · · · | — |
| | All | 100 | 100 | 100 | 100 | · · · | · · · | 100 | 100 | · · · | · · · | 100 |
| All subjects | None | 92 | 42 | — | 36 | 1 | — | 67 | 55 | 3 | 40 | 31 |
| | 1–4 | 7 | 25 | 4 | 31 | 5 | 14 | 15 | 30 | 18 | 26 | 18 |
| | 5–8 | 1 | 30 | 47 | 22 | 15 | 46 | 15 | 12 | 35 | 30 | 21 |
| | 9–12 | — | 3 | 45 | 10 | 42 | 32 | 3 | 1 | 24 | 4 | 19 |
| | 13–16 | — | — | 3 | 1 | 28 | 8 | — | 1 | 14 | — | 9 |
| | 17 and over | — | — | — | — | 7 | — | — | — | 6 | — | 2 |
| | All | 100 | 100 | 100 | 100 | 100 | 100 | 100 | 100 | 100 | 100 | 100 |

SOURCE: Academic Staff Survey.

**Table 273.** *Time spent giving tutorials by post. Michaelmas Term 1964*

OXFORD                    PERCENTAGE

| Tutorials (hours per week) | Professor | Reader | University lecturer with tutorial fellowship | University lecturer without tutorial fellowship | CUF and special lecturer | Other university staff with tutorial fellowship | Other senior research staff | Other university and outside grants staff | College post only: teaching | College post only: research | All posts |
|---|---|---|---|---|---|---|---|---|---|---|---|
| None | 80 | 34 | — | 28 | — | — | 63 | 48 | 3 | 36 | 27 |
| 1–4 | 13 | 27 | 3 | 30 | 5 | 14 | 17 | 31 | 18 | 29 | 18 |
| 5–8 | 5 | 34 | 47 | 30 | 16 | 43 | 17 | 19 | 33 | 31 | 24 |
| 9–12 | 2 | 4 | 45 | 11 | 38 | 32 | 3 | 1 | 24 | 4 | 18 |
| 13–16 | — | — | 4 | 2 | 33 | 11 | — | 1 | 15 | — | 10 |
| 17 and over | — | — | — | — | 8 | — | — | — | 6 | — | 2 |
| All | 100 | 100 | 100 | 100 | 100 | 100 | 100 | 100 | 100 | 100 | 100 |

SOURCE: Academic Staff Survey.

**Table 274.** *Time spent giving tutorials by subject group. Michaelmas Term 1964*

OXFORD                                                           PERCENTAGE

| Tutorials (hours per week) | Arts | Social studies | Science | Medicine | All subjects |
|---|---|---|---|---|---|
| None | 15 | 20 | 31 | 68 | 27 |
| 1–4 | 14 | 15 | 23 | 21 | 18 |
| 5–8 | 21 | 33 | 29 | 7 | 24 |
| 9–12 | 28 | 13 | 13 | 5 | 18 |
| 13–16 | 18 | 13 | 3 | — | 10 |
| 17 and over | 4 | 5 | — | — | 2 |
| All | 100 | 100 | 100 | 100 | 100 |

SOURCE: Academic Staff Survey.

with those for Oxford given above since they are based not on all academic staff, but on those giving some supervision. Corresponding figures for Oxford can, however, be calculated, but no comparison can be made of the proportion of the staff giving some tutorial teaching or supervision. In Oxford, the average hours spent giving tutorials to undergraduates, by those spending some time in this way, was 11 hours for CUF lecturers, about 8 hours for other tutorial fellows, and about 5 hours for others (except professors). It was 10 hours in arts, 8 hours in social studies, 6 hours in science, 4 hours in medicine, and 8 hours over all. The main differences between the Oxford and Cambridge figures are that the averages appear to be considerably higher for Oxford than Cambridge (by up to 50 per cent.) and that for Cambridge there is no systematic difference between holders of fellowships and non-fellows, as there is at Oxford.

### Classes and seminars, lectures, and practicals

458. Distributions according to the time spent on teaching other than tutorials (classes and seminars, lectures, and practical instruction but still excluding postgraduate supervision) are given in Tables 279 and 280. Almost three-quarters did some non-tutorial teaching, and 12 per cent. did at least 7 hours a week. Readers and university lecturers (in particular those with tutorial fellowships) did more than the average of non-tutorial teaching. Although the proportion doing some non-tutorial teaching was highest in arts (82 per cent.), the proportion doing at least 7 hours was low in arts (6 per cent. compared with 22 per cent. in science and 19 per cent. in medicine). Details for the components of non-tutorial teaching are given in Tables 281–5.

Table 275. *Number attending tutorials for undergraduates given by academic staff by post and subject group. Michaelmas Term 1964.*

OXFORD  PERCENTAGE

| Subject group | Percentage of tutorials given to groups of: | Professor | Reader | University lecturer with tutorial fellowship | University lecturer without tutorial fellowship | CUF and special lecturer | Other university staff with tutorial fellowship | Other senior research staff | Other university and outside grants staff | College post only: teaching | College post only: research | All posts |
|---|---|---|---|---|---|---|---|---|---|---|---|---|
| Arts | One | 100 | 91 | 36 | 65 | 65 | 73 | · · · | 65 | 46 | 57 | 62 |
| | Two | — | 6 | 51 | 25 | 31 | 26 | · · · | 27 | 47 | 38 | 33 |
| | Three | — | 3 | 13 | 10 | 4 | 1 | · · · | 8 | 7 | 5 | 5 |
| | All | 100 | 100 | 100 | 100 | 100 | 100 | · · · | 100 | 100 | 100 | 100 |
| Social studies | One | · · · | 52 | 50 | 51 | 49 | 16 | 50 | 38 | 42 | 55 | 47 |
| | Two | · · · | 45 | 48 | 41 | 46 | 47 | 50 | 53 | 56 | 34 | 47 |
| | Three | · · · | 2 | 2 | 8 | 5 | 38 | — | 9 | 2 | 11 | 6 |
| | All | · · · | 100 | 100 | 100 | 100 | 100 | 100 | 100 | 100 | 100 | 100 |
| Science | One | 100 | 57 | 50 | 75 | 56 | 56 | 66 | 72 | 55 | 37 | 59 |
| | Two | — | 38 | 48 | 23 | 27 | 42 | 30 | 25 | 40 | 58 | 36 |
| | Three | — | 5 | 2 | 2 | 17 | 2 | 4 | 2 | 5 | 5 | 5 |
| | All | 100 | 100 | 100 | 100 | 100 | 100 | 100 | 100 | 100 | 100 | 100 |
| Medicine | One | 100 | 86 | 65 | 74 | · · · | · · · | 71 | 70 | · · · | · · · | 72 |
| | Two | — | 14 | 31 | 16 | · · · | · · · | 29 | 27 | · · · | · · · | 23 |
| | Three | — | — | 4 | 10 | · · · | · · · | — | 3 | · · · | · · · | 5 |
| | All | 100 | 100 | 100 | 100 | · · · | · · · | 100 | 100 | · · · | · · · | 100 |
| All subjects | One | 96 | 64 | 47 | 70 | 61 | 57 | 65 | 67 | 47 | 52 | 59 |
| | Two | 4 | 32 | 48 | 25 | 33 | 37 | 32 | 29 | 48 | 42 | 36 |
| | Three | — | 4 | 5 | 5 | 6 | 6 | 3 | 4 | 5 | 6 | 5 |
| | All | 100 | 100 | 100 | 100 | 100 | 100 | 100 | 100 | 100 | 100 | 100 |

SOURCE: Academic Staff Survey.

NOTE: The distributions are based on the number of tutorial hours given for undergraduates by the academic staff.

**Table 276.** *Reasons for giving tutorials to pairs and threes by post. Academic staff (including outside grants staff) who gave tutorials. Michaelmas Term 1964*

OXFORD

PERCENTAGE

| Reasons for giving tutorials to pairs and threes | Professor | Reader | University lecturer with tutorial fellowship | University lecturer without tutorial fellowship | CUF and special lecturer | Other university staff with tutorial fellowship | Other senior research staff | Other university and outside grants staff | College post only: teaching | College post only: research | All posts |
|---|---|---|---|---|---|---|---|---|---|---|---|
| Prefer to teach pairs or threes | 17 | 28 | 39 | 24 | 36 | 54 | 32 | 22 | 41 | 24 | 33 |
| Not enough time | — | 23 | 26 | 14 | 24 | 27 | 11 | 15 | 20 | 31 | 22 |
| College policy | — | 3 | 3 | 3 | 4 | — | 5 | 8 | 9 | 11 | 5 |
| For other reasons | — | — | 7 | 6 | 4 | — | — | — | — | — | 3 |
| Not ascertained | — | 3 | 10 | 3 | 5 | 5 | — | 4 | 8 | 2 | 5 |
| No tutorials to pairs or threes | 83 | 44 | 16 | 50 | 27 | 14 | 53 | 52 | 22 | 33 | 33 |
| All | 100 | 100 | 100 | 100 | 100 | 100 | 100 | 100 | 100 | 100 | 100 |

SOURCE: Academic Staff Survey.

**Table 277.** *Reasons for giving tutorials to pairs and threes by subject group. Academic staff (including outside grants staff) who gave tutorials. Michaelmas Term 1964*

OXFORD                                                                    PERCENTAGE

| Reasons for giving tutorials to pairs and threes | Arts | Social studies | Science | Medicine | All subjects |
|---|---|---|---|---|---|
| Prefer to teach pairs or threes | 34 | 35 | 32 | 23 | 33 |
| Not enough time | 22 | 31 | 20 | 11 | 22 |
| College policy | 4 | 9 | 5 | — | 5 |
| For other reasons | 4 | 1 | 2 | 6 | 3 |
| Not ascertained | 4 | 5 | 5 | 9 | 5 |
| No tutorials to pairs or threes | 32 | 19 | 37 | 51 | 33 |
| All | 100 | 100 | 100 | 100 | 100 |

SOURCE: Academic Staff Survey.

**Table 278.** *Average hours of supervision per week given by those giving some supervision to undergraduates in certain subjects at Cambridge. 1961–2*

CAMBRIDGE                                                                        HOURS

| Academic staff giving some supervision to undergraduates | English | Law | French | Russian | Physics | Bio-chemistry | All six subjects |
|---|---|---|---|---|---|---|---|
| | (average hours per week) | | | | | | |
| University staff holding fellowships | 6·0 | 8·8 | 7·8 | 4·7 | 4·5 | 3·7 | 6·3 |
| University staff not holding fellowships | 6·5 | 7·9 | 5·6 | 7·5 | 5·4 | 2·9 | 5·8 |
| Fellows not holding university posts | 5·0 | 8·0 | 8·7 | . | 4·0 | 2·5 | 5·5 |
| All | 5·6 | 8·6 | 7·9 | 6·3 | 4·5 | 3·2 | 6·0 |

SOURCE: 'Report to the General Board of the Committee on Teaching', *Cambridge University Reporter*, 1 May 1964.

Table 279. *Time spent on teaching other than tutorials and postgraduate supervision by post. Michaelmas Term 1964*

OXFORD

PERCENTAGE

| Teaching, except tutorials and postgraduate supervision (hours per week) | Professor | Reader | University lecturer with tutorial fellowship | University lecturer without tutorial fellowship | CUF and special lecturer | Other university staff with tutorial fellowship | Other senior research staff | Other university and outside grants staff | College post only: teaching | College post only: research | All posts |
|---|---|---|---|---|---|---|---|---|---|---|---|
| None | 7 | 3 | 2 | 9 | 14 | — | 55 | 57 | 38 | 69 | 27 |
| 1–3 | 46 | 42 | 20 | 39 | 60 | 43 | 30 | 19 | 42 | 29 | 39 |
| 4–6 | 34 | 24 | 39 | 32 | 21 | 41 | 7 | 13 | 15 | 2 | 22 |
| 7 and over | 13 | 31 | 38 | 20 | 4 | 16 | 8 | 11 | 5 | — | 12 |
| All | 100 | 100 | 100 | 100 | 100 | 100 | 100 | 100 | 100 | 100 | 100 |

SOURCE: Academic Staff Survey.

**Table 280.** *Time spent on teaching other than tutorials and postgraduate supervision by subject group. Michaelmas Term 1964*

OXFORD                                                                          PERCENTAGE

| Teaching, except tutorials and post-graduate supervision (hours per week) | Arts | Social studies | Science | Medicine | All subjects |
|---|---|---|---|---|---|
| None | 18 | 31 | 30 | 40 | 27 |
| 1–3 | 52 | 52 | 24 | 26 | 39 |
| 4–6 | 25 | 14 | 24 | 15 | 22 |
| 7 and over | 6 | 4 | 22 | 19 | 12 |
| All | 100 | 100 | 100 | 100 | 100 |

SOURCE: Academic Staff Survey.

## Postgraduate supervision

459. Postgraduates reading for the degrees of B.Litt., B.Sc., D.Phil., and B.Phil. and for certain diplomas have a supervisor appointed by the board of the faculty in which their work lies. In addition, some colleges appoint a member of the college to supervise their postgraduates. Because supervision of postgraduates necessarily takes place irregularly, it was not appropriate to seek details of supervision in Michaelmas Term 1964 in the Academic Staff Survey. Information was therefore collected relating to Trinity Term 1964. Some 9 per cent. had not been appointed then, and others were on leave of absence. In all, 12 per cent. were unable to give details of supervision. And others who had given supervision in the Trinity Term had either resigned or were on leave of absence at the time of the survey. The picture of supervision is therefore not complete. Where averages are given, they are based only on those in the survey who were available to supervise in Trinity Term 1964.

460. On average, 1·6 postgraduates were supervised per member of the staff, the great majority for a faculty board (Table 286). If outside grants staff are excluded, the average number supervised was 1·8 (2·0 in science), 53 per cent. supervising at least one. The average was lowest in medicine (0·8) and was highest in social studies because of the relatively large number supervised for colleges (the graduate colleges, many of whose fellows are in social studies, appoint college supervisors). Professors supervised the largest average number (4·2), professors in arts having 5·4. They were followed by readers (3·3) and university lecturers with a tutorial fellowship (2·8) (those in science supervised an average of 3·3). University lecturers without a tutorial fellowship supervised an average of 1·9 and CUF lecturers 1·3.

## Table 281. Time spent giving classes and seminars by post. Michaelmas Term 1964

OXFORD

PERCENTAGE

| Classes and seminars (hours per week) | Professor | Reader | University lecturer with tutorial fellowship | University lecturer without tutorial fellowship | CUF and special lecturer | Other university staff with tutorial fellowship | Other senior research staff | Other university and outside grants staff | College post only: teaching | College post only: research | All posts |
|---|---|---|---|---|---|---|---|---|---|---|---|
| None | 57 | 58 | 58 | 61 | 35 | 41 | 87 | 83 | 47 | 77 | 59 |
| 1–2 | 31 | 30 | 35 | 29 | 40 | 46 | 10 | 12 | 30 | 22 | 28 |
| 3–4 | 9 | 6 | 6 | 9 | 17 | 8 | 3 | 2 | 15 | 1 | 9 |
| 5 and over | 2 | 6 | 1 | 1 | 7 | 5 | — | 3 | 8 | — | 4 |
| All | 100 | 100 | 100 | 100 | 100 | 100 | 100 | 100 | 100 | 100 | 100 |

SOURCE: Academic Staff Survey.

**Table 282.** *Time spent giving classes and seminars by subject group. Michael-mas Term 1964*

OXFORD                                                                    PERCENTAGE

| Classes and seminars (hours per week) | Arts | Social studies | Science | Medicine | All subjects |
|---|---|---|---|---|---|
| None | 39 | 48 | 78 | 79 | 59 |
| 1–2 | 38 | 38 | 19 | 15 | 28 |
| 3–4 | 16 | 10 | 2 | 3 | 9 |
| 5 and over | 7 | 4 | 1 | 4 | 4 |
| All | 100 | 100 | 100 | 100 | 100 |

SOURCE: Academic Staff Survey.

461. The proportion of the staff supervising postgraduates was 50 per cent. 23 per cent. supervised 3 and over, and 8 per cent. 6 and over. Among professors and readers some 85 per cent. did supervision, and 26 per cent. of professors supervised 6 and over. Three-quarters of university lecturers with a tutorial fellowship supervised postgraduates, and about half of other tutorial fellows. Considerably fewer in medicine than in other subject groups did so (see Tables 287 and 288).

462. Distributions showing the amount of supervision postgraduates were given are in Table 289. The amount of supervision is given in hours per term where possible. But this is not always appropriate, particularly in science and medicine where postgraduates often work alongside their supervisor. There is therefore a category for those in 'day-to-day contact' for which the total hours involved cannot be estimated. It is estimated that 41 per cent. of postgraduates fell in this category, the proportion being over 80 per cent. in science and medicine. There is a further category 'other' in Table 289. This includes postgraduates doing field work or studying outside Oxford (in which case supervision was usually carried out by correspondence), and a very small number who were working under someone other than their normal supervisor. Up to 4 hours' supervision per term was received by 13 per cent. of postgraduates, 4–8 hours by 23 per cent., and over 8 hours by 16 per cent. The average hours for these would have been about $7\frac{1}{2}$ hours per term or 0·9 hours per week.[1] These postgraduates for whom a time estimate of the amount of supervision was given comprised about half the total, and each member of the academic staff supervised on

[1] The corresponding estimate from the Postgraduate Survey was lower: about 6 hours per term. The estimates given here may therefore be too high. See Part VI, para. 627.

**Table 283.** *Time spent giving lectures by post. Michaelmas Term 1964*

OXFORD

PERCENTAGE

| Lectures (hours per week) | Professor | Reader | University lecturer with tutorial fellowship | University lecturer without tutorial fellowship | CUF and special lecturer | Other university staff with tutorial fellowship | Other senior research staff | Other university and outside grants staff | College post only: teaching | College post only: research | All posts |
|---|---|---|---|---|---|---|---|---|---|---|---|
| None | 13 | 18 | 34 | 28 | 47 | 43 | 67 | 76 | 83 | 93 | 51 |
| 1–2 | 63 | 57 | 60 | 57 | 50 | 46 | 30 | 18 | 15 | 7 | 41 |
| 3 and over | 24 | 25 | 7 | 16 | 4 | 11 | 3 | 6 | 2 | — | 9 |
| All | 100 | 100 | 100 | 100 | 100 | 100 | 100 | 100 | 100 | 100 | 100 |

SOURCE: Academic Staff Survey.

**Table 284.** *Time spent giving lectures by subject group. Michaelmas Term 1964*

OXFORD                                                                                            PERCENTAGE

| Lectures (hours per week) | Arts | Social studies | Science | Medicine | All subjects |
|---|---|---|---|---|---|
| None | 42 | 58 | 55 | 60 | 51 |
| 1–2 | 50 | 39 | 35 | 31 | 41 |
| 3 and over | 8 | 4 | 10 | 9 | 9 |
| All | 100 | 100 | 100 | 100 | 100 |

SOURCE: Academic Staff Survey.

average 1·6 students. Therefore the time per staff member was 0·9 × 0·8 or 0·7 hours per week. It is impossible to estimate reliably the time involved in day-to-day supervision, but a reasonable assumption might be that it involves a similar amount of time per postgraduate. This would give an average per staff member of about 1½ hours per week supervising 1·6 postgraduates, or, in round numbers, an hour per week per postgraduate supervised. At the time of the survey most supervision was for the University, and these calculations reflect mainly the time involved in university supervision. The amount of supervision for colleges was too small for the time involved to be estimated at all reliably, and the figure of an hour per week per postgraduate supervised should be interpreted as a rough estimate of the time involved in supervising for the University.

### Teaching by faculty lecturers

463. The classification of posts does not show faculty lecturers separately. Some details of their teaching are therefore given here. There were 21 faculty lecturers in the Academic Staff Survey. On average, they spent 8·8 hours per week giving tutorials to undergraduates; 11·6 hours on all forms of teaching for undergraduates; and 12·1 hours on all teaching other than postgraduate supervision. They spent an average of 3·0 hours giving classes and seminars, and lectures. They supervised an average of 0·6 postgraduates.

### Teaching in medicine

464. In the tables on teaching, medicine is shown as a single subject group. If pre-clinical and clinical medicine are considered separately, certain differences between them emerge, and it can be seen that the pattern of teaching in pre-clinical medicine is more similar to that in science than is

Table 285. *Time spent giving practical instruction by post. Michaelmas Term 1964*

OXFORD

PERCENTAGE

| Practical instruction (hours per week) | Professor | Reader | University lecturer with tutorial fellowship | University lecturer without tutorial fellowship | CUF and special lecturer | Other university staff with tutorial fellowship | Other senior research staff | Other university and outside grants staff | College post only: teaching | College post only: research | All posts |
|---|---|---|---|---|---|---|---|---|---|---|---|
| None | 85 | 69 | 35 | 57 | 98 | 59 | 83 | 78 | 92 | 96 | 79 |
| 1–2 | 5 | 4 | 6 | 12 | 1 | 3 | 3 | 2 | 5 | — | 4 |
| 3–4 | 6 | 3 | 6 | 8 | — | 19 | 5 | 7 | 2 | 4 | 5 |
| 5 and over | 5 | 24 | 54 | 23 | — | 19 | 8 | 12 | 2 | — | 13 |
| All | 100 | 100 | 100 | 100 | 100 | 100 | 100 | 100 | 100 | 100 | 100 |

SOURCE: Academic Staff Survey.

Table 286. *Average number of postgraduates supervised by post and subject group. Trinity Term 1964*

OXFORD

| Subject group | Average number of postgraduates supervised: | Professor | Reader | University lecturer with tutorial fellowship | University lecturer without tutorial fellowship | CUF and special lecturer | Other university staff with tutorial fellowship | Other senior research staff | Other university and outside grants staff | College post only: teaching | College post only: research | All posts |
|---|---|---|---|---|---|---|---|---|---|---|---|---|
| Arts | For faculty boards | 5·4 | 3·7 | 2·0 | 1·7 | 1·0 | 0·1 | 0·3 | 0·6 | 0·4 | 0·2 | 1·5 |
| | For colleges | — | 0·1 | — | 0·3 | 0·3 | — | — | — | 0·2 | 0·1 | 0·2 |
| | All | 5·4 | 3·7 | 2·0 | 2·0 | 1·3 | 0·1 | 0·3 | 0·6 | 0·6 | 0·3 | 1·7 |
| | *Percentage of staff supervising* | *93* | *80* | *57* | *52* | *49* | *13* | *33* | *35* | *31* | *19* | *50* |
| Social studies | For faculty boards | 4·4 | 2·8 | . | 5·0 | 1·0 | 0·8 | 2·5 | 0·1 | 1·0 | 0·2 | 1·6 |
| | For colleges | — | 1·0 | . | 0·2 | 0·5 | — | — | 0·3 | 0·8 | — | 0·4 |
| | All | 4·4 | 3·8 | . | 5·2 | 1·6 | 0·8 | 2·5 | 0·4 | 1·8 | 0·2 | 2·0 |
| | *Percentage of staff supervising* | *86* | *80* | *.* | *69* | *55* | *50* | *75* | *20* | *50* | *18* | *51* |
| Science | For faculty boards | 3·4 | 3·1 | 3·1 | 1·6 | 0·3 | 2·1 | 1·1 | 0·3 | 0·8 | 0·7 | 1·6 |
| | For colleges | 0·1 | 0·3 | 0·2 | — | 0·3 | 0·1 | 0·1 | — | — | — | 0·1 |
| | All | 3·5 | 3·4 | 3·3 | 1·6 | 0·6 | 2·2 | 1·2 | 0·3 | 0·8 | 0·7 | 1·7 |
| | *Percentage of staff supervising* | *87* | *83* | *83* | *65* | *25* | *64* | *53* | *20* | *33* | *33* | *54* |
| Medicine | For faculty boards | 1·0 | 2·0 | 0·8 | 0·7 | . | . | 0·4 | 0·5 | . | . | 0·7 |
| | For colleges | — | 0·1 | — | — | . | . | — | — | . | . | — |
| | All | 1·0 | 2·1 | 0·8 | 0·7 | . | . | 0·4 | 0·5 | . | . | 0·8 |
| | *Percentage of staff supervising* | *60* | *100* | *50* | *28* | *.* | *.* | *17* | *20* | *.* | *.* | *35* |
| All subjects | For faculty boards | 4·2 | 3·0 | 2·7 | 1·8 | 1·0 | 1·5 | 0·9 | 0·4 | 0·7 | 0·3 | 1·5 |
| | For colleges | — | 0·3 | 0·1 | 0·1 | 0·4 | 0·1 | 0·1 | — | 0·3 | — | 0·2 |
| | All | 4·2 | 3·3 | 2·8 | 1·9 | 1·3 | 1·6 | 1·0 | 0·4 | 1·0 | 0·3 | 1·6 |
| | *Percentage of staff supervising* | *86* | *85* | *75* | *56* | *49* | *51* | *42* | *21* | *36* | *21* | *50* |

SOURCE: Academic Staff Survey.

NOTE: Only those who were in post and not on leave of absence in Trinity Term 1964 are included in this table.

**Table 287.** *Number of postgraduates supervised by post. Trinity Term 1964*

OXFORD

PERCENTAGE

| Number of postgraduates supervised | Professor | Reader | University lecturer with tutorial fellowship | University lecturer without tutorial fellowship | CUF and special lecturer | Other university staff with tutorial fellowship | Other senior research staff | Other university and outside grants staff | College post only: teaching | College post only: research | All posts |
|---|---|---|---|---|---|---|---|---|---|---|---|
| None | 14 | 15 | 25 | 44 | 51 | 49 | 58 | 79 | 64 | 79 | 50 |
| 1–2 | 27 | 38 | 28 | 32 | 33 | 30 | 25 | 17 | 21 | 19 | 28 |
| 3–5 | 33 | 27 | 34 | 15 | 11 | 14 | 15 | 4 | 11 | 2 | 15 |
| 6 and over | 26 | 20 | 13 | 9 | 5 | 8 | 2 | 1 | 4 | — | 8 |
| All | 100 | 100 | 100 | 100 | 100 | 100 | 100 | 100 | 100 | 100 | 100 |

SOURCE: Academic Staff Survey.

NOTE: See note to Table 286.

**Table 288.** *Number of postgraduates supervised by subject group. Trinity Term 1964*

| OXFORD | | | | | PERCENTAGE |
| --- | --- | --- | --- | --- | --- |
| Number of postgraduates supervised | Arts | Social studies | Science | Medicine | All subjects |
| None | 50 | 49 | 46 | 65 | 50 |
| 1–2 | 29 | 23 | 28 | 26 | 28 |
| 3–5 | 13 | 17 | 18 | 5 | 15 |
| 6 and over | 8 | 11 | 7 | 4 | 8 |
| All | 100 | 100 | 100 | 100 | 100 |

SOURCE: Academic Staff Survey.
NOTE: See note to Table 286.

the pattern in medicine as a whole. In pre-clinical medicine the average of teaching for undergraduates was 5·3 hours, of which 1·7 hours were spent giving tutorials. Both these figures are higher than for medicine as a whole; they are lower than those in science to the extent that fewer tutorials were given. The averages for classes and seminars, lectures, and practicals, 0·2 hours, 0·9 hours, and 2·5 hours, were close to those in science. Teaching for postgraduates occupied an average of 0·8 hours in pre-clinical medicine and 1·1 hours in clinical medicine, while the average number of postgraduates supervised was 0·8 in each case. There was little difference between pre-clinical and clinical medicine in the amount of teaching given by professors and readers, and virtually all the tutorial fellows were in pre-clinical medicine. For university lecturers without a tutorial fellowship the average teaching hours were higher in pre-clinical medicine (8·2 hours for undergraduates and 9·8 hours for all teaching except supervision) than in clinical medicine (for which the corresponding figures were 2·5 hours and 3·9 hours). But in interpreting the figures for clinical medicine it must be borne in mind that both the types of teaching and the time-table of teaching are different in clinical medicine than in other subjects. The usual division of the academic year into three terms does not apply since teaching in clinical medicine is carried on for 46 weeks in the year, and ward rounds (for instance) are difficult to fit into the categories of teaching used. As a result, the survey figures probably do not reflect teaching in clinical medicine as accurately as in other subjects.

### Teaching by outside grants staff

465. Some details of outside grants staff and the teaching they gave are as follows. There were 127 outside grants staff in the survey of whom nearly

OXFORD    PERCENTAGE

| Subject group | Percentage of postgraduates supervised for: | Professor | Reader | University lecturer with tutorial fellowship | University lecturer without tutorial fellowship | CUF and special lecturer | Other university staff with tutorial fellowship | Other senior research staff | Other university and outside grants staff | College post only: teaching | College post only: research | All posts |
|---|---|---|---|---|---|---|---|---|---|---|---|---|
| Arts | 0–4 hours | 23 | 9 | 5 | 16 | 27 | — | — | — | 19 | 22 | 21 |
|  | 4–8 hours | 39 | 48 | 23 | 35 | 40 | — | 100 | 14 | 50 | 11 | 39 |
|  | 8–16 hours | 13 | 20 | 12 | 24 | 14 | — | — | 14 | 6 | 44 | 15 |
|  | 16 hours and over | 3 | — | — | 5 | 5 | — | — | — | — | 11 | 4 |
|  | Day-to-day contact | 5 | — | 2 | 19 | 7 | — | — | 14 | 13 | 11 | 7 |
|  | Other | 17 | 23 | 58 | 2 | 7 | 100 | — | 57 | 13 | — | 15 |
|  | All | 100 | 100 | 100 | 100 | 100 | 100 | 100 | 100 | 100 | 100 | 100 |
| Social studies | 0–4 hours | 13 | 29 | · | 23 | 30 | 100 | — | 17 | 9 | 25 | 23 |
|  | 4–8 hours | 42 | 34 | · | 34 | 33 | — | 80 | 67 | 36 | 25 | 38 |
|  | 8–16 hours | 35 | 29 | · | 25 | 22 | — | 20 | — | 36 | 50 | 26 |
|  | 16 hours and over | — | — | · | — | 1 | — | — | — | — | — | 1 |
|  | Day-to-day contact | — | 3 | · | 13 | — | — | — | 17 | — | — | 1 |
|  | Other | 10 | 5 | · | 5 | 14 | — | — | — | 18 | — | 2 |
|  | All | 100 | 100 | · | 100 | 100 | 100 | 100 | 100 | 100 | 100 | 100 |
| Science | 0–4 hours | 1 | 3 | 2 | 3 | 25 | 2 | 3 | — | — | — | 2 |
|  | 4–8 hours | 4 | 1 | 2 | 7 | 25 | 2 | 3 | — | — | — | 3 |
|  | 8–16 hours | 5 | — | 1 | 15 | — | 2 | — | — | — | — | 4 |
|  | 16 hours and over | 9 | 3 | 2 | 6 | — | — | 3 | — | — | — | — |
|  | Day-to-day contact | 81 | 94 | 93 | 67 | 25 | 94 | 95 | 91 | 100 | 100 | 86 |
|  | Other | — | — | — | 3 | 25 | — | — | 6 | — | — | 1 |
|  | All | 100 | 100 | 100 | 100 | 100 | 100 | 100 | 100 | 100 | 100 | 100 |
| Medicine | 0–4 hours | — | 4 | — | 5 | · | · | · | 6 | · | · | 4 |
|  | 4–8 hours | — | 4 | — | — | · | · | · | — | · | · | 1 |
|  | 8–16 hours | — | 4 | — | 35 | · | · | · | 18 | · | · | 14 |
|  | 16 hours and over | — | — | — | — | · | · | · | — | · | · | — |
|  | Day-to-day contact | 100 | 87 | 100 | 60 | · | · | · | 76 | · | · | 81 |
|  | Other | — | — | — | — | · | · | · | — | · | · | — |
|  | All | 100 | 100 | 100 | 100 | · | · | · | 100 | · | · | 100 |
| All subjects | 0–4 hours | 16 | 10 | 2 | 12 | 27 | 7 | 2 | 3 | 11 | 16 | 13 |
|  | 4–8 hours | 30 | 21 | 6 | 20 | 38 | 2 | 16 | 9 | 36 | 11 | 23 |
|  | 8–16 hours | 13 | 12 | 3 | 21 | 15 | 2 | 5 | 6 | 20 | 32 | 13 |
|  | 16 hours and over | 4 | — | 2 | 3 | 4 | — | — | — | — | 5 | 3 |
|  | Day-to-day contact | 25 | 49 | 77 | 41 | 10 | 88 | 77 | 72 | 29 | 37 | 41 |
|  | Other | 12 | 7 | 10 | 3 | 6 | 2 | — | 9 | 4 | — | 7 |
|  | All | 100 | 100 | 100 | 100 | 100 | 100 | 100 | 100 | 100 | 100 | 100 |

SOURCE: Academic Staff Survey.

NOTES
1. The hours are the total hours during Trinity Term 1964.
2. The distributions are based on the total number of postgraduates supervised.

three-quarters were in science subjects. Their average teaching hours per week were: 1·5 hours for undergraduate tutorials (40 per cent. giving at least one); 2·1 hours on all teaching for undergraduates; and 2·4 hours on all teaching except postgraduate supervision (50 per cent. doing some teaching). They supervised an average of 0·3 postgraduates (18 per cent. supervising at least one).

**Table 290.** *Time spent teaching non-members of the University working for university examinations or teaching for the Delegacy of Extra-Mural Studies by post and subject group. Michaelmas Term 1964*

OXFORD

| | Average hours per week | Percentage doing some |
|---|---|---|
| POST | | |
| Professor | — | 1 |
| Reader | — | 3 |
| Lecturer with tutorial fellowship | — | — |
| Lecturer without tutorial fellowship | 0·1 | 6 |
| CUF and special lecturer | — | 2 |
| Other university staff with tutorial fellowship | — | — |
| Other senior research staff | 0·1 | 2 |
| Other university and outside grants staff | 0·1 | 4 |
| College post only: teaching | — | — |
| College post only: research | 0·4 | 4 |
| | | |
| SUBJECT GROUP | | |
| Arts | 0·1 | 2 |
| Social studies | 0·1 | 7 |
| Science | — | 1 |
| Medicine | 0·1 | 5 |
| | | |
| All | 0·1 | 3 |

SOURCE: Academic Staff Survey.

## Other teaching

466. Teaching given completely outside the University was not within the scope of the Academic Staff Survey. But some teaching is given to non-members of the University working for university examinations (such as students at Ruskin College) and some is done for the Delegacy of Extra-mural Studies. The amounts are small, and involve only 3 per cent. of the staff. Table 290 gives details.

## Comparisons with other estimates

467. The estimates of teaching hours given here may be compared with those published by the Robbins Committee. Our estimate for total teaching

hours (excluding postgraduate supervision) is 8·8 hours a week. If outside grants staff (who were not included in the Robbins Committee Survey) are excluded, the average is 9·6 hours. The Robbins Committee estimate was originally 7·6 hours for Oxford and Cambridge,[1] the national average being the same. But the estimates of discussion periods were subsequently revised, giving an over-all average of 9·4 hours for Oxford and Cambridge and 8·1 hours nationally. But postgraduate supervision falls within the definition of discussion periods, and would therefore have been included in the 9·4 hours. The two estimates differ, therefore, by the time spent on postgraduate supervision, which has been estimated above at about 1·5 hours a week. There are, however, reasons for thinking that average teaching hours at Oxford are higher than at Cambridge, in which case the discrepancy will be less. A comparison of the estimates of the components of the totals shows that the difference between the two estimates (1·7 hours) is the same as the difference between the estimates of tutorials.

468. Our estimate for all forms of teaching, of about 11 hours a week, is substantially higher than the national average of 8 hours. Nationally, the average for tutorials was much lower (1·7 hours against 6·3 hours at Oxford), while the national averages for lectures and practicals were about twice the Oxford figures. (The higher national average for practicals will be largely accounted for by the higher proportion of students in science and medicine.)

### OPINIONS ON TEACHING

469. The Academic Staff Survey contained several questions asking for opinions on certain topics connected with teaching. The answers have been coded and tabulated in order to give an impression of the volume of support for the main views expressed. Tabulation can do no more than this. It cannot bring out the great variety of views and ideas which were expressed; nor can it bring out the reasoning used to support the opinions. This approach is therefore incomplete, and the tables are complemented in Part VII by extracts from some of the comments themselves.

470. The first question asked whether lectures or classes and seminars could be made a better complement to tutorials (Tables 291–3). In coding this and subsequent questions, an attempt was made to distinguish between the more definite answers and those which were qualified in some way. This involves a subjective judgement in deciding what amounts to a qualification, and some of those who simply answered Yes or No may in fact accept the qualifications made by others who replied at greater length. A bare majority thought that lectures or classes and seminars could complement tutorials better, this including 23 per cent. who qualified their answer in a

[1] Robbins Report, Appendix Two (B), Annex Y, and Appendix Three, Annexes P–R are quoted in paras. 467–8. Outside grants staff are excluded from the figures for Oxford.

## Table 291. Answers to question on role of lectures, etc. as complement to tutorials, by post. Michaelmas Term 1964

OXFORD          PERCENTAGE

| Could lectures or classes and seminars be made a better complement to tutorials? | Professor | Reader | University lecturer with tutorial fellowship | University lecturer without tutorial fellowship | CUF and special lecturer | Other university staff with tutorial fellowship | Other senior research staff | Other university and outside grants staff | College post only: teaching | College post only: research | All posts |
|---|---|---|---|---|---|---|---|---|---|---|---|
| Yes | 39 | 27 | 36 | 24 | 27 | 32 | 22 | 24 | 41 | 27 | 28 |
| Qualified yes | 16 | 13 | 27 | 16 | 36 | 27 | 13 | 11 | 27 | 29 | 23 |
| No | 10 | 22 | 17 | 23 | 13 | 14 | 5 | 11 | 3 | 3 | 13 |
| Qualified no | 9 | 4 | 7 | 4 | 13 | 8 | 3 | 3 | 9 | 5 | 7 |
| Tutorials should complement lectures, etc. | 11 | 9 | 4 | 9 | 1 | 5 | 7 | 9 | 2 | 5 | 6 |
| Lectures, etc. already complement tutorials | 3 | 4 | 7 | 11 | 7 | 11 | 2 | 6 | 3 | 3 | 6 |
| No answer | 10 | 19 | 2 | 14 | 3 | 3 | 48 | 35 | 17 | 26 | 17 |
| All | 100 | 100 | 100 | 100 | 100 | 100 | 100 | 100 | 100 | 100 | 100 |

SOURCE: Academic Staff Survey.

**Table 292.** *Answers to question on role of lectures, etc. as complement to tutorials, by subject group. Michaelmas Term 1964*

OXFORD                                                                    PERCENTAGE

| Could lectures or classes and seminars be made a better complement to tutorials? | Arts | Social studies | Science | Medicine | All subjects |
|---|---|---|---|---|---|
| Yes | 27 | 38 | 29 | 19 | 28 |
| Qualified yes | 30 | 18 | 21 | 8 | 23 |
| No | 12 | 12 | 13 | 20 | 13 |
| Qualified no | 10 | 10 | 4 | 3 | 7 |
| Tutorials should complement lectures, etc. | 1 | 5 | 11 | 4 | 6 |
| Lectures, etc. already complement tutorials | 8 | 5 | 5 | 4 | 6 |
| No answer | 12 | 11 | 17 | 43 | 17 |
| All | 100 | 100 | 100 | 100 | 100 |

SOURCE: Academic Staff Survey.

number of ways, the most important of which were: that it should be at the discretion of tutors; that more classes and seminars should be additional to, and not instead of, tutorials; and that it should only be done for special subjects. There is, however, a particular difficulty about interpreting the replies to this question. After the question itself an example was given 'e.g. by covering in classes topics that are now generally dealt with in tutorials'. Some directed their attention to the more general question, and some to this specific example. Where a simple Yes or No was given it is impossible to determine the sense in which it was intended. Some 20 per cent. did not think lectures or classes and seminars could better complement tutorials. 6 per cent. (11 per cent. in science) thought the position should be reversed, with tutorials complementing lectures, etc., while a further 6 per cent. (8 per cent. in arts) stated that lectures, etc., already complemented tutorials. A high proportion of negative answers were given by those who had held a post at Oxford for 21 years and over.

471. The next question asked whether lectures or classes and seminars complementing or replacing tutorials should be compulsory. A third answered Yes in one form or another, while 43 per cent. were against compulsion (Tables 294–6). But only 12 per cent. gave an unqualified Yes, and 14 per cent. specified that only classes and seminars (and often only college classes and seminars) should be compulsory. The other main way in which affirmative answers were qualified was that only classes and seminars *replacing*

**Table 293.** *Answers to question on role of lectures, etc. as complement to tutorials, by years in academic post at Oxford. Michaelmas Term 1964*

OXFORD　　　　　　　　　　　　　　　　　　　　　　　PERCENTAGE

| Could lectures or classes and seminars be made a better complement to tutorials? | Years in academic post at Oxford | | | | | All |
|---|---|---|---|---|---|---|
| | None | 1–5 | 6–10 | 11–20 | 21 and over | |
| Yes | 21 | 32 | 34 | 27 | 18 | 28 |
| Qualified yes | 17 | 22 | 22 | 26 | 25 | 23 |
| No | 8 | 10 | 12 | 15 | 22 | 13 |
| Qualified no | 4 | 5 | 8 | 7 | 15 | 7 |
| Tutorials should complement lectures, etc. | 9 | 7 | 7 | 4 | 2 | 6 |
| Lectures, etc. already complement tutorials | 1 | 8 | 5 | 7 | 5 | 6 |
| No answer | 39 | 17 | 11 | 13 | 15 | 17 |
| All | 100 | 100 | 100 | 100 | 100 | 100 |

SOURCE: Academic Staff Survey.

tutorials should be compulsory. The most common qualification to a negative answer was that lectures, etc., should not be compulsory, but tutors should tell their pupils they must attend. Tutorial fellows were rather less strongly against compulsion than were other staff, but in no post was there a definite majority in favour of it. There were no significant differences between subject groups, except that the proportion giving an unqualified Yes was higher in science than in other subject groups. Nor were there significant differences according to the number of years at Oxford.

472. There was a question which asked whether the number of lectures is too large, and if so, how a reduction should be effected. Nearly half thought there are not too many lectures, 14 per cent. thought they should be better organized rather than reduced in number, and 7 per cent. gave a No qualified in other ways (such as that more seminars are nevertheless needed, or that bad lecturers should be discouraged). About a fifth thought there are too many lectures. This view was strongest among CUF lecturers and in social studies subjects, and grew stronger as the number of years at Oxford increased. The main suggestions for decreasing the number of lectures were to have more classes and seminars instead (10 per cent.) and to reduce lecturing obligations (7 per cent.). Tables 297–9 give details.

473. The last question asking for opinions about teaching was about residence by undergraduates during vacations. The replies are tabulated in

**Table 294.** *Answers to question on whether lectures, etc. complementing or replacing tutorials should be compulsory, by post. Michaelmas Term 1964*

OXFORD                                                                                     PERCENTAGE

| Should lectures or classes and seminars complementing or replacing tutorials be compulsory? | Professor | Reader | University lecturer with tutorial fellowship | University lecturer without tutorial fellowship | CUF and special lecturer | Other university staff with tutorial fellowship | Other senior research staff | Other university and outside grants staff | College post only: teaching | College post only: research | All posts |
|---|---|---|---|---|---|---|---|---|---|---|---|
| Yes | 16 | 15 | 15 | 13 | 10 | 14 | 15 | 13 | 14 | 8 | 12 |
| Qualified yes | 5 | 1 | 6 | 3 | 12 | 5 | 3 | 2 | 8 | 10 | 6 |
| Yes, classes and seminars | 3 | 1 | 10 | 3 | 8 | 14 | 3 | 4 | 6 | 7 | 6 |
| Qualified yes, classes and seminars | 8 | 9 | 10 | 6 | 10 | 14 | 5 | 4 | 14 | 8 | 8 |
| No | 38 | 40 | 44 | 39 | 39 | 30 | 23 | 32 | 35 | 35 | 36 |
| Qualified no | 13 | 4 | 4 | 9 | 9 | 16 | 3 | 2 | 8 | 8 | 7 |
| No answer | 17 | 28 | 11 | 28 | 11 | 8 | 47 | 43 | 17 | 26 | 24 |
| All | 100 | 100 | 100 | 100 | 100 | 100 | 100 | 100 | 100 | 100 | 100 |

SOURCE: Academic Staff Survey.

**Table 295.** *Answers to question on whether lectures, etc. complementing or replacing tutorials should be compulsory, by subject group. Michaelmas Term 1964*

| Should lectures or classes and seminars complementing or replacing tutorials be compulsory? | Arts | Social studies | Science | Medicine | All subjects |
|---|---|---|---|---|---|
| Yes | 9 | 12 | 16 | 11 | 12 |
| Qualified yes | 8 | 10 | 4 | 3 | 6 |
| Yes, classes and seminars | 8 | 4 | 5 | 5 | 6 |
| Qualified yes, classes and seminars | 11 | 9 | 7 | 1 | 8 |
| No | 39 | 39 | 34 | 32 | 36 |
| Qualified no | 8 | 9 | 7 | 3 | 7 |
| No answer | 19 | 16 | 26 | 46 | 24 |
| All | 100 | 100 | 100 | 100 | 100 |

SOURCE: Academic Staff Survey.

**Table 296.** *Answers to question on whether lectures, etc. complementing or replacing tutorials should be compulsory, by years in academic post at Oxford. Michaelmas Term 1964*

| Should lectures or classes and seminars complementing or replacing tutorials be compulsory? | Years in academic post at Oxford | | | | | All |
|---|---|---|---|---|---|---|
| | None | 1–5 | 6–10 | 11–20 | 21 and over | |
| Yes | 7 | 12 | 15 | 13 | 12 | 12 |
| Qualified yes | 7 | 5 | 6 | 7 | 6 | 6 |
| Yes, classes and seminars | 5 | 7 | 4 | 6 | 4 | 6 |
| Qualified yes, classes and seminars | 6 | 10 | 9 | 8 | 5 | 8 |
| No | 27 | 34 | 42 | 38 | 41 | 36 |
| Qualified no | 6 | 7 | 8 | 8 | 5 | 7 |
| No answer | 43 | 24 | 16 | 20 | 27 | 24 |
| All | 100 | 100 | 100 | 100 | 100 | 100 |

SOURCE: Academic Staff Survey.

**Table 297.** *Answers to question on whether the number of lectures should be reduced, and if so, how, by post. Michaelmas Term 1964*

OXFORD

PERCENTAGE

| Should the number of lectures be reduced, and if so, how? | Professor | Reader | University lecturer with tutorial fellowship | University lecturer without tutorial fellowship | CUF and special lecturer | Other university staff with tutorial fellowship | Other senior research staff | Other university and outside grants staff | College post only: teaching | College post only: research | All posts |
|---|---|---|---|---|---|---|---|---|---|---|---|
| Yes, reduce obligations | 8 | 3 | 9 | 8 | 14 | 5 | 8 | 1 | 5 | 6 | 7 |
| Yes, use classes instead | 14 | 6 | 9 | 9 | 15 | 11 | 8 | 5 | 16 | 12 | 10 |
| Yes, by other methods | 1 | 1 | 3 | 3 | 7 | 5 | 2 | 1 | 6 | 7 | 4 |
| No | 49 | 63 | 65 | 63 | 41 | 46 | 27 | 43 | 50 | 34 | 47 |
| No, but could be better organized | 14 | 13 | 13 | 3 | 24 | 19 | 3 | 9 | 14 | 17 | 14 |
| No, qualified in other ways | 14 | 1 | 1 | 6 | 6 | 14 | 12 | 6 | 3 | 8 | 7 |
| No answer | 5 | 12 | 1 | 12 | 2 | — | 45 | 35 | 12 | 22 | 14 |

SOURCE: Academic Staff Survey.

NOTE: The columns do not add to 100 since some mentioned more than one way of reducing the number of lectures.

**Table 298.** *Answers to question on whether the number of lectures should be reduced, and if so, how, by subject group. Michaelmas Term 1964*

OXFORD                                                                    PERCENTAGE

| Should the number of lectures be reduced, and if so, how? | Arts | Social studies | Science | Medicine | All subjects |
|---|---|---|---|---|---|
| Yes, reduce obligations | 9 | 19 | 3 | 1 | 7 |
| Yes, use classes instead | 10 | 21 | 8 | 6 | 10 |
| Yes, by other methods | 5 | 6 | 3 | — | 4 |
| No | 46 | 27 | 56 | 51 | 47 |
| No, but could be better organized | 19 | 19 | 10 | 2 | 14 |
| No, qualified in other ways | 7 | 7 | 7 | 3 | 7 |
| No answer | 8 | 13 | 15 | 38 | 14 |

SOURCE: Academic Staff Survey.

NOTE: The columns do not add to 100 since some mentioned more than one way of reducing the number of lectures.

**Table 299.** *Answers to question on whether the number of lectures should be reduced, and if so, how, by years in academic post at Oxford. Michaelmas Term 1964*

OXFORD                                                                    PERCENTAGE

| Should the number of lectures be reduced, and if so, how? | Years in academic post at Oxford | | | | | All |
|---|---|---|---|---|---|---|
| | None | 1–5 | 6–10 | 11–20 | 21 and over | |
| Yes, reduce obligations | 3 | 5 | 8 | 9 | 14 | 7 |
| Yes, use classes instead | 7 | 9 | 9 | 13 | 15 | 10 |
| Yes, by other methods | 6 | 3 | 6 | 5 | 2 | 4 |
| No | 35 | 49 | 45 | 50 | 52 | 47 |
| No, but could be better organized | 10 | 13 | 20 | 13 | 10 | 14 |
| No, qualified in other ways | 6 | 8 | 7 | 6 | 4 | 7 |
| No answer | 37 | 16 | 8 | 9 | 12 | 14 |

SOURCE: Academic Staff Survey.

NOTE: The columns do not add to 100 since some mentioned more than one way of reducing the number of lectures.

**Table 300.** *Answers to questions on whether undergraduates would benefit from residence in vacation, by post. Michaelmas Term 1964*

OXFORD

PERCENTAGE

| Would undergraduates benefit from residence in vacation? | Professor | Reader | University lecturer with tutorial fellowship | University lecturer without tutorial fellowship | CUF and special lecturer | Other university staff with tutorial fellowship | Other senior research staff | Other university and outside grants staff | College post only: teaching | College post only: research | All posts |
|---|---|---|---|---|---|---|---|---|---|---|---|
| **WITH TEACHING INSTRUCTION** | | | | | | | | | | | |
| Yes | 11 | 10 | 4 | 9 | 6 | 5 | 13 | 16 | 8 | 5 | 9 |
| Yes, but disadvantages for staff too great | 7 | 6 | 12 | 4 | 7 | 5 | 2 | 3 | 5 | 4 | 6 |
| Yes, qualified in other ways | 19 | 11 | 13 | 13 | 10 | 14 | 18 | 15 | 5 | 25 | 14 |
| No | 40 | 48 | 53 | 43 | 62 | 68 | 15 | 22 | 50 | 26 | 43 |
| Qualified no | 13 | 9 | 10 | 3 | 9 | 8 | 5 | 2 | 9 | 9 | 7 |
| No answer | 9 | 15 | 7 | 27 | 6 | — | 47 | 41 | 24 | 30 | 21 |
| **WITHOUT TEACHING INSTRUCTION** | | | | | | | | | | | |
| Yes | 37 | 43 | 51 | 34 | 56 | 41 | 23 | 20 | 33 | 37 | 39 |
| Qualified yes | 30 | 21 | 30 | 15 | 33 | 38 | 15 | 13 | 38 | 24 | 25 |
| No | 15 | 12 | 8 | 18 | 6 | 16 | 13 | 14 | 6 | 10 | 11 |
| No answer | 18 | 24 | 11 | 33 | 5 | 5 | 48 | 53 | 23 | 29 | 25 |
| **FOR SPECIAL PURPOSES** | | | | | | | | | | | |
| Yes | 51 | 49 | 58 | 53 | 42 | 54 | 37 | 42 | 42 | 47 | 46 |
| No | 14 | 10 | 18 | 15 | 17 | 22 | 7 | 5 | 14 | 9 | 13 |
| No answer | 36 | 40 | 24 | 33 | 41 | 24 | 57 | 53 | 44 | 45 | 41 |
| **All** | 100 | 100 | 100 | 100 | 100 | 100 | 100 | 100 | 100 | 100 | 100 |

SOURCE: Academic Staff Survey.

**Table 301.** *Answers to questions on whether undergraduates would benefit from residence in vacation, by subject group. Michaelmas Term 1964*

OXFORD                                                              PERCENTAGE

| Would undergraduates benefit from residence in vacation? | Arts | Social studies | Science | Medicine | All subjects |
|---|---|---|---|---|---|
| WITH TEACHING INSTRUCTION | | | | | |
| Yes | 5 | 6 | 12 | 18 | 9 |
| Yes, but disadvantages for staff too great | 7 | 5 | 7 | 1 | 6 |
| Yes, qualified in other ways | 10 | 15 | 18 | 18 | 14 |
| No | 54 | 47 | 36 | 24 | 43 |
| Qualified no | 9 | 7 | 6 | 1 | 7 |
| No answer | 17 | 20 | 21 | 38 | 21 |
| WITHOUT TEACHING INSTRUCTION | | | | | |
| Yes | 45 | 46 | 36 | 18 | 39 |
| Qualified yes | 29 | 27 | 24 | 9 | 25 |
| No | 10 | 7 | 13 | 17 | 11 |
| No answer | 17 | 20 | 28 | 56 | 25 |
| FOR SPECIAL PURPOSES | | | | | |
| Yes | 44 | 40 | 54 | 36 | 46 |
| No | 12 | 13 | 14 | 11 | 13 |
| No answer | 44 | 47 | 32 | 53 | 41 |
| All | 100 | 100 | 100 | 100 | 100 |

SOURCE: Academic Staff Survey.

Tables 300–2. When asked about vacation residence with teaching instruction, 50 per cent. thought undergraduates would not benefit, the main reason given being that undergraduates needed the vacations for independent reading and thinking. 9 per cent. answered Yes (though they were not necessarily in favour of vacation residence) and 6 per cent. thought that undergraduates would benefit but that the disadvantages for the academic staff would outweigh any advantages to the undergraduates. A further 14 per cent. answered Yes qualified in various ways, such as that vacation residence should be confirmed to the Long Vacation, or that there should be lectures and classes but not tutorials. A substantial majority of tutorial fellows thought that undergraduates would not benefit from vacation residence with teaching, and an above average proportion in science and medicine thought that they would so benefit.

474. Nearly two-thirds thought that undergraduates would benefit from vacation residence without teaching. Where this view was qualified, it was

**Table 302.** *Answers to questions on whether undergraduates would benefit from residence in vacation, by years in academic post at Oxford. Michaelmas Term 1964*

OXFORD                                                                   PERCENTAGE

| Would undergraduates benefit from residence in vacation? | Years in academic post at Oxford | | | | | All |
|---|---|---|---|---|---|---|
| | None | 1–5 | 6–10 | 11–20 | 21 and over | |
| **WITH TEACHING INSTRUCTION** | | | | | | |
| Yes | 6 | 12 | 9 | 7 | 6 | 9 |
| Yes, but disadvantages for staff too great | 5 | 5 | 8 | 6 | 5 | 6 |
| Yes, qualified in other ways | 15 | 17 | 14 | 14 | 10 | 14 |
| No | 27 | 38 | 47 | 51 | 48 | 43 |
| Qualified no | 6 | 7 | 7 | 7 | 10 | 7 |
| No answer | 42 | 22 | 16 | 15 | 19 | 21 |
| **WITHOUT TEACHING INSTRUCTION** | | | | | | |
| Yes | 21 | 32 | 46 | 46 | 48 | 39 |
| Qualified yes | 19 | 25 | 25 | 26 | 25 | 25 |
| No | 14 | 13 | 10 | 11 | 7 | 11 |
| No answer | 46 | 31 | 19 | 17 | 20 | 25 |
| **FOR SPECIAL PURPOSES** | | | | | | |
| Yes | 33 | 51 | 50 | 47 | 38 | 46 |
| No | 11 | 11 | 14 | 13 | 17 | 13 |
| No answer | 56 | 38 | 37 | 40 | 45 | 41 |
| **All** | 100 | 100 | 100 | 100 | 100 | 100 |

SOURCE: Academic Staff Survey.

usually to the effect that libraries should be fully available; or that undergraduates should have access to a tutor for guidance. The idea was welcomed by many as a means of reducing the number of undergraduates who take vacation jobs, and because many undergraduates do not have access to a suitable library or a study at home. A very high proportion of tutorial fellows answered Yes to this question. The proportion answering Yes was relatively high in arts and social studies, and low in medicine.

475. When asked whether undergraduates would benefit from vacation residence for special purposes (such as language courses for scientists) nearly half did not reply. Of those who replied, over three times as many answered Yes as No.

ACADEMIC ACTIVITIES OTHER THAN TEACHING

476. Time spent on teaching and postgraduate supervision has already been discussed. In addition, questions were asked in the Academic Staff Survey about other activities which are part of the academic life. Because the survey was carried out early in Michaelmas Term, a time which was not typical of the whole term or of the whole year, it was not appropriate to base estimates of time spent on these activities on the week or fortnight preceding the survey. In addition, some academic activities, in particular examining and admissions, are concentrated at one or two points in the year. Therefore, with one exception, the questions about time spent on academic activities related to the previous academic year, 1963–4. For work in term average hours per week were asked for, but for vacations the total hours were asked for. The results are presented in terms of hours per week, there being assumed to be 22 working weeks during vacations (i.e. 6 weeks of holiday are allowed for). Where answers were given in terms of days or weeks, an 8-hour day and 42-hour week (this being the working week estimated by the Robbins Committee for Oxford and Cambridge) were assumed.

477. The exception, where the question did not relate to 1963–4, was administration where the time involved is reasonably predictable. This comprises attending university and inter-college committees which meet regularly; attending college governing body and college committee meetings; and carrying out the duties of a college officer such as Dean or Senior Tutor. For these activities the question asked for the expected average hours per week during Michaelmas Term 1964, and the activities are referred to as 'regular administration'. 'Administration' not so qualified should be understood to refer to other administration and to exclude regular administration.

### The validity of the estimates

478. Apart from that on regular administration, the questions on hours of work were extremely difficult to answer and a considerable number of respondents commented to that effect. For three reasons in particular the resulting estimates cannot be regarded as more than rough guides.

479. First, since questions about hours of work are intrinsically difficult to answer, the individual replies are subject to error and may contain systematic biases. When a question refers to a period of a year the errors are likely to be greater than when it refers to the previous week. We recognized the difficulty of giving an answer in the formulation of the question which stated '. . . If, however, you think a meaningful figure can be given, please estimate the time spent. . . .' It is, therefore, impossible fully to assess the reliability of the answers given. The results exhibit the kind of variations between the different activities, between grades, subject groups and between

term and vacations that might be expected, and to this extent are satisfactory. However, the average of 50 hours a week in term for all academic activities is 6 hours higher than the estimate by the Robbins Committee of 43·7 hours a week for Oxford and Cambridge.[1] The Robbins Committee's figure was based on a survey estimate of working time during the 2 weeks when the survey was carried out, and should be less susceptible to unconscious biases than the figures based on the previous year. It therefore seems likely that the average figures for all academic activities from the Academic Staff Survey have been overestimated. There is probably more difficulty in estimating time spent on study and research than that spent on other activities, and it is likely that any bias has affected the figures for study and research rather more than other estimates. The Robbins Committee estimated the average time spent on study and research during term as 16·5 hours for Oxford and Cambridge, and 15·4 hours for all universities.[2] Our figure is 21·4 hours, but outside grants staff are included in this average; when they are excluded the average is 19·7 hours.[3]

480. Secondly, a considerable proportion of the academic staff did not give a full account of their working hours; for example, only 36 per cent. gave complete details of their work in term. If those who did not reply had different hours of work from those who did reply, there will be a distortion in the results. The evidence on this point is discussed below.

481. Thirdly, it was difficult in editing the questionnaires to decide whether blanks should be regarded as zeros or as not ascertained values. This is particularly the case with activities such as university examining in which only a relatively small proportion of the staff take part each year. The rule was adopted that a blank was treated as a not ascertained value. With an activity such as study and research where there is a presumption that virtually all the academic staff take part, this seems unlikely to lead to any distortion. But with activities such as university examining, the rule is likely to lead to an upward bias in the estimates since too few zero values would be included in the calculation of the average. The following paragraphs, however, do give a rough estimate of the maximum bias which could result.

482. Table 303 shows, for each activity, the estimated average, the proportion of the total number who gave an answer, and the proportion (of those giving an answer) who said they had spent some time on the activity. Separate figures are given for term and vacations. Altogether, 74 per cent. completed part of the question and a further 15 per cent. were either not in

---

[1] The published figure is 41·9 hours. To this has been added the correction to teaching hours referred to in paragraph 467.
[2] Robbins Report, Appendix Three, Annex N, Tables N1 and N2, pp. 192–4.
[3] Estimates of the hours of work in term of outside grants staff were 37·0 hours a week for study and research and 46·9 hours a week for all work.

**Table 303.** *Extent to which hours of work were ascertained. 1963–4*

OXFORD

| Type of work | In term | | | In vacations | | |
|---|---|---|---|---|---|---|
| | Average (hours per week) | Percentage ascertained | Percentage non-zero (of those ascertained) | Average (hours per week) | Percentage ascertained | Percentage non-zero (of those ascertained) |
| Preparing teaching | 6·2 | 79 | 91 | 3·0 | 57 | 68 |
| Advising students | 1·8 | 74 | 74 | 0·8 | 55 | 54 |
| Administration (except regular administration) | 3·6 | 73 | 72 | 2·7 | 56 | 61 |
| College admissions | 0·6 | 69 | 30 | 0·8 | 64 | 49 |
| University examining | 0·7 | 67 | 23 | 1·7 | 62 | 39 |
| Study and research | 21·4 | 69 | 96 | 27·3 | 56 | 99 |
| Learned societies and conferences | 1·1 | 69 | 55 | 1·8 | 63 | 77 |
| Other professional work in Oxford | 1·2 | 65 | 34 | 1·3 | 58 | 47 |
| External examining and lecturing | 0·6 | 64 | 27 | 1·1 | 60 | 49 |
| Consulting | 0·5 | 62 | 18 | 0·8 | 57 | 26 |
| Other external work | 0·6 | 58 | 14 | 0·7 | 52 | 22 |
| All above activities | 36·8 | 36 | 100 | 40·2 | 27 | 100 |
| All work including teaching and regular administration | 49·6 | 36 | 100 | .. | .. | .. |

SOURCE: Academic Staff Survey.

NOTES
1. The hours per week in vacations are obtained by assuming 22 working weeks in vacations.
2. The percentage ascertained is the number who gave an estimate as a percentage of all except those who were not in Oxford in 1963–4.
3. The estimates of time spent on teaching (which excludes postgraduate supervision) and regular administration included in the last line of the table are based on Michaelmas Term 1964.

Oxford during 1963–4 or their pattern of work was atypical. The proportion who gave an answer to the individual items was about 70 per cent. for term (except for work outside Oxford for which it was about 60 per cent.) and 60 per cent. for vacations. But only 36 per cent. gave complete details for term, and 27 per cent. for vacations.

483. If the individual averages for activities other than teaching and regular administration are summed, totals of 38·3 hours for term and 42·0 hours for vacations are obtained. These are 1·5 hours and 1·8 hours greater than the estimates based on those who gave complete details. This could be either because the average working hours of those who completed only part

of the question were greater than for those who gave complete details, or because some zero values were incorrectly treated as not ascertained values. A likely upper limit to the error from the latter source may be calculated by assuming that all the not ascertained values were in fact zero for the items which respondents might have disregarded if they spent no time on them, rather than write a zero or a dash. Attending conferences, miscellaneous work in Oxford, and work outside Oxford would come into this category and so might college admissions and university examining. Assuming all the not ascertained values to be zero for these activities gives a total of the individual averages of 36·5 hours for term and 38·9 hours for vacations. This calculation almost certainly over-corrects for any error in distinguishing zeros from values which were not ascertained. The resulting average for work in term is slightly less than the average for those who gave complete details. There is therefore no evidence that those who gave less than complete details differed in their total working hours from those who gave complete details. For vacations the 'corrected' average is 1·3 hours less than that of 40·2 hours for those completing the question. Since the correction is probably excessive, this cannot be regarded as a significant difference. It seems reasonable, therefore, to suppose that the differences between the sum of the individual averages and the averages in the penultimate line of Table 303 are mainly due to zero values having been treated as not ascertained in some cases, and to assume that the average total hours would not have been very different if a complete response had been obtained. But the averages shown in the tables for college admissions, university examining, attending conferences, miscellaneous work in Oxford, and work outside Oxford are likely to contain upward biases (in total) of up to 2 hours for term, and 3 hours for vacations.

484. For the reasons given in the previous six paragraphs, the statistics from the Academic Staff Survey on academic work other than teaching and regular administration are probably less reliable than those on other topics. The results are therefore given in less detail than in other sections.

## Regular administration

485. Almost all respondents to the Academic Staff Survey gave details of time spent on regular administration during Michaelmas Term 1964. The average was 3·6 hours per week, of which 2·7 hours were taken up with college administration (Tables 304 and 305). The average for CUF lecturers was 7·2 hours, of which 3·8 hours were spent carrying out the duties of a college office. Professors (2·6 hours) and readers (1·5 hours) spent the most time on university committees. Considerably more time was spent on regular administration in arts and social studies than in science and medicine, the main reason being that college office holders were mainly in these subject groups.

Table 304. *Average hours per week spent on regular administration during term by post. Michaelmas Term 1964*

OXFORD                                                                                                HOURS

| Regular administration (hours per week) | Professor | Reader | University lecturer with tutorial fellowship | University lecturer without tutorial fellowship | CUF and special lecturer | Other university staff with tutorial fellowship | Other senior research staff | Other university and outside grants staff | College post only: teaching | College post only: research | All posts |
|---|---|---|---|---|---|---|---|---|---|---|---|
| College governing body and college committees | 1·6 | 2·0 | 2·6 | 0·5 | 2·5 | 2·2 | 0·3 | 0·1 | 1·3 | 1·1 | 1·4 |
| University and inter-college committees meeting regularly | 2·6 | 1·5 | 1·0 | 0·8 | 1·0 | 0·5 | 0·7 | 0·2 | 0·2 | 0·1 | 0·8 |
| College office | 0·1 | 0·3 | 1·3 | 0·5 | 3·8 | 0·6 | 0·2 | 0·1 | 0·8 | 1·0 | 1·3 |
| All regular administration | 4·3 | 3·8 | 4·9 | 1·8 | 7·2 | 3·3 | 1·1 | 0·5 | 2·2 | 2·3 | 3·6 |

SOURCE: Academic Staff Survey.

**Table 305.** *Average hours per week spent on regular administration during term by subject group. Michaelmas Term 1964*

OXFORD
HOURS

| Regular administration (hours per week) | Arts | Social studies | Science | Medicine | All subjects |
|---|---|---|---|---|---|
| College governing body and college committees | 1·8 | 1·7 | 1·1 | 0·5 | 1·4 |
| University and inter-college committees meeting regularly | 1·0 | 1·2 | 0·6 | 0·4 | 0·8 |
| College office | 2·3 | 2·0 | 0·4 | 0·2 | 1·3 |
| All regular administration | 5·2 | 4·9 | 2·2 | 1·1 | 3·6 |

SOURCE: Academic Staff Survey.

486. Regular administration was widely dispersed among the academic staff, two-thirds of whom spent some time on it. College offices were held by 56 per cent. of CUF lecturers, 33 per cent. of university lecturers with a tutorial fellowship, and by 22 per cent. over all. Almost all professors, and two-thirds of readers spent time on regular university (and inter-college) committees. The proportion holding a college office was about 30 per cent. in arts and social studies but only 10 per cent. in science. (See Tables 306 and 307.)

487. The distributions for regular administration in Tables 308 and 309 show that 44 per cent. spent 1–4 hours a week and 23 per cent. spent longer than that, 7 per cent. spending 13 hours and over. 29 per cent. of CUF lecturers spent 9 hours and over in this way. The corresponding figure for professors was 10 per cent.

## Work in term

488. The estimated average hours spent in term during 1963–4 on the various academic activities other than teaching and regular administration are given in Tables 310 and 311, and Tables 312–15 give further details of work in term. In the last line of Tables 310 and 311 the averages for teaching and regular administration in Michaelmas Term 1964 have been added to give an estimate of the time spent on all academic activities except postgraduate supervision. This estimate is based on two different time periods, and will only be valid in so far as average hours spent on teaching and regular administration were similar in 1963–4 to those in Michaelmas Term 1964.

Table 306. *Percentage of academic staff spending time on regular administration by post. Michaelmas Term 1964*

OXFORD

PERCENTAGE

| Regular administration | Professor | Reader | University lecturer with tutorial fellowship | University lecturer without tutorial fellowship | CUF and special lecturer | Other university staff with tutorial fellowship | Other senior research staff | Other university and outside grants staff | College post only: teaching | College post only: research | All posts |
|---|---|---|---|---|---|---|---|---|---|---|---|
| College governing body and college committees | 91 | 67 | 100 | 19 | 96 | 100 | 22 | 8 | 70 | 43 | 58 |
| University and inter-college committees meeting regularly | 93 | 65 | 60 | 43 | 45 | 46 | 30 | 10 | 17 | 7 | 39 |
| College office | 3 | 10 | 33 | 9 | 56 | 25 | 3 | 2 | 15 | 12 | 22 |
| All regular administration | 97 | 85 | 100 | 53 | 97 | 100 | 40 | 17 | 71 | 47 | 68 |

SOURCE: Academic Staff Survey.

**Table 307.** *Percentage of academic staff spending time on regular administration by subject group. Michaelmas Term 1964*

OXFORD                                                                PERCENTAGE

| Regular administration | Arts | Social studies | Science | Medicine | All subjects |
|---|---|---|---|---|---|
| College governing body and college committees | 75 | 66 | 46 | 26 | 58 |
| University and inter-college committees meeting regularly | 43 | 47 | 36 | 22 | 39 |
| College office | 35 | 29 | 10 | 4 | 22 |
| All regular administration | 83 | 78 | 59 | 30 | 68 |

SOURCE: Academic Staff Survey.

489. In addition to teaching itself, the estimates show an average of 6·2 hours as spent in preparing teaching and correcting pupils' work, and 1·8 hours as spent in advising students. 3·6 hours were spent on administration other than regular administration. Examining, averaged over the year, took 0·7 hours, and college admissions 0·6 hours. As noted in para. 483 there may be a systematic upward bias in some of these figures.

490. The highest averages for study and research were for readers, senior research staff, other university and outside grants staff, and college research fellows. The lowest was for CUF lecturers. The time spent on study and research was above average in science and (especially) medicine, and below average in arts. As noted in para. 479, there may be a systematic upward bias in these figures.

491. Professors spent nearly three times the average time on administration, and the average was higher in science and medicine than in arts and social studies (presumably because there was more departmental administration). Professors also spent considerably more than the average time on academic work outside Oxford.

492. Tables 312 and 313 give the percentages spending some time on each of the activities. As noted in para. 481, there is likely to be an upward bias in some of the figures.

493. Tables 314 and 315 give distributions for the total time spent on the activities which are necessary adjuncts to university teaching: preparing teaching; advising students; administration; admissions; and university examining. In these tables respondents who did not reply have been excluded.

## Table 308. Time spent on regular administration by post, Michaelmas Term 1964

OXFORD                         PERCENTAGE

| Regular administration (hours per week) | Professor | Reader | University lecturer with tutorial fellowship | University lecturer without tutorial fellowship | CUF and special lecturer | Other university staff with tutorial fellowship | Other senior research staff | Other university and outside grants staff | College post only: teaching | College post only: research | All posts |
|---|---|---|---|---|---|---|---|---|---|---|---|
| None | 3 | 15 | — | 47 | 3 | — | 60 | 83 | 29 | 53 | 32 |
| 1–4 | 68 | 63 | 69 | 42 | 46 | 81 | 35 | 14 | 55 | 35 | 44 |
| 5–8 | 20 | 15 | 20 | 6 | 22 | 14 | 3 | 1 | 6 | 5 | 12 |
| 9–12 | 5 | 3 | 4 | 2 | 10 | 3 | — | 1 | 3 | 2 | 4 |
| 13 and over | 5 | 3 | 7 | 3 | 19 | — | 2 | — | 2 | 4 | 7 |
| Not ascertained | — | 1 | — | — | 1 | 3 | — | — | 6 | 1 | 1 |
| All | 100 | 100 | 100 | 100 | 100 | 100 | 100 | 100 | 100 | 100 | 100 |

SOURCE: Academic Staff Survey.

**Table 309.** *Time spent on regular administration by subject group. Michaelmas Term 1964*

OXFORD PERCENTAGE

| Regular administration (hours per week) | Arts | Social studies | Science | Medicine | All subjects |
|---|---|---|---|---|---|
| None | 17 | 22 | 41 | 70 | 32 |
| 1–4 | 48 | 44 | 46 | 24 | 44 |
| 5–8 | 15 | 18 | 9 | 3 | 12 |
| 9–12 | 7 | 6 | 2 | 2 | 4 |
| 13 and over | 12 | 9 | 2 | 1 | 7 |
| Not ascertained | 1 | 2 | — | — | 1 |
| All | 100 | 100 | 100 | 100 | 100 |

SOURCE: Academic Staff Survey.

494. Most spent some time on these activities, and 9 per cent. spent 25 hours and over per week on them. Over half the total spent between 1 and 12 hours. Professors spent the most time on these activities, 25 per cent. spending 25 hours and over, and 46 per cent. spending 19 hours and over. In arts, a third spent 19 hours and over, the corresponding figures for other subject groups being considerably less.

## Work in vacations

495. Tables 316–21 give similar details for work in vacations. The estimated averages are given in Tables 316 and 317. For all work the estimated average was 40·2 hours a week, but this does not include any teaching which may have been given in vacations. The average for study and research, 27·3 hours, was 6 hours higher than in term, that for preparing teaching was 3 hours lower, while advising students and administration both occupied about an hour less per week in vacations than in term. University examining occupied 1·7 hours a week on average in vacations, compared with 0·7 hours in term. Rather more time was spent on work outside Oxford in vacations than in term.

496. As in term, CUF lecturers had the lowest average for study and research but they spent twice as much time on study and research as in term, and their average was only marginally less than that of professors, who spent only 3 hours more than in term.

497. The percentage of the academic staff spending time on the various academic activities is given in Tables 318 and 319. Tables 320 and 321 give distributions for vacations similar to those in Tables 314 and 315 for term.

**Table 310.** *Average hours of work in term by post. 1963–4*

OXFORD                                                                                                                                                                  HOURS

| Work in term (hours per week) | Professor | Reader | University lecturer with tutorial fellowship | University lecturer without tutorial fellowship | CUF and special lecturer | Other university staff with tutorial fellowship | Other senior research staff | Other university and outside grants staff | College post only: teaching | College post only: research | All posts |
|---|---|---|---|---|---|---|---|---|---|---|---|
| Preparing teaching | 5·4 | 5·7 | 7·2 | 6·2 | 7·4 | 7·3 | 2·7 | 4·1 | 10·1 | 5·4 | 6·2 |
| Advising students | 2·3 | 1·9 | 1·4 | 1·7 | 2·3 | 1·3 | 1·8 | 1·3 | 2·0 | 1·1 | 1·8 |
| Administration | 10·1 | 5·0 | 2·8 | 3·6 | 2·2 | 1·8 | 7·3 | 2·9 | 1·3 | 0·7 | 3·6 |
| College admissions | — | 0·2 | 0·9 | 0·1 | 1·6 | 0·9 | 0·1 | — | 1·1 | — | 0·6 |
| University examining | 1·2 | 0·8 | 0·5 | 0·7 | 1·2 | 0·2 | 0·1 | — | 0·3 | 0·2 | 0·7 |
| Study and research | 19·0 | 26·2 | 18·2 | 21·4 | 10·6 | 21·4 | 33·2 | 32·0 | 17·4 | 34·1 | 21·4 |
| Learned societies and conferences | 2·3 | 0·9 | 0·7 | 1·0 | 0·8 | 0·4 | 1·1 | 1·3 | 1·0 | 1·5 | 1·1 |
| Other professional work in Oxford | 2·1 | 1·4 | 0·9 | 2·2 | 0·6 | 0·6 | 0·8 | 1·0 | 0·7 | 0·9 | 1·2 |
| External examining and lecturing | 1·0 | 0·7 | 0·3 | 1·0 | 0·7 | 0·2 | 0·4 | 0·7 | 0·2 | 0·2 | 0·6 |
| Consulting | 1·5 | 1·0 | 0·3 | 0·4 | 0·3 | 0·1 | 0·9 | 0·3 | 0·4 | 0·6 | 0·5 |
| Other external work | 2·8 | 0·4 | 0·3 | 0·2 | 0·3 | 0·3 | 0·4 | 0·5 | 0·6 | 0·4 | 0·6 |
| All external work | 4·9 | 2·0 | 0·8 | 0·9 | 1·1 | 0·4 | 1·3 | 0·7 | 0·2 | 0·7 | 1·2 |
| All above activities | 44·0 | 40·6 | 31·6 | 37·7 | 29·0 | 37·0 | 46·6 | 41·4 | 30·1 | 45·3 | 36·8 |
| All work including teaching and regular administration | 52·3 | 52·2 | 50·1 | 48·2 | 50·5 | 52·2 | 51·2 | 47·0 | 43·7 | 51·9 | 49·6 |

SOURCE: Academic Staff Survey.

NOTES

1. The estimates of time spent on teaching and regular administration incorporated in the last line of the table are for Michaelmas Term 1964. They relate to those who gave details for all the other activities listed.

2. Time spent supervising postgraduates is excluded.

**Table 311.** *Average hours of work in term by subject group. 1963–4*

OXFORD HOURS

| Work in term (hours per week) | Arts | Social studies | Science | Medicine | All subjects |
|---|---|---|---|---|---|
| Preparing teaching | 8·6 | 6·0 | 4·9 | 2·4 | 6·2 |
| Advising students | 2·1 | 1·7 | 1·7 | 1·0 | 1·8 |
| Administration | 2·7 | 2·9 | 4·5 | 4·3 | 3·6 |
| College admissions | 1·1 | 0·6 | 0·3 | 0·1 | 0·6 |
| University examining | 1·0 | 0·8 | 0·5 | 0·2 | 0·7 |
| Study and research | 14·7 | 21·0 | 25·5 | 29·4 | 21·4 |
| Learned societies and conferences | 1·0 | 0·8 | 1·1 | 1·5 | 1·1 |
| Other professional work in Oxford | 0·8 | 0·9 | 0·8 | 4·6 | 1·2 |
| External examining and lecturing | 0·8 | 0·7 | 0·5 | 0·3 | 0·6 |
| Consulting | 0·2 | 1·3 | 0·5 | 0·7 | 0·5 |
| Other external work | 0·5 | 0·5 | 0·7 | 0·3 | 0·6 |
| All external work | 1·0 | 1·4 | 1·3 | 0·9 | 1·2 |
| All above activities | 33·3 | 32·5 | 39·8 | 40·5 | 36·8 |
| All work including teaching and regular administration | 50·5 | 46·0 | 50·2 | 48·6 | 49·6 |

SOURCE: Academic Staff Survey.

NOTE: See notes to Table 310.

PUBLICATIONS

## Publications during 1959–64

498. During the 5 years 1959–64, members of the academic staff (including outside grants staff) published on average 9·5 articles and reviews and 0·7 books,[1] 36 per cent. having published at least one book (Table 322). The rate of publication was highest in social studies and lowest in science in which the average number of books was 0·3.

499. Professors and readers had the highest rate of publication, each having an average of 1·7 books, and some 70 per cent. in each group having written at least one book. Professors in science had a high average number of articles and reviews and a low average number of books.

[1] Books written jointly with other authors are included.

**Table 312.** *Percentage of academic staff spending time on certain professional activities in term by post. 1963–4*

OXFORD

PERCENTAGE

| Work in term | Professor | Reader | University lecturer with tutorial fellowship | University lecturer without tutorial fellowship | CUF and special lecturer | Other university staff with tutorial fellowship | Other senior research staff | Other university and outside grants staff | College post only: teaching | College post only: research | All posts |
|---|---|---|---|---|---|---|---|---|---|---|---|
| Preparing teaching | 98 | 95 | 100 | 96 | 98 | 100 | 61 | 72 | 97 | 72 | 91 |
| Advising students | 78 | 79 | 81 | 77 | 86 | 85 | 55 | 46 | 90 | 49 | 74 |
| Administration (excluding regular administration) | 92 | 83 | 92 | 82 | 71 | 78 | 90 | 53 | 58 | 25 | 72 |
| College admissions | 2 | 17 | 64 | 6 | 68 | 59 | 8 | 4 | 41 | 5 | 30 |
| University examining | 40 | 30 | 26 | 30 | 30 | 16 | 11 | 4 | 17 | 8 | 23 |
| Study and research | 95 | 98 | 98 | 97 | 94 | 97 | 98 | 98 | 94 | 100 | 96 |
| Learned societies and conferences | 86 | 43 | 46 | 68 | 43 | 30 | 62 | 58 | 63 | 51 | 55 |
| Other professional work in Oxford | 73 | 65 | 34 | 43 | 22 | 19 | 41 | 21 | 22 | 18 | 34 |
| External examining and lecturing | 62 | 40 | 22 | 35 | 22 | 16 | 28 | 15 | 14 | 15 | 27 |
| Consulting | 49 | 29 | 12 | 18 | 9 | 5 | 39 | 13 | 14 | 14 | 18 |
| Other external work | 32 | 31 | 10 | 13 | 12 | 10 | 13 | 9 | 18 | 19 | 14 |
| All external work | 77 | 59 | 28 | 36 | 28 | 16 | 43 | 22 | 16 | 30 | 33 |

SOURCE: Academic Staff Survey.

NOTE: The percentages are based on those for whom the hours of work were ascertained.

**Table 313.** *Percentage of academic staff spending time on certain professional activities in term by subject group. 1963-4*

OXFORD                                                                    PERCENTAGE

| Work in term | Arts | Social studies | Science | Medicine | All subjects |
|---|---|---|---|---|---|
| Preparing teaching | 96 | 90 | 90 | 73 | 91 |
| Advising students | 82 | 81 | 69 | 48 | 74 |
| Administration (excluding regular administration) | 69 | 65 | 76 | 77 | 72 |
| College admissions | 45 | 31 | 21 | 6 | 30 |
| University examining | 30 | 20 | 20 | 13 | 23 |
| Study and research | 95 | 94 | 98 | 99 | 96 |
| Learned societies and conferences | 54 | 40 | 54 | 79 | 55 |
| Other professional work in Oxford | 30 | 23 | 34 | 62 | 34 |
| External examining and lecturing | 27 | 40 | 25 | 22 | 27 |
| Consulting | 11 | 30 | 19 | 23 | 18 |
| Other external work | 16 | 20 | 12 | 6 | 14 |
| All external work | 31 | 51 | 31 | 29 | 33 |

SOURCE: Academic Staff Survey.
NOTE: See note to Table 312.

500. Table 323 shows the relation between the number of years in academic life and authorship.[1] The average number of publications increases with the years in academic life. For those early in an academic career the number of publications is almost bound to be relatively small since they have been 'at risk' for only a short time. Table 323 shows that the rate of publication continues to rise over a period of 20 years or more, which in terms of age means at least into the fifties.

501. Not all the publications during 1959-64 were written while the author was in post at Oxford. 9 per cent. of the staff were newly appointed, and a further 36 per cent. had been in post for up to 5 years (Table 253), so that some of their publications will have been written while in another post. There is the possibility that the publication rate for staff at Oxford may be different from their publication rate before taking up a post at Oxford.

502. Inspection of the first three columns of Table 324 (corresponding to no years, 1-5, and 6-10 years at Oxford) shows no evidence of the

[1] The rate of publication by outside grants staff was roughly the same as that of other academic staff of a similar age.

Table 314. *Time spent on preparing teaching, administration, etc., in term by post. 1963–4*

OXFORD                                  PERCENTAGE

| Preparing teaching, administration, etc., in term (hours per week) | Professor | Reader | University lecturer with tutorial fellowship | University lecturer without tutorial fellowship | CUF and special lecturer | Other university staff with tutorial fellowship | Other senior research staff | Other university and outside grants staff | College post only: teaching | College post only: research | All posts |
|---|---|---|---|---|---|---|---|---|---|---|---|
| None | — | — | — | 3 | — | — | 7 | 24 | — | 17 | 6 |
| 1–6 | 10 | 38 | 22 | 29 | 19 | 18 | 43 | 34 | 17 | 47 | 27 |
| 7–12 | 19 | 21 | 36 | 21 | 35 | 59 | 10 | 22 | 33 | 25 | 27 |
| 13–18 | 25 | 14 | 20 | 26 | 22 | 9 | 13 | 8 | 22 | 6 | 18 |
| 19–24 | 21 | 14 | 9 | 15 | 16 | 9 | 13 | 6 | 17 | 6 | 13 |
| 25 and over | 25 | 14 | 13 | 5 | 8 | 5 | 13 | 6 | 11 | — | 9 |
| All | 100 | 100 | 100 | 100 | 100 | 100 | 100 | 100 | 100 | 100 | 100 |

SOURCE: Academic Staff Survey.

NOTE: The activities included are: preparing teaching; advising students; administration (other than regular administration); college admissions; and internal examining.

**Table 315.** *Time spent on preparing teaching, administration, etc., in term by subject group. 1963–4*

OXFORD                                                          PERCENTAGE

| Preparing teaching, administration, etc., in term (hours per week) | Arts | Social studies | Science | Medicine | All subjects |
|---|---|---|---|---|---|
| None | 1 | 9 | 7 | 15 | 6 |
| 1–6 | 17 | 35 | 26 | 50 | 27 |
| 7–12 | 27 | 22 | 31 | 17 | 27 |
| 13–18 | 22 | 20 | 17 | 7 | 18 |
| 19–24 | 21 | 6 | 9 | 9 | 13 |
| 25 and over | 12 | 8 | 9 | 2 | 9 |
| All | 100 | 100 | 100 | 100 | 100 |

SOURCE: Academic Staff Survey.

NOTE: The activities included are: preparing teaching; advising students; administration (other than regular administration); admissions; and internal examining.

publication rate changing in a systematic way after appointment to a post at Oxford.[1] There is, however, some evidence that, for a given number of years in academic life, the publication rate of those who have spent most or all the time at Oxford (i.e. those in the diagonal entries in the table) is slightly lower than for those who have spent part of the time in another university. Thus each of the averages on the diagonal of the table is less than (in one case equal to) the entry immediately to the left.

503. Tables 325 and 326 give distributions for the number of articles and reviews published during 1959–64. There is considerable dispersion. 15 per cent. published none, 15 per cent. published 1 or 2, and 7 per cent. published 26 and over. (The highest number reported was 255.) Among professors, 21 per cent. had published 26 and over.

504. A fifth of the academic staff had published 1 book, 9 per cent. had published 2, and 8 per cent. had published 3 and over (Tables 327 and 328). The highest proportions having published 3 or more books were 29 per cent. for professors and 18 per cent. for readers. In both arts and social studies, 13 per cent. of all staff had published at least 3 books.

505. Table 329 shows distributions by years in academic life.

[1] The numbers on which are based the figures in the first two columns against 21 years and over in academic life, are very small. See Table 359.

## Table 316. Average hours of work in vacation by post. 1963-4

OXFORD

| Work in vacation (except teaching and regular administration) (hours per week) | Professor | Reader | University lecturer with tutorial fellowship | University lecturer without tutorial fellowship | CUF and special lecturer | Other university staff with tutorial fellowship | Other senior research staff | Other university and outside grants staff | College post only: teaching | College post only: research | All posts |
|---|---|---|---|---|---|---|---|---|---|---|---|
| | | | | | | | | | | | HOURS |
| Preparing teaching | 1·8 | 2·3 | 2·9 | 3·6 | 4·8 | 3·9 | 0·4 | 1·2 | 6·1 | 1·8 | 3·0 |
| Advising students | 1·5 | 0·8 | 0·7 | 0·9 | 0·7 | 0·6 | 1·3 | 0·7 | 0·6 | 0·3 | 0·8 |
| Administration | 7·3 | 2·9 | 2·5 | 2·4 | 1·5 | 1·1 | 6·7 | 2·3 | 0·4 | 0·2 | 2·7 |
| College admissions | 0·1 | 0·3 | 1·6 | 0·2 | 1·8 | 1·3 | — | 0·1 | 1·2 | — | 0·8 |
| University examining | 1·2 | 1·0 | 2·5 | 1·4 | 3·3 | 1·3 | 1·5 | 0·1 | 0·2 | | 1·7 |
| Study and research | 21·9 | 30·0 | 29·1 | 25·5 | 21·7 | 28·8 | 32·6 | 33·7 | 25·3 | 33·3 | 27·3 |
| Learned societies and conferences | 4·3 | 2·1 | 2·3 | 2·1 | 0·6 | 1·6 | 2·4 | 1·6 | 1·6 | 1·1 | 1·8 |
| Other professional work in Oxford | 1·9 | 1·8 | 1·1 | 3·1 | 0·7 | 1·8 | 0·9 | 0·8 | 1·1 | 0·3 | 1·3 |
| External examining and lecturing | 1·8 | 1·7 | 1·3 | 1·0 | 1·0 | 2·1 | 0·6 | 0·8 | 0·9 | 0·2 | 1·1 |
| Consulting | 1·7 | 0·7 | 0·4 | 0·8 | 0·7 | 0·1 | 1·4 | 0·7 | 0·1 | 0·3 | 0·8 |
| Other external work | 1·2 | 0·6 | 0·7 | 0·7 | 0·5 | 0·4 | 0·7 | 1·0 | 0·4 | 0·5 | 0·7 |
| All external work | 3·5 | 2·8 | 2·2 | 2·4 | 1·6 | 2·1 | 1·9 | 1·5 | 0·8 | 0·5 | 1·9 |
| All above activities | 40·3 | 40·9 | 46·5 | 41·2 | 35·5 | 42·5 | 45·8 | 41·8 | 27·1 | 37·6 | 40·2 |

SOURCE: Academic Staff Survey.

**Table 317.** *Average hours of work in vacation by subject group. 1963-4*

OXFORD                                                                    HOURS

| Work in vacation (except teaching and regular administration) (hours per week) | Arts | Social studies | Science | Medicine | All subjects |
|---|---|---|---|---|---|
| Preparing teaching | 5·2 | 3·0 | 1·9 | 0·8 | 3·0 |
| Advising students | 0·6 | 0·5 | 1·1 | 0·8 | 0·8 |
| Administration | 1·7 | 1·3 | 3·5 | 3·6 | 2·7 |
| College admissions | 1·3 | 0·5 | 0·6 | 0·1 | 0·8 |
| University examining | 2·6 | 1·3 | 1·2 | 0·3 | 1·7 |
| Study and research | 24·2 | 26·1 | 29·7 | 29·5 | 27·3 |
| Learned societies and conferences | 1·2 | 1·0 | 2·5 | 1·7 | 1·8 |
| Other professional work in Oxford | 1·0 | 0·3 | 1·3 | 4·1 | 1·3 |
| External examining and lecturing | 1·3 | 1·1 | 0·9 | 0·9 | 1·1 |
| Consulting | 0·4 | 2·3 | 0·7 | 0·6 | 0·8 |
| Other external work | 0·7 | 1·0 | 0·6 | 0·5 | 0·7 |
| All external work | 1·8 | 3·1 | 1·7 | 1·2 | 1·9 |
| All above activities | 38·7 | 37·6 | 42·1 | 38·6 | 40·2 |

SOURCE: Academic Staff Survey.

## Comparisons with other universities

506. The above results from the Academic Staff Survey cannot be directly compared with publication rates at other universities. But a survey carried out by Mr. A. H. Halsey, Head of the Department of Social and Administrative Studies, gives a comparison of total publications at British universities. Table 330 gives details, together with the results of a similar survey carried out by Professor B. R. Clark at the University of California, Berkeley. Each of the distributions is based on total publications over each person's career. They need not have been written while at the particular university or university group shown, and the distributions will depend on the age distribution of staff. Thus the average number of publications at Oxford would be higher than at other universities in Great Britain even if the publication rate were the same since the average age at Oxford is higher. Table 330 shows that the pattern at Oxford is very similar to that at Cambridge, and that the average number of publications is higher at each than at other universities in Great Britain or at Berkeley.

507. The results of a comparison for certain science subjects in 1962-3 between Oxford, Manchester, and University College, London, are given

**Table 318.** *Percentage of academic staff spending time on certain professional activities in vacation by post. 1963–4*

OXFORD                                       PERCENTAGE

| Work in vacation | Professor | Reader | University lecturer with tutorial fellowship | University lecturer without tutorial fellowship | CUF and special lecturer | Other university staff with tutorial fellowship | Other senior research staff | Other university and outside grants staff | College post only: teaching | College post only: research | All posts |
|---|---|---|---|---|---|---|---|---|---|---|---|
| Preparing teaching | 63 | 56 | 79 | 85 | 86 | 75 | 24 | 43 | 100 | 39 | 68 |
| Advising students | 70 | 63 | 67 | 62 | 67 | 50 | 36 | 32 | 39 | 34 | 54 |
| Administration (excluding regular administration) | 86 | 79 | 68 | 68 | 60 | 50 | 76 | 45 | 33 | 11 | 61 |
| College admissions | 9 | 32 | 20 | 20 | 94 | 80 | 8 | 16 | 61 | 8 | 49 |
| University examining | 44 | 51 | 43 | 43 | 54 | 43 | 20 | 9 | 23 | 3 | 39 |
| Study and research | 98 | 100 | 98 | 98 | 99 | 100 | 97 | 98 | 100 | 97 | 99 |
| Learned societies and conferences | 96 | 92 | 90 | 89 | 60 | 89 | 91 | 72 | 62 | 59 | 77 |
| Other professional work in Oxford | 79 | 84 | 63 | 64 | 31 | 36 | 56 | 34 | 24 | 16 | 47 |
| External examining and lecturing | 77 | 68 | 58 | 48 | 53 | 54 | 47 | 33 | 35 | 10 | 49 |
| Consulting | 57 | 50 | 31 | 32 | 17 | 5 | 47 | 17 | 6 | 13 | 26 |
| Other external work | 36 | 48 | 17 | 26 | 17 | 25 | 26 | 18 | 11 | 17 | 22 |
| All external work | 91 | 67 | 63 | 61 | 52 | 55 | 58 | 29 | 29 | 19 | 51 |

SOURCE: Academic Staff Survey.

NOTE: See note to Table 312.

**Table 319.** *Percentage of academic staff spending time on certain professional activities in vacation by subject group. 1963-4*

OXFORD                                                                    PERCENTAGE

| Work in vacation | Arts | Social studies | Science | Medicine | All subjects |
|---|---|---|---|---|---|
| Preparing teaching | 82 | 67 | 64 | 41 | 68 |
| Advising students | 59 | 47 | 57 | 36 | 54 |
| Administration (excluding | | | | | |
| regular administration) | 53 | 42 | 69 | 73 | 61 |
| College admissions | 66 | 46 | 41 | 16 | 49 |
| University examining | 50 | 36 | 34 | 18 | 39 |
| Study and research | 99 | 98 | 99 | 98 | 99 |
| Learned societies and | | | | | |
| conferences | 69 | 61 | 87 | 89 | 77 |
| Other professional work in | | | | | |
| Oxford | 38 | 22 | 55 | 69 | 47 |
| External examining and | | | | | |
| lecturing | 56 | 49 | 43 | 47 | 49 |
| Consulting | 17 | 41 | 29 | 34 | 26 |
| Other external work | 25 | 28 | 19 | 20 | 22 |
| All external work | 51 | 60 | 50 | 44 | 51 |

SOURCE: Academic Staff Survey.
NOTE: See note to Table 312.

in Table 331. The table relates publications to staff at lecturer level and above, as listed in annual reports. The average number of publications at Oxford was 40-60 per cent. higher than in the other two institutions.

### LEAVE OF ABSENCE

508. The regulations for sabbatical leave are set out in full in *Statuta* 1965, pp. 45-47; but in brief they provide that professors, readers, lecturers, senior research officers, and holders of any other post approved by the Visitatorial Board and the General Board may apply for 1 term of leave for every 6 terms of service. The full stipend is normally paid for 2 terms of sabbatical leave in any period of 7 years, and for 3 terms where no stipend from another source is drawn. CUF lecturers are treated slightly differently because their university obligation is merely to carry on advanced study and research and to give 16 lectures or classes a year; their sabbatical entitlement is therefore expressed as being an entitlement to dispensation from up to 16 lectures or classes in any period of 7 years. The main effect of this distinction is that a CUF lecturer can be away from Oxford in practice as much as his college will allow; the University concerns itself only with the delivery of lectures or giving of classes.

**Table 320.** *Time spent on preparing teaching, administration, etc., in vacation by post. 1963–4*

OXFORD            PERCENTAGE

| Preparing teaching, administration, etc., in vacation (hours per week) | Professor | Reader | University lecturer with tutorial fellowship | University lecturer without tutorial fellowship | CUF and special lecturer | Other university staff with tutorial fellowship | Other senior research staff | Other university and outside grants staff | College post only: teaching | College post only: research | All posts |
|---|---|---|---|---|---|---|---|---|---|---|---|
| None | 4 | 4 | — | 7 | — | 7 | 11 | 34 | — | 45 | 13 |
| 1–6 | 37 | 52 | 36 | 44 | 29 | 36 | 50 | 47 | 71 | 48 | 42 |
| 7–12 | 17 | 30 | 24 | 23 | 34 | 29 | 14 | 10 | 21 | 3 | 21 |
| 13–18 | 20 | 4 | 24 | 17 | 18 | 21 | 11 | 3 | 7 | — | 13 |
| 19 and over | 23 | 9 | 15 | 9 | 18 | 7 | 14 | 6 | — | 3 | 11 |
| All | 100 | 100 | 100 | 100 | 100 | 100 | 100 | 100 | 100 | 100 | 100 |

SOURCE: Academic Staff Survey.

NOTE: The activities included are: preparing teaching; advising students; administration (other than regular administration); college admissions; and internal examining.

**Table 321.** *Time spent on preparing teaching, administration, etc., in vacation by subject group. 1963–4*

OXFORD                                                                    PERCENTAGE

| Preparing teaching, administration, etc., in vacation (hours per week) | Arts | Social studies | Science | Medicine | All subjects |
|---|---|---|---|---|---|
| None | 8 | 17 | 14 | 20 | 13 |
| 1–6 | 33 | 44 | 45 | 54 | 42 |
| 7–12 | 26 | 25 | 18 | 17 | 21 |
| 13–18 | 15 | 6 | 15 | 5 | 13 |
| 19 and over | 19 | 8 | 9 | 5 | 11 |
| All | 100 | 100 | 100 | 100 | 100 |

SOURCE: Academic Staff Survey.

NOTE: The activities included are: preparing teaching; advising students; administration (other than regular administration); college admissions; and internal examining.

509. All applications for leave are treated as applications for sabbatical leave until the entitlement is exhausted. Applications for additional (i.e. special) leave are treated *ad hoc*.

510. The practice generally followed by the colleges is similar to that of the University.

511. Table 332 gives details of leave granted by the University and by colleges. The number of cases approved by the University during the academic years 1961–4 was 165 for sabbatical leave, and 63 for special leave; and the University expected 57 people to be on leave in Michaelmas Term 1964. However, many of the people concerned were also tutorial fellows and hence included in the returns from colleges. Table 332 shows the university figures broken down into university staff and university and college staff. The latter should also be included under colleges, and the total number of individuals was 241 for sabbatical leave and 93 for special leave in 1961–4, and 61 in Michaelmas Term 1964.

512. The discrepancy between leave by colleges and leave by the University to university and college staff (which might be expected to be very similar in view of the fact that practically all tutorial fellows also hold a university post) is probably explained by tutorial fellows continuing with their university work even when on leave from their college (e.g. a CUF lecturer

Table 322. *Average number of publications during 1959–64 by post and subject group*

OXFORD

| Subject group | Average number published 1959–64 of: | Professor | Reader | University lecturer with tutorial fellowship | University lecturer without tutorial fellowship | CUF and special lecturer | Other university staff with tutorial fellowship | Other senior research staff | Other university and outside grants staff | College post only: teaching | College post only: research | All posts |
|---|---|---|---|---|---|---|---|---|---|---|---|---|
| Arts | Articles and reviews | 16·0 | 14·2 | 8·7 | 9·7 | 8·3 | 5·8 | 18·0 | 4·0 | 6·7 | 5·5 | 8·7 |
| | Books | 2·1 | 2·6 | 1·2 | 1·3 | 0·8 | 0·4 | 1·0 | 0·7 | 0·6 | 1·0 | 1·1 |
| | *Percentage with at least one book* | 84 | 88 | 57 | 48 | 44 | 13 | 100 | 35 | 25 | 40 | 48 |
| Social studies | Articles and reviews | 13·5 | 39·8 | · | 19·3 | 9·9 | 11·5 | 6·3 | 5·3 | 7·1 | 6·0 | 11·5 |
| | Books | 2·6 | 2·3 | · | 1·3 | 1·1 | 1·0 | 1·3 | 0·3 | 0·7 | 0·7 | 1·1 |
| | *Percentage with at least one book* | 89 | 100 | · | 78 | 50 | 50 | 75 | 25 | 42 | 38 | 53 |
| Science | Articles and reviews | 22·7 | 15·6 | 11·1 | 9·8 | 3·3 | 8·1 | 11·0 | 4·5 | 6·1 | 8·5 | 9·1 |
| | Books | 0·8 | 1·2 | 0·3 | 0·5 | 0·1 | 0·2 | 0·5 | 0·1 | 0·3 | 0·2 | 0·3 |
| | *Percentage with at least one book* | 43 | 52 | 24 | 32 | 9 | 17 | 30 | 7 | 27 | 13 | 22 |
| Medicine | Articles and reviews | 24·2 | 12·8 | 12·4 | 7·2 | · | · | 13·1 | 8·9 | · | · | 10·9 |
| | Books | 1·2 | 0·9 | 0·2 | 0·3 | · | · | 0·1 | 0·1 | · | · | 0·3 |
| | *Percentage with at least one book* | 50 | 55 | 20 | 16 | · | · | 10 | 10 | · | · | 20 |
| All subjects | Articles and reviews | 18·5 | 18·7 | 10·6 | 10·3 | 8·2 | 7·9 | 11·8 | 5·3 | 6·7 | 6·4 | 9·5 |
| | Books | 1·7 | 1·7 | 0·5 | 0·7 | 0·8 | 0·3 | 0·4 | 0·2 | 0·6 | 0·7 | 0·7 |
| | *Percentage with at least one book* | 70 | 69 | 31 | 37 | 43 | 19 | 30 | 13 | 30 | 33 | 36 |

NUMBER

SOURCE: Academic Staff Survey.

**Table 323.** *Average number of publications during 1959–64 by subject group and years in academic life*

OXFORD                                                                                          NUMBER

| Subject group | Average number published 1959–64 of | Years in academic life | | | | | All |
|---|---|---|---|---|---|---|---|
| | | None | 1–5 | 6–10 | 11–20 | 21 and over | |
| Arts | Articles and reviews | 3·2 | 3·0 | 9·1 | 9·6 | 12·6 | 8·7 |
| | Books | 0·2 | 0·3 | 0·8 | 1·2 | 1·6 | 1·0 |
| | Percentage with at least one book | 20 | 18 | 46 | 54 | 70 | 48 |
| Social studies | Articles and reviews | 0·7 | 4·9 | 13·8 | 13·4 | 20·6 | 11·5 |
| | Books | — | 0·4 | 1·1 | 1·6 | 1·8 | 1·1 |
| | Percentage with at least one book | — | 28 | 59 | 76 | 60 | 53 |
| Science | Articles and reviews | 2·1 | 5·9 | 10·7 | 12·1 | 12·9 | 9·1 |
| | Books | — | 0·1 | 0·3 | 0·6 | 0·7 | 0·3 |
| | Percentage with at least one book | — | 7 | 23 | 38 | 44 | 22 |
| Medicine | Articles and reviews | 7·8 | 6·6 | 11·1 | 13·2 | 16·6 | 10·9 |
| | Books | 0·2 | — | 0·1 | 0·4 | 1·0 | 0·3 |
| | Percentage with at least one book | 20 | 2 | 12 | 28 | 50 | 20 |
| All subjects | Articles and reviews | 2·6 | 5·1 | 10·8 | 11·2 | 14·0 | 9·5 |
| | Books | 0·1 | 0·2 | 0·6 | 1·0 | 1·3 | 0·7 |
| | Percentage with at least one book | 6 | 12 | 36 | 50 | 59 | 36 |

SOURCE: Academic Staff Survey.

will fairly commonly deliver his annual quota of lectures even though absent from his college for part of the year; or a scientist might wish to be relieved of his college duties in order to give him more time for his work in the department).

513. The figures in Table 332 do not permit a precise assessment of the extent to which the entitlement to leave is taken up, since the cases approved may have been for 1, 2, 3, or more terms. However, the average number of cases per year in 1961–4 was 110. Since the average period for which leave is granted is almost certainly less than a year, it appears that Michaelmas Term 1964 was not atypical. If the full entitlement had been taken about 160 persons would have been on leave. Thus only about 40

**Table 324.** *Average number of publications during 1959–64 by years in academic life and years at Oxford*

OXFORD                                                                                   NUMBER

| Years in academic life | Average number published 1959–64 of | Years in academic post at Oxford | | | | | All |
|---|---|---|---|---|---|---|---|
| | | None | 1–5 | 6–10 | 11–20 | 21 and over | |
| None | Articles and reviews | 2·6 | . | . | . | . | 2·6 |
| | Books | 0·1 | . | . | . | . | 0·1 |
| | *Percentage with at least one book* | 6 | . | . | . | . | 6 |
| 1–5 | Articles and reviews | 8·5 | 4·7 | . | . | . | 5·1 |
| | Books | 0·6 | 0·1 | . | . | . | 0·2 |
| | *Percentage with at least one book* | 28 | 10 | . | . | . | 12 |
| 6–10 | Articles and reviews | 5·4 | 11·3 | 10·9 | . | . | 10·8 |
| | Books | 0·4 | 0·6 | 0·6 | . | . | 0·6 |
| | *Percentage with at least one book* | 43 | 34 | 37 | . | . | 36 |
| 11–20 | Articles and reviews | 11·8 | 12·5 | 13·9 | 10·4 | . | 11·2 |
| | Books | 1·0 | 1·3 | 1·2 | 0·9 | . | 1·0 |
| | *Percentage with at least one book* | 13 | 63 | 51 | 48 | . | 50 |
| 21 and over | Articles and reviews | 6·0 | 25·0 | 15·2 | 16·3 | 12·1 | 14·0 |
| | Books | 1·0 | 1·1 | 0·8 | 1·6 | 1·3 | 1·3 |
| | *Percentage with at least one book* | 100 | 56 | 45 | 65 | 58 | 59 |
| All | Articles and reviews | 5·0 | 7·2 | 12·0 | 11·4 | 12·1 | 9·5 |
| | Books | 0·3 | 0·4 | 0·8 | 1·0 | 1·3 | 0·7 |
| | *Percentage with at least one book* | 17 | 22 | 42 | 51 | 58 | 36 |

SOURCE: Academic Staff Survey.

per cent. were taking their entitlement. This, coupled with the fact that in 1961–4 a large proportion of the cases were for special leave for individuals who had presumably exhausted their sabbatical entitlement, suggests that there is considerable dispersion in the amount of leave taken.

514. Evidence from Mr. Halsey's survey suggests that the academic staff at Oxford nevertheless have more leave of absence than academic staff at other universities, and are more likely to have paid or partly paid leave.

**Table 325.** *Articles and reviews published during 1959–64 by post*

OXFORD

PERCENTAGE

| Number of articles and reviews published 1959–64 | Professor | Reader | University lecturer with tutorial fellowship | University lecturer without tutorial fellowship | CUF and special lecturer | Other university staff with tutorial fellowship | Other senior research staff | Other university and outside grants staff | College post only: teaching | College post only: research | All posts |
|---|---|---|---|---|---|---|---|---|---|---|---|
| None | — | 4 | 7 | 9 | 11 | 11 | 12 | 28 | 33 | 29 | 15 |
| 1–2 | 5 | 7 | 7 | 8 | 24 | 11 | 5 | 23 | 12 | 17 | 15 |
| 3–5 | 10 | 7 | 20 | 15 | 18 | 27 | 15 | 17 | 18 | 23 | 17 |
| 6–10 | 21 | 22 | 21 | 34 | 22 | 16 | 22 | 18 | 12 | 15 | 22 |
| 11–25 | 39 | 37 | 40 | 28 | 21 | 35 | 35 | 9 | 17 | 9 | 24 |
| 26 and over | 21 | 16 | — | 6 | 5 | — | 12 | 4 | 6 | 5 | 7 |
| Not ascertained | 5 | 4 | — | 1 | — | — | — | — | 2 | 1 | 1 |
| All | 100 | 100 | 100 | 100 | 100 | 100 | 100 | 100 | 100 | 100 | 100 |

SOURCE: Academic Staff Survey.

**Table 326.** *Articles and reviews published during 1959–64 by subject group*

| Number of articles and reviews published 1959–64 | Arts | Social studies | Science | Medicine | All subjects |
|---|---|---|---|---|---|
| None | 15 | 17 | 15 | 15 | 15 |
| 1–2 | 18 | 15 | 14 | 9 | 15 |
| 3–5 | 17 | 17 | 18 | 12 | 17 |
| 6–10 | 21 | 17 | 23 | 23 | 22 |
| 11–25 | 21 | 25 | 24 | 32 | 24 |
| 26 and over | 7 | 9 | 6 | 10 | 7 |
| Not ascertained | 1 | 2 | — | — | 1 |
| All | 100 | 100 | 100 | 100 | 100 |

SOURCE: Academic Staff Survey.

From Table 333, 58 per cent. at Oxford and Cambridge had had leave, compared with 27 per cent. at all universities. The 58 per cent. will not all have taken the leave while holding a post at Oxford or Cambridge, but it is likely that a high proportion did so. It is almost certain that very considerably more leave is taken at Oxford and Cambridge than at other universities in Great Britain. The average length of leave under Oxford and Cambridge was rather shorter than that for all British universities, and those taking it were more likely to have spent it at home. In each group only 8 per cent. spent leave elsewhere in Great Britain. For the Oxford and Cambridge group the ratio of paid or partly paid leave to unpaid leave was 3·1:1. For all universities it was 2·4:1.

## EMOLUMENTS[1]

515. A consequence of the collegiate structure of Oxford is that many members of the academic staff receive a stipend both from the University and from a college. As well as the stipends for university posts, payments are also made by the University for a number of academic activities such as the supervision of postgraduates and university examining. There are also emoluments from colleges over and above fellowship stipends. There are therefore a number of different types of emoluments. The main purpose of this section is to set out the pattern of emoluments in 1964–5 and to make certain comparisons with national figures. First, however, the different types of emolument are described, and the amounts in 1964–5 are summarized in Table 334 below.

[1] Much of the information on emoluments was published before the Commission reported: *Gazette*, vol. cxv, pp. 1077–98.

**Table 327.** *Books published during 1959–64 by post*

OXFORD

PERCENTAGE

| Number of books published 1959–64 | Professor | Reader | University lecturer with tutorial fellowship | University lecturer without tutorial fellowship | CUF and special lecturer | Other university staff with tutorial fellowship | Other senior research staff | Other university and outside grants staff | College post only: teaching | College post only: research | All posts |
|---|---|---|---|---|---|---|---|---|---|---|---|
| None | 30 | 31 | 69 | 63 | 57 | 81 | 70 | 87 | 70 | 67 | 64 |
| 1 | 24 | 30 | 24 | 21 | 25 | 14 | 20 | 8 | 15 | 16 | 20 |
| 2 | 17 | 21 | 6 | 10 | 10 | — | 8 | 3 | 9 | 8 | 9 |
| 3 and over | 29 | 18 | 2 | 6 | 8 | 5 | 2 | 2 | 6 | 9 | 8 |
| All | 100 | 100 | 100 | 100 | 100 | 100 | 100 | 100 | 100 | 100 | 100 |

SOURCE: Academic Staff Survey.

**Table 328.** *Books published during 1959–64 by subject group*

OXFORD                                                           PERCENTAGE

| Number of books published 1959–64 | Arts | Social studies | Science | Medicine | All subjects |
|---|---|---|---|---|---|
| None | 52 | 47 | 78 | 80 | 64 |
| 1 | 22 | 25 | 16 | 15 | 20 |
| 2 | 12 | 16 | 4 | 3 | 9 |
| 3 and over | 13 | 13 | 2 | 3 | 8 |
| All | 100 | 100 | 100 | 100 | 100 |

SOURCE: Academic Staff Survey.

**Table 329.** *Publications during 1959–64 by years in academic life*

OXFORD                                                           PERCENTAGE

| Publications during 1959–64 | Years in academic life | | | | | All |
|---|---|---|---|---|---|---|
| | None | 1–5 | 6–10 | 11–20 | 21 and over | |
| ARTICLES AND REVIEWS | | | | | | |
| None | 56 | 23 | 8 | 8 | 8 | 15 |
| 1–2 | 23 | 23 | 13 | 10 | 12 | 15 |
| 3–5 | 5 | 20 | 20 | 15 | 15 | 17 |
| 6–10 | 10 | 19 | 21 | 26 | 23 | 22 |
| 11–25 | 5 | 11 | 29 | 32 | 28 | 24 |
| 26 and over | 2 | 2 | 9 | 8 | 12 | 7 |
| Not ascertained | — | 1 | — | 1 | 3 | 1 |
| All | 100 | 100 | 100 | 100 | 100 | 100 |
| BOOKS | | | | | | |
| None | 94 | 88 | 64 | 50 | 41 | 64 |
| 1 | 6 | 8 | 23 | 27 | 24 | 20 |
| 2 | — | 2 | 7 | 12 | 17 | 9 |
| 3 and over | — | 1 | 6 | 10 | 18 | 8 |
| All | 100 | 100 | 100 | 100 | 100 | 100 |

SOURCE: Academic Staff Survey.

**Table 330.** *Publications by academic staff of certain universities*

PERCENTAGE

| | Oxford 1963–4 | Oxford and Cambridge 1963–4 | All universities in Great Britain 1963–4 | University of California, Berkeley 1962–3 |
|---|---|---|---|---|
| NUMBER OF ACADEMIC ARTICLES PUBLISHED | | | | |
| None | 9 | 8 | 7 | 14 |
| 1–4 | 17 | 16 | 22 | 22 |
| 5–10 | 10 | 14 | 23 | |
| 11–20 | 25 | 23 | 20 | } 64 |
| 21 and over | 40 | 39 | 28 | |
| | | | | |
| NUMBER OF BOOKS PUBLISHED | | | | |
| None | 40 | 45 | 65 | 60 |
| 1 | } 60 | 23 | 18 | 18 |
| 2 | | 12 | 7 | 7 |
| 3 and over | | 20 | 9 | 15 |
| | | | | |
| WHETHER PREPARING A BOOK FOR PUBLICATION | | | | |
| Yes | 66 | 67 | 50 | 52 |
| No | 34 | 33 | 50 | 46 |
| No answer | — | — | — | 2 |
| | | | | |
| All | 100 | 100 | 100 | 100 |
| | | | | |
| *Number in sample* | *78* | *162* | *1,403* | *286* |

SOURCE: Great Britain: A. H. Halsey.
University of California, Berkeley: Professor B. R. Clark.
NOTES
1. The figures for Great Britain are from a survey (with a response rate of 53 per cent.) of those university teachers who responded to the inquiry by the Robbins Committee in 1961–2 (in which the response rate was 86 per cent.).
2. There were 2 per cent. at the University of California, Berkeley, who stated that they had published books but did not give the number. They have been included under 'one book'.

## Types of emolument

516. *University stipend.* This is based on the annual rates at 1 January 1965; the amount in Table 334 differs from the aggregate of the stipends which were paid during the year because some will have received increments during the year. (University lecturers and senior research officers generally receive increments from the beginning of the quarter following that in which the qualifying age is attained. CUF lecturers receive them from the

**Table 331.** *Publications in certain science subjects by post and subject. Academic staff at lecturer level and above. 1962–3*

NUMBER

| | Oxford | | | Manchester | | | University College, London | | |
|---|---|---|---|---|---|---|---|---|---|
| | Staff | Publica-tions | Average | Staff | Publica-tions | Average | Staff | Publica-tions | Average |
| **POST** | | | | | | | | | |
| Professor | 9 | 34 | 3·8 | 11 | 38 | 3·5 | 15 | 47 | 3·1 |
| Reader | 17 | 67 | 3·9 | 7 | 21 | 3·0 | 25 | 59 | 2·4 |
| Senior lecturer | . | . | . | 18 | 24 | 1·3 | 4 | 7 | 1·8 |
| Lecturer | 104 | 260 | 2·5 | 60 | 79 | 1·3 | 64 | 107 | 1·7 |
| **SUBJECT** | | | | | | | | | |
| Physics | 46 | 94 | 2·0 | 31 | 51 | 1·6 | 32 | 60 | 1·9 |
| Chemistry | 30 | 124 | 4·1 | 28 | 76 | 2·7 | 24 | 57 | 2·4 |
| Biochemistry | 17 | 66 | 3·9 | No separate dept. | | | 13 | 25 | 1·9 |
| Physiology | 14 | 28 | 2·0 | 7 | 3 | 0·4 | 13 | 29 | 2·2 |
| Zoology | 15 | 26 | 1·7 | 13 | 16 | 1·2 | 13 | 22 | 1·7 |
| Botany | 8 | 23 | 2·9 | 17 | 16 | 0·9 | 13 | 27 | 2·1 |
| **All** | 130 | 361 | 2·8 | 96 | 162 | 1·7 | 108 | 220 | 2·0 |

SOURCE: Oxford: Annual Report of the Delegates of the University Museum for the year ended 31 July 1963.
Manchester University and University College, London: Annual Reports.

NOTES
1. The number of staff in Physics at Oxford includes CUF lecturers.
2. The figure for staff in Botany at Oxford relate to 1963–4.
3. Senior research officers at Oxford (for whom the average number of publications was 2·4) are included with lecturers.
4. Some publications by junior staff who are not included in the staff figures may be included.

**Table 332.** *Leave of absence 1961–4 and Michaelmas Term 1964*

OXFORD

NUMBER

| Leave of absence granted | Cases approved during 1961–4 | | Expected to be away in Michaelmas Term 1964 |
|---|---|---|---|
| | Sabbatical | Special | |
| By colleges | 147 | 45 | 34 |
| By University to university staff | 94 | 48 | 27 |
| Total persons | 241 | 93 | 61 |
| By University to university/college staff | 71 | 15 | 30 |

SOURCE: Registry; colleges.

**Table 333.** *Leave of absence*

PERCENTAGE

| | Oxford and Cambridge | All universities in Great Britain |
|---|---|---|
| WHETHER HAD HAD A LEAVE OF ABSENCE FOR A TERM OR MORE WHILE ON THE STAFF OF ANY BRITISH UNIVERSITY (OR CAT) | | |
| Yes | 58 | 27 |
| No | 41 | 73 |
| DURATION OF LEAVE (FOR THOSE HAVING HAD LEAVE) | | |
| 1 term or less | 44 | 40 |
| Between 1 and 3 terms | 28 | 27 |
| 3 terms or more | 28 | 33 |
| WHERE LEAVE WAS SPENT (FOR THOSE HAVING HAD LEAVE) | | |
| At home | 20 | 13 |
| Elsewhere in Great Britain | 8 | 8 |
| America | 33 | 50 |
| Elsewhere | 39 | 29 |
| TYPE OF LEAVE | | |
| Paid or partly paid sabbatical leave | 39 | 10 |
| Unpaid leave of absence | 14 | 8 |
| Paid or partly paid leave of absence | 5 | 9 |
| No leave | 41 | 73 |
| All | 100 | 100 |

SOURCE: A. H. Halsey (see Note 1 to Table 330).

beginning of the month following that in which the qualifying age is attained. Increments for other posts are generally paid from 1 October.) In common with all British universities, the University pays to those appointed before 1 January 1965 (and to those appointed before that date elsewhere who transfer to Oxford without promotion) children's allowances at the rate of £50 a year for each child who is below the age at which compulsory education ceases or being above that age is receiving full-time education; the allowances are not paid to CUF lecturers and are reduced to £25 for other holders of college fellowships with emoluments. These allowances are, however, excluded as they do not form part of stipend.

517. *College fellowship stipend.* This is based on the annual rates at 1 January 1965. The stipends of all fellowships held by the academic staff are included. As with university stipend actual payments were different

to the extent that increments were received during the year. Children's allowances are not included in Table 334 (but details are given in Table 348 of children's allowances paid to tutorial fellows). In three colleges part of the fellowship stipend is deemed an entertainment allowance, and this has been deducted in calculating the total for Table 334.

518. *College lecturership stipend or retaining fee.* College lecturers may be paid a fixed stipend in return for which they teach up to a stated number of hours per week. Alternatively they may receive a retaining fee, and be paid piece-rates for the tutorials they give. The stipends and retaining fees only are included under this head. The average given in Table 334 for those receiving these payments should not be regarded as a typical value. The retaining fees paid to non-stipendiary lecturers rarely exceed £50 a year.

519. *Supervision and other teaching for the University.* The University pays £10 per term for the supervision of postgraduates during their work for a higher degree. These payments account for the major part of this head. Payments are also made for certain tuition for which the University is responsible and for some lecturing and demonstrating where this is not covered by stipend. The amount for 1964–5 has been estimated as the total for 1963–4 revalued at the rates which were introduced in October 1964.

520. *College housing benefits.* It has been the practice of colleges since their foundation to provide their fellows with accommodation. At the present time bachelor tutorial fellows generally live in rooms in the college, while most married tutorial fellows either live in a house provided by the college or receive a housing allowance in lieu; all except five tutorial fellows received one or other of these benefits. Full details of the arrangements for tutorial fellows are given in Table 349. It is extremely difficult to assess the value to fellows of living in college, or in a college house rent free or at a beneficial rent. One approach would be to estimate the housing expenditure of those in otherwise similar circumstances who make their own provision for housing, but insufficient data are available to make this practicable. An alternative approach would be to estimate what a fellow would pay for his accommodation at market prices. This can be faulted on two grounds. First, the market rents of college houses cannot be estimated reliably, even with knowledge of their rateable values. (This is apparent from the details of the college replies on which Table 349 is based on the assumption that colleges do not give markedly better terms to some fellows than to others.) Secondly, a fellow would not necessarily buy or rent a house similar to his college house if he had a free choice and had to meet the total expense himself.

521. The method adopted for valuing college housing benefits has been to assume that colleges approximately equalize the different types of

benefit, and to take the average value within each college as equal to the cash housing allowance paid to those fellows making their own housing provision.[1] The entry in Table 334 thus comprises partly the actual allowances paid to those tutorial fellows (almost half) who receive them and partly a notional figure based on the assumption that the value of the housing benefits of the remaining fellows is equal to the allowances paid to their colleagues.

522. *Other college benefits.* These include college benefits which are available to at least a large proportion of tutorial fellows in a college. The Common Table, which is available to heads of houses and all fellows but which covers the cost of food and service only, is excluded because of the difficulty of estimating the number and value of the meals taken. Payments for college examining are excluded since the available information is incomplete, and the amounts are too small to have warranted a further inquiry. Allowances to cover expenses such as entertainment and books are also excluded from the amount shown in Table 334 (but details of allowances for tutorial fellows are given in Table 348). Three types of benefit are included. Payments for exercising tutorial responsibility are made by several colleges, and for those colleges where a majority of tutorial fellows receive such payments the total amount is included. For the remaining colleges, the payments are included under college offices. A number of colleges pay subscriptions to the British United Provident Association on behalf of fellows (and sometimes of their dependants); and three colleges have pension arrangements more favourable than the normal FSSU arrangement under which the employee contributes 5 per cent. of stipend and the employer a further 10 per cent. In calculating the benefit in these last two cases, account has been taken of income-tax, using the standard rate in force at 1 January 1965.

523. *University examining.* The total amount paid to the staff during 1963–4 is given in Table 334. The payments range from a relatively small number of large payments made to examiners in the major undergraduate Schools to a large number of small payments to examiners of theses.

524. *University offices and allowances.* There is a small number of university offices which are held by members of the academic staff, several of which are held by any individual for only a short time. The most prominent of these offices are the proctorships which are held for one year. Also included under this head are a small number of miscellaneous allowances and fees paid by the University which do not conveniently fall in any other category.

525. *College offices.* Colleges appoint their fellows to offices such as that of Senior Tutor or Dean to carry out academic and administrative duties

---

[1] One college has no cash allowance. An amount equal to the smallest allowance paid by other colleges has been imputed.

which are not normally part of a fellow's duties. The total payment at the rates in force on 1 January 1965 for such offices held by members of the academic staff is given. Particulars of the offices are given in Table 350.

526. *College piece-rate teaching.* College piece-rate teaching payments are made for any college teaching which is not covered by a college stipend; this is mainly teaching given out of college or by college non-stipendiary lecturers. The rates in 1964–5 for 8 hours' tuition (an hour a week for a term) were £14 for 1 pupil, £17. 10s. for a pair, and £21 for 3 pupils. For larger groups, £1 is added for each additional pupil.

527. These payments are the only emolument for which the estimates may contain significant errors. The total paid out by colleges in 1964 was £157,000. But an unknown amount of this was paid to persons other than those on the academic staff. Estimates of the distribution of tutorial teaching obtained from the Tutorial Organizers Survey during Michaelmas Term 1964 suggest that £104,000 was paid to the academic staff plus others who are employed on outside grants or who are college lecturers. But the rates were increased in October 1964. An allowance for this (assuming that 37 per cent. of a year's tutorials are given during Michaelmas Term; this figure is based on details supplied by three colleges) gives £115,000 as the corresponding figure for a year at the current rates. An estimated £10,000 is paid to those employed on outside grants and to college lecturers who have been regarded as part-time. This gives £105,000 as the estimate for payments to the academic staff during 1964–5 if the level of piece-rate teaching was the same as in 1964. The figure rests on a number of assumptions and should be regarded as only a rough estimate.

528. It is impossible with the available information to determine how many individuals received these payments, because there is no accurate means of telling how many of those with a stipendiary tutorial post also did piece-rate teaching. The amount of tutorial teaching reported by other members of the academic staff in the Academic Staff Survey would account for some £56,000 of the total.

## Total emoluments in 1964–5

529. Table 334 gives estimated totals for the emoluments paid to the academic staff (excluding academic staff at the Permanent Private Halls) in 1964–5. The total number of staff concerned was 1,116. Because subsequent analyses are confined to academic staff other than those on clinical scales, two sets of figures are given in this table. (Column (1) includes those —46 in number—on clinical scales; the remainder of the table does not.)

530. The emoluments have been aggregated into three totals on the basis partly of regularity of receipt, and partly of reliability of the estimates. The

**Table 334.** *Sources of emoluments at Oxford. 1964–5 (estimated)*

OXFORD

£

| Emolument | All academic staff | Excluding those on clinical scales | | |
|---|---|---|---|---|
| | | Total amount | Average amount for those receiving | *Percentage receiving* |
| | (1) | (2) | (3) | (4) |
| University stipend | 2,101,600 | 1,985,500 | 2,144 | 87 |
| College fellowship stipend | 731,000 | 729,300 | 1,141 | 60 |
| College lecturership stipend or retaining fee | 41,000 | 41,000 | 265 | 14 |
| Total salary | 2,873,600 | 2,755,800 | | |
| Supervision and other teaching for the University | 36,300 | 36,000 | 72 | 47 |
| College housing benefits | 133,400 | 133,100 | 232 | 54 |
| Other college benefits | 12,800 | 12,800 | 36 | 34 |
| Regular emoluments | 3,056,200 | 2,937,600 | | |
| University examining | 34,500 | 34,000 | 65 | 49 |
| University offices, allowances, and fees | 7,000 | 6,800 | 251 | 3 |
| College offices | 31,500 | 31,200 | 179 | 16 |
| College piece-rate teaching | 105,000 | 103,000 | .. | at least 29 |
| Total emoluments | 3,234,100 | 3,112,600 | | |

SOURCE: Registry; Chest; colleges; Academic Staff Survey.
NOTE: Academic staff at Permanent Private Halls are excluded.

first total is salary. The second is termed regular emoluments, and the third, total emoluments. Regular emoluments include the items in addition to salary which those who receive them at all may expect to receive regularly. This is certainly true of college housing and other benefits. There is more fluctuation in supervision, but it might be expected that most of those supervising in one year also supervise in succeeding years. College piece-rate teaching is similar in this respect and would have been included were the estimate known to be fully reliable. Total emoluments are obtained by adding the remaining items. Payments for university examining are not treated as a regular emolument, although a large proportion receive them, since there is a considerable change in the individuals

taking part in examining from one year to the next, and particularly
among those receiving large amounts from examining. Of the total salary,
73 per cent. was contributed by the University and 27 per cent. by the
colleges. Regular emoluments were 6·4 per cent., and total emoluments
12·5 per cent., above salary. Apart from salary, the largest items were
college housing benefits and college piece-rate teaching.

531. Table I of the Report gives the total expenditure on teaching and
research staff in 1963–4 as £3,497,000. Table 334 shows total emoluments
in 1964–5 as £3,234,000. Apart from the difference in date, Table I
includes employers' FSSU, National Insurance, and Graduated Pension
payments; child allowances; the cost of the Common Table; and payments
for teaching made to persons other than the academic staff. Table 334
includes none of these, but includes payments for examining which are
included under a different head in Table I. In addition, Table 334 includes
some allowance for housing benefits in kind, whereas Table I does not, and
salaries were adjusted in April 1964 as a result of the National Incomes
Commission award. A very approximate reconciliation is as follows:

|  | £'000 | £'000 |
|---|---|---|
| Table 334 | | 3,234 |
| *Add* | | |
| Employers' FSSU | 280 | |
| NI and Graduated Pension | 55 | |
| Child allowances | 66 | |
| Common Table | 57 | |
| Other teaching | 60 | |
|  | —— | |
|  | | 518 |
|  | | 3,752 |
| *Deduct* | | |
| Salary award | 140 | |
| Examining | 35 | |
| Housing in kind | 80 | |
|  | —— | |
|  | | 255 |
| Table I | | 3,497 |

## The estimation of salary distributions for 1964–5

532. Distributions have been estimated of the 1,070 members of the
academic staff, other than those on clinical scales (46 in number) and the
11 academic staff at Permanent Private Halls, by age and salary. Those on
clinical scales are excluded since these are special scales which apply
nationally.[1] The salary groups have been chosen to correspond with the
ranges of the national scales for professors, readers and senior lecturers,
lecturers, and assistant lecturers (except that the range for readers and
senior lecturers is extended to £3,399 instead of £3,250).

[1] In pre-clinical medicine the Oxford salary structure is, in effect, the same as that in
non-medical subjects. Pre-clinical staff are therefore included in the analyses.

533. The distribution for salary is given below in Table 335 while Table 336 gives comparable details for all universities in Great Britain. Table 337 shows the distributions within grades for Oxford and for all universities in Great Britain.

534. Table 336 gives an estimate of the distribution of all full-time academic staff (other than those in clinical medicine, dentistry, and veterinary science) by salary (using groups corresponding to the main grades) within age groups at all universities in Great Britain in October 1964.[1] Part of Table 337 shows, for all ages together, the distribution of these within the three principal salary ranges. These distributions are based on information supplied by the UGC. The information was collected from universities at the beginning of the academic year 1964–5 and will not reflect promotions during the academic year. In addition, the UGC did not collect information about the ages of professors, assistant lecturers, research staff, and 'others'; nor about the distribution of salaries for assistant lecturers, research, and 'other' staff. Finally, the salary groups used by the UGC for medicine were wider than those used for the other faculties and this creates some difficulties in incorporating pre-clinical medical staff in Table 337. In drawing up the tables a number of assumptions and approximations have consequently been made. Where information on age is not available it has been assumed that the age distribution was approximately the same as was found by the Association of University Teachers in their inquiry carried out in 1964–5.[2]

535. The only information on the salaries of research and 'other' staff is the average salary received during the academic year 1963–4. This was £1,004 and £1,416 respectively. The averages for these groups are thus unlikely to have exceeded £1,100 and £1,600 in 1964–5 at the revised salary rates. It seems likely, therefore, that only a very small proportion of research staff, and only a small proportion of 'other' staff, receive a salary above the maximum of the national scale for lecturers.[3] Estimates of the distribution of these persons by salary and estimates of their average salary by age groups must be regarded as very approximate.

536. The salary groups used by the UGC for medicine affect Table 337 but not Table 336. It has been necessary to allocate pre-clinical staff (who form 11 per cent. of readers and senior lecturers and 6 per cent. of lecturers) to one of two possible salary groups for most readers, senior lecturers, and lecturers. This is because the groupings used in medicine have roughly

[1] Full-time university staff at Oxford and Cambridge (and their university, but not their college, salaries) are included.
[2] *The remuneration of university teachers 1964–5*, AUT, 1965. This did not include research and other staff for whom the age distribution found by the Robbins Committee was used (Robbins Report, Appendix Three, Annex H, Table H. 2).
[3] For the assumptions made about this distribution see Note 1 to para. 542 below.

twice the range of those for other subjects. A small distortion between adjacent groups may be introduced in this way.

537. Some lecturers in pre-clinical medicine who should be included among lecturers on the basis of salary may have been included among readers and senior lecturers in the national distributions in Table 336. This is because some scales for pre-clinical medical lecturers have maxima above £2,505 and it is not possible to distinguish between those with a salary of £2,505 and those above that point from the information supplied by the UGC. All have therefore been assumed to have a salary exceeding £2,505. The number involved is small, however, and could not affect more than 0·7 per cent. of all staff.

538. The reader/senior lecturer scales overlap the lecturer scale at many universities in Great Britain. In Tables 336 and 337 staff are allocated to grades according to salary so far as possible. Thus any reader or senior lecturer with a salary of £2,505 or less is included among lecturers in the group £2,300–£2,504. (It is not possible to determine how many have a salary of £2,505, but if there is a significant number the percentage in this group will be understated.) There were 0·5 per cent. of all staff in this position.

## The Oxford and national salary distributions

539. At Oxford 18 per cent. of the academic staff received salaries within the professorial range, though, as Table 337 shows, over a third within the range were only just in it. (Those with salaries of £3,400–£3,649 were mainly tutorial fellows receiving the joint maximum salary of £3,450; those in the range £3,650–£3,899 were mainly readers with tutorial fellowships who receive salaries of up to £3,675; and the remainder were professors.) Nationally there were 11 per cent. in the professorial range.

540. The proportion in the reader/senior lecturer range was 38 per cent. at Oxford and 18 per cent. nationally.[1] At Oxford this group consisted mainly of readers, tutorial fellows, and other university lecturers on one of the three points in the scale above the national maximum. It was more concentrated in the lower range of the scale (see Table 337), but it included some with salaries of £3,251–£3,399, above the maximum of the national reader/senior lecturer range.

541. The proportion receiving salaries less than £1,400 was 13 per cent. at Oxford. Nationally, there were 14 per cent. assistant lecturers, but in addition a large proportion of research and other staff would have had salaries less than £1,400. The proportion in the lecturer range was also lower at Oxford than nationally.

[1] The latter figure is probably a slight understatement since some among research and other staff are likely to have salaries in this range.

**Table 335.** *Salaries of Oxford academic staff by age. All academic staff except those on clinical scales. 1964–5 (estimated)*

OXFORD                                                                                                                    PERCENTAGE

| Age | Salary group | | | | | Number | Average salary (£) | Median salary (£) | Percentage of total |
| --- | --- | --- | --- | --- | --- | --- | --- | --- | --- |
| | Under £1,400 | £1,400 to £2,505 | £2,506 to £3,399 | £3,400 and over | All | | | | |
| Under 30 | 63 | 36 | 1 | — | 100 | 164 | 1,231 | 1,275 | 15 |
| 30–34 | 14 | 80 | 6 | — | 100 | 160 | 1,939 | 1,995 | 15 |
| 35–39 | 3 | 51 | 44 | 2 | 100 | 170 | 2,500 | 2,478 | 16 |
| 40–44 | 2 | 16 | 71 | 12 | 100 | 180 | 2,949 | 2,968 | 17 |
| 45–49 | 3 | 6 | 57 | 34 | 100 | 111 | 3,109 | 3,150 | 10 |
| 50 and over | 1 | 8 | 47 | 45 | 100 | 285 | 3,308 | 3,250 | 27 |
| All | 13 | 31 | 38 | 18 | 100 | 1,070 | 2,575 | 2,723 | 100 |

SOURCE: See source to Table 334.

NOTE: See note to Table 334.

**Table 336.** *Salaries of academic staff at all universities in Great Britain by age. All academic staff except those in clinical medicine, dentistry, and veterinary science. October 1964 (estimated)*

GREAT BRITAIN

| Age | Salary group (where known) or grade | | | | | | | | Number | Average salary (£ per annum) | PERCENTAGE Percentage of total |
|---|---|---|---|---|---|---|---|---|---|---|---|
| | Under £1,400 | £1,400 to £2,505 | £2,506 to £3,399 | £3,400 to £4,750 | Research staff | Others | All | | | |
| Under 30 | 48 | 36 | — | — | 11 | 5 | 100 | 4,108 | 1,287 | 26 |
| 30–34 | 9 | 78 | 3 | 1 | 6 | 4 | 100 | 2,633 | 1,751 | 17 |
| 35–39 | 2 | 61 | 19 | 9 | 5 | 5 | 100 | 2,585 | 2,370 | 16 |
| 40–44 | — | 45 | 31 | 16 | 2 | 7 | 100 | 2,428 | 2,763 | 15 |
| 45–49 | — | 35 | 33 | 22 | 2 | 8 | 100 | 1,345 | 2,966 | 8 |
| 50 and over | — | 26 | 37 | 31 | 2 | 5 | 100 | 2,734 | 3,213 | 17 |
| All | 14 | 46 | 18 | 11 | 5 | 5 | 100 | 15,833 | 2,240 | 100 |

SOURCE: UGC and AUT Remuneration Survey.

NOTE: For details of the construction of this table see paras. 534–8 and 542.

## Table 337. *The distribution of academic staff within salary ranges. 1964–5 (estimated)*

PERCENTAGE

**Lecturer range**

| | £1,400 to £1,484 | £1,485 to £1,699 | £1,700 to £1,949 | £1,950 to £2,099 | £2,100 to £2,299 | £2,300 to £2,504 | £2,505 | All | *Number* |
|---|---|---|---|---|---|---|---|---|---|
| All universities in | | | | | | | | | |
| Great Britain: salary | 9 | 19 | 15 | 11 | 11 | 13 | 23 | 100 | *7,352* |
| Oxford: salary | 8 | 18 | 12 | 17 | 16 | 26 | 2 | 100 | *330* |

**Reader and senior lecturer range**

| | £2,506 to £2,704 | £2,705 to £2,899 | £2,900 to £3,099 | £3,100 to £3,399 | All | *Number* |
|---|---|---|---|---|---|---|
| All universities in | | | | | | |
| Great Britain: salary | 16 | 19 | 24 | 41 | 100 | *2,773* |
| Oxford: salary | 14 | 37 | 15 | 34 | 100 | *409* |

**Professorial range**

| | £3,400 to £3,649 | £3,650 to £3,899 | £3,900 to £4,199 | £4,200 to £4,499 | £4,500 and over | All | *Number* |
|---|---|---|---|---|---|---|---|
| All universities in | | | | | | | |
| Great Britain: salary | 5 | 12 | 42 | 26 | 15 | 100 | *1,761* |
| Oxford: salary | 37 | 9 | 41 | 4 | 8 | 100 | *191* |

SOURCE: Oxford: See source to Table 334.
All universities: UGC.

NOTE: Research staff and others are not included in the distributions for all universities in Great Britain. For details of the construction of these distributions see paras. 532–8.

542. The estimate of average salary at Oxford was £2,575 compared with £2,240 nationally.[1,2] The average age at Oxford is higher, however, and therefore a comparison of average salaries within age groups shows smaller differences between the Oxford and the national figures.

543. Holders of posts on outside grants are excluded from the analyses both for Oxford and for all universities in Great Britain. Of those at Oxford, over half were under 30 years, and a further quarter aged 30–34. Of those under 30 years, two-thirds had salaries in the assistant lecturer range; of those aged 30–34, four-fifths had salaries in the (national) lecturer range; of those aged 35 and over, one-half had salaries in the lecturer range and one-quarter in the senior lecturer range.

## The effects of differences in age

544. It is possible to estimate the effect of the Oxford age distribution on the salary pattern by calculating either a distribution based on the national age pattern, but with the Oxford salary distribution within age groups; or a distribution based on the Oxford age pattern, but with the national salary distribution within age groups. The results are given in Table 338 and show that the proportion in the professorial range is close to the national figure when age differences are allowed for. The proportion in the reader/senior lecturer range is brought closer to the national figure, but a considerable difference remains. The proportion in the lecturer range is correspondingly lower for Oxford than in the national distribution, and the proportion in the assistant lecturer range is not very different from that in the national distribution (after allowing for those in this range among the category 'other'). The average for the reweighted national distribution based on the Oxford age pattern is £2,464. The average salary at Oxford is about 15 per cent. above the national average, but when allowance is made for the higher average age at Oxford, the average salary is only 4½ per cent. above the national average. Thus, over two-thirds of the difference in average salaries can be accounted for by the higher average age at Oxford. These figures only give the order of magnitude of the various quantities, and if a different grouping of the academic staff were to be taken (say, all non-medical staff) no doubt slightly different results would be obtained.

[1] The salaries for those in research and other posts are required for this calculation. The 11 per cent. in these categories were assumed to have salaries thus:

| | |
|---|---|
| Under £1,400 | 6·4 per cent. |
| £1,400–£2,505 | 3·2 |
| £2,506 and over | 1·1 |
| | 11 |

[2] The AUT survey gave an average for all non-medical staff of £2,299, and £2,368 for all academic staff. The survey only included the main teaching grades (professor to assistant lecturer). If research and other staff are excluded from our data on all universities, an average of £2,340 is obtained for non-medical staff, and £2,347 for non-medical and pre-clinical staff. The discrepancy between £2,299 and £2,340 is probably largely accounted for by the inclusion of staff at Oxford and Cambridge in our data, but not in the AUT survey.

**Table 338.** *Salary distributions adjusted for age distributions. 1964–5 (estimated)*

PERCENTAGE

| | Salary group | | | | | All | Average salary (£) |
|---|---|---|---|---|---|---|---|
| | Under £1,400 | £1,400 to £2,505 | £2,506 to £3,399 | £3,400 and over | Others | | |
| ASSUMING OXFORD AGE DISTRIBUTION | | | | | | | |
| Oxford salaries | 13 | 31 | 38 | 18 | — | 100 | 2,575 |
| National salaries | 9 | 45 | 22 | 15 | 9 | 100 | 2,464 |
| ASSUMING NATIONAL AGE DISTRIBUTION | | | | | | | |
| Oxford salaries | 20 | 35 | 32 | 13 | — | 100 | 2,338 |
| National salaries | 14 | 46 | 18 | 11 | 11 | 100 | 2,240 |

SOURCE: Tables 335 and 336.

NOTE: For the assumption made about the distribution by salary of those under 'others' in the national distribution see Note 1 to para. 542.

## Variability between other universities

545. Table 336 gives the average salary distributions for all universities in Great Britain. But, as Table 241 shows, there are wide variations in the proportions of senior posts at different universities. It is not known to what extent average salaries vary as between universities. One of the larger London colleges has, however, supplied us with information which shows that its average salaries in 1964–5 were 8–9 per cent. above the national average. But the average age was also higher than nationally, though not to the same extent as at Oxford. If allowance is made for this, as described in the previous paragraph, salaries were 3 per cent. above the national figure.

## The distribution of regular and total emoluments

546. Tables 339 and 340 give distributions *for Oxford* comparable with those in Table 335 but for regular emoluments and total emoluments respectively (see Table 334 and para. 530). Except for college piece-rate teaching, the amounts included in the distributions are the same as those given in Table 334. But, as explained in paras. 527–8, only £56,000 could reasonably be allocated for piece-rate teaching. It must be emphasized that Tables 339 and 340 are *estimates* of the distributions for 1964–5. In addition to the likely understatement of piece-rate teaching, the notional figure for college housing is used in some cases (as explained in para. 521) and the assumption is made that the pattern for supervision and examining was similar to that in 1963–4. Information is not available to enable comparable tables on a national basis to be prepared.

Table 339. *Regular emoluments of Oxford academic staff by age. All academic staff except those on clinical scales. 1964–5 (estimated)*

OXFORD

| Age | Regular emolument group | | | | | Number | Average regular emoluments (£) | Median regular emoluments (£) | PERCENTAGE Percentage of total |
|---|---|---|---|---|---|---|---|---|---|
| | Under £1,400 | £1,400 to £2,505 | £2,506 to £3,399 | £3,400 and over | All | | | | |
| Under 30 | 58 | 41 | 1 | — | 100 | 164 | 1,345 | 1,300 | 15 |
| 30–34 | 11 | 61 | 28 | 1 | 100 | 160 | 2,132 | 2,225 | 15 |
| 35–39 | 3 | 33 | 57 | 7 | 100 | 170 | 2,691 | 2,708 | 16 |
| 40–44 | 2 | 12 | 51 | 36 | 100 | 180 | 3,140 | 3,240 | 17 |
| 45–49 | 3 | 5 | 41 | 51 | 100 | 111 | 3,308 | 3,460 | 10 |
| 50 and over | 1 | 5 | 40 | 54 | 100 | 285 | 3,460 | 3,540 | 27 |
| All | 12 | 25 | 37 | 27 | 100 | 1,070 | 2,745 | 2,790 | 100 |

SOURCE: See source to Table 334.

NOTE: See note to Table 334.

**Table 340.** *Total emoluments of Oxford academic staff by age. All academic staff except those on clinical scales. 1964–5 (estimated)*

OXFORD | | | | | | | | | PERCENTAGE

| Age | Total emolument group | | | | | Number | Average total emoluments (£) | Median total emoluments (£) | Percentage of total |
|---|---|---|---|---|---|---|---|---|---|
| | Under £1,400 | £1,400 to £2,505 | £2,506 to £3,399 | £3,400 and over | All | | | | |
| Under 30 | 48 | 51 | 1 | — | 100 | 164 | 1,450 | 1,419 | 15 |
| 30–34 | 9 | 54 | 36 | 1 | 100 | 160 | 2,235 | 2,316 | 15 |
| 35–39 | 3 | 21 | 59 | 18 | 100 | 170 | 2,853 | 2,876 | 16 |
| 40–44 | 1 | 8 | 45 | 46 | 100 | 180 | 3,283 | 3,357 | 17 |
| 45–49 | 2 | 5 | 37 | 56 | 100 | 111 | 3,445 | 3,606 | 10 |
| 50 and over | 1 | 5 | 34 | 60 | 100 | 285 | 3,551 | 3,613 | 27 |
| All | 10 | 23 | 35 | 32 | 100 | 1,070 | 2,865 | 2,926 | 100 |

SOURCE: See source to Table 334.

NOTE: See note to Table 334.

547. When total emoluments are included, there were 32 per cent. within the professorial range, and 35 per cent. within the reader/senior lecturer range.

## Differences between fellows and non-fellows

548. No distinction is made in Tables 335, 339, and 340 between fellows and non-fellows, but the salary structure for tutorial fellows is different from that for university lecturers without a fellowship. There are altogether three groups to be considered. The first comprises tutorial fellows. The second comprises those with university posts but not college fellowships. The third is an intermediate group comprising those with non-tutorial fellowships. Comparisons are made between these three groups below, but it should not be inferred that the three groups are in all ways comparable. The sense in which comparability is attempted is that only those in the main 'career grades' are included in the analyses.

549. A tutorial fellowship is taken to be a career in itself, and all tutorial fellows are included, regardless of the university post held (if any). For the other two groups, only those with university posts of reader, full-time and part-time lecturer, and senior research officer and equivalent are included. Professors are excluded since the apex of a career in any of the three groups is taken to be a professorship. Other posts such as departmental demonstratorships and junior research fellowships, for instance, are excluded as being posts from which an individual may enter any one of the career groups.

550. The distinction between non-tutorial fellows and non-fellows is somewhat artificial and a brief description of non-tutorial fellows is necessary. Rather more than half held professorial, supernumerary, and other non-stipendiary fellowships. Twelve of these were fellows of Linacre College and most of the remainder were readers. Nearly all those receiving stipends held college research fellowships. But a few in the last category also held a lecturership at the same college as their fellowship, and the stipend may be paid for the lecturership. The numbers are given in Table 341.

551. Averages, by age group, for the three groups described are given for the three classes of emoluments in Table 342. The age distributions and the numbers in each age group are also given. It will be seen that the numbers of non-tutorial fellows in the two lowest age groups are small, and the corresponding averages may be affected by individuals with special circumstances.

552. Three points may be made about Table 342. First, it presents a static picture applying to 1 January 1965. It does not take account of the mobility

**Table 341.** *Non-tutorial fellows. 1 January 1965*

OXFORD                                                              NUMBER

|  | Stipendiary fellows | Non-stipendiary fellows | All |
|---|---|---|---|
| Readers | 8 | 28 | 36 |
| Others | 27 | 19 | 46 |
| All non-tutorial fellows | 35 | 47 | 82 |

SOURCE: Colleges.

NOTE: Only non-tutorial fellows holding a university post as reader, lecturer, or equivalent are included.

**Table 342.** *Average emoluments for tutorial fellows, and for others who were readers, university lecturers (full-time or part-time), senior research officers, and equivalent. 1964–5 (estimated)*

OXFORD                                                                      £

|  |  | Age | | | | | | |
|---|---|---|---|---|---|---|---|---|
|  |  | Under 30 | 30–34 | 35–39 | 40–44 | 45–49 | 50 and over | All |
| Salary | Tutorial fellows | 1,566 | 2,153 | 2,594 | 3,019 | 3,162 | 3,144 | 2,695 |
|  | Non-tutorial fellows | 1,711 | 2,373 | 2,855 | 2,877 | 2,900 | 3,178 | 2,886 |
|  | Non-fellows | 1,516 | 1,860 | 2,354 | 2,653 | 2,758 | 2,859 | 2,465 |
| Regular emoluments | Tutorial fellows | 1,835 | 2,448 | 2,891 | 3,316 | 3,468 | 3,444 | 2,991 |
|  | Non-tutorial fellows | 1,754 | 2,524 | 2,966 | 2,971 | 3,003 | 3,241 | 2,972 |
|  | Non-fellows | 1,526 | 1,881 | 2,382 | 2,685 | 2,791 | 2,894 | 2,494 |
| Total emoluments | Tutorial fellows | 1,874 | 2,529 | 3,054 | 3,456 | 3,590 | 3,548 | 3,106 |
|  | Non-tutorial fellows | 1,912 | 2,667 | 3,192 | 3,220 | 3,436 | 3,342 | 3,169 |
|  | Non-fellows | 1,692 | 2,051 | 2,566 | 2,832 | 2,889 | 2,992 | 2,636 |
| *Percentage of total* | *Tutorial fellows* | *8·9* | *18·2* | *19·0* | *20·0* | *12·1* | *21·8* | *100·0* |
|  | *Non-tutorial fellows* | *6·1* | *7·3* | *15·9* | *19·5* | *12·2* | *39·0* | *100·0* |
|  | *Non-fellows* | *5·3* | *15·8* | *22·1* | *21·1* | *10·5* | *25·3* | *100·0* |
| *Number* | *Tutorial fellows* | *45* | *92* | *96* | *101* | *61* | *110* | *505* |
|  | *Non-tutorial fellows* | *5* | *6* | *13* | *16* | *10* | *32* | *82* |
|  | *Non-fellows* | *10* | *30* | *42* | *40* | *20* | *48* | *190* |

SOURCE: See source to Table 334.

NOTE: Those on clinical scales are excluded.

between groups, and particularly between non-fellows and non-tutorial fellows. The high average age of non-tutorial fellows (over half were age 45 and over) suggests that non-fellows tend to be elected to non-tutorial fellowships during their late thirties or forties. Furthermore, the position was changing particularly rapidly at the time. Secondly, a comparison between non-tutorial fellows and non-fellows is complicated by the distribution of readers. The proportion on the reader scale was 44 per cent. among non-tutorial fellows and 9 per cent. among non-fellows. A man who is promoted to reader is more likely to be elected to a non-tutorial fellowship. Thirdly, the table does not show the effect on an individual's emoluments of appointment to a non-tutorial fellowship. This is partly on account of the distribution of readers, and partly because some non-tutorial fellowships are non-stipendiary, and some fellowship stipends appear to replace college lecturership stipends or fees.

**Table 343.** *Average emoluments for tutorial fellows (other than readers), and for others who were university lecturers (full-time or part-time), senior research officers, and equivalent. 1964–5 (estimated)*

OXFORD             £

| | | Age | | | | | | |
| --- | --- | --- | --- | --- | --- | --- | --- | --- |
| | | Under 30 | 30–34 | 35–39 | 40–44 | 45–49 | 50 and over | All |
| Salary | Tutorial fellows | 1,566 | 2,141 | 2,579 | 3,006 | 3,138 | 3,067 | 2,654 |
| | Non-tutorial fellows | 1,439 | 2,287 | 2,541 | 2,825 | 2,596 | 2,888 | 2,587 |
| | Non-fellows | 1,516 | 1,860 | 2,328 | 2,565 | 2,758 | 2,756 | 2,391 |
| Regular emoluments | Tutorial fellows | 1,835 | 2,437 | 2,874 | 3,301 | 3,443 | 3,358 | 2,947 |
| | Non-tutorial fellows | 1,480 | 2,468 | 2,635 | 2,916 | 2,641 | 2,940 | 2,669 |
| | Non-fellows | 1,526 | 1,881 | 2,358 | 2,591 | 2,791 | 2,792 | 2,419 |
| Total emoluments | Tutorial fellows | 1,874 | 2,519 | 3,040 | 3,443 | 3,567 | 3,472 | 3,065 |
| | Non-tutorial fellows | 1,623 | 2,613 | 2,910 | 3,140 | 2,968 | 3,059 | 2,876 |
| | Non-fellows | 1,692 | 2,051 | 2,544 | 2,751 | 2,889 | 2,902 | 2,569 |
| *Percentage of total* | *Tutorial fellows* | 9·3 | 18·8 | 19·5 | 20·5 | 12·0 | 19·9 | 100·0 |
| | *Non-tutorial fellows* | 8·7 | 10·9 | 15·2 | 30·4 | 13·0 | 21·7 | 100·0 |
| | *Non-fellows* | 5·8 | 17·4 | 23·3 | 19·8 | 11·6 | 22·1 | 100·0 |
| *Number* | *Tutorial fellows* | 45 | 91 | 94 | 99 | 58 | 96 | 483 |
| | *Non-tutorial fellows* | 4 | 5 | 7 | 14 | 6 | 10 | 46 |
| | *Non-fellows* | 10 | 30 | 40 | 34 | 20 | 38 | 172 |

SOURCE: See source to Table 334.

NOTE: Those on clinical scales are excluded.

553. To meet the difficulties of comparison due to the distribution of readers, Table 343 gives the same details as Table 342 but with all those holding a university post on the reader scale excluded. Thus Table 342

shows the average emoluments received by all those in 'career' posts. Promotion to a readership is a possibility for non-fellows and such promotion has in the past increased an individual's chance of a non-tutorial fellowship. The comparison between non-tutorial fellows and non-fellows is thereby obscured and Table 343 gives comparisons for more homogeneous groups by excluding readers.

**Table 344.** *Emoluments of Oxford academic staff on clinical scales. 1964–5 (estimated)*

OXFORD | | | | | | PERCENTAGE

| Type of emolument | Emolument group | | | | | Average emoluments (£) |
|---|---|---|---|---|---|---|
| | Under £1,400 | £1,400 to £2,505 | £2,506 to £3,399 | £3,400 and over | All | |
| Salary | 7 | 52 | 15 | 26 | 100 | 2,562 |
| Regular emoluments | 7 | 52 | 13 | 28 | 100 | 2,577 |
| Total emoluments | 4 | 50 | 17 | 28 | 100 | 2,643 |

SOURCE: See source to Table 334.

## Staff on clinical scales

554. The 46 members of the academic staff on clinical salary scales have been excluded above. Table 344 gives details of their emoluments.

## Details of college emoluments

555. Colleges were asked to give details of the emoluments of their academic staff,[1] and their replies are summarized in this section. Summaries of the information given by colleges and other societies are in Tables 345–52. That on heads of houses is given in Table 345, on tutorial fellows in Tables 346–9, and on college offices in Table 350. Details of payments for piece-rate teaching are given in Table 351, and of teaching norms for tutorial fellows in Table 352. In these tables colleges are referred to by number, and not by name. The numbering has been determined at random and three different orderings are used: one for heads of houses; one for tutorial fellows (and for piece-rate teaching payments); and one for college offices. The colleges are grouped thus:

| | Heads of houses | Tutorial fellows | College offices |
|---|---|---|---|
| Men's colleges | 101–23 | 1–23 | 201–23 |
| Women's colleges | 131–5 | 31–35 | 231–5 |
| Graduate colleges | 141–3 | 41–43 | 241–3 |
| Permanent Private Halls | 151–2 | 51–52 | |

[1] The Permanent Private Halls were invited to reply to the questionnaire sent to colleges and two availed themselves of this opportunity. The questionnaire is reproduced in the Annex to this Part.

556. The information in Tables 345–52 and in paras. 557–68 relates to the position at 1 January 1965 except where otherwise specified. All money amounts are in £ per annum. No definition of 'tutorial fellow' was given in the questionnaire. Most colleges have interpreted the term in the same kind of way, so as, in general, to include anyone who might be described as 'fellow and tutor' or 'fellow and lecturer'. In some colleges, however, the term is not in official use, while in others it has a rather special meaning. A very small number of fellows have been classified in a different way than that returned by their college in order to achieve consistency between colleges. Notes on the tables are given in paras. 557–65.

557. *Heads of houses* (Table 345). The estimates of the value of emoluments in kind given were made by the colleges concerned. They may, therefore, not all have been made on the same basis. The university posts held by heads of houses were as follows:

| Post | No. holding | Stipend £ |
|---|---|---|
| Vice-Chancellor | 1 | 2,250 |
| Pro-Vice-Chancellor | 4 | 250 |
| Clerk of Market | 1 | 5 |
| CUF lecturer | 1 | 1,350 |
| Special teaching | 1 | 425 |

558. *Scales for tutorial fellows* (Tables 346 and 347). Scales are given for CUF lecturers and also for university lecturers for those colleges which have such scales. The combined college and university stipend is given. It should be noted that the University stipulates that the joint university plus college stipend for university lecturers may not exceed £3,450. The corresponding joint maximum for readers is £3,675.

559. In three colleges part of the stipend is deemed an entertainment allowance. Details are:

| College number | Amount (£) |
|---|---|
| 6 | 50 |
| 7 | 30 |
| 15 | 25 |

The scales in Table 346 are inclusive of these amounts.

560. Tutorial fellows holding university posts other than reader, lecturer or CUF lecturer, or holding no university post, generally receive a college stipend such that their total stipend is comparable with, or a little below, that of a CUF lecturer (in arts subjects) or a lecturer (in science subjects). Some colleges have more than one scale depending on the amount of teaching undertaken, and this is indicated in the table by the number of hours. The stipends of a number of tutorial fellows are fixed *ad personam*; for example, fellows with major college offices of a permanent or semi-permanent nature such as bursar often receive a lower college stipend and, correspondingly, reduced teaching hours.

| College number | Stipend | Expenses and entertainment allowance | Lodgings (provision by college) | | | | | | | |
| --- | --- | --- | --- | --- | --- | --- | --- | --- | --- | --- |
| | | | Service and/or establishment allowance | Rent | Rates | Heat and light | Maintenance | Decorating | Furnishing | Gardening |
| 101 | 3,050 | 300 | 550 | — | — | 600 est. | — | — | — | Incl. in service |
| 102 | 3,280 | 600 | 800 app. | Yes | Yes | ¾ of cost | Yes | Yes | No | Incl. in service |
| 103 | 3,400 | 400 | 250 (max.) | Yes | Yes | Up to 50 | Yes | Yes | No | ¼ gardener |
| 104 | 3,000 | 550 | None | Yes | Yes | 300 app. | Yes | Yes | | |
| 105 | 2,000 | 500 | 1 scout free +78 | Yes | Yes | 150 (max.) | | | | |
| 106 | 2,000 | 600 | | | | 400 est. (d) | | | | |
| 107 | 4,250 | 500 | 350 (max.) | Yes | Yes | 378 | Yes | Yes | Some | 220 |
| 108 | 4,750 | 750 | 750 | Yes | Yes | 200 (max.) | Yes | Yes | | |
| 109 | 3,000 | 400 | 400 | Yes | Yes | 550 est. | Yes | Yes | Some | Incl. in service |
| 110 | 3,800 | 500 | 1,380 | — | 260 est. | 200 | | | | |
| 111 | 3,280 | 500 | 800 | Yes | Yes | Up to 250 | | Yes | | |
| 112 | 245 (a) | 820 | 300 (max.) | Yes | Yes | 80 est. | Incl. in rent and rates | Yes | | Gardener |
| 113 | | 450 | | — | 375 est. | | | | | |
| 114 | 3,600 | 750 (max.) (b) | 300 | Yes | Yes | Total less 75 Incl. in exp. | Yes | External | 2,000 (e) | Yes |
| 115 | 3,000 (b) | 600 (max.) | | Yes | Yes | 300 (max.) | | External | | |
| 116 | 3,000 | 500 (max.) | 300 (f) | Yes | Yes | 1,200 (max.—never fully expended. Includes service) | Yes | | | No |
| 117 | 3,500 (c) | 500 (max.) | 950 | Yes | Yes | 400 | | Public rooms | Public rooms | Yes |
| 118 | 3,750 | 600 | | Yes | Yes | 400 app. | | Once in 7 years | Public rooms | Yes |
| 119 | 3,500 | 500 | Yes | Yes | Yes | | Yes | Some | Some | |
| 120 | 3,850 | 500 | | — | — | 800 est. | | | | |
| 121 | 3,280 | 400 | | | | | | | | |
| 122 | 3,500 | 800 | 800 | Yes | Yes | Yes | Yes | Yes | | |
| 123 | 3,500 | 400 (max.) | | Yes | Yes | Central heating + prop. of elec. | Public rooms | Public rooms | | |
| 131 | 2,600 | 550 | | 1,400 app. | | Yes | | | Some | |
| 132 | 3,000 | 500 | 202 | Yes | Yes | | | | No | |
| 133 | 3,000 | 650 | No | — | 1,100 est. | | | | | |
| 134 | 3,150 | 500 | Yes | 500 | | | | | | |
| 135 | 3,000 | 500 | No | 400 | | | | | | |
| 141 | 2,800 | 700 | No | Yes | Yes | 350 | Yes | Yes | Some | Yes |
| 142 | 4,150 | 500 | | Yes | Yes | No | Yes | Yes | No | No |
| 143 | 3,000 | 650 | 400 app. | Yes | Yes | 400 app. | Yes | Yes | No | 50 app. |
| 151 | 1,050 | 200 | | Yes | Yes | 70 app. | Yes | Yes | | |
| 152 | 2,508 | 410 | | Yes | Yes | | Yes | Yes | | |

SOURCE: Colleges.

NOTES

(a) The college states that 'The college is of the opinion that the salary of the Head should approximate that paid to a professor who is head of a department. The continued and insistent generosity of the present Head, who refuses to accept a stipend commensurate with his position, has relieved the college of the necessity of introducing such a scale.'

(b) To be revised or reviewed.

(c) £1,000 of this has been renounced.

(d) Most of the lodgings is given over to undergraduate accommodation. The estimate given is for that part occupied by the head of house.

(e) Initial allowance.

(f) Excludes service.

**Table 346.** *Scales for tutorial fellows by age. Combined college and university stipend. 1 January 1965*

OXFORD       £ PER ANNUM

[continued

| Age | College number and university post | | | | | | | | | | | |
|---|---|---|---|---|---|---|---|---|---|---|---|---|
| | 2 CUF lect. | 2 Univ. lect. | 3 CUF lect. | 3 Univ. lect. | 4 CUF lect. | 4 Univ. lect. | 5 CUF lect. and univ. lect. | 6 CUF lect. and univ. lect. | 7 CUF lect. | 7 Univ. lect. | 8 CUF lect. | 8 Univ. lect. |
| 25 | 1,450 | | | 1,750 | 1,400 | 1,650 | 1,300 (a) | 1,500 | 1,650 | 1,900 | 1,500 | 1,775 |
| 26 | 1,500 | | 1,650 | 1,750 | 1,450 | 1,650 | 1,400 | 1,500 | 1,650 | 1,900 | 1,500 | 1,775 |
| 27 | 1,550 | 1,750 | 1,650 | 1,750 | 1,500 | 1,650 | 1,500 | 1,500 | 1,650 | 1,900 | 1,500 | 1,775 |
| 28 | 1,625 | 1,835 | 1,650 | 1,835 | 1,600 | 1,785 | 1,600 | 1,600 | 1,650 | 1,985 | 1,600 | 1,860 |
| 29 | 1,700 | 1,920 | 1,650 | 1,920 | 1,650 | 1,870 | 1,650 | 1,700 | 1,650 | 2,070 | 1,600 | 1,945 |
| 30 | 1,885 | 2,005 | 2,300 | 2,155 | 1,850 | 2,005 | 1,875 | 1,800 | 2,005 | 2,155 | 1,700 | 2,030 |
| 31 | 1,970 | 2,090 | 2,300 | 2,240 | 1,950 | 2,090 | 2,000 | 1,900 | 2,090 | 2,240 | 2,100 | 2,115 |
| 32 | 2,055 | 2,175 | 2,300 | 2,325 | 2,025 | 2,175 | 2,066 | 2,000 | 2,175 | 2,325 | 2,100 | 2,200 |
| 33 | 2,140 | 2,260 | 2,300 | 2,410 | 2,100 | 2,260 | 2,120 | 2,100 | 2,260 | 2,410 | 2,100 | 2,285 |
| 34 | 2,225 | 2,345 | 2,300 | 2,495 | 2,200 | 2,345 | 2,180 | 2,200 | 2,345 | 2,495 | 2,200 | 2,370 |
| 35 | 2,325 | 2,430 | 2,700 | 2,580 | 2,300 | 2,430 | 2,340 | 2,300 | 2,445 | 2,580 | 2,300 | 2,455 |
| 36 | 2,385 | 2,515 | 2,700 | 2,665 | 2,350 | 2,515 | 2,400 | 2,400 | 2,515 | 2,665 | 2,300 | 2,500 |
| 37 | 2,465 | 2,600 | 2,700 | 2,750 | 2,450 | 2,600 | 2,460 | 2,500 | 2,600 | 2,750 | 2,400 | 2,675 |
| 38 | 2,545 | 2,685 | 2,700 | 2,835 | 2,525 | 2,685 | 2,520 | 2,600 | 2,685 | 2,835 | 2,400 | 2,760 |
| 39 | 2,625 | 2,770 | 2,700 | 2,920 | 2,625 | 2,770 | 2,580 | 2,700 | 2,770 | 2,920 | 2,400 | 2,845 |
| 40 | 2,725 | 2,855 | 3,100 | 3,005 | 2,725 | 2,855 | 2,740 | 2,900 | 2,870 | 3,005 | 2,600 | 2,930 |
| 41 | 2,785 | 2,940 | 3,100 | 3,090 | 2,800 | 2,940 | 2,800 | 3,000 | 2,940 | 3,090 | 2,600 | 3,065 |
| 42 | 2,870 | 3,025 | 3,100 | 3,175 | 2,875 | 3,025 | 2,866 | 3,100 | 3,025 | 3,175 | 2,600 | 3,150 |
| 43 | 2,950 | 3,110 | 3,100 | 3,260 | 2,950 | 3,110 | 2,920 | 3,200 | 3,110 | 3,260 | 2,700 | 3,235 |
| 44 | 2,975 | 3,110 | 3,100 | 3,260 | 2,950 | 3,110 | 2,980 | 3,300 | 3,110 | 3,260 | 2,700 | 3,235 |
| 45 | 3,075 | 3,160 | 3,450 | 3,450 | 3,050 | 3,110 | 3,140 | 3,400 | 3,260 | 3,260 | 2,800 | 3,235 |
| 46 | | | | | | | 3,200 | | | | 2,900 | |
| 47 | | | | | | | 3,260 | | | | 2,900 | |
| 48 | | | | | | | 3,320 | | | | 2,900 | |
| 49 | | | | | | | 3,380 | | | | 3,000 | |
| 50 and over | | | | | | | 3,450 | | | | 3,000 | |

NOTE: (a) £1,400 for university lecturers.

| Age | College number and university post | | | | | | | | | | | | |
|---|---|---|---|---|---|---|---|---|---|---|---|---|---|
| | 9 CUF lect. | 9 Univ. lect. | 10 CUF lect. | 10 Univ. lect. | 11 CUF lect. | 11 Univ. lect. | 12 CUF lect. | 12 Univ. lect. | 13 CUF lect. and univ. lect. (b) | 14 CUF lect. | 14 Univ. lect. | 15 CUF lect. and univ. lect. | 16 CUF lect. and univ. lect. |
| 25 | 1,410 | 1,650 | 1,450 | 1,800 | 1,650 | 1,775 | 1,450 | 1,650 | 1,500 | 1,600 | 1,760 | 1,300 (a) | 1,400 |
| 26 | 1,470 | 1,650 | 1,500 | 1,800 | 1,650 | 1,775 | 1,500 | 1,650 | 1,540 | 1,600 | 1,760 | 1,400 | 1,500 |
| 27 | 1,530 | 1,650 | 1,550 | 1,800 | 1,650 | 1,775 | 1,550 | 1,650 | 1,580 | 1,600 | 1,760 | 1,500 | 1,550 |
| 28 | 1,590 | 1,735 | 1,600 | 1,885 | 1,650 | 1,875 | 1,600 | 1,735 | 1,620 | 1,600 | 1,845 | 1,585 | 1,600 |
| 29 | 1,650 | 1,820 | 1,650 | 1,970 | 1,650 | 1,980 | 1,650 | 1,820 | 1,660 | 1,600 | 1,930 | 1,670 | 1,650 |
| 30 | 1,860 | 1,915 | 1,950 | 2,105 | | 2,085 | | 1,905 | 1,910 | 1,850 | 2,015 | 1,800 | 1,900 |
| 31 | 1,970 | 2,010 | 2,070 | 2,190 | | 2,190 | | 1,990 | 2,060 | 1,850 | 2,100 | 1,850 | 2,150 |
| 32 | 2,080 | 2,105 | 2,140 | 2,275 | | 2,290 | | 2,075 | 2,210 | 1,850 | 2,185 | 1,950 | 2,350 |
| 33 | 2,190 | 2,200 | 2,210 | 2,360 | | 2,395 | | 2,160 | 2,360 | 1,850 | 2,270 | 2,100 | 2,550 |
| 34 | 2,290 | 2,295 | 2,280 | 2,445 | | 2,495 | | 2,250 | 2,510 | 1,850 | 2,355 | 2,250 | 2,750 |
| 35 | 2,390 | 2,390 | 2,430 | 2,580 | | 2,605 | | 2,350 | 2,610 | 2,200 | 2,440 | 2,400 | 2,850 |
| 36 | 2,500 | 2,505 | 2,480 | 2,665 | | 2,715 | | 2,450 | 2,710 | 2,200 | 2,525 | 2,500 | 2,950 |
| 37 | 2,610 | 2,620 | 2,550 | 2,750 | | 2,825 | | 2,550 | 2,810 | 2,200 | 2,610 | 2,600 | 3,050 |
| 38 | 2,720 | 2,735 | 2,650 | 2,835 | | 2,935 | | 2,650 | 2,910 | 2,200 | 2,695 | 2,700 | 3,150 |
| 39 | 2,830 | 2,850 | 2,750 | 2,920 | | 3,040 | | 2,750 | 3,010 | 2,200 | 2,780 | 2,800 | 3,250 |
| 40 | 2,940 | 2,955 | 2,850 | 3,055 | | 3,150 | | 2,850 | 3,110 | 2,450 | 2,865 | 2,900 | 3,300 |
| 41 | 3,040 | 3,060 | 2,950 | 3,140 | | 3,260 | | 2,950 | 3,170 | 2,450 | 2,950 | 2,950 | 3,350 |
| 42 | 3,140 | 3,165 | 3,050 | 3,225 | | 3,365 | | 3,050 | 3,230 | 2,450 | 3,035 | 3,000 | 3,400 |
| 43 | 3,240 | 3,270 | 3,150 | 3,350 | | 3,450 | | 3,150 | 3,290 | 2,450 | 3,120 | 3,050 | 3,450 |
| 44 | 3,340 | 3,360 | 3,150 | 3,350 | | 3,450 | | 3,250 | 3,350 | 2,450 | 3,120 | 3,100 | 3,450 |
| 45 | 3,450 | 3,450 | 3,250 | 3,350 | | 3,450 | | 3,350 | 3,450 | 2,825 | 3,120 | 3,150 | 3,450 |
| 46 | | | | | | | | | | | | 3,150 | |
| 47 | | | | | | | | | | | | 3,150 | |
| 48 | | | | | | | | | | | | 3,150 | |
| 49 | | | | | | | | | | | | 3,150 | |
| 50 and over | 3,450 | 3,450 | | | | | | | | | | 3,250 | |

NOTES

(a) £1,400 for university lecturers.

(b) For university lecturers the scale is not a strict age scale. The stipend is related to age, but also depends upon the duties of the fellowship.

[continued

**Table 346.** *Scales for tutorial fellows by age. Combined college and university stipend. 1 January 1965 (continued)*

£ PER ANNUM

| Age | College number and university post | | | | | | | | | | | | |
|---|---|---|---|---|---|---|---|---|---|---|---|---|---|
| | 17 CUF lect. | 17 Univ. lect. | 18 CUF lect. | 18 Univ. lect. | 19 CUF lect. | 19 Univ. lect. | 20 CUF lect. | 20 Univ. lect. | 21 CUF lect. (c) | 22 CUF lect. and univ. lect. Scale I (d) | 22 CUF lect. and univ. lect. Scale II (d) | 23 CUF lect. | 23 Univ. lect. |
| 25 | | | 1,600 | 1,875 | 1,650 | 1,550 | 1,550 | 1,700 | | 1,450 | 1,450 | 1,450 | 1,650 |
| 26 | | | 1,625 | 1,900 | 1,650 | 1,550 | 1,575 | 1,700 | | 1,500 | 1,500 | 1,500 | 1,650 |
| 27 | 1,650 | 2,000 | 1,650 | 1,925 | 1,650 | 1,550 | 1,600 | 1,700 | 1,550 | 1,550 | 1,550 | 1,550 | 1,650 |
| 28 | 1,650 | 2,085 | 1,650 | 1,925 | 1,650 | 1,635 | 1,625 | 1,785 | 1,600 | 1,600 | 1,600 | 1,600 | 1,735 |
| 29 | 1,650 | 2,170 | 1,650 | 1,925 | 1,650 | 1,720 | 1,650 | 1,870 | 1,650 | 1,650 | 1,650 | 1,650 | 1,820 |
| 30 | 2,100 | 2,255 | 2,225 | 2,500 | 2,165 | 2,155 | 2,000 | 2,155 | 1,800 | 2,000 | 2,000 | 1,900 | 1,905 |
| 31 | 2,190 | 2,340 | 2,300 | 2,575 | 2,300 | 2,240 | 2,050 | 2,240 | 1,900 | 2,125 | 2,150 | 2,000 | 2,000 |
| 32 | 2,280 | 2,425 | 2,375 | 2,650 | 2,350 | 2,325 | 2,150 | 2,325 | 1,950 | 2,250 | 2,300 | 2,100 | 2,100 |
| 33 | 2,370 | 2,510 | 2,450 | 2,725 | 2,400 | 2,410 | 2,250 | 2,410 | 2,000 | 2,375 | 2,450 | 2,200 | 2,200 |
| 34 | 2,450 | 2,595 | 2,525 | 2,800 | 2,450 | 2,495 | 2,350 | 2,495 | 2,050 | 2,500 | 2,600 | 2,300 | 2,300 |
| 35 | 2,550 | 2,680 | 2,580 | 2,855 | 2,600 | 2,580 | 2,500 | 2,630 | 2,200 | 2,600 | 2,700 | 2,400 | 2,400 |
| 36 | 2,640 | 2,765 | 2,635 | 2,910 | 2,650 | 2,665 | 2,600 | 2,715 | 2,300 | 2,700 | 2,800 | 2,500 | 2,500 |
| 37 | 2,730 | 2,850 | 2,690 | 2,965 | 2,750 | 2,750 | 2,700 | 2,800 | 2,350 | 2,800 | 2,900 | 2,600 | 2,600 |
| 38 | 2,820 | 2,935 | 2,745 | 3,020 | 2,850 | 2,835 | 2,800 | 2,885 | 2,400 | 2,900 | 3,000 | 2,700 | 2,700 |
| 39 | 2,900 | 3,020 | 2,800 | 3,075 | 2,950 | 2,920 | 2,900 | 2,970 | 2,450 | 3,000 | 3,100 | 2,800 | 2,800 |
| 40 | 3,000 | 3,105 | 2,855 | 3,130 | 3,100 | 3,055 | 3,050 | 3,105 | 2,600 | 3,100 | 3,200 | 2,900 | 2,900 |
| 41 | 3,100 | 3,190 | 2,910 | 3,185 | 3,150 | 3,140 | 3,100 | 3,190 | 2,700 | 3,150 | 3,250 | 3,000 | 3,000 |
| 42 | 3,180 | 3,275 | 2,990 | 3,265 | 3,200 | 3,225 | 3,150 | 3,275 | 2,750 | 3,200 | 3,300 | 3,100 | 3,085 |
| 43 | 3,270 | 3,450 | 3,125 | 3,400 | 3,250 | 3,360 | 3,200 | 3,360 | 2,800 | 3,250 | 3,350 | 3,150 | 3,170 |
| 44 | 3,350 | 3,450 | 3,175 | 3,450 | 3,350 | 3,330 | 3,250 | 3,360 | 2,850 | 3,300 | 3,400 | 3,150 | 3,170 |
| 45 | 3,450 | 3,450 | 3,225 | 3,450 | 3,450 | 3,450 | 3,450 | 3,450 | 3,000 | 3,350 | 3,450 | 3,250 | 3,250 |
| 46 | | | 3,225 | | | | | | 3,100 | | | | |
| 47 | | | 3,225 | | | | | | | | | | |
| 48 | | | 3,225 | | | | | | | | | | |
| 49 | | | 3,225 | | | | | | | | | | |
| 50 and over | | | 3,250 | | | | | | | | | | |

NOTES
(c) The stipends of university lecturers are approximately £110 higher than those of CUF lecturers at each age.

[continued

OXFORD

£ PER ANNUM

| Age | College number and university post | | | | | | | 43 CUF lect. (f) |
|---|---|---|---|---|---|---|---|---|
| | 32 CUF lect. (e) | 34 CUF lect. A Scale (6 hours) | 34 CUF lect. B Scale (10 hours) | 34 CUF lect. C Scale (12 hours) | 34 CUF lect. D Scale (15 hours) | 35 CUF lect. (e) A Scale (12–18 hours) | 35 CUF lect. (e) B Scale (8–11 hours) | |
| 25 | 1,350 | 1,375 | 1,585 | 1,690 | 1,848 | | | 1,325 |
| 26 | 1,400 | 1,375 | 1,585 | 1,690 | 1,848 | | | 1,400 |
| 27 | 1,450 | 1,375 | 1,585 | 1,690 | 1,848 | 1,375 | 1,275 | 1,475 |
| 28 | 1,500 | 1,375 | 1,585 | 1,690 | 1,848 | 1,375 | 1,275 | 1,575 |
| 29 | 1,550 | 1,375 | 1,585 | 1,690 | 1,848 | | | 1,675 |
| 30 | 1,700 | 1,475 | 1,685 | 1,790 | 1,948 | 1,520 | 1,420 | 1,875 |
| 31 | 1,750 | 1,475 | 1,685 | 1,790 | 1,948 | 1,520 | 1,420 | 1,975 |
| 32 | 1,800 | 1,475 | 1,685 | 1,790 | 1,948 | 1,620 | 1,470 | 2,075 |
| 33 | 1,850 | 1,475 | 1,685 | 1,790 | 1,948 | 1,620 | 1,470 | 2,150 |
| 34 | 1,900 | 1,525 | 1,735 | 1,840 | 1,998 | 1,720 | 1,520 | 2,225 |
| 35 | 2,050 | 1,625 | 1,835 | 1,940 | 2,098 | 1,820 | 1,620 | 2,400 |
| 36 | 2,100 | 1,625 | 1,835 | 1,940 | 2,008 | 1,920 | 1,670 | 2,475 |
| 37 | 2,150 | 1,675 | 1,885 | 1,990 | 2,148 | 1,920 | 1,670 | 2,550 |
| 38 | 2,200 | 1,775 | 1,985 | 2,090 | 2,248 | 2,020 | 1,720 | 2,625 |
| 39 | 2,250 | 1,775 | 1,985 | 2,090 | 2,248 | 2,020 | 1,720 | 2,700 |
| 40 | 2,400 | 1,875 | 2,085 | 2,190 | 2,348 | 2,220 | 1,870 | 2,875 |
| 41 | 2,450 | 1,925 | 2,135 | 2,240 | 2,398 | 2,220 | 1,870 | 2,950 |
| 42 | 2,500 | 1,925 | 2,135 | 2,240 | 2,398 | 2,320 | 1,920 | 3,025 |
| 43 | 2,550 | 1,925 | 2,135 | 2,240 | 2,398 | 2,320 | 1,920 | 3,025 |
| 44 | 2,600 | 1,925 | 2,135 | 2,240 | 2,398 | 2,420 | 1,970 | 3,025 |
| 45 | 2,750 | 2,075 | 2,285 | 2,390 | 2,548 | 2,520 | 2,120 | 3,125 |
| 46 | | 2,075 | 2,285 | 2,390 | 2,548 | 2,620 | 2,170 | |
| 47 | | 2,075 | 2,285 | 2,390 | 2,548 | 2,670 | 2,220 | |
| 48 | | 2,075 | 2,285 | 2,390 | 2,548 | 2,720 | 2,270 | |
| 55 and over | | 2,175 | 2,385 | 2,490 | 2,648 | | | |

SOURCE: Colleges.

NOTES

(e) A fellow's position on the scale is determined by age and experience.

(f) The scale for special CUF lecturers (see para. 401) is £50 less at each age.

**Table 347.** *Salary scales for tutorial fellows which are not age scales.*
*1 January 1965*

OXFORD                                                                    £ PER ANNUM

| Age | College number and university post | | Year | College number and university post | | | |
| --- | --- | --- | --- | --- | --- | --- | --- |
| | 1 CUF lecturer teaching 12–15 hours (see note) | 1 University lecturer teaching up to 9 hours (see note) | | 31 CUF lecturer | 33 CUF lecturer Scale A 13 hours or more | 33 CUF lecturer Scale B 11–12 hours | 33 CUF lecturer Scale C 10 hours or less |
| 25 and under | 1,550 | 1,650 | Probationary | | 450 | 315 | 225 |
| 26 | 1,575 | 1,650 | 1 | 450 | 510 | 375 | 285 |
| 27 | 1,600 | 1,650 | 2 | 450 | 545 | 410 | 320 |
| 28 | 1,625 | 1,735 | 3 | 500 | 580 | 445 | 355 |
| 29 | 1,650 | 1,820 | 4 | 560 | 615 | 480 | 390 |
| 30 | 2,010 | 2,005 | 5 | 620 | 675 | 540 | 450 |
| 31 | 2,085 | 2,090 | 6 | 680 | 710 | 575 | 485 |
| 32 | 2,160 | 2,175 | 7 | 740 | 745 | 610 | 520 |
| 33 | 2,235 | 2,260 | 8 | 800 | 780 | 645 | 555 |
| 34 | 2,310 | 2,345 | 9 | 860 | 815 | 680 | 590 |
| 35 | 2,485 | 2,480 | 10 | 920 | 850 | 715 | 625 |
| 36 | 2,560 | 2,565 | 11 | 980 | 885 | 750 | 660 |
| 37 | 2,635 | 2,650 | 12 | 1,040 | 945 | 810 | 720 |
| 38 | 2,710 | 2,735 | 13 | 1,100 | 1,005 | 870 | 780 |
| 39 | 2,785 | 2,820 | 14 | 1,160 | 1,065 | 930 | 840 |
| 40 | 2,960 | 2,955 | 15 | 1,220 | 1,125 | 990 | 900 |
| 41 | 3,040 | 3,040 | 16 | 1,280 | 1,185 | 1,050 | 960 |
| 42 | 3,120 | 3,125 | 17 | 1,340 | 1,245 | 1,110 | 1,020 |
| 43 | 3,200 | 3,210 | 18 | 1,400 | 1,305 | 1,170 | 1,080 |
| 44 | 3,200 | 3,210 | 19 | | 1,365 | 1,230 | 1,140 |
| 45 and over | 3,300 | 3,300 | 20 | | 1,420 | 1,285 | 1,195 |

SOURCE: Colleges.

NOTES

*College 1.* The college stipend is made up of a fellowship stipend and a tutorship. The former is based on length of service, and is £50 on election rising by quinquennial increments to £200. The tutorship is paid on one of three age scales according to the university post held. The scales for CUF lecturers and university lecturers (including the university stipend and the *first £50 of the fellowship stipend*) are given in the table. The total combined stipend is thus the amount given by the scales above, plus any quinquennial increments in fellowship stipend.

*College 31.* The college stipend for CUF lecturers is based on length of service and is given in the table. The college stipend is increased by £550 in the first two years if no CUF lecturership is held.

*College 33.* The college stipend for CUF lecturers is based on length of service and teaching hours. The stipend is supplemented by a research grant of the value of a CUF lecturership for the appropriate age group for fellows not holding a CUF lecturership or comparable university post. The three scales are given in the table.

*College 42.* Official fellows receive a stipend on the scale £350 × 50–700 × 25–800 × 50–1,750. Official fellows not holding a university post normally hold a college Ordinary Lecturership, the stipend of which is £200 × 50–400 × 100–900. A fellow is placed at a point on the scale which the governing body considers appropriate to his qualifications and experience.

561. With the exception of colleges 41 and 52, salary scales had been revised in the light of the National Incomes Commission award. With the exception of college 51, the new scales were in effect by 1 January 1965. The majority came into effect on 1 April (or 25 March) 1964. Exceptions are:

| Date | College |
|------|---------|
| 1 January 1964 | 7 |
| 1 October 1964 | 4, 10, 14, 23, 31–35, 42 |
| 1 January 1965 | 9 |
| 1 April 1965 | 51 |

The age scales given in Table 346 for the undergraduate colleges are shown in Figs. 1 and 2.

562. *Allowances for tutorial fellows* (Table 348). The allowances mentioned in para. 522 are given in detail. College provision of office accommodation and telephone is not included since this is normally provided by universities for their staff. But in some cases it appears that fellows have to pay, at least in part, for the heating and lighting of their working rooms. It should be noted that all the colleges have agreed not to pay children's allowances to anyone appointed after 31 December 1964 (except to someone already entitled who transfers to Oxford without promotion); Council has also suggested to the colleges that they should restrict allowances, where payable, to £50, and it is understood that the majority of colleges have agreed to do so.

563. *College offices* (Table 350). All college offices are included. The majority are held by tutorial fellows. The principal offices are listed individually. Other offices are shown in one of three groups according to the value of the stipend. The offices which occur in these groups are as follows:

*Others (£0–49)*
Camerarius
Decanal duties
Financial adviser and auditor
Fire Officer
Garden Master
Keeper of Archives
Keeper of Minutes
Registrar
Secretary to Governing Body or college committees
Treasurer (JCR) or Senior Treasurer (clubs)

*Others (£50–90)*
Appointments Committee representative
Camerarius
Editor of college journal
Garden Master
Keeper of Archives
Keeper of Minutes
Science supervisor
Secretary to Governing Body or college committees
Treasurer (JCR) or Senior Treasurer (clubs)

*Others (£100 and over)*
Building fellow
Clerk to college
Curator of Pictures
Junior Censor
Praefectus of Holywell Manor
Precentor
Secretary to Governing Body or college committees

564. *Piece-rate teaching* (Table 351). Payments during 1964 for the teaching described in para. 526 are given. Not all the payments shown as being made to 'others' will have been made to members of the academic staff.

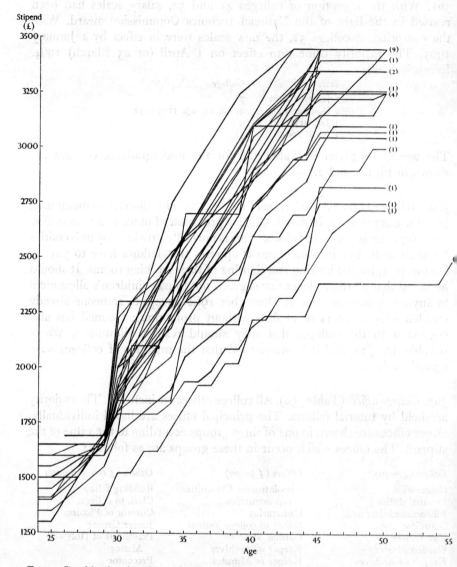

FIG. 1. Combined university and college stipend scales for CUF lecturers by age for 22 men's and 3 women's colleges.

NOTES: (i) the number of colleges at each end point is shown in brackets;
(ii) graduate colleges are not included;
(iii) for college 22 Scale I is plotted;
(iv) for college 34 Scale C is plotted;
(v) for college 35 Scale A is plotted.

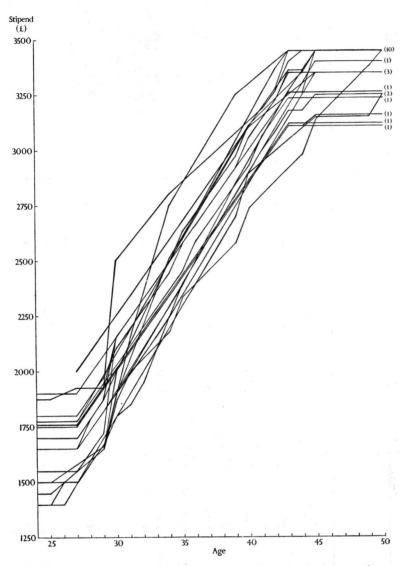

FIG. 2. Combined university and college stipend scales for university lecturers by age for 21 men's colleges.

NOTES: (i) the number of colleges at each end point is shown in brackets;
(ii) graduate colleges are not included;
(iii) for college 22 Scale I is plotted.

# Table 348. Allowances (and other benefits) for tutorial fellows. 1 January 1965

OXFORD

£ PER ANNUM

| College number | Tutorial responsibility (number receiving in brackets) | Children (per child) (if elected before 1 Jan. 1965) (b) | Entertainment (maximum) | Books (maximum) | Meals | BUPA F—fellows D—dependants (total for 1964 in brackets) | FSSU college contribution other than ⅔ (y) | College admissions and examining (number receiving in brackets) | Other |
|---|---|---|---|---|---|---|---|---|---|
| 1 | — | 50 | (f) | 30 (x) | D | — | — | — | |
| 2 | — | 50 | 10 (g)(h) | 30 | D | F (286) | — | — | £5 (£2 if resident for part of year). £10 to 9 senior tutorial fellows. |
| 3 | — | 80 (c) | | | | F (137) | — | — | |
| 4 | 50 (7) | 50 | 20 (i) | 10 (x) | L+D | — | — | 10 (14) | 11 garages rented to 9 fellows at half rent. |
| 5 | | 50 (d) | 40 (j) | | L or D | — | — | 25 (14) | |
| 6 | | 50 | | | L+D | F+D (266) | — | — | |
| 7 | | 50 | (k)(m) | 10 (x) | L+D | (236) | — | — | |
| 8 | | 50 | 30 (n) | 20 (x) | L+D | (353) | (z) | — | |
| 9 | | 50 (e) | 30 | | D | — | — | — | |
| 10 | | 80 | (f) | | D | — | — | 10 | |
| 11 | | | | 100 on commencing fellowship | L+D | F (275) | — | — | Schools dinners—£2 per head allowance. |
| 12 | | 50 | 30 (p) | 80 over first 2 years of fellowship | D | (216) | — | — | Free garaging for 4 bachelor fellows and 1 married fellow. |
| 13 | 100 (16) | 50 under age 12 / 100 age 12 and over | 2 per pupil (q) | 30 (x) | L+D | (380) | — | — | |
| 14 | | 75 | 15 | 15 | L+D | — | — | — | |
| 15 | | 50 up to 4 children | 25 (g)(r) | | L+D | — | — | 5 | |
| 16 | | 100 | 60 (g) | 30 (x) | All | (424) | — | — | Trust fund yielding approx. £475 to facilitate travel. Limited secretarial, duplicating, etc., services provided for fellows by the college office. Fellows under 30 already receiving a marriage allowance will continue to do so until they reach 30. |
| 17 | 50 (6)(a) | 75 | 45 (g) | — | D+part L | (454) | — | 5–15 | A variable amount (£25–£60 in recent years) to senior tutorial fellows (19 in 1964). |
| 18 | — | 80 | 30 | | L+D | (252) | — | 30 (17) | |
| 19 | | 50 | 20 | | L+D | (522) | — | — | |
| 20 | 70 (17) | 50 | 30 (s)(t) | | L+D | (141) (coll. pays ½) | ⅚(c) | — | |
| 21 | | 50 | 20 | 15 (x) | L+D | (270) | ⅘ | — | |
| 22 | — | 80 up to age 10 / 130 over age 10 | 40 | 40 (x) | L+D | — | — | — | Vacation allowance of £100 per annum to unmarried fellows living in college since college is closed for part of vacation. |
| 23 | — | 50 up to 3 children | 30 | 20 | All | — | — | — | |

| | | | | All in term; B+(L or D) in vacation / All | F (152) | |
|---|---|---|---|---|---|---|
| 33 | | | | | | |
| 34 | —————— 25 —————— | | | All | | — / · / — |
| 35 | — | — | 30 (u) | L+D in full term | F (152) | — |
| 41 | — | · | 25 (v) | 50 | L+D in full term (120) | · / — |
| 42 | — | — | 35 (w) | 50 | L+D (163) | — |
| 43 | | | 75 | | D | — | Up to £100 over 3-year period for expenses of attendance at conferences. |
| 51 | | | — | | | — | £10 for expenses of attendance at conferences. |
| 52 | — | — | — | | L+D if living out; all if living in | — | £5 for each Sunday sermon in college chapel. |

SOURCE: Colleges.

NOTES

(a) Departmental senior tutors.

(b) Reduced by amount received in children's allowance from University unless otherwise specified.

(c) Reduced by £50 if children's allowance is received from the University.

(d) An allowance of £100 for children over 13 ceased on 31 December 1964, but continues for those children for whom it had already begun.

(e) Only applies to children born before 1 October 1964.

(f) Approved entertainment paid for by college.

(g) Allowance off battels.

(h) Up to £20 for Vicegerent, Senior Tutor, Dean, and Chaplain.

(i) £50 for Chaplain.

(j) £50 of stipend is deemed an entertainment allowance. The Dean receives an additional £50.

(k) £30 of stipend is deemed an entertainment allowance.

(m) Plus £50 for Dean and £25 for Chaplain.

(n) Plus £1 per moral pupil other than those for whom a fellow is tutorially responsible (normally 6 per fellow).

(p) £40 for Dean and Tutor for Graduates.

(q) Paid to 16 moral tutors. In addition £40 is paid to the Dean and £60 to the Chaplain.

(r) £25 of stipend is deemed an entertainment allowance.

(s) Paid to 17 moral tutors.

(t) £50 for Vicegerent and Tutor for Graduates.

(u) £70 for Vicegerent.

(v) For fellows who act as college supervisors. The Senior Tutor and some other Official Fellows receive £50.

(w) Plus £15 for Dean of Degrees and £25 for Librarian.

(x) Books remain property of college.

(y) One college is not a member of the FSSU scheme for fellows and lecturers appointed before June 1963. It has its own scheme under which the college contributes four-fifths of the cost of providing for the pension of a tutorial fellow and two-thirds for the pension of a lecturer. One permanent private hall is not a member of the FSSU.

(z) College pays full contribution for fellows elected before 1952.

**Table 349.** *Housing (tutorial fellows). 1 January 1965*

OXFORD

| College number | Housing (or marriage) allowance for tutorial fellows living out of college (£ per annum) | Number living in college rent free | Number assisted in buying and how—(also rec. housing or marriage allowance) | Number recvg. housing or marr. allowance only | College houses — Number occupying college houses (k) | Rent paid or reduction in stipend (rents indicated by †) (£ per annum) | College responsibility for repairs and decoration | Responsibility for rates | Arrangements about capital improvements | Net rateable value (p) (rented houses indicated by †) (£) |
|---|---|---|---|---|---|---|---|---|---|---|
| 1 | 175 | 2 | 2 loans @ 6% | 11 | 4 | 200, 336, 307, 372 | External and structural | Added to reduction | Rent inc. by 6% of cost | 122, 222, 214, 278 |
| 2 | 200 | 2 | 13 loans @ 4% | 4 | 7 | Nil | External (internal by negotiation) | College | Has not arisen | 138, 122, 122, 138, 142, 142, 126 |
| 3 | 300 (a) | 6 | 3 (†) int. free loans | — | — | | | | | |
| 4 | 150 (b) | 1 | — | 10 | 4 | 328, 399, 400, 293 | All | College | Has not arisen | 126, 146, 186, 146 |
| 5 | 150 (a); 200 (a) | 2 | 3 loans @ ½% over bank rate on balance not obtd. on mtge. | 6 | — | | | | | |
| 6 | 200 (b)(c); 250 (a)(c) | 6 | —(j) | 1 | 10 (m) | 332, 283, 325, 290, 378, 320, 220, 329, 212, 230 | All | College | Rent inc. by int. charged at half market rate | 388, 198, 372, 306, 266, 190, 234, 250, 150, 242 |
| 7 | 200 (c) | 1 | 1 loan of up to £1,000 at overdraft rate | 13 | 1 | 200 | External | College | If any, paid by college | Not rated separately |
| 8 | 150 (a) | 1 | 2 loans @ 4% | 12 | 3 | Nil (2), 50 | All | 1) college 2) part pd. by college 3) fellow | If any, paid by college | 174, 126, 178 |
| 9 | 300 (c) | 3 | — | 12 | 1 | 300 | Added to reduction | Added to reduction | — | 110 |
| 10 | 150 (c) | 5 | — | 6 | — | | | | | |
| 11 | 300 (d) | 3 | — | 2 | 15 | 285†, 105 (2), 92, 165, 115, 175, 43 (2), 150, 137, 77, 50, 73, 52 | Maintenance | Fellow if rent paid; college otherwise | Rent inc. by 5% of cost | 130†, 302 (2), 254, 250, 202, 208, 250 (2), 110, 242, 162, 194, 134, 182 |
| 12 | 200 | 4 | 1 loan @ 4½% | 4 | 4 | 175, 115, 260, 150 | Sums of £26, £30, £32, £16 added to reduction | College | 6% int. and 1/15 of cap. added to reduction | 150, 384, 298, not rated separately |
| 13 | 150 (a) | 3 | — (under consideration) | 11 | 9 | 335, 274, 426, 213, 337, 300, 342, 395, 355 | All | College | 3% plus proportion of cap. plus repairs added to reduction | 194, 174, 276, 138, 184, 194, 222, 264, 230 |
| 14 | 250 (a) | 4 | 1 loan @ 3½% | 9 | 2 | Nil | External and structural | College | Normal landlord/tenant basis | 190, 258 |
| 15 | 350 (a) | 8 | — | 2 | 8 | Nil (4), 225, 155, 200, 345 | All | Rent free: coll.; added to reduction otherwise (n) | Paid by college | 306, 270, 294, 82, 258, 166, 242, 154 |

# Table 349. Housing (tutorial fellows). 1 January 1965 (continued)

OXFORD

| College number | Housing (or marriage) allowance for tutorial fellows living out of college (£ per annum) | Number living in college rent free | Number assisted in buying and how—(also rec. housing or marriage allowance) | Number recvg. housing or marr. allowance only | College houses | | | | | |
|---|---|---|---|---|---|---|---|---|---|---|
| | | | | | Number occupying college houses (h) | Rent paid or reduction in stipend (rents indicated by †) (£ per annum) | College responsibility for repairs and decoration | Responsibility for rates | Arrangements about capital improvements | Net rateable value (p) (rented houses indicated by †) (£) |
| 16 | 350 (a)(e) | 3 | — | 4 | 19 | Nil | Major repairs and decoration | College | Paid by college | 451, 162, 250, 214, 146, 286, 146, 355, 258, 190, 170, 280, 338, 178, 306, 166, 367, 146, not rated separately |
| 17 | 100 (b) 150 (a) | 3 | — | 11 | 11 | 470, 459, 437, 172, 357, 211, 268, 305, 416, 636, 383 | External and major internal repairs | College | Int. usually added to reduction | 313, 298, 388, 126, 286, 178, 218, 230, 306, 304, 198 |
| 18 | 300 (200 if *) | 2 | — | 8 | 6 | 150†, 259*, 451, 257*, 233*, 348 | Normal repairs | Fellow if rent paid; college otherwise | Rent inc. by 9% of capital cost | 202 (3), 154, 134 |
| 19 | 350 (a) | 5 | — | 13 | 8 | Nil (7), 160† | Rent free: college; rented: normal landlord/tenant agreement | Rent free: college; rented: fellow | Has not arisen | 202, 226, 278, 388, 106, 298, 290, 146† |
| 20 | 200 | 4 (f) | 1 loan @ 4¾% | 5 | 12 | 310, 315, 300, 470, 235, 270, 300, 542, 430, 259, 335, 350 | All | College | Reduction inc. by 8% of cost | 266, 262, 70, 158, 50, 178, 174, 430 (2), 77, 50, 266 |
| 21 | 500 (a) | 5 | — | 1 | 5 | Nil | Structural repairs; external decoration; materials for internal decoration | College | College, if of value to future occupants | 226, 322, 262, 214, 206 |
| 22 | 175 (b) 350 (a) | 4 | — | 5 | 12 | 238, 178, 210, 307, 327, 175, 280, 220, 200, 150, 210, 189 | Repairs and external decoration; internal up to 15% of reduction | College | Int. free loans (up to 10 years) to fellow | 246, 242, 218, 266, 210, 218, 272, 159, 198, 130, 162, 126 |
| 23 31 | 300 (a) 50 for 2 fellows with vested int. occupying college houses | 2 (g) 10 | — — | 16 — | 1 5 | Nil 200 (4), 60 | External Maintenance and repairs but not decoration | Fellow College | No fixed policy Rent increased | 170 178 (2), 186, 82, approx. 80 |
| 32 33 | 150 200 | 10 3 | — — | 4 10 | — — | — — | — — | — — | — — | — — |

[continued

**Table 349.** *Housing (tutorial fellows). 1 January 1965 (continued)*

OXFORD

| College number | Housing (or marriage) allowance for tutorial fellows living out of college (£ per annum) | Number living in college rent free | Number assisted in buying and how—(also rec. housing or marriage allowance) | Number recvg. housing or marr. allowance only | College houses | | | | | Net rateable value (p) (rented houses indicated by †) (£) |
|---|---|---|---|---|---|---|---|---|---|---|
| | | | | | Number occupying college houses (k) | Rent paid or reduction in stipend (rents indicated by †) (£ per annum) | College responsibility for repairs and decoration | Responsibility for rates | Arrangements about capital improvements | |
| 34 | By age: under 30  50; 30–39  100; 40–49  150; 50 & over  200 | 5 (h) | — | 9 | 3 | 200, 250, 275. | No arrangements | Added to reduction in two cases | No arrangements | 118, 68, not known |
| 35 | 150 | 8 | — | 5 | — | — | — | — | — | — |
| 41 | — | 3 | · | 2 | 3 | Nil | All | College | Has not arisen | 64, 48, 134 |
| 42 | 300 (a) | 2 | — | 7 | 1 | 312 | Repairs but not decoration | College | No arrangements | 146 |
| 43 | 275 | — | — | — | 2 | Nil | All | College | Paid by college | 194, 142 |
| 51 | — | 1 | — | — | | | | | | |
| 52 | — | 2 | — | — | 1 | Nil | External | College | Int. free loan | 114 |

SOURCE: Colleges.

NOTES

(a) Except those occupying a college house.
(b) For those occupying a college house.
(c) Marriage allowance.
(d) Except those occupying a college house and suffering a reduction in stipend.
(e) Fellows with a vested interest receive a marriage allowance to age 30.
(f) One pays rent of £200 but receives a housing allowance.
(g) One, resident part-week, receives the housing allowance.
(h) Two pay £100 rent for an extra room. One, resident part-week, receives part of the housing allowance.
(i) Includes one who is living in a college house and who does not receive the housing allowance.
(j) College would loan at 1% below market rate.
(k) In many cases fellows have tenancy agreements which oblige them to occupy the houses as one of the conditions of their employment, and the value of the accommodation is therefore not part of their taxable income.
(m) Rents for those occupying college houses are equal to half market rent plus an allowance for internal decoration.
(n) In one case the college pays one-third of the rates.
(p) Houses are listed in the same order as under 'rent paid or reduction in stipend' wherever possible.

565. *College teaching norms* (Table 352). Included in the questionnaire about emoluments were questions on teaching norms (question 18) and on whether a tutorial fellow who does piece-rate teaching keeps the proceeds (question 19). The replies are summarized in Table 352.

566. There were also two questions on the placing of fellows in salary scales, and one on the provision of college accommodation for fellows and lecturers. The answers of the colleges (referred to by the numbers given in para. 555) are reproduced in the Annex to this Part, together with the questionnaire.

567. *Research fellows.* There are two broad classes of research fellow in the colleges. There are junior research fellows who are at the beginning of their academic career, and who form a fairly homogeneous group so far as their salary and other emoluments from colleges are concerned. And there are senior research fellows who are established academics, often holding a university post, and to whom a wide variety of college arrangements apply. These range from non-stipendiary fellowships to posts which are hardly distinguishable from tutorial fellowships. In the undergraduate colleges there were about 40 junior research fellows, and 40 senior research fellows of whom three-fifths also held a university post. In the graduate colleges the distinction between junior and senior research fellows is less clear-cut. In all, there were 43 research fellows at graduate colleges of whom 13 held a university post. The stipends of junior research fellows were normally non-incremental, and ranged between £600 and £1,000, except that the college stipend was reduced if another post was held. Most junior research fellows were entitled to rooms in college if unmarried, and many who were married received a housing allowance in the range £100–£250, the usual figure being £100 or £125. The stipends of senior research fellows not holding a university post were in the range £450–£2,050 at the undergraduate colleges, but included in this group are some whose fellowship was not full-time; at the graduate colleges the highest scale had a maximum of £2,750, and 9 research fellows had stipends above £2,000. Most of the salary arrangements at the undergraduate colleges were made *ad personam*; only one college had a salary scale for research fellows. The graduate colleges had a scale or scales for research fellows not holding a university post. Senior research fellows holding university posts received stipends ranging from £50 to £600, and some had non-stipendiary fellowships; most stipends were in the range £100–£450. The other emoluments of senior research fellows varied according to their college responsibilities. A majority received housing benefits similar to those of tutorial fellows.

568. *College lecturers.* There is a very wide range in the arrangements which colleges make with their lecturers, and in the duties involved. There are

**Table 350.** *Payments for college offices. 1 January 1965*

Holders are tutorial fellows unless otherwise specified

OXFORD

| College number | Vicegerent | Senior Tutor (incl. Tuition Secretary and Senior Censor) | Bursar (incl. Estates, Finance, and Domestic Bursar) | Dean (incl. Principal of Post-masters and Junior Dean) | Dean of Degrees | Dean of Post-graduate Students | Tutor for Admissions | Chaplain | Librarian | Others (£0–49) | Others (£50–99) | Others (£100 and over) |
|---|---|---|---|---|---|---|---|---|---|---|---|---|
| | | | | | | | | | | | | £ PER ANNUM |
| 201 | 150 (j)(x) | 200 | 300 | 50 | 60 | | | | 100 | 20 | 50 | 100 |
| 202 | | 500 (e) | 350 (b) | 75 (a) / 125 (x) / 150 | 60 | 75 | 300 | | 400 (f) | | | 200 (2) / 300 |
| 203 | Nil (x) | 200 | | | | | | | 75 | 25 | | |
| 204 | 50 (x) | 300 (e) | 500 (e)(x) | 200 | 40 | 75 | | | 100 (y) / 120 | 10 (y) / 25 | | |
| 205 | | 400 | 330 | 200 | 10 + capitation fees | | | | | | | |
| 206 | | 150 | | 110 (y) | | 80 | 150 | | 110 | 11 / 16 / 30 (x) | 55 (x) / 55 (y) / 55 (x) / 75 / 75 | |
| 207 | 25 (x) | 150 | 150 | 50 | 75 | | 125 | Nil (g) | 75 | | 50 (x) / 50 (y) / 75 | |
| 208 | | 200 (e) | 175 (g)(x) / 250 | 100 / 150 | 150 | | 150 | 200 (y) | 200 (x) | | 50 (x) / 50 (y) / 75 | |
| 209 | Nil | 200 | 1,450 | 100 (x) | 75 | | | Nil | Nil (y) / 100 | | | |
| 210 | 50 | 50 | 75 / 150 / 60 | 50 | | | | | 75 | | 60 / 90 | |
| 211 | | 200 | | 75 | 60 (x) | | | 300 (x) | 80 | | | |
| 212 | 100 (x) | 350 | 175 | 150 | 40 (2) | | 350 | Nil | 100 (y) | | | 120 (2 |
| 213 | | 200 | Nil (g) / 600 (f) | 140 / 175 / 200 | | | | | 200 | | | |

| College | | | | | | | | | | |
|---|---|---|---|---|---|---|---|---|---|---|
| 214 | Nil (x) | 200 | 250 | 20 (x) / 100 | 80 | 200 (e)(x) | 100 (x) | 100 | 20 | 150 |
| 215 | 100 (x) | 100 (x) | 250 | 100 | Nil | | Nil | | | |
| 216 | 350 | 350 | | 125 (b) / 25 (y) | 25 / 25 | 350 | | 250 (x) | 35 | 50 (2)(x) |
| 217 | 75 (x) | 250 | | 250 | | | 100 (y) | 250 (y) | | 50 (y) |
| 218 | 250 (x) | 350 (x) | 150 (z) / 1,250 (z) / 150 (y) / 200 | 270 (y) / 400 / 150 / 200 | 125 | 200 (x) | Nil (x)(e) | 75 / 100 | | 50 (y) / 150 (a) |
| 219 | 50 | 150 (y) / 200 | | | 50 (x) / 5 per ceremony | | | | | |
| 220 | | | | | | | | | | |
| 221 | 150 (x) | 400 (x) | 600 | 150 / 150 + 5 per degree day | | | | 100 (c) / 300 | | |
| 222 | 175 | 175 | 400 (e) | 200 | 15 + 3 per session after the first in a term | 125 | | 60 | | |
| 223 | 200 | 300 | | 50 / 200 / 60 / 100 | 30 (x) / 20 | | | 250 (b) | | 200 |
| 231 | 60 (c) | 60 | | 75 / Nil (f)(x) / 40 (c) / 80 | 30 | | | 60 / 60 (x)(i) / 75 (c) | Nil (f)(x) | |
| 232 | 100 (j) | | | | | | | | | |
| 233 | 80 | | 350 (h) | | | | | | | |
| 234 | 30 | 30 | | | | | | | | |
| 235 | | | | | | | | | | |
| 241 | 75 | 75 incl. post of Dean | 400 / 450 (2) | (1) 50 (a) / (2) see Sr. Tutor | 25 (b) | | 75 | 75 / 100 (b) | 30 | 50 (a) / 50 |
| 242 | | | | | | | | | | |
| 243 | 100 (b) | 100 | 1,100 (a) / 1,150 (b) | | | | | 600 (b) | | 200 |

SOURCE: Colleges.

NOTES
(a) Research fellow.
(b) Other non-tutorial fellow.
(c) Stipendiary lecturer.
(e) Reduction in duties permitted.
(f) Teaching h.p.w. reduced to 6.
(g) Teaching h.p.w. reduced to 9.
(h) Teaching h.p.w. reduced to 8–11.
(i) Teaching h.p.w. reduced to 12.
(j) Temporary and exceptional.
(x) (y) or (z) Indicates offices held by the same individual for the time being.

# THE ACADEMIC STAFF

**Table 351.** *Piece-rate teaching payments in 1964*

OXFORD                                                                                      £

| College number | Payments to | | | | Total |
|---|---|---|---|---|---|
| | Fellows of college | Lecturers of college | Fellows of other colleges | Others | |
| 1 | 166 | 375 | 979 | 1,127 | 2,647 |
| 2 | 1,188 | 117 | 1,304 | 6,572 | 9,181 |
| 3 | 379 | 444 | 1,154 | 2,157 | 4,134 |
| 4 | 575 (a) | 1,243 (a) | 932 (a) | 3,067 (a) | 5,817 |
| 5 | 474 | 1,477 (b) | 1,145 | 2,065 | 5,161 |
| 6 | 280 | 1,115 | 430 | 1,658 | 3,483 |
| 7 | — | 452 | - - - - - - - - 4,797 - - - - - - - - - - - | | 5,249 |
| 8 | 538 | 884 | 1,633 | 4,384 | 7,439 |
| 9 | 93 | 839 | 1,312 | 2,568 | 4,812 |
| 10 | 1,048 | 1,100 | 770 | 3,877 | 6,795 |
| 11 | 222 | 657 | 523 | 2,280 | 3,682 |
| 12 | 255 | 396 | 851 | 1,520 | 3,022 |
| 13 | 605 | — | 456 | 3,887 (c) | 4,948 |
| 14 | — | - - - - - - - - - - - - - - - 3,500 - - - - - - - - - - - | | | 3,500 |
| 15 | 678 | 147 | 890 | 2,840 | 4,555 |
| 16 | 544 | - - - - - - - - - - - - - - 3,949 (d) - - - - - - - - - - | | | 4,493 |
| 17 | 213 | 833 | 701 | 3,929 | 5,676 |
| 18 | 137 | 1,482 | - - - - - - - - 2,280 - - - - - - - - - - - | | 3,899 |
| 19 | 1,857 | 1,033 | 681 | 2,505 | 6,076 |
| 20 | 28 | 1,568 | 1,123 | 2,839 | 5,558 |
| 21 | 1,252 | 1,452 | 1,152 | 1,337 | 5,193 |
| 22 | 542 | 526 | 1,606 | 3,080 | 5,754 |
| 23 | — | 350 | 1,700 | 3,700 | 5,750 |
| 31 | — | 1,310 | 2,204 | 3,040 | 6,554 |
| 32 | 932 | 925 | 3,743 | 3,653 | 9,253 |
| 33 | 108 | 810 | 1,425 | 3,550 | 5,893 |
| 34 | 925 | 2,570 (e) | - - - - - - - - - 5,401 (e) - - - - - - - - | | 8,896 |
| 35 | 60 | 908 | 3,169 | 2,858 | 6,995 |
| 41 | — | — | — | — | — |
| 42 | — | — | - - - - - - - - - - - - 60 - - - - - - - - - - - | | 60 |
| 43 | — | — | — | — | — |
| 51 | — | — | - - - - - - - - - - - 669 - - - - - - - - - - - | | 669 |
| 52 | — | — | - - - - - - - - - 1,564 - - - - - - - - - - - | | 1,564 |
| Total | 13,099 | 23,013 | 29,883 | 22,220  68,493 | 156,708 |

SOURCE: Colleges.

NOTES
(a) Exceeds normal.
(b) Includes non-stipendiary fellows who are lecturers.
(c) Includes payments to Instructors.
(d) Includes retaining fees.
(e) Based on academic year 1963–4.

1. It has been assumed that retaining fees paid to non-stipendiary lecturers are *not* in-cluded, unless the answer stated otherwise.
2. Piece-rates for teaching were increased on 1 October 1964. Before that date the **rates** for eight hours' tuition were £12 for one pupil, £15 for a pair, and £18 for **three** pupils. For larger groups £1 is added for each additional pupil. For the rates from 1 October 1964 see para. 526.
3. Some of the payments to college fellows ('own' college or 'other' colleges) were made to emeritus and other non-stipendiary fellows.

two broad groups: stipendiary lecturers (defined as those brought into the FSSU) and non-stipendiary lecturers; but the distinction between the two groups is not clear-cut, as some lecturers appear to receive a stipend although they are not in the FSSU and others are paid a relatively large fee plus piece-rates for teaching over a given number of hours. Among stipendiary lecturers there was considerable variation in the salary for a given number of hours of teaching because of variations in responsibilities other than teaching (e.g. responsibilities for organizing teaching) and because colleges took account of other posts held. In many cases where the lecturer was a tutorial fellow of another college the payments were made to his college and not to the lecturer himself. The most usual rates were about £350 a year for 6 hours teaching a week during term; £800–£900 for 12 hours; and £1,000–£1,300 for 14–16 hours. About half the stipendiary lecturers lived in rooms in college or received a housing allowance. A few colleges paid child allowances to stipendiary lecturers in some cases. Non-stipendiary lecturers received a retaining fee of usually between £15 and £45 a year, and were, in addition, paid at piece-rates for the teaching they did. It is a common practice to allow lecturers to dine free of charge on one or two nights a week during term.

### LOCATION OF RESIDENCE OF THE ACADEMIC STAFF

569. Analysis of the location of residence of the academic staff shows the extent to which colleges are able to ensure that their fellows live near the college through the provision of accommodation or of housing assistance. Tables 353–5 give distributions of the academic staff in the main grades in post at 1 January 1965 according to both the distance of their residence from their work-place (Tables 353 and 354), and the district in which they lived (Table 355). Table 356 gives some information on the age of tutorial fellows living in college.

570. Place of work has been taken as the college for all tutorial fellows. For other staff it has been taken as the university department or institution where appropriate; as the office or teaching room provided by the University where appropriate; as the college for others holding a fellowship; and as the Radcliffe Camera for others.

571. Residence has been taken mainly from the Michaelmas Term 1964 list of *Resident Members*, but other directories were used and the Registry and the Chest gave assistance.

572. The academic staff included are: professors; readers; university lecturers; senior research officers and equivalent; CUF and special lecturers; faculty lecturers; and any others who were tutorial fellows. Staff at the Permanent Private Halls are not included.

## Table 352. *Teaching norms for tutorial fellows. 1 January 1965*

OXFORD

| College number | Teaching norm (CUF lecturer) (hours per week) | Teaching norm (university lecturer) | Additional payments if norm exceeded | Deduction if norm not reached | Who keeps payments for piece-rate teaching for other colleges | Restrictions on teaching (hours per week) |
|---|---|---|---|---|---|---|
| 1 | 12–15 (a) | 9 | Tutors—no Lecturers—yes | No (b) | Fellow (b) | None |
| 2 | 15 (c) | 6 | Yes | No (b) | Fellow (b) | None |
| 3 | 12 | (d) | Yes | No | College | Max. of 20 |
| 4 | At least 15 | At least 4 or 5 | Yes—univ. lect. No—CUF lect. | (e) | Fellow | Max. of 5 for other colleges |
| 5 | 16 (f) | (d) | Yes | No | College | Max. of 20 (f) |
| 6 | 12 | 8 | No | No | Fellow | (g) |
| 7 | No norm | No norm | . | . | Fellow | None |
| 8 | 12–14 | 6 | Yes—univ. lect. No—CUF lect. | No | Fellow | None |
| 9 | 14 | 9 | No | No | Fellow (h) | None |
| 10 | 14 (i) | 6 | Yes | No | Fellow | None |
| 11 | 12 | 7–9 | No | No | Fellow (h) | None |
| 12 | 14 | (d) | No | No | Fellow | None |
| 13 | 10–14 | (d) | No | No (j) | Fellow | Max. of 4 for other colleges |
| 14 | No norm | No norm | . | . | Fellow (h) | None |
| 15 | 12 (k) | 7½ | No | No | College | None |
| 16 | 14–15 | (d) | No | No | Fellow | None (m) |
| 17 | 12–16 | 9 | No | No | Fellow | (g) |
| 18 | No norm | No norm | . | . | Fellow | None (m) |
| 19 | 14 | (d) | Yes | No | Fellow | None |
| 20 | 15 (max.) | 10 (s) | No | No | Fellow | None |
| 21 | 12–15 (n) | 7–11 (s) | No | No | Fellow (b) | (g) |
| 22 | 12 (min.) 15 (max.) (p) | 10 (arts) 6 (science) | (d) | (d) | Fellow (b) | None |
| 23 | No norm | No norm | . | . | Fellow | None |
| 31 | 12–15 (f) | (d) | No | No | College | None |
| 32 | 10–12 | (d) | Yes | Yes | College | None (q) |
| 33 | Scale A: 13 or more Scale B: 11–12 Scale C: 10 or less | (d) | No | No | Fellow (b) | Max. of 18 |
| 34 | Scale A: 6 Scale B: 10 Scale C: 12 Scale D: 15 | (d) | Yes | No | College | Max. of 18 |
| 35 | Scale A: 12–18 Scale B: 8–11 | (d) | No | No | College | None (r) |
| 41 | . | . | . | . | Fellow | None |
| 42 | . | . | . | . | Fellow | Max. of 6 for other colleges |
| 43 | . | . | . | . | Fellow | |
| 51 | No norm | No norm | . | . | Fellow | None |
| 52 | No norm | No norm | . | . | Fellow | None |

SOURCE: Colleges.

NOTES

(a) 12 for faculty lecturers.

(b) Piece-rate receipts paid to college until norm is reached.

(c) To be reduced to 12 from M.T. 1965. Given in terms of *tutorial hours* calculated thus:

    1 hour with single pupil = 1 tutorial hour.

    1 hour with two pupils = 1¼ tutorial hours.

    1 hour with three or more pupils = 1½ tutorial hours.

[continued

573. Tutorial fellows at the women's colleges are shown separately; those at the men's and graduate colleges are divided into three groups thus:

Group (1): tutorial fellows of colleges housing at least two-thirds of the tutorial fellows living out of college; i.e. colleges with code numbers 3, 6, 11, 15, 16, 20, 21, 22 for the purpose of the tables giving college emoluments (see para. 555).

Group (2): tutorial fellows not in groups (1) or (3).

Group (3): tutorial fellows of the four colleges with the lowest salary scales; i.e. colleges with code numbers 2, 4, 8, 14.

574. The districts within Oxford (i.e. within the proposed city boundaries) are defined thus:

(i) Central: the area bounded by the Cherwell, Isis, South Parks Road, Keble Road, Little Clarendon Street, Walton Street, Worcester Street, Hythe Bridge Street, Oxpens Road;

(ii) North-central: the area bounded by the Oxford Canal, St. Margaret's Road (not itself included), Woodstock Road (not itself included), and the Central area;

(iii) North: the area bounded by the Oxford Canal, the city boundary, the Cherwell, and the North-central and Central areas;

(iv) East: the part of the City east of Magdalen Bridge (and including Headington and Iffley);

(v) West: the remainder of the City west of Magdalen Bridge (and including Cumnor Hill, North and South Hinksey, and Binsey).

continued]

(d) Not stated.
(e) Has not arisen.
(f) Including lecturing.
(g) Permission required.
(h) Some fees are paid to the college by fellows voluntarily.
(i) 10 for faculty lecturers.
(j) But fellows can be asked to undertake additional work.
(k) A maximum of 15 including university teaching other than postgraduate supervision.
(m) Unless such teaching interfered with fellow's college duties.
(n) Including classes. For the purposes of Note (b) the norm is 12 hours.
(p) Including university undergraduate teaching.
(q) Tutors of less than five years' standing may not normally teach for more than 12 hours a week.
(r) But fellows are expected not to exceed the maximum number of hours of their scale.
(s) For scientists. There is no norm for other university lecturers.
   1. The hours under restrictions on teaching are the maximum including teaching for the college unless specified otherwise.
   2. Outside tuition is often done on an exchange basis with no money changing hands.
   3. Only formal, or near-formal, restrictions are noted. In some colleges there may be an understanding that a fellow keeps his total teaching within a limit.

**Table 353.** *Distance of residence from work-place. 1964–5*

OXFORD

| | Academic staff living | | | | | | | | PERCENTAGE | Number |
| | In college | Within ¼ mile (but not in college) | ¼ mile to ½ mile | ½ mile to 1 mile | Within Oxford but over 1 mile | Boars Hill and Hinksey Hill | Elsewhere outside Oxford | Address not known | All | All |
|---|---|---|---|---|---|---|---|---|---|---|
| Tutorial fellows, Group (1) | 26 | 16 | 17 | 12 | 21 | — | 7 | — | 100 | 153 |
| Tutorial fellows, Group (2) | 19 | 6 | 2 | 10 | 44 | 4 | 15 | — | 100 | 217 |
| Tutorial fellows, Group (3) | 16 | 2 | — | 8 | 55 | 3 | 17 | — | 100 | 64 |
| Tutorial fellows, men's and graduate colleges | 21 | 9 | 7 | 11 | 38 | 2 | 13 | — | 100 | 434 |
| Tutorial fellows, women's colleges | 51 | 10 | 15 | 14 | 7 | — | 3 | — | 100 | 72 |
| All tutorial fellows | 25 | 9 | 8 | 11 | 33 | 2 | 11 | — | 100 | 506 |
| Professors | 12 | 8 | 4 | 14 | 43 | 6 | 13 | — | 100 | 104 |
| Readers, lecturers, and equivalent other than tutorial fellows | 3 | 4 | 4 | 12 | 44 | 4 | 28 | 2 | 100 | 305 |
| All except tutorial fellows | 5 | 5 | 4 | 13 | 44 | 4 | 24 | 1 | 100 | 409 |
| All | 16 | 7 | 6 | 12 | 38 | 3 | 17 | 1 | 100 | 915 |

SOURCE: Michaelmas Term 1964 list of *Resident Members*, local directories, and source to Table 235.

NOTES

1. See para. 573 for the grouping of tutorial fellows.
2. Academic staff at the Permanent Private Halls and junior academic staff are excluded. See para. 572.
3. Academic staff in post at 1 January 1965 are included, but some of the addresses used may relate to an earlier date.

Table 354. *Percentage of academic staff living within various distances from work-place. 1964–5*

OXFORD

PERCENTAGE

| | Academic staff living | | | | | | | | All | Number |
|---|---|---|---|---|---|---|---|---|---|---|
| | In college | Within ¼ mile | Within ½ mile | Within 1 mile | Within Oxford | Boars Hill and Hinksey Hill | Elsewhere outside Oxford | Not known | | |
| Tutorial fellows, Group (1) | 26 | 42 | 59 | 72 | 93 | — | 7 | — | 100 | *153* |
| Tutorial fellows, Group (2) | 19 | 25 | 27 | 37 | 81 | 4 | 15 | — | 100 | *217* |
| Tutorial fellows, Group (3) | 16 | 17 | 17 | 25 | 80 | 3 | 17 | — | 100 | *64* |
| Tutorial fellows, men's and graduate colleges | 21 | 30 | 37 | 47 | 85 | 2 | 13 | — | 100 | *434* |
| Tutorial fellows, women's colleges | 51 | 61 | 76 | 90 | 97 | — | 3 | — | 100 | *72* |
| All tutorial fellows | 25 | 34 | 42 | 54 | 87 | 2 | 11 | — | 100 | *506* |
| Professors | 12 | 20 | 24 | 38 | 82 | 6 | 13 | — | 100 | *104* |
| Readers, lecturers, and equivalent other than tutorial fellows | 3 | 6 | 10 | 23 | 67 | 4 | 28 | 2 | 100 | *305* |
| All except tutorial fellows | 5 | 10 | 14 | 27 | 71 | 4 | 24 | 1 | 100 | *409* |
| All | 16 | 23 | 30 | 42 | 80 | 3 | 17 | 1 | 100 | *915* |

SOURCE: See source to Table 353.

NOTE: See notes to Table 353.

**Table 355.** *District in which academic staff live. 1964-5*

OXFORD

| | District in which living | | | | | | | | | PERCENTAGE All | Number |
|---|---|---|---|---|---|---|---|---|---|---|---|
| | College | Central Oxford | North-central Oxford | North Oxford | East Oxford | West Oxford | Boars Hill and Hinskey Hill | Elsewhere outside Oxford | Address not known | All | Number |
| Tutorial fellows, Group (1) | 26 | 32 | 1 | 25 | 5 | 3 | — | 7 | — | 100 | 153 |
| Tutorial fellows, Group (2) | 19 | 7 | — | 37 | 15 | 2 | 4 | 15 | — | 100 | 217 |
| Tutorial fellows, Group (3) | 16 | 2 | — | 36 | 16 | 11 | 3 | 17 | — | 100 | 64 |
| Tutorial fellows, men's and graduate colleges | 21 | 15 | — | 33 | 12 | 4 | 2 | 13 | — | 100 | 434 |
| Tutorial fellows, women's colleges | 51 | 8 | 3 | 31 | 4 | — | — | 3 | — | 100 | 72 |
| All tutorial fellows | 25 | 14 | 1 | 32 | 11 | 3 | 2 | 11 | — | 100 | 506 |
| Professors | 12 | 11 | 1 | 41 | 13 | 3 | 6 | 13 | — | 100 | 104 |
| Readers, lecturers, and equivalent other than tutorial fellows | 3 | 5 | 1 | 39 | 12 | 8 | 4 | 28 | 2 | 100 | 305 |
| All except tutorial fellows | 5 | 6 | 1 | 40 | 12 | 6 | 4 | 24 | 1 | 100 | 409 |
| All | 16 | 11 | 1 | 36 | 11 | 5 | 3 | 17 | 1 | 100 | 915 |

SOURCE: See source to Table 353.
NOTE: See notes to Table 353.

OXFORD

PERCENTAGE

**Table 356.** *Age of tutorial fellows living in college and out of college. 1964–5*

| Age | Men's and graduate colleges | | | | Women's colleges | | | | All colleges | | | |
|---|---|---|---|---|---|---|---|---|---|---|---|---|
| | Living in college | Living out of college | All | Those living in college as percentage of age group | Living in college | Living out of college | All | Those living in college as percentage of age group | Living in college | Living out of college | All | Those living in college as percentage of age group |
| Under 30 | 17 | 8 | 10 | 38 | 5 | 3 | 4 | 67 | 14 | 7 | 9 | 40 |
| 30–34 | 25 | 18 | 19 | 28 | 19 | 6 | 13 | 78 | 23 | 16 | 18 | 33 |
| 35–39 | 14 | 21 | 19 | 15 | 19 | 17 | 18 | 54 | 16 | 20 | 19 | 21 |
| 40–44 | 11 | 22 | 21 | 15 | 16 | 17 | 17 | 50 | 15 | 22 | 20 | 19 |
| 45–49 | 18 | 12 | 12 | 20 | 16 | 14 | 15 | 55 | 12 | 12 | 12 | 26 |
| 50 and over | 15 | 20 | 20 | 20 | 24 | 43 | 33 | 38 | 20 | 22 | 22 | 24 |
| All | 100 | 100 | 100 | 21 | 100 | 100 | 100 | 51 | 100 | 100 | 100 | 25 |
| Number | 92 | 342 | 434 | | 37 | 35 | 72 | | 129 | 377 | 506 | |

SOURCE: See source to Table 353.

NOTES

1. Tutors at the Permanent Private Halls are not included.
2. See Note 3 to Table 353.

575. The great majority of tutorial fellows and of professors lived in Oxford. Among tutorial fellows two groups lived particularly close to their college; those in Group (1) and those at the women's colleges (half of whom lived in the college itself). Three-quarters of the former and 90 per cent. of the latter lived within one mile. The proportion living within one mile was substantially less for the other groups of tutorial fellows, and was only a quarter for Group (3).

576. The proportion of readers, lecturers, etc. (other than tutorial fellows), living within Oxford was considerably less than for the other groups (two-thirds against 80–95 per cent.). The main differences between this and other groups were in the proportions living in college and outside Oxford. A larger proportion lived out of college but within a mile of their work than did tutorial fellows in Group (2) or in Group (3).

577. The proportion of professors, readers, lecturers, etc. (other than tutorial fellows), living in college may be overstated since if the list of *Resident Members* gave a college address only, and no other address could be found, it has been assumed the person lived in college. A number of professors have a London address, and appear to live in college when in Oxford.

578. Most of those living in Oxford, but not in college, lived either in central Oxford, north Oxford, or east of Magdalen Bridge. A little over a third lived in north Oxford, the proportion not varying much between the different groups. 11 per cent. lived in central Oxford, but there was great variation between the groups of staff, with 32 per cent. of tutorial fellows in Group (1) living in this district. The majority of those living east of Magdalen Bridge lived in Headington (7 per cent.) with 2 per cent. in Iffley and 1 per cent. elsewhere.

579. Table 356 shows the age distribution of tutorial fellows living in college and living out of college, and the proportion of each age group living in college.

# ANNEX

580. The replies of colleges (referred to by the numbers given in para. 555) to questions 16, 17, and 24 of the questionnaire about emoluments and related matters, and the questionnaire itself are reproduced.

581. *Questions 16 and 17*

16. Where a scale is not a strict age scale, how is the position of a fellow or lecturer on a scale determined?
17. If there is more than one scale for tutorial fellows, what is the reason for this policy?

*College no. 1*

Qu. *16*. Scales are either (*a*)  age scales, or
                       (*b*)  length-of-service scales, or
                       (*c*)  fixed.

We wish to avoid any system of remuneration which is not automatically determined.

Qu. *17*. Scale A applies to official fellows and tutors, being university lecturers who undertake to teach up to 9 hours a week (on average) for the college.

Scale B applies to official fellows and tutors, being CUF lecturers, who undertake college teaching of 12–15 hours per week (on average).

Scale B+ applies to official fellows and tutors with the same duties as those on Scale B, but holding no university appointment.

Scale C applies to official fellows and tutors, being faculty lecturers, who undertake to teach up to 12 hours a week (on average) for the college.

Scale D applies to an official fellow and tutor, being a university reader, who undertakes to teach up to 6 hours a week for the college.

Note: As the fellowship scale is a length-of-service scale, and the tutorship is an age scale, it has been necessary to state them separately.

*College no. 2*

Qu. *16*. Not applicable. It is a strict age scale for fellows and there is no *scale* for lecturers.

Qu. *17*. The college has felt itself unable to afford to pay the sums necessary to equate the salaries earned by the two groups of fellows.

*College no. 3*

Qu. *16*. Not applicable, since all our scales are age scales.

Qu. *17*. The reason is the differing payments made by the University to those with university appointments.

*College no. 4*

Qu. *16*. Not applicable.

Qu. *17*. The college would prefer to have one scale only of combined emoluments and this is its ultimate aim. In its latest revision of salary scales the previously existing differences between the two scales for university lecturers and CUF lecturers have been appreciably reduced. The new scales are a compromise in recognition of the fact that we cannot yet afford to pay any of our fellows on a scale which would bring their college and university salaries up to the joint maximum laid down by the University for a university lecturer who also holds a college post.

*College no. 5*

Qu. *16*. All scales are age scales.

Qu. *17*. No.

*College no. 6*

Qu. *16*. There are no such scales.

Qu. *17*. Special scales are necessary for tutors who are not yet CUF or university lecturers. The college usually pays a tutor in this position such sum as will bring his combined college and university stipend to £100 p.a. less than a tutor/lecturer of the same age.

### College no. 7

*Qu. 16.* Not applicable for fellows; for lecturers either by negotiation with other colleges with whom the lecturer is shared or by reference to the amount of teaching a lecturer undertakes.

*Qu. 17.* Differential between science and arts fellows, plus the fact that the former receive a larger proportion of their salaries from the University.

### College no. 8

*Qu. 16.* Not applicable.

*Qu. 17.* Our Class A scale is for fellows who hold CUF lecturerships. Our Class B scale for fellows who hold university lecturerships. Our Class C scale is for fellows who hold university lecturerships and will normally do less than 6 hours' teaching for the college.

### College no. 9

*Qu. 16.* The only scales are age scales.

*Qu. 17.* Scales A and B bring the total college and university stipend to the same level as far as possible with a smooth college scale. (Difference of age definition for various university posts have to be considered.)

### College no. 10

*Qu. 16.* The only two stipend scales are strict age scales.

*Qu. 17.* Scale B provides a fellow holding a 'full-time' university post with what in the college's view is the minimum fellowship stipend which would make worth while his holding of a fellowship with its extra duties alongside his university appointment. The college singly could not afford to equate Scale A of which it contributes so much greater a share with Scale B. It is, however, content to acquiesce in a moderate discrepancy between Scale A and B in view of the difference between the obligations to the University of the tutorial fellow who is a full-time university lecturer and those of a tutorial fellow with a part-time university post.

### College no. 11

*Qu. 16.* The only scales are strict age scales.

*Qu. 17.* Only one scale.

### College no. 12

*Qu. 16.* Our scales for fellows are strictly by age. We have no scales for lecturers.

*Qu. 17.* The difference in our two scales, for university lecturers and for CUF, is due to our policy of producing the same combined salary.

### College no. 13

*Qu. 16.* Not applicable.

*Qu. 17.* There is basically one combined scale, but there are divergences from it according to university appointments held and the amount of college teaching done.

*College no. 14*

Qu. 16. Not applicable.

Qu. 17. Not applicable.

*College no. 15*

Qu. 16. Not applicable.

Qu. 17. Not applicable.

*College no. 16*

Qu. 16. Our scale for tutorial fellows is based strictly on age.

Qu. 17. We have only one scale.

*College no. 17*

Qu. 16. We have no such scales. Research lecturers receive a minimum of £650 plus a free set of rooms and dining rights.

Qu. 17. Only one scale with diminishing differences as between CUF and other university lecturers. *Object*: to get as even a scale as possible, bringing about a gradual approximation between joint total payments to CUF and other lecturers, and their ultimate equalization.

*College no. 18*

Qu. 16. Not applicable.

Qu. 17. We have two scales for tutorial fellows, one for those holding university lecturerships, mainly in the experimental sciences, and one for those holding CUF lecturerships, mainly in arts. This issue has been seriously considered and debated several times by the college in recent years. The present scheme is not universally supported, but has a substantial majority in favour of it. The majority agreed that the formal demands made upon fellows who hold university lecturerships in the experimental sciences are more substantial and more specific both during term and during vacation than those imposed on CUF lecturers. The latter have considerably greater choice of time in arranging for their vacation studies, etc. For this reason a higher combined scale has been accepted for science fellows.

*College no. 19*

Qu. 16. The college scales are strict age scales.

Qu. 17. The scale for tutorial fellows (CUF lecturers) differs from the scale for tutorial fellows (university lecturers) for the reason that the corresponding university scales are different. At present the college scales are so fixed that the total combined stipends of fellows on each scale are, at each age point, equal or nearly equal. The college is not, however, committed as a matter of principle to the policy of equating the total combined stipends of tutorial fellows (CUF), for whom there is no mandatory joint maximum, with the total combined stipends of university lecturers, for whom there is.

*College no. 20*

*Qu. 16.* Only in two cases (Groups A and C) can there be said to be salary 'scales': remuneration in the other cases is mostly fixed *ad hoc*.

[Group A comprises fellows teaching for 15 hours a week for the college and holding, or about to receive, a CUF lecturership; Group C comprises fellows teaching for 10 hours and holding a university lecturership.]

*Qu. 17.* The reason for the existence of a separate scale for university lecturers (Group C) is that these fellows receive a larger salary from the University than fellows holding CUF lecturerships, and can do only 10 hours of college teaching a week, instead of 15.

*College no. 21*

*Qu. 16.* The only scales are age scales.

*Qu. 17.* All tutorial fellows are on the same tutorial and fellowship scales. However, a science tutor's stipend from the college is adjusted so that his total stipend is about £150 per annum more than that of an arts tutor of the same age.

*College no. 22*

*Qu. 16.* (*a*) Tutorial fellows are paid strictly according to the age scales in qu. 13 above.

(*b*) The stipends of research fellows and lecturers are fixed *ad hoc* by reference to such factors as:

(i) The university stipend and research grants, if any, of the fellow or lecturer.

(ii) The duties of the fellowship or lecturership.

(iii) The funds available, particularly in the case of a research fellowship endowed by a trust fund.

*Qu. 17.* (*a*) The conditions governing the operation of the scales detailed in qu. 13 above are as follows:

(i) Fellows be paid on Scale II only if they are not receiving children's allowances.

(ii) Fellows elected before 31 December 1964 be given a once and for all option between the scales.

(iii) Fellows, elected after 31 December, be paid on Scale II.

(iv) The differential between the two scales be permanently maintained.

This scheme was adopted by the college to overcome the difficulties created by the ending of children's allowances.

(*b*) Any tutorial fellow who is a university reader or of equivalent rank be paid on Scale II with a supplement of £200 p.a.

*College no. 23*

*Qu. 16.* Does not arise.

*Qu. 17.* There are separate scales only in relation to different university appointments (i.e. CUF, faculty, or university lecturers); the scales are so arranged as to make the total emoluments (college plus university) as nearly as possible the same for each category.

*College no. 31*

Qu. *16*. It is determined by age and experience.

Qu. *17*. Not more than one. Any appointments not on the tutorial salary scale are made *ad hoc*. We have none at present.

*College no. 32*

Qu. *16*. When a tutor is appointed her initial stipend may be fixed at any point on the scale, according to her experience. There is no college scale for lecturers.

Qu. *17*. There is only one scale.

*College no. 33*

Qu. *16*. In determining the position of a newly appointed fellow on the scale, the college takes into account the years of service in this or some other university previous to the appointment. If the new fellow comes from a lecturer's post in another university, an attempt is made to approximate her position on the college scale to her previous salary, bearing in mind that the college can offer full residence. If the new fellow has previously been a lecturer of the college, or a research fellow, these points are taken into consideration.

Qu. *17*. We have three scales for tutorial fellows based on differences in hours of teaching. We consider it most important that fellows should have opportunities for doing their own research and wish them to feel free to make tutorial arrangements enabling them to do this without unfairness to the college.

*College no. 34*

Qu. *16*. The salary scale for tutorial fellows is based on:
   (i) fellowship stipend: age scale;
   (ii) tutorial stipend: hourly option per week, i.e. A 6-hour (only allowed in certain circumstances), B 10-hour, C 12-hour, D 15-hour options.

Qu. *17*. To allow flexibility in teaching hours according to the number of students in a given school and for tutorial fellows working on research.

*College no. 35*

Qu. *16*. By reference to age and experience.

Qu. *17*. Different hours.

*College no. 41*

Qu. *16*. By reference to the date of his election to the particular fellowship.

Qu. *17*. Not applicable.

*College no. 42*

Qu. *16*. The college scale for official fellowships is not an age scale. A fellow is brought on to the scale at a point which the Governing Body considers suitable for his qualifications and experience.

Qu. *17*. Fellows of this college are not appointed to CUF lecturerships unless they also hold lecturerships at undergraduate colleges. In order that the salaries of official fellows who do not hold CUF or other university lecturerships should bear comparison with the salaries of those fellows who do, official fellows are appointed to college lecturerships.

*College no. 43*

*Qu. 16.* Strict age scale.

*Qu. 17.* Only one scale. The reason for the difference in the scale between official and research fellows (housing allowance for the former, but not for the latter) is that official fellows carry general responsibility concerning the college.

*College no. 52*

*Qus. 16 and 17.* Salaries are fixed by College Salaries Committee, based on age, qualification, experience, and the financial position of the college. As the college finances improve, it is hoped to bring tutorial salaries up to the university level.

### 582. *Question 24*

24. Is accommodation [in houses of which the college is landlord] normally available for any fellow or lecturer wanting it? If not, on what basis is the accommodation allocated?

*College no. 1*

Such accommodation is only provided for official fellows. In principle the college is prepared to buy houses for the accommodation of married official fellows, but in recent years few such requests have been received. All fellows who have expressed a wish to be accommodated in a college house have in fact been provided with one. We are at present planning to build a house for a fellow, and should propose to meet any future needs by further building.

*College no. 2*

Not applicable. [College provides no housing accommodation.]

*College no. 3*

No. The college owns a certain number of houses which (so far as they are not required for college servants) are available to married tutorial fellows in order of seniority.

Owing to the age and character of the college houses, the tendency is for older married fellows to purchase their own houses. It was to encourage this tendency that the college decided to make loans available for house purchase, in the belief that it is the younger, newly elected fellow who derives most benefit from a college house or flat.

*College no. 4*

Not applicable. [College provides no housing accommodation.]

*College no. 5*

There is at present accommodation for 5 fellows and lecturers. The college considers the purchase of accommodation for lease to fellows who desire it.

*College no. 6*

The college has recently been able to provide a house for any fellow or lecturer provided reasonable notice is given. For certain houses priority is given to tutors.

*College no. 7*

The college possesses two houses and one flat suitable for fellows. When a vacancy occurs, fellows are invited to apply; preference would be given in order of seniority.

*College no. 8*

Accommodation is offered on the rare occasions when it becomes available. The college owns the lease of only two houses which are divided into flats.

*College no. 9*

No.

*College no. 10*

Not applicable. [College provides no housing accommodation.]

*College no. 11*

Normally available.

*College no. 12*

Accommodation is normally available to a tutorial fellow, but he may have to wait for it. The accommodation is allocated by decision of the Governing Body on an *ad hominem* basis. The college has recently acquired some flats, among the purposes of which is to provide temporary accommodation for newly elected fellows.

*College no. 13*

College houses or flats are normally available for any tutorial fellow but not for a lecturer.

*College no. 14*

No—if one of our few houses becomes available, the fellows normally have the choice in order of seniority unless the college should decide otherwise.

*College no. 15*

No—accommodation is limited; allocation made by seniority.

*College no. 16*

Accommodation is available to satisfy most requests by married tutorial fellows for occupation of a college house or flat. The allocation is in the complete discretion of the college, but consideration is given to the relative seniority of fellows seeking such accommodation. Requests for such accommodation made by fellows other than tutorial fellows or by lecturers can seldom be satisfied.

*College no. 17*

No. Thirteen houses are available for tutorial fellows and are offered to tutorial fellows who apply for them in order of seniority. Two of the houses available are momentarily vacant. There are no houses 'available' for other fellows or for lecturers.

*College no. 18*

No. The number of college houses available is considerably less than the number of married fellows. As and when a house falls vacant it is offered to fellows in order of seniority. Nevertheless, if the college so decides after consultation with its Finance Committee, a house may be purchased for a fellow and occupied by him at a strictly economic rent fixed by an independent valuer.

*College no. 19*

No. Applications for vacant accommodation are considered in the following order of preference:

(i) Tutors, lecturers, and officers of the college, in order of seniority in the college.
(ii) Other fellows, in order of seniority in the college.

*College no. 20*

For any fellow, yes. For lecturers who are not fellows, rarely, and not at present.

*College no. 21*

No fellow has a statutory entitlement to be accommodated. Normally a college house is available for a married tutor.

*College no. 22*

The policy of the college is, in the long-term, to make accommodation available for all tutorial fellows requiring it. As accommodation becomes free, the Bursar reports to the college. It is allocated according to seniority.

*College no. 23*

No. No fixed policy; each case determined *ad hoc*.

*College no. 31*

To date we have been able to make accommodation available to any fellow wanting it. We have no full-time lecturers and do not make accommodation available to part-time lecturers.

*College no. 32*

The question does not apply as the college has no houses.

*College no. 33*

No.

*College no. 34*

Yes.

*College no. 35*

No.

*College no. 41*

When a vacancy in a local college house occurs fellows are notified and may apply for tenancy. The property hitherto available is not city property and there is little demand for it.

*College no. 42*

No. Accommodation is allotted as available.

*College no. 43*

The college has 14 flats in north Oxford, mainly for married students, but several are available for married research fellows who, because of their short tenure, might find it difficult to obtain a house. Allocation is broadly by seniority and need.

*College no. 51*

Houses are supplied to all our tutors.

*College no. 52*

Yes.

583. *Questionnaire to the colleges*

On 19 November 1964 the Chairman of the Commission sent a letter to the heads of all colleges containing questions on the organization of Oxford. Many of the questions, and the replies to them, were reproduced in Part XIII of *Written Evidence*. The remainder dealt with emoluments and are reproduced here, together with the preamble to that section of the questionnaire.

## ARTICLES V (*b*) and (*c*)

(*b*) whether the present position about the emoluments of persons holding university posts along with college fellowships on the one hand and of persons holding university posts without college fellowships on the other is satisfactory;

(*c*) whether the present obscurity about the emoluments of college fellows and the disparity of these emoluments should be removed;

*Note.* In order to deal adequately with Articles V (*b*) and (*c*) of our terms of reference, it is necessary for us to have information about the present general practice; and we are asking questions now in order that we may have this information in time for our oral hearings over the next two terms. If your college has not yet revised its arrangements in the light of the new salaries for universities generally following from the recommendations made by the National Incomes Commission last spring, please indicate this clearly in your reply.

We shall have to come back at a later stage to those colleges which have not as yet completed their 'N.I.C. revision'. Until the replies to the present questions have been received and considered, it is impossible to say whether some of the complex and *ad hoc* arrangements with individuals (especially those involving payment from several sources simultaneously) will make it necessary for us to come back to all colleges for some further help.

(12) (a) What is the stipend of the head of the college?
    (b) What allowances does he receive? Please specify, and estimate if possible the value of allowances in kind.
    (c) What are the financial arrangements for his lodgings (other than those included under (b))?
    (d) Does he hold a paid university appointment? Please specify.

(13) What are the salary scales for
    (a) tutorial fellows (if there is more than one scale, please make clear to which category of tutorial fellow each applies; if tutorial fellows receive separate salaries in respect of their fellowship and in respect of their tutorship, please combine these when answering this question);
    (b) research fellows;
    (c) other stipendiary fellows (excluding holders of full-time college administrative posts);
    (d) stipendiary lecturers (i.e. lecturers brought into the FSSU)?

    For each scale in (a)–(d), please
    (i) make clear whether or not the university element in a joint stipend is included;
    (ii) give the date on which it came/will come into effect;
    (iii) list each point separately and show against each point the number of fellows or lecturers on that point on 1 January 1965 and give for each fellow or lecturer
        1. his age;
        2. the university (including departmental) post(s) he holds (if any);
        3. the appointment(s) he holds at other colleges (if any), making clear whether these are held under a joint arrangement or independently and whether the stipend shown is the total joint stipend or merely the contribution of the college towards it;
        4. the college office(s) he holds, together with the stipend of the office and whether any reduction is made in his fellowship or lecturership duties;
        5. (for non-tutorial fellows only) whether he holds a lecturership in the college, and if so the stipend of it;
        6. (for lecturers only) the duties for which the salary is paid.

(14) What retaining fees (or non-pensionable stipends) does the college pay its non-stipendiary lecturers? For each fee or stipend please give where possible the details asked for under (13) (iii) above.

(15) How much did the college pay for piece-rate teaching in 1964? If possible, please show separately the total amounts paid to
    (a) fellows of the college;
    (b) lecturers of the college;
    (c) fellows of other colleges;
    (d) others.

(16) Where a scale is not a strict age scale, how is the position of a fellow or lecturer on a scale determined?

(17) If there is more than one scale for tutorial fellows, what is the reason for this policy?

(18) Is there a norm laid down by regulation or convention governing the hours of teaching covered by a tutorial fellow's salary? If so, what is the norm? Is additional payment made if the norm is exceeded? Is a deduction made if the norm is not reached?

(19) If a tutorial fellow does piece-rate teaching for other colleges
   (a) does the fellow keep the payments;
   (b) does the college keep the payments?
   In either case, is there any restriction on the amount that may be done?

(20) What payments (over and above the scales quoted in (13)) are made to tutorial fellows
   (a) for exercising tutorial responsibilities other than teaching; please specify the duties and the numbers of tutorial fellows receiving each kind of payment;
   (b) for marriage;
   (c) for children;
   (d) for entertainment;
   (e) for books;
   (f) for any other purpose (excluding housing—see (22) below)? Please specify.

(21) Are any of the payments given in (20) made to
   (a) other classes of fellow, stipendiary or non-stipendiary (including professorial);
   (b) lecturers?
   Please specify.

(22) How many tutorial fellows
   (a) live in college rent free?
   (b) live in college paying rents? Please state the rents paid.
   (c) live in houses of which the college is landlord? Please state in each case
      (i) the net rateable value;
      (ii) *either* the rent paid (if any)
      (iii) *or* the reduction made in salary;
      (iv) the arrangements for repairs and decoration;
      (v) the arrangements about the payment of rates;
      (vi) the arrangements about capital improvements (e.g. the installation of central heating).
   (d) are assisted by the college in buying their own house? Please describe the nature of the assistance.

    (*e*) receive a housing allowance

       (i) in addition to (*a*);
       (ii) in addition to (*b*);
       (iii) in addition to (*c*);
       (iv) in addition to (*d*);
       (v) instead of (*a*), (*b*), (*c*), or (*d*)?

    In each case, please state the allowance made.

(23) To what extent are the arrangements described in (22) extended to

    (*a*) other classes of fellow, stipendiary or non-stipendiary (including profes-
    sorial);
    (*b*) lecturers?

Please specify.

(24) Is accommodation under (22) (*c*) normally available for any fellow or lecturer wanting it? If not, on what basis is the accommodation allocated?

(25) What other benefits are available to tutorial fellows?

    (*a*) to what free meals are they entitled?
    (*b*) does the college pay a subscription to the British United Provident
    Association on behalf of tutorial fellows and their families? If so, what
    is the total subscription for tutorial fellows for 1964?
    (*c*) does the college pay more than two-thirds of the FSSU contributions
    of tutorial fellows? If so, what proportion does it pay?
    (*d*) any others? Please specify.

(26) To what extent are the benefits described in (25) extended to

    (*a*) other classes of fellow, stipendiary or non-stipendiary (including pro-
    fessorial);
    (*b*) lecturers?

      Please specify.

# PART VI

---

# THE MAIN SOURCES OF STATISTICAL INFORMATION

---

584. The material in Parts I–V is based both upon university records, and on the inquiries carried out by the Commission. The main sources are described below, and the forms on which records are kept, and the questionnaires issued by the Commission, are reproduced in the Annex.

585. There are three main records of students. Every student must complete a matriculation form when he matriculates; the Registry maintains a card index containing details of the academic record of each student; and the colleges and other societies make returns to the University giving numbers of students in residence for the purpose of the returns which must be made to the UGC.

586. The matriculation forms record name, college or society, proposed course of study at Oxford, whether a college scholarship or exhibition is held, and date of matriculation. They also record father's name and occupation, address of parent or guardian, and date and place of birth, nationality, and education of the candidate for matriculation. The forms are completed by all students (except the small number of diploma and clinical students who do not become members of a college or society) and by any other persons who become members of the University, usually members of the academic staff who are not Oxford graduates, and who take a degree by incorporation (if graduates of Cambridge or Trinity College, Dublin) or by decree. At the end of each academic year the matriculation forms for the year are bound in alphabetical order, with those for men and women in separate volumes. No details are added to matriculation forms subsequent to matriculation. A copy of the matriculation form in use in 1964–5 is included in the Annex.

587. The Registry maintains a card index of each matriculated member of the University,[1] on which details of academic successes are recorded. The

---

[1] There is also a card index of non-matriculated diploma students.

cards are filed alphabetically, and no distinction is made between students in residence and others, since the University has no official information on this. There is a white card for each member of the University. This is reproduced in the Annex. On it are recorded name, college or society, and date of matriculation. Details are added of examination successes, prizes, and degrees taken, as these occur. Postgraduates reading for higher degrees (and medical students) also have a second, coloured, card, which gives appropriate details of their work, such as the name of the supervisor, the title of the thesis, the date at which the thesis was presented, and with what result. There are several of these cards. That for the B.Litt., B.Sc., and D.Phil. is reproduced in the Annex.

588. Each postgraduate reading for a higher degree has a time-limit within which he must take the examination or submit his thesis, or his status will lapse. The cards for postgraduates reading for higher degrees are kept separately until this time-limit has expired, and a list of them is published each term by the Committee for Advanced Studies.[1] The published list does not distinguish between students in residence and others, and some persons included in it may have given up their studies altogether. And it does not give all postgraduates, since most diploma students are not included.

589. The UGC requires returns of student numbers from universities twice a year.[2] The first, in summary form, is of the number of students at the beginning of the academic year. The second, which is much more detailed, relates to the whole academic year (that is, all students who had been in residence at some time during the year), and is submitted in the following October. For each return the Registry collects information from each college or society. For the main return details are collected of the number of first-degree students by School and year, and of other students by course or subject group. In addition, information required by the UGC on university and home residence is collected, and there are questions on the financial assistance received by students. The Michaelmas Term return collects student numbers by type of course and subject group, and the numbers of those entering the University for the first time by type of course. (A more detailed analysis of the latter group is possible using the matriculation forms and is published in the *Gazette*.) The forms used are reproduced in the Annex.

590. In addition to the above university records of students, the University

---

[1] Candidates for the Diploma in Law and Diploma in Geochemistry, and for Part II Chemistry and Metallurgy are also included in the list.

[2] The description relates to the position in 1964–5. The arrangements for 1965–6 are different.

maintains a list of members of the University,[1] and colleges publish lists of their members receiving tuition or supervision. Both lists are published each year in the *Calendar*. The college lists do not distinguish undergraduates and postgraduates and, for 1964–5, all postgraduates registered for a higher degree, whether in residence or not, are included.

591. Some of the statistics given in Parts II, III, and IV are based on a sample of 1958 matriculations. A one-in-two sample of names was taken from the matriculation forms for 1958–9, and further information was recorded from the matriculation forms, the card indexes, and the records of the Appointments Committee.

### COLLEGE ADMISSIONS

592. The university records about individuals admitted by colleges are those given at matriculation. But for admissions of men since 1963–4 the Admissions Office (which was set up by the colleges and is not a university body) has more detailed records. For each candidate for the entrance competition for admission as an undergraduate there is a record card. Most of the analyses of 1964–5 admissions of men given in Part II are based on these record cards. Each card gives name, school, age, number of terms in sixth form, subject for entrance examination, intended subject at Oxford, college of first choice, whether also a candidate for Cambridge, and results of GCE O, A, and S level examinations (or the equivalent). For candidates who are accepted, the college and whether a scholarship or exhibition was awarded are entered on the card. The card is reproduced in the Annex.

### THE COMMISSION'S SURVEYS

593. Four surveys were carried out during Michaelmas Term 1964.[2] One was of organizers of tutorial work in the colleges and other societies. One was of all members of the academic staff. The remaining two consisted of samples of undergraduates and postgraduates respectively.

594. In each survey the questionnaires were sent to the respondents for completion by them. The dispatch of the questionnaires, and of reminders

[1] The list gives term of matriculation and degrees with the year in which received. It includes:
- (a) all members of the University under supervision or instruction;
- (b) all members of Convocation;
- (c) all non-graduates for one year after going out of residence;
- (d) all graduates other than members of Convocation for eight years from matriculation;
- (e) other members who went down before 1 October 1963, who had paid dues continuously from the time of their matriculation until 1 October 1963, and who are nominated for inclusion by their college.

[2] A questionnaire was also addressed to schools (see Part II, para. 182); it is reproduced in the Annex. In addition, part of one questionnaire addressed to colleges dealt with emoluments. The questions are reproduced in Part V, para. 583.

to those who did not reply by the date given, and the editing of the questionnaires was carried out by the Commission's staff. The questionnaires were then sent to the Atlas Computer Laboratory, Harwell, where, by courtesy of the Director, the information was transferred to punched cards and processed on the Atlas Computer. The first questionnaires were sent out on 7 October 1964 and the field work and editing were completed by 23 November 1964. Computing time for the processing was 113 minutes. Details of each survey are given below, followed by a comparison of those estimates which can be obtained from more than one survey or from official university records. The questionnaires are reproduced in the annex.

## THE TUTORIAL ORGANIZERS SURVEY

595. The survey covered the college teaching arrangements in Michaelmas Term 1964 for all undergraduates reading for an Honour School. There was a questionnaire for each of the 24 Honour Schools, and for Classical Honour Moderations, in each college or society. The persons who would be able to complete the questionnaires could not be identified beforehand, and the arrangements for the field work were therefore different from those for the other surveys. A set of 25 questionnaires was sent to each Senior Tutor (or the corresponding college officer) with a request that he distribute them appropriately for completion, and collect and return the completed questionnaires. This was done in all cases.

596. While the survey was in process Professor Beeston pointed out that the inquiry was inappropriate to Oriental Studies where teaching is organized by the faculty rather than by the colleges. It was agreed that Professor Beeston would provide details of teaching in Oriental Studies, and that the Oriental Studies returns would be excluded from the survey proper.

## THE ACADEMIC STAFF SURVEY

597. The survey covered all members of the academic staff (including outside grants staff) in post at 1 October 1964, except those on leave of absence. The information from which the list of names was compiled was obtained mainly from the Chest, but for some departmental and outside grants posts information was obtained from the department concerned. And for holders of college, but not of university, posts names were taken from the 1965 *Calendar* (which was in proof when the list was compiled).

598. The categories of staff who were included were all teaching and research staff in the main grades whose salaries are a charge on central university funds (or on trust funds such as the Nuffield Medical Benefaction),[1] i.e. professors, readers, lecturers,[2] senior research officers, tutors, and

---

[1] Except those known to have leave of absence from the University.
[2] Except that one head of house holding a CUF lecturership was excluded.

equivalent posts; departmental and outside grants teaching and research posts; and all college fellows and lecturers other than honorary or emeritus fellows and those holding purely administrative posts. A few junior posts such as research assistant were excluded, however. Departmental and outside grants staff were only included if their post was in the 'teaching and research' category used by the Chest, and their salary was at least the minimum of the national scale for assistant lecturers (except that a few exceptions were made in the case of slightly lower salaries where the post appeared to be of the same nature as those with salaries above the assistant lecturer minimum).

599. Heads of houses were excluded, as were library and other staff in the academic community. At the editing stage 36 persons were judged to be part-time and were not included in the analyses. They include college non-stipendiary lecturers who did not hold any other post, part-time university lecturers also holding a university library or museum post, holders of part-time university posts and no college post, and staff in clinical medicine holding joint appointments with the hospital.

600. The questionnaires were sent out on 13 October 1964 with a request for a reply by 24 October. A letter signed by the Chairman was sent to those who had not replied by that date, and about a week later members of the Commission contacted all those from whom a questionnaire had still not been received. As a result a very high response rate was achieved. To check-in replies as they arrived, and to keep track of the response, use was made of a method devised at the Social Survey,[1] in which there is a 'control envelope' for each person which can be used to keep duplicate address slips and any correspondence which may be received. By moving the envelopes from one file to another as the questionnaire was received, edited, and dispatched there was always an up-to-date record of the state of the field work. This method was also used in the Undergraduate and Postgraduate Surveys, and proved most effective.

601. Of the 1,292 in the survey, 66 proved either to be on leave of absence or not to fall within the definition of the academic staff adopted, and there were a further 36 non-respondents. Thus the response rate was 92·1 per cent. of all questionnaires sent out, and 97·1 per cent. of those within the scope of the survey. Of the 1,190 returns, 1,154 were from full-time staff.[2] Table 357 gives details of response.

[1] Scott, C., 'Research on mail surveys', *J. R. Statist. Soc.* A, vol. 124, 1961. See Appendix 1.
[2] For the purpose of the analysis of emoluments in Part V, some 14 of these were, however, treated as part-time. They were stipendiary college lecturers with a stipend below £500 per annum, and no other post, and fellows with stipends substantially below the usual rates.

**Table 357.** *Details of response in Academic Staff Survey*

| OXFORD | | NUMBER |
|---|---|---|
| Questionnaires sent out | | 1,292 |
| Outside scope of survey | | 66 |
| on leave of absence | 41 | |
| not teaching and research post | 10 | |
| retired or taken post elsewhere | 14 | |
| not yet taken up appointment | 1 | |
| Non-respondents | | 36 |
| refusals | 5 | |
| questionnaire not completed | 2 | |
| deceased since 1 October | 3 | |
| reply received late | 2 | |
| no reply received | 24 | |
| Questionnaires completed | | 1,190 |
| by full-time staff | 1,154 | |
| by part-time staff | 36 | |

SOURCE: Academic Staff Survey.

602. There was a total of 99 persons in the survey who were registered as students for a higher degree in 1963–4. Details are:

| | |
|---|---|
| Central university post | 18 |
| university lecturer | 6 |
| senior research officer | 2 |
| CUF lecturer | 3 |
| faculty lecturer | 3 |
| others | 4 |
| Departmental post | 5 |
| Outside grants post | 17 |
| College post only | 59 |
| tutorial fellow | 8 |
| junior research fellow or research fellow | 34 |
| lecturer | 17 |

603. The sample numbers in the main breakdowns used in Part V are given in Tables 358 and 359. Where cells in these and other breakdowns would contain only one individual, he has been transferred to the most closely comparable cell. The total numbers in the two tables do not agree because some values of the classifying variables were not ascertained. And the tabulations in Part V may be based on different numbers where the variable tabulated may sometimes be not ascertained.[1] The differences are trivial except in the case of time spent on academic activities, the estimates of which are discussed in paras. 478–84 of Part V. Tables 360–3 give fuller details of the proportion of ascertained values than is given in Table 303.

[1] The numbers on which are based tabulations of the Undergraduate and Postgraduate Surveys also vary slightly because of values which were not ascertained in a trivial number of cases.

**Table 358.** *Numbers in Academic Staff Survey by post and subject group*

OXFORD

NUMBER

| Subject group | Professor | Reader | University lecturer with tutorial fellowship | University lecturer without tutorial fellowship | CUF and special lecturer | Other university staff with tutorial fellowship | Other senior research staff | Other university and outside grants staff | College post only: teaching | College post only: research | All posts |
|---|---|---|---|---|---|---|---|---|---|---|---|
| Arts | 45 | 16 | 21 | 33 | 210 | 8 | 3 | 26 | 32 | 45 | 439 |
| Social studies | 9 | 11 | — | 18 | 54 | 4 | 4 | 20 | 19 | 24 | 163 |
| Science | 23 | 29 | 64 | 78 | 22 | 25 | 33 | 123 | 15 | 23 | 435 |
| Medicine | 10 | 11 | 5 | 31 | — | — | 20 | 40 | — | — | 117 |
| All subjects | 87 | 67 | 90 | 160 | 286 | 37 | 60 | 209 | 66 | 92 | 1,154 |

SOURCE: Academic Staff Survey.

P

**Table 359.** *Numbers in Academic Staff Survey by subject group, years in academic life, and years at Oxford*

OXFORD                                                                                        NUMBER

|  | Years in academic life | | | | | All |
| --- | --- | --- | --- | --- | --- | --- |
|  | None | 1–5 | 6–10 | 11–20 | 21 and over |  |
| SUBJECT GROUP |  |  |  |  |  |  |
| Arts | 15 | 82 | 63 | 171 | 105 | 436 |
| Social studies | 11 | 40 | 37 | 55 | 20 | 163 |
| Science | 31 | 147 | 74 | 117 | 58 | 427 |
| Medicine | 5 | 41 | 18 | 29 | 23 | 116 |
| YEARS IN ACADEMIC POST AT OXFORD |  |  |  |  |  |  |
| None | 62 | 29 | 7 | 8 | 1 | 107 |
| 1–5 | — | 281 | 64 | 54 | 9 | 408 |
| 6–10 | — | — | 121 | 53 | 11 | 185 |
| 11–20 | — | — | — | 257 | 54 | 311 |
| 21 and over | — | — | — | — | 131 | 131 |
| All | 62 | 310 | 192 | 372 | 206 | 1,142 |

SOURCE: Academic Staff Survey.

604. Details of the main classification of posts as used in Table 358 and in presenting the survey results in Part V are as follows. The category 'university lecturer' comprises full-time university lecturers and lecturers in clinical medicine on Scales II and III. 'Other senior research staff' includes all senior non-teaching staff: directors, senior research officers (and others paid on the same scale such as graduate assistants), research officers in clinical medicine paid on Scales II and III, and some senior research appointments made *ad personam*.[1] 'Other university and outside grants staff' includes, besides outside grants staff: first assistants; tutors in the Department and Institute of Education, in the Department of Social and Administrative Studies, and in clinical medicine; faculty lecturers, departmental demonstrators, junior lecturers in mathematics, and lecturers in clinical medicine paid on Scale I, other than those holding a tutorial fellowship; research officers in the Institute for Research in Agricultural Economics and the Institutes of Economics and Statistics, and of Commonwealth Studies; and holders of departmental research posts.

### THE UNDERGRADUATE SURVEY

605. The survey covered a one-in-six sample of first-, second-, and third-year undergraduates reading for the B.A. The sample was drawn from the 1963–4 and 1962–3 matriculation forms for second- and third-year undergraduates, and from lists supplied by the colleges for the first year.

[1] Other than those holding a tutorial fellowship.

Table 360. *Percentage of academic staff for whom hours of work in term were ascertained, by post. 1963–4*

OXFORD

PERCENTAGE

| Work in term | Professor | Reader | University lecturer with tutorial fellowship | University lecturer without tutorial fellowship | CUF and special lecturer | Other university staff with tutorial fellowship | Other senior research staff | Other university and outside grants staff | College post only: teaching | College post only: research | All posts |
|---|---|---|---|---|---|---|---|---|---|---|---|
| Preparing teaching | 82 | 73 | 85 | 80 | 82 | 100 | 80 | 68 | 74 | 81 | 79 |
| Advising students | 76 | 65 | 83 | 75 | 76 | 97 | 75 | 62 | 67 | 72 | 74 |
| Administration | 79 | 68 | 76 | 79 | 69 | 79 | 82 | 68 | 60 | 70 | 73 |
| Admissions | 71 | 68 | 71 | 76 | 65 | 85 | 76 | 62 | 63 | 75 | 69 |
| Examining | 73 | 62 | 74 | 69 | 68 | 74 | 71 | 59 | 56 | 68 | 67 |
| Preparing teaching, admin., etc. | 59 | 48 | 54 | 61 | 48 | 56 | 57 | 51 | 42 | 61 | 53 |
| Study and research | 72 | 67 | 65 | 70 | 66 | 82 | 75 | 67 | 74 | 70 | 69 |
| External examining | 74 | 58 | 71 | 64 | 64 | 74 | 63 | 59 | 51 | 60 | 64 |
| Consulting | 68 | 57 | 72 | 61 | 65 | 62 | 65 | 57 | 49 | 61 | 62 |
| Other external work | 56 | 48 | 63 | 59 | 62 | 62 | 61 | 53 | 51 | 56 | 58 |
| External work | 50 | 45 | 57 | 54 | 54 | 56 | 55 | 52 | 44 | 53 | 51 |
| Learned societies and conferences | 74 | 62 | 77 | 72 | 68 | 79 | 73 | 64 | 63 | 68 | 69 |
| Other professional work in Oxford | 71 | 67 | 76 | 69 | 64 | 76 | 57 | 59 | 53 | 67 | 65 |
| Other work | 45 | 38 | 52 | 51 | 51 | 53 | 49 | 47 | 37 | 47 | 48 |
| All above activities | 33 | 33 | 38 | 40 | 35 | 32 | 45 | 38 | 28 | 32 | 36 |

SOURCE: Academic Staff Survey.

NOTES

1. The percentage ascertained is the number who gave an estimate as a percentage of all except those who were not in Oxford in 1963–4.
2. 'Other work' comprises external work, learned societies and conferences, and other professional work in Oxford.

**Table 361.** *Percentage of academic staff for whom work in term was ascertained, by subject group.* 1963–4

OXFORD                                                                    PERCENTAGE

| Work in term | Arts | Social studies | Science | Medicine | All subjects |
|---|---|---|---|---|---|
| Preparing teaching | 79 | 76 | 84 | 68 | 79 |
| Advising students | 71 | 72 | 80 | 60 | 74 |
| Administration | 68 | 61 | 82 | 71 | 73 |
| Admissions | 66 | 66 | 75 | 63 | 69 |
| Examining | 63 | 64 | 74 | 60 | 67 |
| Preparing teaching, administration, etc. | 46 | 49 | 62 | 51 | 53 |
| Study and research | 65 | 61 | 74 | 73 | 69 |
| External examining | 62 | 54 | 72 | 51 | 64 |
| Consulting | 59 | 57 | 71 | 52 | 62 |
| Other external work | 54 | 53 | 66 | 49 | 58 |
| External work | 48 | 43 | 59 | 41 | 51 |
| Learned societies and conferences | 68 | 56 | 76 | 66 | 69 |
| Other professional work in Oxford | 64 | 54 | 73 | 56 | 65 |
| Other work | 45 | 44 | 56 | 39 | 48 |
| All above activities | 30 | 33 | 43 | 37 | 36 |

SOURCE: Academic Staff Survey.
NOTE: See notes to Table 360.

606. In drawing the sample stratification by college and subject was used to the greatest possible extent. For the first year colleges were asked to classify expected matriculands into arts (including social studies) and science undergraduates. For the second year matriculation forms were used. Since they had not been bound it was possible to stratify by college and proposed subject. For the third year bound matriculation forms (in alphabetical order) were used and a one-in-six sample was drawn, until a series of 'quotas' by college and proposed subject were filled so as to give approximately the same balance by subject as in the published figures on student numbers (*Gazette*, vol. xciv, p. 308), and by college as in the Registry records.

607. The method of selection will have led to under-representation of (the very small number of) those who originally intended to work for a

**Table 362.** *Percentage of academic staff for whom hours of work in vacation were ascertained, by post. 1963–4*

OXFORD

PERCENTAGE

| Work in vacation | Professor | Reader | University lecturer with tutorial fellowship | University lecturer without tutorial fellowship | CUF and special lecturer | Other university staff with tutorial fellowship | Other senior research staff | Other university and outside grants staff | College post only: teaching | College post only: research | All posts |
|---|---|---|---|---|---|---|---|---|---|---|---|
| Preparing teaching | 51 | 53 | 59 | 65 | 50 | 71 | 67 | 56 | 53 | 63 | 57 |
| Advising students | 59 | 50 | 60 | 60 | 49 | 65 | 65 | 53 | 42 | 67 | 55 |
| Administration | 64 | 55 | 54 | 61 | 47 | 53 | 67 | 59 | 49 | 61 | 56 |
| Admissions | 55 | 62 | 70 | 68 | 65 | 74 | 71 | 56 | 53 | 67 | 64 |
| Examining | 58 | 58 | 68 | 66 | 65 | 62 | 69 | 53 | 51 | 63 | 62 |
| Preparing teaching, admin., etc. | 37 | 38 | 39 | 47 | 30 | 32 | 53 | 47 | 33 | 53 | 40 |
| Study and research | 55 | 62 | 55 | 59 | 49 | 65 | 65 | 59 | 63 | 58 | 56 |
| External examining | 60 | 62 | 73 | 58 | 60 | 76 | 63 | 58 | 47 | 54 | 60 |
| Consulting | 56 | 57 | 66 | 57 | 57 | 59 | 63 | 53 | 40 | 56 | 57 |
| Other external work | 50 | 42 | 56 | 52 | 53 | 71 | 61 | 51 | 44 | 51 | 52 |
| External work | 41 | 40 | 52 | 48 | 48 | 59 | 51 | 48 | 40 | 47 | 47 |
| Learned societies and conferences | 62 | 63 | 73 | 69 | 58 | 79 | 69 | 60 | 60 | 56 | 63 |
| Other professional work in Oxford | 60 | 53 | 68 | 59 | 56 | 74 | 53 | 56 | 49 | 56 | 58 |
| Other work | 35 | 33 | 46 | 43 | 42 | 56 | 43 | 42 | 37 | 40 | 42 |
| All above activities | 24 | 30 | 26 | 30 | 23 | 24 | 41 | 32 | 19 | 25 | 27 |

SOURCE: Academic Staff Survey.
NOTE: See notes to Table 360.

**Table 363.** *Percentage of academic staff for whom hours of work in vacation were ascertained, by subject group. 1963–4*

OXFORD                                                                    PERCENTAGE

| Work in vacation | Arts | Social studies | Science | Medicine | All subjects |
|---|---|---|---|---|---|
| Preparing teaching | 48 | 52 | 70 | 50 | 57 |
| Advising students | 49 | 45 | 67 | 50 | 55 |
| Administration | 49 | 47 | 67 | 53 | 56 |
| Admissions | 61 | 54 | 73 | 52 | 64 |
| Examining | 60 | 53 | 71 | 48 | 62 |
| Preparing teaching, admin., etc. | 29 | 36 | 53 | 39 | 40 |
| Study and research | 50 | 46 | 65 | 63 | 56 |
| External examining | 57 | 50 | 72 | 42 | 60 |
| Consulting | 51 | 52 | 68 | 41 | 57 |
| Other external work | 48 | 47 | 63 | 38 | 52 |
| External work | 42 | 42 | 59 | 33 | 47 |
| Learned societies and conferences | 58 | 54 | 73 | 60 | 63 |
| Other professional work in Oxford | 54 | 46 | 69 | 46 | 58 |
| Other work | 38 | 38 | 50 | 30 | 42 |
| All above activities | 20 | 25 | 35 | 30 | 27 |

SOURCE: Academic Staff Survey.

NOTE: See notes to Table 360.

postgraduate qualification, but subsequently changed to a B.A. course. Otherwise there is no evidence that the sample does not reflect the characteristics of all first-degree students (except those in their fourth year) fairly closely.

608. For the sample selection, the year of an undergraduate was year from matriculation. But undergraduates with Senior Status usually take one fewer than the normal number of years, and begin their course with second-year work. For the analyses these undergraduates were classified as second year in their first year of residence, etc.

609. The questionnaires were sent out on 29 October 1964, and return was requested by 2 November. Those who had not returned a questionnaire by then were contacted by one of a team of postgraduates and recent graduates employed for this purpose, and encouraged to do so.

**Table 364.** *Details of response in Undergraduate Survey*

| OXFORD | | NUMBER |
|---|---|---|
| Questionnaires sent out | | 1,172 |
| Outside scope of survey | | 37 |
| did not come up | 4 | |
| gone down | 24 | |
| deceased | 2 | |
| not an undergraduate | 6 | |
| fourth year | 1 | |
| Non-respondents | | 66 |
| refusals | 4 | |
| questionnaire not completed | 1 | |
| away from Oxford | 16 | |
| no reply received | 45 | |
| Questionnaires completed | | 1,069 |

SOURCE: Undergraduate Survey.

610. Of the 1,172 questionnaires sent out, 1,069 were completed. Of the remainder, 37 were outside the scope of the survey, and there were 66 non-respondents. Table 364 gives details. Among those outside the scope of the survey was one man in his fourth year. He was an undergraduate with Senior Status, in his third year of residence, but having Senior Status was assumed to be doing fourth-year work. Those 'away from Oxford' include linguists spending a year in the country of the language they were studying. The over-all response rate was 91·2 per cent. Among those within the scope of the survey the response was 94·2 per cent.

**Table 365.** *Numbers in Undergraduate Survey by subject group and year*

| OXFORD | | | | NUMBER |
|---|---|---|---|---|
| Subject group | Year | | | All years |
| | First | Second | Third | |
| Arts | 173 | 172 | 151 | 496 |
| Social studies | 79 | 65 | 72 | 216 |
| Science | 127 | 124 | 106 | 357 |
| All subjects | 379 | 361 | 329 | 1,069 |

SOURCE: Undergraduate Survey.

611. Table 365 gives the sample numbers in the main breakdown used in Part III. Sample numbers by School and college are given in Tables 100 and 102.

THE POSTGRADUATE SURVEY

612. The survey covered a one-in-two sample of students reading for higher degrees who in Michaelmas Term 1964 were in their second or subsequent year of research in Oxford, and who were in residence at the time of the survey. The method of selection was to take every second name from the list of students under the Committee for Advanced Studies on the first day of Hilary Term 1964 (*Gazette*, vol. xciv, pp. 579–661), as amended to the end of Hilary Term (*Gazette*, vol. xciv, pp. 923–32). This method of selection achieved stratification by faculty board and degree since the lists are arranged in this way, but in addition the names under Social Studies were further stratified according to college thus: Nuffield, St. Antony's, and others. Candidates for the Diplomas in Law and Geochemistry and for Part II Chemistry and Part II Metallurgy, 1963, were excluded. Candidates for Part II Chemistry and Part II Metallurgy, 1964, were included. This preliminary sample therefore included all those who might have been working for a higher degree during 1963–4 (except those working for B.Mus., B.C.L., or B.D.) plus those working for Part II Chemistry or Part II Metallurgy.

613. The preliminary sample was arranged by colleges, and lists circulated to colleges during August 1964. College secretaries were asked (*a*) to indicate those on the lists who were expected to be in residence during Michaelmas Term 1964, and (*b*) to add the names of those who were expected to be in residence during Michaelmas Term 1964 for their second or subsequent year of work for the degrees of B.Mus., B.C.L., or B.D. (every other one of which was included in the final sample list). Annotated returns were received from every society except one Permanent Private Hall. Although not asked to do so, several colleges indicated individuals who would be in residence but had been elected to tutorial fellowships. Such names were not included in the final sample. The preliminary sample contained 1,015 names, and the final sample to whom questionnaires were sent contained 488 names.

614. The sampling process was the best that could be devised in the circumstances. It had the shortcomings that colleges could not have been sure in August who would come into residence in Michaelmas Term and the names of some who did come into residence may have been excluded. There are no reliable tests that can be applied to the sample to discover how adequately it represents the population from which it was intended it should be drawn.

615. The questionnaires were sent out on 19 October 1964 with a request for their return by 26 October. Those who did not reply were contacted during the following week by the same team of assistants as referred to in para. 609.

**Table 366.** *Details of response in Postgraduate Survey*

| OXFORD | | NUMBER |
|---|---|---|
| Questionnaires sent out | | 488 |
| Outside scope of survey | | 41 |
| completed degree | 3 | |
| gone down | 30 | |
| not reading for higher degree | 4 | |
| holders of posts | 4 | |
| Non-respondents | | 61 |
| refusals | 2 | |
| questionnaire not completed | 2 | |
| away from Oxford | 20 | |
| no reply received | 34 | |
| not known in college | 3 | |
| Questionnaires completed | | 386 |

SOURCE: Postgraduate Survey.

616. Details of response are in Table 366. Of the 488 questionnaires sent out, 386 were completed satisfactorily, giving an over-all response rate of 79·1 per cent. But 41 were certainly not within the scope of the survey. When these are allowed for the response rate is 86·4 per cent. Among those excluded there was a small number who had changed to an undergraduate or diploma course, or had obtained appointment to a full-time teaching post such as a tutorial fellowship, university lecturership, or a full-time departmental demonstratorship. The remainder had either completed their degree, or had gone down. The total number who had completed their degree or gone down was, however, almost certainly greater than the 33 shown in Table 366. It was impossible to contact a number of the non-respondents, and it is likely that a high proportion of those out of Oxford at the time of the survey or shown as not known at their college had gone down, and that some of the others from whom no reply was received had also gone down. The true response rate was therefore almost certainly higher than 86 per cent.

617. There was some overlap between the Postgraduate Survey and the Academic Staff Survey, since junior research fellows, college lecturers, and holders of departmental and outside grants research posts who were registered as reading for higher degrees were included in the former. There were altogether 12 who were included in both the surveys for this reason.

618. The sample numbers for the main breakdowns used in Part IV are given in Tables 367–9.

**Table 367.** *Numbers in Postgraduate Survey by subject group, year, and degree aimed at*

OXFORD                                                                                          NUMBER

| | Subject group | | | All subjects |
|---|---|---|---|---|
| | Arts | Social studies | Science and medicine | |
| YEAR (MICHAELMAS TERM 1964) | | | | |
| Second | 89 | 28 | 75 | 192 |
| Third | 40 | 11 | 87 | 138 |
| Fourth | 10 | 2 | 28 | 40 |
| Fifth and subsequent | 5 | — | 11 | 16 |
| DEGREE AIMED AT | | | | |
| B.Litt. | 22 | 8 | — | 30 |
| B.Sc. | — | — | 7 | 7 |
| B.Phil. | 24 | 4 | — | 28 |
| B.C.L. | — | 3 | — | 3 |
| D.Phil. | 98 | 26 | 194 | 318 |
| All | 144 | 41 | 201 | 386 |

SOURCE: Postgraduate Survey.

### COMPARISONS BETWEEN THE SURVEY RESULTS AND OTHER SOURCES

619. It is possible to compare some of the estimates of teaching given by the teachers in the Tutorial Organizers and Academic Staff Surveys with each other, and with estimates given by the taught in the Undergraduate and Postgraduate Surveys. It is also possible to compare the estimates of undergraduate numbers from the Tutorial Organizers and Undergraduate Surveys with the official university figures obtained from the college student numbers returns.

### Student numbers

620. According to the college returns there were 7,171 first-degree students (other than those reading for the Second B.M.) in 1964–5. The Tutorial Organizers Survey gave a total of 7,129 in the Michaelmas Term, but this total excludes 33 reading for the Pass School. The two totals are thus in very good agreement. Those reading for the Pass School were all men, and are included under arts. Thus the college returns show almost the same distribution by subject group as the Tutorial Organizers Survey, but the number of men is slightly higher, and the number of women slightly lower. The distributions by year are different because of the different treatment

**Table 368.** *Numbers in Postgraduate Survey by college group, first degrees, and marital status.*

OXFORD                                                                                    NUMBER

| | College group | | | | All societies |
|---|---|---|---|---|---|
| | Men's societies | Women's colleges | Nuffield and St. Antony's | Linacre | |
| UNIVERSITY OF FIRST DEGREES | | | | | |
| Oxford | 149 | 14 | 4 | — | 167 |
| Oxford and another U.K. university | 7 | — | 3 | — | 10 |
| Another U.K. university | 35 | 12 | 3 | 13 | 63 |
| Other U.K. universities (two degrees) | 5 | 1 | — | — | 6 |
| Overseas | 43 | 10 | 7 | 9 | 69 |
| Overseas and Oxford | 7 | 1 | 2 | — | 10 |
| Overseas and another U.K. university | 1 | — | — | 2 | 3 |
| Overseas (two degrees) | 33 | 5 | 4 | 13 | 55 |
| No degree | 1 | 1 | — | 1 | 3 |
| MARITAL STATUS | | | | | |
| Single | 184 | 28 | 13 | 18 | 243 |
| Married, husband or wife not in Oxford | 3 | 3 | — | 1 | 7 |
| Married with children, family not in Oxford | 2 | 1 | 1 | 3 | 7 |
| Married, husband or wife in Oxford | 59 | 7 | 3 | 4 | 73 |
| Married with children, family in Oxford | 33 | 5 | 6 | 12 | 56 |
| All | 281 | 44 | 23 | 38 | 386 |

SOURCE: Postgraduate Survey.

**Table 369.** *Numbers in Postgraduate Survey by age*

| OXFORD | NUMBER |
|---|---|
| Under 22 | 4 |
| 22–25 | 232 |
| 26–29 | 98 |
| 30 and over | 52 |
| All | 386 |

SOURCE: Postgraduate Survey.

**Table 370.** *Estimates of undergraduate numbers from different sources. Michaelmas Term 1964*

OXFORD                                                                    NUMBER

| Undergraduates reading for B.A. | College returns to University | Tutorial Organizers Survey | Undergraduate Survey | |
|---|---|---|---|---|
| YEAR | | | | |
| First | 2,445 | 2,340 | 2, 414 | |
| Second | 2,331 | 2,363 | 2,300 | |
| Third | 2,042 | 2,117 | 2,096 | |
| Fourth and subsequent | 353 | 309 | — | (353) |
| SUBJECT GROUP | | | | |
| Arts | 3,478 | 3,435 | 3,160 | (3,407) |
| Social studies | 1,342 | 1,344 | 1,376 | (1,399) |
| Science | 2,351 | 2,350 | 2,274 | (2,357) |
| SEX | | | | |
| Men | 6,002 | 5,981 | 5,695 | (5,991) |
| Women | 1,169 | 1,148 | 1,115 | (1,172) |
| All | 7,171 | 7,129 | 6,810 | (7,163) |

SOURCE: Registry; Tutorial Organizers Survey; Undergraduate Survey.

NOTES

1. The numbers based on college returns are for the year 1964–5.
2. The entries under Tutorial Organizers Survey include the undergraduates in Oriental Studies as given in Table 132. They exclude the 33 undergraduates reading for the Pass School.
3. The sample numbers in the Undergraduate Survey have been multiplied by 6·37 to give estimates of the total population allowing for non-response. The figures in brackets include those in the fourth and subsequent years as given in the college returns.

of undergraduates with Senior Status. In the college returns they are classified by year of residence, and in the survey according to the probable year of the course they were taking. The survey gives a smaller total in the first year for this reason. In all, 152 of those entering the University in Michaelmas Term 1964 took Senior Status. Since not all these will necessarily have embarked on an undergraduate course, the discrepancy for the first year can be explained in this way. The higher totals from the survey for the second and third years will also be a consequence of the treatment of Senior Status, but not the lower total for the fourth and subsequent years. The reason for this is probably that some tutors classified undergraduates who were spending a fourth year through changing course or for some similar reason according to the year of the work they were doing instead of their year of residence.

621. Undergraduates in the fourth and subsequent years were excluded from the Undergraduate Survey. If they are added to the estimates based on the survey, a total of 7,163 is obtained, in very good agreement with the college returns and the Tutorial Organizers Survey. There is very close agreement with the college returns on the number of men and women, but arts subjects are slightly under-represented (by about 2 per cent.) and social studies slightly over-represented (by about 4 per cent.). Undergraduates with Senior Status were classified by year in the same way in the Undergraduate Survey as in the Tutorial Organizers Survey. Table 370 shows, therefore, that in the Undergraduate Survey the first year was somewhat over-represented and the second and third years slightly under-represented. Sampling fluctuations will account for part of the discrepancies, but the method of drawing the sample will also be partly responsible. The sampling fraction was the same for each year, and the sample was drawn from those who had matriculated, without taking account of wastage since matriculation in the second- and third-year samples. This would be expected to lead to discrepancies in the direction observed.

**Table 371.** *Estimates from different sources of tutorial hours given to undergraduates. Michaelmas Term 1964*

OXFORD                                                                                    NUMBER

| Tutorial hours given to undergraduates by | Tutorial Organizers Survey | Academic Staff Survey | Undergraduate Survey | Postgraduate Survey |
|---|---|---|---|---|
| Academic staff | 6,687 | 6,552 | .. | .. |
| Postgraduates | 429 | .. | .. | 464 |
| Others | 351 | .. | .. | .. |
| All | 7,467 | .. | 6,720 | .. |

SOURCE: The surveys specified in the heading.

NOTES

1. The entries under Tutorial Organizers Survey do not include tutorials given to the 33 undergraduates reading for the Pass School, but tutorials given in Oriental Studies are included.
2. The figure from the Academic Staff Survey includes tutorials given by part-time staff, and the actual hours reported have been multiplied by 1·03 to allow for non-response.
3. The figure from the Undergraduate Survey is the estimated tutorial hours (of teachers) for the sample multiplied by 6·37 to give an estimate (allowing for non-response) for all undergraduates other than those in the fourth and subsequent years.
4. The figure from the Postgraduate Survey is the estimated tutorial hours from the sample multiplied by 2 to give an estimate for all postgraduates. There is no allowance for non-response since no accurate figure can be obtained, but if such an allowance were made the figure in the table would be somewhat larger. Tutorials given by postgraduates in their first year, or by diploma students (which are likely to be few in number) are not included.

## Tutorials

622. Estimates of tutorials given to undergraduates can be obtained (in part at least) from each of the four surveys. Table 371 gives details, all in the form of total hours given by the teachers. From the Tutorial Organizers Survey[1] 7,467 hours were reported (excluding those given to undergraduates reading for the Pass School), of which 6,687 were given by members of the academic staff. The estimate from the Academic Staff Survey[2] is 2 per cent. less than this (after making an allowance for non-response).

623. According to the Tutorial Organizers Survey, 429 hours were given by postgraduates. A fully comparable estimate from the Postgraduate Survey cannot be obtained, since first-year postgraduates were not included, and an accurate allowance for non-response cannot be made. The survey figures give an estimate of 464 hours, without an allowance for non-response. Thus the survey figure is of the order of 10 per cent. higher than that from the Tutorial Organizers Survey. The discrepancy is likely to be largely accounted for by the members of the academic staff in the Postgraduate Survey who gave tutorials.

624. The estimate of tutorial hours from the Undergraduate Survey is 6,720 hours. An allowance for non-response is included, but the survey did not cover undergraduates in the fourth and subsequent years. The figure from the Tutorial Organizers Survey excluding the fourth and subsequent years is 6,997. The estimate from the Undergraduate Survey is 4 per cent. lower than this.

## Classes and seminars

625. Estimates of the total number of classes and seminars can be obtained from the Tutorial Organizers Survey, the Undergraduate Survey, and the Academic Staff Survey. Undergraduates in the Undergraduate Survey reported attending an average of 0·84 classes or seminars per week, with an average attendance of about 9 persons. This would require about 680 classes and seminars per week altogether. The average length of these classes and seminars is difficult to estimate precisely, but is likely to be in the region of 1½ hours. This would give about 1,020 class hours in all. 61 per cent. or 620 class hours were reported as attended by undergraduates of one college only. In the Tutorial Organizers Survey, tutors reported about 720 teachers' hours for college classes and seminars attended by undergraduates of one college only. Some of these classes and seminars would have been given by more than one teacher, so the total of class hours would have been less. Tutors reported a total of about 230 teachers' hours giving inter-college classes and seminars (i.e. college organized classes and

---

[1] Plus the information on teaching in Oriental Studies. See Table 132.
[2] Tutorials given by part-time academic staff are included.

THE MAIN SOURCES OF STATISTICAL INFORMATION 431

seminars attended by undergraduates of more than one college). Each of these hours should have been reported by as many tutors as there were colleges represented; thus each hour should have been reported at least twice. Therefore, 100 teachers' hours might be taken as a reasonable figure for inter-college classes. This gives a total of 820 teachers' hours for all college and inter-college classes and seminars. The total of class hours would be less, and perhaps about 700 hours. Thus, college and inter-college classes and seminars comprised about 70 per cent. of all classes and seminars. The estimate for all class and seminar teaching for undergraduates from the Academic Staff Survey is 790 teachers' hours. This is not directly comparable with the above figures, as some class teaching is given by persons other than the academic staff; the Tutorial Organizers Survey shows the total as about 165 teachers' hours. The Undergraduate Survey and Tutorial Organizers Survey yield an estimate of about 1,000 class hours,

**Table 372.** *Estimates from different sources of the amount of supervision postgraduates receive, by subject group. Trinity Term 1964*

OXFORD                                                           PERCENTAGE

| Amount of supervision | Arts and social studies | Science and medicine | All sub-jects |
|---|---|---|---|
| FROM ACADEMIC STAFF SURVEY | | | |
| Under 4 hours | 21 | 2 | 13 |
| 4 but under 8 hours | 38 | 3 | 23 |
| 8 but under 16 hours | 18 | 5 | 13 |
| 16 hours and over | 3 | 3 | 3 |
| In day-to-day contact | 8 | 85 | 41 |
| Other | 11 | 1 | 7 |
| All | 100 | 100 | 100 |
| FROM POSTGRADUATE SURVEY | | | |
| Under 4 hours | 55 | 19 | 36 |
| 4 but under 8 hours | 25 | 17 | 21 |
| 8 but under 16 hours | 13 | 7 | 10 |
| 16 hours and over | 3 | 7 | 5 |
| In day-to-day contact | 3 | 50 | 27 |
| All | 100 | 100 | 100 |

SOURCE: Academic Staff Survey and Table 193.

NOTES

1. The distributions based on the Academic Staff Survey include supervision for a college as well as for a faculty board. Those based on the Postgraduate Survey include supervision by the faculty supervisor only.
2. The distributions based on the Postgraduate Survey exclude postgraduates who were in residence in Trinity Term 1964 but not in Michaelmas Term 1964.

or 1,100–1,150 teachers' hours in all, and hence about 960 teachers' hours given by the academic staff. This is 170 hours, or 22 per cent., above the estimate from the Academic Staff Survey. One possible explanation of the discrepancy is that some members of the academic staff gave the number of classes and seminars, rather than the number of hours, for classes and seminars which lasted for over one hour. Another is that some university classes and seminars recorded in the Academic Staff Survey as given for postgraduates may have been attended by undergraduates also, and hence included in the estimate from the Undergraduate Survey.

## Postgraduate supervision

626. The academic staff (including outside grants staff and part-time staff) reported they supervised 1,510 postgraduates for faculty boards, and 173 for colleges in Trinity Term 1964. In 1963–4 the University paid rather less than £18,000 in supervision fees to members of the academic staff. The rates were £5 per term, so that fees were paid for an average of about 1,200 postgraduates. Some postgraduates receive supervision although no fee is paid. The survey figure[1] of 1,510 is therefore consistent with the payments made by the University.

627. Table 372 shows distributions according to the amount of supervision reported in the Academic Staff Survey and in the Postgraduate Survey. Both in arts and social studies and in science and medicine, the postgraduates reported a smaller proportion of supervision through day-to-day contact than did the academic staff. And where the time was estimated, the postgraduates gave lower estimates than did the academic staff. The averages, for all subjects, were about 7½ hours a term from the Academic Staff Survey, and about 6 hours a term from the Postgraduate Survey. Within the subject groups, the discrepancy was somewhat larger than this.

[1] The figure would be somewhat higher if those on leave in Michaelmas Term 1964 and those who had resigned between Trinity Term and Michaelmas Term could be included.

# ANNEX

628. The following documents are reproduced:

(*a*) Matriculation form used in 1964–5.

(*b*) Record card (general).

(*c*) Record card (B.Litt., B.Sc., and D.Phil.).

(*d*) Form for Michaelmas Term returns of student numbers from colleges.

(*e*) Form for annual returns of student numbers from colleges.

(*f*) List of subjects for returns of student numbers.

(*g*) Record card used by Admissions Office.

(*h*) Covering letter and questionnaire for Tutorial Organizers Survey.

(*i*) Questionnaire for Academic Staff Survey.

(*j*) Questionnaire for Undergraduate Survey.

(*k*) Questionnaire for Postgraduate Survey.

(*l*) Questionnaire for Schools Survey.

## (a) Matriculation form used in 1964–5

N.B.—This form must be filled up by the candidate for Matriculation in his own handwriting and in ink

# UNIVERSITY OF OXFORD

| | | |
|---|---|---|
| Date of matriculation <br> (To be left blank) | | **FOR COMPLETION BY A COLLEGE OFFICER** <br> State whether the candidate is |
| College, Hall, or Society | | Scholar     } *Strike* <br> Exhibitioner } *out* <br> Commoner  } *two* |
| Surname <br> (To be written in capital letters) | | **NOTE:** <br> The names here given will be entered in the University records exactly as shown. |
| Other names in full <br> (To be written in capital letters) | | |

| | YEAR | MONTH | DAY OF MONTH |
|---|---|---|---|
| Date of birth | | | |

| | NATIONALITY | PLACE OF BIRTH | |
|---|---|---|---|
| Nationality and place of birth | | | |

| | |
|---|---|
| Schools or other places of education attended during the *last six years* (With dates) | |
| Father's names in full | |
| Father's profession or occupation | |
| Present residence of parent or guardian (The guardian's name should also be stated) | |
| Proposed course of study at Oxford | If reading for:   1. B.A. Degree, state proposed Honour School (if Natural Science, state which branch): ........................ <br> 2. Any other degree, state board of faculty and degree concerned................ <br> 3. A diploma, state which one: ........................ <br> 4. Any other course, give details: ........................ |
| Full names in candidate's own handwriting (Not in capital letters) | |

## (b) Record card (general)

| MATRICULATED: | |
| --- | --- |
| DATE OF BIRTH: | SECOND PUBLIC EXAMINATION (PASS) |
| ADMISSION QUALIFICATION | |
| | |
| | |
| | |
| | |
| FIRST PUBLIC EXAMINATION | SECOND PUBLIC EXAMINATION (HONOURS) |
| HONOUR MODERATIONS: | |
| | |
| | |
| | |
| | |
| | B.A. Degree: |

| OTHER DEGREES | DIPLOMAS, CERTIFICATES, SCHOLARSHIPS, PRIZES |
| --- | --- |
| M.A. | |
| B.LITT. | |
| D.LITT. | |
| B.SC. | |
| D.SC. | |
| B.PHIL. | |
| D.PHIL. | OPTIONAL SUBJECTS |
| B.D. | First Public Examination: |
| D.D. | |
| B.C.L. | |
| D.C.L. | |
| B.M. | Second Public Examination: |
| D.M. | |
| M.CH. | |
| B.MUS. | |
| D.MUS. | |

## (c) Record card (B.Litt., B.Sc., and D.Phil)

Previous Degrees:

| | DOCTOR OF PHILOSOPHY | |
|---|---|---|
| Board: | | Supervisor: |
| Admission date (first fee paid): | | |
| Subject: | | |

Modified on ............................ to read

| Leave of absence for | Terms | Referred back: |
|---|---|---|
| Examiners: | | Examiners after being referred back: |
| *Leave to supplicate given: refused: | | Date of Degree: |

2,000:—8.64          * If B.Litt. or B.Sc. Certificate issued, see overleaf.          [P.T.O.

Previous Degrees:

| Board: | Branch of Study: |
|---|---|
| Prob. B.LITT. admission: | Supervisor: |
| B.LITT. or B.SC. admission: | |
| Subject: | |

Modified.........................to read

| Leave of absence for | Terms | Referred back: |
|---|---|---|
| Examiners: | | Examiners after being referred back: |
| B.Litt. B.Sc. Certificate issued: refused: | | B.Litt. or B.Sc. Degree: |

[P.T.O.

# d) Form for Michaelmas Term returns of student numbers from colleges

University Registry,
Oxford.

Ref. No. UG/2

8 October 1964

To the Heads of all Colleges

Dear Sir,
The University Grants Committee requires certain information about the students in residence during the present term, to be supplied by 31 October.
Please therefore complete the appended schedule and return it by *Monday, 19 October 1964,* addressed to the Head Clerk, University Registry.

Yours sincerely,
R. E. Clifford

---

. Number of students reading for any degree, diploma or examination, or undertaking any course of study, in residence in Michaelmas Term, 1964. See attached list for the division of subjects.

| Subject | B.A. and B.M. degree | Chem. Pt. II or Metallurgy Pt. II | Research (B.Litt., B.Sc., & D.Phil.) | Other higher degrees | Diplomas | Any others |
|---|---|---|---|---|---|---|
| Arts | | | | | | |
| Social Studies | | | | | | |
| Pure Science | | | | | | |
| Applied Science—Engineering | | | | | | |
| Applied Science—Metallurgy | | | | | | |
| Medicine | | | | | | |
| Agriculture and Forestry | | | | | | |
| Overseas Services Course | | | | | | |
| Totals: | | | | | | |
| TOTAL of all the above: | | | | | | |

2. Number of students entering the University *for the first time* in Michaelmas Term 1964.
(a) Who are reading for the B.A. and B.M. Degree .........
(b) Who are reading for B.Litt., B.Sc. or D.Phil. .........
(c) Who are reading for other higher degrees .........
(d) Who are reading for a diploma or certificate .........
(e) Who are taking an Overseas Service Course .........
(f) Any others .........

TOTAL:

REC/EMA
23.9.64

## (e) *Form for annual returns of student numbers from colleges*

------------------------------------------------------------------

### Students in Residence during the
### Academic Year 1964–65

**IMPORTANT.** It is essential that the total shown under (1) *University residence* should agree with the total of (2) *Home residence*; and also with the *combined* totals of (3), (4), (5), (6) and (7), but excluding B.M. candidates working elsewhere.

**1.** University Residence

Number of Students residing

| | |
|---|---|
| In College | ———— |
| In Lodgings | ———— |
| At Home | ———— |
| Total | ———— |

**2.** Home Residence

Number of Students whose homes are situated

    (i) Within 30 miles of Oxford ————

    (ii) In other parts of Great Britain ————

    (iii) Outside Great Britain but within the Commonwealth:

        (a) Reading for B.A. degree ————

        (b) Reading for Higher Degree or Diploma ————

        (c) Reading for any other course ————

    (iv) In Foreign Countries:

        (a) Reading for B.A. degree ————

        (b) Reading for Higher Degree or Diploma ————

        (c) Reading for any other course ————

**[OVER**

**3.** Number of Students reading for the DEGREE OF B.A.

| Subject | First Year | Second Year | Third Year | Fourth Year | Fifth or Later Year |
|---|---|---|---|---|---|
| Literae Humaniores | | | | | |
| Jurisprudence | | | | | |
| Modern History | | | | | |
| Theology | | | | | |
| Oriental Studies | | | | | |
| English Lang. and Literature | | | | | |
| Modern Languages | | | | | |
| Geography | | | | | |
| Phil., Pol., and Economics | | | | | |
| Music | | | | | |
| Groups of the Pass School | | | | | |
| Mathematics | | | | | |
| Physics | | | | | |
| Physiology: (1) B.M. Students (2) Others | | | | | |
| Chemistry, Pt. I | | | | | |
| Zoology | | | | | |
| Botany | | | | | |
| Geology | | | | | |
| Biochemistry | | | | | |
| Engineering Science | | | | | |
| Metallurgy, Pt. I | | | | | |
| Psychol., Phil., and Physiol. | | | | | |
| Agriculture | | | | | |
| Forestry | | | | | |
| Engineering and Economics | | | | | |

**4.** Number of Students reading for RESEARCH DEGREES

| | ARTS | SOCIAL STUDIES | PURE SCIENCE | TECHNOLOGY (ENGINEERING) | TECHNOLOGY (METALLURGY) | MEDICINE | AGRICULTURE and FORESTRY |
|---|---|---|---|---|---|---|---|
| B.Litt. | | | | | | | |
| B.Sc. (Ordinary) | | | | | | | |
| B.Sc. (Chemistry, Pt. II) | | | | | | | |
| B.Sc. (Metallurgy, Pt. II) | | | | | | | |
| B.Phil. | | | | | | | |
| D.Phil. | | | | | | | |

**5.** Number of Students reading for other HIGHER DEGREES

        B.D.                                        _____

        B.C.L.                                   _____

        B.M. (*other than those entered under Physiology in Table* (3)):

                (*a*) Working in Oxford             _____

                (*b*) Working elsewhere            _____

        B.Mus.                                 _____

**6.** Number of Students reading for a DIPLOMA

        Advanced Mathematics      _____

        Agricultural Economics      _____

        Anthropology      _____

        Celtic Studies      _____

        Classical Archaeology      _____

        Comparative Philology      _____

        Economic Development      _____

        Economics and Political Science      _____

        Education      _____

        European Archaeology      _____

        Fine Art (Certificate)      _____

        Forestry      _____

        Geochemistry      _____

        History of Art      _____

        History and Philosophy of Science      _____

        Law      _____

        Slavonic Studies      _____

        Social and Administrative Studies      _____

        Soil Science      _____

        Statistics Diploma or Certificate      _____

        Theology      _____

**7.** Number of Students NOT reading for any Degree or Diploma (if any)

        (*a*) Overseas Services Courses      _____

        (*b*) Any others      _____

[OVER

**8.** State number of students in residence who hold

| | Reading for B.A. or B.M. Degrees | Reading for D.Phil., B.Phil., B.Litt., B.Mus., B.Sc., B.C.L., B.D. Degrees, and Diplomas |
|---|---|---|
| (a) A college scholarship or exhibition (*excluding* those entered under (b) or (c)) | _____ | _____ |
| (b) A college scholarship or exhibition *together with* a state scholarship (supplemental) | _____ | _____ |
| (c) A college scholarship or exhibition *together with* a local education authority award | _____ | _____ |
| (d) A local education authority award (excluding those entered under (c)) | _____ | _____ |
| (e) A state scholarship (G.C.E.) | _____ | _____ |
| (f) A state studentship | _____ | _____ |
| (g) A D.S.I.R. studentship | _____ | _____ |
| (h) Any other type of award or grant (*other than contributions from family, relations, or friends*) | _____ | _____ |

**9.** State number of those given in 8 above who receive in total from all sources named:

| | | |
|---|---|---|
| (a) £10 a year or less | _____ | _____ |
| (b) More than £10 but less than £75 a year | _____ | _____ |
| (c) £75 a year or more | _____ | _____ |

## (f) List of subjects for returns of student numbers

University Registry,
Oxford.

## LIST OF SUBJECTS USED FOR STATISTICAL PURPOSES

### Arts subjects

Literae Humaniores
Philosophy as a Lit.Hum. or B.Phil. subject
(other than P.P.E. or P.P.P.)
Modern History
Theology
Oriental Studies
English
Modern Languages
General and Comparative Literature (for B.Phil.)
Geography
Music
Education
Pass School

### Social Studies subjects

Anthropology
Jurisprudence
Philosophy, Politics, and Economics
Politics (for B.Phil.)
Economics (for B.Phil.)
Statistics

### Pure Science subjects

Mathematics
Physics
Chemistry
Physiology (other than B.M. students)
Zoology
Botany
Geology
Biochemistry
Psychology
Psychology, Philosophy, and Physiology

### Applied Science subjects

Engineering Science
Engineering Science and Economics
Metallurgy

### Medicine subjects

All medical subjects
Physiology (for those reading for B.M. degree)

### Agriculture subjects

Agriculture
Forestry
Agricultural Economics

REC/JL
27.4.65.
545/65

## (g) *Record card used by Admissions Office*

-------------------------------------------------------------------

**II. THIS SIDE IS TO BE COMPLETED BY THE CANDIDATE**
PLEASE USE BLACK INK AND WRITE IN BLOCK CAPITALS

| | | |
|---|---|---|
| 1. FULL NAME | FIRST NAMES | SURNAME |
| 2. SCHOOL | | |
| 3. PROPOSED COURSE OF STUDY AT OXFORD (*a*) | | |
| 4. COLLEGE OF FIRST CHOICE (*b*) | | GROUP |
| 5. SUBJECT TO BE OFFERED IN THE EXAMINATION (*c*) | | |
| 6. HOW MANY TERMS OF 'A' LEVEL WORK WILL YOU HAVE COMPLETED BY JULY 1964? (*d*) | | Age on 1 November 1964<br>Years    Months |
| 7. IF UNSUCCESSFUL AT OXFORD, DO YOU WISH TO BE CONSIDERED AT CAMBRIDGE? (*e*) | | |

8. SUBJECTS PASSED AT 'O' LEVEL OR ITS EQUIVALENT (*f*)

SUBJECTS offered at 'A' or 'S' level in June/July 1964

| Board (*g*) | Date | Subjects | Pass | Fail | Board (*g*) | Subjects (*h*) | Level | | 'A' grade | 'S' grade | Date |
|---|---|---|---|---|---|---|---|---|---|---|---|
| | | USE OF ENGLISH | | | | | A | S | | | |
| | | LATIN | | | | | A | S | | | |
| | | | | | | | | | | | |
| | | | | | | | | | | | |

SUBJECTS previously taken at 'A' or 'S' level and grades obtained (*j*)

| | | | | | | | A | S | | | |
|---|---|---|---|---|---|---|---|---|---|---|---|
| | | | | | | | A | S | | | |
| | | | | | | | A | S | | | |
| | | | | | | | | | | | |

*(h) Covering letter and questionnaire for Tutorial Organizers Survey*

## UNIVERSITY OF OXFORD · COMMISSION OF INQUIRY

### 74 HIGH STREET · OXFORD

*Chairman:* LORD FRANKS, Provost of Worcester College

*Secretary:* B. G. CAMPBELL    *Assistant Secretary:* P. H. BROWN    *Second Assistant Secretary:* MISS J. S. WATLING

*Telephone:* Oxford 43302

7 October 1964

*To all Senior Tutors*

It has become clear to us from our own discussions that there are considerable variations in the practice of the tutorial system. We consider that it is essential for us to have full information about the tutorial system if we are to form an accurate picture of Oxford as it is today, and we have asked some questions about it in the questionnaires we are addressing to each member of the teaching and research staff and to a sample of undergraduates. It is, however, impossible from either of these sources to obtain information about the extent to which undergraduates are sent out of college for instruction or about the extent to which instruction is given by people who hold neither a university nor a college post; and that these points may be of importance is clear from the report recently published at Cambridge (Report to the General Board of the Committee on Teaching—*Reporter* of 1 May 1964).

I accordingly enclose a questionnaire (together with a copy of this letter) for each Honour School (the Pass School we consider too small to be worth troubling you about) and for Classical Honour Moderations (other First Public Examinations should be combined with the appropriate Honour School). We should be most grateful if you could arrange for each to be completed by the person in the college responsible for the tutorial arrangements in the School. We appreciate that in certain Schools more than one person may be responsible; in such cases, we hope those responsible will combine to produce one form in respect of their School. Alternatively, separate forms can be returned by each (additional forms can be obtained from the Secretary of the Commission). But however the forms are completed it is most important that the teaching received by each undergraduate should be included ONCE and ONLY ONCE.

We are sorry to have to inflict this further questionnaire on you, but we see no other way of obtaining this information. May we ask you to collect and return the completed forms to us by 24 OCTOBER?

# UNIVERSITY OF OXFORD
# COMMISSION OF INQUIRY

## *To those responsible to a College or other Society for the arrangement of Tutorial Work*

**The purpose of this questionnaire is to ascertain who teaches the undergraduates. A similar investigation has recently been concluded at Cambridge, and the Commission would be most grateful if Tutors would assist it by completing this form.**

Please write your answers in the tables or spaces provided but do not make any entries in the right-hand margin, which will be used in preparing the information for machine tabulation.

COLLEGE .......................................................................................................

HONOUR SCHOOL .....................................................................................

1. For how many undergraduates in each year in the above college and School are you organizing teaching this term? (These undergraduates will be referred to as 'your undergraduates' in subsequent questions.)

*Note* In this and subsequent questions an undergraduate with **Senior Status** should be classed as **second year in the year in which he matriculates**, as third year in the subsequent year, &c.

    1st year                    ........................

    2nd year                   ........................

    3rd year                   ........................

    4th and subsequent years ........................

2. By whom is their tutorial teaching (i.e. teaching of not more than three persons at one time) being given? Allocate the total of **hours per week** being given this term to your undergraduates (including hours given by yourself) between the categories below.

*Notes*
  (i) Each tutorial should be reckoned at its 'nominal' length, and no adjustment should be made for any that last longer than the arranged time. Time spent on preparation and correcting work should **not** be included in this return.

  (ii) The hours should be the hours spent by **teachers** on your undergraduates—not hours received by undergraduates. For example, an hour's tutorial to a pair of your undergraduates in the same year should be returned as **one** hour (since the teacher has spent only one hour) NOT as two (even though two undergraduates have each received an hour's teaching). If a pair are in different years, return one-half hour under each year. If one of a pair is from another college, return one-half hour only. (The other half-hour will be returned by the other college.) Similarly, tutorials given fortnightly should be entered as one-half hour per week.

| | For undergraduates in their | | | |
|---|---|---|---|---|
| | 1st year | 2nd year | 3rd year | 4th and subsequent years |
| (a) Fellows of undergraduates' college | | | | |
| (b) Lecturers of undergraduates' college | | | | |
| (c) Fellows or lecturers of other colleges [not included in (a) or (b)] | | | | |
| (d) Persons holding a university but not a college post | | | | |
| (e) Postgraduate students [not included in (a)–(d)] | | | | |
| (f) Other persons not holding any university or college post | | | | |

**3.** How many of the total hours specified under **2. (c), (d), (e), and (f)** do your undergraduates receive

    (a) because the college has appointed no teacher in the subject;   .........................

    (b) because the college teacher is on leave;   .........................

    (c) because the college teacher has reached his maximum hours;   .........................

    (d) for teaching for optional or special papers;   .........................

    (e) for other reasons? Please specify.

.........................................................................................

**4.** By whom is their class and seminar teaching (i.e. teaching of more than three persons at one time) being given? Allocate the total of **hours per week** being given this term to your undergraduates (including hours given by yourself) between the categories below.

*Notes*

    (i) Exclude classes or seminars announced in the lecture list.

    (ii) Each class or seminar should be reckoned at its 'nominal' length, and no adjustment should be made for any that last longer than the arranged time. Time spent on preparation and correcting work should **not** be included in this return.

    (iii) The hours should again be the hours spent by the **teachers**. For example, an hour's class given by one teacher should be returned as one hour, regardless of how many undergraduates attend; an hour's class given by two teachers should be returned as two hours, &c. For classes given less frequently than once a week, the average hours **per week** should be entered.

    (iv) Where your undergraduates attend classes or seminars with undergraduates from other colleges, return the hours in the second table below, but do **not** make any reduction on account of joint attendance.

| (a) CLASSES AND SEMINARS ATTENDED SOLELY BY YOUR UNDER-GRADUATES | For undergraduates in their | | | |
|---|---|---|---|---|
| | 1st year | 2nd year | 3rd year | 4th and subsequent years |
| (i) Fellows or lecturers of undergraduates' college | | | | |
| (ii) Fellows or lecturers of other colleges [not included in (i)] | | | | |
| (iii) Jointly by persons in (i) and (ii) | | | | |
| (iv) Persons holding a university but not a college post | | | | |
| (v) Persons not holding any university or college post | | | | |
| (vi) Jointly by any combination other than (i) and (ii) | | | | |

| (b) CLASSES AND SEMINARS ATTENDED BY YOUR UNDERGRADUATES TOGETHER WITH UNDERGRADUATES FROM OTHER COLLEGES | For undergraduates in their | | | |
|---|---|---|---|---|
| | 1st year | 2nd year | 3rd year | 4th and subsequent years |
| (i) Fellows or lecturers of your undergraduates' college | | | | |
| (ii) Fellows or lecturers of other colleges [not included in (i)] | | | | |
| (iii) Jointly by persons in (i) and (ii) | | | | |
| (iv) Persons holding a university but not a college post | | | | |
| (v) Persons not holding any university or college post | | | | |
| (vi) Jointly by any combination other than (i) and (ii) | | | | |

5. (a) Is the progress of your undergraduates regularly tested by written college examinations (Collections)?

..................................................................................................................

(b) If so, are there penalties for bad performance in Collections?

# (*i*) *Questionnaire for Academic Staff Survey*

## UNIVERSITY OF OXFORD · COMMISSION OF INQUIRY

### 74 HIGH STREET · OXFORD

*Chairman:* LORD FRANKS, Provost of Worcester College

*Secretary:* B. G. CAMPBELL   *Assistant Secretary:* P. H. BROWN   *Second Assistant Secretary:* MISS J. S. WATLING

*Telephone:* Oxford 43302

13 October 1964

*To all members of the teaching and research staff*

In the statement I made in Congregation on 2 June, I gave a warning that the Commission would be unable to avoid some questionnaires since many of the facts essential to our inquiry are not known. We appreciate the inconvenience of questionnaires at this time, and we have therefore made them as few and as short as we can. There are, however, some questions we feel we must ask of all members of the teaching and research staff.

The earlier questions are designed to enable us to form an accurate picture of the time spent in teaching, supervision, and other academic activities by the holders of the various different kinds of post. Subsequent questions are asked because it is already clear to us

(*a*) that there are considerable variations in the practice of the tutorial system; and

(*b*) that the post-war extension of the C.U.F. lecturer system has led to a greatly increased number of lectures.

We therefore wish to inquire about present tutorial practices, whether the present number of lectures is desirable, whether certain parts of the Honour School requirements could be, or should be, exclusively covered by lecture courses, and about what part is being played, or could be played, by the use of seminars or class teaching. Question 8 is asked because in no other way can we obtain the information about publications at Oxford that is more readily obtainable at other universities.

The enclosed questions cover some of the points arising out of those of our terms of reference which concern teaching and research. Others will be covered by a further short questionnaire addressed only to those responsible for the arrangement of undergraduate teaching. We hope, however, that if you wish to make any general comments on teaching and research you will do so; space has been left at the end of the questionnaire for this purpose.

We hope the questions are clear and cover the ground; but if any points of difficulty arise, please get in touch with the Secretary of the Commission. We shall be most grateful if your reply could reach us by 24 October.

Yours sincerely,

FRANKS

The information obtained from these questionnaires will not be used in oral evidence or published in a form which would enable any individual to be identified. They are numbered so that if any recipients have not replied by 24 October they can be reminded in order that the Commission may receive replies from everyone and obtain an accurate picture of present-day Oxford.

The questionnaire probably does not cater for the full variety of academic work encountered in Oxford. If you feel that your activities are not adequately covered by the questions, please explain any special circumstances that will help in interpreting your replies. Include these comments on a separate sheet if there is not sufficient space on the questionnaire.

Please write in your answers or tick the appropriate category. **Do not** make any entries in the right-hand margin which will be used for coding some of the information for machine tabulation.

## PART I

1. (a) Are you a matriculated member of the University?...........

   (b) Are you a member of a university faculty? List the faculties or sub-faculties to which you belong. If there is more than one, **underline** the one in which your work principally lies.

   ..............................................................................

2. What is your subject? .........................................................................................

3. (a) What is your university appointment (or appointments)?

       (i) professor;

       (ii) reader;

       (iii) university lecturer (or senior university lecturer);

       (iv) C.U.F. lecturer;

       (v) special lecturer;

       (vi) faculty lecturer (i.e. a faculty lecturer appointed as such by the General Board);

       (vii) departmental demonstrator;

       (viii) holder of a university research post (please specify);

       ..............................................................................

       (ix) holder of some other university post (please specify);

       ..............................................................................

       (x) no university appointment.

   (b) Are any of your university appointments part-time? Please specify each part-time appointment (except C.U.F. and special lecturerships).

   ..............................................................................

   (c) If you are a professor, are you in Schedule A, Schedule B, or

   Schedule C? ....................................................................................

(*d*) Are you a fellow of a college or other society? If so, please give the following details:

    (i) college;   ......   .............. .............. .................................................. ......

    (ii) year of election to a fellowship at the college in (i);.....................

    (iii) type of fellowship presently held (e.g. Tutorial, Senior Research, Professorial) and the main teaching and other duties attached to it. (Do not give college offices unless the fellowship is held specifically in respect of the office, e.g. Full-time Bursar or Librarian.)

(*e*) Are you a lecturer of a college or other society? (List each lecturership you hold other than one at a college of which you are a fellow.)

| stipendiary (i.e. qualifying for F.S.S.U.) lecturerships | non-stipendiary (i.e. not qualifying for F.S.S.U.) lecturerships |
|---|---|
| | |

**4.** (*a*) What was your age at 1 October 1964?.................................................

    (*b*) For how many years have you held an academic appointment in any university?   .................................................

    (*c*) Since what year have you continuously held an academic appointment or appointments in Oxford (apart from leaves of absence)?...................

## 5. TEACHING

*Notes*

    (i) Where teaching is intended for both undergraduates and postgraduates, please return it under the section for which it is primarily intended; do not return it under both categories in (*a*).

    (ii) A 'tutorial' is to be taken to mean teaching of not more than three people at one time; a 'class' or 'seminar' is to be taken to mean teaching of more than three people at one time (other than lectures).

    (iii) In (*a*) and (*b*) give 'nominal' hours, rather than 'actual' hours, for any teaching that lasts longer than the arranged time. Where classes (or other teaching) have no set length, enter the average actual hours which you expect them to last.

    (iv) Do **not** include time spent in preparing teaching and correcting pupils' work outside the hours of actual teaching. Question 10 is concerned with this.

    (v) Do **not** include postgraduate supervision. Question 7 is concerned with this.

    (vi) Please give as accurate estimates as you can for your average weekly load **this term,** even if it is not a typical Michaelmas Term. You are invited in (*c*) to explain any special circumstances.

(*a*) How many **hours, on average, per week this term** are you spending on the following types of teaching?

| | For undergraduates (i.e. those reading for a B.A.—with the exception of Part II Chemists and Metallurgists—or B.M. and members of Overseas Service Courses) | For postgraduates (including diploma students who are members of the University and Part II Chemists and Metallurgists) |
|---|---|---|
| (i) giving lectures (including lecture demonstrations) | | |
| (ii) giving tutorials | | |
| (iii) giving classes or seminars | | |
| (iv) giving practical instruction to regular classes | | |

(*b*) How many hours per week this term are you spending teaching non-members of the University working for examinations of the University or teaching for the Delegacy of Extra-mural Studies? ..........................

(*c*) Is this a reasonably representative Michaelmas Term for you? If not, please explain the ways in which it is atypical.

**6.** (*a*) How many of the undergraduate tutorials are given

    (i) to single undergraduates; .............................................

    (ii) to pairs; .............................................

    (iii) to threes? .............................................

(*b*) If some of the tutorials in (*a*) are given to pairs or threes, is this

    (i) because you prefer to teach thus;

    (ii) for other reasons (for instance, you would prefer to teach more undergraduates singly but cannot afford the time)? Please specify.

**7.** (*a*) How many postgraduates (including diploma students) were you supervising under a faculty board **last term**? .....................

(*b*) Do you give academic supervision to postgraduates on behalf of a college? If so, to how many **last term**? .........................

(*c*) Please divide the postgraduates entered in (*a*) and (*b*) into the following categories:

| | Part II Chemists and Metallurgists | Other Post-graduates |
|---|---|---|
| (i) supervised for less than 4 hours last term | ........... | ............... |
| (ii) supervised for at least 4 hours but less than 8 hours last term | ............. | ............... |
| (iii) supervised for at least 8 hours but less than 16 hours last term | ........... | ............... |
| (iv) supervised for 16 hours or more last term | ........... | ............... |
| (v) in day-to-day contact, problems discussed as they arise | ............... | ............... |
| (vi) if any postgraduates cannot be fitted into these categories please give separate details for them: | | |

**8.** During the academic years 1959–64, how many of the following did you have published under your own name or jointly:

   (*a*) books; .............

   (*b*) articles and reviews (other than brief notices)? .............

**9.** How many **hours per week this term** do you expect **on average** to spend

   (*a*) attending your college governing body and college committees; ...............

   (*b*) attending university and inter-college committees which meet **regularly** (include, for instance, meetings of Council, the General Board, faculty boards, and their committees); ...............

   (*c*) carrying out the duties of a college office; ...............

**10.** Questions 5, 6, and 9 cover time which will be regularly spent this term on teaching and administration. There are other activities for which it may be difficult to give, in advance, an average weekly figure for this term. In addition, work during vacations has not been included. If, however, you think a meaningful figure can be given, please estimate the time spent on the other activities which accounted for your working time **during the last academic year,** in terms and vacations.

| | Average hours per week during term | Total hours during vacations |
|---|---|---|
| (*a*) Preparing teaching (including lectures) and correcting pupils' work (include setting, marking, and returning Collections other than during tutorials) | ................. | ................. |
| (*b*) Advising students on both academic and personal matters | ................. | ................. |
| (*c*) Administration not entered in Question 9. Include university and departmental administration, faculty and departmental meetings, correspondence and interviews (including interviewing students on behalf of a faculty board) and meetings of *ad hoc* committees | ................. | ................. |
| (*d*) College admissions | ................. | ................. |
| (*e*) University examining | ................. | ................. |
| (*f*) Study and research | ................. | ................. |
| (*g*) Meetings of learned societies and conferences. | ................. | ................. |
| (*h*) Other professional work in Oxford (e.g. editing or refereeing for journals). | ................. | ................. |
| (*j*) Professional work outside Oxford | | |
|    (i) External examining and lecturing | ................. | ................. |
|    (ii) As a consultant or adviser (to governments, international organizations, industry &c.) | ................. | ................. |
|    (iii) Other | ................. | ................. |

## PART II

Your answers will be assumed to relate to your own faculty only, unless you make it clear that you are expressing wider opinions.

If you wish to give longer answers than space allows please give them at the end of the questionnaire or on a separate sheet.

11. (a) Could lectures or classes and seminars be made a better complement to tutorials (e.g. by covering in classes topics that are now generally dealt with in tutorials)?

☐

(b) If so, do you think attendances at either lectures or classes and seminars specifically designed to replace or complement tutorials should be made compulsory?

☐

12. (a) Is the number of lectures offered too large?

(b) If so, how should a reduction be effected (e.g. by reducing lecturing obligations; or by encouraging lecturers to give classes or seminars rather than lectures)?

☐

**13.** Do you think undergraduates would benefit from residence in vacation

    (*a*) with teaching instruction;

    (*b*) without teaching instruction;

    (*c*) for special purposes (e.g. courses in languages for scientists)?

**14.** Have you any general comments on teaching and research?

## (j) Questionnaire for Undergraduate Survey
# UNIVERSITY OF OXFORD
# COMMISSION OF INQUIRY

## Survey of Undergraduates

The University recently appointed a Commission, under the chairmanship of Lord Franks, the Provost of Worcester College, to inquire into the existing organization of the University and the colleges for the purposes of research, teaching, and administration. The Commission wishes to build up an accurate picture of the present teaching arrangements in Oxford, and it has addressed questionnaires to those responsible for arranging and giving the teaching. It feels, however, that the picture would not be complete without information from those receiving the teaching. It is therefore sending this questionnaire to a random sample of 1,000 under-graduates. Your name was included in the sample, and the Commission would be most grate-ful if you would complete the questionnaire and return it to the Secretary of the Commission at 74 High Street by **Monday, 2 November.**

The information obtained from these questionnaires will not be used in any way which would enable any individual to be identified. They are numbered so that if any recipients have not replied by 2 November they can be reminded in order that the Commission may receive replies from everyone and obtain an accurate picture of present-day Oxford.

It may be that you are no longer an undergraduate because you have changed to a post-graduate course since you matriculated. If so, please answer questions 1–4 and 14 only.

Please write your answers in the spaces or boxes provided or place a tick in the appropriate box. But **do not** make any entries in the right-hand margin, which will be used to prepare some of the information you give for machine tabulation.

1. What is your college? ........................................................................................

2. Have you Senior Status (i.e. are you exempt from the First Public Examina-tion), and if so, on what grounds?

    (a) No Senior Status      0

    (b) Senior Status because you are a graduate of another university in the United Kingdom      1

    (c) Senior Status because you are a graduate of an overseas university      2

    (d) Senior Status for other reasons      3

3. Are you in your

    (a) first,

    (b) second,

    (c) third,

    year at Oxford? ........................................................................................

**4.** Are you at present reading for

    (*a*) a Preliminary Examination or Moderations (state which School);

.........................................................................................................................

    (*b*) a Final Honour School (state which);................................................................

    (*c*) the Pass School (state which Groups);............................................................

    (*d*) some other course (state which)?....................................................................

**Questions 5–12 all relate to the week 25–31 October inclusive**

**5.** (*a*) How many tutorials (i.e. teaching of not more than three persons at one time) did you go to during the week

        (i) alone;

        (ii) with one other;

        (iii) with two others?

    (*b*) For how many of the tutorials **returned under (*a*) (ii) and (iii)** were the others attending

        (i) all of your own college;

        (ii) all of your own sex?

    (*c*) Did you miss any tutorials during the week? If so, how many?....................

**6.** (*a*) How many classes or seminars (i.e. teaching of more than three persons at one time but excluding lectures) did you attend during the week?

        ...........................................................

    (*b*) For how many of the classes or seminars returned under (*a*) were the total number of pupils present

        (i). 5 or less;

        (ii) 6–10;

        (iii) more than 10?

    (*c*) How many of the classes or seminars were composed exclusively of members of

        (i) your own college;

        (ii) your own sex?

**7.** If you attended classes or seminars during the week, how many were for

    (*a*) proses or other exercises in language for those reading modern or ancient languages;

    (*b*) teaching in any 'ancillary' or 'tool' subject (e.g. languages for historians or mathematics for economists);

    (*c*) teaching in optional or special subject papers;

    (*d*) other purposes? Please specify.

    ..............................................................................................

**8.** How many lectures did you attend during the week?.................................... ☐☐

**9.** How many of the following did you write during the week:

    (*a*) essays;

    (*b*) exercises (e.g. proses, verses, unseens, etc.);

    (*c*) other written pieces for a tutorial, class, or seminar?

**10.** Did you receive during the week any additional teaching **for your subject** for which you yourself paid?

    (*a*) No additional teaching     0

    (*b*) From Extra-Mural Delegacy classes     1

    (*c*) From an educational establishment that is not part of the University. Please specify....................     2

    (*d*) From private individuals     3

    (*e*) From any other source. Please specify

    ....................................................................................     4

**11.** How many hours did you spend during the week in laboratories doing practical work? ................ ☐☐

**12.** During the week did you work in, or use books belonging to,

    (*a*) the Bodleian Library (including the Camera, the Radcliffe Science Library, and the Law Library); ................

    (*b*) college libraries; ................

    (*c*) departmental or faculty libraries;................

    (*d*) the City libraries; ................

    (*e*) any other libraries?................

**13.** (*a*) How many books related to your work have you bought this term?

    ....................................................................................

    (*b*) What was their approximate total cost?....................

**14.** (*a*) Have you changed your Final Honour School (or other course)

        (i) between your acceptance by your college and the middle of your first term of residence; ................

        (ii) subsequently? ................

    (*b*) If so, what was your former Final Honour School (or other course)?

    ....................................................................................

    (*c*) Did you wish to change but were unable to do so

        (i) because you were advised that you did not have the basic knowledge necessary to read the alternative subject;................

        (ii) because you were advised it was too late;................

        (iii) for other reasons? ................

    (*d*) If so, to which Final Honour School (or other course) did you wish

    to change? ....................................................................................

952425.2          R

*(k) Questionnaire for Postgraduate Survey*

# UNIVERSITY OF OXFORD
# COMMISSION OF INQUIRY

## *Survey of Students reading for Higher Degrees*

The University recently appointed a Commission, under the chairmanship of Lord Franks, the Provost of Worcester College, to inquire into the existing organization of the University and the colleges for the purposes of research, teaching, and administration. The Commission wishes to build up an accurate picture of the way in which the work of those reading for higher degrees is organized, and it has addressed questionnaires to those responsible for the organization. It feels, however, that the picture would not be complete without information from the students themselves. It is therefore sending this questionnaire to a random sample of 500 from those in their second and subsequent years. Your name was included in the sample, and the Commission would be most grateful if you would complete the questionnaire and return it to the Secretary of the Commission at 74 High Street by **Monday, 26 October.**

The information obtained from these questionnaires will not be used in any way which would enable any individual to be identified. They are numbered so that if any recipients have not replied by 26 October they can be reminded in order that the Commission may receive replies from everyone and obtain an accurate picture of present-day Oxford.

Please write your answers in the spaces provided or place a tick in the appropriate box. But **do not** make any entries in the right-hand margin, which will be used to prepare some of the information you give for machine tabulation. If you wish to give extended answers for which there is not room please include them on a separate sheet.

1. College .............................................................

2. Age at 1 October 1964.............................

3. Details of first degree(s).
    (*a*) Name (e.g. B.A., B.Sc.)..................................
    (*b*) Country ...............................................
    (*c*) University ............................................
    (*d*) Subject(s) ...........................................
    (*e*) Class ................................................
    (*f*) Year taken .........................................

4. Are you married or single?..................

5. Do you have any children? If so, how many? .................

6. Are your wife (or husband) and family living with you in Oxford?.................

7. (*a*) For which Oxford degree are you registered? ......................
    (*b*) Which Oxford degree do you hope finally to take? ..........................

**8.** Under which faculty are you registered? ................................................................

**9.** When did you begin to work for a higher degree in Oxford?

       Term ...................................................

       Year ...................................................

**10.** (a) Do you hold a fellowship at a college or other society? If so, please state category of fellowship. ...................................................................

    (b) Do you hold a lecturership at a college or other society? ...................

    (c) Do you hold a university or departmental post? If so, please specify and state whether it is full-time or part-time.

    ................................................................................................

**11.** During the year October 1963–September 1964 for how many weeks were you in residence in Oxford? ...................

## SUPERVISION AND TUITION

**12.** (a) How often **last term** did you see your faculty supervisor to discuss your work? You should **not** include tutorials here; they are covered in Question 15.

      (i) Not at all     0

     (ii) Once     1

    (iii) Once a month     2

    (iv) Once a fortnight     3

     (v) Once a week     4

    (vi) More than once a week     5

   (vii) In day-to-day contact     6

    (b) Approximately how long did you spend discussing your work with your faculty supervisor during last term?

      (i) Less than 4 hours     1

     (ii) At least 4 hours but less than 8 hours     2

    (iii) At least 8 hours but less than 16 hours     3

    (iv) 16 hours or more     4

     (v) In day-to-day contact     5

    (c) Would you have wished to see your faculty supervisor more often?

    If so, how often? ...................................................................

**13.** Over the **last three vacations** estimate the **total** number of hours you spent discussing your work with your faculty supervisor.

    (a) Less than 1 hour     1

    (b) At least 1 hour but less than 5 hours     2

    (c) At least 5 hours but less than 10 hours     3

    (d) At least 10 hours but less than 20 hours     4

    (e) 20 hours or more     5

**14.** Is there any senior member of the University other than your faculty supervisor whom you consult regularly about your work? If so, with how many people and how often?

☐

**15.** (*a*) How often did you have a tutorial (i.e. teaching of not more than three persons at one time) **last term**? **Do not** include any teaching already entered in Question 12.

    (i) Not at all      ☐ 0

    (ii) Once a fortnight      ☐ 1

    (iii) Once a week      ☐ 2

    (iv) More than once a week      ☐ 3

(*b*) Did you attend alone or with other students?

    (i) Alone      ☐ 1

    (ii) With others      ☐ 2

    (iii) Did not have tutorials      ☐ 3

(*c*) Are you satisfied with the number of tutorials you received?

    (i) Satisfied      ☐ 1

    (ii) Prefer more      ☐ 2

    (iii) Prefer fewer      ☐ 3

**16.** (*a*) Did your first degree course adequately equip you for postgraduate work?............................

(*b*) If not, what further instruction did you need?

☐

(*c*) Have you received at Oxford any formal instruction in research methods and sources? Please specify.

☐

## LECTURES, SEMINARS, AND CLASSES

**17.** (*a*) Do you regularly attend seminars and/or classes? (That is, teaching of more than three persons at one time but excluding lectures.)...........

(*b*) If so, how many did you attend during the week 19–24 October?

☐

**18.** (*a*) Do you regularly attend lectures?........................

(*b*) If so, how many did you attend during the week 19–24 October?

☐

**19.** Do you consider that the classes, seminars, and lectures provided in your subject for those reading for higher degrees are adequate for your needs? If not, what changes would you suggest?

☐

GENERAL

**20.** How many hours a week will you spend **this term** (**excluding** time spent on preparation and marking)

    (*a*) teaching at tutorials or classes; .................................

    (*b*) demonstrating in a laboratory; .................................

    (*c*) doing any other teaching inside the University; .................................

    Please specify.

    (*d*) doing any teaching outside the University? .................................

    Please specify.

**21.** Are there adequate opportunities for you to make contact with

    (*a*) other students reading for higher degrees in your general field;

    (*b*) senior members in your field?

**22.** Do you consider that the library facilities are adequate for your needs? If not, what are their deficiencies?

**23.** Are the general conditions under which you do your work satisfactory? If not, what is unsatisfactory?

**24.** Do you live

        (*a*) in college;      I

        (*b*) in accommodation provided by your college;      2

        (*c*) elsewhere?      3

**25.** What facilities does your college provide for those reading for higher degrees? Please indicate for each what use you make of it.

**26.** Is there anyone in your college or department whom you can consult, other than your supervisor, on non-academic problems?

........................................................................................................................

**27.** Do you think the needs of postgraduates are best met by:

(*a*) **the existing collegiate system,** which includes societies for both undergraduates and postgraduates, postgraduate societies specialized as to fields of study (i.e. Nuffield and St. Antony's), and postgraduate societies not specialized as to fields of study (i.e. Linacre House), the University in all cases taking the primary responsibility for the postgraduates' academic work;

(*b*) postgraduate societies, the University still taking the primary responsibility for the postgraduates' academic work,
   (i) specialized as to fields of study;
   (ii) not specialized as to fields of study;

(*c*) postgraduate societies which would themselves take full responsibility for the postgraduates' academic work,
   (i) specialized as to fields of study;
   (ii) not specialized as to fields of study;

(*d*) the organization of work through university departments or institutes, non-academic needs being met by optional membership of
   (i) a social centre on the lines of Halifax House; or
   (ii) a postgraduate society; or
   (iii) a combined postgraduate and undergraduate society?

If you would like to give reasons for your choice, please do so here:

**28.** Have you any other observations on the general position of those reading for higher degrees in Oxford?

# (*l*) *Questionnaire for Schools Survey*

The Commission would find it very helpful to have the following information about the structure and work of your Sixth Forms before the proposed meeting on 14 June. Wherever relevant, will you kindly give the information separately for boys and girls.

———

1. How many pupils were in each year of the Sixth Form in the Autumn Term 1964?

2. How many of these pupils have 'O' Level qualifications in two languages?

3. Third and Fourth Year Sixth Forms
   Please state of pupils in each of these forms in the Autumn Term 1964:
   (*a*) what were their ages;
   (*b*) what had been their performance in 'A' Level examinations (subjects attempted and grades achieved);
   (*c*) how many have since left school.

4. Do you operate an express stream to 'O' Level? If so, please say in what year of their course pupils make the decision to specialise in the Arts or the Sciences.

5. For how many periods in the week do you find it possible to give separate teaching to pupils in the Third and Fourth Year Sixth Forms?

6. Is the teaching in the Second and Third Year Sixth Forms geared in any way to the requirements of the Oxford and Cambridge special entrance examinations?

7. How many candidates have you submitted to all United Kingdom universities during the academic year beginning in September 1964?

8. How many candidates did you submit to Oxford and Cambridge for the 1964 special entrance examination from the Second, Third and Fourth Year Sixth Forms respectively?

9. If the number of candidates submitted was small, why was this so? Was it due, for example, to the style and content of the papers as compared with 'A' or 'S' Level papers, to the difficulty of providing suitable teaching for a small number of pupils, to the reluctance of pupils to apply to a university with an unfamiliar 'image', or for other reasons?

10. In what circumstances do you advise pupils to try for a place at Oxford or Cambridge
    (*a*) in the Second Year
    (*b*) in the Third Year of the Sixth Form?

11. How many Oxford and Cambridge graduates have you on your staff, and for how long have they been members of it?

12. Have you any other comments which you would like to have circulated before the discussion on 14 June?

# PART VII

## OPINIONS OF THE ACADEMIC STAFF
## AND OF POSTGRADUATES

629. Some of the questions which were asked, both in the Academic Staff Survey and in the Postgraduate Survey, were put in a form which invited comment. In addition, postgraduates were invited to make general observations about the circumstances of those reading for higher degrees at Oxford. And the academic staff were asked similarly for observations about teaching and research.

630. Comment of this kind is not susceptible to reliable statistical treatment and it is therefore given separately from the statistical results of the surveys. It is volunteered by an unrepresentative, because self-selected, group of individuals and the selection of illustrative remarks is open in any case to the risk of bias, both in the choice of replies and in the numbers of instances presented to illustrate any particular point. The Commission chose to incur this risk. It was considered that some of the answers were so interesting and gave so much illumination to certain of the matters discussed in the main report, that it would be a loss to those who may read it if they were omitted.

631. Those readers who are unaccustomed to social surveys should remember that 'it takes all sorts to make a world', even a university one. It seems clear from the replies as a whole that, as might have been expected, postgraduates' needs are more diverse than those of undergraduates, and that academics in large numbers see all sides of a question. It follows that in matters where individual habits or tastes differ widely, changes designed to meet one complaint are likely to provoke another, from someone who values the practice complained about. We have illustrated contrasting views where it seemed to us fair to do so. It should, however, be remembered also that, where complainants outnumber those satisfied with some practice, it is probable that the practice could be improved in the sense that a change would reduce the volume of complaint or increase that of approval.

632. We have endeavoured to select passages which either represent a substantial volume of opinion, or which in our own judgement illustrate in a particularly apt manner some matter on which we make a recommendation in the main body of the report. We have also tried, where it seemed appropriate, to indicate the statistical distribution of the replies to allied questions which could be treated in this way.

## ACADEMIC STAFF

633. In the Academic Staff Survey respondents were invited to give their general comments on teaching and research, as well as for their views on certain specific points concerned with teaching. Some tabulations of the latter are given in Part V, paras. 469–75. Here, the views and arguments put forward are illustrated through the comments themselves.

634. An attempt has been made to represent the main points which were made, and to reflect the balance of opinion where it was divided, but selection of the individual comments must to a considerable extent be arbitrary. Nor is it possible to assess just how widely held each viewpoint was. Over half the respondents did not make any comment and, of those who did so, most confined themselves to one or two topics. Since many topics were touched on, only a relatively small number discussed any particular one. A very approximate assessment of the over-all balance of views is that, of those commenting, a fifth were generally satisfied with teaching and research in Oxford; a quarter were critical of the heavy teaching load with its consequent adverse effects on research; a third were critical of other aspects of arrangements for teaching and research, and a sixth were critical of the tutorial system itself and/or of the college organization of undergraduate teaching.

635. A great deal of the comment centred around the tutorial system. A very large number thought that too many tutorials are given and that the results are harmful to undergraduates, tutors, and research.

636. A CUF lecturer in social studies represented many in arts and social studies when he wrote:

Properly used, the tutorial system is unrivalled as a method of dealing with the problems of the individual undergraduate in assimilating, organizing, presenting, and evaluating his material. Oxford should preserve it jealously, for once lost it will never be regained. Misused as a means of imparting information to 'cover a syllabus', it is absurdly wasteful and inefficient. When the undergraduate is expected to write two essays a week he has no time to investigate any subject properly, and it becomes impossible for his overworked tutor to train him in method so as to make him capable without tutorial assistance of dealing with new subjects on his own—the original object of the system.

637. For some the remedy lay in more extensive use of classes:

I agree with the recently published comments by R. N. W. Blake about spoon-feeding and specialization, and about too much *preparing* people for examinations. I disapprove, for example, of 'revision-classes' and in my own subject dislike the growing practice of sending undergraduates out to so-called specialists. I think it would be much better if tutors taught what they can teach and enjoy teaching and think they teach well, and could send their pupils to small classes, run by experts or specialists, for areas of the field which they themselves don't or can't teach. Too many undergraduates go to too many tutorials, and have to write too many essays.                                (CUF lecturer in arts.)

638. The undergraduate's point of view was put by a CUF lecturer in arts:

My impression is that undergraduates are very much over-taught. During my first year as an undergraduate (when I was reading mathematics) I had one tutorial a week, and this was about right for me, a reasonably able and energetic man. Some others of my year were wasting (and in one case quite deliberately) a lot of our tutor's time. During the rest of my undergraduate life I was having two tutorials (in some cases three) a week, and could never manage to keep up, and often (without much deliberate ill will) wasted my tutor's time. Friends in New College, where the rule was three tutorials a fortnight, used to reckon that they had one good week, when they could think, and one crisis week when life was impossible. I think we all should have done much better if we had had not more than one essay a week to produce, either for an individual tutorial or for a seminar.

639. The effects on tutors were put by a junior research fellow in arts:

They teach too wide a period, covering the ground at too great a pace, often competing with another tutor teaching simultaneously a quite different subject. The tutorial system is excellent: its operation is a scandal. Fewer hours are an urgent need. For pupils to appear every hour, on the hour, destroys the tutor's liveliness and this lack of verve is quickly sensed by pupils whose interest quickly falls and whose performance flags. Tired tutors (the majority) are slow to praise. They tend to take little account of the problems of individual pupils, to make the same comments whatever the essay, and to prepare set-pieces on topics which they produce as giving a lecture, irrespective of the pupil's knowledge. As an undergraduate I found most tutorials impersonal. Now, as a tutor, I find that I give of my best only when taking one tutorial in a morning, perhaps two. This is true of many tutors, yet some of my colleagues are forced to do four hours a morning. Given less rushed conditions, they could really stimulate pupils. They know this, and you must help them to be able to give of their (very remarkable) best.

A CUF lecturer in social studies wrote:

The incessant routine of tutorial upon tutorial is very wearing. Many of Darlington's strictures upon college fellows are true enough, and the defects he mentioned are all attributable, in one way or another, to the fact that we are kept at a grindstone for too long.

640. The degree to which tutors should specialize was discussed. The view that tutors should specialize was more widespread in science, but not absent in arts. Two comments were:

I think that the college system of organizing teaching has serious disadvantages for the teacher. It forces the tutor (especially in the smaller colleges) to teach over a much wider range than he can keep up with or maintain interest in—a limited amount of skating on thin ice may be stimulating, but to do it constantly is demoralizing and boring. The college tutor under the present system carries three obligations (of teaching, administration, and research) which he cannot carry out with equal efficiency, and he is forced into a choice of which he will neglect. Two of them can be done efficiently together, but not three.

(CUF lecturer in arts.)

Even as a recent graduate it is difficult to be fully competent to teach the wide range of subjects demanded of a tutorial fellow. The teaching would be more efficient if tutors specialized as they do in research, and the undergraduates went to different tutors every term. This would involve co-operation between colleges, but should not prove too difficult. Taking chemistry as an example: this system now does largely operate by dividing the subject into its three main divisions (physical, organic, and inorganic). Students go in rotation to three tutors, each a specialist. I would further divide the subjects so that the tutors would have a more detailed knowledge of their teaching subjects.

(Junior research fellow in science.)

But a junior research fellow in arts wrote:

Giving general tuition has kept horizons wide in my own research field, and has presented interesting challenges to notions born and bred within the confines of a thesis.

641. There were some criticisms that tutorials are not always conducted as effectively as they might be. A research fellow in arts had these comments:

While the tutorial system *can* be the most stimulating form of instruction, in practice this is very often not so. This is partly because there is much time-wasting in the Oxford tutorial. Firstly, instead of distributing roneo'd booklists, 10 minutes of each hour is wasted in dictating (usually inaccurately) a booklist from memory. Secondly, another 20 minutes is wasted during which one of the undergraduates reads out his essay; though there are certain advantages in hearing one's own literary work read aloud, this is a complete waste of time for the other undergraduate present; it also means that the tutor never gets a view of the essay as a whole, and is thus constantly interjecting with criticisms, which if he had read it beforehand he would have realized were catered for later on in the essay. Certainly any advantage from the reading-aloud system is fully counteracted by the waste of the tutor's 'talking-time', which is clearly only half the nominal hour of the Oxford tutorial, even assuming that the tutorial does not begin or end with 'chit-chat'. Tutors should take in all essays beforehand and comment fully on them, so that the *whole* hour can be spent in discussion. This may mean increasing the number of tutors, or reducing their non-academic duties, so that they can give more time to each individual pupil's work.

642. The relationship between tutorials and other forms of teaching attracted a great deal of comment. The better use of classes and lectures (especially the former) commanded a good deal of support. A junior research fellow in arts wrote:

I have had to teach students who have reached a high standard in the common range of topics taught in the tutorial system, and canonized by the Final Honours Examination, yet retaining a primitiveness in the handling of ideas, a parochialism, a narrowness of frame of reference, which appals me. I feel that behind a dyke of academic sophistication, there still lies a large area that has been kept, intellectually, on a very underdeveloped level. We, as conscientious tutors, must, I am afraid, bear some of the responsibility for this state of affairs. The only way out I can see is to organize lectures and classes in such a way as to ensure that the undergraduate really knows that there is more to his subject than what he receives from us in his tutorials. At the present the organization of the lecture system is a matter of wilful amateurism. Quite simple measures, such as the formation of a selected lecture list—a 'Humanities list', ranging over the History, Lit. Hum., Theology, English, and Modern Languages faculties would give the student a new sense of richness.

But a CUF lecturer in arts put a quite different view:

I believe that the *average* Oxford undergraduate may acquire through the tutorial method rather less technical knowledge than he might through lectures, or at any rate a much more patchy knowledge. But the effort of having to compose a respectable essay, virtually from scratch, for a tutorial, without the help of previously acquired lecture notes, is a very valuable intellectual exercise; in my experience in Scotland the mind of the average student was seldom if ever exercised in the same way, and certainly not in the regular fashion of the continuous flow of tutorials in the Oxford system. He could generally get by by serving up the professorial notes. It is not the tutorial system, but the tutorial system unrelated to lectures which is unique to Oxford; and, however accidental historically, is, I believe, the most valuable feature of the Oxford system in which the imparting of technical information is *not* the main function.

A professor in social studies thought that the tutorial system led to too little contact of professors with undergraduates:

The divorce of professors from the teaching of undergraduates (except through lectures, which are despised) is a thoroughly unhealthy and wrong practice. It results from the fact that the tutorial system, a very good thing in itself, is in Oxford carried to absurd lengths. It attempts, quite unjustifiably, to be self-sufficient, and gives no credit to other forms of teaching. A great deal of taxpayers' money spent on lectures is thus wasted, college tutors are overworked, and undergraduates are deprived of the opportunity to exchange ideas with professors.

643. A minority (perhaps a sixth of those making comments) were critical of the tutorial system itself. Such criticism was more frequent in science

than in other subjects, and was particularly strong in Physics. Two scientists wrote as follows:

I am convinced that the traditional college system is ill-suited to the teaching of Physics—or, at any rate, it is enormously wasteful. The necessary instruction could be given perfectly well by means of lectures which should include the provision of problems for students to work. The problems could then be dealt with in classes. I regard the standard weekly tutorial in Physics as an anachronism. What I would really like to see is something like the American system with which I am familiar as I taught at Harvard for nearly three years. Harvard probably turns out more top-grade physicists than any other university in the world and does this without the benefits of the tutorial system and with a relatively small lecturing staff. The practice in the best American universities seems to me to be so conspicuously more efficient than our own that I am astonished that we have not yet moved closer towards it. A consequence of the system I am advocating is that the admission of undergraduates to the University and questions such as their subsequent removal due to inability to maintain the required academic standard would have to be taken out of the hands of colleges, but I can think of no good reason why this should not be done.

(University lecturer and tutorial fellow.)

For most students the tutorial system is a waste of time and money. It is a benefit only to the very gifted and *sometimes* to the very weak but willing student. The idea of close contact and exchange with the mature scholar is largely eyewash. (University lecturer.)

A senior research fellow in arts wrote:

With considerable experience of both Manchester and Oxford, I do not believe that the Oxford tutorial system is either a good form of education or necessary for personal relations between teachers and taught.

644. One way of easing the pressure on undergraduates during term is to increase the period of residence. Of a number of suggestions on ways of doing this, one was:

I suggest that we are trying to cram too much teaching into 8-week terms. Further, the vacations are too long, serving mainly to distract undergraduates from habits of work acquired with difficulty during term. I suspect that in the first year the alternation of 8-week terms with 6-week vacations accentuates the problem of transition from home to university life which affects many undergraduates, especially those who come from day schools and from social backgrounds remote from that which is predominant here. These arguments point to an extension of at least the first 2 terms to 10 weeks, the number of tutorials, etc., *not being increased*, with a corresponding reduction in the length of the short vacations. (CUF lecturer in arts.)

645. Small subjects in which colleges do not usually appoint tutors present problems which were stressed by staff in these subjects. Psychology is an example:

Undergraduates wishing to read relatively new subjects like Psychology are particularly badly served by the colleges. It is not uncommon for an undergraduate from a smaller college or hall (in days gone by, from larger colleges too) to turn up at the Institute of Experimental Psychology forlornly badgering the secretary or members of the staff to find him a tutor 'as his college told him they haven't got a tutor and they expected the Institute would fix him up'. But this is not, and should not be, the responsibility of the Institute (or of any scientific department); it is properly the responsibility of a college to provide tuition for its men, and when it ceases to do that there is little left to excuse it. Colleges now meet their needs by appointing psychologists as part-time tutors or lecturers. They do not usually consult them in relation to admissions. Tutors, correspondingly, may teach for a number of colleges. The consequence of a small increase in numbers admitted to read Psychology by each college may then be an unexpected and large increase in the load thrown on an individual tutor. He may meet this by shifts: teaching pairs when he thinks this inferior to teaching individuals singly; farming people out to inferior helpers; or he may resign from some of his colleges, precipitating a crisis. They may then appoint a fresh tutor, if one can be found. Thus only in a series of lurches from crisis to crisis is the tutorial force available adjusted to the need for it.

646. When lectures were discussed, the great majority of comments were against compulsion though many thought there was scope for improving the organization of lectures (see Tables 294–9). The viewpoint of many college tutors was expressed by a CUF lecturer in arts:

I believe that we should stick to our tradition that, in general, students are *not* compelled to get their instruction through certain prescribed channels, but *are* compelled in tutorials to produce evidence of having been instructed. (There must, of course, be some exceptions in the shape of required classes, etc.) To establish a system of required lectures would impair the training in independent work on which we set such high value, would place a disastrous emphasis on prepackaged instruction, and reduce the importance of the tutorial and therefore the responsibility of the student. It is true, however, that the lecture provision could be much better organized, and therefore probably much better used, without resorting to compulsion.

647. There were a considerable number of comments that the standard of lecturing is not as high as it might be and suggesting that training be given. For example:

Steps should be taken to improve the quality of lecturing. Most professional men are not too proud to learn the techniques of their profession. Lecturing technique can be taught; for instance, the Army through courses in 'Methods of Instruction' train most unlikely people to be competent teachers. Lecturers in the University of Oxford should know how to use a black-board, how to organize their material, not to play with the chalk, and to speak up. They might even be encouraged to use occasionally the odd teaching aid.

(Departmental demonstrator.)

648. The balance between teaching and research attracted a great deal of discussion. A tutorial fellow in science expressed a view which was shared by many:

My own subject is advancing very rapidly. New concepts and new techniques develop very quickly and a tutor cannot hope to keep abreast of his subject unless he has adequate time for study and research. For such study and research he needs to be intellectually alive and fresh—he cannot do it at the end of a serious day of teaching. In my view teaching and research must be complementary in a university and it is vital to keep both of these aspects in their correct proportion.

A university lecturer with a tutorial fellowship in science did not regard the problems of teaching and research as affecting Oxford only:

The whole system of teaching and research in the University and, as far as my very limited knowledge goes, in the country needs reorganizing. In my opinion many of the criticisms made of Oxford in these matters, while valid, are really criticisms of the whole British academic system highlighted by an Oxford background.

Several with experience of other universities made comparisons between the teaching load at Oxford and elsewhere. A CUF lecturer in arts wrote:

The most desirable division of time between teaching and research must be a matter of opinion. It is, however, a fact that Oxford expects much more teaching than either of the other universities in which I have taught: the largest number of hours per week I taught at one coincides almost exactly with the minimum to be expected in a summer term (the lightest for a Mods. tutor) here, while the normal week's teaching at the other constitutes just over half my average week's teaching in the lightest of the three years I have taught in Oxford.

649. It was frequently stressed that it is not only the total amount of teaching which is important; but the fragmentation of the day which results. This is especially important in science where lengthy experiments are necessary, but the point was also made in other subjects:

Under the present system it is almost impossible for a college tutor in a large subject to do continuous research. Yet for many kinds of subject intermittent research is either inefficient or inadequate. It is therefore necessary that tutors should be protected against the pressure to engage in teaching and administration to excess. Since colleges care little about research, and since it is in their interests (as institutions) to get as much teaching out of their tutorial fellows as possible, the initiative probably has to come from the University.

(CUF lecturer in arts.)

A possible solution was put forward by a college lecturer in arts:

Some individuals may indeed work better teaching all their lives or doing research. However, for most people what is wanted is more opportunity to write without removal from the stimulus to thought and clarification which teaching has as its most valuable side-product. The obvious solution is to institute more jobs, college and university, in which two terms rather than three are spent teaching, the other being free if desired for the man's own work. This system is already being employed in London, e.g. in the Institute of Archaeology, with satisfactory results for both teachers and taught in removing the commonly felt tension between teaching and research.

650. Many considered the creation of more senior (and other) posts with limited teaching duties as the best way to ease the pressure on research time. For example:

The don who remains interested in his subject but who for one reason or another does not seek a chair outside Oxford, in time comes to find great frustration. There seems to be very little time for one's own research, and an immense amount of repetition in tutoring. Inevitably one becomes to some extent bored. A cure of some sort could be effected if there were more university posts of the grade of reader and lecturer to which more senior dons could aspire, even if they were to be held for only limited periods of time.          (CUF lecturer in arts.)

Both [teaching and research] would profit greatly by the introduction of a large new category of staff, namely, *research workers with limited teaching commitments*. If a large number of such posts were created both in colleges and university departments, the teaching load would be spread and the quality and sophistication of teaching enhanced.                    (Professor in medicine.)

651. Difficulties in financing research in the sciences were mentioned by those responsible. A professor wrote:

The University must find out how to initiate research. At the moment in this department no General Board un-earmarked money *whatever* is used for buying research equipment and this means that any new developments must be undertaken by seeking outside help. This is true of the technical and other staff that such developments might entail; it would be a great help if the University would accept that it is its responsibility to staff laboratories that it builds or allows to be built, but it does not. This is true not only of academic posts but also of technical and secretarial posts. In this department we have even had to seek outside money for a telephone operator and for janitors and cleaners. The University obviously cannot finance great new ventures, but it should at least provide the irreducible background support that the very scale of the buildings implies and should provide some money that can be used to finance first investigations at the growing points of the subject.

652. The needs of postgraduates were mentioned quite frequently, particularly in arts and social studies subjects. A university lecturer and tutorial fellow in arts discussed their needs for instruction:

There is a lack of proper attention to instruction in basic research techniques at the immediate postgraduate stage. A weaker man gets confused and discouraged at the seeming inadequacy of his undergraduate approach, and the better man wastes a lot of time finding his own way through the wood. The change from undergraduate to research work is the biggest single jump in secondary-plus education—far bigger than that from school to university. Few people seem to realize the need for what guidance is possible in the *isolation* of the early stages of research. Something analogous to (if not in detail identical with) the English Faculty's basic graduate course is needed in other faculties as well as close contact between graduates and teaching staff.

A professor in arts was one of several respondents who stressed the need for faculty entres:

If one analyses this problem I think one is bound to conclude that it exists here partly because of the ambiguity of the postgraduate's position in a largely collegiate university where, however, responsibility for research lies not with colleges but with the University. I think there is a very real need to give postgraduate students generally centres where they can meet informally others working in similar fields and, equally important, have chances of meeting teachers in those fields. It is easy to deride the value of, say, a cup of coffee in a common room where one is working, but I have been impressed by the usefulness of such facilities in universities where they are available to postgraduate students. We value very highly in Oxford the role of the college common room in the education of undergraduates. I think similar possibilities ought to be available to postgraduates, either in faculty research institutes or, possibly, attached to all the major libraries. There are, of course, other reasons than this for considering the establishment of such research centres.

653. The cross-fertilization which is facilitated by the college system was generally recognized and welcomed. A number complained, however, of inadequate opportunities of meeting others in the same subject:

The collegiate system, as at present organized, has in practice the effect of atomizing the non-scientific faculties: colleagues in the same field do not and cannot meet frequently and informally to exchange information and ideas. Each member of a faculty is in effect isolated from every other: occasional dinner engagements, infrequent faculty meetings, and the meetings of societies seem to me no substitute for the regular day-to-day contact which the existence of departmental or quasi-departmental institutions would promote. The present system also has the effect of militating against the sort of combined research which is increasingly desirable in the social sciences.

(Junior research fellow in social studies.)

654. Some scientists considered that the college system is detrimental to research. A professor in Physical Sciences wrote:

The research atmosphere at Oxford is probably the thinnest I have experienced anywhere. This appears to result primarily from the college system, for the following reasons:

(i) The dominance of the college system means that research is not considered of real importance at Oxford, in so far as personal judgements are concerned. In other words, the prevailing attitudes do not lead to the encouragement of research.

    (ii) The college-centred system inhibits the close contacts between people of related interests which would normally stimulate discussion and generate research activity. In most universities these contacts take place at the luncheon table. In Oxford these contacts scarcely exist; I can scarcely think of a more positive action that could be taken by the University to stimulate research in Oxford than to set up an adequate cafeteria close to the Museum's site. Any factor which could break down the distance between individuals in Oxford (greater here than I have ever seen anywhere else) would be beneficial.

    (iii) The majority of Oxford appointments are primarily of college teachers. In fact, research activity on the part of an applicant even appears to be something of a positive disqualification, on the grounds that such an applicant is 'too specialized' to be appropriate for a college tutorial fellowship, or that he would be unwilling to give the necessary attention to the tutorial work.

655. A considerable number of research workers (many of whom are employed on outside grants) have no college connexion or only a nominal one, and some felt they lost something of importance thereby:

My contacts with scientific colleagues in several university departments are most stimulating and helpful. But one misses any common meeting ground with the corporate life of the University, my college, and with scholars in other disciplines. My own college is small with very limited facilities for senior members of the University, so that I have had no contact with the college since taking my M.A. by incorporation. I regret very much that there is at present no basis for regularly meeting with other members of my college. I consider such contacts with members of the University outside my special field to be of the greatest importance for the maintenance of one's intellectual drive, and to give a sense of corporate belonging to Oxford, which is difficult under the present arrangements. I would support whole-heartedly the proposals for the development of non-collegiate facilities for senior members of the University not involved in general teaching duties.                     (Research officer in medicine.)

I am a full-time research worker with a grant from BECC. I am not a member of a college or any society. I have worked here since January of this year. I feel it is regrettable that there is at present no way in which I can participate in university life.                             (Research worker on outside grant.)

656. The salary and career structure came in for a certain amount of comment, particularly by scientists. A college lecturer and non-tutorial fellow in science attributed over-teaching to the salary structure:

This [high teaching] load has to be undertaken in order that one's salary can approach that of a man of comparable age and standing elsewhere. Even so, 9 hours' tuition a week, together with college retaining fees and examining fees, produces a salary which is often still some £300–£500 per annum less than could be obtained elsewhere as a senior lecturer or reader—unless one has an official fellowship at one of the richer colleges. Moreover, this extra income is not eligible for FSSU, which is unjust since the work performed in earning it is elsewhere a salaried part of one's university duties and therefore superannuable. The basic reason why scientists teach too much is, in my opinion, financial and this is the core of the problem. Oxford has no senior lecturerships into which men of 38 or above can be promoted, and readerships are only given to men of such seniority that they would have senior chairs in large departments elsewhere. In most universities an active man at this stage has a more than even chance of being promoted senior lecturer or reader between the ages of 38 and 45.

The career structure at Oxford was discussed by a CUF lecturer in arts:

The egalitarianism of the University has good effects on its teaching. It is accepted that a man may wish to stay as a tutorial fellow for the whole of his working life and that the distinction between tutorial fellows and professors and readers should be more of function than of status. Bad effects can follow. Vegetating idleness is not unknown; though more hierarchical systems do not appear more successful in averting it and magnify its consequences when it strikes men in power. The good effects are numerous. Able and experienced men are not all removed into spheres where they do not perform the more time-consuming and important parts of undergraduate teaching.

A university lecturer and tutorial fellow in science was more critical:

Once in a senior position, the lack of further promotion opportunities removes a strong incentive for excellence in either teaching or research. I do not feel that the rigid age-wage scale is entirely satisfactory. There seems to be no organized system of review once one is hired. This promotes the attitude of settling back and feeling one has now 'arrived' which has been typical of Oxford. The intellectual output of many Oxford dons is very low, and they are content to spend their time on petty administrative details (either for the University or a college) for which they are either ill- or over-qualified.

657. Administration was referred to in the previous extract. The relation between the academic structure and the administrative structure was commented on by a CUF lecturer in arts:

The assumptions made governing the exercise of power in this University correspond to those of scholarship, for example, that all are equally entitled to offer their views and that these should be judged by the evidence offered, not according to the status of the proponent. A fault of our system is that questions of policy and administration are often treated as if they were of scholarship: not only must debate precede decision, but it is often regarded as preferable. But systems departing too far from ours can lead to questions of scholarship being treated as questions of power. The spirit of a university should be one of the greatest freedom and it is not easy or safe to separate one kind of freedom from another.

A senior research fellow in arts was perhaps making a similar point:

I have never seen or imagined a place so badly organized as Oxford but notice with pleased astonishment that it works after a fashion, although not nearly so well as it thinks it does.

The amount of administration was commented on adversely many times, but not all thought it a bad thing:

Some people complain about the amount of administration that a tutorial fellow at Oxford is called upon to undertake at times. In my view this is a mistaken attitude. Most of the administration that fellows find themselves doing brings them into contact with undergraduate problems, and that seems to me entirely desirable. I would even regard it as almost a part of the task of teaching.
(CUF lecturer in arts.)

The need for more secretarial assistance was mentioned many times:

Secretarial and research assistance is derisory for the average staff-member. It is humiliating to have to beg for it.          (Reader in social studies.)

658. There were widespread criticisms of library facilities (and especially of opening hours, too many separate buildings, insufficient access to stacks, and limited borrowing facilities). Criticisms in PPE subjects were particularly strong:

The other despair-generating factor in the teaching and researching of my subject is DESPERATE library facilities. It is a scrimmage for any don or under-graduate to lay his hands on any such ordinary periodical as the *Philosophical Review* during term-time. (May I suggest that the Commission visit the Social Studies reading room any Monday–Friday morning and *witness* the conditions there?) People have been complaining of them, and opening hours, for years. Nothing happens. Bodley should certainly be open on Sunday evenings, and on all evenings till 11.0 p.m. or midnight. (Concerning the staffing problem which would arise, U.S. universities have had excellent results with part-time graduate and undergraduate paid assistance. Why haven't Bodley tried this?) In philosophy there is a crying need for a proper sub-faculty library. At the moment books I need are to be found in (1) Classics reading room, Old Bodley; (2) Radcliffe Camera; (3) Social Studies; (4) Ashmolean Museum; (5) Radcliffe Science Library. The undergraduates have to go to almost as many places and they have borrowing facilities only for unspecialized material.          (CUF lecturer.)

659. The lack of recognition of the degrees of other universities was criticized by a senior research officer in social studies:

As a graduate of Oxford who has returned after twenty years abroad, I find our attitude to the degrees of other universities arrogant, antiquated, and offensive. This is symbolized by the regulations regarding the wearing of gowns and hoods. Nothing has done more than this to create the impression abroad that Oxford, whose own M.A. degrees can be bought for a few pounds but which does not recognize those of Harvard or the Sorbonne, is still living in the eighteenth century.

660. Among the comments on more specialized points was one on the position of staff in clinical medicine:

Could I please draw attention to the anomalous position of lecturers appointed by the Nuffield Committee for the Advancement of Medicine? Although we take a full and active part in university medical teaching (some of it undergraduate) and in research, we are not 'University Lecturers'; our names are not among those of other lecturers within the Faculty; our appointments are not announced in the *Gazette* and elsewhere. Nor do we have security of tenure, though many of us have been with the University for many years, are senior members of the University and often of a college, and are serious students of, and authorities in, our own specialities.

661. Few features of Oxford life escaped comment by the academic staff, and the Commission, and its inquiries, were no exception. A philosopher wrote:

Out of thirteen questions, one, namely 8, and bits of 10, are concerned with the advancement of their subject by dons. All the rest are questions about pedagogy and administration. Neither in the questionnaire nor in that to be answered by faculties and sub-faculties is any serious attempt made to find out whether our subjects are vigorous, alive, half-alive, or dead; whether other universities send their products to us for graduate work; whether their teachers come to us as Recognized Students, or on their sabbatical leaves, etc. Or whether, if there is some life in our subjects, we find it hard or easy to make our contributions. Or whether the University or the colleges do enough—or anything—to assist such contributions. My own sub-faculty has, and I think deserves, a world-wide reputation for its productivity of philosophical ideas. Its members are constantly being invited to visiting and permanent professorships overseas. We receive a constant stream of philosophers from overseas who wish to spend a term, two terms, or a year in our midst. *But* all that the Commission seems to want to know is how many books and articles we have produced since 1959—with no further evidence being requested to show whether they have mattered to the subject—much less whether anything has made it difficult for us to write any more. Its interest in vacation courses seems to be concentrated on its potential effects on undergraduates. Nothing is said about its effects on, for example, our philosophers. If the Commission's report is based merely on the answers to its questions, it will say a lot about our performance or non-performance of our teaching duties to undergraduates and graduates and almost nothing about our performance or non-performance of our duties to our subject. It will mention, perhaps, the fact that last term we coped, or tried to cope, with over 100 postgraduates in Philosophy without giving any idea why they ever came to Oxford rather than to Cambridge or Edinburgh. Harvard, say, or Melbourne University would say 'Oxford is full of active philosophers'. The Commission's report is, I fear, going to say 'Oxford has a lot of busy philosophy tutors'. And of course it *has*. But does the Commission care *nothing* about what Harvard, say, cares hugely about?

### POSTGRADUATES

662. A high proportion of the respondents in the postgraduate survey made comments on the adequacy of teaching arrangements, of library facilities, and of working conditions. In addition, some two-thirds responded to the invitation for their observations on the general position of those reading for higher degrees in Oxford. As with the academic staff, these observations

covered a very wide range of topics, and the same qualifications as were mentioned in the introduction to the comments of the academic staff should be borne in mind. Some 6 per cent. expressed general satisfaction with conditions, and presumably most of the third who did not comment were reasonably satisfied.

663. There was a considerable body of opinion that more teaching should be provided. When asked explicitly about the adequacy of seminars, classes, and lectures, about a third stated a need for more teaching in these forms (see Table 205). The main demand was for more seminars. But at least one American warned against going too far:

> In general I must say that, as compared with my experience of graduate study in the U.S.A., I very much value the freedom and at least implicit emphasis on and encouragement of individual initiative and responsibility, and so feel very wary of making any criticisms lest Oxford become, in this sense, 'Americanized', (required lectures, required course work, continual required exams, etc.). But I would come out strongly for more seminars. (D.Phil. student in arts.)

664. There were comparatively few adverse comments on supervision, although a few stated that though their own supervisor was satisfactory, some of their friends had been less fortunate. (23 per cent. of the sample were not satisfied with the amount of supervision they received—see Table 197.) Many recognized the importance of a good supervisor, for instance a D.Phil. student in Physical Sciences:

> In conclusion, I think that the most important single factor in successful post-graduate work is a good supervisor—who must encourage and advise, but leave his pupils to organize and think for themselves—and I have been lucky in having a first-class one.

One form of complaint was expressed by a D.Phil. student in Social Studies:

> The major problem here lies in the first year of research, when very close super-vision is required, but rarely given, so that a wasted first year is a very general complaint.

Some complained about the difficulty of changing one's supervisor, a difficulty which can be particularly great in the sciences:

> Particularly in the experimental sciences, research studentships are tied from the beginning to a particular supervisor, frequently by the fact that the apparatus is provided by a contract to which he specifically is a party. In such cases, change of supervisor requires a change of research topic which is likely to incur risk of losing the supporting studentship. Research is a much more personal matter than pursuit of an undergraduate course, but whereas undergraduates can change tutors by arrangement through the college, research students are faced with the choice of giving-up, or seeing their supervisors as little as possible, when personal incompatibility arises. There is need of administrative machinery to deal with this problem. (D.Phil. student in Physical Sciences.)

In at least one case a failure in communication caused a complaint:

It would have helped me a great deal if at the beginning of my two years in Oxford I had been told that B.Phil. students can ask to see other senior members besides the supervisor to whom they are allotted.

(B.Phil. student in Literae Humaniores.)

665. It is a characteristic of Oxford that a great deal of the responsibility for a research degree should fall on the student. This was welcomed by a D.Phil. student in arts:

As far as my personal experience goes I must say that I have found the conditions for research here more than adequate. My supervisor and college have always been most generous in terms of time, finance, and general assistance. As to the approach to the problems of research itself my own feeling is that at Oxford it is essentially an adult pursuit. Here the burden is placed fairly and squarely on the shoulders of the student himself; he is compelled to accept the maximum amount of responsibility for his work; he must do the research, locate the sources, explore the material, and formulate his conclusions in an articulate and coherent manner. Unhappily there seems to be a growing opinion that the student, even the mature student, should be 'guided' all the way. Frankly I feel that any attempt at 'formal instruction' in research methods and sources (who can instruct in sources but the supervisor?) would lead to a sacrifice of the spontaneity which the present Oxford approach to research allows. What is the point to formal instruction in method? If after three years at a university a man cannot use a library, collect, compare, and collate his material, he has no right to be doing research.

666. That loneliness is to a certain extent an inevitable part of the postgraduate's life was recognized in many other comments, but many of these (especially in arts and social studies) felt that it is accentuated in Oxford; that the postgraduate has no recognized place in the academic community; and that a cause of the trouble is that Oxford is organized predominantly for undergraduate studies. For a number it was evident that Oxford had not come up to their (high) expectations. It was granted that the ingredients are here—world-renowned scholars, first-class research, an agreeable setting, etc.—and this made the disappointment the greater when the expected intellectual excitement failed to materialize. To a large extent the problem was seen as one of communication—with both senior members and other postgraduates.

667. One comment was 'postgraduates are treated as undergraduates by the dons, and as dons by the undergraduates', and this view recurred repeatedly:

Generally they fall between two stools. Neither dons nor undergraduates—for both of whom facilities seem reasonable—they wander in a no-man's land with no adequate organization of their academic, social, and material needs.

(B.Phil. student in Literae Humaniores.)

There is a popular song which tells of a certain 'Mr. In-Between'. This applies well to the position of the higher degree student in Oxford. He hardly has the opportunity to meet senior members of the University on a social level: for example, his presence would not normally be welcome at a high table, unless he has a fellowship. On the other hand, contacts with undergraduates are difficult because of difference in age and the quaint respect that they have for postgraduates.

(B.Litt. student in Modern Languages.)

Briefly, they can best be described as stepsons. The University is neither interested in their general welfare nor in providing them with facilities and arrangements which would make it possible for students to have discussions and seminars with senior members in their particular fields. The gulf between a research student and the expert in his field is so great that it has made really creative study of a subject, on an advanced level, quite impossible. For an overseas student the whole affair is quite painful. He comes in the hope of meeting and discussing and reading with people whose views and ideas seem to matter. But when he comes up he finds that he can hardly have more than 18 hours of contact with a dry, disinterested 'supervisor'. One must admit that postgraduate studies in Oxford are still in a primitive state. It is a university for the first degree. Here, you have libraries adequate for advanced study—in fact, fit only for advanced work (Bodleian's resources have no meaning for an undergraduate)—but no method, no atmosphere, no organization.

(D.Phil. student in English.)

668. The disappointment and isolation expressed by many, and the view that too much importance attaches to undergraduate study, are illustrated in the following extracts:

I think the worst aspect of Oxford for a postgraduate is the feeling that no one really cares what you are doing; your supervisor sees you and is very helpful but he's got lots of other commitments and the contact is superficial, academically and socially. A research student must necessarily be isolated to some extent by virtue of the kind of work he's doing; but while the scientists seem to find some sort of community with others working in the same lab., the arts man has no such opportunities. On the whole I feel that my time at Oxford has been intellectually fruitless; all being well I'll get my meal-ticket (the D.Phil.), but there's been so little intellectual stimulation that I'll be very glad to get back to Australia. The academic world there may be provincial in the continental sense, but it is at least possible to meet and get to know other people with similar interests; and while postgraduate students in Australia may be over-taught, surely this is better than not being taught at all. (D.Phil. student in Modern History.)

I have found that the general position of those reading for higher degrees is not a very happy one. The college authorities and tutors often have little specialized knowledge about research topics and one can't help but form the opinion that researchers are second-class students—in the eyes of the college—whose perversity has led them to deviate from the 'norm' of the undergraduate, tutorial-style degree. This, I feel, comes from the positive obsession with Schools results, there is more rejoicing in the SCR at one first in Schools than two successful D.Phils. or B.Litts. Researchers have little opportunity (in the humanities, at least) to get to know each other and discuss work. There is no social centre where researchers can get together, no café, no refectory, where researchers can congregate. If the School of Social Studies had its own centre, equipped with cafeteria and bar, I am sure that research students would tend to frequent it, and benefit from the cross-fertilization of the different subjects that are included in the School. (D.Phil. student in Social Studies.)

Many postgraduates coming from North America expect a thriving community for postgraduate work at a university as renowned as Oxford, yet they find a university which is traditionally undergraduate in organization. There is little catering to the needs of the postgraduate, and the lack of co-ordination of graduate faculties is inbred by a complacent collegiate system. Standards and degree requirements seem to be poorly outlined and vary extensively from faculty to faculty or even between tutors within the same faculty. The postgraduate student is left feeling lost in a complacent, over decentralized world; often he feels the only way to obtain a degree is to somehow fight to reorganize the rather vague system in which he is trapped. This is particularly true of students in arts subjects. (B.Phil. student in Social Studies.)

I can only repeat for emphasis (I hope). The *isolation* is most depressing, especially when one assumes that there are a great many interesting people doing research in the same field. The general attitude seems to be that married students should be ignored in the hope that they will go away, which I would suggest is an extremely short-sighted view in light of the obvious trend. (B.Litt. student in arts.)

Although I have been very fortunate in my postgraduate career at Oxford, none the less, in general, the condition of the postgraduate researcher is completely determined by the attitude of his supervisor to research. The status of research in the University, in the humanities, is perhaps reflected in the attention paid to the undergraduates' final examinations both in university publications and in the colleges. It would appear that a don's reputation rests first on his undergraduate results, second on his publications, and third, if this is relevant at all, on his postgraduate supervision. Furthermore, those dons who are genuinely interested in postgraduate research and supervision are hampered by excessive undergraduate teaching, which leaves them little time for their own research, let alone supervising that of others. (D.Phil. student in Modern Languages.)

669. The part that the colleges play, and might play, in the life of postgraduates came in for a great deal of comment. There were many divisions of view, and the positions of those who had already been undergraduates at Oxford were understandably different from those of graduates of other universities. Some complained mainly that the colleges do not do enough:

I think that the biggest argument against the present system is that too few colleges provide facilities for graduate students. A number of colleges extract a large amount of money from their graduate students and provide virtually nothing in return. (D.Phil. student in Physical Sciences.)

Others were well content:

The existing collegiate system seems admirable in all ways; it offers membership of a society composed of men of different ages, subjects, religions, and backgrounds. It is this basic variety combined with a unity of purpose and historical environment which is its most satisfying feature. As such it caters for individual development set within a community. It is a microcosm of society. Because of its varied make-up it provides stimulus to thought and encourages the process of cross-fertilization.                    (D.Phil. student in Modern History.)

But not always for the same reasons:

Since the reason for the presence of postgraduates here is for research not 'general education', the present system, whereby postgraduates in colleges tend to be very separated from the remainder of their colleges, has much to commend it. Though a mixing of study and non-study is essential to get the best from an undergraduate degree, this is not so with a higher degree, and so the present 'neglect' of postgraduates achieves a desirable end. If one wishes to work here for a higher degree sufficiently strongly, then one will be prepared to put up with hardship; too much fostering of 'postgraduate spirit' in postgraduate colleges, corresponding to 'undergraduate spirit' in present colleges, cannot help but lead to a decrease in research productivity, a lowering of standards, and the loss of the good name of Oxford in academic and other circles.

(D.Phil. student in Physical Sciences.)

A good many scientists, and some others in subjects with a university institution which serves the functions of a department, felt little need for a college connexion at all (about a fifth, over all, thought college membership should be optional—see Tables 229–31). An arts student wrote:

The desire of a student to enter into collegiate life will clearly vary from individual to individual. After four years of collegiate life at Cambridge and knowing Oxford well, collegiate life has had no special attractions for me nor supplied any needs. I have found that both my academic and non-academic needs have been adequately filled through the university department where I have been working. Nevertheless, I suppose many feel that being a member of a college supplements contacts gained through departments and faculties, and it might have done so in my case had I not been turned against the college by the exorbitant fees and the demand made during my first term to eat 46 dinners in hall (since reduced to 16).

(B.Litt. student in arts.)

670. A number, however, were more radical in their views, and considered that the roles of the colleges (particularly the traditional colleges) in respect of postgraduates should be altered, and some thought university institutions should be founded. Not surprisingly, suggestions were various and often conflicting. A selection is given:

Where graduates are concerned the college system has patently failed. The recent creation of Middle Common Rooms attempts to meet a great need, but will serve only to perpetuate a system which is basically unsatisfactory. The only way to adapt the colleges to the needs of research students is to create graduate colleges. Accordingly, colleges which have failed academically at the under-graduate level should be closed down and reopened as mixed graduate colleges. Remaining colleges admitting undergraduates should be prohibited from admit-ting students for higher degrees. However, unless these new graduate colleges can exist as adult communities—and not as extensions of the present 'inflated boarding school' system, or as snobbish, introverted establishments such as Nuffield—they may do more harm than good. I would agree with the findings of the Committee on Graduates, Council of Junior Members, published as 'Oxford Graduates, Survey 1962', but not necessarily with their suggested solutions to problems. (D.Phil. student in Physical Sciences.)

The college has made great efforts—but are they in the right direction?
(Student at a college whose MCR attracted more favourable comment than most.)

One would put in a special plea for a non-specialized postgraduate centre. The Sutherland Committee proposed an arts graduate centre on academic grounds; they ignored the non-academic reasons. The two main ones are:
(i) it would be a meeting place for postgraduates of both sexes;
(ii) it would bring together postgraduates of all disciplines.
This point is often ignored. (D.Phil. student in Social Studies.)

The present system is unsatisfactory in providing for the social needs of graduates (and in particular of those from other universities) as there are too many colleges and societies. This results in numerous small and isolated groups of postgraduates. A postgraduate society (or a few postgraduate societies) will only solve this problem satisfactorily if *all* postgraduate students automatically became members of the society rather than their undergraduate colleges. Socie-ties of this nature should certainly not be specialized as to fields of study.
(B.Sc. student in Agriculture and Forestry.)

I feel that it is a good safeguard for the graduate student not to be entirely dependent on his department. On the other hand, it seems unfair that those who have gained degrees good enough to gain them State Studentships should not all be able to take advantage of the kind of benefits conferred by such institutions as St. Antony's and Nuffield. I have felt for a long time that all college revenue should be centralized under the University's control, with grants from the Uni-versity to the colleges for fabric and *per capita* teaching/taught upkeep. On such a basis, presumably, a few colleges would not be unable to find money while others are largely unable to spend it. Also, on such a basis, other colleges besides Nuffield and St. Antony's might be brought into being by the University, rather than on individual initiative, for graduate studies. This might avoid the localism which one suspects will overtake a Balliol–St. Anne's joint graduate society, as well as providing a more equal advantage to graduate students who otherwise have only the social life of their college Junior or Middle Common Rooms, or are outside the college system altogether. (B.Phil. student in Social Studies.)

The chief problem is that they [postgraduates] are scattered at random through-out a large town, and there are inadequate social facilities for them. They cannot meet and cross-fertilize each other's ideas. For those who enjoy the college atmosphere and who belong to a college which has a MCR *and* which is usefully situated in relation to their living accommodation or place of work, this can largely supply their need. For the remainder, who are in the majority, there is no satisfactory alternative. One possibility would be to create a postgraduate colony—for example, in north Oxford by some central administration of the property owned by St. John's College—and arrange for a number of small postgraduate restaurants or other such meeting places within that geographic area. Large social centres such as Halifax House are too institutional to be humanly satisfactory solutions to the problem: they are too reminiscent of the NAAFI social centres of the Armed Forces! (D. Phil. student in Physical Sciences.)

671. There were a number of more particular points which were made comparatively frequently.

672. The position of graduates of other universities has already been mentioned. Further comments are:

Graduate students, especially those who do not come up through the Oxford undergraduate system are, as it were, allowed to use the facilities of this great university but otherwise stand outside it. (D.Phil. student in arts.)

Oxford should be disabused of its Rip van Winkle idea that it is the centre of the universe. It should extend elementary courtesies to graduates of other universities. Doctorates of other universities should be recognized in the style of address and should not be referred to in studied fashion as Mr. ——. This does not affect me personally and the actual status is unimportant. The thing that does matter is the regrettable attitude of mind that allows this to continue.
(D.Phil. student in Medicine.)

The position of those reading for higher degrees who graduated at Oxford would seem to me to be much happier than those from other universities. In forming a graduate common room in Keble, we made a particular effort to welcome graduates from other universities, who otherwise had virtually no opportunity to meet other graduates at a social level in college. Already this term I have been approached by several such members, who had difficulty in appreciating the impeccable logic of a system which places their names on the college list as undergraduates, and which obliges them to wear undergraduate gowns.
(B. Litt. student and Oxford graduate.)

Graduates of other universities who have to wear those appalling advanced students' gowns have my deepest sympathy.
(D.Phil. student in Physical Sciences.)

673. Accommodation difficulties were mentioned many times. They can be especially severe for overseas and married students. (Many colleges try to give unmarried postgraduates the opportunity of a first year in college. The Postgraduate Survey was taken from postgraduates in their second or subsequent years, among whom 7 per cent. of graduates of other U.K. universities and 24 per cent. of overseas graduates lived in college or college accommodation—see Table 222):

The accommodation situation in Oxford is a major drawback to life here. Provision of suitable accommodation (perhaps at cost) would seem to be a function which the University could well undertake and in which respect Oxford compares unfavourably with many provincial universities and CAT's.

(D.Phil. student in Biological Sciences.)

The accommodation position is bad and deteriorating. The Delegacy of Lodgings is hidebound by restrictions which they must enforce, e.g. I was forced to leave cheap and comfortable lodgings in the country near Oxford and shift to the City. (B.Phil. student in Literae Humaniores.)

The accommodation system is very chancy—I should like to see blocks of flats owned by the University for graduates married and single. (The University organization for digs. often won't help women.)

(Woman D.Phil. student in Science.)

674. A particular form of accommodation problem is vacation residence. Most postgraduates spend much of the vacations in Oxford, but they may have to vacate college rooms out of term to make room for conferences, etc.:

For most graduates there is very little distinction between term and vacation, and it would be a great step forward if colleges were to make less of the distinction also. (D.Phil. student in Physical Sciences.)

The position of those reading for higher degrees with regard to term and vacation time must be realized by college authorities. Two terms ago one postgraduate was fined for being in Oxford at a time when the terms of his grant and nature of his research made it impossible for him to be elsewhere. When graduates live in college they must be able to remain there out of term and without having hindrances placed in their way. The term-vacation categories are not applicable to postgraduate work. (D.Phil. student in Physical Sciences.)

675. A problem for married postgraduates is that they often cannot take their wives into college, and this is one reason why over half the married postgraduates in the survey (see Table 228) rarely used college facilities:

A married postgraduate feels the need of a graduate centre of some kind, to which he can at any time take his wife, whether or not she is a member of the University. (B.Phil. student in Literae Humaniores.)

676. College fees were mentioned as excessive by a number:

The college fees (amounting so far to £340 including caution money and with one more bill to come) I regard as exorbitant because they far exceed anything the college offers in return. Of course some of the items are indisputably just, e.g. B.Litt. tutor's fee, degree fees, meals. However, I feel that for postgraduates some system of paying college bills should be arranged so that the graduate could pay more directly for what he in fact uses. I would feel that, for instance, a £10–£20 fee for using the Bodleian would be far more reasonable than a £20 college establishment charge. My dissatisfaction with both college and library has been of an administrative and not a personal nature. The collegiate system may well be suited to integrating postgraduates into the life of the university, but will only achieve this when it really devotes itself to finding an efficient and cheap way of providing social and academic contacts and when it ceases to regard postgraduates as an easy source of revenue.            (B.Litt. student in arts.)

677. Among scientists there were a number of complaints about working conditions in their departments. These complaints generally concerned poorly maintained equipment, poor workshop facilities, and overcrowding. The absence of a central purchasing body was criticized at least once.

678. When asked about library facilities, rather more than half made no comment, or were satisfied with them. The proportion with no adverse comment was higher in science and medicine (about two-thirds) than in arts and social studies (just under half). Adverse comments covered a wide range of topics. College libraries, where they were mentioned at all, were usually reckoned as of very little use to postgraduates. The main comments were directed at the Bodleian and departmental libraries, and criticism of one often went together with satisfaction with another. Possibly the most frequent criticism (especially in arts and social studies) was that books and periodicals (often highly specialized) were not available, and that the procedure for obtaining books from other libraries was slow. Frequent criticisms were made of opening hours (especially out of term), and—less frequently—of the standards of service, in particular of the catalogues and the apparent lack of co-ordination between libraries in Oxford. Some unfavourable comparisons were made with library facilities at American universities.

PRINTED IN GREAT BRITAIN
AT THE UNIVERSITY PRESS, OXFORD
BY VIVIAN RIDLER
PRINTER TO THE UNIVERSITY